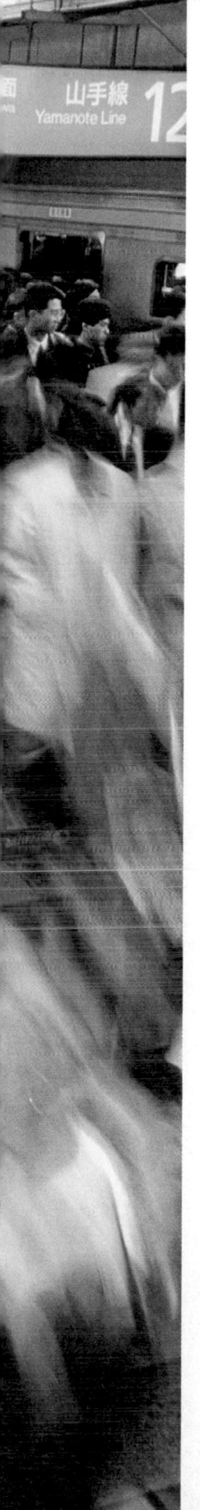

WELCOME TO TOKYO

Lights, sushi, manga! Sprawling, frenetic, and endlessly fascinating, Japan's capital is a city of contrasts. Shrines and gardens are pockets of calm between famously crowded streets and soaring office buildings. Mom-and-pop noodle houses share street space with Western-style chain restaurants and exquisite fine dining. Shopping yields lovely folk arts as well as the newest electronics. And nightlife kicks off with karaoke or sake and continues with techno clubs and more. Whether you seek the traditional or the cutting edge, Tokyo will provide it.

TOP REASONS TO GO

★ **Ultimate cityscape:** A skyline of neon-lighted streets and vast high-rises awes the senses.

★ **Incredible eats:** From humble ramen to sumptuous sushi, Tokyo is foodie heaven.

★ **Green havens:** Pristine gardens and lush city-center parks soften the urban scene.

★ **Fashion-forward shops:** From Muji to Miyake, Tokyo is a playground for shopaholics.

★ **Contemporary art:** The Mori Art Museum caps a stunningly diverse scene.

★ **Sacred spaces:** Senso-ji Complex and Meiji Shrine offer spiritual retreats.

Fodor's TOKYO

Design: Tina Malaney, *Associate Art Director*; Erica Cuoco, *Production Designer*

Photography: Jennifer Arnow, *Senior Photo Editor*

Maps: Rebecca Baer, *Senior Map Editor*; Mark Stroud, Henry Colomb (Moon Street Cartography), David Lindroth, *Cartographers*

Production: Angela L. McLean, *Senior Production Manager*; Jennifer DePrima, *Editorial Production Manager*

Sales: Jacqueline Lebow, *Sales Director*

Business & Operations: Chuck Hoover, *Chief Marketing Officer*; Joy Lai, *Vice President and General Manager*; Stephen Horowitz, *Head of Business Development and Partnerships*

Writers: Brett Bull, Rob Goss, Misha Janette, Noriko Kitano, Robert Morel, Annamarie Sasagawa

Editors: Amanda Sadlowski (lead editor), Róisin Cameron, Mike Dunphy

Production Editor: Elyse Rozelle

6th Edition

ISBN 978–0–14–754654–8

ISSN 1554–5881

PRINTED IN THE UNITED STATES OF AMERICA

10 9 8 7 6 5 4 3 2 1

Fodor's

TOKYO

11
中央・総武線
各駅停車
Chūō・Sōbu Line (Local)
千駄ヶ谷・千葉方面
for Sendagaya & Chiba

CONTENTS

Fodor's Features

CONTENTS

MAPS

ABOUT THIS GUIDE

Fodor's Recommendations

Everything in this guide is worth doing—we don't cover what isn't—but exceptional sights, hotels, and restaurants are recognized with additional accolades. **Fodor's**Choice★ indicates our top recommendations; and **Best Bets** call attention to notable hotels and restaurants in various categories. Care to nominate a new place? Visit Fodors.com/contact-us.

Trip Costs

We list prices wherever possible to help you budget well. Hotel and restaurant price categories from **$** to **$$$$** are noted alongside each recommendation. For hotels, we include the lowest cost of a standard double room in high season. For restaurants, we cite the average price of a main course at dinner or, if dinner isn't served, at lunch. For attractions, we always list adult admission fees; discounts are usually available for children, students, and senior citizens.

Hotels

Our local writers vet every hotel to recommend the best overnights in each price category, from budget to expensive. Unless otherwise specified, you can expect private bath, phone, and TV in your room. For expanded hotel reviews, facilities, and deals visit Fodors.com.

Top Picks
★ **Fodor's**Choice

Listings
- Address
- Branch address
- Telephone
- Fax
- Website
- E-mail
- Admission fee
- Open/closed times
- Subway
- Directions or Map coordinates

Hotels & Restaurants
- Hotel
- Number of rooms
- Meal plans
- Restaurant
- Reservations
- Dress code
- No credit cards
- Price

Other
- See also
- Take note
- Golf facilities

Restaurants

Unless we state otherwise, restaurants are open for lunch and dinner daily. We mention dress code only when there's a specific requirement and reservations only when they're essential or not accepted.

Credit Cards

The hotels and restaurants in this guide typically accept credit cards. If not, we'll say so.

EUGENE FODOR

Hungarian-born Eugene Fodor (1905–91) began his travel career as an interpreter on a French cruise ship. The experience inspired him to write *On the Continent* (1936), the first guidebook to receive annual updates and discuss a country's way of life as well as its sights. Fodor later joined the U.S. Army and worked for the OSS in World War II. After the war, he kept up his intelligence work while expanding his guidebook series. During the Cold War, many guides were written by fellow agents who understood the value of insider information. Today's guides continue Fodor's legacy by providing travelers with timely coverage, insider tips, and cultural context.

EXPERIENCE TOKYO

1

TOKYO TODAY

Tokyo can often seem to have been frozen in time—especially in the traditions that underpin many Tokyoites' lives or the temples and gardens that have survived centuries of upheaval—yet in many ways the city never stands still, and change of some kind—gradual and rapid—is always afoot.

2020 Olympics

In 2013 Tokyo got the exciting news that it would host the 2020 summer games, beating out cities like Madrid and Buenos Aires. Tokyo was deemed a "safe" choice by much of the media, capable of hosting the world event without political drama or economic upheaval. The decision is also seen as a supportive rally by the international community after the devastation of the earthquake and tsunami in 2011. Overall, the city has embraced its role as host: 2020 posters have appeared all over the city, from *izakaya* to office buildings, and every current major redevelopment or government plan seems to be slated for completion by 2020.

The Green Movement

Japan still has a penchant for overpackaging and pesticides, but Tokyo is gradually becoming a greener city. In the last few years eco-friendly hybrid taxis have become a familiar sight in central Tokyo, while offices and public buildings have been sprouting rooftop gardens. After the energy shortages that followed the 2011 earthquake and tsunami, *setsuden* (energy saving) became a prominent buzzword. These efforts come to the fore in the summer months as people look for alternatives to energy-guzzling air-conditioning—look out for people growing "green curtains" (usually vinous plants) on their balconies to block out the heat of the midday sun. You will also see the eco-boom reflected in menus. While Japan still lags behind other developed nations when it comes to the production and consumption of organic produce, organic food is much easier to find than it once was in Tokyo's restaurants and cafés.

Dining

Judge a city by Michelin stars alone and Tokyo is the undisputed culinary capital of the world. In 2015, the guide handed out 303 stars to a total of 226 restaurants in Tokyo, double the number given to restaurants in Paris and New York combined. The culinary culture in Japan, however, runs far deeper than Michelin's elevated focus, and there's been a renewed appreciation among Japanese for what's been

ON THE CALENDAR

January Basho: This tournament at Kokugikan Sumo Hall sees the sport's best get in their first licks of the year. Two 15-day tournaments take place in the same venue in May and September.

Opening Day: Japan's 12 baseball teams kick off their season at the end of March. Tokyo teams include the Yakult Swallows and Yomiuri Giants, while the Chiba Lotte Marines, Seibu Lions, and Yokohama DeNA Baystars are based in neighboring prefectures.

Roppongi Art Night: In late April, Roppongi's numerous art venues stay open through the night and the streets are overrun with artists and revelers.

dubbed *B-kyu gurume* (literally B-grade gourmet)—low-cost, fairly no-frills dishes such as ramen and *okonomiyaki* (a savory pancake filled with various ingredients).

Pollution

A decade ago you would have struggled to find a smoke-free café or bar, but quite a shift has taken place in recent years. Although some coffee shop chains still only have token nonsmoking areas, where smoke from neighboring tables fills the air, the major international brands and many small, local cafés are frequently smoke-free or at least keep smokers in a separate, closed room or on different floors. Izakaya are as smoky as ever, yet a growing number of Tokyo's pubs and bars are smoke-free zones. Many of Tokyo's wards, including Chiyoda and Shinjuku, have also banned smoking on the street. This all ties in with a steady decline in cigarette sales in Japan, which has been aided by regular increases in the price of cigarettes in recent years. Japan's 30 million or so smokers still get through an incredible 20 billion cigarettes a year, but that number is still less than half the amount consumed in the mid-'90s.

Population

With a population of just over 13 million, Tokyo knows crowds. Commuters get squashed in the morning and evening rush hours, while shoppers in areas like Shibuya and Shinjuku are buffeted by shoulder bumps. But with an aging population and declining birthrate, Tokyo's population is soon expected to stop growing. It might peak at the 14 million mark in the next decade, but after that, one government report predicts there will be just 8 million Tokyoites by 2100.

Craft Beer

Sake and mass-produced beer brands like Asahi might be Japan's most famous tipples, but the country has started to embrace craft beer in recent years. To be fair, there have been small-scale brewers in Japan for years—some great, like Baird Brewing and the Shiga Kogen Brewery, others less so—but what's new is the number of places in Tokyo where hopheads can sample their wares. Joining older pubs, such as the magnificent Popeye in Ryogoku, are hip venues in Shibuya like Goodbeer Faucets, which is drawing a once unimaginable eclectic mix of drinkers to artisanal beer.

Sanja Festival: Asakusa's streets see dozens of portable shrines hoisted through huge crowds for three days in May.

Sumida River Fireworks: The skies of eastern Tokyo burst with color on the last Saturday of July.

Tokyo International Film Festival: Over 10 days in late October, more than 130 films from around the world are screened at the theaters in the Roppongi Hills complex.

WHAT'S WHERE

1 Imperial Palace District. This is the center of Tokyo, where Edo Castle once stood.

2 Akihabara. Akihabara is famed for its electronics stores, manga shops, video arcades, and cultish maid cafés.

3 Ueno and Yanaka. Ueno Park is home to three museums, a university of fine arts, and a zoo. Adjoining Yanaka is a charming old neighborhood with an abundance of temples.

4 Asakusa. The sacred merges with the secular and ancient tradition with modernity in Asakusa. The area is home to Tokyo's oldest temple, Senso-ji.

5 Tsukiji and Shiodome. Tsukiji is home to what is purportedly the world's largest fish market. Its neighbor, Shiodome, is a massive development zone, with plenty of shops, hotels, and restaurants.

6 Nihombashi, Ginza, and Marunouchi. Nihombashi lays claim as the geographical and financial center of Tokyo. Slightly southwest is Ginza, where you'll find Tokyo's traditional high-end stores and equally expensive restaurants. On the other side of Tokyo Station, Marunouchi is home to plush retail and office complexes.

7 Aoyama, Harajuku, and Shibuya. Aoyama and Harajuku are chic neighborhoods saturated with shopping options. To the south is Shibuya, an urban teen's dream packed with people and hip shops.

8 Roppongi. With a rich and sometimes sordid history of catering to foreign nightlife, Roppongi now has the massive Roppongi Hills and Tokyo Midtown developments.

9 Shinjuku. The train station here is supposedly the busiest in the world. And when the sun sets, the bars and clubs in the red-light area of Kabuki-cho come to life.

10 Odaiba. An artificial island in Tokyo Bay, Odaiba is an isolated hub for shops, restaurants, family-oriented amusements, and parks.

11 Greater Tokyo. Covering all of Tokyo plus large parts of its neighboring prefectures, the Greater Tokyo metropolitan area is home to destinations such as the ancient capital Kamakura and the port city of Yokohama.

12 Side Trips from Tokyo. Ancient temples, shrines, national parks, and Mt. Fuji are all day-trip options from Tokyo.

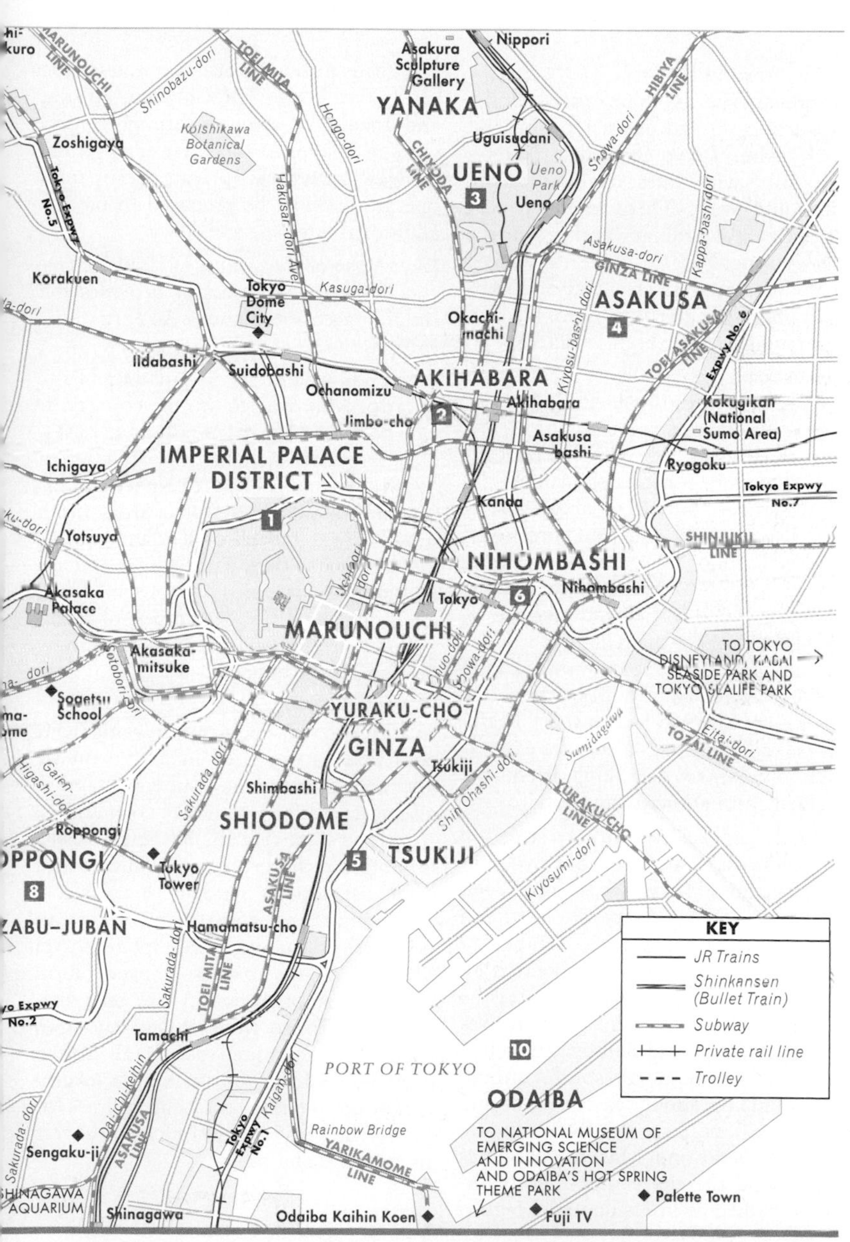
Nippori
Asakura Sculpture Gallery
YANAKA
Uguisudani
UENO
Ueno Park
Ueno
3
Zoshigaya
Koishikawa Botanical Gardens
Shinobazu-dori
MARUNOUCHI LINE
TOEI MITA LINE
Hongo-dori
CHIYODA LINE
HIBIYA LINE
Showa-dori
Tokyo Expwy No.5
Hakusan-dori Ave.
Kappa-bashi-dori
Asakusa-dori
GINZA LINE
Korakuen
Tokyo Dome City
Kasuga-dori
Okachi-machi
ASAKUSA
4
Kiyosu-bashi-dori
TOEI ASAKUSA LINE
Expwy No. 6
Iidabashi
Suidobashi
Ochanomizu
AKIHABARA
Akihabara
2
Jimbo-cho
Kokugikan (National Sumo Area)
Asakusa bashi
IMPERIAL PALACE DISTRICT
Ichigaya
Ryogoku
Tokyo Expwy No.7
Kanda
1
Yotsuya
SHINJUKU LINE
NIHOMBASHI
Uchibori-dori
Akasaka Palace
Tokyo
6
Nihombashi
MARUNOUCHI
Chuo-dori
Showa-dori
TO TOKYO DISNEYLAND, KASAI SEASIDE PARK AND TOKYO SEALIFE PARK
Akasaka-mitsuke
Sotobori-dori
Sogetsu School
YURAKU-CHO
GINZA
Sumidagawa
TOZAI LINE
Eitai-dori
Gaien-Higashi-dori
Sakurada-dori
Tsukiji
Shin Ohashi-dori
Shimbashi
YURAKU-CHO LINE
SHIODOME
Roppongi
ROPPONGI
Tokyo Tower
ASAKUSA LINE
5
TSUKIJI
Kiyosumi-dori
8
AZABU-JUBAN
Hamamatsu-cho
Sakurada-dori
TOEI MITA LINE
KEY
JR Trains
Shinkansen (Bullet Train)
Subway
Private rail line
Trolley
Tokyo Expwy No.2
Tamachi
10
PORT OF TOKYO
Dai-ichi-Keihin
Kaigan-dori
ODAIBA
Sakurada-dori
Sengaku-ji
ASAKUSA LINE
Tokyo Expwy No.1
Rainbow Bridge
YURIKAMOME LINE
TO NATIONAL MUSEUM OF EMERGING SCIENCE AND INNOVATION AND ODAIBA'S HOT SPRING THEME PARK
Palette Town
SHINAGAWA AQUARIUM
Shinagawa
Odaiba Kaihin Koen
Fuji TV

TRANSPORTATION PRIMER

Getting Around by Train

Shinkansen: The JR Shinkansen bullet trains travel up and down Honshu and into Kyushu. Tokyo Station is Tokyo's main hub, with lines heading north, south, and west. There are two seat classes offered: ordinary and green; the latter is roughly 30% more expensive, but the cars are less crowded and marginally more comfortable. Smoking and nonsmoking cars are both available.

Regional trains: About 70% of Japan's railways are owned by Japan Railways (JR Group), the other 30% are owned by private companies. In Tokyo, the Japan Railways Yamanote Line loops around the city, while its Sobu and Chuo lines split that circle into east and west directions. Tokyu's Toyoko Line travels between Shibuya Station and Yokohama to the south. For Tokyo Disneyland take the JR Keiyo Line east. The main line of the Odakyu company and Keio Inokashira Line use Shinjuku and Shibuya, respectively, as hubs to serve Tokyo to the west. Many of these rail companies also offer express trains, similar to the Shinkansen, for extended destinations away from Tokyo.

Subways: The easiest way to explore Tokyo is via subway. There are two subway companies: Tokyo Metro and Toei. Each system operates separate lines and has separate fares, and it's cheaper to complete a journey on lines operated by one company. Tokyo Metro operates the majority of lines. The Ginza Line moves between Asakusa and Shibuya, which is also served by the north–south-running Fukutoshin Line and the east–west-bound Hanzomon Line. Like the JR Yamanote Line, the Oedo and Marunouchi lines loop around the city center. The Namboku Line begins in residential Meguro and heads through Korakuen, the station for Tokyo Dome. The Chiyoda, Hibiya, and Tozai lines also cut through central parts of Tokyo. At the outer edges of the subway networks, private companies operate the line; be prepared to pay an additional fare.

Tokyo Monorail: Beginning at Hamamatsucho Station, the monorail provides the simplest access to Haneda Airport.

JR Pass

Japan Railways offers the Japan Rail Pass, an affordable way to see the country. It can be used on all JR railways, buses, and ferryboats including the Shinkansen "bullet" trains—except for Nozomi trains on the Tokaido and Sanyo Shinkansen lines. Slower Hikari or Kodama trains, however, serve these same routes and are included. Passes must be purchased at an authorized JR outlet outside of Japan before your trip and are available for 7-, 14-, or 21-day periods.

Prepaid Subway Cards

JR East offers **Suica**, a rechargeable debit card that can be used in Tokyo on JR and non-JR trains and subways, and is also accepted for payment at convenience stores and some vending machines. **PASMO** is another rechargeable prepaid card and offers the same as Suica. Both cards cost a nonrefundable ¥500 each, but it can be worth it for the flexibility to travel between all of Tokyo's transportation networks. Another option is to get a one-day pass; Tokyo Metro's **One-Day Open Ticket** gives unlimited use of all Tokyo Metro lines for ¥600, while the **Tokunai Pass** offers unlimited use of all JR lines for ¥750. The ¥1,590 **Tokyo Furii Kippu** covers JR subways and buses.

HOW TO USE A TICKET MACHINE

Use the map above the ticket machine to determine how much money to put on your ticket. The numbers next to each stop indicate the price from your current station.

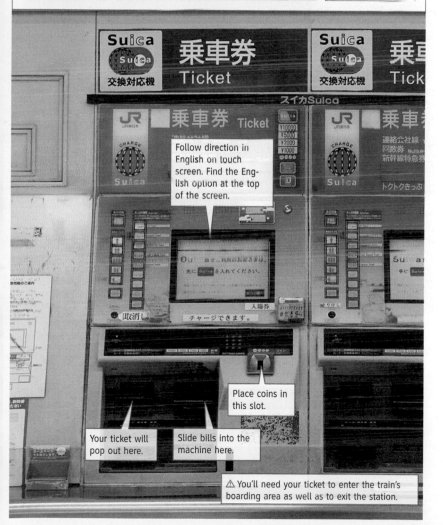

Follow direction in English on touch screen. Find the English option at the top of the screen.

Place coins in this slot.

Your ticket will pop out here.

Slide bills into the machine here.

⚠ You'll need your ticket to enter the train's boarding area as well as to exit the station.

TOKYO TOP ATTRACTIONS

Tokyo Skytree

At 2,092 feet in height, the world's second-tallest structure towers over eastern Tokyo, providing breathtaking views across the city from its observation decks. Opinion is split on the design merits of Tokyo Skytree and its white-metallic lattice frame, but what can't be disputed is how the communications tower and entertainment complex has transformed the city's skyline.

Tosho-gu Shrine

This beautiful UNESCO World Heritage–designated complex set within a forest in Nikko, 130 km (81 miles) north of Tokyo, is the mausoleum of Ieyasu Tokugawa, who began the Tokugawa Shogunate that reigned over the nation between 1603 and 1868. Decorated with gold leaf and numerous wood carvings, the compound also includes multiple Shinto and Buddhist buildings, many of which are acknowledged by the government as Important Cultural Properties.

Art Triangle Roppongi

Roppongi's two modern urban developments, the towering Roppongi Hills and Tokyo Midtown complexes, are home to several major art venues (Mori Art Museum, the Suntory Art Museum, and 21_21 Design Sight), while a short walk away is the sleekly designed National Art Center. This bastion of artistic and architectural gems hosts the fantastic Roppongi Art Night festival every spring.

Senso-ji (Senso Temple)

Tokyo's oldest temple—supposedly founded in the 600s to hold a statue of Kannon found by two fishermen in the nearby Sumida River—is a marvelous piece of architecture. On the way to the main building, visitors walk under two roofed gateways (one 40 feet high and the other 73 feet) that are separated by a colorful shopping street, before passing a five-story pagoda. All this makes the perfect backdrop for the numerous

festivals held here, including the Sanja Matsuri in May.

Tsukiji Fish Market

If it lives in the sea, chances are that it can be found at Tsukiji, affectionately referred to as "Tokyo's kitchen." Thousands of wholesalers and buyers broker deals for crabs piled in buckets, squirming eels, bagged clams, and endless varieties of fish at this chaotic market.

Takeshita-dori in Harajuku

This pedestrian-only street outside JR Harajuku Station features various shops selling some of Japan's trendiest and most garish clothing to swarms of Tokyo youth. Since the target is teenagers, prices are low, at least in comparison to the upscale boutiques found in nearby Aoyama and Omotesando. Takeshita-dori is only about 500 yards long, but the shopping hordes are so dense and relentless on weekends that it can take 20 minutes to navigate from one end to the other.

Mt. Fuji

At an elevation of 12,388 feet, Mt. Fuji is the nation's highest peak. It's also one of Japan's most famous symbols and is a point of inspiration for the Japanese and their visitors. The dormant volcano sits between Yamanashi and Shizuoka prefectures, dominating the skyline from miles away. In nice weather, it can also be viewed from Tokyo and Yokohama. For a closer peek, head to the Hakone region or Fuji Five Lakes area; you can also climb it in summer or see it from a Shinkansen bullet train traveling between Tokyo and Kyoto.

TOP EXPERIENCES

Stay at a ryokan

The *ryokan* offers one of Japan's most unforgettable experiences. The rooms at these traditional inns are outfitted with Japanese-style interiors, such as tatami flooring, sliding screen doors, and paper (*shoji*) blinds, while floor cushions and small tables make sitting for the in-room tea service and multicourse dinner comfortable. At bedtime, futons are rolled out onto the tatami. The room rate usually includes breakfast and dinner. Hakone, near Mt. Fuji, has a wonderful selection of these inns, as do the Fuji Five Lakes area and Nikko; these are all easily reached from Tokyo.

Relax in a Japanese garden

Gardens in the traditional Japanese style can be found across Tokyo, from standalone landscaped gardens featuring stone lanterns, rocks, ponds, and rolling hedges, such as Kiyosumi Teien and Hamarikyu, to smaller affairs attached to shrines and temples or found on castle grounds. Many of the principles that influence Japanese garden design come from religion. Shintoism, Taoism, and Buddhism all stress the contemplation and re-creation of nature as part of the process of achieving understanding and enlightenment.

Sing some karaoke

Karaoke is a Japanese institution and its rabid popularity cannot be understated. Whether after work or with the whole family, millions of locals enjoy this recreation, in which they sing popular songs into a microphone as the instrumental track plays on the in-room sound system and its lyrics roll across a monitor. Rooms, referred to as karaoke boxes, can be rented by the hour and seat between 2 and 10 customers. Choose a song from the song selection book, fortify yourself for your performance with drinks and light snacks, and let loose your inner diva.

Taste seafood and sushi

As might be expected of a nation consisting of more than 4,000 islands, Japan is synonymous with the fruits of the sea. Sashimi and sushi have gained popularity with restaurant-goers around the world, but it's hard to imagine some other so-called delicacies catching on. The northern island of Hokkaido boasts of the quality of its creamy *uni* (sea urchin), while Akita Prefecture is famous for *shiokara* (raw squid intestines). In Tokyo, you can see just about anything that lives in the sea at the fish market at Tsukiji. Domestic tourism and television schedules are dominated by food, and it's not uncommon for city dwellers to travel the length and breadth of the country on weekend excursions to taste regional specialties.

Participate in a tea ceremony

The tea ceremony, or *chanoyu* (the way of tea), is a precisely choreographed program that started more than 1,000 years ago with Zen monks. The ritual begins as the server prepares a cup of tea for the first guest. This process involves a strictly determined series of movements and actions, including the cleansing of each utensil to be used. One by one, the participants slurp up their bowl of tea and then eat a sweet confectionary served with it. In Tokyo, the teahouse at Hamarikyu Gardens offers a wonderful chance to enjoy this tradition. Some hotels, such as the New Otani and Imperial Hotel, also have tearooms where you can try the ceremony with English guidance.

Sip o-sake

Whether you're out with friends, with clients, or belting out a tune at the local karaoke bar, you're sure to have a drink at least once during your stay. Rice-based sake, pronounced *sa*-kay, is the alcoholic beverage most associated with Japan, and more than 2,000 different brands are available. The sake bar Amanogawa, in the Keio Plaza Hotel Tokyo, provides a wonderful opportunity to sample different varieties. *Shochu,* a much stronger drink than sake at 20% to 40% ABV, is usually made from grain or potato and is served straight, on the rocks, or mixed with juice or water. As for beer, Asahi and Kirin are the two heavyweights, constantly battling for the coveted title of Japan's leading brewer, but many beer fans rate Suntory's The Premium Malts brand and Sapporo's Yebisu brand as the tastiest mass produced brews in the land. Be sure to try some of Japan's fantastic craft beers at specialist bars like Goodbeer Faucets in Shibuya or Beer Club Popeye in Ryogoku.

Take a dip in an onsen

Soaking in an *onsen* (hot spring bath) is one of Japan's greatest and oldest pleasures. The country's earliest records contain accounts of onsen bathing by both humans and animals. The tradition has endured partly because the mineral-rich waters, which are found all over Japan, are said to alleviate all manner of ailments. More than that, immersing yourself in the piping hot water just feels so good, whether it's at one of Tokyo's onsen theme parks, like Oedo Onsen Monogatari or LaQua, or soaking surrounded in nature in Hakone and Nikko, where most of the ryokan have natural hot spring baths.

Chow down at a basement food hall

Entire basement floors (*depachika*) of many Japanese department stores (*depato*) are often occupied by grocery sections featuring high-end food. Entire sections are dedicated to fish (including sushi), meats, cheese, and tea. At least one bakery will serve fresh baguettes, and there will be dozens selling fine chocolates and patisseries. Imported foods, like German sausages, are here as well, often alongside regional specialties from various parts of Japan. Many of the deli counters will have free bite-size samples available, which makes for a great way to try some local flavors.

Watch a sumo match

Sumo pits two extremely large athletes against each other in a ring (*dohyo*). A wrestler who breaches the ring's boundary or touches the ground with a body part (other than the sole of his foot) loses. Originally intended as entertainment for Shinto gods, single bouts usually last less than a minute. Tournaments, running 15 days, are held three times a year in Tokyo. Novice wrestlers (*jonokuchi*) compete in the morning and top athletes (*ozeki* and *yokozuna*) wrestle in the late afternoon. Crowds get pretty boisterous, especially for the later matches.

A WALK THROUGH EVERYDAY TOKYO

Tokyo's soul is found in its *shitamachi,* the neighborhoods that define much of the city's east side. Spend a few hours walking here to discover old neighborhoods, ancient temples, and cultural riches.

Yanaka

The central shopping street **Yanaka Ginza** is crammed with mom-and-pop stores and small eateries that feel as if they've remained unchanged since the Meiji era of the late 1860s through the early 1910s. Leave behind Yanaka's main street and you will soon be lost in a captivating maze of back alleys that lead past quiet temples and shrines, many eventually skirting the sprawling **Yanaka Cemetery,** a beautiful spot in cherry blossom season. The last of the Tokugawa shoguns is buried here, as are many other colorful characters in Tokyo's history.

Ueno

Walking southeast from Yanaka, it's a fairly short walk to **Ueno Park** (or you can walk to JR Nippori Station and take the Yamanote Line to Ueno). Here you'll find the city's biggest zoo, an ancient temple, and plenty of green spaces, but the main reason the park stands out is the museums that dot the grounds. On the north end, **Tokyo National Museum** holds an unparalleled collection of Japanese and Asian artifacts, dating from as far back as the Jomon period. Moving south, the **National Science Museum** is a great hands-on stop for kids, while at the southern end of the park the **Shitamachi Museum** does a wonderful job of revealing the history and development of Tokyo's working-class areas. Across the road from the park's southeast end, the vendors of the bustling **Ameyoko** street market sell everything from knock-off designer clothing to fine teas.

Kappabashi

Leaving Ueno and walking east, the next highlight is Kappabashi. In the early 1900s, merchants selling culinary wares began to converge on this half-mile-long street, and it is now where Tokyo's restaurant trade goes to stock up on everything from disposable chopsticks to hanging lanterns. Among the 170 shops here are several that specialize in the plastic replicas of food that many restaurants display in their windows. The most famous of these, **Maizuru**, near the southern end of the street, has been selling realistic mock-ups of sushi, pints of lager, and the like for more than 50 years.

Asakusa

East of Kappabashi's southern end is Asakusa. At the heart of this district is the mighty **Senso temple complex**, with its grand five-story pagoda, giant gateways, and colorful street stalls. A several-minute walk west of Senso's main temple building is **Hanayashiki**, a tiny amusement park that's home to Japan's oldest roller coaster. In the streets south of Hanayashiki are historic theaters like **Engei Hall,** which, like Hanayashiki, serve as reminders of Asakusa's prewar days as Tokyo's main entertainment district. The *yakitori-ya* that spill out on the street around here are great places to grab some grilled chicken and a beer and rest your feet.

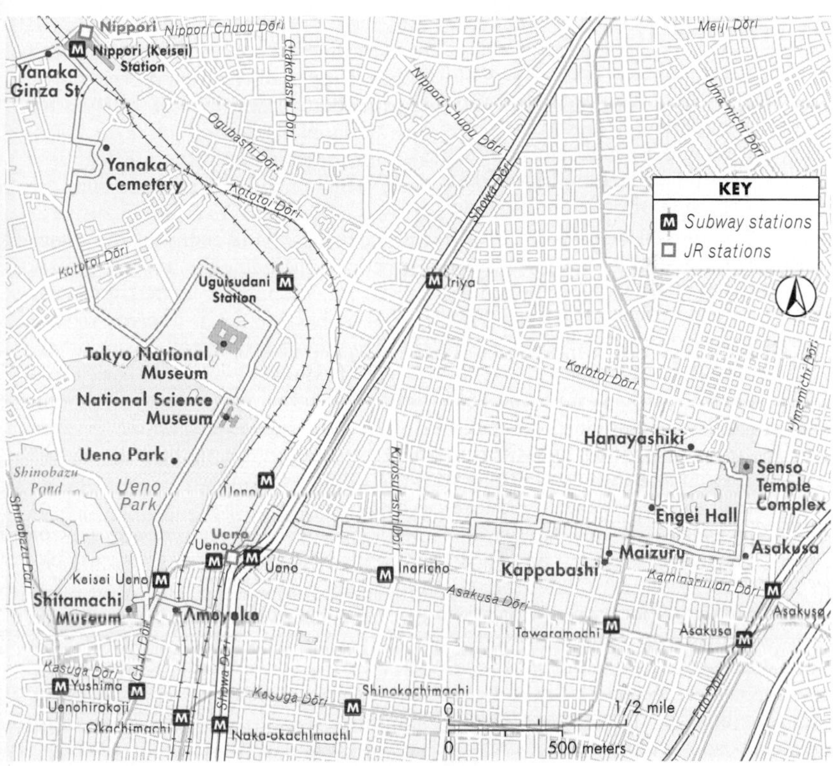

Highlights	The old, narrow streets of Yanaka, the museums and street market of Ueno, the culinary-ware stores of Kappabashi, historic Senso-ji, and the historic Asakusa district.
Where to Start	Start at the Yanaka Ginza shopping street, a couple of minutes' walk from the west exit of Nippori Station on the JR Yamanote Line.
Time/Length	6 km (4 miles); duration about 3 hours without food stops.
Where to End	At Asakusa Station on the Ginza Line.
Best Time to Go	Weekdays are best to avoid the worst crowds.
Worst Time to Go	Mid-July to mid-September, when the summer heat and humidity can make being outside for more than 10 minutes very unpleasant.
Getting Around	The walk is best done entirely on foot, but an alternative is to take the Ginza subway line from Ueno Station to Kappabashi (Tawaramachi Station) and from there to Asakusa Station.

GREAT ITINERARIES

TOKYO IN 3 DAYS

Tokyo is a metropolis that confounds with its complexity: 35 million people occupy a greater metropolitan area that includes soaring towers of glass and steel, rolling expressways, numerous temples, parks, and mile after mile of concrete housing blocks. Since the end of World War II, the city has constantly reinvented itself. Few things have remained static other than Tokyo's preeminence as Japan's economic center.

Day 1: Tsukiji & Daiwa Sushi

Start *very* early with a visit to the **Fish Market** in the Tsukiji district to catch the lively tuna auctions and then taste the finest, freshest sushi at **Daiwa Sushi.** Take a morning stroll through **Ginza** to explore its fabled shops and *depato* (department stores). Then hit a chic restaurant or café for lunch (more reasonably priced ones are found on the upper floors of most department stores). The skyscrapers of **Shiodome** are just down the street, in the direction of **Shimbashi.** Take a peek on the first floor of the **Shiodome Media Tower**; aerial photographs show Ginza as it was roughly 100 years ago—a network of canals. In the skyscrapers' shadows are the charming Hama Rikyu Tei-en Gardens, whose pathways and ponds are ideal for a late-afternoon stroll. In the evening, head back up toward Ginza and enjoy *yakitori* (grilled chicken) at one of the many small restaurants under the elevated railway lines in **Yurakucho**.

Day 2: Asakusa and Ueno

Spend the morning at **Senso-ji** and adjacent **Asakusa Jinja** in Asakusa. If you're looking for souvenir gifts—sacred or secular—allow time and tote space for the abundant selection the local vendors along **Nakamise-dori** have to offer. A 10-minute walk west is **Kappabashi**, a street dedicated to outfitting restaurants and bars with dishes, cups, chopsticks, and even plastic food models. From there go to **Ueno** for an afternoon of museums, markets, vistas, and historic sites, and take a break at **Ueno Park**. Keep in mind that in the evening the crowds in Asakusa are not as intrusive as during the day, and many of the major attractions, including the five-tier pagoda of Senso-ji, are brightly lighted. It's worth it to loop back to get a different view of the area and end the evening with dinner at one of Asakusa's izakaya (basically, a drinking den that serves food).

Day 3: Shibuya and Shinjuku

Start off at Shibuya's **Hachiko Square** and the famous "Scramble Crossing" intersection and hit nearby stores like **Shibuya 109**, which is crammed with teen fashion boutiques. Inside the station building is the once-lost masterpiece by avant-garde artist **Taro Okamoto**, *Myth of Tomorrow*, while towering over the east side of the station is the 34-story **Shibuya Hikarie building**, one of the latest redevelopments filled with shops, restaurants, and businesses to hit Tokyo. In the afternoon see the Shinto shrine, **Meiji Jingu**, and walk through the nearby Harajuku and **Omotesando** fashion districts. Spend the rest of the afternoon on the west side of **Shinjuku**, Tokyo's 21st-century model city, and savor the view from the observation deck of architect Kenzo Tange's monumental **Tokyo Metropolitan Government Office**; cap off the day by visiting **Shinjuku Gyo-en National Garden**. For those seeking a bit of excitement, the red-light district of **Kabuki-cho**, just to the east of **JR Shinjuku Station**, comes alive once the sun goes down; Kabuki-cho and neighboring Golden Gai are full of good places to eat and drink.

TOKYO IN 5 DAYS

Add these two days onto the three-day itinerary.

Day 4: Akihabara and Imperial Palace

Spend the morning browsing in **Akihabara**, Tokyo's electronics quarter, and see the nearby Shinto shrine **Kanda Myojin**. In the afternoon, tour the **Imperial Palace** and the grounds surrounding it. The **Chidorigafuchi National Cemetery** has a wonderful park and a boat-rental facility—both great for unwinding. If the **Yomiuri Giants** are in town, catch a game at **Tokyo Dome** in the evening. If not, try a traditional hot spring bath or ride the roller coaster at LaQua amusement park next to Tokyo Dome.

Day 5: Get Out of Town to Kamakura

For a different perspective of Japan, spend a day out of Tokyo. Easily accessible by train is **Kamakura**, the 13th-century military capital of the country. The **Great Buddha** (Daibutsu) of **Kotoku-in Temple** in nearby **Hase** is but one of many National Treasures of art and architecture in and around Kamakura. An early start will allow you to see most of the important sights in a full day and make it back to Tokyo by late evening. As Kamakura is one of the most popular of excursions from Tokyo, avoid the worst of the crowds by going on a weekday, but time it to avoid rush-hour commuting that peaks roughly at 8 am and just after 6 pm.

If You Have More Time

With a week or more, you can make Tokyo your base for more side trips (*see Chapter 9, Side Trips from Tokyo*). An easy day trip is to take a train out to **Yokohama**, with its scenic port and Chinatown. Farther off, but again an easy train trip, is **Nikko**, where the founder of the Tokugawa Shogun dynasty is enshrined. The decadently designed **Tosho-gu** shrine complex is a monument unlike any other in Japan, and the picturesque **Lake Chuzenji** is in forests nearby. Two full days, with an overnight stay, would allow you an ideal, leisurely exploration of both. Another option would be a trip to **Hakone**, where you can soak in a traditional onsen or climb to the summit of **Fuji-san** (Mt. Fuji). You could also potter around Tokyo some more to fill in the missing pieces: see the Buddhist temple, **Sengaku-ji**, in Shinagawa; the remarkable **Edo-Tokyo Hakubutsukan** in Ryogoku; a tea ceremony; a Kabuki play; or a sumo tournament, if one is in town. Or head to Odaiba in Tokyo Bay for attractions that include the **National Museum of Emerging Science and Innovation**, **Palette Town's** malls and Ferris wheel, and the **Oedo Onsen** baths.

WHEN TO GO

Spring and fall are the best times to visit. *Sakura* (cherry blossoms) begin blooming in Tokyo by early April, while fall has clear blue skies, albeit punctuated by the occasional typhoon. The short *tsuyu* (rainy season) in June brings humidity and rain that can linger into early July. July and August bring heat, mostly blue skies, and stifling humidity. Winter can be gray and chilly some days, mild and sunny others, with Tokyo and other areas along the coast receiving very little snow. Japanese vacation during three holiday periods: the few days before and after New Year's; Golden Week in early May; and the mid-August week for Obon. Travel's not advised during these times, as plane and train tickets book up fast.

JAPANESE ETIQUETTE

Many Japanese expect foreigners to behave differently and are tolerant of faux pas, but they are pleasantly surprised when people acknowledge and observe their customs. The easiest way to ingratiate yourself with the Japanese is to take time to learn and respect Japanese ways.

General Tips

■ Bow upon meeting someone, but don't go over the top. Outside of formal situations a slight nod of the head will suffice.

■ Pointing at someone is considered rude. To make reference to someone or something, gently wave your hand up and down in his or her direction.

■ Direct expression of opinions isn't encouraged. It's more common for people to gently suggest something.

■ Avoid physical contact with people you don't know closely. A slap on the back or hand on the shoulder could be uncomfortable for a Japanese person.

■ Avoid too much eye contact when speaking. Direct eye contact is a show of aggression and rudeness.

At Someone's Home

■ Most entertaining is done in restaurants and bars. Don't be offended if you're not invited to someone's home.

■ Should an invitation be extended, a small gift—perhaps a bottle of alcohol or box of sweets, ideally from your country—should be presented.

■ At the entryway, remove your shoes and put on the provided slippers (if any). Remove your slippers if you enter a room with tatami flooring. Before entering the bathroom, remove your house slippers and switch to those found near the bathroom doorway.

■ It's not customary for Japanese businessmen to bring wives along. If you're traveling with your spouse, don't assume that an invitation includes both of you. If you want to bring your spouse, ask in a way that eliminates the need for a direct refusal.

While Shopping

■ After entering a store, the staff will greet you with *irasshaimase,* which is a welcoming phrase. A simple smile is an appropriate acknowledgment. After that, polite requests to view an item or try on a piece of clothing should be followed as anywhere in the West. Bargaining is common at flea markets, but not in regular stores.

■ There's usually a plastic tray at the register for you to place your money or credit card. Your change and receipt, however, will usually be placed in your hand. It should be noted that many small shops do not accept credit cards.

Giving Gifts

■ Gift giving is a year-round national pastime, peaking during summer's *ochugen* and the year-end *oseibo*. Common gifts between friends, family, and associates include elegantly wrapped packages of fruit, noodles, or beer.

■ On Valentine's Day, women give men chocolate, but on White Day in March the roles are reversed. On both of these days it's common to give small gifts to coworkers and friends, not just partners.

■ For weddings and funerals, cash gifts are the norm. Convenience stores carry special envelopes in which the money (always crisp, new bills) should be inserted.

BUDGET TRAVEL TIPS

Tokyo can be painfully expensive, but here are some tips that can help ease the strain on the travel budget.

Lodging

Big Western or Japanese hotel chains can be expensive, but Japan also has "business hotels" that provide small, basic rooms at very reasonable prices. Look out for chains like Toyoko Inn, Dormy Inn, and Comfort Inn. With some business hotel chains, you can get discounted rates by signing up for free membership cards. For example, Toyoko Inn's membership card offers 20% off on Sunday and 5% off on other days.

Another saving option, if you or someone you know can read Japanese, is to book via a hotel's own Japanese website, which usually gives the best rates and options.

If there are four of you traveling together, youth hostels can be an attractive budget option—rooms are often set up for four people, so there will be no sharing with strangers. Hostels also tend to be very clean, usually offer meals at a good price, and are often in popular tourist areas.

Transportation

If you are traveling around Japan, the JR Pass will save you a fortune in fares and allow you to use most Shinkansen services. It will also get you on JR sleeper trains, which can save on accommodation costs. If you are just planning a weekend out of Tokyo, stop by a major train station and ask about passes for the area. The Hakone Free Pass, which can be bought at Shinjuku Station, covers the train fare to and from Hakone on the Odakyu Line as well as unlimited use of otherwise expensive buses, sightseeing boats, cable cars, and local trains for two or three days in Hakone.

Food

Eating takeout from department store basement food halls is an excellent way to save money. You will save even more if you wait until an hour before closing, when many prepared foods are marked down 25%–50%. Even better deals on ready-made lunches and dinners can be found at supermarkets like Aeon and Ito Yokado (and many smaller local ones) and convenience stores like Lawson and 7-Eleven. They all sell bento and pasta dishes for under ¥500, as well as *onigiri* (rice balls) and sandwiches for under ¥500.

To save on higher-end dining, eat at lunch. Many expensive restaurants do smaller, but still extremely good, lunches at a fraction of the price of their evening courses.

Shopping

For deals on the (almost) latest Japanese cameras and accessories, try somewhere like Map Camera in Shinjuku. Many Japanese amateur photographers frequently upgrade to the newest models, so you will find plenty of very modern but well-priced used gear in great condition.

For more bargain-hunting, head to the Ameyoko Street Market by JR Ueno Station. You can find everything from the freshest seafood to a can of Spam, real Rolex watches to fake Gucci bags, and everything else in between, lots of it at fairly decent prices.

Flea markets can also be a good place to find great souvenirs at budget-friendly prices. There's a major antiques market held the first and third Sunday of the month at Tokyo International Forum in Yurakucho, as well as many other flea markets set up at shrines, such as the Sunday market at Hanazono Jinja in Shinjuku.

TOKYO LIKE A LOCAL

Izakaya

Wining and dining, cocktails with class, clubbing and carousing—you'll find it all, and more, beneath Tokyo's neon-soaked night sky. Of all the drinking options nothing is as local as an izakaya—Japan's answer to the English pub. These ubiquitous watering holes provide a great way to mix with locals and sample a wide range of food and drinks. Shinjuku, Shimbashi, and Yurakucho are particularly good izakaya hunting grounds.

Shin Hinomoto (aka Andy's Place), Yurakucho. There are no issues with language barriers at this bustling izakaya under the railway tracks in Yurakucho. It's a quintessential izakaya with fish sourced daily at Tsukiji market, albeit run by a Brit.

Kamiya Bar, Asakusa. The convivial locals make this old-fashioned pub a great place to soak up the shitamachi atmosphere, especially if you loosen up with some Denki Bran, a mix of brandy, gin, and curaçao first served here in the 1880s.

Onsen

Japan is perched on a geothermal gold mine and onsen are everywhere. Locals have made bathing in these hot springs a near-ritualistic experience, with unique healing properties attributed to the water. These baths are more about self-pampering than getting clean, but give yourself a thorough shower and rinse before your soak, as proper etiquette demands it. There are indoor and outdoor pools of different sizes, with varying temperatures to choose from, but the ones outside are best if you want to admire the natural setting.

Oedo Onsen Monogatari, Odaiba. This onsen near Yurikamome Telecom Center Station on the Yurikamome Line pays homage to this tradition at an Edo period–style facility with all the trimmings; it's the city's finest.

Hakone Kowakien Yunessun Resort, Kanagawa Prefecture. Just 90 minutes by train from Tokyo, Hakone is famed for its abundance of onsen resorts and inns, from the budget to the lavish. The resort offers an exquisite traditional onsen, a water amusement park, and bathing-suit-only grounds. Visitors can even soak in green tea and sake.

Baseball

It's fair to say that baseball is as much a national pastime in Japan as it is in the United States. The Japanese have adopted and adapted the sport in a way that makes it a fascinating and easy-to-grasp microcosm of both their culture and their relationship to the West. The team names alone—the Yakult Swallows and the Hiroshima Carp, for example—amuse Westerners accustomed to such monikers as the Yankees and Indians, and the fans' cheers are more in unison than in United States ballparks. The season runs from late March through October. Same-day baseball game tickets are hard to come by for the most popular teams, such as Tokyo's Yomiuri Giants; try the respective stadiums or various ticket agencies. You can buy tickets for most events at convenience stores, such as Lawson, 7-Eleven, and Family Mart. Depending on the stadium, the date, and the seat location, expect to pay from ¥1,500 to ¥8,000.

ISOLATION AND ENGAGEMENT: A HISTORY OF JAPAN

By Robert Morel

A century and a half after opening its shores to outsiders, Japan is still a mystery to many Westerners. Often misunderstood, Japan's history is much deeper than the stereotypes of samurai and geisha, overworked businessmen, and anime. Its long tradition of retaining the old while embracing the new has captivated visitors for centuries.

Much of Japanese history has consisted of the ongoing tension between its seeming isolation from the rest of the world and a desire to be a part of it. During the Edo period, Japan was closed to foreigners for some 250 years. Yet while the country has always had a strong national identity, it has also had a rapacious appetite for all things foreign. Just 50 years after opening its borders, parts of Tokyo looked like London, and Japan had become a colonial power in Asia. Much earlier, the Japanese imported Buddhism, tea, and their first writing system from China.

In the 19th century, the country incorporated Western architecture, technology, and government. More recently, the Japanese have absorbed Western fashion, music, and pop culture. Nevertheless, the country's history lives on in local traditions, festivals, temples, cities, music, and the arts.

Senso-ji Complex in Tokyo's Asakusa neighborhood

593–622 Prince Shotoku encourages the Japanese to embrace Chinese culture

710–784 Japan has first permanent capital at Nara

500 | 650 | 800 | 950

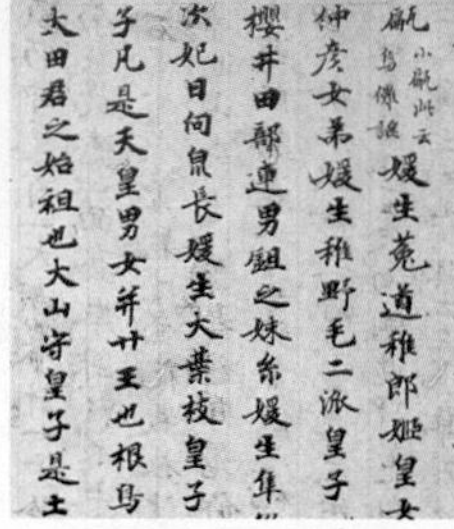

甂小甂此云烏儒誤媛生菟道稚郎姫皇女
仲彥女弟媛生稚野毛二派皇子
櫻井田部連男鉏之妹糸媛生隼總
次妃日向泉長媛生大葉枝皇子
子凡是天皇男女并廿王也根鳥
大田君之始祖也大山守皇子是土

(top) Horyu-ji Inner Gate and pagoda, (bottom) Nihon Shoki, (right) Large Buddha statue at Todai-ji Temple

10,000 BC–AD 622 Ancient Japan

The first people in Japan were the hunters and fishers of the Jomon period, known for their pottery. In the following Yayoi period, hunting and fishing gave way to agriculture, as well as the introduction of rice farming and metalworking. Around AD 500 the Yamato tribe consolidated power in what is now the Kansai plain, with Yamato leaders claiming descent from the sun goddess Amaretsu and taking the title of emperor. Prince Shotoku promoted the spread of Buddhism from China and commissioned Horyu-ji Temple in Nara in 607.

- Horyu-ji Temple (Nara)
- National Museum (Tokyo)

710–784 Nara Period

As Japan's first permanent capital and urban center, Nara is often considered the birthplace of Japanese culture. Under the Emperor Shomu, who commissioned the Great Buddha at Todai-ji Temple, Buddhism rose to prominence. The first Japanese written histories, the *Kojiki* and *Nihon Shoki,* were compiled during this period, as was the *Manyoshu,* Japan's first collection of poetry. Since the country was the Eastern terminus of the Silk Road, Japan's royal family amassed an impressive collection of treasures from mainland Asia, many of which are still on display at Todai-ji Temple's Shoso-in.

- The Great Buddha at Todai-ji Temple (Nara)

794–1160 Heian Period

Partly to escape intrigues and the rising power of the Nara's Buddhist Priests, in 794 the Emperor Kammu moved the capital to Heian-kyo (now Kyoto). *Heian* translates roughly as "peace and tranquility," and during this time the Imperial court expanded its power throughout Japan. Inside the court, however, life was far from calm. This was a period of great courtly intrigue, and struggles for power between aristocrats, the powerful Fujiwara clan (the most powerful of Japan's four great noble families), and the new military class known as *bushi.* Though some emperors managed to maintain control of the court, the Heian period saw the

794–1160 The capital is moved from Nara to Heian-kyo (now Kyoto)

1467–77 The Onin Wars initiate a 100-year period of civil war

1100 | 1250 | 1400 | 1550

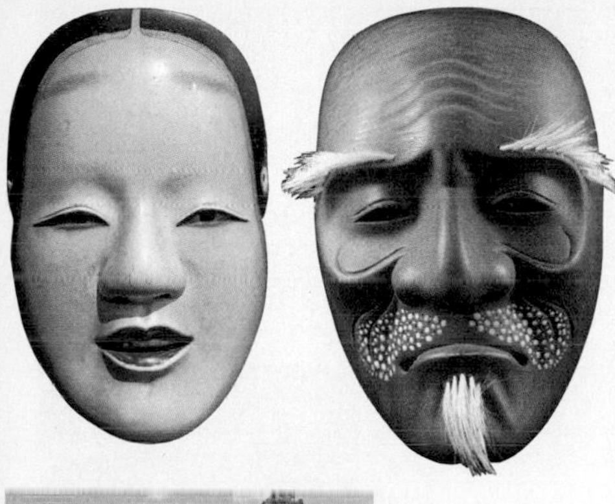

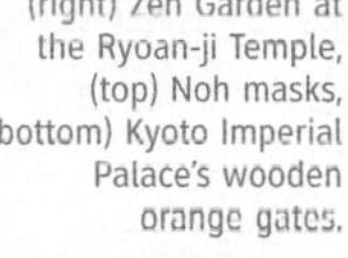

(right) Zen Garden at the Ryoan-ji Temple, (top) Noh masks, (bottom) Kyoto Imperial Palace's wooden orange gates.

slow rise of the military class, leading to a series of wars that established them as the ruling class until well into the 19th century. Considered Japan's great classical period, this was a time when courtly arts flourished. The new Japanese *kana* script gave rise to a boom in literature. Compiled in 990, Sei Shonagon's *Pillow Book* gave a window into courtly life, and Shibuki Murasaki's *Tale of Genji* is often regarded as the world's first classic novel. Japanese *waka* poetry experienced a revival, breeding the new forms of poetry such as *tanka* that are still in use today.

- The Imperial Palace (Kyoto)

1185–1335 Kamakura Period

As the Imperial Court lost control, the Genpei War (1180–1185) resulted in the defeat of clans loyal to the emperor in Kyoto and the rise of a new government in Kamakura. Yoritomo Minamoto named himself *Sei-i Tai Shogun* and established the *Kamakura bakufu*, a spartan military government. During this time, Japan repelled two Mongol invasions, thanks to timely typhoons that were later dubbed *kamikaze*, or divine wind. In this militaristic climate, Zen Buddhism, with its focus on self-reliance and discipline, exploded in popularity.

- Eihiji Temple (Fukushima)
- Hachimangu Shrine and the Great Buddha (Kamakura)

1336–1568 Muromachi (Ashikaga) Period

The heyday of the samurai, the Muromachi period was one of near constant civil war. Feudal lords known as *daimyo* consolidated their power in local fiefdoms. Peasant rebellions and piracy were common. Nevertheless, trade flourished. The movement of armies required *daimyo* to build roads, while improved communications gave birth to many merchant and artisan guilds. Trade with China grew, and in 1543 Portugal began trading with Japan, introducing firearms and Christianity. Noh theater and the tea ceremony were founded, and Kyoto's most famous temples were built in this period.

- Kinkaku-ji Temple (Kyoto)
- Ryoan-ji Temple (Kyoto)

TIMELINE

1637 Japan is closed to the outside world except for a Dutch trading post in Nagasaki

1720 Ban on Western literature lifed

1600 | 1650 | 1700 | 1750

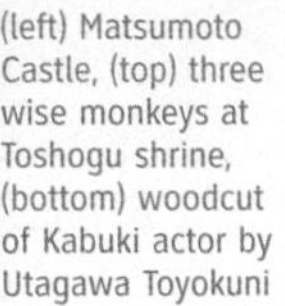

(left) Matsumoto Castle, (top) three wise monkeys at Toshogu shrine, (bottom) woodcut of Kabuki actor by Utagawa Toyokuni

1568–1600 National Unification (Momoyama Period)

In 1568 Oda Nobunaga, a lord from Owari in central Japan, marched on Kyoto and took the title of Shogun. He controlled the surrounding territories until his death in 1582, when his successor, Toyotomi Hideyoshi, became the new Shogun. After unifying much of central and western Japan, he attempted unsuccessful invasions of Korea before his death in 1598. In 1600 Tokugawa Ieyasu, a top general, defeated Hideyoshi's successor in the battle of Sekihagara.

- Osaka Castle (Osaka)
- Matsumoto Castle (Matsumoto)

1600–1867 Edo (Tokugawa) Period

The Edo period ushered in 250 years of relative stability and central control. After becoming Shogun, Ieyasu Tokugawa moved the capital to Edo (present-day Tokyo). A system of *daimyo*, lords beholden to the Shogun, was established along with a rigid class system and legal code of conduct. Although Japan cut off trade with the outside world, cities flourished. By the mid-18th century, Edo's population had grown to more than 1 million, and urban centers like Osaka and Kyoto had become densely populated. Despite such rapid growth, urban life in the Edo period was highly organized, with districts managed by neighborhood associations that have persisted (in a modified way) to the present day. Popular entertainment and arts arose to satisfy the thriving merchant and artisan classes. Kabuki, flashy and sensational, overtook Noh theater in popularity, and Japan's famed "floating world" (*ukio*), with its theaters, drinking houses, and geishas emerged. Sumo, long a Shinto tradition, became a professional sport. Much of what both Japanese and foreigners consider "Japanese culture" dates to this period. But by 1853, the Shogun's hold on power was growing tenuous.

- Toshogu (Nikko)
- Katsura Imperial Villa (Kyoto) Muhammad Ali Mosque

1800	1850	1900	1950
	1853 U.S. Commodore Matthew Perry reopens Japan to foreign trade	1868 Meiji Restoration begins	1941 Japan attacks Pearl Harbor

(top) Tokyo University, (left) wedding in Meiji Shrine, (bottom) A6M5 fighter plane at Yusyukan museum.

1868–1912 Meiji Period

The Tokugawa Shogunate's rigid class system and legal code proved to be its undoing. After U.S. Commodore Matthew Perry opened Japan to trade in March 1854, the following years were turbulent. In 1868, the last Shogun, Tokugawa Yoshinobu, ceded power to Emperor Meiji, and Japan began to modernize after 250 years of isolation. Adopting a weak parliamentary system from Germany, rulers moved quickly to develop national industry and universities. Victories over China and Russia also emboldened Japan.

- Tokyo University (Tokyo)
- Heian Shrine (Kyoto)
- Nara National Musuem (Nara)

1912–1925 Taisho Period

In the early 20th century, urban Japan was beginning to look a lot Europe and North America.

Fashion ranged from traditional *yukata* and kimono to zoot suits and bobbed hair. In 1923 the Great Kanto Earthquake and its resulting fires destroyed Yokohama and much of Tokyo. Although city planners saw this as an opportunity to modernize Tokyo's maze of streets, residents were quick to rebuild, ensuring that many neighborhood maps look much the same today as they did a century ago.

- Asakusa (Tokyo)
- The Shitamachi Museum (Tokyo)
- Meiji Shrine (Tokyo)

1926–1945 Wartime Japan

Although Japan was was increasingly liberal throughout the 1920s, the economic shocks of the 1930s helped the military gain greater control, resulting in crackdowns on left-leaning groups, the press, and dissidents. In 1931 Japan invaded Manchuria; in 1937 Japan captured Nanking, killing many civilians. Joining the Axis powers in 1936, Japan continued its expansion in Asia and in 1941 attacked Pearl Harbor. After the atomic bombings of Hiroshima and Nagasaki, the Emperor announced Japan's surrender on August 15, 1945.

- Hiroshima Peace Memorial Park (Hiroshima)
- Yasukuni Shrine Museum (Tokyo)

1964 Tokyo hosts the Summer Olympic games

1989 Emperor Hirohito dies

2006 Shinzo Abe elected as the country's youngest prime minister

2009 Liberal Democratic Party loses power

2012 LDP's Shinzo Abe re-elected as prime minister

1970 | 1990 | 2010 | 2030

(top) 1964 Summer Olympics, Tokyo, (bottom) manga comic books, (right) Shinjuku, Tokyo

1945–1989

Postwar Japan and the Economic Miracle

The initial postwar years were hard on Japan. More than half of Japan's total urban area was in ruins, its industry in shambles, and food shortages common. Kyoto was the only major metropolitan area in the country that escaped widespread damage. Thanks to an educated, dedicated population and smart planning, however, Japan was soon on the road to recovery. A new democratic government was formed and universal suffrage extended to all adult men and women. Japan's famous "Peace Constitution" forbade the country from engaging in warfare. With cooperation from the government, old companies like Matsushita (Panasonic), Mitsubishi, and Toyota began exporting Japanese goods en masse, while upstarts like Honda pushed their way to the top. In 1964 Japan joined the Organization for Economic Cooperation and Development's group of "rich nations" and hosted the Tokyo Olympics. At the same time, anime began gaining popularity at the box office and on TV, with Osamu Tezuka's classic *Tetsuwan Atom* (*Astro Boy*) making a splash when it aired in 1963. In the 1970s and '80s Japan became as well known for its electronics as its cars, with Nintendo, Sony, and Panasonic becoming household names abroad.

- Showa-Kan (Takayama)
- National Stadium (Yoyogi Park)

1990–PRESENT

From Goods to Culture

Unfortunately, much of Japan's rapid growth in the 1980s was unsustainable. By 1991 the bubble had burst, leading to 20 years of limited economic expansion. Japan avoided an economic crisis, and most people continued to lead comfortable, if somewhat simpler, lives. After decades of exporting goods, Japan has—particularly since 2000—become an exporter of culture in the form of animation, video games, and cuisine. Japan, famous for importing ideas, has begun to send its own culture to the world.

- Shinjuku, Harajuku, and Shibuya, (Tokyo)
- Akihabara (Tokyo)
- Manga Museum (Kyoto)

2

A JAPANESE CULTURE PRIMER

Updated by Annamarie Sasagawa

Something about Japanese culture must have led you to pick up this book and contemplate a trip to Japan. Perhaps it was a meal at your favorite sushi bar back home. It could have been the warm tones of an exquisite piece of Japanese pottery. Maybe it was a Japanese novel you read in translation—or a film. Whatever it was that sparked your interest, it's a good bet that something you find in this chapter will make your trip unforgettable.

There is a display of horsemanship called *yabusame* (now to be seen mainly at shrine festivals) in which a mounted archer, in medieval costume, challenges a narrow roped-off course lined at 260-foot intervals with small wooden targets on bamboo posts: the rider has to come down the course at full gallop, drop the reins, nock an arrow, aim and release, and take the reins again—with only seconds to set up again for the next target. Few archers manage a perfect score—but "for us," explains a yabusame official, "merely hitting the target is secondary."

Therein lies the key to understanding pretty nearly every expression of traditional Japanese culture: the passionate attention to *form* and *process*. The results are important, of course; otherwise the forms would be empty gestures. But equally important—perhaps more important—is *how you get there*. Not for nothing are so many of these disciplines, from the tea ceremony to calligraphy to the martial arts, presented to us as Ways; excellence in any one of them depends on *doing it the way it's supposed to be done*, according to traditions that may be centuries old. Philosophically, this is all about how rules can liberate: spend enough time and effort on the mastery of forms, and one day they leave the realm of conscious thought and become part of you. Not for nothing, either, are so many elements of Japanese culture rooted in the teachings of Zen Buddhism, about breaking free from the limits of the rational Self.

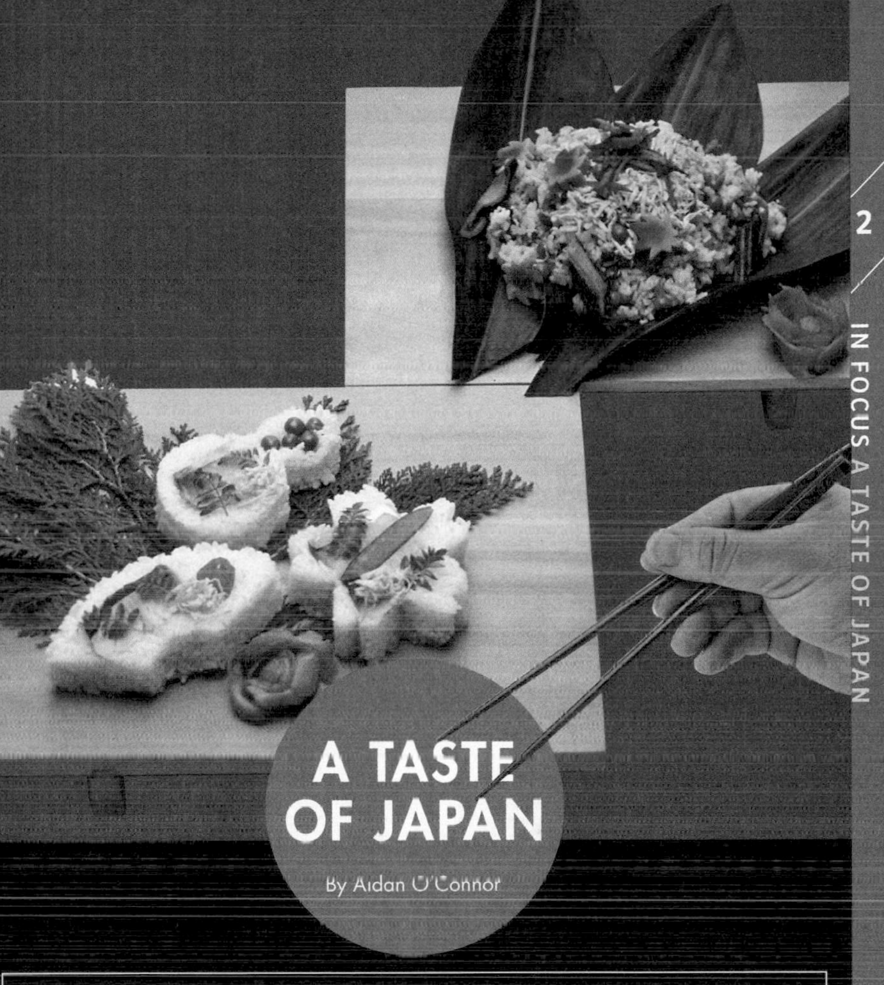

A TASTE OF JAPAN

By Aidan O'Connor

Get ready for an unparalleled eating adventure: from humble bowls of ramen to elaborate kaiseki feasts, a vast culinary universe awaits visitors to food-obsessed Japan.

Japan's food offerings are united by a few key philosophies. Presentation is paramount—a dedication to visual appeal means that colors and shapes are just as important as aromas, textures, and flavors. Details count—food is prepared with pride and care, and everything from a bowl's shape to a dish's finishing garnish carries meaning. Natural flavors shine through—seasonal ingredients star in minimally processed preparations, with condiments used to enhance flavors rather than mask them.

You'll find these culinary philosophies at all levels, from tiny noodle shops to lively robatayaki grills to elegant sushi restaurants. Here's what you need to know to make the most of your meals. As they say in Japan, *itadakimasho* (let's eat)!

Pressed sushi (oshizushi) and Japanese-style fried rice

THE JAPANESE MEAL

Breakfast (*asa-gohan*, literally "the morning rice") is typically eaten at home and features rice, fried fish, and miso soup. Lunch (*hiru-gohan*), mostly eaten out of the home at school or work, involves a bento lunch box of rice, grilled fish, vegetables, and pickles. The evening meal (*ban-gohan*) has the broadest range, from restaurant meals of sushi to traditional meals cooked at home.

For home-prepared meals, the basic formula consists of one soup and three dishes—a main dish of fish or meat and two vegetable side dishes. These are served together with rice, which is part of every meal. When entertaining guests, more dishes will be served. Classical Japanese cooking follows the principle of "fives." An ideal meal is thought to use five cooking methods—boiling, grilling, frying, steaming, and serving raw; incorporate five colors—black or purple, white, red or orange, yellow, and green; and feature five tastes—sweet, sour, salty, bitter, and *umami* (the Japanese are credited with discovering umami, or savoriness). Ingredient quality is key, and cooking techniques are intended to coax out an ingredient's maximum natural flavor.

Staple ingredients include seafood, which plays a leading role in Japanese cuisine, with dozens of species available,

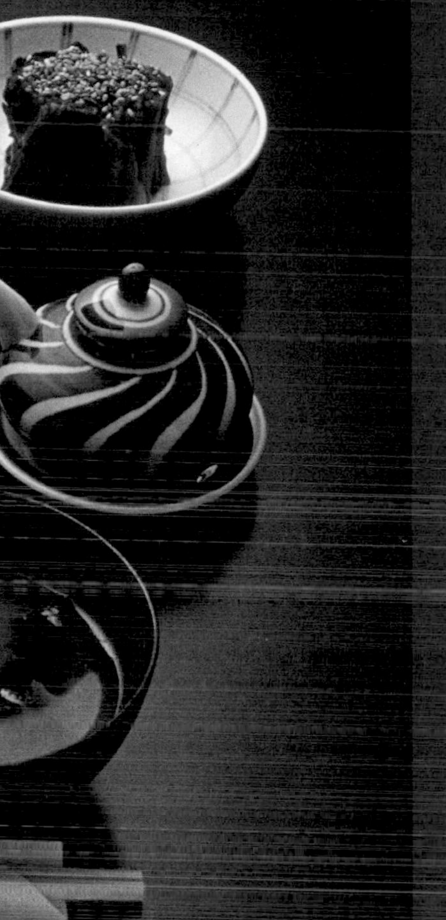

from familiar choices like *maguro* (tuna) and *ebi* (shrimp) to more exotic selections like *anago* (conger eel) and *fugu* (blowfish). Meat options include chicken, pork, beef, and—in rural areas—venison and wild boar. Then there is a huge variety of vegetables and fungi (both wild and cultivated) such as *renkon* (lotus root), *daikon* (white radish), and matsutake mushrooms. Finally there is the soy bean, eaten whole as edamame, or fermented in tofu or miso.

Condiments range from tangy *shiso* (a member of the mint family) to spicy wasabi and savory soy sauce.

DINING ETIQUETTE

Here are a few tips to help you fit in at the Japanese table:

- Don't point or gesture with chopsticks.
- Avoid lingering over communal dishes with your chopsticks while you decide what to take. Do not use the end you have been eating with to remove food from the dish—use the serving chopsticks provided or the thick end of your own chopsticks.
- When not in use, place your chopsticks on the chopstick rest.
- Never pass food from your chopsticks to someone else's or leave chopsticks standing in your rice bowl (it resembles incense sticks at a funeral).
- There is no taboo against slurping your noodle soup, though women are generally less boisterous about it than men.
- Pick up the soup bowl and drink directly from it. Take the fish or vegetables from it with your chopsticks. Return the lid to the soup bowl when you are finished eating. The rice bowl, too, is to be held in your free hand while you eat from it.
- When drinking with a friend don't pour your own. Pour for the other person first. He will in turn pour yours.
- Japanese don't pour sauce on their rice. Sauces are intended for dipping foods into it lightly.
- It is still considered tacky to eat as you walk along a public street.

Pouring sake into a traditional Japanese cup

SUSHI

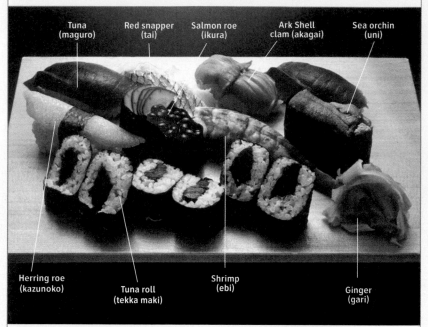

Tuna (maguro)
Red snapper (tai)
Salmon roe (ikura)
Ark Shell clam (akagai)
Sea orchin (uni)
Herring roe (kazunoko)
Tuna roll (tekka maki)
Shrimp (ebi)
Ginger (gari)

■ Sushi actually refers to anything, seafood or otherwise, served on or in vinegared rice. It is not raw fish. **Nigiri-zushi** (the sushi best known overseas) is actually a fairly recent development from Tokyo.

■ **Makizushi** is a sushi roll. These can be fat, elaborate rolls or simple sticks.

■ Other types of sushi include **chirashi-zushi** with fish and vegetables scattered artfully into the rice and, in Kyoto and Osaka, **oshizushi** in which preserved mackerel, among other fish, is pressed onto the rice. This is served in slices.

■ **Funazushi**, from around Lake Biwa near Kyoto, is perhaps the oldest type. The fish and rice are buried for six months. The rice is thrown away and the fish is eaten. This technique was historically used as a means of preserving protein. It is an acquired taste.

■ **Kaitenzushi** (conveyor belt sushi) outlets abound and are cheap. However, for the real experience, nothing matches a traditional sushi-ya.

Hand-rolled sushi

■ Using your hands is acceptable. Dip the fish, not the rice, lightly in the soy.

■ The **beni-shoga** (pickled ginger) is a palate freshener. Nibble sparingly.

■ **Wasabi** may not be served with your sushi, as the chef often dabs a bit on the rice when making your sushi. If you want extra wasabi, ask for it.

■ Customers will often request **omakase** (tasting menu). The chef will then choose and serve the best fish, in the order he deems appropriate.

RAMEN

Shoyu ramen

■ Ramen is practically Japan's national dish. A ramen restaurant is never far away.

■ There are four main types: from the chilly north island of Hokkaido, there is **shio ramen** (salt ramen) and **miso ramen** (ramen in a miso broth). **Shoyu ramen** made with soy sauce is from Tokyo, while **tonkotsu ramen** (ramen in a white pork broth) is from Kyoto. Note that most ramen stocks contain meat or fish.

■ Each area has its own variation—corn and butter ramen in Sapporo; a stock made from pork and dried anchovies in northern Honshu; or Fukuoka's famed **Hakata ramen** with its milky tonkotsu broth and thin noodles with myriad toppings.

■ The reputation of a ramen restaurant depends on its stock, often a closely guarded secret.

■ Ramen is meant to be eaten with gusto. Slurping is normal.

■ Typical toppings include sliced roast pork, bean sprouts, boiled egg, **shinachiku** (fermented bamboo shoots), spring onion, **nori** (dried seaweed) and **kamaboko** (a fishcake made from white fish).

■ Beyond ramen, udon shops and soba shops also offer noodle dishes worth trying.

Miso ramen

Shio ramen

ROBATAYAKI

Grilled fish (tsukeba)

■ **Robata** means fireside, and the style of cooking is reminiscent of old-fashioned Japanese farmhouse meals cooked over a charcoal fire in an open hearth.

■ Robatayaki restaurants and izakaya taverns serving grilled foods can be found near any busy station.

■ It's easy to order at a robatayaki, because the selection of food to be grilled is lined up at the counter. Fish, meat, vegetables, tofu—take your pick.

■ Some popular choices are **yaki-zakana** (grilled fish), particularly **karei-shio-yaki** (salted and grilled flounder) and **asari saka-mushi** (clams simmered in sake).

■ Try the grilled Japanese **shiitake** (mushrooms), **ao-to** (green peppers), and the **hiyayakko** (chilled tofu sprinkled with bonito flakes, diced green onions, and soy sauce).

Matsutake mushroom

■ **O-tsukuri** (sashimi) and **katsuono tataki** (seared bonito) are very popular. The fish will vary according to the season.

■ Dipping sauces are concocted using soy, **dashi** (soup stock), and a hint of citrus such as yuzu.

■ Many robatayaki pride themselves on their wide selection of sake and shochu.

■ Most Japanese people will finish their meal with a rice dish.

TEMPURA

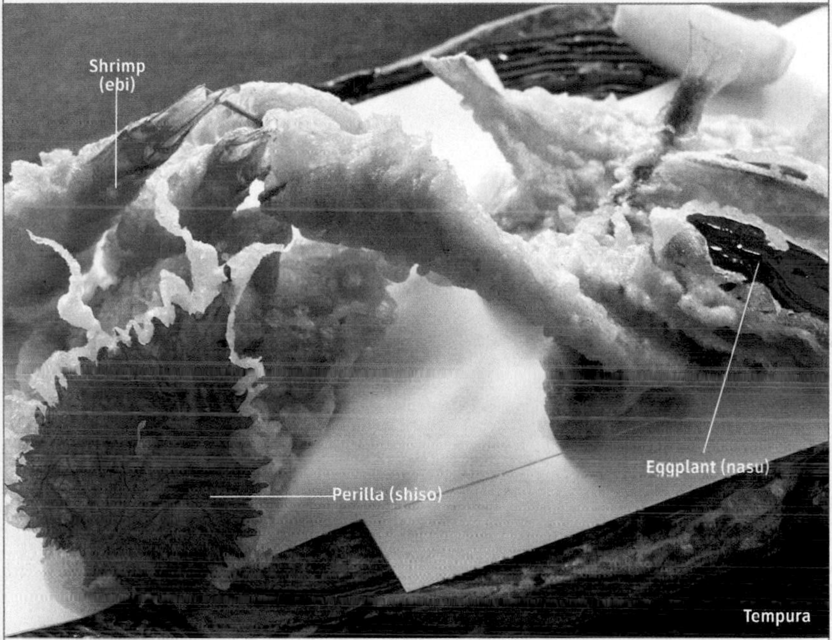

Shrimp (ebi)
Eggplant (nasu)
Perilla (shiso)

Tempura

■ Though tempura features in many busy eateries as part of a meal, it bears little resemblance to the exquisite morsels produced over the course of a full tempura meal at an intimate specialty restaurant.

■ The secret of good tempura lies in the quality of the ingredients, the freshness and temperature of the oil, and the lightness of the batter.

■ Good tempura is light and crispy, not crunchy like fried chicken.

■ Tempura is most often fried in soybean oil, but cottonseed or sesame oil also may be used.

■ Because only the freshest of ingredients will do, the menu changes with the season. Baby corn, green peppers, sweet potato, lotus root, shiitake mushrooms, and shiso leaves are the most common vegetables. In spring expect **sansai** (wild vegetables) picked that morning.

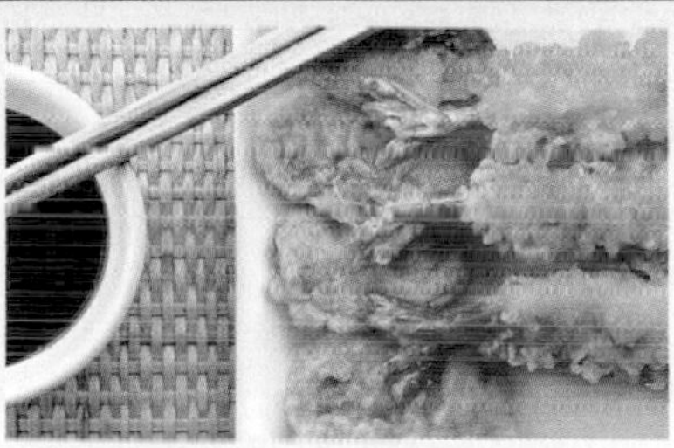

Shrimp Tempura with sweet potatoes

■ Prawns and white fish are also popular tempura items.

■ **Tsuyu** (dipping sauce) is made from dashi seasoned with soy and **mirin** (sweet rice wine). You may see a white mound of grated daikon on your plate. Add that to the tsuyu for a punch of flavor.

■ Alternatively, mixtures of salt and powdered green tea or salt and yuzu may be sprinkled on the tempura.

BENTO

Assorted fruit (kudamono)

Miso soup (miso shiru)

Salad

Assorted tempura (tempura no moriawase)

Beef teriyaki (gyu no teriyaki)

Grilled salmon (sake)

Rice (gohan)

Dipping sauce for tempura (tsuyu)

Pickles (tsukemono)

Assorted bento

■ Bento boxes, the traditional Japanese box lunch, can be bought everywhere from the basement level of a luxurious department store to a convenience store.

■ A typical bento will contain rice, grilled fish, a selection of vegetable dishes, some pickles, and perhaps a wedge of orange or other fruit.

■ Every region has its **meibutsu**, or speciality dish. These are often showcased in lunch boxes available at stations or local stores.

■ Though the humble bento is usually relatively inexpensive, more ornate and intricate boxes featuring kaiseki dishes or sushi are often bought for special occasions.

■ The bento exists in an almost limitless number of variations according to the region and the season.

Bento lunch box

■ A bento is designed to be taken out and eaten on the move. They are perfect on long-distance train rides or for a picnic in the park.

BEVERAGES

Sake

■ There are more than 2,000 different brands of sake produced throughout Japan. It is often called rice wine but is actually made by a fermenting process that is more akin to beer-making. The result is a fantastically complex drink with an alcoholic content just above wine (15–17% alcohol). It is the drink of choice with sashimi and traditional Japanese food.

■ There are four main types of sake: **daiginjo, ginjo, junmai,** and **honjozo**. The first two are the most expensive and made from highly polished rice. The latter two, however, also pack flavor and character.

■ Like wine, sake can be sweet (*amakuchi*) or dry (*karakuchi*). Workaday sake may be drunk warm (*atsukan*) while the higher grades will be served chilled. Sake is the only drink that can be served at any temperature.

■ Another variety is **nama-zake.** This is unpasteurized sake and is prized for its fresh, zingy taste.

■ **Shochu** is a distilled spirit that is often 25% alcohol or more. Like vodka, it can be made from potato, sweet potato, wheat, millet, or rice. It is drunk straight, on the rocks, with water, or in cocktails.

■ Any good izakaya or robatayaki will stock a diverse selection of both sake and shochu, and staff will make recommendations.

■ Beer is, perhaps, the lubricant of choice for most social situations. Japanese beer is of a high standard and tends to be lager. It has a relatively high alcohol content at 5% or more. Recently there has been a boom in microbreweries.

JAPANESE FINE ARTS

(this page above) Japanese lacquerware; (opposite page upper right) a calligrapher at work; (opposite page bottom left) traditional Japanese papermaking

What raises Japanese handicrafts to the level of fine arts? It is, one could argue, the standards set by the nation's *Ningen kokuho*: its Living National Treasures, who hand down these traditional skills from generation to generation.

Legally speaking, these people are "Holders of Important Intangible Cultural Properties." A law, enacted in 1950, establishes two broad categories of Intangible Property. One comprises the performing arts: Kabuki, Noh, Bunraku puppet theater, and traditional music and dance. The other embraces a wide range of handicrafts, most of them in the various forms and styles of textiles, pottery, lacquerware, papermaking, wood carving, and metalworking—from all over the country. The tiny cohort of individuals and groups who exemplify these traditions at the highest levels (there are a maximum of 70 designees at any given time) receive an annual stipend; the money is intended not so much to support the title holders (Living National Treasures command very healthy sums for their work) as to help them attract and train apprentices, and thus keep the traditions alive.

CARRYING ON

Official sponsorship has proven itself a necessity in more than a few craft traditions. The weaving of *bashofu*, for example, a fabric from Okinawa, is on its way to becoming a lost art—unless the present Living National Treasure can encourage enough people to carry on with the craft. Papermaking, a cottage industry that once supported some 28,500 households nationwide, now supports only a few hundred.

LACQUERWARE

Japanese lacquerware has its origins in the Jomon period (10,000–300 BC), and by the Nara period (710–794) most of the techniques we recognize today, such as *maki-e* (literally, "sprinkled picture"), the use of gold or silver powder to underlay the lacquer, had been developed. The Edo period (1603–1868) saw the uses of lacquer extended to vessels and utensils for the newly prosperous merchant class.

The production of lacquerware starts with refining sap from the Japanese sumac (*urushi*). The lacquer is layered on basketry, wood, bamboo, metal, and even paper. The polished black and red surfaces may have inlays of mother-of-pearl or precious metals, creating motifs and designs of exquisite beauty and delicacy. Many regions in Japan are famous for their distinct lacquerware styles, among them Kyoto, Wajima, and Tsugaru. Hint: tableware with lacquer over plastic bases, rather than wood, are no less beautiful, but far less expensive.

PAPERMAKING

Washi, Japanese paper, can have a soft translucent quality that seems to belie its amazing strength and durability. It makes a splendid material for calligraphy and brush painting, and it can be fashioned into a wide variety of traditional decorative objects. The basic ingredient is the inner bark of the paper

mulberry, but leaves, fiber threads, and even gold flake can be added in later stages for a dramatic effect. The raw mulberry branches are first steamed, then bleached in cold water or snow. The fibers are boiled with ash lye, rinsed, beaten into pulp, and soaked in a tank of starchy taro solution. A screen is dipped into the tank, pulled up, and rocked to drain the solution and crosshatch the fibers. The wet sheets of paper are stacked to press out the excess liquid, then dried in the sun.

The best places to watch the papermaking process are Kurodani, near Kyoto; Mino, in central Japan; and Yame, near Kurume. Many are known for their unique washi products: Gifu for umbrellas and lanterns, Nagasaki for its distinctive kites, Nara for calligraphy paper.

CALLIGRAPHY

Calligraphy arrived in Japan around AD 500 with the sacred texts of Buddhism, written in *kanji* (Chinese ideograms). By 800, the *kana* syllabic alphabets of the Japanese language had also developed, and the writing of both kanji and kana with a brush, in india ink, had become an art form—a wedding of meaning and emotion that was (and still is) regarded as a revelation of the writer's individual character. The flow of the line from top to bottom, the balance of shapes and sizes, the thickness of the strokes, the

About 30 different styles of porcelain are made in Japan.

amount of ink on the brush: all contribute to the composition of the work. There are five main styles of calligraphy in Japan. Two are based on the Chinese: *tensho*, typically used for seal carving; and *reisho*, for the copying of sutras. Three are solely Japanese: *kaisho*, the block style often seen in wood carving; and the flowing *sosho* (cursive) and *gyosho* styles. Sosho is especially impressive—an expression of freedom and spontaneity that takes years of discipline to achieve; retouching and erasing is impossible.

CERAMICS

There are some 30 traditional styles of pottery in Japan, from unglazed stoneware to painted porcelain. Since the late 1600s, when Imari and Kakiemon porcelain were exported to Europe, the achievements of Japanese potters have delighted collectors.

Although the Japanese have been making pottery for some 12,000 years, the styles we know today were developed by Chinese and Korean craftsmen who immigrated (or were forcibly brought) to Japan in the 17th century. Some of them discovered deposits of fine kaolin clay in northern Kyushu, and founded the tradition in that region of porcelains like Arita-yaki, with brilliantly colored enamel decoration over cobalt blue underglaze. Other porcelain wares include Tobe-yaki from Ehime Prefecture, Kutani-yaki from Ishikawa Prefecture, and Kiyomizu-yaki from Kyoto.

These apart, most Japanese pottery is stoneware—which has an earthier appeal, befitting the rougher texture of the clay. Stoneware from Mashiko, where celebrated potter Hamada Shoji (1894–1978) worked, is admired for its rustic brown, black, and white glazes, often applied in abstract patterns. Many regional potters use glazes on stoneware for coloristic effects, like the mottled, crusty Tokoname-yaki, with its red-iron clay. Other styles, among them the rough-surfaced Shigaraki-yaki made near Kyoto; the white or blue-white Hagi-yaki; and Bizen-yaki from Okayama Prefecture, are unglazed: their warm tones and textures are accidents of nature, achieved when the pieces take their colors from the firing process, in wood-burning through-draft kilns called *anagama* or *nobori-gama*, built on the slopes of hills. The effects depend on the choice of the wood the potter uses, where he places a particular piece in the kiln, and how he manipulates the heat, but the results are never predictable.

Main pottery towns include Hagi, Bizen, and Arita, but you can always find their products in Kyoto and Tokyo. If you do go on a pilgrimage, call ahead to local kilns and tourist organizations to verify that what you want to see will be open and to ask about sales. Recommended reading: *Inside Japanese Ceramics* by Richard L. Wilson.

TEXTILES

Run your fingers over a Japanese textile, and you touch the fabric of Japanese social history. As the caste system took shape under Buddhist and Confucian influences, it created separate populations of samurai, farmers, artisans, and merchants (in descending order). Rules and conventions emerged—enforced in the Edo period by strict sumptuary laws—about who could wear what, and on what occasions. Appearances identified people. One glance at a kimono, and you knew the wearer was a woman of middle age, the wife of a prosperous tradesman, on her way to the wedding of a family connection. Order was maintained. You were what you wore. Courtesans and actors, of course, could dress over the top; their roles gave them the license. And little by little, the merchants also found ways around the laws, to dress as befit their growing wealth and power. Evolving styles and techniques of making fabrics gave weavers and dyers and designers new opportunities to show their skills.

Western clothing follows the body line in a sculptural way; the kimono is meant as a one-size-fits-all garment in which gender matters, but size and shape are largely unimportant. Whatever the wearer's height or weight, a kimono is made from one bolt of cloth cut and stitched into panels that provide ample surface for decoration.

Regional styles proliferate. Kyoto's *Nishijin-ori* silk brocade is as sumptuous as a Japanese textile can be. Okinawa produces a variety of stunning fabrics; one, called *bashofu*, is made of plantain fiber threads, dyed and woven in intricate motifs, and feels like linen. Kyoto's and Tokyo's stencil dyeing techniques yield subtle, elegant geometric patterns and motifs from nature. Kanazawa's *Kaga yuzen* paste-resist dyeing on silk is famous for its flower and bird motifs, in elegant rainbow colors.

The used kimonos you often see in Kyoto or Tokyo flea markets can be bargains. Also look for lighter-weight *yukata* (robes), *obi* (sashes), or handkerchiefs from Arimatsu, near Nagoya, for example. Good introductions to these craft traditions can be seen at Kyoto's Fuzoku Hakubutsukan (Costume Museum) and Nishijin Orimono (Textile Center), and the Edo-period dress collection in Tokyo's National Museum

Kaga yuzen textiles from Kanazawa exhibit a traditional flower motif

PERFORMING ARTS

Gorgeous costumes, sword fights and tearful reunions, acrobatics and magical transformations, spectacular makeup and masks, singing and dancing, ghosts and goblins, and star-crossed lovers: never let it be said that traditional Japanese culture is short on showmanship.

(this page above) A highly stylized Noh theater performance; (opposite page upper right) the Oshika Kabuki troupe; (opposite page bottom left) a Kabuki mannequin from the Edo-Tokyo Museum

The performing arts all have roots in continental Asia. Kabuki makeup as well as *gagaku* ceremonial court music and dance are Chinese-inspired; the four-string *biwa* shares a Silk Road ancestry with the Persian *oud*. Collectively, the theater traditions generate work for artisans—weavers and dyers, instrument makers, woodcarvers, and more—who make a special contribution of their own. Common features aside, the differences among them are astonishing. Kabuki is great showbiz, translatable and appreciable pretty much anywhere in the world. Gagaku is virtually inaccessible, even to the vast majority of the Japanese themselves. Most of an audience that will sit riveted by the graceful, suggestive movements of *buyo* (traditional dance) will fall asleep at a dance-recitation of Noh.

MASTER PERFORMERS

The performing arts also have National Treasures, but filling the 70 allotted slots is easier than in the fine arts. The worlds of Japanese theater are mainly in the grip of small oligarchies—"schools"—where traditions are passed down from father to son. Some of these master performers are 9th- and even 22nd-generation holders of hereditary family stage names and specializations.

KABUKI

Tradition has it that Kabuki was created around 1600 by an Izumo shrine maiden named Okuni; it was then performed by troupes of women, who were often available as well for prostitution (the authorities soon banned women from the stage as a threat to public order). Eventually Kabuki cleaned up its act and developed a professional role for female impersonators, who train for years to project a seductive, dazzling femininity. By the latter half of the 18th century it had become Everyman's theater par excellence—especially among the townspeople of bustling, hustling Edo. Kabuki had spectacle; it had pathos and tragedy; it had romance and social satire. It had legions of fans, who spent all day at the theater, shouting out the names of their favorite actors at the stirring moments in their favorite plays.

Kabuki flowered especially in the "floating world" of Edo's red-light entertainment district. The theater was a place to see and be seen, to catch the latest trends in music and fashion, where people of all classes came together under one roof—something that happened nowhere else in the city. Strict censorship laws were put in place and just as quickly circumvented by clever playwrights; Kabuki audiences could watch a *jidai-mono* (historical piece) set in the distant past, where the events and characters made

thinly veiled reference to troublesome contemporary events.

The Genroku era (1673–1841) was Kabuki's golden age, when the classic plays of Chikamatsu Monzaemon and Tsuruya Namboku were written, and most of the theatrical conventions and stage techniques we see today were honed to perfection. The *mie*, for example, is a dramatic pose the actor strikes at a certain moment in the play, to establish his character. The use of *kumadori* makeup, derived from Chinese opera and used to symbolize the essential elements of a character's nature, also dates to this period. The exaggerated facial lines of the kumadori, in vivid reds and blues and greens over a white rice-powder base, tell the audience at once that the wearer is a hero or villain, noble or arrogant, passionate or cold. To the Genroku also date revolving stages, trapdoors, and—most importantly—the *hanamichi*: a long, raised runway from the back of the theater, through the audience, to the main stage, where characters enter, exit, and strike their mie poses.

Kabuki traditions are passed down through generations in a small group of families; the roles and great stage names are hereditary. The repertoire does not really grow, but stars like Ichikawa Ennosuke and Bando Tamasaburo have developed unique performance styles that still draw audiences young and old.

The principal character in a Noh play wears a carved, wooden mask.

This ancient art now has a stylish home in the Kengo Kuma–designed Kabuki-za theater in Tokyo's Ginza district, which opened in 2013. Recommended reading: *The Kabuki Guide* by Masakatsu Gunji.

NOH

Noh is a dramatic tradition far older than Kabuki; it reached a point of formal perfection in the 14th century and survives virtually unchanged from that period. Where Kabuki was Everyman's theater, Noh developed for the most part under the patronage of the warrior class. It is dignified, ritualized, and symbolic. Many of the plays in the repertoire are drawn from classical literature or tales of the supernatural. The texts are richly poetic, and even the Japanese find them difficult to understand. (Don't despair: the major Noh theaters usually provide synopses of the plays in English.) The action—such as it is—develops at nearly glacial pace.

The principal character in a Noh play wears a carved wooden mask. Such is the skill of the actor, and the mysterious effect of the play, that the mask itself may appear expressionless until the actor "brings it to life," at which point the mask can express a considerable range of emotions. As in Kabuki, the various roles of the Noh repertoire all have specific costumes—robes of silk brocade with intricate patterns that are works of art in themselves. Noh is not a very "accessible" kind of theater: its language is archaic; its conventions are obscure; and its measured, stately pace can put even Japanese audiences to sleep.

More accessible is the *kyogen,* a short comic interlude traditionally performed between two Noh plays in a program. The pace is quicker, the costumes (based on actual dress of the medieval period) are simpler, and most kyogen do not use masks; the comedy depends on the satiric premise—a clever servant who gets the best of his master, for example—and the lively facial expressions of the actors.

Like Kabuki, Noh has a number of schools, the traditions of which developed as the exclusive property of hereditary families. The major schools have their own theaters in Tokyo and

Kyoto, with regular schedules of performances—but if you happen to be in Kyoto on June 1–2, don't miss the Takigi Noh: an outdoor performance given at night, by torchlight, in the precincts of the Heian Shrine. There are other torchlight performances as well in Tokyo, at the Meiji Shrine (early October) and Zojoji Temple (late May), and in Nara at the Kasuga Shrine (May).

BUNRAKU

The third major form of traditional Japanese drama is Bunraku puppet theater. Itinerant puppeteers were plying their trade in Japan as early as the 10th century; sometime in the late 16th century, a form of narrative ballad called *joruri,* performed to the accompaniment of a three-string banjolike instrument called the *shamisen,* was grafted onto their art, and Bunraku was born. The golden age of Bunraku came some 200 years later, when most of the great plays were written and the puppets themselves evolved to their present form, so expressive and intricate in their movements that they require three people acting in unison to manipulate them.

The puppets are about two-thirds human size and elaborately dressed in period costume; each one is made up of interchangeable parts—a head, shoulder piece, trunk, legs, and arms. The puppeteer called the *omozukai* controls the expression on the puppet's face and its right arm and hand. The *hidarizukai* controls the puppet's left arm and hand along with any props that it is carrying. The *ashizukai* moves the puppet's legs. The most difficult task belongs to the omozukai—a role it commonly takes some 30 years to master.

Creating the puppet heads is an art in itself, and today there are only a handful of carvers still working. As a rule, the heads are shaped and painted for specific figures—characters of different sex, age, and personality—and fitted with elaborate wigs of human hair in various styles to indicate the puppet's social standing. Able to roll their eyes and lift their eyebrows, the puppets can achieve an amazing range of facial expression.

The chanters, who provide both the narration of the play and the voices of the puppets, deliver their lines in a kind of high-pitched croak from deep in the throat. The texts they recite are considered to be among the classics of Japanese dramatic literature; the great playwright Chikamatsu Monzaemon (1653–1725) wrote for both Bunraku and Kabuki, and the two dramatic forms often adapted works from each other.

The most important Bunraku troupe is the government-supported National Bunraku Theatre in Osaka, but there are amateur and semiprofessional companies throughout the country—the most active of them on Awaji Island, near Shikoku. Periodically there are also performances in Tokyo in the small hall of the National Theater.

Bunraku puppets are about two-thirds human size.

2

ONSEN AND BATHING

(above) A lakeside rotenburo made from natural rocks; (opposite upper right) Gakenoyu Onsen in Nagano; (opposite bottom left) a spa in Shirahama Onsen

A chain of volcanic islands on the fiery Pacific Rim, Japan has developed a splendid subculture around one of the more manageable manifestations of this powerful resource: the *onsen* thermal spa.

The benchmark Japanese weekend excursion—be it family outing, company retreat, or romantic getaway—is the hot spring resort. Fissured from end to end with volcanic cracks and crannies, the country positively wheezes with geothermal springs. Hot water gushes and sprays almost everywhere—but most especially in the mountains; there are hot springs in every prefecture, on every offshore island—even in cities built, incautiously, above the very fault lines themselves. And to all these superheated hollows flock the Japanese in endless enthusiasm, putting many thousands of people to work, catering to their needs; onsen are as nearly recession-proof an industry as the nation has. It's not too much to say that to understand the Japanese, to discover their innermost nature, you need to get naked with them a while in hot mineral water.

YUDEDAKO

The Japanese have a special term for that blissful state of total immersion: *yudedako*—literally "boiled octopus"—and Japanese people of all ages and both sexes will journey for miles to attain it. Getting boiled is a step on the road to sound health, good digestion, clear skin, marital harmony—to whatever it is that gives you a general sense of being at one with the universe.

If you're new to Japan, you might be astounded by the popularity of thermal baths. It can seem like the only way for a town to hope to bring in Japanese tourists is to have an onsen. Quite naturally, the Japanese have developed a subculture around one of the more relaxing side benefits of its geographic circumstances.

THE ONSEN EXPERIENCE

An *onsen* can refer to a particular region or subregion, like Yufuin in Oita Prefecture, Kinugawa in Tochigi, or Hakone in Kanagawa: a resort destination especially well endowed with thermal springs. Or it can mean more specifically a public bathhouse with a spring-fed pool, where you pay an admission fee and soak at your leisure. (At last count, there were some 6,700 of these nationwide.) Or it could mean a lodging—one of two basic varieties—with a spring of its own. One type is the *kanko* hotel: a mega-onsen with multiple baths, in grand pharaonic styles with mosaics and waterfalls, and banquet halls and dinner shows, as well as tatami guest rooms that sleep six—and, inevitably, discos and karaoke bars and souvenir shops. The other type is the onsen of everyone's dreams: the picture-perfect traditional inn, a ryokan of half a dozen rooms, nestled up somewhere in the mountains all by itself, with a spectacular view and a *rotenburo*—an outdoor pool—to enjoy it from.

THE ROTENBURO

Ah! the rotenburo! At smaller onsen, you can book the exquisitely crafted pool, with its stepping-stones and lanterns, and bamboo screens, for a private soak: an hour or so of the purest luxury, especially by moonlight. The rotenburo is a year-round indulgence; the view from the pool might be a mountainside white with cherry blossoms in spring, or a lakefront brilliant in the red and gold of maples in autumn, or—best of all, perhaps—a winter panorama, with the snow piled high on the pines and hedges that frame the landscape, to contemplate from your snug, steamy vantage point while you slowly wrinkle yourself like a prune. Be warned: whatever the season, you'll need to make reservations well in advance, for onsen accommodations of any sort. Japan has more than 3,000 registered spas; collectively, they draw nearly 140 million visitors a year, and hotel space is not easy to come by.

WHAT IS AN ONSEN?

By law, an onsen is only an onsen if the water comes out of the ground at a specified minimum temperature, and contains at least one of 19 designated minerals and chemical compounds—which makes for a wide range of choices. There are iron springs with red water; there are silky-smooth alkali springs; there are springs with radon and sulphur sodium bicarbonate; there are springs with water at a comfortable

Most onsen have single-sex bathing, a few have mixed bathing.

100°F (37.8°C), and springs so hot they have bath masters to make sure you stay only for three minutes and not a fatal second longer.

One reason many Westerners are reluctant to go bathing in Japan is the fact that you have to take all your clothes off. *In front of everyone else.* There is that issue—no getting around it: Japanese communal bathing is done in the buff—but that shouldn't deter you from the experience of a truly good thing. The bath is a great equalizer: in a sense the bath *is* Japan, in its unalloyed egalitarianism. Here, rank and title are stripped away: there is no way to tell if the body boiling beside you belongs to a captain of industry or his humble employee, to an ambassador, to a pauper, to a mendicant priest—and each bather offers the other an equal degree of respect and regard; no one ever behaves in a way that might spoil the enjoyment of any other bather; no one is embarrassed or causes embarrassment.

ONSEN ETIQUETTE

Another reason you might have for your reluctance is the worrisome conviction that bathing with a bunch of strangers comes with a raft of rules—rules all those strangers know from childhood, but at least one of which you're bound to break, to your everlasting horror and shame. "What if I drop the soap in the bath?" is a typical fear.

In fact, the pitfalls are not at all so awful. There certainly are protocols to follow, but it's a short list.

1. While there are still a few spas that keep alive the old custom of *konyoku* (mixed bathing), all of them have separate entrances for men and women, announced in Japanese characters on hangings over the doors. If in doubt, ask.

2. A word of warning: body tattoos, in Japan, are indelibly associated with the *yakuza*—organized crime families and their minions—and spas commonly refuse entry to tattooed visitors, to avoid upsetting their regular clientele. The rule is strictly enforced—and could extend to that little butterfly you got on

your shoulder when you were young and reckless. Put a bandage over it.

3. The first room you come to inside is the dressing room. It's almost always tatami-floored: take your shoes or slippers off in the entryway. The dressing room will have lockers for your keys and valuables, and rows of wicker or plastic baskets on shelves; pick one, and put your clothes in it. If you're staying overnight at an inn with a spa of its own, you'll find a cotton kimono called a *nemaki* in your room—you sleep in it, in lieu of pajamas—and a light quilted jacket called a *hanten*. Night or day, this is standard gear to wear from your room to the spa, anywhere else around the inn, and even for a stroll out of doors. Leave them in the basket.

The spa should provide—or you should bring—two towels: leave the bigger one in the basket, to dry off with, and take the smaller one with you next door, to the pools. (Holding this towel modestly over your nether parts is the accepted way of moving around in the spa.)

4. The pool area will have rows of washing stations along the walls: countertops with supplies of soap and shampoo, a mirror, taps and showerhead, a stool, and a bucket. Here's where you get clean—and that means *really* clean. Soap up, shower, scrub off every particle of the day's wear and tear. Take your time; use your wash towel. Leave no trace of soap. Then take your towel modestly to the pool.

You can bring the towel with you into the bath, but the onsen really would rather you didn't. Most people leave theirs at poolside or set them folded on top of their heads. (Another item of protocol: spas don't insist on bathing caps, but they do want you to keep your head above water.)

And that's all there is to it. Find a pleasant spot; soak in blissful silence, if you prefer (but not too long, if you're not used to it), or feel free to strike up a conversation with a fellow soaker: *atsui desu ne*—the local equivalent of "Hot enough for you?"—is a good start. The Japanese call their friendliest, most relaxing acquaintances *hadaka no o-tsukiai*: naked encounters.

Staying at a mega-onsen? Conviviality reigns in the pools of these establishments, with all sorts of amenities to help it along. At some inns, for example, you can order a small floating table for yourself and your fellow boilers, just big enough for a ceramic flask of sake or two, and a suitable number of cups. You get to warm your insides and outsides at the same time: how bad can that be?

When you've soaked to your heart's content, dry yourself off with your smaller towel and head back to the dressing room. Grab your larger towel from the basket, wrap it around yourself, and rest a bit until your body temperature drops back to normal. Get dressed and head out to the post-bath rest area to have a cold glass of water and lounge on the tatami mats before heading back out into the world.

You clean yourself thoroughly before setting foot in the onsen.

THE RYOKAN

You're likely to find Japanese hospitality polished, warm, and professional pretty much anywhere you stay—but nowhere more so than in a *ryokan*: a traditional inn.

(above) A traditional tatami-mat room in a ryokan; (opposite upper right) a ryokan meal served in myriad little dishes; (opposite bottom left) bedding for a ryokan, which is laid out nightly

Ryokans are typically one- or two-story wooden buildings where the guest rooms have tatami mat floors; the bedding—stowed by day in a closet—is rolled out at night. The rooms have hardly any furniture—perhaps one low dining table and cushions on the floor, a chest of drawers with a mirror, and a scroll painting or a flower arrangement in the *tokonoma* (alcove)—but every room in a proper ryokan will have windows with sliding paper screens looking out on an exquisite interior garden. Rates are per person and include the cost of breakfast and dinner. Some inns are reluctant to accept foreign guests: the assumption is that you don't know the language or the rules of ryokan etiquette. Call well ahead for reservations: better yet, have somebody Japanese make the call for you. The venerable, top-of-the-line ryokans expect even first-time Japanese guests to have introductions from a known and respected client.

COSTS

Ryokans of august lineage and exemplary service are expensive: expect to pay ¥30,000 or even ¥50,000 per person per night with two meals. There are plenty of lesser-priced ryokan in Japan, which start from ¥10,000 per person, including breakfast and dinner, though these may not have garden views. The Japan National Tourism Organization has a listing of some of the latter.

RYOKAN ETIQUETTE

Remove your shoes as you step up from the entryway of your ryokan, and change into slippers. A maid will escort you to your room. (It might take you two or three tries thereafter to find it on your own. Ryokans pride themselves on quiet and privacy, and the rooms are typically laid out in a labyrinth of corridors, where you're seldom aware of the presence of other guests.) Slippers come off at the door; on tatami, only socks/stockings or bare feet are acceptable. Relax first with a cup of green tea, and then head for the bath. In ryokans with thermal pools (not all have them), you can take to the waters pretty much anytime between 6 am and 11 pm; otherwise—unless you have in-room facilities—guests must stagger visits to the communal bath. The maid will make these arrangements. Be mindful of Japanese bathing rules *(Onsen and Bathing, above)*; wash and rinse off thoroughly before you get in the tub for a long hot soak. After your bath, change into a nemaki, the simple cotton kimono you'll find in your room, that doubles as sleepwear—or as standard garb for an informal stroll. These days, ryokans often have private baths, but especially in more venerable establishments (even those with astronomical rates), all facilities may be shared.

Ryokans don't have legions of staff, and will appreciate it if you observe their routines and schedules. Guests are expected to arrive in the late afternoon and eat around 6. The front doors are usually locked at 10, so plan for early evenings. Breakfast is served around 8, and checkout is at 10.

FOOD

Not every inn that calls itself a ryokan offers breakfast and dinner. Indeed, some offer only breakfast; some inns have no meals at all. Seek out those that do; it's an important part of the experience. And while some ryokans will allow you to pay a lesser rate and skip dinner, why would you do that? Dinner—a feast of local specialties in beautiful dishes of all shapes and sizes—is sometimes served in your room. When you're finished, your maid will clear the table and lay out your futon bedding: a mattress filled with cotton wadding and (in winter) a heavy, thick comforter. In summer the comforter is replaced with a thinner quilt. In the morning the maid will clear away the futon and bring in your Japanese-style breakfast: grilled fish, miso soup, pickled vegetables, and rice. If you prefer, the staff will usually be able to come up with coffee and toast, not to mention a fried egg.

JAPANESE POP CULTURE

(top left) Manga is a Japan-wide obsession; (top right) distinctive manga style; (bottom right) matriarch of Japanese kawaii, Hello Kitty

Step onto the streets of Shibuya—or brave the crowds of preening high-school fashionistas populating Harujuku's Takeshita-dori—and you'll get a crash course on Japanese pop culture that extends way beyond familiar exports like Hello Kitty and Godzilla. Japanese pop culture has long been a source of fascination—and sometimes bewilderment—for foreign visitors. New fashion styles, technology, and popular media evolve quickly here, and in something of a vacuum.

That leads to a constant turnover of wholly unique, sometimes wacky trends you won't find anywhere outside Japan. Luckily, you don't have to go out of your way to explore Japan's popular obsessions. You can have an immersion experience just walking through neighborhoods like Shibuya, Shinjuku, Harujuku, and Akihabara.

DID YOU KNOW?

There are more than 5 million vending machines in Japan, making it the most dense population of machines, per capita, anywhere in the world. Here, automated machines sell everything from hot drinks to live lobsters. Some use facial recognition to verify age for tobacco and beer and even offer indecisive customers age-appropriate drink recommendations.

KAWAII

Kawaii, or "cute," isn't just a descriptor you'll hear coming out of the mouths of teenage girls, it's an aww-inducing aesthetic you'll see all over Tokyo; major airlines plaster depictions of adorable animation characters like Pikachu across the sides of their planes, and even at local police stations it's not unusual for a fluffy, stuffed-animal mascot to be on display. Duck into an arcade photo booth to take *purikura*—stickers pictures that let you choose your own kawaii background—or head to Sanrio Puroland, an entire theme park dedicated to cuteness.

J-POP IDOLS

The age of the boy band—or the girl band for that matter—is not over in Japan. "Idol" groups are hot. Over-the-top outfits, sugar-sweet synthesized beats, and love-professing lyrics (with the occasional English word thrown in) dominate the Japanese pop charts. AKB-48, one of Tokyo's hottest groups of idols, is 48 girls strong, and performs daily at its own theater complex in Akihabara. Beloved pop groups like all-male SMAP have been pumping out hits for more than 20 years.

ANIME AND MANGA

Peek over the shoulder of a comic-book-reading businessman and you'll quickly discover that, in Japan, cartoons aren't just kids' stuff. Animation (*anime*) and

comic books (*manga*) are extremely popular with readers both young and old. Comic book addicts, known as *otaku*, claim Tokyo's Akihabara as their home base. Though otaku can be translated as "nerd" or "obsessive," the term has been embraced by some. Former prime minister Taro Aso declared himself an otaku and confessed to reading 10 to 20 manga a week.

VIDEO GAMES

Japan is the cradle of the video game industry, and ever since the early 1970s it's been a dominant force in the gaming market. As companies like Namco gave way to Sega, Nintendo, and Sony, the gaming systems also continued to evolve and become more sophisticated. Like manga and anime, games enjoy a mainstream following. If you're a gamer, you'll be happy to find games that are unreleased in the United States alongside rebooted arcade classics like Legend of Zelda and Super Mario Bros.

BASEBALL IN JAPAN

Sumo may be the national sport, but without question, the most popular sport in Japan is baseball. It was first introduced in 1872 by Horace Wilson and has been popular ever since.

(above) Hanshin Tiger fans releasing balloons after the seventh inning; (opposite upper right) a night game at Yokohama Stadium; (opposite bottom left) players from the Japanese Little League

Each October, two major-league teams in the United States (or one major-league team from the United States and one major-league team from Canada) play the best of seven games to decide the World Series. But judging from the results of the World Baseball Classic (WBC) that Japan has won twice, any true world series of baseball would have to include Japan. While the Japanese professional-league season is shorter than its American counterpart (130–140 games versus 162 games), the major-league season's brevity is more than made up for by the company-league season, the university circuit, and the spring and summer high school tournaments. In addition, there are junior high school and elementary school leagues. Many municipalities and towns even have senior leagues for people over 60 years old. The game is played everywhere: from the southern islands of Okinawa to the northern tip of Hokkaido.

CATCHING A GAME

Even if you're not a baseball fan, you should try to take in a game on any level for the spectacle. Like the players, the fans come prepared. From team colors and fan paraphernalia to songs and boxed lunches, the Japanese fans have it down. The cheering starts with the first pitch and doesn't end until the last out. Wherever you go to see a game, you will be made to feel welcome and your interest or curiosity will be rewarded.

2

BASEBALL-DO

Martial arts in Japan (judo, kendo, kyudo) and many other activities including the tea ceremony (*chado*) and calligraphy (*shodo*) end in the suffix *do* (pronounced "doe" as in the female deer and meaning "way"). In Japan, baseball is also a *do*, an art rather than a sport. Of course, the Japanese watch baseball as they watch any sport, but in terms of their preparation and mental approach to the game, it is a do.

All of Japan's active arts require years of practice to achieve the level of intense concentration and mindlessness that mastery requires. The idea is that if you practice something long enough and hard enough, it will become pure reflex. Then you won't have to think about what to do and when to do it. You will just do it. Major players like Toritani and Sakamoto, Nishioka and Makajima play with a fluidity and grace that is beyond athleticism, exhibiting true mastery of the sport, and the result can be breathtaking.

SPRING AND SUMMER HIGH SCHOOL TOURNAMENTS

If you're fortunate enough to be in Japan in either March or August, you can attend the high school baseball tournament held annually at Koshien Stadium in Nishinomiya (near Osaka), the mecca of Japanese baseball. In what regard is high school baseball held?

Well, the pro team that normally plays at Koshien (the Hanshin Tigers) has to hit the road for two weeks in August to make way for the summer tournament. Both high school tournaments last about two weeks. Many of the star high school players go on to be standout players in both Japan and the United States. Both Boston Red Sox pitcher Koji Uehara and Miami Marlins star Ichiro Suzuki were star high school players.

TICKET PRICES

Tickets for a professional baseball game (the season runs from late March/early April to October) are a relatively good buy. At Koshien, home of the Hanshin Tigers, prices range from ¥1,900 for a seat in the outfield to ¥4,000 for a reserved seat on a lower level. When box seats are offered for sale, you can expect to pay around ¥6,000. Prices are similar at Tokyo Dome, where the Yomiuri Giants play.

Tickets for the high school baseball tournaments are even more affordable. Prices range from ¥500 for upper-reserved to ¥1,200 for lower-reserved to ¥1,600 for box seats. Seats in the bleachers are free throughout the tournaments.

Most other games (school, community, or company) are either free or, in the case of a championship game, require only a nominal fee.

JAPANESE MARTIAL ARTS

(above) A practice kendo session; (opposite upper right) practicing aikido throws; (opposite bottom left) competitors at a judo tournament

Take all that chop-socky stuff in the movies with a grain of salt: the Japanese martial arts are primarily about balance—mental, spiritual, and physical—and only incidentally about attack and self-defense.

Judo and karate are now as much icons of Japanese culture as anime or consumer electronics, and just as enthusiastically embraced abroad. Judo, karate, and aikido, all essentially 20th-century developments, have gone global; it would be hard to name a country anywhere without a network of *dojos* (martial arts academies or training halls) and local organizations, affiliates of the governing bodies in Japan, certifying students and holding competitions. Judo has been an Olympic sport for men since the 1964 games in Tokyo, and for women since 1988. An estimated 50 million people worldwide practice karate, in one or another of the eight different forms recognized by the World Union of Karate-do Federations. Aikido was first introduced abroad in the 1950s; the International Aikido Federation now has affiliates in 44 member nations. Korea and Taiwan have instruction programs in kendo (fencing) that begin at the secondary school level.

LEVELS

Levels of certification are as much a part of the martial arts as they are in other traditional disciplines—the difference being that marks of rank are clearly visible. Students progress from the 10th *kyu* level to the 1st, and then from 1st *dan* to 8th (or 10th, depending on the system or school). Beginners wear white belts, intermediates wear brown, dan holders wear black or black-and-red.

KYUDO: THE WAY OF THE BOW

Archery is the oldest of Japan's traditional martial arts, dating from the 12th century, when archers played an important role in the struggles for power among samurai clans. Today it is practiced as a sport and a spiritual discipline. The object is not just to hit the target (no mean feat), but to do so in proper form, releasing the arrow at the moment the mind is empty of all extraneous thought.

KENDO: THE WAY OF THE SWORD

Fencing was a mainstay of feudal Japan, but the roots of modern kendo date to the early 18th century, with the introduction of the *shinai*—a practice sword made of bamboo slats—and the distinctive armor (*bogu*) still in use to protect the specific target areas the fencer must strike to earn points in competition. Matches are noisy affairs; attacks must be executed with foot stamping and loud spirited shouts called *kiai*.

JUDO: THE GENTLE WAY

Dr. Kano Jigoro (1860–1938) was the proverbial 90-pound weakling as a teenager; to overcome his frailty, he immersed himself at the University of Tokyo in the martial arts, and over a period of years developed a reformed version of *jujutsu* on "scientific principles," which he finally codified in 1884. The *ju*of judo means "softness" or "gentleness"—a reference to its techniques of using one's opponent's strength against him—but belying the fact that this really is a rough-and-tumble contact sport.

KARATE: THE EMPTY HAND

Odd as it may sound, karate (literally: "the empty hand") doesn't quite qualify as a traditional Japanese martial art. Its origins are Chinese, but it was largely developed in the Ryukyu Kingdom (Okinawa before it was annexed), and didn't come to Japan proper until 1922. It lays stress on self-defense, spiritual and mental balance, and *kata*—formal, almost ritual sequences of movement. But it is as much about offense as defense: most of the movements end in a punch, a kick, or a strike with the knee or elbow.

AIKIDO: THE WAY OF HARMONY

The youngest of the Japanese martial arts was developed in the 1920s by Ueshiba Morihei (1883–1969), incorporating elements of both jujutsu and kendo, with much bigger doses of philosophy and spirituality. Aikido techniques consist largely of throws; the first thing a student learns is how to fall safely. Partner practice begins with a stylized strike or a punch; the intended receiver counters by getting out of the way, leading the attacker's momentum, pivoting into a throw or an arm/shoulder pin. The essential idea is to do no damage.

SUMO

This centuries-old national sport of Japan is not to be taken lightly—as anyone who has ever seen a sumo wrestler will testify.

(above) Two wrestlers battle in the ring; (opposite upper right) a wrestler in traditional dress outside the arena; (opposite bottom left) the ceremonial entrance of the tournament participants

Sheer mass, mind you, isn't necessarily the key to success—though it might seem that way. There are no weight limits or categories in sumo; contenders in the upper ranks average 350 pounds. But Chiyonofuji, one of the all-time great *yokozuna* (grand champions), who tipped the scales at a mere 280 pounds, regularly faced—and defeated—opponents who outweighed him by 200 pounds or more. That said, sumo wrestlers do spend a lot of their time just bulking up, consuming enormous quantities of a high-protein stew called *chanko nabe*, washed down with beer. Akebono, the first foreign-born yokozuna, weighed more than 500 pounds; current Grand Champion Hakuho, from Mongolia (the profusion of non-Japanese at the top of this most traditional of Japanese institutions is no small embarrassment to the Sumo Association), started his career at 160 pounds and doubled his weight in four years.

SUMO RULES

The official catalog of sumo techniques include 82 different ways of pushing, pulling, tripping, tossing, or slapping down your opponent, but the basic rules are exquisitely simple: Except for hitting below the belt (which is all a sumo wrestler wears) and striking with a closed fist, almost anything goes. Touch the sand with anything but the soles of your feet, or get forced out of the ring, and you lose.

SUMO HISTORY

The earliest written references to sumo date back to the year 712; for many centuries it was not so much a sport as a Shinto religious rite, associated with Imperial Court ceremonies. Its present form—with the raised clay *dohyo* (platform) and circle of rice straw bales to mark the ring, the ranking system, the referee and judges, the elaborate costumes and purification rituals—was largely developed in the 16th and early 17th centuries.

THE SUMO WORLD

Sumo is very much a closed world, hierarchical and formal. To compete in it, you must belong to a *heya* (stable) run by a retired wrestler who has purchased that right from the association. The stable master, or *oyakata*, is responsible for bringing in as many new wrestlers as the heya can accommodate, for their training (every stable has its own practice ring) and schooling in the elaborate etiquette of sumo, and for every facet of their daily lives. Youngsters recruited into the sport live in the stable dormitory, doing all the community chores and waiting on their seniors while they learn. When they rise high enough in tournament rankings, they acquire servant-apprentices of their own.

All the stables in the association—now some 50 in number—are in Tokyo. Most are clustered on both sides of the

Sumida River near the green-roofed *Kokugikan* (National Sumo Arena), in the areas called Asakusabashi and Ryogoku. Come early in the day, and you can peer through the windows of the heya to watch them practice; with luck—and good connections—you might even get invited in.

There are six official sumo tournaments throughout the year: three in Tokyo (January, May, and September); one each in Osaka (March), Nagoya (July), and Fukuoka (November). Wrestlers in the upper divisions fight 15 matches over 15 days. A few weeks before each tournament, a panel of judges and association *toshiyori* (elders) publish a table called a *banzuke*, which divides the 800-plus wrestlers into six ranks and two divisions, East and West, to determine who fights whom. Rankings are based on a wrestler's record in the previous tournament: win a majority of your matches and you go up in the next banzuke; lose a majority and you go down.

If you can't attend one of the Tokyo sumo tournaments, you may want to at least pay a short visit to the practice sessions (⇨ *Greater Tokyo in Chapter 3*). Sometimes tours can be arranged in advance.

THE GEISHA

(above) A traditional geisha performance in Kanazawa; (opposite upper right) geishas in Kyoto; (opposite bottom left) geishas on the streets of Kyoto

The geisha—with her white makeup and Cupid's-bow red lip rouge, her hair ornaments, the rich brocade of her kimono—is as much an icon of Japan, instantly recognizable the world over, as Mt. Fuji itself.

Gei stands for artistic accomplishment (*sha* simply means "person"), and a geisha must be a person of many talents. As a performer, she should have a lovely voice and a command of traditional dance, and play beautifully on an instrument like the *shamisen*. She must have a finely tuned aesthetic sense, and excel at the art of conversation. In short, she should be the ultimate party hostess and gracious companion. Geisha (or *geiko* in Kyoto dialect) begin their careers at a very young age, when they are accepted into an *okiya*, a sort of guildhall where they live and learn as *maiko* (apprentices). The okiya is a thoroughly matriarchal society; the owner/manager is called *o-kami-san*, who is addressed as *okaasan* ("mother"), to underscore the fact that the geishas have given up one family for another.

GEISHA LIFE

The okiya provides the apprentices with room and board, pays for their training and clothing (the latter a staggering expense), and oversees their daily lives. The maiko in turn do household chores; when they have become full-fledged geisha, they contribute a part of their income to the upkeep of the house and its all-female staff of teachers, dressers, and maids.

2

THE GEISHA BUSINESS

There are no free agents in the geisha world; to engage one for a party you need a referral. Geisha work almost exclusively at traditional inns (ryokan), restaurants (*ryotei*), and teahouses (*chaya*); the owners of one will contact an okiya with which they have a connection and make the engagement—providing, of course, that you've established yourself as a trustworthy client. That means you will understand and be prepared to pay the bill, when it shows up sometime later. Fees for a geisha's or maiko's time are measured in "sticks"—generally, one hour: the time it would take a stick of incense to burn down—and the okiya can really stick it to you. Bills are based on the number of guests at the party, and can run as high as ¥25,000 per person or more, for a two-hour engagement.

There were as many as 80,000 geisha in the 1920s; today there may be 1,000 left, most of them living and working in the Gion district of Kyoto; in Kanazawa; and in the Shimbashi, Akasaka, and Ginza districts of Tokyo. Fewer and fewer young Japanese women are willing to make the total commitment this closed world demands (even a geisha who opts to live independently will remain affiliated with her okiya for the rest of her career); fewer and fewer Japanese men

of means have the taste or inclination to entertain themselves or important guests in this elegant fashion. On the other hand, the profession—while it lasts—does provide considerable job security. A geisha is valued, not solely for her beauty, but for her artistic and social skills—and her absolute discretion (what she might see and hear, for example, at a party hosted by a political bigwig for his important business connections, could topple empires). A geisha with these accomplishments will still be in demand long after the bloom of youth has fled.

A geisha will establish a variety of relations with men. She will try to develop a roster of repeat clients, and may choose one among them as a patron, for financial support and—although she is by no means, as some people imagine, a prostitute—for sexual intimacy. When a geisha marries, most often to such a client, she leaves the profession.

THE TEA CEREMONY

(above) Guests participating in a tea ceremony; (opposite upper right) a bowl of matcha green tea; (opposite bottom left) an outdoor garden tea ceremony

The Way of Tea—in Japanese, *Cha-no-yu* or *Sado*—is more than a mere ceremonial occasion to have a cuppa: it is a profound spiritual and philosophical ritual. It's also a ritual you can experience easily and relatively inexpensively.

Tea came to Japan from China in the late 8th century, first as a medicinal plant; it was the Zen monks of the 12th century who started the practice of drinking tea for a refresher between meditation sessions. Rules and customs began to evolve regarding how to drink this precious beverage, and they coalesced in the Muromachi period of the 14th and 15th centuries as the earliest form of the Cha-no-yu. The Way of Tea developed an aesthetic of its own, rooted in the Zen sense of discipline, restraint, and simplicity: an aesthetic in which the most valued tea bowls, vessels, and utensils were humble, unadorned—and even imperfect. The choreographed steps and movements of the tea ceremony were devised to focus the appreciation—in Japanese, called *wabi*—for this subdued and quiet refinement.

THE TEA PAVILION

Contemplate a Japanese tea pavilion long enough, and you begin to see how much work and thought can go into the design of something so simple. A stone path through a garden, a thatched roof, a low doorway into a single room with a *tokonoma* (alcove) and tatami floor are barely big enough for the tea master and a few guests, and yet are a gateway to the infinite.

THE WAY OF TEA

The poet-priest Sen no Rikyu (1522–91) is the most revered figure in the history of Cha-no-yu. Three traditional schools of the tea ceremony, the Ura Senke, the Omote Senke, and the Mushakoji Senke—with some variations among them—maintain the forms and aesthetic principles he developed.

A full-scale formal tea ceremony, called a *chaji*, is like a drama in two acts, involving a multicourse *kaiseki* meal, two different kinds of powdered green tea, and an intermission—and can take as long as four hours to perform. Most ceremonies are less formal, confined to the serving of *usucha* ("thin tea") and a confection, for an intimate group; these are called *o-chakai*. Both forms demand a strictly determined, stately series of moves to be made by both guests and hosts.

Participants gather first in the *machiai*, a kind of waiting room or shelter in the garden, until they are invited to proceed to the teahouse. They remove their shoes, and enter the teahouse through a low doorway. It is customary to comment on the flower arrangement or scroll in the alcove. The guests sit in *seiza*, their legs tucked under them; the host enters from another small doorway, greets them, and carefully cleans the utensils: bowl, tea scoop, caddy, ladle, whisk. No matter that they are spotless already; cleaning them is part of the ritual.

When the tea is prepared, it is served first to the principal guest, who turns the bowl in the palm of his hand, drains it in three deep, careful sips, and returns it to the host. The other participants are served in turn. The guests comment on the presentation, and the ceremony is over; when they leave the pavilion, the host bows to them from the door.

You won't be expected to have the same mastery of the etiquette as a Japanese guest, but the right frame of mind will get you through, if you are invited to a tea ceremony. Make conversation that befits the serenity of the moment. (A well-known haiku poetess once said that what she learned most from Cha-no-yu was to think before she spoke.) Above all, pay close attention to the practiced movements of the host, and remember to praise the *wabi*—the understated beauty—of the utensils he or she has chosen.

Recommended reading: *The Book of Tea* by Okakura Kakuzo; *Cha-no-Yu: The Japanese Tea Ceremony* by A. L. Sadler.

2

JAPANESE GARDENS

Oases of calm and contemplation—and philosophical statements in their own right—Japanese gardens are quite unlike the arrangements of flowers, shrubs, and trees you find in the West.

(above) The garden of Hogon-in, Kyoto; (opposite upper right) the gardens of Kinkaku-ji, Kyoto; (opposite bottom left) Koishikawa Korakuen Garden, Tokyo

One key to understanding—and more fully enjoying—a Japanese garden is knowing that its design, like all traditional Japanese arts, emerged out of the country's unique mixture of religious and artistic ideas. From Shintoism comes the belief in the divinity or spirit that dwells in natural phenomena like mountains, trees, and stones. The influence of Taoism is reflected in the islands that serve as symbolic heavens for the souls of those who achieve perfect harmony. Buddhist gardens—especially Zen gardens, expressions of the "less is more" aesthetic of the warrior caste—evolved in medieval times as spaces for meditation and the path to enlightenment. The classic example from this period is the *karesansui* (dry landscape) style, a highly abstract composition of meticulously placed rocks and raked sand or gravel, sometimes with a single pruned tree, but with no water at all.

SHAKEI

Shakei ("borrowed landscape") is a way of extending the boundaries of the visual space by integrating a nearby attractive view—like a mountain or a sweeping temple roofline, for example—framing and echoing it with plantings of similar shape or color inside the garden itself. A middle ground, usually a hedge or a wall, blocks off any unwanted view and draws the background into the composition.

GARDEN DESIGN

Historically, the first garden designers in Japan were temple priests; the design concepts themselves were originally Chinese. Later, from the 16th century on, the most remarkable Japanese gardens were created by tea masters, who established a genre of their own for settings meant to deepen and refine the tea ceremony experience. Hence the *roji*: a garden path of stepping-stones from the waiting room to the teahouse itself, a transition from the ordinary world outside that prepares participants emotionally and mentally for the ceremony. Gradually, gardens moved out of the exclusive realm to which only nobles, wealthy merchants, and poets had access, and the increasingly affluent middle class began to demand professional designers. In the process, the elements of the garden became more elaborate, complex, and symbolic.

The "hide-and-reveal" principle, for example, dictates that there should be no point from which all of a garden is visible, that there must always be mystery and incompleteness in its changing perspectives. The garden *unfolds* as you walk from one view to another along the winding path. References to celebrated natural wonders and literary allusions, too, are frequently used design techniques. Mt. Fuji might be represented by a truncated cone of

stones; Ama-no-Hashidate, the famous pine-covered spit of land across Miyazu Bay, near Kyoto, might be rendered by a stone bridge; a lone tree might stand for a mighty forest. Abstract concepts and themes from myths and legends, readily understood by the Japanese, are similarly part of the garden vocabulary. The use of boulders in a streambed, for example, can represent life's surmountable difficulties; a pine tree can stand for strength and endurance; islands in a pond can evoke a faraway paradise.

Seasonal change is a highlight of the Japanese garden: the designer in effect choreographs the different plants that come into their glory at different times of year: cherry and plum blossoms and wisteria in spring; hydrangeas, peonies, and water lilies in summer; the spectacular reds and orange of the Japanese maple leaves in autumn. Even in winter, the snow clinging to the garden's bare bones makes an impressive sight. In change, there is permanence; in permanence, there is fluid movement—often represented in the garden with a water element: a pond or a flowing stream, or an abstraction of one in raked gravel or stone.

RELIGION IN JAPAN

(above) A Shinto shrine near Tokyo; (opposite upper right) a statue of Buddha at Todai-ji, Nara; (opposite bottom left) the gates at Futura-san Jinja, Nikko

Although both Buddhism and Shinto permeate Japanese society and life, most Japanese are blissfully unaware of the distinction between what is Shinto and what is Buddhist. A wedding is often a Shinto ceremony, while a funeral is a Buddhist rite.

There's a saying in Japan that you're Shinto at birth (marked with a Shinto ceremony), Christian when you marry (if you choose a Western-style wedding), and Buddhist when you die (honored with a Buddhist funeral). The Japanese take a utilitarian view of religion and use each as suits the occasion. One prays for success in life at a shrine and for the repose of a deceased family member at a temple. There is no thought given to the whys for this—these things simply are. The neighborhood shrine's annual *matsuri* is a time of giving thanks for prosperity and for blessing homes and local businesses. *O-mikoshi*, portable shrines for the gods, are enthusiastically carried around the district by young local men. Shouting and much sake drinking are part of the celebration. But it's a celebration first and foremost.

RELIGION IN NUMBERS

While most Japanese—some 90 million people out of some 128 million total—identify themselves as Buddhist, most also practice and believe in Shinto, even if they don't identify themselves as Shinto followers per se. The two religions overlap and even complement each other, even though most Japanese people would not consider themselves "religious."

SHINTO

Shinto—literally, "the way of the *kami* (god)"—is a form of animism or nature worship based on myth and rooted to the geography and holy places of the land. It's an ancient belief system, dating back perhaps as far as 500 BC, and is indigenous to Japan. The name is derived from a Chinese word, *shin tao,* coined in the 8th century AD, when divine origins were first ascribed to the royal Yamato family. Fog-enshrouded mountains, pairs of rocks, primeval forests, and geothermal activity are all manifestations of the *kami-sama* (honorable gods). For many Japanese, the Shinto aspect of their lives is simply the realm of the kami-sama and is not attached to a religious framework as it would be in the West. In that sense, the name describes more a way of thinking than a religion.

BUDDHISM

A Korean king gave a statue of Shaka—the first Buddha, Prince Gautama—to the Yamato Court in AD 538. The Soga clan adopted the foreign faith, using it as a vehicle to change the political order of the day. After battling for control of the country, they established themselves as political rulers, and Buddhism took permanent hold. Simultaneously, Japan sent its first ambassadors to China, inaugurating the importation of Chinese culture, writing, and religion into

Japan. By the 8th century, Buddhism was well established.

Japanese Buddhism developed in three waves. In the Heian period (794–1185), Esoteric Buddhism was introduced primarily by two priests, both of whom studied in China: Saicho and Kukai. Saicho established a temple on Mt. Hie near Kyoto, making it the most revered mountain in Japan after Mt. Fuji. Kukai established the Shingon sect of Esoteric Buddhism on Mt. Koya, south of Nara. In Japanese temple architecture, Esoteric Buddhism introduced the separation of the temple into an interior for the initiated and an outer laypersons' area.

Amidism (Pure Land) was the second wave, introduced by the monk Honen (1133–1212), and it flourished in the late 12th century until the introduction of Zen in 1185. Its adherents saw the world emerging from a period of darkness during which Buddhism had been in decline, and asserted that salvation was offered only to the believers in *Amida,* a Nyorai (Buddha) or enlightened being. Amidism's promise of salvation and its subsequent versions of heaven and hell earned it the appellation "Devil's Christianity" from visiting Christian missionaries in the 16th century.

In the Post-Heian period (1185 to the present) the influences of Nichiren and Zen Buddhist philosophies pushed Japanese Buddhism in new directions.

The Senso-ji Complex is the heart at soul of the Asakusa district of Tokyo.

Nichiren (1222–82) was a monk who insisted on the primacy of the Lotus Sutra, the supposed last and greatest sutra of Shaka. Zen Buddhism was attractive to the samurai class's ideals of discipline and worldly detachment and thus spread throughout Japan in the 12th century. It was later embraced as a nonintellectual path to enlightenment by those in search of a direct experience of the sublime. More recently, Zen has been adopted by a growing number of people in the West as a way to move beyond the subject/object duality that characterizes Western thought.

SHRINE AND STATE

While the modern Japanese constitution expressly calls for a separation of church and state, it hasn't always been this way. In fact, twice over the last 150 years, Shinto was the favored religion and the government used all of its influence to support it.

During the Meiji Restoration (1868), the emperor was made sovereign leader of Japan, and power that had been spread out among the shoguns was consolidated in the Imperial House. Shinto was favored over Buddhism for two reasons. First, according to Shinto, the members of the Imperial Family were direct descendants of the kami who had formed Japan. The second reason was more practical: many of the Buddhist temples were regional power bases that relied upon the shoguns for patronage. Relegating Buddhism to a minor religion with no official support would have a weakening effect on the shoguns, while the government could use Shinto shrines to strengthen its power base.

Indeed, Buddhism was actively suppressed. Temples were closed, priests were harassed, and priceless art was either destroyed or sold. The collections of Japanese art at the Museum of Fine Arts, Boston and the Freer Gallery in Washington, DC, were just two of the indirect beneficiaries of this policy.

During the Pacific War (the Japanese term for World War II), Shinto was again used by the military (with the complicity of the Imperial House) to justify an aggressive stance in Asia. (It should be noted that Kokuchukai Buddhism was also used to sanction the invasion of other countries.) The emperor was a god and therefore infallible. Since the Japanese people were essentially one family with the emperor at the head, they were a superior race that was meant to rule the lesser peoples of Asia.

Once ancestor worship was allied with worship of the emperor, the state became something worth dying for. So potent was this mix that General Douglas MacArthur identified state Shinto as one of the first things that had to be dismantled upon the surrender of Japan. The emperor could stay, but shrine and state had to go.

RELIGIOUS FESTIVALS

Although there are religious festivals and holy days observed throughout the year, the two biggest events in the Japanese religious calendar are New Year's (*Oshogatsu*) and *Obon*. New Year's is celebrated from January 1 to 3. Many people visit temples the night of December 31 to ring in the New Year or in the coming weeks. Temple bells are struck 108 times to symbolize ridding oneself of the 108 human sins. This practice is called *hatsumode*. Food stalls are set up close to the popular places, and the atmosphere is festive and joyous. Many draw fortune slips called *omikuji* to see what kind of a year the oracle has in store for them.

The other major religious event in the Japanese calendar is the Obon holiday, traditionally held from August 13 to 15. Obon is the Japanese festival of the dead when the spirits come back to visit the living. Most people observe the ritual by returning to their hometown or the home of their grandparents. Graves are cleaned and respects are paid to one's ancestors. Family ties are strengthened and renewed.

VISITING A BUDDHIST TEMPLE

The first thing to do when visiting a temple is to stop at the gate (called *mon* in Japanese), put your hands together, and bow. Once inside the gate, you should stop to wash your hands at the stone receptacle usually found immediately upon entering the temple grounds. Fill one of the ladles with water using your right hand and wash your left hand first. Then refill the ladle with water using your left hand and wash your right hand. Some people also pour water in their right hand to rinse their mouth, but this is not necessary.

After washing your hands, you can ring the temple bell if you choose.

Next, light a candle in front of the main altar of the temple and place it inside the glass cabinet. Then put your hands together and bow. You can also light three sticks of incense (lighting them together is customary) and put them in the large stone or brass stand. This action is also followed with a prayer and a bow. It is important to note, however, that while some people may light both a candle and three sticks of incense, others may just do one or the other. Some may skip this part entirely.

After you finish, you can proceed to the main altar, put your hands together, bow, and pray. Many people recite one of the Buddhist sutras.

A worshipper bows at the Meiji Shrine in the Shibuya District of Tokyo.

(Above) The massive torii (entrance gates) of the Meiji Shrine are over 40 feet tall.

If you'd like to have a closer look at the interior of the altar building, you can climb the steps and look inside. At this time, you can also throw a coin inside the wooden box on the top step as an offering, again putting your hands together and bowing.

Most temples have sub-altars dedicated to different Buddhist saints or deities, and you can repeat the candle, incense, and prayer steps observed at the main altar if you choose.

After praying at the main altar and/or sub-altar, you'll probably want to spend some time walking around the temple grounds. Most temples are incredibly beautiful places. Many have gardens and sculpture worthy of a visit in their own right.

Upon leaving the temple, you should stop at the gate, turn, put your hands together, and bow to give thanks.

VISITING A SHINTO SHRINE

Shrines, like temples, have gates, though they are called *torii* and are often painted bright orange. In terms of their appearance, torii look much like the mathematical symbol for pi. As with the gates of temples, one enters and exits through the torii, bowing on the way in and again on the way out. However, when visiting a shrine one claps twice before bowing. This is to summon the kami. Once you have their attention, you clap twice again to pay them homage.

Inside the shrine, you wash your hands as you would at a temple (left hand and then right hand). You then proceed to the main altar, clap twice, and bow. In a shrine, clapping twice and bowing is often repeated, as there may be special trees, stones, and other holy objects situated throughout the grounds.

After you have finished visiting the shrine, you should turn around at the torii, clap twice, and bow upon leaving.

3

EXPLORING TOKYO

Updated by Robert Morel

From the crush of the morning commute to the evening crowds flowing into shops, restaurants, and bars, Tokyo's image is that of a city that never stops and rarely slows down. It is all too often portrayed as a strange carousel of lights, sounds, and people set on fast-forward, but these days there is a greater focus on cultural development and quality of life.

For a time it seemed that Tokyo was becoming the city of the future—compact urban life, surrounded by high-tech skyscrapers, the world's densest rail system, and a 3-D network of highways overlapping and twisting above the city. Twenty years of gradual economic stagnation have cooled that vision, but if Tokyo no longer sees itself as the city of the future, it seems to have settled comfortably into being a city of the present.

While parts of the city such as Shibuya or Shinjuku's Kabuki-cho continue to overwhelm with a 24-hour cacophony of light, sound, and energy, other neighborhoods are surprisingly relaxed. In Ometesando and Aoyama, people are more likely to be sipping wine or coffee with friends at an outdoor café than downing beer and sake with coworkers in an *izakaya* (a bar that serves food). The people are as varied as their city. Residents of Aoyama may wear European fashion and drive fancy imports, but those residing in Asakusa prefer to be decidedly less flashy.

Even the landscape is varied. The city hosts some of the most unsightly sprawls of concrete housing—extending for miles in all directions—in the world, but offsetting all the concrete and glass is a wealth of green space in the form of parks, temple grounds, and traditional gardens.

Whether you're gazing at the glow of Tokyo's evening lights or the green expanse of its parks, this is a city of astonishing and intriguing beauty. If you're a foodie, artist, design lover, or cultural adventurer, then Tokyo, a city of inspiration and ideas, is for you.

ORIENTATION AND PLANNING

GETTING ORIENTED

Greater Tokyo incorporates 23 wards, 26 smaller cities, five towns, and eight villages—altogether sprawling 88 km (55 miles) from east to west and 24 km (15 miles) from north to south with a population of 35 million people. The wards alone enclose an area of 590 square km (228 square miles), which comprise the city center and house 8 million residents. Chiyoda-ku, Chuo-ku, Shinjuku-ku, and Minato-ku are the four central business districts.

DID YOU KNOW?

Space is the greatest luxury in Tokyo and affordable housing is found only in the suburbs. An average Tokyo family probably lives in a cramped apartment that averages 80 square meters (860 square feet). A one-bedroom apartment situated inside the Roppongi Hills residential complex is approximately ¥600,000 (around $7,000) per month to rent.

3

PLANNING

ATMS AND MONEY

The ATMs at most 7-Eleven and Lawson convenience stores have English menus and accept Visa and MasterCard debit and credit cards. Additionally, Seven Bank, Citibank, Shinsei Bank (in some subway stations), and Japan Post ATMs allow international bank card transactions. Tokyo is a safe city, so you may carry cash without fear of street crime.

BUDGET TIPS

If you plan on visiting a lot of the city's sites, purchasing a **GRUTT Pass** (🌐 *www.museum.or.jp/grutto*) is the way to go. The pass, which is only ¥2,000 (¥2,800 with a one-day Tokyo Metro pass), gives visitors free or discounted admission to 78 sites throughout the city including museums, zoos, aquariums, and parks. Passes can be purchased at participating sites, as well as the Tokyo Tourist Information Center. Keep in mind that passes expire two months after the date of purchase.

TOKYO ADDRESSES

The simplest way to decipher a Tokyo address is to break it into parts. For example, in 6-chome 8–19, Chuo-ku, the "chome" indicates a precise area (a block, for example), the numbers following chome indicate the building within the area, and "ku" refers to the ward (a district) of a city.

Even Japanese people cannot quickly find a building based on the address alone. If you get in a taxi with a written address, do not assume the driver will be able to locate your destination even with the onboard navigation system. Usually, people provide very detailed instructions or maps to explain their exact locations. It's always good to know the location of your destination in relation to a major building or department store; most hotels can provide this information before you head out.

IMPERIAL PALACE DISTRICT 皇居近辺

The Imperial Palace district is the core of Japan's government. It is primarily comprised of the *Nagata-cho* (surrounding neighborhood), the Imperial Palace (*Kokyo-gaien*), the Diet (national parliament building), the prime minister's residence (*Kantei*), and the Supreme Court. The Imperial Palace and the Diet are both important for visitors to see, but the Supreme Court is rather nondescript. Unfortunately, the prime minister's residence is only viewable from afar, hidden behind fortified walls and trees.

The Imperial Palace was built by the order of Ieyasu Tokugawa, who chose the site for his castle in 1590. The castle had 99 gates (36 in the outer wall), 21 watchtowers (of which 3 are still standing), and 28 armories. The outer defenses stretched from present-day Shimbashi Station to Kanda. Completed in 1640 (and later expanded), it was at the time the largest castle in the world.

The Japanese Imperial Family resides in heavily blockaded sections of the palace grounds. Tours are conducted by reservation only, and restricted to designated outdoor sections, namely, the palace grounds and the East Gardens. While the East Gardens are open to visitors daily, the main grounds are open to the general public only twice a year, on January 2 and December 23 (the Emperor's birthday), when thousands of people assemble under the balcony to offer their good wishes to the Imperial Family.

TOP ATTRACTIONS

Chidorigafuchi National Cemetery (千鳥ヶ淵戦没者墓苑 *Chidorigafuchi Senbotsusha Boen*). High on the edge of the Imperial Palace moat, this cemetery holds the remains of thousands of unknown soldiers and is famous for its springtime cherry blossoms. The adjacent **Chidorigafuchi Boathouse** rents out rowboats and pedal boats. Only a small part of the Palace's outer moat is accessible, but a walk here makes for a refreshing 30 minutes. The entrance to the garden is near Yasukuni Jinja. ✉ *2 Sanban-cho, Chiyoda-ku, Imperial Palace* ☎ *03/3234–1948* 🎫 *Park free, boat rental ¥500 for 30 mins during regular season, ¥800 for 30 mins during cherry blossom season* ⏲ *Park daily sunrise–sunset; boathouse early Apr.–late Nov., Tues.–Sun. 11–5:30* Ⓜ *Hanzo-mon and Shinjuku subway lines, Kudanshita Station (Exit 2).*

Fodor's Choice ★ **Imperial Palace East Garden** (皇居東御苑 *Kokyo Higashi Gyo-en*). Tokyo's most central yet most overlooked oasis of green and quiet is more a relaxed, spacious park than a traditional Japanese garden, making it a good picnic spot as well. Formerly part of the grounds of Edo Castle, it was claimed for the Imperial Family after the 1868 Meiji Restoration. Though most of the old castle was torn down or lost to fire, the stone foundations hint at the scale of the country's former seat of power.

The entrance to the East Garden is the Ote-mon, once the main gate of Ieyasu Tokugawa's castle. Here, you will come across the National Police Agency *dojo* (martial arts hall) and the Ote Rest House, where you can buy a simple map of the garden. The **Museum of the Imperial Collection** next door features rotating exhibits of imperial household treasures.

The **Hundred-Man Guardhouse** was once defended by four shifts of 100 soldiers each. Past it is the entrance to what was once the *ni-no-maru*, the "second circle" of the fortress. It's now a grove and garden. At the far end is the **Suwa Tea Pavilion,** an early-19th-century building relocated here from another part of the castle grounds.

The steep stone walls of the **hon-maru** (the "inner circle"), with the Moat of Swans below, dominate the west side of the garden. Halfway along is **Shio-mi-zaka,** which translates roughly as "Briny View Hill," so named because in the Edo period the ocean could be seen from here.

Head to the wooded paths around the garden's edges for shade, quiet, and benches to rest your weary feet. In the southwest corner is the Fujimi Yagura, the only surviving watchtower of the hon-maru; farther along the path, on the west side, is the **Fujimi Tamon,** one of the two remaining armories.

The odd-looking octagonal tower is the **Tokagakudo Concert Hall.** Its mosaic tile facade was built in honor of Empress Kojun in 1966. ✉ *1–1 Chiyoda, Chiyoda-ku, Imperial Palace* ☎ *03/3213–1111* 🎫 *Free* ⏲ *Mar.–Apr. 14 and Sep.–Oct., Tues.–Thurs. and weekends 9–4:30; Apr. 15–Aug., Tues.–Thurs. and weekends 9–5; Nov.–Feb., Tues.-Thurs. and weekends 9–4* Ⓜ *Tozai, Marunouchi, and Chiyoda subway lines, Ote-machi Station (Exit C13B).*

National Diet Building (国会議事堂 *Kokkai-Gijido*). The Japanese parliament occupies a perfect example of post–World War II Japanese architecture; on a gloomy day it seems as if it might have sprung from the screen of a German Expressionist movie. Started in 1920, construction took 17 years to complete. Guided tours are available most days, but it's best to call ahead to confirm times. The Prime Minister's residence,

GETTING ORIENTED

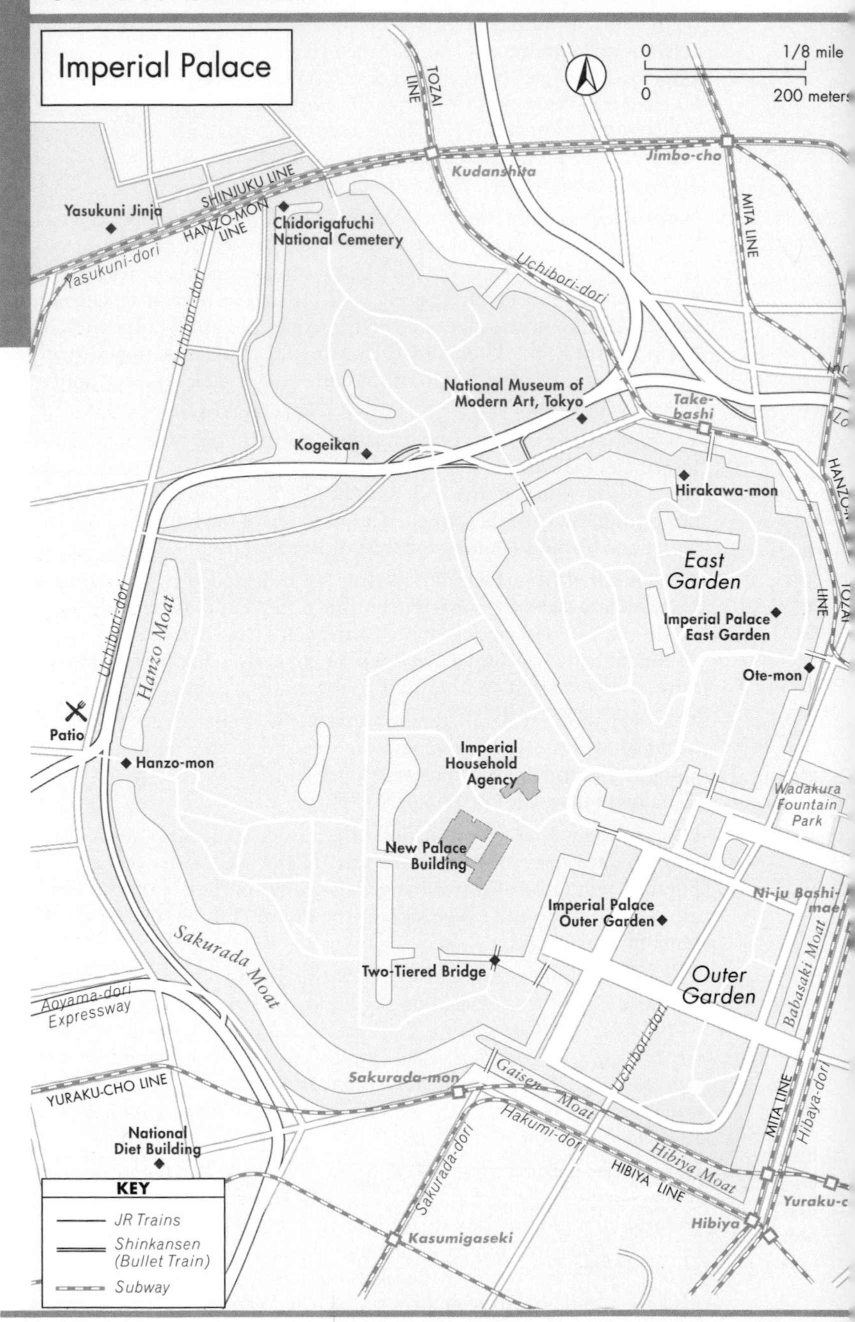
Imperial Palace
0 1/8 mile
0 200 meters
TOZAI LINE
Kudanshita
Jimbo-cho
MITA LINE
SHINJUKU LINE
HANZO-MON LINE
Yasukuni Jinja
Chidorigafuchi National Cemetery
Yasukuni-dori
Uchibori-dori
National Museum of Modern Art, Tokyo
Take-bashi
Kogeikan
Hirakawa-mon
East Garden
Imperial Palace East Garden
Ote-mon
Hanzo Moat
Patio
Hanzo-mon
Imperial Household Agency
Wadakura Fountain Park
New Palace Building
Ni-ju Bashi-mae
Imperial Palace Outer Garden
Sakurada Moat
Two-Tiered Bridge
Outer Garden
Babasaki Moat
Aoyama-dori Expressway
Sakurada-mon
Gaisen Moat
YURAKU-CHO LINE
Hakumi-dori
Sakurada-dori
Hibiya Moat
Hibiya-dori
National Diet Building
HIBIYA LINE
Hibiya
Kasumigaseki
KEY
JR Trains
Shinkansen (Bullet Train)
Subway

ORIENTATION

The Imperial Palace is located in the heart of central Tokyo, and the city's other neighborhoods branch out from here. The palace, where the Imperial Family still resides, is surrounded by a moat that connects through canals to Tokyo Bay and Sumida River (Sumida-gawa) to the east.

PLANNING

Imperial Household Agency (宮内庁). The best way to discover the Imperial Palace is to take part in one of the free tours offered by the Imperial Household Agency. There are four different tours: Imperial Palace Grounds, the East Gardens (*Higashi Gyo-en*), Sannomaru Shozokan, and Gagaku Performance (autumn only). Tour registration is required a day in advance; hours change according to the season. ✉ *1-1 Chiyoda, Chiyoda-ku, Imperial Palace* ☎ *03/3213–1111* 🌐 *www.kunaicho.go.jp.*

If going on your own, allow at least an hour for the East Garden and Outer Garden. Visit Yasukuni Jinja after lunch and spend at least an hour there, taking half an hour each for the small Yushukan (at Yasukuni Jinja) and Kogeikan museums. The modern art museum requires a more leisurely visit.

■ **TIP→ Avoid visiting the Imperial Palace on Monday, when the East Garden and museums are closed; the East Garden is also closed Friday. In July and August, heat will make the palace walk grueling—bring a hat and bottled water.**

GETTING HERE AND AROUND

The best way to get to the Imperial Palace is by subway. Take the Chiyoda Line to Nijubashimae Station (Exit 6) or the JR lines to Tokyo Station (Marunouchi Central Exit). There are three entrance gates—Ote-mon, Hirakawa-mon, and Kita-hane-bashi-mon. You can also easily get to any of the three from the Ote-machi or Takebashi subway stations.

QUICK BITES

Patio (パティオ). Before exploring the Imperial Palace, enjoy breakfast at Patio, located inside the Grand Arc Hanzomon Hotel. On summer evenings, the restaurant also offers a relaxed beer garden with a reasonably priced set menu and all-you-can-drink option. ✉ *1-1 Hayabusa-cho, Chiyoda-ku, Imperial Palace* ☎ *03/3288–1636* 🌐 *www.grandarc.com/english/restaurant.html.*

TOP REASONS TO GO

Enjoy a city oasis. Located in the middle of the city, the Imperial Palace East Garden is a wonderful place to escape the hustle and bustle of the city.

Visit a controversial shrine. The Yasukuni Shrine (Shrine of Peace for the Nation), which represents Japan's militaristic past, has long been the source of political tension between Japan, Korea, and China.

See some of Japan's finest art. The finest collection of Japanese modern art is housed in the National Museum of Modern Art, including works by such renowned painters as Taikan Yokoyama, Gyoshu Hayami, Kokei Kobayashi, and Gyokudo Kawai.

Kantei, is across the street; you can try and get a glimpse of it, but it's quite hidden by walls and trees. ✉ *1–7–1 Nagata-cho, Chiyoda-ku, Imperial Palace* ☎ *03/5521–7445* 🌐 *www.sangiin.go.jp* ⏲ *Mon.–Fri. 8–5* Ⓜ *Marunouchi subway line, Kokkai-Gijido-mae Station (Exit 2).*

National Museum of Modern Art, Tokyo (国立近代美術館 *Tokyo Kokuritsu Kindai Bijutsukan*). Founded in 1952 and moved to its present site in 1969, this was Japan's first national art museum. Twentieth- and 21st-century Japanese and Western art is featured throughout the year, but the museum tends to be rather lackadaisical about how these exhibitions are organized and presented, and the exhibitions are seldom on the cutting edge. The second through fourth floors house the permanent collection, which includes the painting, prints, and sculpture by Rousseau, Picasso, Tsuguji Fujita, Ryuzaburo Umehara, and Taikan Yokoyama. ✉ *3–1 Kitanomaru-koen, Chiyoda-ku, Imperial Palace* ☎ *03/5777–8600* 🌐 *www.momat.go.jp* 🎫 *¥430* ⏲ *Tues.–Thurs. and weekends 10–5, Fri. 10–8* Ⓜ *Tozai subway line, Takebashi Station (Exit 1B); Hanzo-mon and Shinjuku subway lines, Kudanshita Station (Exit 2).*

Yasukuni Jinja (靖国神社 *Shrine of Peace for the Nation*). Founded in 1869, this shrine is dedicated to approximately 2.5 million Japanese, Taiwanese, and Koreans who have died since then in war or military service. As the Japanese constitution expressly renounces both militarism and state sponsorship of religion, Yasukuni has been a center of stubborn political debate, particularly since 1978 when a shrine official added the names of several class-A war criminals to the list. Numerous prime ministers have visited the shrine since 1979, causing a political chill between Japan and its close neighbors, Korea and China who suffered under Japanese colonialism. Despite all this, hundreds of thousands of Japanese come here every year, simply to pray for the repose of friends and relatives they have lost. These pilgrimages are most frenzied on August 15, the anniversary of the conclusion of World War II, when former soldiers and ultra-right-wing groups descend upon the shrine's grounds en masse.

The shrine is not one structure but a complex of buildings that include the **Main Hall** and the **Hall of Worship**—both built in the simple, unadorned style of the ancient Shinto shrines at Ise—and the **Yushukan,** a museum of documents and war memorabilia. Also here are a Noh theater and, in the far western corner, a sumo-wrestling ring. Sumo matches are held at Yasukuni in April, during the first of its three annual festivals. You can pick up a pamphlet and simplified map of the shrine, both in English, just inside the grounds.

Refurbished in 2002, the Yushukan presents Japan at its most ambivalent—if not unrepentant—about its more recent militaristic past. Critics charge that the newer exhibits glorify the nation's role in the Pacific War as a noble struggle for independence; certainly there's an agenda here that's hard to reconcile with Japan's firm postwar rejection of militarism as an instrument of national policy. Many Japanese visitors are moved by such displays as the last letters and photographs of young

Once the site of the Imperial Palace's innermost defense circles, the East Garden now offers respite in a beautiful setting.

kamikaze pilots, while others find the Yushukan a cautionary, rather than uplifting, experience.

Although some of the exhibits have English labels and notes, the English is not very helpful; most objects, however, speak clearly enough for themselves. Rooms on the second floor house an especially fine collection of medieval swords and armor. Visiting on a Sunday offers a chance to forage at the flea market that runs from morning until sundown. ✉ *3–1–1 Kudankita, Chiyoda-ku, Imperial Palace* ☎ *03/3261–8326* 🌐 *www.yasukuni.or.jp* 🎫 *Shrine free, Yushukan ¥800* 🕐 *Grounds Mar.–Oct., daily 8:15–5; Nov.–Feb., daily 8:15–4; Museum daily, 9–4:30* Ⓜ *Hanzo-mon and Shinjuku subway lines, Kudanshita Station (Exit 1).*

WORTH NOTING

Hanzo-mon (半蔵門 *Hanzo Gate*). The house of Hattori Hanzo (1541–96) once sat at the foot of this small wooden gate. Hanzo was a legendary leader of Ieyasu Tokugawa's private corps of spies and infiltrators—and assassins, if need be. They were the menacing, black-clad ninja—perennial material for historical adventure films and television dramas. The gate is a minute's walk from the subway. ✉ *Chiyoda-ku, Imperial Palace* Ⓜ *Hanzo-mon subway line, Hanzo-mon Station (Exit 3).*

CLOSE UP

Stretch Your Legs

The venue of choice for runners is the **Imperial Palace Outer Garden**. At the west end of the park, *Sakurada-mon's* (Gate of the Field of Cherry Trees) small courtyard is the traditional starting point for the 5-km (3-mile) run around the palace, though you can join in anywhere along the route. Jogging around the palace is a ritual that begins as early as 6 am and goes on throughout the day, no matter what the weather. Almost everybody runs the course counterclockwise, but now and then you may spot someone going the opposite way.

Looking for a challenge? Japan hosts a number of marathons throughout the year and one of the most famous is the **Tokyo Marathon** (🌐 *www.tokyo42195.org*), which is held in February. Plan ahead if you're going to sign up, because the registration deadline is at the end of August of the previous year (most of the country's running events require signing up and qualifying far more in advance than their counterparts on other shores). The marathon starts at one of Tokyo's most prominent landmarks, the Tokyo Metropolitan Government Office in Shinjuku-ku, winds its way through the Imperial Palace, past the Tokyo Tower and Asakusa Kaminarimon Gate, and finishes at Tokyo Big Sight Exhibition Center in Koto Ward.

Hirakawa-mon (平川門 *Hirakawa Gate*). The approach to this gate crosses the only wooden bridge that spans the Imperial Palace moat. The gate and bridge are reconstructions, but Hirakawa-mon is especially beautiful, looking much as it must have when the shogun's wives and concubines used it on their rare excursions from the harem. ✉ *Imperial Palace* Ⓜ *Tozai subway line, Takebashi Station (Exit 1A).*

Imperial Palace Outer Garden (皇居外苑 *Kokyo-Gaien*). When the office buildings of the Meiji government were moved from this area in 1899, the whole expanse along the east side of the palace was turned into a public promenade and planted with 2,800 pine trees. The Outer Garden affords the best view of the castle walls and their Tokugawa-period fortifications: Ni-ju-bashi and the Sei-mon, the 17th-century Fujimi Yagura watchtower, and the Sakurada-mon gate. From 10 to 3 on Sundays, the road between the Outer Garden and Palace is closed to traffic and the reception desk near the south end of the garden lends bicycles for free. ✉ *Chiyoda-ku, Imperial Palace* 🎫 *Free* Ⓜ *Chiyoda subway line, Ni-ju-bashi-mae Station (Exit 2).*

NEED A BREAK?

Wadakura Funsui Koen Restaurant (和田倉噴水公園レストラン). Stop by the Wadakura Funsui Koen Restaurant for pasta, sandwiches, and soup with lovely water fountain views. English menus are available upon request, but the signs are only in Japanese. ✉ ***3–1 Kokyo Gaien, Chiyoda-ku, Imperial Palace*** ☎ ***03/5224–6062*** Ⓜ ***Otemachi Station (Exit D2 or D3).***

Kogeikan (工芸館 *Crafts Gallery at the National Museum of Modern Art*). This Gothic Revival redbrick structure from 1910 is worth seeking out. The exhibits of modern and traditional Japanese crafts inside are all too few, but many master artists are represented here in the traditions of lacquerware, textiles, pottery, bamboo, and metalwork. ✉ *1–1 Kitanomaru-koen, Chiyoda-ku, Imperial Palace* ☎ *03/5777–8600* 🌐 *www.momat.go.jp/english/cg* 🎫 *¥210; additional fee for special exhibits; admission to National Museum of Modern Art is separate* 🕑 *Thurs.–Tues. 10–5* Ⓜ *Hanzo-mon and Shinjuku subway lines, Kudanshita Station (Exit 2); Tozai subway line, Takebashi Station (Exit 1B).*

Ote-mon (大手門 *Ote Gate*). The main entrance to the Imperial Palace East Garden was in former days the principal gate of Ieyasu Tokugawa's castle. Most of the gate was destroyed in 1945 but was rebuilt in 1967 based on the original plans. The outer part of the gate survived and offers an impressive entrance into the Palace's East Gardens. ✉ *Chiyoda-ku, Imperial Palace* Ⓜ *Tozai, Marunouchi, and Chiyoda subway lines, Ote-machi Station (Exit C10).*

Two-Tiered Bridge (二重橋 *Ni-ju-bashi*). Making a graceful arch across the moat, this bridge is surely the most photogenic spot on the grounds of the former Edo Castle. Mere mortals may pass through only on December 23 (the Emperor's birthday) and January 2 to pay their respects to the Imperial Family. The guards in front of their small, octagonal, copper-roof sentry boxes change every hour on the hour—alas, with nothing like the pomp and ceremony at Buckingham Palace. ✉ *Chiyoda-ku, Imperial Palace* Ⓜ *Chiyoda subway line, Ni-ju-bashi-mae Station (Exit 2).*

3

AKIHABARA 秋葉原

Sightseeing ★★★
Dining ★★
Lodging ★★
Shopping ★★★★
Nightlife ★

Akihabara is techno-geek heaven. Also known as Akihabara Electric Town, or just Akiba, this district was once a dizzying collection of small, ultra-specialized electronics and computer shops, but has now become the center of Japan's anime, manga, and computer-focused *otaku* (nerd) culture.

More recently, the area has gained mainstream appeal among shoppers and tourists, with large all-in-one electronics shops crowding out many of the smaller and unique stores. Even so, the area has stayed true to its roots. Venture off the main road to see the real Akiba, where maid cafés (where servers are yes, dressed as maids and treat their customers as "masters and mistresses") mix with computer and hi-fi audio stores filled with dedicated fans searching for computer parts, rare comics, or techno-accessories they can't find anywhere else. For visitors, seeing the subculture and energy of Akiba is as much a draw as the shopping.

If you're looking for something a little more cerebral, head to Jimbo-cho, where family-run specialty bookstores of every genre abound. A number of antiquarian booksellers carry rare typeset editions, wood-block-printed books of the Edo period, and individual prints. The bookstores run for ½ km (¼ mile) on Yasukuni-dori beginning at the Surugadai-shita intersection. Many of Japan's most prestigious publishing houses make their home in Jimbo-cho as well, and the area is also home to Meiji University and Nihon University.

TOP ATTRACTIONS

Radio Kaikan (ラジオ会館). Eight floors featuring a variety of independent vendors selling mini-spy cameras, cell phones disguised as stun guns, manga comics, adult toys, gadgets, and oddball hobby supplies draw otaku, other shoppers, and visitors alike. And that's just the main building. Start browsing from the top floor and work your way down. There are two annexes across the street as well. ✉ *1–15–16 Soto-Kanda, Chiyoda-ku, Akihabara* ☎ *03/3251–3711 office* Ⓜ *JR Yamanote Line, Akihabara Station (Akihabara Electric Town Exit).*

WORTH NOTING

Kanda Shrine (神田明神 *Kanda Myojin*). This shrine is said to have been founded in 730 in a village called Shibasaki, where the Ote-machi financial district stands today. The shrine itself was destroyed in the Great Kanto Earthquake of 1923, and the present buildings reproduce in concrete the style of 1616.

You will never be able to see every shrine in the city and the ones in Akihabara are of minor interest, unless you are around for the **Kanda Festival**—one of Tokyo's three great blowouts—in mid-May. (The other two are the Sanno Festival of Hie Jinja in Nagata-cho and the Sanja Festival of Asakusa Shrine.) Some of the smaller buildings you see as you come up the steps and walk around the Main Hall contain the *mikoshi*—the portable shrines that are featured during the festival. Kanda Myojin is on Kuramae-bashi-dori, about a five-minute walk west of the Suehiro-cho subway stop. ✉ *2–16–2 Soto-Kanda, Chiyoda-ku, Akihabara* ☎ *03/3254–0753* Ⓜ *Ginza subway line, Suehiro-cho Station (Exit 3).*

SHRINE FESTIVAL 411

Every town, city, or village in Japan has a shrine festival at least once a year that essentially airs out their gods. The mid-May Kanda Festival began in the early Edo period. The floats that lead the procession today move in stately measure on wheeled carts, attended by the shrine's priests and officials. The portable Shinto shrines (*mikoshi*), some 70 of them, follow behind, carried on the shoulders of the townspeople. Shrine festivals are a peculiarly competitive form of worship: piety is a matter of who can shout the loudest, drink the most beer, and have the best time.

Holy Resurrection Cathedral (ニコライ堂 *Nikolai-do*). It's curious that a Russian Orthodox cathedral was built in Tokyo's Electric Town, but it's a place to stop for a quick snapshot. Formally, this is the Holy Resurrection Cathedral, derived from its founder, St. Nikolai Kassatkin (1836–1912), a Russian missionary who came to Japan in 1861 and spent the rest of his life here. The building, planned by a Russian engineer and executed by a British architect, was completed in 1891. Heavily damaged in the earthquake of 1923, the cathedral was restored with a dome much more modest than the original. Even so, the cathedral endows this otherwise featureless part of the city with unexpected charm. ✉ *4–1–3 Surugadai, Chiyoda-ku, Akihabara* ☎ *03/3291–1885* Ⓜ *Chiyoda subway line, Shin-Ochanomizu Station (Exit B1).*

Tokyo Anime Center (東京アニメセンター). As an information source and exhibitor of images and films, the center attracts tens of thousands of visitors each year. An on-site shop sells a wide range of anime goods that will satisfy even the most ardent of fans. ✉ *4F UDX Bldg., 4–14–1 Soto-Kanda, Chiyoda-ku, Akihabara* ☎ *03/5298–1188* 🌐 *www.animecenter.jp* ⏲ *Tues.–Sun. 11–7* Ⓜ *JR Yamanote Line, Akihabara Station (Akihabara Electric Town Exit).*

Yushima Seido (湯島 *Yushima Shrine*). The origins of this shrine date to a hall, founded in 1632, for the study of the Chinese Confucian classics. Its headmaster was Hayashi Razan, the official Confucian scholar

GETTING ORIENTED

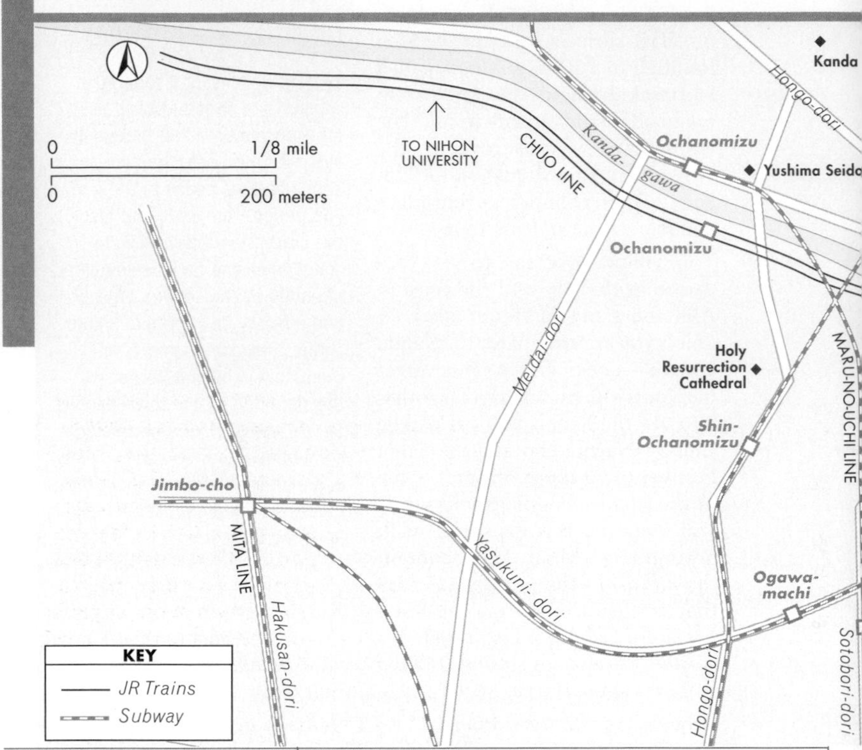

ORIENTATION

Akihabara is east of the Imperial Palace, right below Ueno and Asakusa. Akihabara Station is located north of Tokyo Station, on the JR Yamanote, Hibiya, and Tsukuba lines. It's right below Asakusa and Ueno districts.

Located just to the west of Akihabara, Jimbo-cho should be a very short stopover either before or after an excursion to Akihabara. The best way to get there is by taxi, which should cost about ¥800 to or from Akihabara Station.

GETTING HERE AND AROUND

Take the train to Akihabara Station on the JR Yamanote Line. Akihabara is a 20- to 30-minute ride from most hotels in Shinjuku or Minato-ku.

PLANNING

Keep in mind that most stores in Akihabara do not open until 10 am. Weekends draw hordes of shoppers, especially on Sunday, when the four central blocks of Chuo-dori are closed to traffic and become a pedestrian mall.

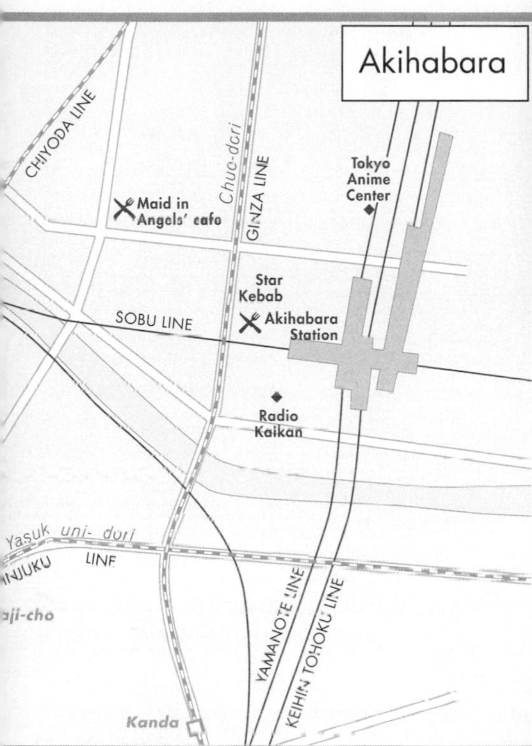

TOP REASONS TO GO

Be addressed as "master." At maid cafés, largely popularized in Akihabara, waitresses dress in maid costumes and address patrons as "master." Once limited to Japanese *otaku* (nerd) culture, these have gone mainstream and can make for a fun if silly stop.

Dance in the streets. A visit in May must include the Kanda Festival—one of Tokyo's major street celebrations. More than 200 portable shrines are carried in a parade towards the ground of the Kanda Myojin.

Browse an eccentric collection. Check out the toys, electronic gadgets, and hobby items at Radio Kaikan, a vertical bazaar.

QUICK BITES

Star Kebab. If you need a break from shopping for electronics and games, a spicy kebab sandwich from Star Kebab should do the trick. This branch and other outlets in the area offer beef strips, lettuce, and tomatoes in pita pockets. ✉ *1–8–10 Soto-Kanda, Chiyoda-ku* ☎ *03/6804–8330* 🌐 *www.kebab.co.jp* ▭ *No credit cards.*

Maid in Angels' (M.I.A.) Cafe (ミアカフェ). The Maid in Angels' (M.I.A.) Cafe is not exceptional by any standard, but it's a glimpse inside the world of the *otaku.* Waitresses in frilly dresses serve beer, juice, tea, pasta, curries, and desserts at simple wood tables and booths. Check the event board outside the front door for special café happenings, like when the girls change costumes based on the holidays. Santa suits, anyone? ✉ *2–19–36 Suda-cho, Chiyoda-ku* ☎ *03/5294–0078* 🌐 *www.mia-cafe.com* Ⓜ *JR Yamanote Line, Akihabara Station (Akihabara Electric Town Exit).*

Even in hyper-modern Tokyo, women still dress in traditional kimonos on special occasions.

to the Tokugawa government. Moved to its present site in 1691 (and destroyed by fire and rebuilt six times), the hall became an academy for the ruling elite. In a sense, nothing has changed: in 1872 the new Meiji government established the country's first teacher-training institute here, and that, in turn, evolved into Tokyo University—the graduates of which still make up much of the ruling elite. The hall looks like nothing else you're likely to see in Japan: painted black, weathered, and somber, it could almost be in China. ✉ *1–4–25 Yushima, Bunkyō-ku, Akihabara* ☎ *03/3251–4606* 🌐 *www.seido.or.jp* 🎫 *Free* 🕒 *Weekdays 9–5, weekends 10–5; closed Aug. 13–17 and Dec. 29–31* Ⓜ *JR Sobu Line, Marunouchi subway line, Ochanomizu Station (Exit B2).*

UENO AND YANAKA

Sightseeing ★★★★
Dining ★★★★
Lodging ★★★
Shopping ★★★
Nightlife ★★

Located in the heart of Ueno, JR Ueno Station is Tokyo's version of the Gare du Nord: the gateway to and from Japan's northeast provinces. Since its completion in 1883, the station has served as a terminus in the great migration to the city by villagers in pursuit of a better life.

Ueno was a place of prominence long before the coming of the railroad. After Ieyasu Tokugawa established his capital here in 1603, 36 subsidiary temples were erected surrounding the Main Hall, and the city of Edo itself expanded to the foot of the hill where the main gate of the Kan-ei-ji once stood. Some of the most important buildings in the temple complex have survived or have been restored and should not be missed.

A short walk from the north end of Ueno Park, Yanaka is one of Tokyo's most charming neighborhoods. It began as a temple town in the Edo period when the city moved a number of prominent temples here to save them from the rather frequent fires that broke out in more populated parts of town. The sheer abundance of temples (more than 70 in a small area) makes for an excellent walk. Most temples are found on the streets to the west of Yanaka Cemetery and south of Yanaka Ginza, a colorful shopping street where merchants cater to locals with groceries and daily goods. Wander down the winding backstreets to enjoy the surprise and sense of wonder as you turn a corner to find a quiet temple garden or a Buddhist service in session. Over time, craftsmen made the neighborhood home, and galleries and cafés have joined the traditional wooden houses and temples, giving the area a feel of being tourist-friendly without being overdone. In October, the area hosts the Yanaka Geikoten, a three-week-long art-and-craft festival when artisans open the doors to their workshops, and galleries hold special events.

UENO 上野

TOP ATTRACTIONS

Ame-ya Yoko-cho Market (アメヤ横丁). The sprawling stalls have become especially famous for the traditional prepared foods of the New Year, and, during the last few days of December, as many as half a million people crowd into the narrow alleys under the railroad tracks to stock up for the holiday. The market dates to World War II, when not much besides Ueno Station survived the bombings. Anyone who could make it here from the countryside with rice and other small supplies of food could sell them at exorbitant black-market prices. Sugar was a commodity that couldn't be found at any price in postwar Tokyo. Before long, there were hundreds of stalls in the black market selling various kinds of *ame* (confections), most made from sweet potatoes. These stalls gave the market its name, Ame-ya Yoko-cho (often shortened to Ameyoko), which means "Confectioners' Alley." Shortly before the Korean War, the market was legalized, and soon the stalls were carrying watches, chocolate, ballpoint pens, blue jeans, and T-shirts that had somehow been "liberated" from American PXs. In years to come the merchants of Ameyoko diversified even further—to fine Swiss timepieces and fake designer luggage, cosmetics, jewelry, fresh fruit, and fish. For a break, the area also features numerous small restaurants specializing in raw slices of tuna over rice (*maguro-don*)—cheap, quick, and very good. ✉ *Ueno 4-chome, Taito-ku, Ueno* ⏲ *Most shops and stalls daily 10–7* Ⓜ *JR Ueno Station (Hiroko-ji Exit).*

Kannon Hall (清水観音堂 *Kiyomizu Kannon-do*). This National Treasure was a part of Abbot Tenkai's attempt to build a copy of Kyoto's magnificent Kiyomizu-dera in Ueno. His attempt was honorable, but failed to be as impressive as the original. The principal Buddhist image of worship here is the Senju Kannon (Thousand-Armed Goddess of Mercy). Another figure, however, receives greater homage. This is the Kosodate Kannon, who is believed to answer the prayers of women having difficulty conceiving children. If their prayers are answered, they return to Kiyomizu and leave a doll, as both an offering of thanks and a prayer for the child's health. In a ceremony held every September 25, the dolls that have accumulated during the year are burned in a bonfire. ✉ *1–29 Ueno Koen, Taito-ku, Ueno* ☎ *03/3821–4749* 🎫 *Free* ⏲ *Daily 7–5* Ⓜ *JR Ueno Station (Koen-guchi/Park Exit).*

National Museum of Western Art (国立西洋美術館 *Kokuritsu Seiyo Bijutsukan*). Along with castings from the original molds of Rodin's *Gate of Hell, The Burghers of Calais,* and *The Thinker,* the wealthy businessman Matsukata Kojiro (1865–1950) acquired some 850 paintings, sketches, and prints by such masters as Renoir, Monet, Gauguin, van Gogh, Delacroix, and Cézanne. Matsukata kept the collection in Europe, but he left it to Japan in his will. The French government sent the artwork to Japan after World War II, and the collection opened to the public in 1959 in a building designed by Swiss-born architect Le Corbusier. Since then, the museum has diversified a bit; more recent acquisitions include works by Reubens, Tintoretto, El Greco, Max Ernst, and Jackson Pollock. The Seiyo is one of the best-organized, most pleasant museums to visit in Tokyo. ✉ *7–7 Ueno Koen, Taito-ku, Ueno* ☎ *03/5777–8600* 🌐 *www.nmwa.go.jp* 🎫 *¥430; additional fee for special exhibits* ⏲ *Tues.–Thurs. and weekends 9:30–5:30, Fri. 9:30–8* Ⓜ *JR Ueno Station (Koen-guchi/Park Exit).*

FAMILY **Shinobazu Pond** (不忍池). When an inlet of Tokyo Bay receded around the 17th century, Shinobazu became a freshwater pond. Abbot Tenkai, founder of Kan-ei-ji on the hill above the pond, had an island made for Benzaiten, the goddess of the arts. Later improvements included a causeway to the island, embankments, and even a racecourse (1884–93). Today the pond is in three sections. The first, a wildlife sanctuary, is home to the ciy's locust flowers; this is the only place in Tokyo you can see them bloom from mid-June through August. Some 5,000 wild ducks migrate here from as far away as Siberia, sticking around from September to April. The second section, to the north, belongs to Ueno Zoo; the third, to the west, is a small lake for boating. In July, the Ueno *matsuri* (festival) features food stalls and music events in the small at the pond's edge. At the pond's southwestern corner, there is also a bandshell with various music events throughout the year. ✉ *Shinobazu-dori, Taitō-ku* 🎫 *Free* Ⓜ *JR Ueno Station (Koen-guchi/Park Exit); Keisei private rail line, Keisei-Ueno Station (Higashi-guchi/East Exit).*

Shinobazu Pond Bentendo (不忍池弁財天). Perched in the middle of Shinobazu Pond, this shrine is dedicated to the goddess Benten, one of the Seven Gods of Good Luck that evolved from a combination of Indian, Chinese, and Japanese mythology. As matron goddess of the arts, she is depicted holding a lutelike musical instrument called a *biwa*. The shrine, built by Abbot Tenkai, was destroyed in the bombings of 1945; the present version, with its distinctive octagonal roof, is a faithful copy. You can rent rowboats and pedal boats at a nearby boathouse. ✉ *2–1 Ueno Koen, Taito-ku, Taito-ku* ☎ *03/3828–9502 boathouse* 🎫 *Rowboats ¥600 for 1 hr, pedal boats ¥600 for 30 mins, swan boats ¥700 for 30 mins* ⏲ *Boathouse daily 9–5* Ⓜ *JR Ueno Station (Koen-guchi/Park Exit); Keisei private rail line, Keisei-Ueno Station (Ikenohata Exit).*

Tokudai-ji (徳大寺 *Tokudai Temple*). This is a curiosity in a neighborhood of curiosities: a temple on the second floor of a supermarket. Two deities are worshipped here. One is the bodhisattva Jizo, and the act of washing this statue is believed to safeguard your health. The other is of the Indian goddess Marici, a daughter of Brahma; she is believed to help worshippers overcome difficulties and succeed in business. ✉ *4–6–2 Ueno, Taitō-ku, Ueno* Ⓜ *JR Yamanote and Keihin-tohoku lines, Okachi-machi Station (Higashi-guchi/East Exit) or Ueno Station (Hiroko-ji Exit).*

Tokyo Metropolitan Art Museum (東京都美術館 *Tokyo-to Bijutsukan*). By far the most ecclectic of Ueno's art museums, the Tokyo Metropolitan hosts large-scale exhibitions ranging from classic masterpieces to modern architecture. The museum's smaller galleries often play home to group exhibitions of painting, photography, calliraphy, sculpture, and nearly any other kind of art one can dream up. Many smaller exhibits are free. ✉ *8–36 Ueno Koen, Taitō ku, Ueno* ☎ *03/3823–6921* 🌐 *www.tobikan.jp* 🎫 *Permanent collection free; fees vary for*

GETTING ORIENTED

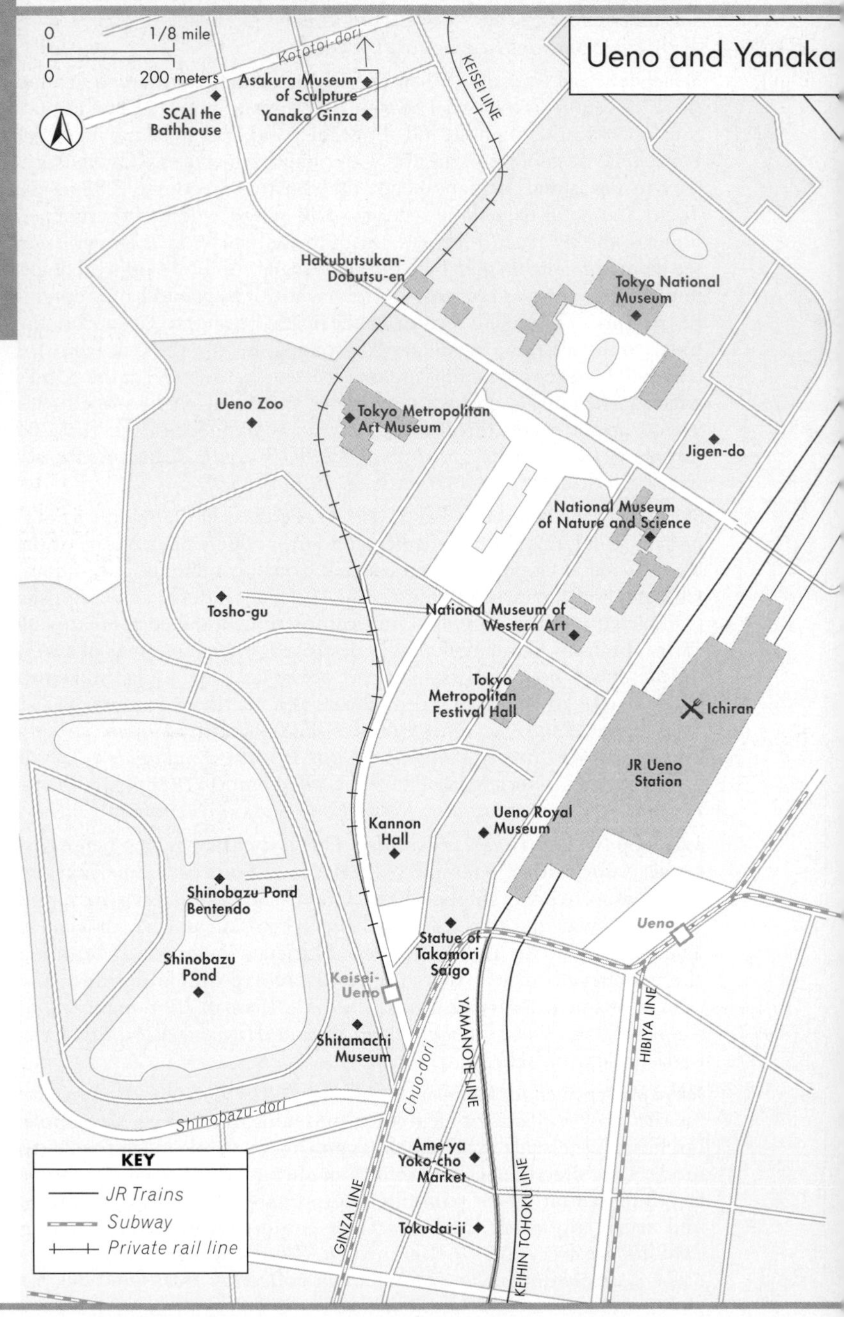

Ueno and Yanaka
0 1/8 mile
0 200 meters
Kototoi-dori
Asakura Museum of Sculpture
Yanaka Ginza
SCAI the Bathhouse
KEISEI LINE
Hakubutsukan-Dobutsu-en
Tokyo National Museum
Ueno Zoo
Tokyo Metropolitan Art Museum
Jigen-do
National Museum of Nature and Science
Tosho-gu
National Museum of Western Art
Tokyo Metropolitan Festival Hall
Ichiran
JR Ueno Station
Ueno Royal Museum
Kannon Hall
Shinobazu Pond Bentendo
Statue of Takamori Saigo
Ueno
Shinobazu Pond
Keisei-Ueno
YAMANOTE LINE
HIBIYA LINE
Shitamachi Museum
Chuo-dori
Shinobazu-dori
Ame-ya Yoko-cho Market
GINZA LINE
KEIHIN TOHOKU LINE
Tokudai-ji
KEY
JR Trains
Subway
Private rail line

ORIENTATION

Ueno and Yanaka, along with Asakusa, make up the historical enclave of Tokyo. Though the Tokyo Sky Tree transmission tower can be seen from nearly all parts of these neighborhoods, traditional architecture and way of life are preserved here at the northeastern reaches of the city. If you are pressed for time all three areas can be explored in a single day, though if you want to visit Ueno's museums, it is best to devote an entire day to fully appreciate the area.

PLANNING

Ueno and Yanaka can be explored on one excursion or two: an afternoon of cultural browsing or a full day of cultural discoveries in one of the great centers of the city. Museums can get crowded later in the day, so it is a good idea to start at Ueno Station in the morning and make your way toward Yanaka in the early afternoon. ■ **TIP→ Avoid Monday, when most of the museums are closed**. In April, the cherry blossoms of Ueno Koen are glorious.

QUICK BITES

Ichiran (一蘭). At Ueno Station is a branch of Japan's most amusing ramen chain. Ichiran serves *tonkotsu* (pork broth) noodles 24 hours a day. Rather than receiving a menu upon entry, guests are given survey sheets (English forms are available) on which they tick boxes expressing the flavor, appearance, and style they desire in the meal. Then they settle down in a stall with a curtain. Like magic—presto!—the curtain rises and made-to-order steaming bowls appear. ✉ *7-1-1 Ueno* ☎ *03/5826-5861* 🌐 *www.ichiran.co.jp* 💳 *No credit cards.*

TOP REASONS TO GO

Hit the top museums. Ueno has Tokyo's top museums, including the Tokyo National Museum and the National Museum of Western Art.

Get a glimpse of old Tokyo. Stroll through Yanaka, taking in the temples and old houses, galleries, and cafés of one of Tokyo's best-remaining traditional neighborhoods.

See a shining shrine. Dating back to 1627, the Tosho-gu Shrine is a National Treasure that houses a priceless collection of historical art and is one of the few remaining early-Edo-period buildings in Tokyo.

Witness a lotus display. From mid-June through August, *Shinobazu-ike* (Shinobazu Pond) is the only place in Tokyo where you'll see such a vast expanse of lotus flowers in bloom

GETTING HERE AND AROUND

Ueno Station can be accessed by train on the Hibiya Line, Ginza Line, and JR Yamanote Line (Koen Entrance). Yanaka is a short walk from the north end of Ueno Park and can also be accessed from Nippori Station (West Exit). Be sure to avoid rush hours in the morning (8–9) and evening (6–9) and bring plenty of cash for admission fees to museums and food for the day as finding an ATM may be challenging. Museums accept some major credit cards for admission and in their stores.

3

The "ame" in Ame-ya Yoko-cho Market also means "American," referencing the many American products sold during the area's black market era.

other exhibits (usually ¥800–¥1,400) ⏲ Daily 9:30–5; closed 1st and 3rd Mon. of month Ⓜ JR Ueno Station (Koen-guchi/Park Exit).

Fodor's Choice ★ **Tokyo National Museum** (東京国立博物館 *Tokyo Kokuritsu Hakubutsukan*). This complex of four buildings grouped around a courtyard is one of the world's great repositories of East Asian art and archaeology. Altogether, the museum has some 87,000 objects in its permanent collection, with several thousand more on loan from shrines, temples, and private owners.

The Western-style building on the left (if you're standing at the main gate), with bronze cupolas, is the **Hyokeikan.** Built in 1909, it was devoted to archaeological exhibits; aside from the occasional special exhibition, the building is closed today. The larger **Heiseikan,** behind the Hyokeikan, was built to commemorate the wedding of crown prince Naruhito in 1993 and now houses Japanese archaeological exhibits. The second floor is used for special exhibitions.

In 1878, the 7th-century Horyu-ji (Horyu Temple) in Nara presented 319 works of art in its possession—sculpture, scrolls, masks, and other objects—to the Imperial Household. These were transferred to the National Museum in 2000 and now reside in the **Horyu-ji Homotsukan** (Gallery of Horyu-ji Treasures), which was designed by Yoshio Taniguchi. There's a useful guide to the collection in English, and the exhibits are well explained. Don't miss the hall of carved wooden *gigaku* (Buddhist processional) masks.

The central building in the complex, the 1937 **Honkan,** houses Japanese art exclusively: paintings, calligraphy, sculpture, textiles, ceramics, swords, and armor. Also here are 84 objects designated by the government as National Treasures. The Honkan rotates the works on display several times during the year. It also hosts two special exhibitions annually (April and May or June, and October and November), which feature important collections from both Japanese and foreign museums. These, unfortunately, can be an ordeal to take in: the lighting in the Honkan is not particularly good, the explanations in English are sketchy at best, and the hordes of visitors make it impossible to linger over a work you especially want to study. The more attractive **Toyokan,** to the right of the Honkan, was completed in 1968 and recently renovated; it is devoted to the art and antiquities of China, Korea, Southeast Asia, India, the Middle East, and Egypt. ✉ *13–9 Ueno Koen, Taitō-ku, Ueno* ☎ *03/3822–1111* 🌐 *www.tnm.jp* 🎫 *Regular exhibits ¥620, special exhibits ¥1,500* ⏲ *Tues.–Sun. 9:30–5, times vary during special exhibitions* Ⓜ *JR Ueno Station (Koen-guchi/Park Exit).*

3

Fodor's Choice ★ **Tosho-gu** (東照宮 *Tosho Shrine*). This shrine, built in 1627, is dedicated to Ieyasu, the first Tokugawa shogun. It miraculously survived all major disasters that destroyed most of Tokyo's historical structures—the fires, the 1868 revolt, the 1923 earthquake, the 1945 bombings—making it one of the few early-Edo-period buildings left in Tokyo. The shrine and most of its art are designated National Treasures.

Two hundred *ishidoro* (stone lanterns) line the path from the stone entry arch to the shrine itself. One of them, just outside the arch to the left, and more than 18 feet high, is called *obaketoro* (ghost lantern). Legend has it that one night a samurai on guard duty slashed at a ghost (*obake*) that was believed to haunt the lantern. His sword was so strong, it left a nick in the stone, which can be seen today.

The first room inside the shrine is the **Hall of Worship;** the four paintings in gold on wooden panels are by Tan'yu, a member of the famous Kano family of artists, dating from the 15th century. Behind the Hall of Worship, connected by a passage called the *haiden,* is the sanctuary, where the spirit of Ieyasu is said to be enshrined.

The real glory of Tosho-gu is its so-called **Chinese Gate,** at the end of the building, and the fence on either side that has intricate carvings of birds, animals, fish, and shells of every description. The two long panels of the gate, with their dragons carved in relief, are attributed to Hidari Jingoro, a brilliant sculptor of the early Edo period whose real name is unknown (*hidari* means "left"; Jingoro was reportedly left-handed). ✉ *9–88 Ueno Koen, Taitō-ku, Ueno* ☎ *03/3822–3455* 🎫 *¥200* ⏲ *Daily 9–5* Ⓜ *JR Ueno Station (Koen-guchi/Park Exit).*

WORTH NOTING

FAMILY **National Museum of Nature and Science** (国立科学博物館 *Kokuritsu Kagaku Hakubutsukan*). The six buildings of the complex house everything from fossils to moon rocks—the 30-meter (98-foot) model of a blue whale perched at the entrance is a huge hit with kids. And what self-respecting science museum wouldn't have dinosaurs? Look for them in the B2F Exhibition Hall, in the newest annex. Although the museum occasionally outdoes itself with special exhibits, it's pretty conventional and provides few hands-on learning experiences. Kids seem to like it,

The Tokyo National Museum offers not only a huge collection of Japanese artifacts, but its buildings are a study in traditional and foreign architecture.

but this is not a place to linger if your time is short. ✉ *7–20 Ueno Koen, Taitō-ku, Ueno* ☎ *03/5777–8600* 🌐 *www.kahaku.go.jp* 🎫 *¥620; additional fee for special exhibits* 🕑 *Tues.–Sun. 9–5* Ⓜ *JR Ueno Station (Koen-guchi/Park Exit).*

FAMILY **Shitamachi Museum** (下町風俗資料館 *Shitamachi Fuzoku Shiryokan*). Japanese society in the days of the Tokugawa shoguns was rigidly stratified. Some 80% of the city's land was allotted to the warrior class, temples, and shrines. The remaining 20%—between Ieyasu's fortifications on the west, and the Sumida-gawa on the east—was known as *shitamachi*, or "downtown" or the "lower town" (as it expanded, it came to include what today constitutes the Chuo, Taito, Sumida, and Koto wards). It was here that the common, hardworking, free-spending folk, who made up more than half the population, lived. The Shitamachi Museum preserves and exhibits what remained of that way of life as late as 1940.

The two main displays on the first floor are a merchant house and a tenement, intact with all their furnishings. This is a hands-on museum: you can take your shoes off and step up into the rooms. On the second floor are displays of toys, tools, and utensils donated, in most cases, by people who had grown up with them and used them all their lives. There are also photographs and video documentaries of craftspeople at work. Occasionally various traditional skills are demonstrated, and you're welcome to take part. This small but engaging museum makes great use of its space, and there are even volunteer guides (available starting at 10) who speak passable English. ✉ *2–1 Ueno Koen, Taitō-ku,*

Ueno ☎ 03/3823–7451 🌐 www.taitocity.net/taito/shitamachi 🎫 ¥300 ⏲ Tues.–Sun. 9:30–4:30 Ⓜ JR Ueno Station (Koen-guchi/Park Exit).

Statue of Takamori Saigo (西郷隆盛像). As chief of staff of the Meiji Imperial army, Takamori Saigo (1827–77) played a key role in forcing the surrender of Edo and the overthrow of the shogunate. Ironically, Saigo himself fell out with the other leaders of the new Meiji government and was killed in an unsuccessful rebellion of his own. The sculptor Takamura Koun's bronze, made in 1893, sensibly avoids presenting Saigo in uniform. Entering Ueno Park from the south, the statue is on the right after climbing the large staircase on your way to Kiyomizu Kanon-do Temple. ✉ *Ueno Park, Taito-ku, Ueno* Ⓜ *JR Ueno Station (Koen-guchi/Park Exit); Keisei private rail line, Keisei-Ueno Station (Higashi-guchi/East Exit).*

3

Ueno Royal Museum (上野の森美術館 *Ueno-no-Mori Bijutsukan*). Although the museum has no permanent collection of its own, it hosts an interesting selection of temporary exhibits. The museum often focuses on group exhibitions and work by contemporary artists, but often working within the bounds of more traditional media. Thanks to its manageable size and pleasant atmosphere, the Ueno Royal Musem is a relaxing alternative to Ueno's larger (and more crowded) museums. ✉ *1–2 Ueno Koen, Taitō-ku, Ueno* ☎ *03/3833–4191* 🌐 *www.ueno-mori.org* 🎫 *Prices vary depending on exhibit, but usually ¥500–¥1,000* ⏲ *Open only during exhibitions, 10–5* Ⓜ *JR Ueno Station (Koen-guchi/Park Exit).*

FAMILY **Ueno Zoo** (上野動物園 *Ueno Dobutsuen*). The two main gardens of Japan's first zoo, built in 1882, host an exotic mix of more than 900 species of animals. The giant panda is the biggest draw, but the tigers from Sumatra, gorillas from the lowland swamp areas of western Africa, and numerous monkeys, some from Japan, make a visit to the East Garden worthwhile. The West Garden is highlighted by rhinos, zebras, and hippopotamuses, and a children's area. The process of the zoo's expansion somehow left within its confines the 120-foot, five-story Kanei-ji Pagoda. Built in 1631 and rebuilt after a fire in 1639, the building offers traditional Japanese tea ceremony services. ✉ *9–83 Ueno Koen, Taitō-ku, Ueno* ☎ *03/3828–5171* 🌐 *www.tokyo-zoo.net/english/ueno* 🎫 *¥600, free on Mar. 20, May 4, and Oct. 1* ⏲ *Tues.–Sun. 9:30–5* Ⓜ *JR Ueno Station (Koen-guchi/Park Exit).*

YANAKA 谷中

Asakura Museum of Sculpture (朝倉彫刻館 *Asakura Chosokan*). Reopened in 2014 after years of renovation, the museum houses the most famous works of local sculptor Fumio Asakura. Formerly Asakura's home and studio, the building and garden are a lovely stop when wandering through the Yanaka area. The tearoom on the opposite side of the courtyard is a quiet place, where you can appreciate the beauty and calmness of his garden. ✉ *7–18–10 Yanaka, Taito-ku, Yanaka* ☎ *03/3821–4549* 🌐 *www.taitocity.net/taito/asakura* 🎫 *¥500* ⏲ *Tues.–Thurs. and weekends 9:30–4:30* Ⓜ *JR Yamanote Line, Nippori Station.*

The National Museum of Western Art pays homage to great painters and sculptors from Europe and the United States.

SCAI the Bathhouse. A contemporary art gallery housed in a 200-year-old building, SCAI is a symbol of Yanaka's blend of old and new. The exterior of the building, established in 1787 as a bathhouse, has been well preserved, while the inside is a light and airy gallery featuring rotating exhibits of contemporary art. Although it is a small gallery, the exhibitions are impressive and it is worth a peek just to see the building itself. ✉ *Kashiyu-ato, 6–1–23 Yanaka, Taitō-ku, Yanaka* ☎ *03/3821–1144* 🌐 *www.scaithebathhouse.com* 🎫 *Free* 🕒 *Tues.–Sat., noon–6 during exhibitions.*

NEED A BREAK?

Kayaba Coffee (カヤバ珈琲). Standing on the border of Ueno and Yanaka, this historic café is a popular stop for lunch or a light snack. A century old, the café has been stylishly renovated and serves homemade sandwiches, curries, cakes, and *kaki gori*, a traditional treat of flavored shaved ice. The first floor has a bar and dark wood tables, while the second is an airy Japanese style tatami room with low tables. ✉ *6–1–29 Yanaka, Taitō-ku* ☎ *03/3823–3545* 🌐 *kayaba-coffee.com* Ⓜ *JR Nippori Station, JR Ueno Station.*

Yanaka Ginza (谷中銀座). It used to be that every neighborhood in Tokyo had its own small shopping street, but with the rise of supermarkets and convenience stores in the 1980s, they began to vanish. Thanks to a forward-thinking shopkeepers' and residents' association, Yanaka Ginza not only survived but has flourished. The street is now an interesting mix of shops selling groceries and daily goods for locals, as well as sweets, snacks, and crafts. ✉ *3 Yanaka, Taito-ku, Yanaka.*

ASAKUSA 浅草

Sightseeing ★★★★
Dining ★★★★
Lodging ★★★
Shopping ★★★
Nightlife ★★

If there is one must-visit neighborhood in Tokyo, this is it. Asakusa brings together cultural sites, dining, and entertainment in vibrant surroundings that are at once historic and modern.

Cars make room for the rickshaw drivers who sometimes outpace the motorized traffic. On the neighborhood's backstreets, neo French and Italian cafés mix with generations-old soba and tempura shops while customers in the latest fashions sit with those in traditional kimonos. Kaminari-mon, the gateway to Senso-ji—Tokyo's oldest temple—is a backdrop for artisans and small entrepreneurs, children and grandmothers, hipsters, hucksters, and priests. It is hard not to be swept away by the relaxed energy that pulses through the area. If you have any time to spend in Tokyo, make sure you devote at least a day to exploring Asakusa.

Historically, Asakusa has been the city's entertainment hub. The area blossomed when Ieyasu Tokugawa made Edo his capital, and it became the 14th-century city that never slept. For the next 300 years it was the wellspring of almost everything we associate with Japanese culture. In the mid-1600s, it became a pleasure quarter in its own right with stalls selling toys, souvenirs, and sweets; acrobats, jugglers, and strolling musicians; and sake shops and teahouses—where the waitresses often provided more than tea. Then, in 1841, the Kabuki theaters moved to Asakusa. The theaters were here for only a short time, but it was enough to establish Asakusa as *the* entertainment quarter of the city—a reputation it held unchallenged until World War II, when most of the area was destroyed.

After the war, development focused on areas to the west like Shinjuku and Shibuya. In a way, this saved Asakusa from becoming yet another neighborhood filled with neon, concrete, and glass instead mostly keeping to the same style of low buildings and tiny independent shops that existed before the war. Seven decades have certainly changed the neighborhood, but many of the smaller side streets retain the charm and feel of old Tokyo. Although the area has become dramatically more popular in recent years, tourists usually keep to the main streets and line up at the same restaurants around the Senso-ji Temple Complex. Venture a few minutes away from the temple area and the crowds thin out and souvenir shops give way to quiet storefronts selling traditional crafts. Although Senso-ji Temple is well worth seeing, taking the time to wander through the neighborhood gives you a hint of what it may have been like years ago.

TOP ATTRACTIONS

Asakusa Jinja (浅草神社 *Asakusa Shrine*). Several structures in the famous Senso-ji shrine complex survived the bombings of 1945. The largest, to the right of the Main Hall, is this Shinto shrine to the Hikonuma brothers and their master, Naji-no-Nakamoto—the putative founders of Senso-ji. In Japan, Buddhism and Shintoism have enjoyed a comfortable coexistence since the former arrived from China in the 6th century. The shrine, built in 1649, is also known as Sanja Sama (Shrine of the Three Guardians). Near the entrance to Asakusa Shrine is another survivor of World War II: the original east gate to the temple grounds, **Nitenmon,** built in 1618 for a shrine to Ieyasu Tokugawa and designated by the government as an Important Cultural Property. ✉ *2–3–1 Asakusa, Taitō-ku, Asakusa* ☎ *03/3844–1575* 🌐 *www.asakusajinja.jp.*

Belfry (時の鐘鐘楼 *Toki-no-kane Shoro*). The tiny hillock Benten-yama, with its shrine to the goddess of good fortune, is the site of this 17th-century belfry. The bell here used to toll the hours for the people of the district, and it was said that you could hear it anywhere within a radius of some 6 km (4 miles). The bell still sounds at 6 am every day, when the temple grounds open. It also rings on New Year's Eve—108 strokes in all, beginning just before midnight, to "ring out" the 108 sins and frailties of humankind and make a clean start for the coming year. Benten-yama and the belfry are at the beginning of the narrow street that parallels Nakamise-dori. ✉ *Taitō-ku, Asakusa.*

Dembo-in (伝法院 *Dembo Temple*). Believed to have been made in the 17th century by Kobori Enshu, the genius of Zen landscape design, the garden of Dembo-in is part of the living quarters of the abbot of Senso-ji and the best-kept secret in Asakusa. The garden is usually empty and always utterly serene, an island of privacy in a sea of pilgrims. Spring, when the wisteria blooms, is the ideal time to be here.

A sign in English on Dembo-in-dori—you'll see it about 150 yards west of the intersection with Naka-mise-dori—leads you to the entrance, which is a side door to a large wooden gate. For permission to see the abbot's garden, you must first apply at the temple administration building, between Hozo-mon and the Five-Story Pagoda, in the far corner. ✉ *2–3–1 Asakusa, Taitō-ku, Asakusa* ☎ *03/3842–0181 for reservations* 🎫 *Free* 🕓 *Daily 9–4; may be closed if abbot has guests* Ⓜ *Ginza subway line, Asakusa Station (Exit 1/Kaminari-mon Exit).*

FAMILY **Hanayashiki** (花やしき). Dubbing itself "the old park with a smile," Tokyo's premier retro amusement park was established in 1853. Think Coney Island: a haunted house, Ferris wheel, and merry-go-round await the kids who will likely be a little tired of Asakusa's historic *areas.* ✉ *2–28–1 Asakusa, Taitō-ku, Asakusa* ☎ *03/3842–8780* 🌐 *www.hanayashiki.net* 🎫 *¥900–¥2,200* ⏲ *Daily 10–6, but check schedule for later closing times* Ⓜ *Ginza subway line, Asakusa Station (Exit 1/Kaminari-mon Exit).*

Kaminari-mon (雷門 *Thunder God Gate*). The main entryway to Senso-ji's grounds towers above the ever-present throng of tourists and passing rickshaw drivers. With its huge red-paper lantern hanging in the center, this landmark of Asakusa is picture-perfect, provided you can find a clear shot. The original gate was destroyed by fire in 1865; the replica you see today was built after World War II. Traditionally, two fearsome guardian gods are installed in the alcoves of Buddhist temple gates to ward off evil spirits. The Thunder God (Kaminari-no-Kami) is on the left with the Wind God (Kaze-no-Kami) on the right. Want to buy some of Tokyo's most famous souvenirs? Stop at **Tokiwa-do,** the shop on the west side of the gate for *kaminari okoshi* (thunder crackers), made of rice, millet, sugar, and beans.

Kaminari-mon marks the southern extent of **Nakamise-dori,** the Street of Inside Shops. The area from Kaminari-mon to the inner gate of the temple was once composed of stalls leased to the townspeople who cleaned and swept the temple grounds. This is now kitsch-souvenir central, so be prepared to buy a few key chains, dolls, and snacks. ✉ *2–3–1 Asakusa, Taitō-ku, Asakusa* Ⓜ *Ginza subway line, Asakusa Station (Exit 1/Kaminari-mon Exit).*

Kappabashi (かっぱ橋). In the 19th century, according to local legend, a river ran through the present-day Kappabashi district. The surrounding area was poorly drained and was often flooded. A local shopkeeper began a project to improve the drainage, investing all his own money, but met with little success until a troupe of *kappa*—mischievous green water sprites—emerged from the river to help him. A more prosaic explanation for the name of the district points out that the lower-ranking retainers of the local lord used to earn extra money by making straw raincoats, also called *kappa,* that they spread to dry on the bridge.

Today, Kappabashi's more than 200 wholesale dealers sell everything the city's restaurant and bar trade could possibly need to do business, from paper supplies and steam tables to the main attraction, plastic food. ✉ *Nishi-Asakusa 1-chome and 2-chome, Taitō-ku, Asakusa* ⏲ *Most shops daily 9–6* Ⓜ *Ginza subway line, Tawara-machi Station (Exit 1).*

THE SANJA FESTIVAL

The Sanja Festival, held annually over the third weekend of May, is said to be the biggest, loudest, wildest party in Tokyo. Each of the areas in Asakusa has its own mikoshi, which, on the second day of the festival, are paraded through the streets of Asakusa to the shrine. Many of the "parishioners" take part naked to the waist, or with the sleeves of their tunics rolled up, to expose fantastic red-and-black tattoo patterns that sometimes cover their entire backs and shoulders. These are the markings of the Japanese underworld.

Asakusa's heart and soul is the Senso-ji Complex, famous for its 17th-century Shinto shrine, Asakusa Shrine, as well as its garden and the wild Sanja Festival in May.

NEED A BREAK?

Nakase (中清). Nakase is a lovely retreat from the overbearing crowds at the Senso-ji Complex. The building, which is 130 years old, lends a truly authentic Japanese experience: food is served in lacquerware bento boxes and there are an interior garden and a pond, which is filled with carp and goldfish. Across Orange-dori from the redbrick Asakusa Public Hall, Nakase is expensive, but the experience is worth it. ✉ ***1-39-13 Asakusa, Taitō-ku, Asakusa*** ☎ ***03/3841-4015*** ⏲ ***Closed Thurs.*** Ⓜ ***Ginza subway line, Asakusa Station (Exit 1/Kaminari-mon Exit).***

Fodor's Choice ★

Senso-ji Complex. Even for travelers with little interest in history or temples, this complex in the heart and soul of Asakusa is without a doubt one of Tokyo's must-see sights. Come for its local and historical importance, its garden, its 17th-century Shinto shrine, and Tokyo's most famous festival: the wild Sanja Matsuri in May. The area also offers a myraid of interesting shops, winding back streets, and an atmosphere unlike anywhere else in Tokyo. ✉ *2–3–1 Asakusa, Taitō-ku, Asakusa* ☎ *03/3842–0181* 🌐 *www.senso-ji.jp* 🎟 *Free* ⏲ *Temple grounds daily 6–sunset* Ⓜ *Ginza subway line, Asakusa Station (Exit 1/Kaminari-mon Exit).*

Senso-ji Main Hall (浅草観音堂). Established in 645, the bright red Main Hall has long been the center of Asakusa, though what you see today is a faithful replica of the original that burned in the fire raids of 1945. It took 13 years to raise money for the restoration of the beloved Senso-ji, which is much more than a tourist attraction. Kabuki actors still come here before a new season of performances, and sumo wrestlers visit before a tournament to pay their respects. The large lanterns were donated by the geisha associations of Asakusa and nearby Yanagibashi. Most Japanese stop at the huge bronze incense burner, in front of the Main Hall, to bathe their hands and faces in the smoke—it's a charm to ward off illnesses—before climbing the stairs to offer their prayers.

Unlike in many other temples, however, part of the inside has a concrete floor, so you can come and go without removing your shoes. In this area hang Senso-ji's chief claims to artistic importance: a collection of 18th- and 19th-century votive paintings on wood. Plaques of this kind, called *ema,* are still offered to the gods at shrines and temples, but they are commonly simpler and smaller. The worshipper buys a little tablet of wood with the picture already painted on one side and inscribes a prayer on the other. The temple owns more than 50 of these works, which were removed to safety in 1945 to escape the air raids. Only eight of them, depicting scenes from Japanese history and mythology, are on display. A catalog of the collection is on sale in the hall, but the text is in Japanese only.

DID YOU KNOW?

Kamiya Bar, the first drinking establishment in Japan to call itself a "bar," was started in Asakusa in 1880 and it still stands today. Stop by for a jolt of Denki Bran, a drink that dates back to the Meiji Era. A mixture of a few different liquors and brandy, the brew—the recipe is a secret—is sold in bottles at the bar and is definitely an acquired taste. Be prepared with a chaser.

Lighting is poor in the Main Hall, and the actual works are difficult to see. One thing that visitors cannot see at all is the holy image of Kannon itself, which supposedly lies buried somewhere deep under the temple. Not even the priests of Senso-ji have ever seen it, and there is in fact no conclusive evidence that it actually exists.

Hozo-mon, the gate to the temple courtyard, is also a repository for sutras (Buddhist texts) and other treasures of Senso-ji. This gate, too, has its guardian gods; should either god decide to leave his post for a stroll, he can use the enormous pair of sandals hanging on the back wall—the gift of a Yamagata Prefecture village famous for its straw weaving. ✉ *2 3–1 Asakusa, Taitō-ku, Asakusa* 🌐 *www.senso-ji.jp.*

Tokyo Sky Tree (スカイツリー). Opened in 2011 to mixed reviews, this 2,000-plus-foot-tall skyscraper has become a symbol of the ongoing revival of the eastern side of the city. When it opened, tickets to the observation decks were booked for months in advance and the tower, along with the adjacent Solamachi shopping complex, continues to draw shoppers and tourists to the area. On a clear day, the views from the 1,155-foot-high Tembo Deck observation area are impressive. For an extra fee, visitors can go to the Tembo Galleria, another 330 feet up. ✉ *1-1-2 Oshiage, Sumida-ku, Asakusa* 🌐 *www.tokyo-skytree.jp/en* 🎫 *¥2,500 (plus ¥1,000 for top observation deck)* 🕐 *Daily 8 am–10 pm* Ⓜ *Tobu Skytree Line Skytree Station, Tobu Skytree Line Oshiage Station.*

GETTING ORIENTED

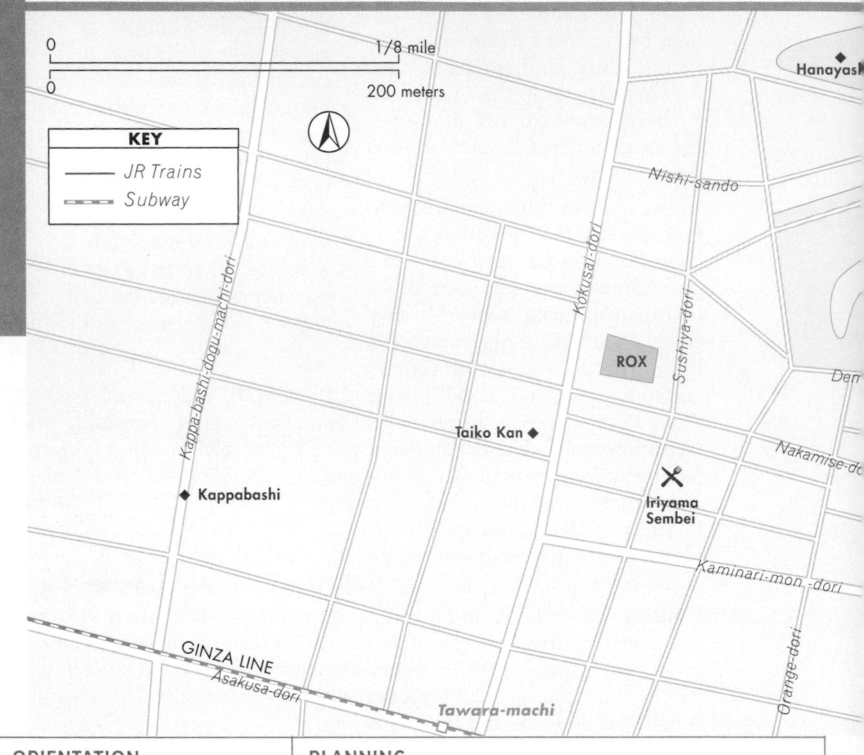

ORIENTATION	PLANNING
Asakusa is a border city ward that separates central Tokyo from its suburban areas. It's a unique spiritual and commercial, tourist, and residential area, where locals walk their dogs on the Asakusa Jinja grounds or give offerings and pray at Kannon Temple. Asakusa is just east of Ueno and can be explored in a half day, whether you go straight from Ueno or on a separate excursion.	Unlike most of the other areas to explore on foot in Tokyo, Senso-ji is admirably compact. You can easily see the temple and explore the area surrounding it in a morning. The garden at Dembo-in is worth a half hour. If you decide to include Kappabashi, allow yourself an hour more for the tour. Some of the shopping arcades in this area are covered, but Asakusa is essentially an outdoor experience. Be prepared for rain in June and heat and humidity in July and August. The Asakusa Tourist Information Center (Asakusa Bunka Kanko Center) is across the street from Kaminari-mon. English-speaking volunteers are on duty here daily 10–5 and will happily load you down with maps and brochures.

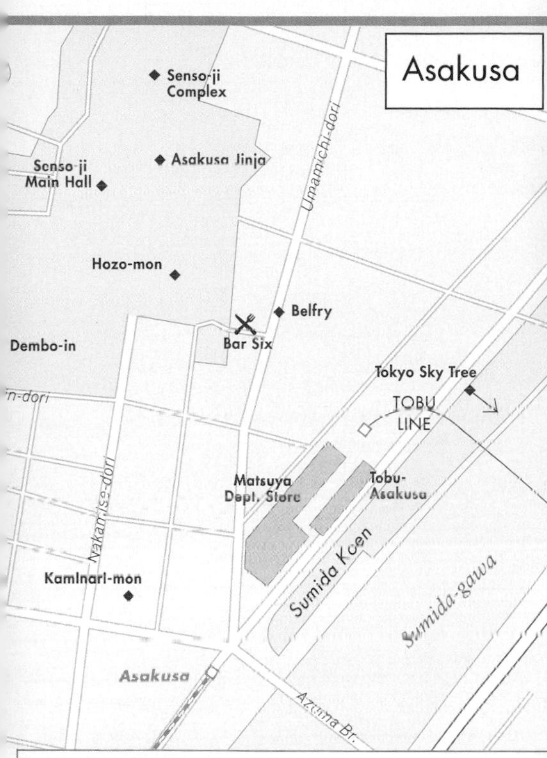

3

GETTING HERE AND AROUND

Getting here by subway from Ueno Station (Ginza Line, Ueno Station to Asakusa Station, ¥170) or taxi (approximately ¥1,000) is most convenient. Asakusa is the last stop (eastbound) on the Ginza Line.

Another way to get to Asakusa is by river-bus ferry from Hinode Pier, which stops at the south-west corner of Sumida Koen.

QUICK BITES

Iriyama Sembei (入山煎餅). For a little local flavor, stop at Iriyama Sembei for a baked rice cracker. Dried for three days and baked for a few minutes, the soy-dipped snacks are a real treat. ✉ *1–13–4 Asakusa, Taitō-ku, Asakusa* ☎ *03/3844–1376* ▭ *No credit cards* ⏲ *Closed Wed. and Thurs.*

Bar Six. Should a cocktail be on your mind, hit up Bar Six, on the sixth floor of the Amuse Museum, and enjoy the views of the Senso-ji Complex. ✉ *2–34–3 Asakusa, Taitō-ku* ☎ *03/5806–5106* ▭ *No credit cards* ⏲ *Closed Mon.*

TOP REASONS TO GO

Make a wish. Visit the Asakusa Jinja, where the souls of the three men who built Senso-ji are enshrined. If you have a special wish, purchase a wooden placard, write your message on it, and leave it for the gods.

Go wild. Drunken people? Loud crowds? Brilliant colors? It's all part of the Sanja Festival, which happens every May.

Grab a photo-op. Want to show your friends that you saw the Thunder God Gate? Then make sure you take a photograph in front of the giant red-paper lantern of Kaminari-mon.

Wander the backstreets. The streets to the west of the Senso-ji Complex are full of restaurants, cafés, and shops. Many of the streets have a wonderfully retro feel hard to find in other parts of Tokyo.

Shop 'til you drop. Looking for souvenirs? Visit more than 80 shops on Nakamise-dori that sell everything from rice crackers to *kiriko* (cut and colored glassware).

The Dembo Shrine offers a bit of solitude inside the otherwise bustling Senso-ji Complex.

WORTH NOTING

FAMILY **Taiko Kan** (太鼓館 *Drum Museum*). Become a *taiko* (drum) master for a day as you pound away on the exhibits at this fourth-floor museum dedicated to traditional Japanese and foreign drums. More than 200 instruments can be played, making it a great place for kids. Just make sure their hands remain off the antique instruments, which are carefully marked. Should you feel inspired, there is a shop on the ground floor of the same building that sells various Japanese drums and festival accessories, which make great souvenirs. ✉ *2–1–1 Nishi-Asakusa, Taitō-ku, Asakusa* ☎ *03/3842–5622* 🌐 *www.miyamoto-unosuke.co.jp/taikokan* 🎫 *¥500* 🕑 *Wed.–Sun. 10–5* Ⓜ *Ginza subway line, Tawara-machi Station.*

3

TSUKIJI AND SHIODOME

Sightseeing ★★★
Dining ★★★★
Lodging ★★★★
Shopping ★★★
Nightlife ★★

Although it's best known today as the former site of the largest wholesale fish market in the world, Tsukiji is also a reminder of the awesome disaster of the great fire of 1657.

In the space of two days, it killed more than 100,000 people and leveled almost 70% of Ieyasu Tokugawa's new capital. Ieyasu was not a man to be discouraged by mere catastrophe, however; he took it as an opportunity to plan an even bigger and better city, one that would incorporate the marshes east of his castle. Tsukiji, in fact, means "reclaimed land," and a substantial block of land it was, laboriously drained and filled, from present-day Ginza to the bay

Now a redeveloped business district, Shiodome (literally "where the tide stops") was once an area of saltwater flats where the Meiji government built the Tokyo terminal in 1872—the original Shimbashi Station—on Japan's first railway line. By 1997, long after the JR had run out of use for the land, an urban renewal plan for the area evolved, and the land was auctioned off. Among the buyers were Nippon Television and Dentsu, the largest advertising agency in Asia.

In 2002, Dentsu consolidated its scattered offices into the centerpiece of the Shiodome project: a 47-story tower and annex designed by Jean Nouvel. With the annex, known as the Caretta Shiodome, Dentsu created an "investment in community": a complex of cultural facilities, shops, and restaurants that has turned Shiodome into one of the most fashionable places in the city.

TSUKIJI 築地

TOP ATTRACTIONS

Fodor's Choice ★ **Backstreet shops of Tsukiji** (築地6丁目). If you have time for only one market, this is the one to see. The three square blocks between the Tokyo Central Wholesale Market and Harumi-dori have scores of fishmongers, but also shops and restaurants. Stores sell pickles, tea, crackers and snacks, cutlery (what better place to pick up a professional sushi knife?), baskets, and kitchenware. Hole-in-the-wall sushi bars here have

GETTING ORIENTED

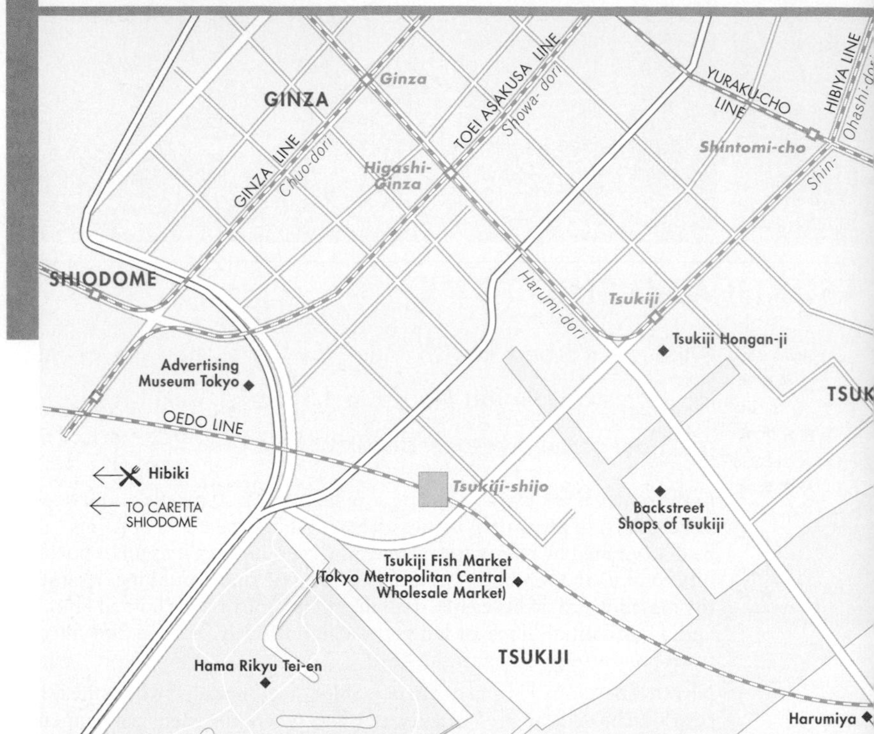

ORIENTATION	PLANNING
Shiodome is the southeastern transportation hub of central Tokyo while Tsukiji is a sushi-lover's dream. Perhaps getting up at 5 am to eat fish at the market isn't your idea of breakfast, but this is definitely an excellent place to taste the freshest sushi on Earth, located just east of Shiodome.	Tsukiji has few places to spend time *in*; getting from point to point, however, can consume most of a morning. The backstreet shops will probably require no more than an hour. Allow yourself about an hour to explore the fish market; if fish in all its diversity holds a special fascination for you, take two hours. Remember that in order to see the fish auction in action, you need to get to the market before 5:30 am; by 9 am the business of the market is largely finished for the day. Sushi and sashimi will be cheaper here than in other parts of Tokyo, with sushi sets at most sushi stalls costing between ¥1,000 to ¥2,100. This part of the city can be brutally hot and muggy in August; during the O-bon holiday, in the middle of the month, Tsukiji is comparatively lifeless. Mid-April and early October are best for strolls in the Hama Rikyu Tei-en.

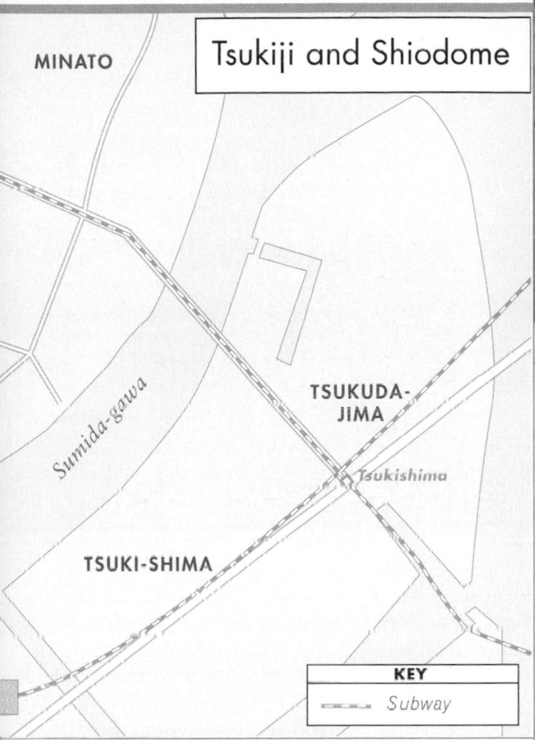

3

TOP REASONS TO GO

Discover an urban oasis. Settle into a lovely traditional garden and old teahouse surrounded by skyscrapers and concrete at Hama Rikyu Tei-en.

Feast on fish. You'll dine on the freshest sushi in the world at Tsukiji fish market.

Get off the beaten path. Discover the local charm of old sushi and sashimi restaurants, and small markets in the backstreets of Tsukiji.

Regard ads as art. Get a glimpse at ad formats, from radio to magazines, dating back to the Edo period (1603–1868) at the Advertising Museum Tokyo.

GETTING HERE AND AROUND

Shiodome is easily accessed by public transport: JR lines and Yurikamome Line at Shimbashi Station, Toei Oedo Line to Shiodome Station, and Asakusa Line and Ginza Line to Shimbashi Station. The connection station to the Yurikamome Monorail, a scenic ride that takes you to Odaiba in approximately 30 minutes, is also here. You can also get around quite easily on foot. There are elevated walkways that connect all the major buildings and subway and train stations. To visit the fish market, take the subway to Tsukiji Station, which will always be the more dependable and cost-efficient option.

QUICK BITES

Hibiki (響). Perched on the 46th floor of the Carretta Shiodome Building overlooking Tokyo Bay, this seafood-focused izakaya is a nice escape from the chaotic frenzy below. Specialties include grilled fish and housemade tofu. ✉ *Carretta Shiodome, 46F, 1-8-1 Higashi, Shimbashi, Mintao-ku, Shiodome* ☎ *03/6215-8051* 🌐 *www.dynac-japan.com/hibiki.*

Cherry blossoms bloom at Hama Rikyu garden.

set menus ranging from ¥1,000 to ¥2,100; look for the plastic models of food in glass cases out front. The area includes the row of little counter restaurants, barely more than street stalls, under the arcade along the east side of Shin-Ohashi-dori, each with its specialty. If you haven't had breakfast by this point in your walk, stop for *maguro donburi*—a bowl of fresh raw tuna slices served over rice and garnished with bits of dried seaweed. Some 100 of the small retailers and restaurants in this area are members of the Tsukiji Meiten-kai (Association of Notable Shops) and promote themselves by selling illustrated maps of the area for ¥50; the maps are all in Japanese, but with proper frames they make great souvenirs. There are currently plans to move part of the fish market to a new location in Toyosu, and it's unclear what will happen to these streets once the move occurs. Check the Tokyo tourism website before making plans to visit. ✉ *Tsukiji 4-chome, Chūō-ku, Tsukiji* Ⓜ *Toei Oedo subway line, Tsukiji-shijo Station (Exit A1); Hibiya subway line, Tsukiji Station (Exit 1).*

Harumiya. As during the time of the samurai, cruising in a roof-topped boat, or *yakatabune*, is the perfect means to relax amid bursting fireworks or cherry blossoms. The charm remains intact: guests are treated like royalty and are entertained while floating on the gentle waves of the Sumida or Arakawa River. Hosts within the cabin serve multiple courses of tempura and sushi and pour beer and whiskey while the boats cruise past historic bridges and along the riverbanks that make up the bay front. When the *shoji* (paper blinds) are opened, panoramic views of the illuminated Tokyo nightscape are a sight to behold. Observation decks offer even better viewing opportunities. Boats accommodate groups of

20 to 350, and tours run day and night, year-round. Nighttime is the best time to take a ride, to see the spectacle of light that Tokyo becomes after dark. There are launch locations on the bay and the Arakawa River. ✉ *Harumi Josenba, 3-1 Harumi, Chuo-ku, Tsukiji* ☎ *03/3644–5445* 🌐 *www.harumiya.co.jp* 🎫 *Around ¥10,000 per person for 2 hrs of touring* Ⓜ *Oedo subway line, Kachidoki Station (Exit A3).*

Fodor's Choice ★ **Tsukiji Fish Market** (中央卸売市場 *Tokyo Metropolitan Central Wholesale Market, Tsukiji Shijo*). The world's biggest and busiest fish market was moved to from Nihonbashi to Tsukiji after the Great Kanto Earthquake of 1923, and part of it occupies the site of what was once Japan's first naval training academy. Today the market sprawls over some 54 acres of reclaimed land and employs approximately 15,000 people. Its warren of buildings houses about 1,200 vendors, supplying 90% of the seafood (and some of the vegetables, meat, and fruit) consumed in Tokyo every day—some 2,000 metric tons of it. Most of the seafood sold in Tsukiji comes in by truck, arriving through the night from fishing ports all over the country. A big attraction for tourists is the early-morning tuna auction. Limited to 120 visitors a day, people line up in front of the Fish Information Center well before it opens at 5 am. There are currently plans to move the market to Toyosu, an island in Tokyo Bay, sometime in 2017 or early 2018, but these plans have been continually delayed over the past few years. Check the Tokyo tourism website before making plans to visit. ✉ *5–2–1 Tsukiji, Chūō-ku* ☎ *03/3542–1111* 🌐 *www.tsukiji-market.or.jp* 🎫 *Free* ⏲ *Mon.–Sat. (except 2nd and 4th Wed. of month) 5 am–3 pm* Ⓜ *Toei Oedo subway line, Tsukiji-shijo Station (Exit A1); Hibiya subway line, Tsukiji Station (Exit 1).*

WORTH NOTING

Tsukiji Hongan-ji (築地本願寺 *Tsukiji Hongan Temple*). Disaster seemed to follow this temple, which is an outpost of Kyoto's Nishi Hongwan-ji. Since it was first located here in 1657, it was destroyed at least five times, and reconstruction in wood was finally abandoned after the Great Kanto Earthquake of 1923. The present stone building dates from 1935. It was designed by Chuta Ito, a pupil of Tokyo Station architect Tatsuno Kingo. Ito's other credits include the Meiji Shrine in Harajuku; he also lobbied for Japan's first law for the preservation of historic buildings. Ito traveled extensively in Asia; the evocations of classical Hindu architecture in the temple's domes and ornaments were his homage to India as the cradle of Buddhism. But with stained-glass windows and a pipe organ as well, the building is nothing if not eclectic. Talks in English are held on the third Saturday of the month at 5:30. ✉ *3–15–1 Tsukiji, Chūō-ku, Tsukiji* ☎ *03/3541–1131* 🌐 *www.tsukijihongwanji.jp* 🎫 *Free* ⏲ *Daily services at 7 am and 4 pm* Ⓜ *Hibiya subway line, Tsukiji Station (Exit 1).*

SHIODOME 汐留

Advertising Museum Tokyo (アド・ミュージアム東京). The unique Japanese gift for graphic and commercial design comes into historical perspective in these exhibits featuring everything from 18th-century wood-block prints to contemporary fashion photographs and videos. The museum is maintained by a foundation established in honor of Hideo Yoshida, fourth president of the mammoth Dentsu Advertising Company, and includes a digital library of some 130,000 entries and articles on everything you ever wanted to know about hype. There are no explanatory panels in English—but this in itself is a testament to how well the visual vocabulary of consumer media can communicate across cultures. ✉ *B1F–B2F Caretta Shiodome, 1–8–2 Higashi-Shimbashi, Minato-ku, Shiodome* ☎ *03/6218–2500* 🌐 *www.admt.jp* 🎫 *Free* ⏲ *Tues.–Fri. 11–6:30, weekends 11–4:30* Ⓜ *Toei Oedo subway line, Shiodome Station (Exit 7); JR (Shiodome Exit) and Asakusa and Ginza lines (Exit 4), Shimbashi Station.*

Hama Rikyu Tei-en (浜離宮庭園 *Detached Palace Garden*). A tiny sanctuary of Japanese tradition and nature that's surrounded by towering glass buildings is a great place to relax or walk off a filling Tsukiji sushi breakfast. The land here was originally owned by the Owari branch of the Tokugawa family from Nagoya, and it extended to part of what is now the fish market. When a family member became shogun in 1709, his residence was turned into a palace—with pavilions, ornamental gardens, pine and cherry groves, and duck ponds. The garden became a public park in 1945, although a good portion of it is fenced off as a nature preserve. None of the original buildings have survived, but on the island in the large pond is a reproduction of the pavilion where former U.S. president Ulysses S. Grant and Mrs. Grant had an audience with the emperor Meiji in 1879. The building can now be rented for parties. The stone linings of the saltwater canal work and some of the bridges underwent a restoration project that was completed in 2009. The path to the left as you enter the garden leads to the "river bus" ferry landing, from which you can cruise up the Sumida-gawa to Asakusa. Note that you must pay the admission to the garden even if you're just using the ferry. ✉ *1–1 Hamarikyu-Teien, Chūō-ku, Shiodome* ☎ *03/3541–0200* 🎫 *¥300* ⏲ *Daily 9–4:30* Ⓜ *Toei Oedo subway line, Shiodome Station (Exit 8).*

NIHOMBASHI, GINZA, AND MARUNOUCHI

Tokyo is a city of many centers. The municipal administrative center is in Shinjuku. The national government center is in Kasumigaseki while Nihombashi is the center of banking and finance.

When Ieyasu Tokugawa had the first bridge constructed at Nihombashi, he designated it the starting point for the five great roads leading out of his city, the point from which all distances were to be measured. His decree is still in force: the black pole on the present bridge, erected in 1911, is the Zero Kilometer marker for all the national highways and is considered the true center of Tokyo.

Long known as Tokyo's ritzy shopping district, Ginza was originally the city's banking district, and the district owes its name to the business of moneymaking: in 1912 Ieyasu Tokugawa relocated a plant making silver coins to a patch of reclaimed land west of his castle. The area soon came to be known informally as Ginza (Silver Mint). Today the neighborhood is still home to most of the country's major security companies, but it's best known as the place where high-end shopping first took root in Japan. Before the turn of the 20th century, Ginza was home to the great mercantile establishments that still define its character. The side streets of Ginza's Sukiya-bashi enclave also have many art galleries, where artists or groups pay for the gallery by the week, publicize their shows themselves, and in some cases even hang their own work.

As a neighborhood that is largely devoted to business, Marunouchi has stronger options for dining than sightseeing. It is home to the recently restored historic Tokyo Station, which is well worth a look.

Marunouchi lies west of Tokyo Station and extends between Hibiya Park and the Outer Garden of the Imperial Palace. In the late 19th century, Iwasaki Yanosuke, the second president of Mitsubishi Corporation, bought the land. Today it houses numerous office and retail complexes as well as the headquarters of various companies within the Mitsubishi group.

The clock atop Ginza's Wako department store commemorates the Hattori Clock Tower, which stood at the same location from 1894 to 1921.

NIHOMBASHI 日本橋

TOP ATTRACTIONS

Mitsukoshi (三越). Even if you don't plan to shop, this branch of Tokyo's first *depato* (department store), also called *hyakkaten* (hundred-kinds-of-goods emporium) merits a visit. Two bronze lions, modeled on those at London's Trafalgar Square, flank the main entrance and serve as one of Tokyo's best-known meeting places. Inside, a sublime statue of Magokoro, a Japanese goddess of sincerity, rises four stories through the store's central atrium. ✉ *1–4–1 Nihombashi-muromachi, Chūō-ku, Nihombashi* ☎ *03/3241–3311* 🌐 *www.mitsukoshi.co.jp* ⏲ *Daily 10–7, basements until 8* Ⓜ *Ginza and Hanzo-mon subway lines, Mitsukoshi-mae Station (Exits A3 and A5).*

WORTH NOTING

Bank of Japan (日本銀行 *Nihon Ginko*). The older part of the complex is the work of Tatsuno Kingo, who also designed Tokyo Station. Completed in 1896, on the site of what had been the Edo-period gold mint, the bank is one of the few surviving Meiji-era Western-style buildings in the city. The annex building houses the **Currency Museum,** a historical collection of rare gold and silver coins from Japan and other East Asian countries. There's little English information here, but the setting of muted lighting and plush red carpets evokes the days when the only kind of money around was heavy, shiny, and made of precious metals. ✉ *2–1–1 Nihombashi-Hongokucho, Chuo-ku, Nihombashi* ☎ *03/3277–3037* 🌐 *www.imes.boj.or.jp* 🎫 *Free* ⏲ *Tues.–Sun. 9:30–4:30* Ⓜ *Ginza (Exit A5) and Hanzo-mon (Exit B1) subway lines, Mitsukoshi-mae Station.*

FAMILY **Kite Museum** (凧の博物館 *Tako no Hakubutsukan*). Kite flying is an old tradition in Japan. The collection here includes examples of every shape and variety from all over the country, hand-painted in brilliant colors with figures of birds, geometric patterns, and motifs from Chinese and Japanese mythology. You can call ahead to arrange a kite-making workshop (in Japanese) for groups of children. ✉ *1–12–10 Nihombashi, Chūō-ku, Nihombashi* ☎ *03/3275–2704* 🌐 *www.taimeiken.co.jp/museum.html* 🎫 *¥210* 🕑 *Mon.–Sat. 11–5* Ⓜ *Tozai subway line, Nihombashi Station (Exit C5); JR Tokyo Station (Yaesu Exit).*

Nihombashi Bridge (日本橋). Originally built in 1603, this was the starting point of Edo Japan's five major highways and the point from which all highway distances were measured. Even today one sees signs noting the distance to Nihombashi. Rebuilt in stone in 1911, the structure's graceful double arch, ornate lamps, and bronze Chinese lions and unicorns are unfortunately marred by an expressway running directly overhead. In the rush to relieve traffic congestion in preparation for the 1964 Olympics, city planners ignored the protestations of residents and preservation groups and pushed ahead with construction. ✉ *Nihombashi* Ⓜ *Tozai and Ginza subway lines, Nihombashi Station (Exits B5 and B6); Ginza and Hanzo-mon subway lines, Mitsukoshi-mae Station (Exits B5 and B6).*

GINZA 銀座

Kabuki-za (*Kabuki Theater*). Soon after the Meiji Restoration and its enforced exile in Asakusa, Kabuki began to reestablish itself in this part of the city. The first Kabuki-za was built in 1889, with a European facade. In 1912 the Kabuki-za was taken over by the Shochiku theatrical management company, which replaced the old theater building in 1925; it was damaged during World War II but restored soon thereafter. The most recent iteration of the building retains its classic architecture—until one notices the looming office building coming out of the middle. The interior has been vastly improved, though. Tickets are sold only at the theater's ticket booth. Reservations by phone are recommended. If you want to see what all of the hype is about, this is the place to see a Kabuki show. For a short 15 to 30 minute sampling, get a single act ticket; the final act usually provides the best spectacle. English Earphone Guides are available for a small fee and provide explanations and comments in English about the performance. ✉ *4–12–15 Ginza, Chuo-ku, Ginza* ☎ *03/3545–6800* 🌐 *www.kabuki-bito.jp/eng* 🎫 *¥2,500–¥17,000* 🕑 *Box office daily 10–4, matinees 11–3:45, evening shows 4:30–9* Ⓜ *Hibiya or Asakusa subway line, Higashi-Ginza Station (Exit 3).*

MARUNOUCHI 丸の内

Tokyo International Forum (東京国際フォーラム). This postmodern masterpiece, the work of Uruguay-born American architect Raphael Viñoly, is the first major convention and art center of its kind in Tokyo. Viñoly's design was selected in a 1989 competition that drew nearly 400 entries from 50 countries. The plaza of the Forum is that rarest of

The Tokyo International Forum's glass atrium is the centerpiece of this arts- and culture-oriented building.

Tokyo rarities: civilized open space. There's a long central courtyard with comfortable benches shaded by trees, the setting for an antiques flea market the first and third Sunday of each month. The Forum itself is actually two buildings. Transit fans should take a stroll up the catwalks to the top, which concludes with a view of the Tokyo Station JR lines. ✉ *3–5–1 Marunouchi, Chiyoda-ku, Marunouchi* ☎ *03/5221–9000* 🌐 *www.t-i-forum.co.jp* Ⓜ *Yuraku-cho subway line, Yuraku-cho Station (Exit A-4B).*

Idemitsu Museum of Arts (出光美術館 *Idemitsu Bijutsukan*). The strength of the collection in these four spacious, well-designed rooms lies in the Tang- and Song-dynasty Chinese porcelain and in the Japanese ceramics—including works by Nonomura Ninsei and Ogata Kenzan. On display are masterpieces of Old Seto, Oribe, Old Kutani, Karatsu, and Kakiemon ware. The museum also houses outstanding examples of Zen painting and calligraphy, wood-block prints, and genre paintings of the Edo period. Of special interest to scholars is the resource collection of shards from virtually every pottery-making culture of the ancient world. The museum is on the ninth floor of the Teikoku Gekijo building, which looks down upon the lavish Imperial Garden. ✉ *Teigeki Bldg. 9F, 3–1–1 Marunouchi, Chiyoda-ku, Marunouchi* ☎ *03/5777–8600* 🌐 *www.idemitsu.com/museum* 🎫 *¥1,000* 🕒 *Tues.–Thurs. and weekends 10–5, Fri. 10–7* Ⓜ *Yurakucho subway line, Yurakucho Station (Exit B3); Yamanote Line, Yurakucho Station.*

Tokyo Station (東京駅 *Tokyo Eki*). This work of Kingo Tatsuno, one of Japan's first modern architects, was completed in 1914, with Tatsuno modeling his creation on the railway station of Amsterdam. The

A GOOD WALK: NIHOMBASHI AND GINZA

Tokyo's east side routinely plays second fiddle to the trendier and hipper areas out west. But that shouldn't stop you from wandering through the ever-changing streets of Nihombashi and Ginza.

NIHOMBASHI

Nihombashi was the commercial center of Tokyo during the Edo period. For a peek at a company that started during that time, enter Mitsukoshi department store, which is the original outlet of this venerable chain. Check out the massive supermarket in the basement—the perfect place to grab a snack to take with you on the rest of the walk. From there head south on Chuo-dori to the Nihombashi Bridge, which was built during the Edo period to be the origin of five national highways. Unfortunately, it is also well known for being obscured by an overhead freeway built for the 1964 Olympics.

GINZA

The intersection of Harumi-dori and Chuo-dori is swamped with visitors on weekends, when the area becomes a pedestrian mall (known as a Pedestrian Paradise) and benches and umbrellas spring up in the street. Historically Ginza has been regarded as Tokyo's ritziest area, and it still is, but the landscape has changed. Yes, Wako (identifiable by the large clock on top) still has its legendary luxury-goods store positioned proudly at the intersection, but retailers like Uniqlo and Abercrombie & Fitch have opened outlets a bit farther south. There's even a name for browsing this area: Gin-bura, or "Ginza wandering." The best time to wander here is Sunday from noon to 5 or 6 (depending on the season), when Chuo-dori is closed to traffic between Shimbashi and Kyo-bashi.

CHICKEN UNDER THE TRACKS

Move back up at the intersection, turn left, and keep going until you pass beneath the large freeway overpass. Off to the right is the Yuraku-cho Mullion Building, which includes a selection of shops and the Marunouchi Piccadilly movie theater. Hungry? Stop in at one of the *yakitori* restaurants in Yakatori Alley, the area underneath railroad tracks.

HIBIYA PARK

If tea is more of your thing, stop in the lobby of Peninsula Hotel for the famous Peninsula Traditional Afternoon Tea. When finished, cross Hibiya-dori; Hibiya Park, which was converted from a military facility more than 100 years ago, is off to the left. Nearly each weekend, the park hosts a festival, fair, or music event. Cap off the day with a stroll through its meandering paths while viewing its ponds, greenery, and fountain.

building lost its original top story in the air raids of 1945, but was promptly repaired. In the late 1990s, a plan to demolish the station was impeded by public outcry. The highlight is the historic and luxurious Tokyo Station Hotel, on the second and third floors. The area around the station is increasingly popular for dining, shopping, and entertainment. ⊠ *1–9–1 Marunouchi, Chiyoda-ku, Marunouchi* Ⓜ *Marunouchi subway line and JR lines.*

GETTING ORIENTED

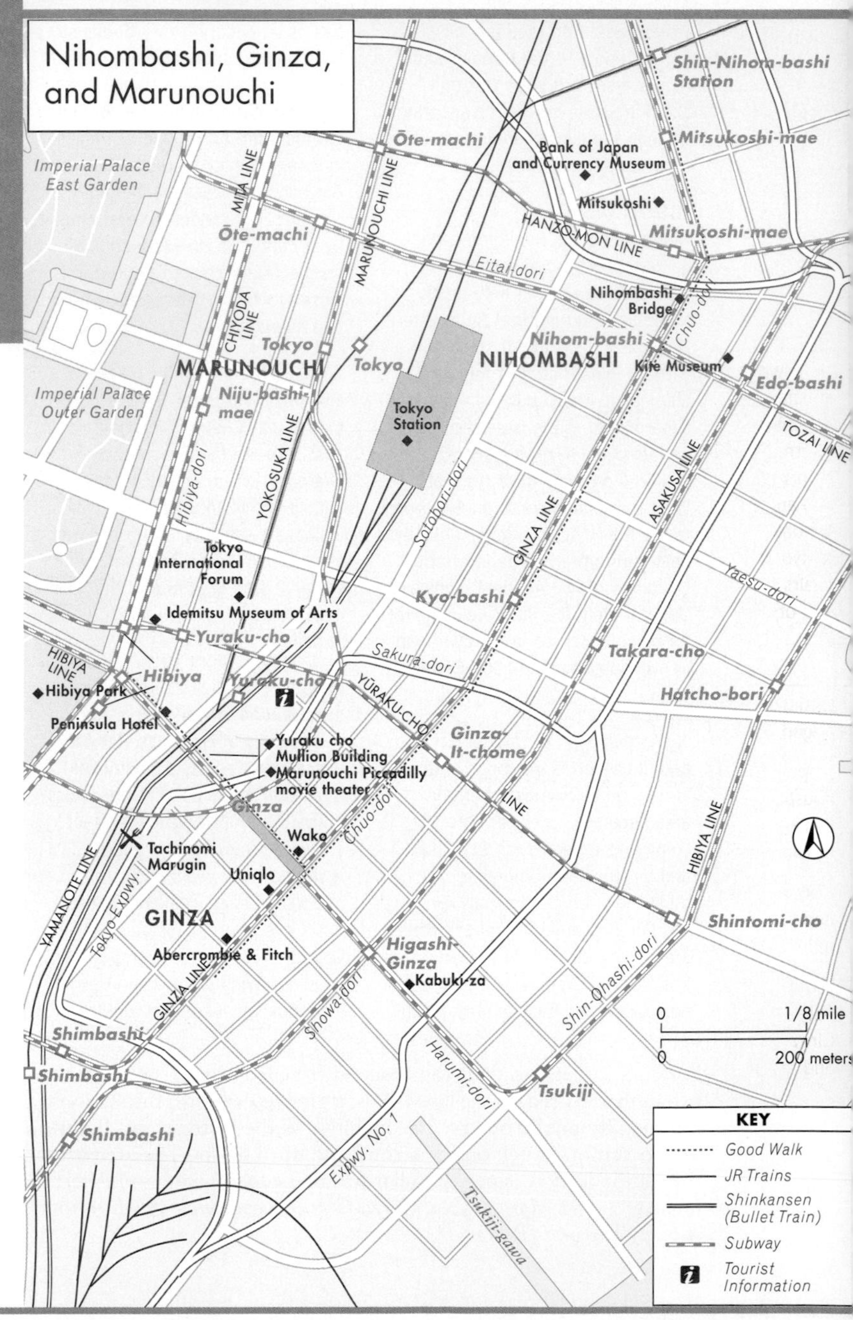
Nihombashi, Ginza, and Marunouchi
Imperial Palace East Garden
Imperial Palace Outer Garden
MARUNOUCHI
NIHOMBASHI
GINZA
Shin-Nihom-bashi Station
Mitsukoshi-mae
Ōte-machi
Bank of Japan and Currency Museum
Mitsukoshi
HANZO-MON LINE
Eitai-dori
Nihombashi Bridge
Chuo-dori
Nihom-bashi
Kite Museum
Edo-bashi
TOZAI LINE
MITA LINE
MARUNOUCHI LINE
CHIYODA LINE
Tokyo
Niju-bashi-mae
YOKOSUKA LINE
Tokyo Station
Hibiya-dori
Sotobori-dori
GINZA LINE
ASAKUSA LINE
Yaesu-dori
Tokyo International Forum
Idemitsu Museum of Arts
Kyo-bashi
Yuraku-cho
Takara-cho
HIBIYA LINE
Hibiya
Hibiya Park
Peninsula Hotel
Sakura-dori
YŪRAKU-CHO LINE
Hatcho-bori
Ginza-It-chome
Yuraku cho Mullion Building
Marunouchi Piccadilly movie theater
Ginza
Wako
Tachinomi Marugin
Uniqlo
YAMANOTE LINE
Tokyo Expwy.
Abercrombie & Fitch
Higashi-Ginza
Kabuki-za
Showa-dori
Shintomi-cho
Shin-Ohashi-dori
Shimbashi
Harumi-dori
Tsukiji
Expwy. No. 1
Tsukiji-gawa
0 1/8 mile
0 200 meters
KEY
Good Walk
JR Trains
Shinkansen (Bullet Train)
Subway
Tourist Information

PLANNING

Attack this area early in the morning but avoid rush hour (8–9) if you plan on taking the subway. None of the area's sites, with the possible exception of the Idemitsu Museum, should take you more than 45 minutes; the time you spend shopping is up to you. In summer start early or in the late afternoon, because by midday the heat and humidity can be brutal. On weekend afternoons (October–March, Saturday 3–5 and Sunday noon–5; April–September, Saturday 2–6 and Sunday noon–6), Chuo-dori is closed to traffic from Shimbashi to Kyo-bashi and becomes a pedestrian mall with tables and chairs set out along the street. Note that some museums and other sights in the area close Sunday.

TOP REASONS TO GO

Satisfy a yen for yen. See where the history of the yen began, in the Bank of Japan and Currency Museum.

Appreciate Tang and Song. The Idemitsu Museum of Art houses a collection of Tang- and Song-dynasty Chinese porcelain and Japanese ceramics. Also on display are masterpieces of Old Seto, Oribe, Old Kutani, Karatsu, and Kakiemon ware.

Take a leisurely stroll. On weekends, see the historic Wako department store, and explore the small side streets of this old shopping district without fear of traffic.

Indulge in a feeding frenzy. Check out the basement food halls in Mitsukoshi department store in Nihombashi and Ginza, where you will find hundreds of delicious desserts and prepared foods.

ORIENTATION

The combined areas of Marunouchi, Ginza, and Nihombashi are located beside the Imperial Palace district, to the southeast of central Tokyo. Marunouchi lies west of Tokyo Station and extends between Hibiya Park and the Outer Garden of the Imperial Palace.

GETTING HERE AND AROUND

To access Marunouchi, multiple north-south-running JR lines run between Tokyo and Yurakucho stations. The Yuraku-cho subway line, too, rolls through from Nagata-cho and Shin Kiba. To the east, the Ginza and Hibiya subway lines stop at Ginza Station. Slightly north is Nihombashi, which is also on the Ginza Line and only a few minutes from the bustling Ote-machi Station on the Tozai Line (¥170). By walking west from Yuraku-cho, Hibiya Park is reachable in five minutes. So is Ginza, in the opposite direction.

QUICK BITES

Tachinomi Marugin (立呑みマルギン). An ideal place inside this area for a short stop is the *yakitori* (grilled chicken) restaurant Tachinomi Marugin. Skewered chicken breasts, small salads, and sausages are sure to put a smile on the face of even the weariest shopper. *✉ 7-1-105 Ginza, Chūō-ku ☎ 03/3571-8989 ▭ No credit cards ⏲ Closed Mon.*

3

AOYAMA, HARAJUKU, AND SHIBUYA

Sightseeing ★★★★
Dining ★★★★
Lodging ★★★★★
Shopping ★★★★★
Nightlife ★★★★★

As late as 1960, the area between the Meiji Shrine and the Aoyama Cemetery wasn't considered to be a very happening tourist hot spot; the municipal government zoned a chunk of it for low-cost public housing. Another chunk, called Washington Heights, was being used by U.S. occupation forces who spent their money elsewhere. The few young Japanese people in the area were either hanging around Washington Heights to practice their English or attending the Methodist-founded Aoyama University, and sought entertainment farther south in Shibuya.

When Tokyo won its bid to host the 1964 Olympics, Washington Heights was turned over to the city for the construction of Olympic Village. Aoyama-dori, the avenue through the center of the area, was renovated and the Ginza and Hanzo-mon subway lines were built under it. Suddenly, Aoyama became attractive for its Western-style fashion houses, boutiques, and design studios. By the 1980s, the area had become one of the hippest parts of the city. Today, the low-cost public housing along Omotesando is long gone, replaced by the glass-and-marble emporia of *the* preeminent fashion houses of Europe: Louis Vuitton, Chanel, Armani, and Prada. Their showrooms here are cash cows of their worldwide empires. Superb shops, restaurants, and amusements in this area target a population of university students, wealthy socialites, young professionals, and people who like to see and be seen.

The heart of Tokyo's youth and street-fashion scene, Harajuku is home to a plethora of stores, boutiques, and cafés. But it isn't only a place for trendy teenagers; Omotesando Dori, the wide, tree-lined avanue leading through the neighborhood, is home to many high-fashion and designer brands. A walk through the neighborhood's winding backstreets also reveals a range of more sophisticated restaurants and cafés. Meanwhile Yoyogi Park and Meiji Shrine offer a respite from Tokyo's crowds and concrete, with a variety of museums and galleries that give a taste of Japanese art and history.

Once a small town on the road from Edo to Kamakura, it was only in the early 20th century that Harajuku started to become a central part of Tokyo. In 1919, the Meiji Shrine was unveiled and Omotesando Dori turned into the bustling boulevard it is today. These two additions brought more visitors, residents, and shops throughout the years. Like much of Tokyo, nearly all of Harajuku was destroyed in the bombings of 1945, with only Meiji Shrine remaining intact. After the war, Harajuku, along with nearby Aoyama, was home to an area called Washington Heights, which housed U.S. military soliders and several shops catering to these Americans. After the occupation, the area received a boost as the central location of many events in the 1964 Tokyo Olympics.

One of Tokyo's busiest shopping and entertainment areas, Shibuya is a sometimes overwhelming mix of shops, restaurants, bars, and clubs. Shibuya Scramble is known as one of the world's busiest pedestrian crossings and nearly a tourist site in its own right. While most smaller shops tend to be youth-focused, the area's department stores, restaurants, and nightlife draw in people of all ages. Unlike many other parts of Tokyo, Shibuya offers little in way of museums, temples, or traditional culture, but more than makes up for it with its pure energy and atmosphere.

Shibuya gets its name from the samurai family who presided over the area in the 11th century; the family name Shibuya and the land was granted to a Heian Era general as a gift for thwarting an attack on the Imperial Palace in Kyoto. For the next six centuries, Shibuya remained a small hamlet of the city. With the opening of Shibuya Station in 1885, the area began to grow, taking off in the 1930s when it became a key terminal linking Tokyo and Yokohama. After being leveled in the war, Shibuya was quickly rebuilt and reestablished its reputation as an entertainment district. In the 1980s and '90s, it was the center of Tokyo's youth and fashion culture as well as the center of the technology industry.

AOYAMA 青山

Fodor's Choice ★ **Nezu Museum** (根津美術館 *Nezu Bijutsukan*). On view are traditional Japanese and Asian works of art owned by Meiji-period railroad magnate and politician Kaichiro Nezu. For the main building, architect Kengo Kuma designed an arched roof that rises two floors and extends roughly half a block through this upscale Minami Aoyama neighborhood. At any one time, the vast space houses a portion of the 7,000 works of calligraphy, paintings, sculptures, bronzes, and lacquerware that comprise the Nezu's collection. The museum is also home to one of Tokyo's finest gardens, featuring 5 acres of ponds, rolling paths, waterfalls, and teahouses. ✉ *6–5–1 Minami-Aoyama, Minato-ku, Aoyama* ☎ *03/3400–2536* 🌐 *www.nezu-muse.or.jp* 🎫 ¥*1,200* ⏲ *Tues.–Sun. 10–5* Ⓜ *Ginza and Hanzo-mon subway lines, Omotesando Station (Exit A5).*

Gothic styles influence the striking outfits worn by Harajuku Girls.

Sogetsu Ikebana School (草月会館 *Sogetsu Kaikan*). The schools of *ikebana* (flower arranging), like those of other traditional arts, are highly stratified organizations. Students rise through levels of proficiency, paying handsomely for lessons and certifications as they go, until they can become teachers themselves. At the top of the hierarchy is the *iemoto,* the head of the school, a title usually held within a family for generations. The Sogetsu school of flower arrangement is a relative newcomer to all this. It was founded by Sofu Teshigahara in 1927, and, compared to the older schools, it espouses a style flamboyant, free-form, and even radical. Two-hour introductory lessons in flower arrangement are given in English a few times each month. Reservations must be made in advance. The main hall of the Sogetsu Kaikan, created by the late Isamu Noguchi, one of the masters of modern sculpture, is well worth a visit. Additionally, the school holds rotating *ikebana* exhibitions throughout the year. Sogetsu Kaikan is a 10-minute walk west on Aoyama-dori from the Akasaka-mitsuke intersection or east from the Aoyama-itchome subway stop. ✉ *7–2–21 Akasaka, Minato-ku, Akasaka* ☎ *03/3408–1151* 🌐 *www.sogetsu.or.jp* ☞ *¥40,000 for a 1½-hour lesson for up to 4 people* Ⓜ *Ginza and Marunouchi subway lines, Akasaka-mitsuke Station; Ginza and Hanzo-mon subway lines, Aoyama-itchome Station (Exit 4).*

Yamatane Museum of Art (山種美術館 *Yamatane Bijutsukan*). The museum specializes in *Nihon-ga* (traditional Japanese painting) from the Meiji period and has a private collection of masterpieces by such painters as Taikan Yokoyama, Gyoshu Hayami, Kokei Kobayashi, and Gyokudo Kawai. Exhibits, which sometimes include works borrowed from other collections, change seven or eight times a year. Visitors can take a break at Café Tsubaki, which offers coffee and cake sets. ✉ *3–12–36 Hiroo, Shibuya-ku, Akasaka* ☎ *03/5777–8600* 🌐 *www.yamatane-museum.jp* 🎫 *¥1,000* ⏲ *Tues.–Sun. 10–5* Ⓜ *Hibiya subway line, Ebisu Station (Exit 2); JR Yamanote Line, Ebisu Station (West Exit).*

HARAJUKU 原宿

3

TOP ATTRACTIONS

Japanese Sword Museum (刀剣博物館 *Token Hakabutsukan*). It's said that in the late 16th century, before Japan closed its doors to the West, the Spanish tried to establish a trade here in weapons made from famous Toledo steel. The Japanese were politely uninterested; they had been making blades of incomparably better quality for more than 600 years. At one time there were some 200 schools of sword-making in Japan; swords were prized not only for their effectiveness in battle but for the beauty of the blades and fittings and as symbols of the higher spirituality of the warrior caste. There are few inheritors of this art today and the Sword Museum's mission is to maintain the knowledge and appreciation of sword-making. While the collection has swords made by famous craftsmen such as Nobufusa (a living cultural asset) and Sanekage (a famous 14th-century sword-maker), the focus here is on the swords as objects of beauty. The swords are individually displayed as works of art, giving visitors a chance to appreciate the detail, creativity, and skill involved in creafting each one. ✉ *4–25–10 Yoyogi, Shibuya-ku, Harajuku* ☎ *03/3379–1386* 🌐 *www.touken.or.jp* 🎫 *¥600* ⏲ *Tues.–Sun. 10–4:30* Ⓜ *Odakyu private rail line, Sangu-bashi Station.*

Fodor's Choice ★ **Meiji Shrine** (明治神宮 *Meiji Jingu*). This shrine honors the spirits of Emperor Meiji, who died in 1912, and Empress Shoken. It was established by a resolution of the Imperial Diet the year after the Emperor's death to commemorate his role in ending the long isolation of Japan under the Tokugawa Shogunate and setting the country on the road to modernization. Virtually destroyed in an air raid in 1945, it was rebuilt in 1958.

A wonderful spot for photos, the mammoth entrance gates (*torii*), rising 40 feet high, are made from 1,700-year-old cypress trees from Mt. Ari in Taiwan; the crosspieces are 56 feet long. Torii are meant to symbolize the separation of the everyday secular world from the spiritual world of the Shinto shrine. The buildings in the shrine complex, with their curving, green, copper roofs, are also made of cypress wood. The surrounding gardens have some 100,000 flowering shrubs and trees.

An annual festival at the shrine takes place on November 3, Emperor Meiji's birthday, which is a national holiday. On the festival and New Year's Day, as many as 1 million people come to offer prayers and pay their respects. Several other festivals and ceremonial events are held here throughout the year; check by phone or on the shrine website to see what's scheduled during your visit. Even on a normal weekend the shrine draws thousands of visitors, but this seldom disturbs its mood of quiet serenity.

GETTING ORIENTED

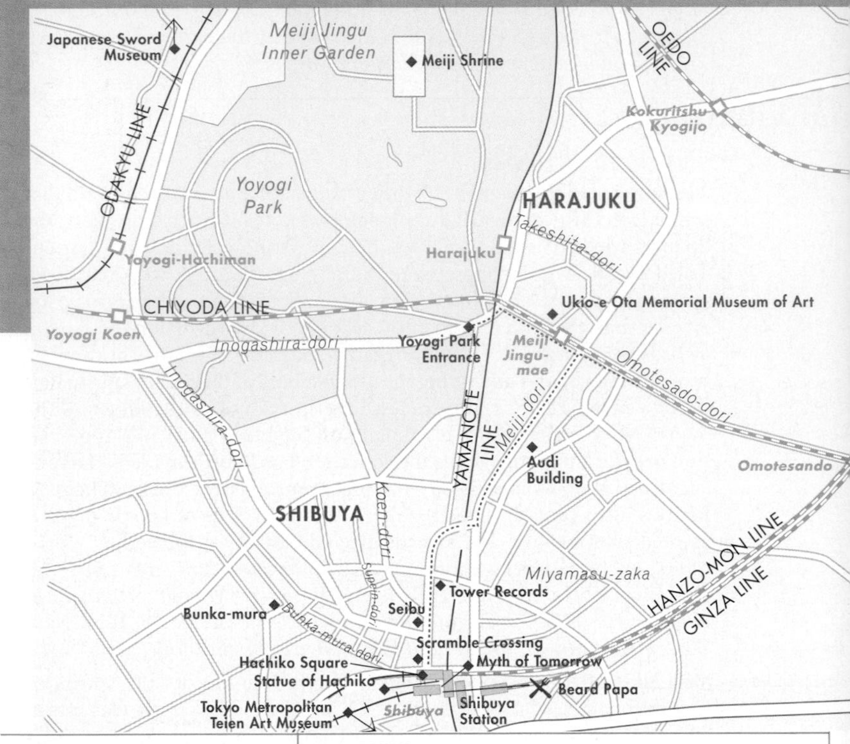

ORIENTATION	PLANNING
Aoyama and Harajuku, west of the Imperial Palace and just north of Roppongi, are the trend-setting areas of youth culture and fashion. Aoyama and nearby Omotesando contain European fashion houses' flagship stores while Harajuku is the young, bohemian fashion district. Shibuya, an entertainment district, is not as clean or sophisticated as Tokyo's other neighborhoods. Shops, cheap restaurants, karaoke lounges, bars, and nightclubs are everywhere.	Trying to explore Aoyama and Harajuku together will take a long time because there is a lot of area to cover. Ideally, spend an entire day here, allowing for plenty of time to browse the shops. You can see Meiji Shrine in less than an hour; the Nezu Museum and its gardens warrant a leisurely two-hour visit. The best way to enjoy this area is to explore the tiny shops, restaurants, and cafés in the backstreets. Shibuya seems chaotic and intimidating at first, but it is fairly compact. You can easily cover it in about two hours. Be prepared for huge crowds: Shibuya crossing is one of the busiest intersections in the world and at one light change, hundreds rush to reach the other side. Unless you are shopping, no particular stop should occupy you for more than a half hour; allow an hour for the NHK Broadcasting Center if you decide to take the guided tour. Sunday is the best day to visit Shibuya and Yoyogi Koen, as it affords the best opportunity to observe Japan's younger generation.

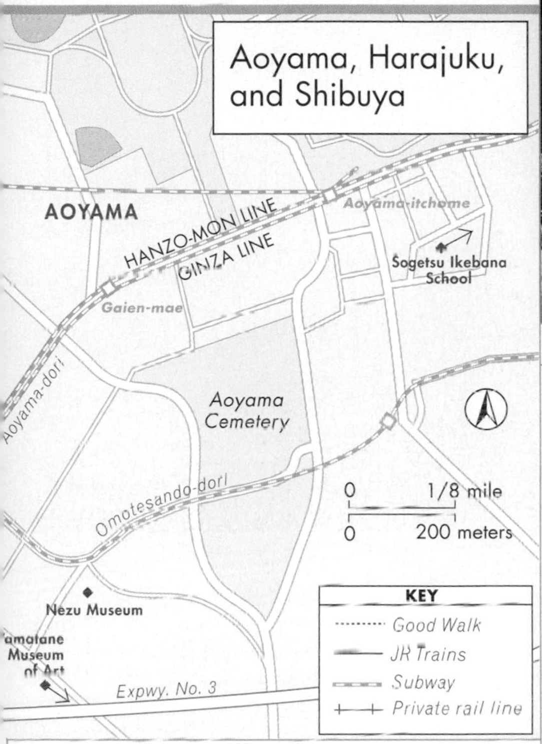

TOP REASONS TO GO

Behold some Tokyo street style. Japanese street fashion may be less out there than in years past, but Shibuya and Harajuku are still the places to see the newest trends.

See a national treasure. Stop inside Shibuya Station for a peek at *Myth of Tomorrow,* the large, 14-panel mural by avant-garde artist Taro Okamoto.

Find a place for prayers and picnics. The beautiful Meiji Shrine and more lively Yoyogi Koen offer a refreshing bit of green amidst the concrete, crowds, and neon.

QUICK BITES

Beard Papa. While long lines in Shibuya are often due to trendiness rather than quality, Beard Papa makes some genuinely good cream puffs. Pick up a single or a six-pack of piping-hot pastries. Follow the vanilla smell near the Toyoko Line ticket gate. ✉ *1–12–1 Shibuya* (still near the Tokyo Line gate).

GETTING HERE AND AROUND

Primary access to Shibuya is via the looping JR Yamanote Line, but the Fukutoshin subway line also goes north from Shibuya up through Shinjuku and onto Ikebukuro. Old standbys are the Hanzo-mon and Ginza lines, both of which stop in Omotesando Station (¥170). The Inokashira railway goes toward Kichijoji, home to Inokashira Park, and the Toyoko railway reaches Yokohama in about 30 minutes. Hachiko Exit will be swarmed with people. Just next to it is the "scramble crossing," which leads from the station to the area's concentration of restaurants and shops. Two bus stops provide service to Roppongi to the east and Meguro and Setagaya wards to the west. On Meiji-dori, Harajuku is walkable to the north in 15 minutes, and Ebisu takes about the same going south.

A Harajuka boutique shows off loud costumed looks.

The peaceful **Inner Garden** (Jingu Nai-en), where the irises are in full bloom in the latter half of June, is on the left as you walk in from the main gates, before you reach the shrine. Beyond the shrine is the **Treasure House,** a repository for the personal effects and clothes of Emperor and Empress Meiji—perhaps of less interest to foreign visitors than to the Japanese. *1–1 Yoyogi-kamizono-cho, Shibuya, Harajuku* *03/3379–9222* *www.meijijingu.or.jp* *Shrine free, Inner Garden ¥500, Treasure House ¥500* *Shrine daily sunrise–sunset; Inner Garden Mar.–Nov., daily 9–4; Treasure House daily 10–4; closed 3rd Fri. of month* *Chiyoda and Fukutoshin subway lines, Meiji-Jingu-mae Station; JR Yamanote Line, Harajuku Station (Exit 2).*

Ukio-e Ota Memorial Museum of Art (太田記念美術館 *Ota Kinen Bijutsukan*). The gift of former Toho Mutual Life Insurance chairman Seizo Ota, this is probably the city's finest private collection of *ukiyo-e*, traditional Edo-period wood-block prints. Ukiyo-e (pictures of the floating world) flourished in the 18th and 19th centuries. The works on display are selected and changed periodically from the 12,000 prints in the collection, which include some extremely rare work by artists such as Hiroshige, Hokusai, Sharaku, and Utamaro. *1–10–10 Jingumae, Shibuya-ku, Harajuku* *03/3403–0880* *www.ukiyoe-ota-muse.jp* *¥700–¥1,000, depending on exhibit* *Tues.–Sun. 10:30–5:30; closed a few days at the end of each month; call ahead or check website* *Chiyoda and Fukutoshin subway lines, Meiji-Jingu-mae Station (Exit 5); JR Yamanote Line, Harajuku Station (Omotesando Exit).*

A GOOD WALK: SHIBUYA AND HARAJUKU

Shibuya and Harajuku are extremely popular with teenagers, hipsters, and those who love to watch the latest fashions walk by.

SHIBUYA

Begin at Shibuya Station, where the once-lost mural *Myth of Tomorrow* is mounted inside the plaza that leads to the Keio Inokashira Line. Hachiko Square is at street level below. Made famous for its statue of loyal dog Hachiko, the plaza is Shibuya's most common meeting place, and to say it is usually packed would be an understatement. The intersection fronting the plaza is the famous Scramble Crossing, which at peak times accommodates more than a thousand people during a single light change. Cross with the masses and turn right onto the adjoining street to get to Seibu Department. Stop inside for whatever clothing and footwear you may fancy. Tower Records—go for the selection of J-pop—is on the opposite side of the street.

ON TO MEIJI-DORI

At Meiji-dori go right towards Harajuku. This area is known for its high-end boutiques from international and domestic clothing makers. After a few minutes, you'll see the Audi Building, whose multi-sloped glass exterior, resembling an iceberg, ought to catch the eye of any fan of architecture. Farther north is a large outlet for clothing chain Uniqlo, a very popular label that offers inexpensive jeans, T-shirts, and jackets.

UP TO HARAJUKU

The intersection where Meiji-dori meets Omotesando-dori presents several possibilities. You can head down Omotesando to take in the pretty tree-lined street with its cafés and designer shops. On Sunday head in the other direction, to the entrance of Yoyogi Park, and check out the leather-clad, 1960s-style street dancers, who offer no shortage of photo ops. The huge park is worth a visit any day of the week. Another option is to cross the intersection and head to the Laforet building on the left, which has many small boutiques filled with the trendiest fashions in the city.

FAMILY **Yoyogi Park** (代々木公園 *Yoyogi Koen*). This park is the perfect spot to have a picnic on a sunny day. On Sunday, people come to play music, practice martial arts, and ride bicycles on the bike path (rentals are available). From spring through fall there are events, concerts, and festivals most weekends. While the front half of the park makes for great people-watching, farther along the paths it is easy to find a quiet spot to slip away from the crowds of Harajuku. ✉ *2–1 Yoyogi-mizono-cho, Shibuya-ku, Harajuku* ☎ *03/3469–6081* Ⓜ *Chiyoda and Fukutoshin subway lines, Meiji-Jingu-mae Station (Exit 2); JR Yamanote Line, Harajuku Station (Omotesando Exit).*

SHIBUYA 渋谷

Myth of Tomorrow (明日の神話 *Ashita no Shinwa*). This once-lost mural by avant-garde artist Taro Okamoto has been restored and mounted inside Shibuya Station. Often compared to Picasso's *Guernica,* the 14 colorful panels depict the moment of an atomic bomb detonation. The painting was discovered in 2003 in Mexico City, where in the late '60s it was to be displayed in a hotel but was misplaced following the bankruptcy of the developer. Walk up to the Inokashira Line entrance; the mural is mounted along the hallway that overlooks Hachiko plaza. ✉ *2 Dogenzaka, Shibuya-ku, Shibuya* Ⓜ *JR Shibuya Station (Hachikō Exit).*

TEENYBOPPER SHOPPERS

On weekends the heart of Harajuku, particularly the street called Takeshita-dori, belongs to high school and junior high school shoppers, who flock there for the latest trends. Entire industries give themselves convulsions just trying to keep up with adolescent styles. Slip into Harajuku's less-crowded backstreets—with their outdoor cafés, designer-ice-cream and Belgian-waffle stands, and a profusion of stores with names like A Bathing Ape and the Virgin Mary—and you may find it impossible to believe that Japan's the most rapidly aging society in the industrial world.

NEED A BREAK?

Les Deux Magots (デュ・マゴ・パリ). Sister of the famed Paris café, Les Deux Magots, on the Garden Floor of the Bunkamura complex, serves a good selection of beers and wines, sandwiches, salads, quiches, tarts, and coffee. There's a fine-arts bookstore next door, and the tables in the courtyard are perfect for people-watching. ✉ ***Bunka-mura, lower courtyard, 2–24–1 Dogen-zaka, Shibuya-ku*** ☎ ***03/3477–9124*** 🌐 ***www.bunkamura.co.jp*** Ⓜ ***JR Yamanote Line, Ginza and Hanzo-mon subway lines, and private rail lines; Shibuya Station (Exits 5 and 8 for Hanzo-mon subway line, Kita-guchi/North Exit for all others).***

Statue of Hachiko (ハチ公像). Hachiko is the Japanese version of Lassie; he even starred in a few heart-wrenching films. Every morning, Hachiko's master, a professor at Tokyo University, would take the dog with him as far as Shibuya Station and Hachiko would go back to the station every evening to greet him on his return. In 1925 the professor died of a stroke. Every evening for the next seven years, Hachiko would go to Shibuya and wait there until the last train had pulled out of the station. When loyal Hachiko died, his story made headlines. A handsome bronze statute of Hachiko was installed in front of the station, funded by fans from all over the country. The present version is a replica—the original was melted down for its metal in World War II. This Shibuya landmark is one of the most popular meeting places in the city. Look for the green train car fronting the JR station; the statue is off the side, where everyone is standing. ✉ *2-1 Dogenzaka, Shibuya-ku, Shibuya* Ⓜ *JR Shibuya Station (Hachikō Exit).*

Commuters arriving at Shibuya Station view Taro Okamoto's *Myth of Tomorrow.*

Tokyo Metropolitan Teien Art Museum (東京都庭園美術館). Once home to Japan's Prince Asaka, this lavish 1930s art-deco building hosts a range of fine arts exhibits throughout the year. With shows ranging from classic paintings to contemporary sculpture, it seems the exhibits are chosen for their ability to harmoniously mix with the building's lush interior. If you visit, be sure to leave time for a stroll through the Teien's Japanese Garden, which is particularly lovely when the leaves change in the fall or during cherry blossom season in April. ✉ *5–21–9 Shirokanedai, Minato-ku, Shibuya* ☎ *03/3443–0201* ⊕ *www.teien-art-museum.ne.jp* 🎫 *Usually ¥800–¥1,200, but varies by exhibit* Ⓜ *JR Yamanote Line or Toei Mita Line, Meguro Station (Central Exit).*

ROPPONGI 六本木

Roppongi, once known for its clubs, bars, and nightlife, has become one of Tokyo's major shopping, dining, and art districts. The area is abuzz with shoppers, tourists, and office workers throughout the day and evening. As the clock inches closer to the last train, the crowd changes to young clubbers and barhoppers staying out until sunrise.

For many travelers, the lure of the neighborhood is the shopping on offer in ritzy developments like Roppongi Hills and Tokyo Midtown. In addition, though, there's the three points of what's known as Art Triangle Roppongi—the National Art Center, Mori Art Museum, and Suntory Museum of Art. The neighborhood is also home to the Fujifilm Square photo gallery, 21_21 Design Sight, and many other art and cultural events.

TOP ATTRACTIONS

Mori Art Museum (森美術館). Occupying the 52nd and 53rd floors of Mori Tower, this museum is one of the leading contemporary art showcases in Tokyo. The space is well designed (by American architect Richard Gluckman), intelligently curated, diverse in its media, and hospitable to big crowds. The nine galleries showcase exhibits that rotate every few months and tend to focus on leading contemporary art, architecture, fashion, design, and photography. ✉ *6–10–1 Roppongi, Minato-ku, Roppongi* ☎ *03/5777–8600* 🌐 *mori.art.museum/eng* 🎫 *Admission fee varies with exhibit* ⏲ *Wed.–Mon. 10–10, Tues. 10–5* Ⓜ *Hibiya subway line, Roppongi Station (Exit 1C).*

National Art Center, Tokyo (国立新美術館). Tokyo's largest rotating exhibition space is home to major international modern and contemporary exhibits as well as smaller shows (usually free) and is worth visiting for the architecture alone. Architect Kisho Kurokawa's stunning facade shimmers in undulating waves of glass, and the bright exhibition space with its soaring ceilings feels a bit like being inside the set of a utopian sci-fi movie. The building houses seven exhibition areas; a library; a museum shop; and a restaurant, Brasserie Paul Bocuse Le Musée, offering fine French dishes. ✉ *7–22–2 Roppongi, Minato-ku, Roppongi* ☎ *03/5777–8600* 🌐 *www.nact.jp* 🎫 *Admission fee varies with exhibit* ⏲ *Mon., Wed., Thurs., and weekends 10–6, Fri. 10–8* Ⓜ *Toei Oedo and Hibiya lines, Roppongi Station (Exit 7).*

Suntory Museum of Art (サントリー美術館). Based on the principle of dividing profits three ways, Suntory, Japan's beverage giant, has committed a third of its profits to what it feels is its corporate and social responsibility to provide the public with art, education, and environmental conservation. The establishment of the Suntory Art Museum in 1961 was just one of the fruits of this initiative, and the museum's current home at Tokyo Midtown Galleria is a beautiful place to view some of Tokyo's finest fine art exhibitions. Past displays have included everything from works by Picasso and Toulouse-Lautrec to fine kimonos from the Edo period. ✉ *Tokyo Midtown Galleria, 3F, 9–7–4 Akasaka, Minato-ku, Roppongi* ☎ *03/3479–8600* 🌐 *www.suntory.com/sma* 🎫 *Around ¥1,300 but varies by exhibit* ⏲ *Mon., Wed., Thurs., Sun. 10–6, Fri.–Sat. 10–8* Ⓜ *Toei Oedo Line, Roppongi Station; Hibiya Line, Roppongi Station (Exit 8).*

FAMILY **Tokyo Tower** (東京タワー). In 1958 Tokyo's fledgling TV networks needed a tall antenna array to transmit signals. Trying to emerge from the devastation of World War II, the nation's capital was also hungry for a landmark—a symbol for the aspirations of a city still without a skyline. The result was the 1,093-foot-high Tokyo Tower, an unabashed knockoff of Paris's Eiffel Tower, complete with great views of the city. The Main Observatory, set at 492 feet above ground, and the Special Observatory, up an additional 330 feet, quickly became major tourist attractions; they still draw many visitors a year, the vast majority of them Japanese youngsters on their first trip to the big city. A modest art gallery, the Guinness Book of World Records Museum Tokyo, and view-filled dining round out the tower's appeal as an amusement complex. ✉ *4–2–8 Shiba-Koen, Minato-ku, Roppongi* ☎ *03/3433–5111* 🌐 *www.tokyotower.co.jp* 🎫 *Main Observatory ¥900, Special Observatory ¥700 extra* ⏲ *Tower daily 9 am–10:30 pm; museums and art gallery daily 10–9* Ⓜ *Hibiya subway line, Kamiyacho Station (Exit 2).*

WORTH NOTING

Fujifilm Square (フジフイルムスクエア). The Fujifilm Photo Salon hosts rotating photography exhibits with a strong focus on landscapes, while the Photo History Museum is a showcase of cameras and prints dating back to the mid-19th century. While the salon and history museum are on the small side, it is a good stop while visiting Roppongi's larger galleries. ✉ *9–7–3 Akasaka, Minato-ku, Roppongi* ☎ *03/6271–3350* 🌐 *fujifilmsquare.jp* 🎫 *Free* ⏲ *Daily 10–7* Ⓜ *Hibiya subway line, Roppongi Station (Exit 6).*

GETTING ORIENTED

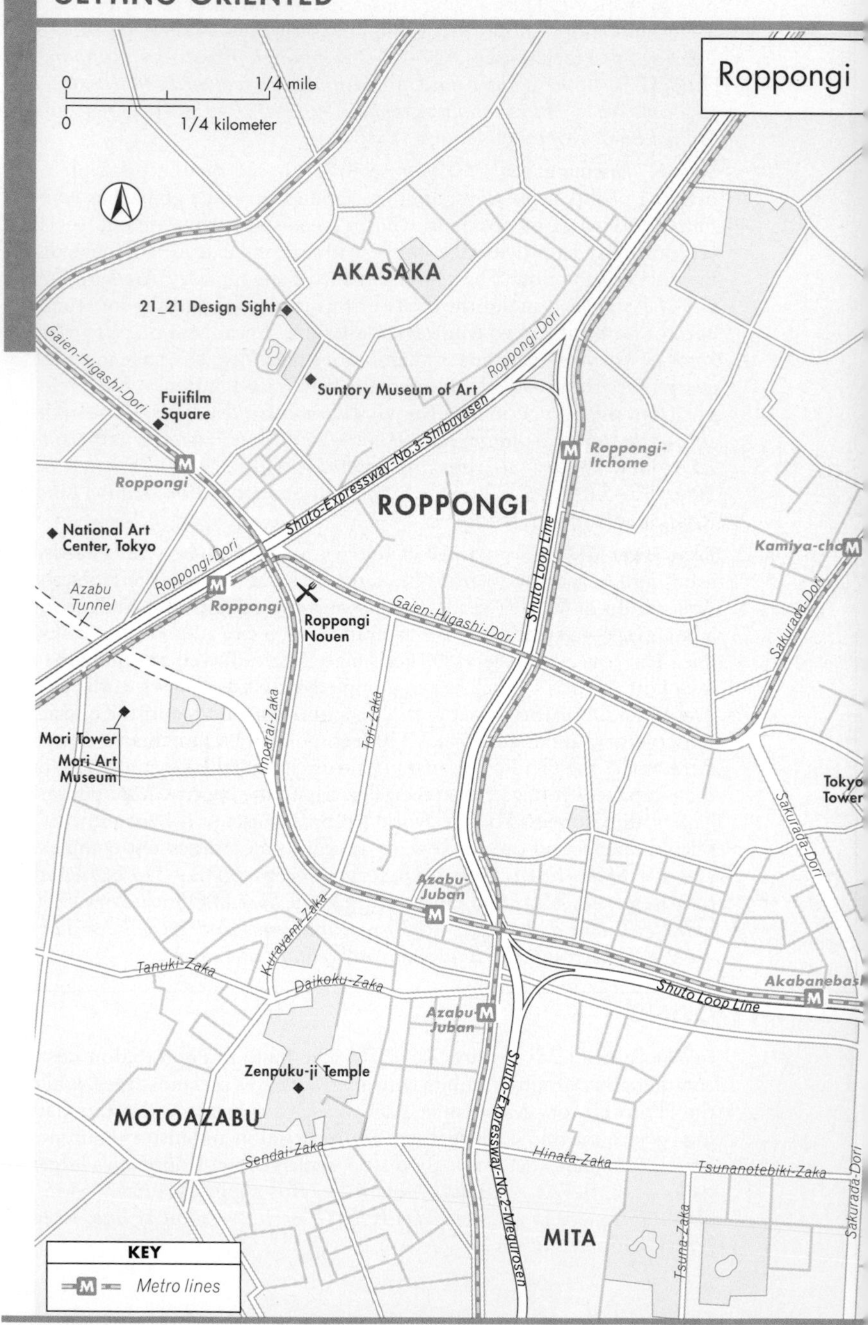

Roppongi
0
1/4 mile
0
1/4 kilometer
AKASAKA
21_21 Design Sight
Suntory Museum of Art
Fujifilm Square
Roppongi
National Art Center, Tokyo
Azabu Tunnel
Roppongi
Roppongi Nouen
ROPPONGI
Roppongi-Itchome
Kamiya-cho
Mori Tower
Mori Art Museum
Tokyo Tower
Azabu-Juban
Azabu-Juban
Akabanebashi
Zenpuku-ji Temple
MOTOAZABU
MITA
Gaien-Higashi-Dori
Roppongi-Dori
Shuto-Expressway-No.3-Shibuyasen
Shuto Loop Line
Sakurada-Dori
Imoarai-Zaka
Tori-Zaka
Kurayami-Zaka
Tanuki-Zaka
Daikoku-Zaka
Sendai-Zaka
Hinata-Zaka
Tsunanotebiki-Zaka
Tsuna-Zaka
Shuto-Expressway-No.2-Megurosen
KEY
Metro lines

PLANNING

There are ATMs and currency-exchange services at Roppongi Hills and Tokyo Midtown shopping complexes, as well as family- and kid-friendly activities, such as small parks and sculptures.

Azabu Juban is a quick visit and a good place to sit in a café and people-watch. The best time to visit is in August, during the **Azabu Juban Summer Festival**, one of the biggest festivals in Minato-ku. The streets, which are closed to car traffic, are lined with food vendors selling delicious international fare and drinks. Everyone wears their nicest summer *yukatas* (robes) and watches live performances. Check the online *Minato Monthly* newsletter (🌐 *www.city.minato.tokyo.jp*) in August for a list of summer festivals.

TOP REASONS TO GO

See Tokyo's top art. With the National Art Center, Tokyo, the Mori and Suntory Art Museums, and 21_21 Design Sight, Roppongi has become the place for Tokyo's top art exhibitions.

Hit the heights. Take in the view from one of two observation decks atop the Tokyo Tower, an unabashed knockoff of Paris's Eiffel Tower.

Watch how the locals do it. Wander into the adjoining residential enclave of Azabu Juba to observe everyday life for Tokyoites, along with some nice café sitting.

ORIENTATION

Roppongi is located just east of Shibuya and Aoyama, and south of the Imperial Palace.

GETTING HERE AND AROUND

The best way to get to Roppongi is by subway, and there are two lines that'll take you to Roppongi Station: the Hibiya Line, which takes you right into the complex of Roppongi Hills, or the Oedo Line, with exits convenient to Tokyo Midtown.

QUICK BITES

Roppongi Nouen (六本木農園). This perfect place for a refreshing mid-day break shows that sustainable dining can be both delicious and affordable, even in the heart of Roppongi. Nouen uses ingredients from local farms and has a list of organic sake and wine, as well as lunch sets from ¥1,500. In the spring and fall, the restaurant's garden patio offers a quiet place to relax after a morning at one of the many museums in the area. ✉ *6-6-15 Roppongi, Minato-ku, Roppongi* ☎ *03/3405-0684* ⏲ *No lunch Mon.*

The Mori Art Museum curates temporary contemporary art exhibitions in a sky-high space.

Mori Tower (森タワー). When it opened in 2003, the Roppongi Hills complex was the center of Tokyo opulence, with the shimmering, 54-story Mori Tower as its main showpiece. Though no longer a unique skyscraper, the tower still outclasses most with the Tokyo City View observation promenade on the 52nd floor and the open-air Sky Deck on the tower rooftop; the views from both are wonderful and extend all the way to Mt. Fuji on a clear day. ✉ *6–10–1 Roppongi, Minato-ku, Roppongi* ☎ *03/5777–8600* 🌐 *www.roppongihills.com/tcv/en* 🎫 *¥1,800, additional ¥500 for Sky Deck* ⏲ *Daily 10 am–11 pm (Sky Deck 10–8)* Ⓜ *Hibiya subway line, Roppongi Station (Exit 1C).*

21_21 Design Sight. This low-slung building hosts rotating exhibitions focused on cutting-edge art and design. Designed by architect Tadao Ando, the subdued exterior belies the expansive and bright gallery space, where exhibits are often interactive and focus on presenting the world of design in an exciting and accessible light. ✉ *9–7–6 Akasaka, Minato-ku, Roppongi* ☎ *03/3475–2121* 🌐 *2121designsight.jp/en* 🎫 *¥1,000* ⏲ *Wed.–Mon. 11–8* Ⓜ *Hibiya subway line, Roppongi Station (Exit 6).*

Zenpuku-ji Temple (麻布山善福寺). This temple, just south of the Ichinohashi Crossing, dates back to the 800s. In the 1200s, the temple was converted to the Shinran school of Buddhism. When Consul-General Townsend Harris arrived from the Americas in 1859, he lived on the temple grounds. ✉ *1–6–21 Moto-Azabu, Minato-ku, Roppongi* ☎ *03/3451–7402* Ⓜ *Toei Oedo and Namboku subway lines, Azabu Juban Station (Exits 1 and 7).*

SHINJUKU 新宿

Sightseeing ★★★
Dining ★★★
Lodging ★★★★★
Shopping ★★★
Nightlife ★★★★★

If you love the grittiness and chaos of big cities, you're bound to love Shinjuku. Come here, and for the first time Tokyo begins to seem *real:* all the celebrated virtues of Japanese society—its safety and order, its grace and beauty, its cleanliness and civility—fray at the edges.

To be fair, the area has been on the fringes of respectability for centuries. When Ieyasu, the first Tokugawa shogun, made Edo his capital, Shinjuku was at the junction of two important arteries leading into the city from the west. It became a thriving post station, where travelers would rest and refresh themselves for the last leg of their journey; the appeal of this suburban pit stop was its "teahouses," where the waitresses dispensed a good bit more than sympathy with the tea.

When the Tokugawa dynasty collapsed in 1868, 16-year-old Emperor Meiji moved his capital to Edo, renaming it Tokyo, and modern Shinjuku became the railhead connecting it to Japan's western provinces. It became a haunt for artists, writers, and students; in the 1930s Shinjuku was Tokyo's bohemian quarter. The area was virtually leveled during the firebombings of 1945—a blank slate on which developers could write, as Tokyo surged west after the war.

Now, by day the east side of Shinjuku Station is an astonishing concentration of retail stores, vertical malls, and discounters of every stripe and description. By night much of the activity shifts to the nearby red-light quarter of Kabuki-cho, which is an equally astonishing collection of bars and clubs, strip joints, hole-in-the-wall restaurants, *pachinko* parlors (an upright pinball game), and peep shows—just about anything that amuses, arouses, alters, or intoxicates is for sale. Recent crackdowns by police have limited this sort of adult activity but whatever you're after is probably still there if you know where to look.

Among the bright lights of Kabuki-cho you may glimpse Yakuza members in the crowds of revelers.

TOP ATTRACTIONS

Shinjuku Gyoen National Garden (新宿御苑). This lovely 150-acre park was once the estate of the powerful Naito family of feudal lords, who were among the most trusted retainers of the Tokugawa shoguns. After World War II, the grounds were finally opened to the public. It's a perfect place for leisurely walks: paths wind past ponds and bridges, artificial hills, thoughtfully placed stone lanterns, and more than 3,000 kinds of plants, shrubs, and trees. There are different gardens in Japanese, French, and English styles, as well as a greenhouse (the nation's first, built in 1885) filled with tropical plants. The best times to visit are April, when 75 different species of cherry trees—some 1,500 trees in all—are in bloom, and the first two weeks of November, during the chrysanthemum exhibition. ✉ *11 Naito-machi, Shinjuku-ku, Shinjuku* ☎ *03/3350–0151* 🎫 *¥200* 🕒 *Tues.–Sun. 9–4:30; also Mon. 9–4:30 in cherry-blossom season (late Mar.–early Apr.)* Ⓜ *Marunouchi subway line, Shinjuku Gyo-en-mae Station (Exit 1).*

Shinjuku Park Tower Building (新宿パークタワー). Kenzo Tange's Shinjuku Park Tower has in some ways the most arrogant, hard-edged design of any of the skyscrapers in Nishi-Shinjuku, but it does provide any number of opportunities to rest and refuel. Some days there are free chamber-music concerts in the atrium. There are many international and Japanese restaurants to choose from in the building, and the sky-lighted bamboo garden of the Peak Lounge on the 41st floor of the Park Hyatt Hotel, part of the tower, was the set location of the Oscar-winning film *Lost in Translation.* ✉ *3–7–1 Nishi-Shinjuku, Shinjuku* Ⓜ *JR Shinjuku Station (Nishi-guchi/West Exit).*

NEED A BREAK?

Humax Pavilion (ヒューマックスパビリオン). Need a break from the sensory overload? At the Humax Pavilion, you can shoot a few games of pool, recline in a sauna, relax in a karaoke box, or sharpen your skills at Grand Theft Auto. This multifloor entertainment center is smack-dab in the middle of Kabuki-cho's chaos. ✉ ***1–20–1 Kabuki-cho, Shinjuku-ku, Shinjuku*** ☎ ***03/3200–2213*** 🌐 ***www.humax.co.jp*** Ⓜ ***JR Shinjuku Station (Higashi-guchi/East Exit) and Marunouchi subway line (Exits B10, B11, B12, and B13).***

3

WORTH NOTING

Hanazono Jinja (花園神社 *Hanazono Shrine*). Constructed in the early Edo period, Hanazono is not among Tokyo's most imposing shrines, but it does have one of the longest histories. Prayers offered here are believed to bring prosperity in business. The shrine is a five-minute walk north on Meiji-dori from the Shinjuku-san-chome subway station. The shrine grounds are at their most lively during the spring and autumn festivals. The block just to the west (5-chome 1) has the last, embattled, remaining bars of the "Golden Gai," a district of tiny, somewhat seedy *nomiya* (bars) that in the '60s and '70s commanded the fierce loyalty of fiction writers, artists, freelance journalists, and expat Japanophiles— all the city's hard-core outsiders. ✉ *5–17–3 Shinjuku, Shinjuku-ku, Shinjuku* ☎ *03/3209–5265* 🎫 *Free* ⏲ *Daily sunrise–sunset* Ⓜ *Marunouchi and Fukutoshin subway lines, Shinjuku-san-chome Station (Exits B2 and B3).*

Seiji Togo Memorial Sompo Japan Museum of Art (東郷青児美術館 *Sompo Japan Togo Seiji Bijutsukan*). The painter Seiji Togo (1897–1978) was a master of putting on canvas the grace and charm of young maidens. More than 100 of his works from the museum collection are on display here at any given time, along with works by other Japanese and Western artists, such as Gauguin and Cezanne. The museum also houses van Gogh's *Sunflowers*. The gallery includes an especially good view of the old part of Shinjuku. ✉ *42F Sompo Japan Headquarters Bldg., 1–26–1 Nishi-Shinjuku, Shinjuku* ☎ *03/5405–8686* 🌐 *www.sjnk-museum.org/en* 🎫 *¥1,000; additional fee for special exhibits* ⏲ *Tues.–Sun. 10–6* Ⓜ *Marunouchi and Shinjuku subway lines, JR rail lines; Shinjuku Station (Exit A18 for subway lines, Nishi-guchi/West Exit or Exit N4 from the underground passageway for all others).*

GETTING ORIENTED

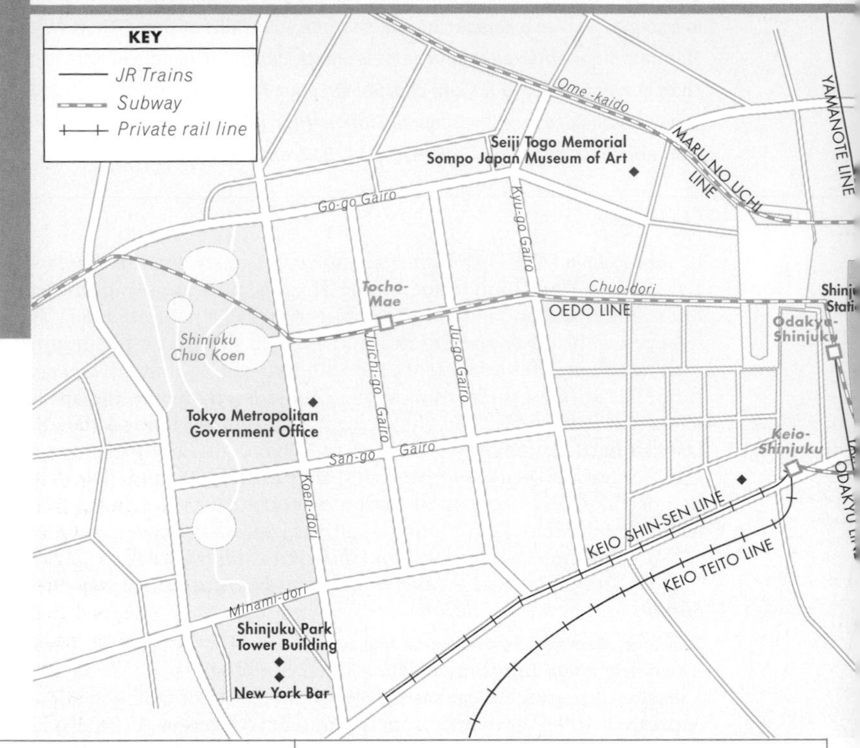

ORIENTATION	PLANNING
By day, Shinjuku is a bustling center of business and government where office workers move in droves during rush hour. By night, people are inundated with flashing signs, and a darker side of Tokyo emerges, when hordes leave their offices to go out for drinks, food, and sometimes, sex. Perhaps this is a rougher side of town, but Shinjuku is a fascinating place to discover at night.	Every day three subways, seven railway lines, and more than 3 million commuters converge on Shinjuku Station, making this the city's busiest and most heavily populated commercial center. The hub at Shinjuku—a vast, interconnected complex of tracks and terminals, department stores and shops—divides the area into two distinctly different subcities, Nishi-Shinjuku (West Shinjuku) and Higashi-Shinjuku (East Shinjuku). Plan at least a full day for Shinjuku if you want to see both the east and west sides. Subway rides can save you time and energy as you're exploring, but don't rule out walking. The Shinjuku Gyo-en National Garden is worth at least an hour, especially if you come in early April during *sakura* (cherry blossom) season. The Tokyo Metropolitan Government Office complex can take longer than you might expect as lines for the elevators to the observation decks are often excruciatingly long. Sunday, when shopping streets are closed to traffic, is the best time to tramp around Higashi-Shinjuku.

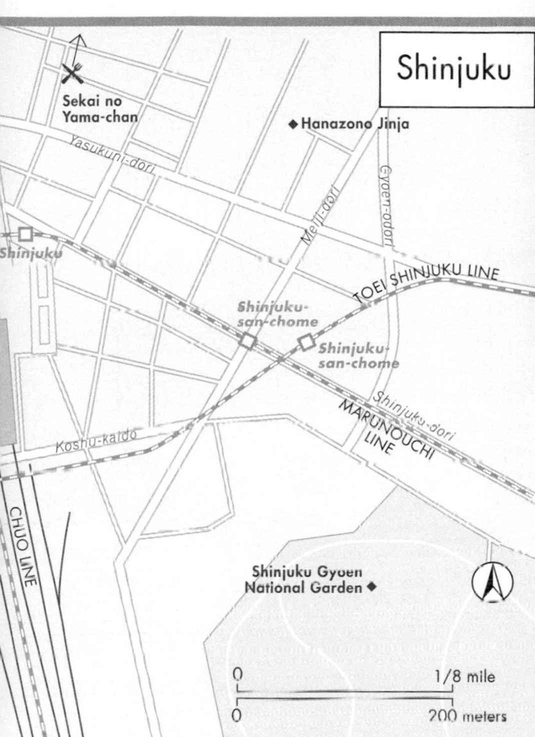

3

TOP REASONS TO GO

Gaze at Japan's most famous mountain. The observation deck of Tokyo Metropolitan Government Office has a great view of Mt. Fuji, and the complex hosts open-air concerts and exhibitions.

Get a dose of van Gogh. The Seiji Togo Memorial Sompo Japan Museum of Art has van Gogh's *Sunflowers*, and the work of Japanese painter Seiji Togo.

Drink like a movie star. No, you haven't fallen down the rabbit hole: the famous New York Bar now calls the Park Hyatt home. You might recognize it from the movie *Lost in Translation.*

GETTING HERE AND AROUND

From Shibuya to the south and Ikebukuro to the north, the JR Yamanote Line is one of the more common ways to reach Shinjuku Station. The Saikyo Line travels the same path but less frequently. The Keio and Odakyu lines serve destinations to the west. Subway lines, like the Marunouchi, Shinjuku, and Toei Oedo, are best used to move to destinations in the center of the city, such as Ote-machi, Kudanshita, and Roppongi. On foot, Kabuki-cho is accessible in minutes to the east. For the forest of office-building skyscrapers, go through the underground passage to the west.

QUICK BITES

Sekai no Yama-chan. Chicken wings, or *tebasaki*, are not rare in Tokyo, but the basket served up by Nagoya-based *izakaya* (traditional bar) chain Sekai no Yama-chan is perhaps the spiciest. The outlet near the Seibu Shinjuku Station ticket gate is often crowded but the food is delicious, fast, and cheap. ✉ *2–45–2 Kabuki-cho, Shinjuku* ☎ *03/3232–1035.*

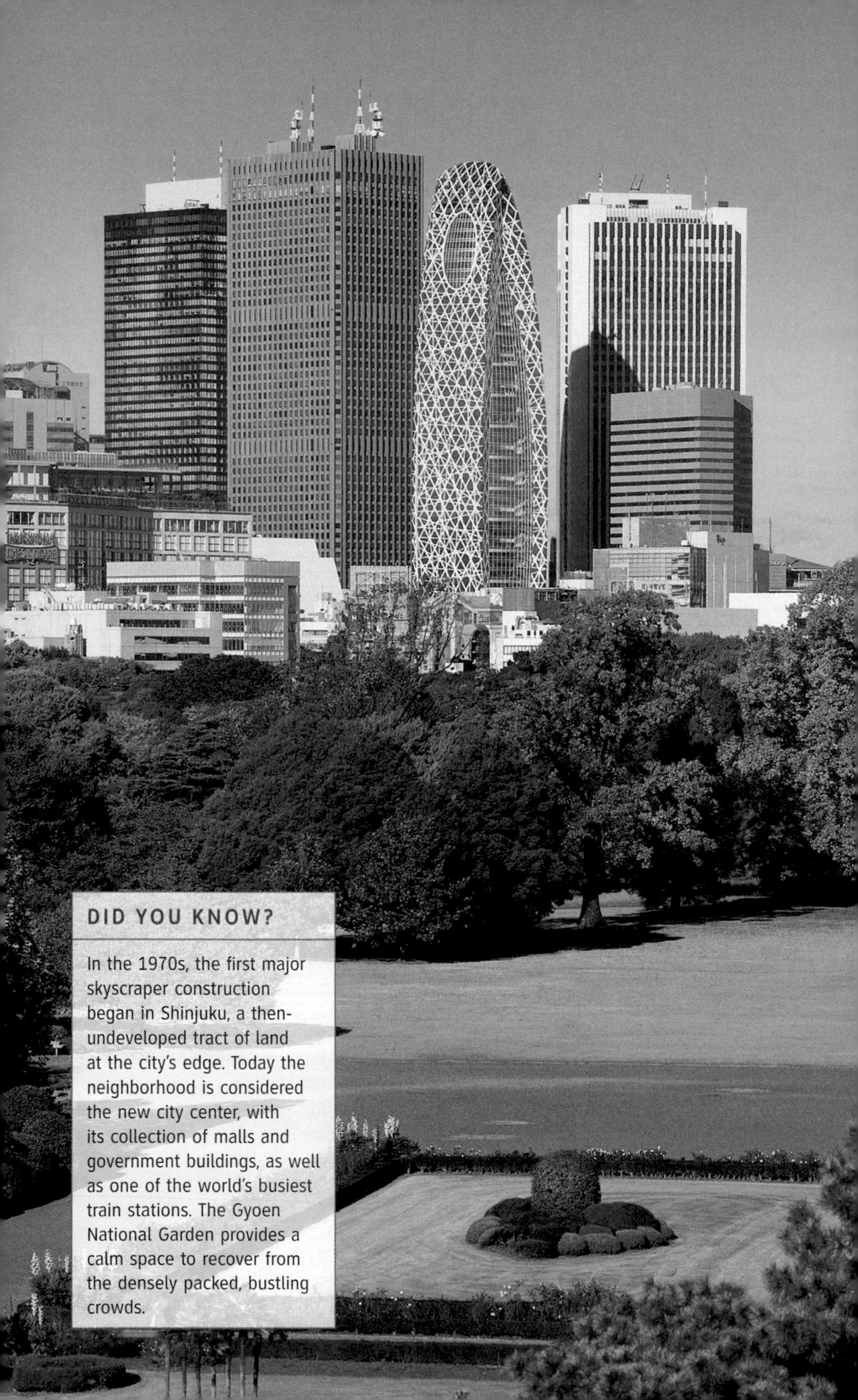

DID YOU KNOW?

In the 1970s, the first major skyscraper construction began in Shinjuku, a then-undeveloped tract of land at the city's edge. Today the neighborhood is considered the new city center, with its collection of malls and government buildings, as well as one of the world's busiest train stations. The Gyoen National Garden provides a calm space to recover from the densely packed, bustling crowds.

Tokyo Metropolitan Government Office (東京都庁 *Tokyo Tocho*). Dominating the western Shinjuku skyline and built at a cost of ¥157 billion, this Kenzo Tange–designed, grandiose, city-hall complex is clearly meant to remind observers that Tokyo's annual budget is bigger than that of the average developing country. The late-20th-century complex consists of a main office building, an annex, the Metropolitan Assembly building, and a huge central courtyard, often the venue of open-air concerts and exhibitions. The building design has raised some debate: Tokyoites either love it or hate it. On a clear day, from the observation decks on the 45th floors of both towers (663 feet above ground), you can see all the way to Mt. Fuji and to the Boso Peninsula in Chiba Prefecture. Several other skyscrapers in the area have free observation floors—among them the Shinjuku Center Building and the Shinjuku Sumitomo Building—but city hall is the best of the lot. The Metropolitan Government website, incidentally, is an excellent source of information on sightseeing and current events in Tokyo. ✉ *2–8–1 Nishi-Shinjuku, Shinjuku* ☎ *03/5321–1111* 🌐 *www.metro.tokyo.jp* 🎫 *Free* ⏲ *South observation deck, daily 9:30–5:30; North observation deck, daily 9:30–10:30 pm* Ⓜ *ToeiOedo subway line, Tocho-mae Station (Exit A4).*

ODAIBA お台場

Sightseeing ★★★★
Dining ★★★
Lodging ★★★
Shopping ★★★★
Nightlife ★

Odaiba is a man-made peninsula in Tokyo Bay, with its beginnings dating back to the Edo period (1603–1868), when various fortifications were constructed for protection from attacks by ships.

As a result of Japan's rapidly expanding economy in the 1980s, the area became a target location for a number of flamboyant and futuristic-looking development projects. Today, 1,000 acres of landfill are home to various leisure, corporate, and commercial complexes.

Connected to the city by the Yurikamome monorail from Shimbashi and the Rinkai Line from Osaki, Odaiba is known to tourists for its arcades, hotels, shopping malls, and museums, as well as the city's longest (albeit artificial) stretch of sandy beach, along the boat harbor (swimming is not recommended because of high levels of pollution). There's also a large Ferris wheel, a neon phantasmagoric beacon for anyone driving into the city across the Rainbow Bridge. The exhibition halls at the Tokyo Big Sight, the entrance of which is beneath four large upside-down pyramids, hosts numerous conventions, trade shows, and fairs.

At the foot of the Rainbow Bridge, one can walk out onto the diamond-shape Odaiba Park that juts out into the bay, or stroll over the bridge itself to get an amazing view of what is certainly one of the most diverse megaprojects in Tokyo.

TOP ATTRACTIONS

Fuji Television Building (フジテレビ). Architecture buffs should make time for Odaiba if only to contemplate this futuristic building, designed by Kenzo Tange and completed in 1996. From its fifth-floor Studio Promenade, you can watch television programs being produced. The observation deck on the 25th floor affords a spectacular view of the bay and the graceful curve of the Rainbow Bridge. ✉ *2–4–8 Daiba, Minato-ku, Odaiba* ☎ *0180/993–188* 🌐 *www.fujitv.co.jp* 🎫 *¥550* 🕒 *Tues.–Sun. 10–6* Ⓜ *Rinkai Line, Tokyo Teleport Station; Yurikamome Line, Odaiba-kaihin Koen Station.*

Odaiba Kaihin Koen (お台場海浜公園). This artificial beach and its boardwalk are home to a small replica of the Statue of Liberty and, for many strolling couples, a wonderful evening view of the Rainbow Bridge. ✉ *1–4–1 Daiba, Minato-ku, Odaiba* Ⓜ *Yurikamome Line, Odaiba-kaihin Koen Station.*

Palette Town (パレットタウン). This complex of malls and amusements is located at the east end of the island. The uncontested landmark here is the 377-foot-high Palette Town Ferris Wheel, one of the world's largest and modeled after the London Eye. Just opposite is Mega Web, a complex of rides and multimedia amusements that's also a showcase for the Toyota Motor Corporation. You can ride a car (hands off—the ride is electronically controlled) over a 1-km (½-mile) course configured like a roller coaster but moving at a stately pace. You can drive any car you want, of course, as long as it's a Toyota. ✉ *1–3–15 Aomi, Koto-ku, Odaiba* ☎ *03/5500–2655* 🌐 *www.palette-town.com* 🎫 *Ferris wheel ¥900* 🕑 *Daily 10–10* Ⓜ *Yurikamome Line, Odaiba-kaihin Koen Station.*

3

WORTH NOTING

Museum of Maritime Science (船の科学館 *Fune-no-Kagakukan*). This museum houses an impressive collection of models and displays on the history of Japanese shipbuilding and navigation. Built in the shape of an ocean liner, the museum is huge; if you're interested in ships, plan at least a couple of hours here to do it justice. There are no English-language explanations at the museum. Anchored alongside the museum are the ferries: *Yotei-maru,* which for some 30 years plied the narrow straits between Aomori and Hokkaido, and the icebreaker *Soya-maru,* the first Japanese ship to cross the Arctic Circle. ✉ *3–1 Higashi-Yashio, Shinagawa-ku, Odaiba* ☎ *03/5500–1111* 🌐 *www.funenokagakukan.or.jp* 🎫 *¥700* 🕑 *Tues.–Sun. 10–5* Ⓜ *Yurikamome Line, Funeno-Kagakukan Station.*

FAMILY **Miraikan** (日本科学未来館 *National Museum of Emerging Science and Innovation*). Make sure to stop by the third floor of the museum known locally as Miraikan, where you will meet the most famous intelligent robot in the world, ASIMO, and a host of other experimental robots in development. This hands-on museum has three different areas focusing on humans' relationship to the planet, the frontiers of outer space and the deep sea, and our life in the near future. There is also a special theater with planetarium and 3-D shows (reservations required). ✉ *2–3–6 Aomi, Koto-ku, Odaiba* ☎ *03/3570–9151* 🌐 *www.miraikan.jst.go.jp* 🎫 *¥620* 🕑 *Wed.–Mon. 10–5* Ⓜ *Yurikamome Line, Funeno-Kagakukan Station.*

GETTING ORIENTED

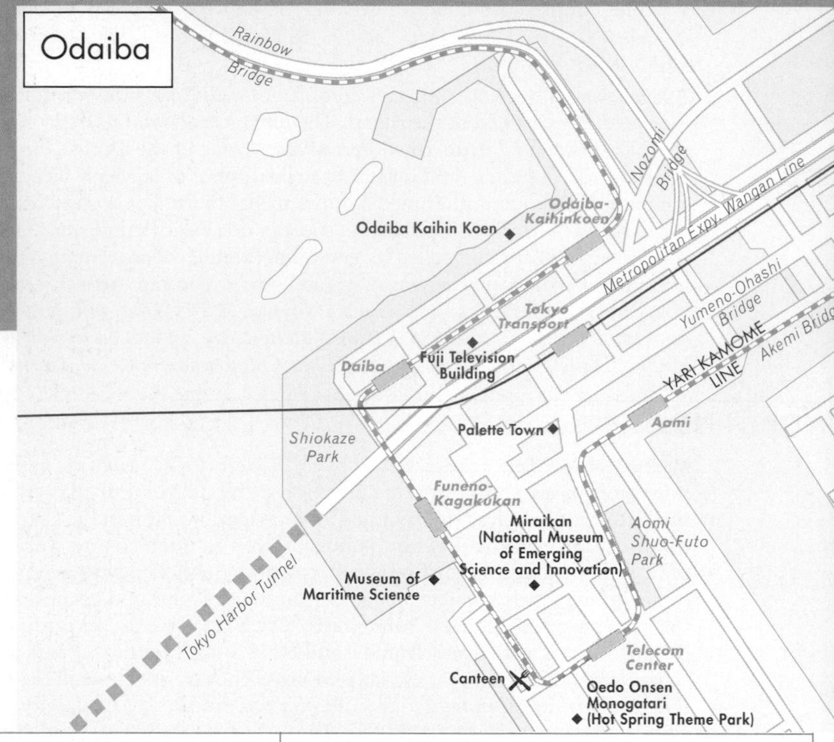

ORIENTATION

Located on the southernmost point of Tokyo, this is a popular weekend destination for families. The lack of historical monuments or buildings in Odaiba separates it from Tokyo's other districts.

PLANNING

If you can, visit Odaiba during the week, as weekends are frenzied and crammed with families. Though a bit isolated, its entertainment facilities make for a good half-day excursion.

GETTING HERE AND AROUND

The best way to get here is via the fully automated Yurikamome Line. From Shimbashi Station you can take the JR, Karasumori Exit; Asakusa subway line, Exit A2; or the Ginza subway line, Exit 4—follow the blue seagull signs to the station entrance. You can pick up a map of Odaiba in English at the entrance. The Yurikamome Line makes 10 stops between Shimbashi and the terminus at Ariake; fares range from ¥320 to ¥380, but the best strategy is to buy an ¥800 one-day unlimited-use pass that allows you to make multiple stops at different points. The line runs every three to five minutes. The JR Rinkai Line also serves the area from Osaki Station, which is a part of the Yamanote Line loop. Perhaps the most interesting means of arrival is via the Tokyo Cruise Ship, which operates a boat service between Hinode Pier (at Hinode Station on the Yurikamome Line) and the Odaiba Seaside Park.

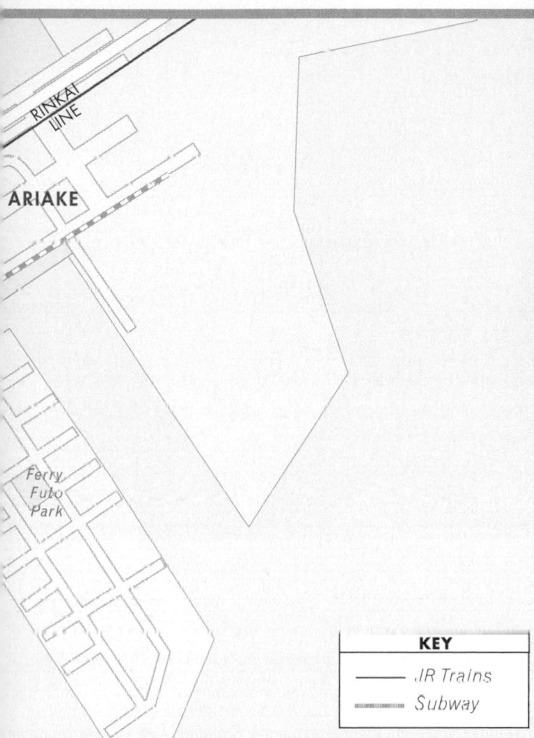

TOP REASONS TO GO

Go on a date, Japanese-style. With its fake Statue of Liberty, giant Ferris wheel, game centers with rides and puri-kura photo booths, and slew of theme restaurants, Odaiba is a good destination for kitsch-loving couples.

Soak sore muscles. Oedo Onsen Monogatari (Odaiba's Hot Spring Theme Park) is a memorable onsen experience in Edo-era surroundings; that is, if you don't mind being naked in a crowd.

Meet ASIMO. Honda's famous humanoid robot resides at Miraikan (the National Museum of Emerging Science and Innovation).

QUICK BITES

Canteen. Shopping and entertainment are two attractive points for Odaiba, but the chance for a short escape from Tokyo's madness is another. To enhance that, stop in at Canteen, a café operated by Transit General Office. The terrace seating is a fine choice for enjoying a cup of coffee and an ice cream cake. ✉ *2–7–4 Aomi, Odaiba* ☎ *03/5530–0261* ⏲ *Closed Sun.*

Head to the beach without leaving town at Odaiba's Decks Tokyo Beach.

Oedo Onsen Monogatari (大江戸温泉物語 *Odaiba's Hot Spring Theme Park*). Once upon a time, when bathtubs in private homes were a rarity, the great defining social institution of Japanese urban life was the relaxing *sento*: the local public bath. And if the sento was also an *onsen*—a thermal spring—with waters drawn from some mineral-rich underground supply, the delight was even greater. No more than a handful of such places survive in Tokyo, but the Oedo Onsen managed to tap a source some 4,600 feet below the bay. Visitors can choose from several indoor and outdoor pools, each with different temperatures and motifs—but remember that you must soap up and rinse off (including your hair) before you enter any of them. Follow your soak with a massage and a stroll through the food court—modeled after a street in Yoshiwara, the licensed red-light district of the Edo period—for sushi or noodles and beer. Charges include the rental of a yukata and a towel. ⚠ **Guests with tattoos are not allowed inside the park.** ✉ *2–6–3 Aomi, Koto-ku, Odaiba* ☎ *03/5500–1126* 🌐 *www.ooedoonsen.jp* 🎫 *¥2,480–¥2,880; ¥2,000 surcharge after midnight* 🕒 *Daily 11 am–9 am; front desk closes at 2 am* Ⓜ *Rinkai Line, Tokyo Teleport Station; Yurikamome Line, Odaiba-kaihin Koen Station.*

3

GREATER TOKYO

Sightseeing ★★★
Dining ★★
Lodging ★★
Shopping ★★
Nightlife ★

The size of the city and the diversity of its institutions make it impossible to fit all of Tokyo's interesting sights into neighborhoods. Plenty of worthy places—from Tokyo Disneyland to sumo stables to the old Oji district—fall outside the city's neighborhood repertoire. Yet no guide to Tokyo would be complete without them.

Central Tokyo is routinely described as a concrete haven, yet the Kasai Seaside Park offers numerous flora at the edge of Tokyo Bay. Tokyo has a few traditional areas remaining, but if the sport of sumo tickles your fancy, the largest collection of training stables is in the Ryogoku area. Two things make this working-class shitamachi neighborhood worth a special trip: this is the center of the world of sumo wrestling as well as the site of the extraordinary Edo-Tokyo Museum. Also outside the city center are some theme parks, like Tokyo Disneyland and Sanrio Puroland, whose numerous kitsch attractions celebrate Japan's love for all that is cute. Creatures from the sea abound at the Shinagawa Aquarium and Sunshine International Aquarium. If land mammals are more to your liking, the Tama Zoo is a fine choice for kids.

TOP ATTRACTIONS

Fodor's Choice ★ **Edo-Tokyo Museum.** From an open plaza on massive pillars an escalator takes you directly to the sixth floor—and back in time 300 years. You cross a replica of the Edo-period Nihombashi Bridge into a truly remarkable collection of dioramas, scale models, cutaway rooms, and even whole buildings: an intimate and convincing experience of everyday life in the capital of the Tokugawa shoguns. Equally elaborate are the fifth-floor re-creations of early modern Tokyo, the "enlightenment" of Japan's headlong embrace of the West, and the twin devastations of the Great Kanto Earthquake and World War II. If you only visit one non-art museum in Tokyo, make this it.

Both modern and traditional, the facade of Edo-Tokyo Museum hints at the collection inside.

To get to the museum, leave Ryogoku Station by the West Exit, immediately turn right, and follow the signs. The moving sidewalk and the stairs bring you to the plaza on the third level; to request an English-speaking volunteer guide, use the entrance to the left of the stairs instead, and ask at the General Information counter in front of the first-floor Special Exhibition Gallery. ⊠ *1–4–1 Yokoami, Sumida-ku, Greater Tokyo* ☎ *03/3626–9974* 🌐 *www.edo-tokyo-museum.or.jp* 🎫 *¥600; additional fees for special exhibits* 🕒 *Tues.–Fri. and Sun. 9:30–5:30, Sat. 9:30–7:30.*

Sumo Museum. (相撲博物館 *Sumo Hakubutsukan)* If you can't attend one of the Tokyo sumo tournaments, you may want to at least pay a short visit to this museum, in the south wing of the arena. There are no explanations in English, but the museum's collection of sumo-related wood-block prints, paintings, and illustrated scrolls includes some outstanding examples of traditional Japanese fine art. ⊠ *1–3–28 Yokoami, Sumida-ku, Greater Tokyo* ☎ *03/3622–0366* 🌐 *www.sumo.or.jp* 🎫 *Free* 🕒 *Weekdays 10–4:30.*

Fodor's Choice ★ **Sengaku-ji** (泉岳寺 *Sengaku Temple*). In 1701, a young provincial baron named Asano Takumi-no-Kami attacked and seriously wounded a courtier named Yoshinaka Kira. Asano, for daring to draw his sword in the confines of Edo Castle, was ordered to commit suicide, so his family line was abolished and his fief confiscated. Forty-seven of Asano's loyal retainers vowed revenge; the death of their leader made them *ronin*—masterless samurai. On the night of December 14, 1702, Asano's ronin stormed Kira's villa in Edo, cut off his head, and brought it in triumph to Asano's tomb at Sengaku-ji, the family temple. The ronin were sentenced to commit suicide—which they accepted as the reward, not the price, of their honorable vendetta—and were buried in the temple graveyard with their lord.

Through the centuries this story has become a national epic and the last word on the subject of loyalty and sacrifice, celebrated in every medium from Kabuki to film. The temple still stands, and the graveyard is wreathed in smoke from the bundles of incense that visitors still lay reverently on the tombstones. There is a collection of weapons and other memorabilia from the event in the temple's small museum. One of the items derives from Kira's family desire to give him a proper burial. The law insisted this could not be done without his head, so they asked for it back. It was entrusted to the temple, and the priests wrote a receipt, which survives even now in the corner of a dusty glass case. "Item," it begins, "One head." ✉ *2–11–1 Takanawa, Minato-ku, Greater Tokyo* ☎ *03/3441–5560* 🌐 *www.sengakuji.or.jp* 🎫 *Temple and grounds free, museum ¥200* ⏲ *Temple Apr.–Sept., daily 7–6; Oct.–Mar., daily 7–5. Museum daily 9–4* Ⓜ *Asakusa subway line, Sengakuji Station (Exit A2).*

3

FAMILY **Tokyo Disneyland** (東京ディズニーランド). Mickey-san and his coterie of Disney characters entertain here at Tokyo Disneyland the same way they do in the California and Florida Disney parks. When the park was built in 1983 it was much smaller than its counterparts in the United States, but the construction in 2001 of the adjacent DisneySea and its seven "Ports of Call," all with different nautical themes and rides, added more than 100 acres to this multifaceted Magic Kingdom.

There are several types of admission tickets. Most people buy the One-Day Passport (¥6,900), which gives you unlimited access to the attractions and shows at one or the other of the two parks. See the park website for other ticketing options. You can buy tickets in advance from any local travel agency, such as the Japan Travel Bureau (JTB). ✉ *1–1 Maihama, Urayasu, Greater Tokyo* ☎ *0570/00–8632* 🌐 *www.tokyodisneyresort.co.jp* ⏲ *Disneyland, daily 9:30–6:30; Disney Sea, daily 10–10; seasonal closings in Dec. and Jan.* Ⓜ *JR Keiyo Line, Maihama Station.*

FAMILY **Tokyo Sea Life Park** (葛西臨海水族館 *Kasai Rinkai Suizokan*). The three-story cylindrical complex of this aquarium houses more than 540 species of fish and other sea creatures within three different areas: "Voyagers of the Sea" ("Maguro no Kaiyu"), with migratory species; "Seas of the World" ("Sekai no Umi"), with species from foreign waters; and the "Sea of Tokyo" ("Tokyo no Umi"), devoted to the creatures of the bay and nearby waters. To get here, take the JR Keiyo Line local train from Tokyo Station to Kasai Rinkai Koen Station; the aquarium is a 10-minute walk from the South Exit. ✉ *6–2–3 Rinkai-cho, Edogawa-ku, Greater Tokyo* ☎ *03/3869–5152* 🌐 *www.tokyo-zoo.net/english/kasai* 🎫 *¥700* ⏲ *Thurs.–Tues. 9:30–5* Ⓜ *JR Keiyo Line, Kasai Rinkai Koen Station.*

GETTING ORIENTED

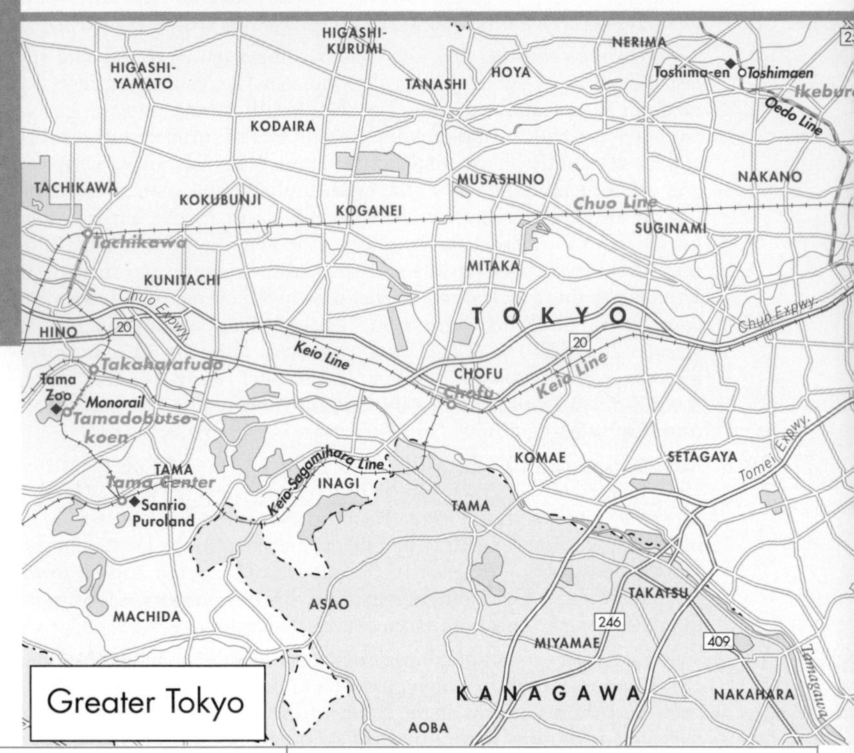

Greater Tokyo

ORIENTATION	PLANNING
Since they are so accessible, the central wards of Tokyo are often the focus for visitors. Of course, there is much more to discover in the city. The areas that lie to the west of Shibuya, south of Shinagawa, north of Ikebukuro, and east of Tokyo Station offer amusement parks, zoos, galleries, and museums.	For the amusement parks and zoos, visitors will want to plan to spend the entire day. The galleries and parks will only take a few hours. Be sure to plan ahead: some destinations can take over an hour to reach by train. Also keep in mind that the farther away from the city one moves the more spread out the city becomes, so plan on taking a taxi from the train station.

GETTING HERE AND AROUND

From central Tokyo, the city spreads out like the spokes of a wheel; various railways serve areas in all cardinal directions. For Chiba Prefecture, where Tokyo Disneyland is located, take Keiyo Line, which originates at Tokyo Station. Use the same line to access Kasai Seaside Park. Multiple JR lines and the Keihin Kyuko Line chug south from Shinagawa Station in the direction of Yokohama and to the Shinagawa Aquarium. To the west, the Chuo Line passes through Shinjuku to reach Tachikawa Station; transfer to the Tama Monorail here for the Tama Zoo. The Keio Line, too, starts at Shinjuku Station; Sanrio Puroland is accessible from Tama Center Station on this line. The Namboku Line is a subway line that moves north through Komagome Station on the Yamanote Line before reaching the throwback town of Oji.

TOP REASONS TO GO

Meet a Japanese Mickey. Tokyo Disneyland mimics the California original in amazing detail. It also adds Tokyo Disney Sea, a park with a nautical theme.

Supersize yourself. Head to Ryogoku to see sumo wrestlers grapple in the ring. There's also a wonderful museum dedicated to Tokyo's history (the Edo-Tokyo Museum) just around the corner.

Get in the samurai spirit. At Sengaku-ji, learn the story of the deaths of 47 samurai, often portrayed in Kabuki theater plays, and visit a museum dedicated to the men.

CLOSE UP

A Mostly Naked Free-For-All

Sumo wrestling dates back some 1,500 years. Originally a religious rite performed at shrines to entertain the harvest gods, a match may seem like a fleshy free-for-all to the casual spectator, but to the trained eye, it's a refined battle. Two wrestlers square off in a dirt ring about 15 feet in diameter and charge straight at each other in nothing but silk loincloths. There are various techniques of pushing, gripping, and throwing, but the rules are simple: except for hitting below the belt, grabbing your opponent by the hair (which would certainly upset the hairdresser who accompanies every sumo ringside), or striking with a closed fist, almost anything goes. If you're thrown down or forced out of the ring, you lose. There are no weight divisions and a runt of merely 250 pounds can find himself facing an opponent twice his size.

You must belong to one of the roughly two dozen *heya* (stables) based in Tokyo to compete. Stables are run by retired wrestlers who have purchased the right from the Japan Sumo Association. Hierarchy and formality rule in the sumo world. Youngsters recruited into the sport live in the stable dormitory, do all the community chores, and wait on their seniors. When they rise high enough in tournament rankings, they acquire their own servant-apprentices.

Most of the stables are concentrated on both sides of the Sumida-gawa near the Kokugikan. Wander this area when the wrestlers are in town (January, May, and September) and you're more than likely to see some of them on the streets, in their wood clogs and kimonos. Come 7 am–11 am and you can peer through the doors and windows of the stables to watch them in practice sessions. One that offers tours is the **Michinoku Stable** (*1–18–7 Ryogoku*). Have a Japanese speaker complete the application form on the website in advance (🌐 *michinokubeya.com*) and you might be able to gain access.

When: Of the six Grand Sumo Tournaments (called *basho*) that take place during the year, Tokyo hosts three: in early January, mid-May, and mid-September. Matches go from early afternoon, when the novices wrestle, to the titanic clashes of the upper ranks at around 6 pm.

Where: Tournaments are held in the Kokugikan, the National Sumo Arena, in Ryogoku, a district in Sumida-ku also famed for its clothing shops and eateries that cater to sumo sizes and tastes. 1–3–28 Yokoami, Sumida-ku ☎ *03/3623–5111* 🌐 *www.sumo.or.jp* JR Sobu Line, Ryogoku Station (West Exit).

How: The most expensive seats, closest to the ring, are tatami-carpeted boxes for four people, called *sajiki.* The boxes are terribly cramped and cost ¥9,500–¥11,700 per person. Cheap seats start as low as ¥3,800 for advance sales, ¥2,200 for same-day box office sales for general admission seats. For same-day box office sales you should line up an hour before the tournament. You can also get tickets through Family Mart, Circle K Sunkus, and Lawson convenience stores.

WORTH NOTING

Asuka-yama Oji Paper Museum. (紙の博物館 *Kami no Hakubutsukan*) The original paper mill that once stood here (Japan's first) is long gone, but the memory lingers on through exhibits that cover 2,000 years of the history of paper and show the processes for milling paper from pulp and recycling and include a number of the machines used. Other exhibits illustrate the astonishing variety of products that can be made from paper. ✉ *1–1–3 Oji, Kita-ku, Greater Tokyo* ☎ *03/3916–2320* 🌐 *www.papermuseum.jp* 🎫 *¥300* 🕒 *Tues.–Sun. 10–5* Ⓜ *Arakawa Toden Line, Asukayama-koen Station; JR Keihin-Tohoku Line, Oji Station.*

3

FAMILY **Kasai Rinkai Park** (葛西臨海公園 *Kasai Seaside Park*). The star attraction here is the Diamonds and Flowers Ferris Wheel (Daia to Hana no Dai-kanransha), which takes passengers on a 17-minute ride to the apex, 384 feet above the ground, for a spectacular view of the city. On a clear day you can see all the way to Mt. Fuji; at night, if you're lucky, you reach the top just in time for a bird's eye view of the fireworks over the Magic Kingdom, across the river. If you don't want to take the Ferris-wheel ride, the park also has an observatory looking out over Tokyo Bay. For visitors more inclined to look at fish than eat them, the park has a nice aquarium, but it gets crowded on weekends and school holidays. ✉ *6 Rinkai-cho, Edogawa-ku, Greater Tokyo* ✣ *Take the JR Keiyo Line local train from Tokyo Station to Kasai Rinkai Koen Station; the park is a 5-minute walk from the South Exit* ☎ *03/5696–1331* 🎫 *Free, Ferris wheel ¥700* 🕒 *Most park attractions closed Wed.; Ferris wheel Sept.–July, weekdays 10–8, weekends 10–9.*

FAMILY **Sanrio Puroland** (サンリオピューロランド). As a theme park dedicated to the world's most famous white cat with no mouth—Hello Kitty, of course—Sanrio Puroland is effectively a shrine to the concept of cuteness. An all-day passport allows for unlimited use of multiple attractions, including three theaters, a boat ride, and the Kitty Lab, where guests are allowed to experiment with what exactly is "cute." Pens, packaged snacks, and plush toys are readily available so guests don't leave empty-handed. ✉ *1–31 Ochiai, Tama-shi, Greater Tokyo* ☎ *042/339–1111* 🌐 *en.puroland.jp* 🎫 *¥3,300–¥3,800* 🕒 *Mon.–Wed. and Fri. 10–5, summer until 6; weekends 10–8* Ⓜ *Keio Line, Tama Center Station.*

FAMILY **Shinagawa Aquarium** (品川水族館 *Shinagawa Suizokukan*). The fun part of this aquarium in southwestern Tokyo is walking through an underwater glass tunnel while some 450 species of fish swim around and above you. There are no pamphlets or explanation panels in English, however, and do your best to avoid Sunday, when the dolphin and sea lion shows draw crowds in impossible numbers. Take the local Keihin-Kyuko private rail line from Shinagawa to Omori-kaigan Station. Turn left as you exit the station and follow the ceramic fish on the sidewalk to the first traffic light; then turn right. ✉ *3–2–1 Katsushima, Shinagawa-ku, Greater Tokyo* ☎ *03/3762–3433* 🌐 *www.aquarium.gr.jp* 🎫 *¥1,300* 🕒 *Wed.–Mon. 10–5; dolphin and sea lion shows 3 times daily, on varying schedule* Ⓜ *Keihin Kyuko Line, Omori Kaigan Station.*

FAMILY **Sunshine International Aquarium** (サンシャイン国際水族館). This aquarium has some 750 kinds of sea creatures on display, plus sea lion performances four times a day (except when it rains). An English-language pamphlet is available, and most of the exhibits have some English explanation. If you get tired of the sea life, head to the Sunshine Starlight Dome planetarium, where you can see 400,000 stars. And if that still isn't enough to keep you occupied, try the 60th-floor observatory for great views of the city. ✉ *3–1–3 Higashi-Ikebukuro, Toshima-ku, Greater Tokyo* ☎ *03/3989–3331* 🌐 *www.sunshinecity.co.jp* 🎫 *Aquarium ¥2,000, planetarium ¥1,100, observatory ¥620; tickets may be purchased in combination* ⏲ *Aquarium weekdays 10–6, weekends 10–6:30; planetarium daily 11–7; observation deck daily 10–9:30* Ⓜ *JR Yamanote Line, Ikebukuro Station (East Exit); Yurakucho subway line, Ikebukuro Station (Exit 35).*

FAMILY **Tama Zoo** (多摩動物園 *Tama Dobutsu Koen*). More a wildlife park than a zoo, this facility in western Tokyo gives animals room to roam; moats typically separate them from you. You can ride through the Lion Park in a minibus. To get here, take a Keio Line train toward Takao from Shinjuku Station and transfer at Takahata-Fudo Station for the one-stop branch line that serves the park. ✉ *7–1–1 Hodokubo, Hino, Greater Tokyo* ☎ *042/591–1611* 🌐 *www.tokyo-zoo.net/english/tama* 🎫 *¥600; Lion Bus ¥350* ⏲ *Thurs.–Tues. 9:30–5* Ⓜ *Keio Line or Tama Monorail, Tamadobutsu-koen Station.*

Toden Arakawa Trolley. Take the JR Yamanote Line to Otsuka, cross the street in front of the station, and change to the Toden Arakawa Line—Tokyo's last surviving trolley. Heading east, for ¥170 one-way, the trolley takes you through the back gardens of old neighborhoods on its way to Oji, once the site of Japan's first Western-style paper mill, built in 1875 by Oji Paper Company, the nation's oldest joint-stock company.

T ✉ *Oji, Greater Tokyo.*

FAMILY **Toshima-en** (としまえん). This large, well-equipped amusement park in the northwestern part of Tokyo has four thrill rides, a haunted house, and six swimming pools. What makes it special is the authentic Coney Island carousel—left to rot in a New York warehouse, discovered and rescued by a Japanese entrepreneur, and lovingly restored down to the last gilded curlicue on the last prancing unicorn. ✉ *3–25–1 Koyama, Nerima-ku, Greater Tokyo* ☎ *03/3990–8800* 🌐 *www.toshimaen.co.jp* 🎫 *Day pass ¥4,200* ⏲ *Thurs.–Mon. 10–5* Ⓜ *Toei Oedo subway line, Toshimaen Station.*

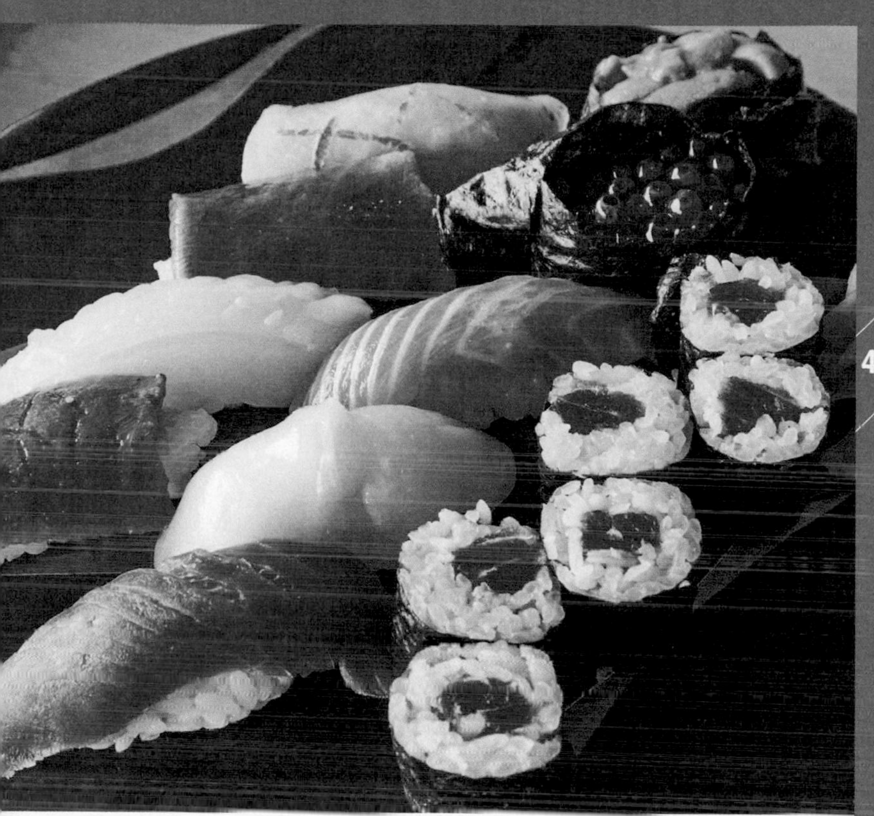

4

WHERE TO EAT

TOKYO'S VENDING MACHINES AND CONVENIENCE STORES

With a brightly lighted convenience store on practically every corner and a few well-stocked vending machines in between, quick shopping is truly hassle-free in Tokyo—and with items ranging from novel to bizarre, an impulse buy can turn into a journey of discovery.

(top left) Ubiquitous vending machines provide fast, cheap drinks, snacks, and more; (top right) limited-edition potato chip flavors; (bottom right) convenience stores give a taste of Japanese culture.

While vending machines and convenience stores did not originate in Japan, their popularity in the country seems to have no limit. Today Japan has the world's highest density of vending machines per capita, with one machine for every 23 people. Those looking for a wider selection can head to one of the 40,000 or so convenience stores in the country. Canned drinks, both cold and hot, are the main staple of vending machines, but it is not uncommon to find ones with cigarettes, batteries, snacks, ice-cream cones, toiletries, fresh fruit, customized business cards, or even umbrellas. For North Americans used to convenience stores that sell little more than junk food and magazines, the Japanese equivalent can be a source of amazement, boasting everything from postal and courier services and digital photo printing to full hot meals.

DID YOU KNOW?

Vending machines hold a dizzying array of options from water and fruit juice to sugar-laden coffee, colas, and even alcohol. If you need a healthy snack, Dole installed banana dispensers around Shibuya train station, targeting hurried commuters with no time for breakfast. Need something like a quick change for work? Shinjuku Station even has machines selling white business shirts and ties.

VENDING MACHINES

If you visit Tokyo during the hot and humid summer months, you'll quickly understand why there is a machine selling cool drinks on every sidewalk. In winter, hot drinks warm both the stomach and hands. Popular drinks include Pocari Sweat, a noncarbonated sports drink with a mild grapefruit taste; Aquarius, a similar drink by Coca-Cola; and *Ito En*, a variety of cold green tea in plastic bottles. Machines sell beer and other alcoholic beverages, but you may want to avoid *shochu*, alcohol sold in glass jars or paper cartons—not only is it fairly strong at typically 20% ABV, but the variety sold in vending machines is usually of very low, throat-burning quality. Coffee—both hot and cold—comes in small cans. You'll see locals buy one, suck it down, and dispose of the can, all during the two-minute wait for the subway. Hot drinks have a red strip below them on the vending machine and cold drinks are marked with blue. If red Japanese text appears below an item, the machine is sold out. Edible items aren't the only things for sale, as shrines and temples use vending machines to sell *omikuji*, fortunes written on slips of paper.

CONVENIENCE STORES

The first convenience store opened in Japan in 1973, and like so many other imported concepts, the Japanese have embraced the *konbini*, turning it into something of their own. Beyond the usual products you might expect, Japanese convenience stores also carry *bento* (boxed meals), basic clothing items, and event tickets. Services available include digital photo printing, faxing, and utility bill payments. Convenience stores are actually a great option for a quick meal, including sandwiches, noodle dishes, fresh fruit, and a variety of salads. Peek into the freezer and Haagen-Dazs tempts you with flavors like matcha green tea. Near the cash register are hot food options, including fried chicken and steamed buns stuffed with meat or a sweet bean paste. Step into a 7-Eleven, Lawson, or Family Mart and see familiar brands with a Japanese twist such as salty watermelon Pepsi or soy sauce Pringles.

TOP BUYS

Japanese Pringles potato chips have come in flavors such as cheese and bacon and seaweed, and new surprising combinations are rolled out every season. Another international brand that often adds a local twist is Kit Kat, which in the past has released matcha green tea, wasabi, and passion fruit versions of its candy bars. New varieties of Kit Kat debut throughout the year, some only available in certain regions. If you are traveling with children, a fun purchase is *Ramune*, a carbonated drink sold in a glass bottle sealed with a glass marble held in place by the pressure of the gas—push the marble down with your thumb to break the seal. One convenience store treat you cannot leave Japan without trying at least once is *onigiri*, a triangular rice ball containing canned tuna with mayonnaise, pickled plum, or other fillings, and wrapped in sheets of dried seaweed.

Updated by
Rob Goss

Tokyo is undoubtedly one of the most exciting dining cities in the world. Seasonal ingredients reign supreme here, and there's an emphasis on freshness—not surprising given raw seafood is the cornerstone of sushi. And though Tokyoites still stubbornly resist foreign concepts in many fields, the locals have embraced outside culinary styles with gusto.

While newer restaurants targeting younger diners strive for authenticity in everything from New York–style bagels to Neapolitan pizza, it is still not uncommon to see menus serving East-meets-West concoctions such as spaghetti topped with cod roe and shredded seaweed. That said, the city's best French and Italian establishments can hold their own on a global scale. Naturally, there's also excellent Japanese cuisine available throughout the city, ranging from the traditional to nouveau, which can be shockingly expensive.

That is not to imply that every meal in the city will drain your finances—the current rage is all about *"B-kyu gurume"* (B-class gourmet), restaurants that fill the gap between nationwide chains and fine cuisine, serving tasty Japanese and Asian food without the extra frills of tablecloths and lacquerware. All department stores and most skyscrapers have at least one floor of restaurants that are accessible, affordable, and reputable.

Asakusa is known for its tempura, and Tsukiji prides itself on its fresh sashimi, which is available in excellent quality throughout the city. Ramen is a passion for many locals, who travel across town or stand in line for an hour in order to sit at the counter of a shop rumored to have the perfect balance of noodles and broth. Even the neighborhood convenience stores will offer colorful salads, sandwiches, and a selection of beer and sake. There have been good and affordable Indian and Chinese restaurants in the city for decades. As a result of increased travel by the Japanese to more exotic locations, Thai, Vietnamese, and Turkish restaurants have popped up around the city. ■ **TIP→ When in doubt, note that Tokyo's top-rated international hotels also have some of the city's best places to eat and drink.**

DINING PLANNER

DRESS

Dining out in Tokyo does not ordinarily demand a great deal in the way of formal attire. If you are attending a business meal with Japanese hosts or guests, dress conservatively: for men, a suit and tie; for women, a dress or suit in a basic color and minimal jewelry. Minimal should also apply to cologne and perfume. On your own, follow the unspoken dress codes you'd observe at home. We mention dress only when men are required to wear a jacket or a jacket and tie.

ORDER FOOD WITHOUT SPEAKING JAPANESE

English OK! (*www.englishok.jp*) lists restaurants where English is spoken so people with limited or no Japanese can order food without worrying about the language barrier. Before heading out, check the website for maps, sample menus, and printable coupons.

4

For Japanese-style dining on tatami floors, keep two things in mind: wear shoes that slip on and off easily and presentable socks, and choose clothing you'll be comfortable in for a few hours with your legs gathered under you.

ETIQUETTE

⇨ *For tips on dining etiquette, see the Japanese Cultural Primer in Chapter 2.*

MENUS

Many less-expensive restaurants have picture menus or plastic replicas of the dishes they serve, displayed in their front windows, so you can always point to what you want to eat if the language barrier is insurmountable.

RESERVATIONS

Reservations are always a good idea: we mention them only when they're essential or not accepted. Book as far ahead as you can, and reconfirm as soon as you arrive.

PRICES

Eating at hotels and famous restaurants is costly; however, you can eat well and reasonably at standard restaurants that may not have signs in English.

Good places to look for moderately priced dining spots are in the restaurant concourses of department stores and larger office buildings, usually on the basement levels and the top floors.

All restaurants charge 8% tax, and by law, the price on the menu includes tax. *Izakaya* (Japanese pubs) often charge a flat table fee (around ¥500 per person), which includes the tiny appetizer that's served to all guests. More expensive restaurants typically add a service charge of 10%, as do some other restaurants when serving large parties. This is usually indicated at the bottom of menus.

Japanese-style restaurants often serve set meals called *teishoku,* which may include rice, soup, and pickled vegetables in addition to the main course—this can drive up the cost. You can sometimes request the main dish without the sides, but then you'd be missing out on the beauty and harmony of a Japanese meal.

	WHAT IT COSTS IN YEN			
	$	$$	$$$	$$$$
At Dinner	Under ¥1,000	¥1,000–¥2,000	¥2,001–¥3,000	over ¥3,000

Prices in the reviews are the average cost of a main course at dinner or, if dinner is not served, at lunch.

RESTAURANT REVIEWS

Restaurant reviews are listed in alphabetical order within neighborhood. Use the coordinate (⊕ B2) at the end of each listing to locate a site on the Where to Eat in Tokyo map.

IMPERIAL PALACE 皇居近辺

In the heart of the city near the Imperial Palace, this district has many upscale restaurants, but happily there are also many affordable places for lunch, thanks to all the hungry office workers in the area.

$$$$ CHINESE

✕ **Heichinrou** (聘珍楼). A short walk from the Imperial Hotel, this branch of one of Yokohama's oldest and best Chinese restaurants commands a spectacular view of the Imperial Palace grounds from 28 floors up. Call ahead to reserve a table by the window. The cuisine is Cantonese; pride of place goes to the *kaisen ryori,* a banquet of steamed sea bass, lobster, shrimp, scallops, abalone, and other seafood dishes. Much of the clientele comes from the law offices, securities firms, and foreign banks in the building. The VIP room at Heichinrou, with its soft lighting and impeccable linens, is a popular venue for power lunches. $ *Average main: ¥13000* ✉ *28F Fukoku Seimei Bldg., 2–2–2 Uchisaiwai-cho, Chiyoda-ku* ☎ *03/3508–0555* 🌐 *www.heichin.com* ⏲ *Closed Sun.* Ⓜ *Mita Line, Uchisaiwai-cho Station (Exit A6)* ⊕ *E4.*

AKIHABARA 神保町

$ JAPANESE

✕ **Kanda Matsuya** (神田まつや). Soba—thin buckwheat noodles often served chilled in summer and hot in winter—are available everywhere, even convenience stores. The family-run Matsuya serves authentic soba in a rustic atmosphere. A simple soba meal costs ¥650, or, for a bit more, get noodles topped with tempura or other goodies. $ *Average main: ¥1000* ✉ *1–13 Kanda Sudacho, Chiyoda-ku* ☎ *03/3251–1556* 💳 *No credit cards* ⏲ *Closed Sun.* Ⓜ *Marunouchi Line, Awajicho Station (Exit A3)* ⊕ *F2.*

$ **Kanda Yabu Soba** (かんだやぶそば). Soba—thin noodles made from
JAPANESE buckwheat flour and quickly dipped into a hot broth or cold dipping sauce—are the lighter cousin of udon. Because it can be eaten so quickly, soba is often sold at small stands in train stations, where it can be slurped down while waiting to change trains. The ever-popular Kanda Yabu Soba, located in a recently built but traditional building that replaced the original 130-year-old restaurant after a fire in 2013, is a great place to sit down and savor the dish—be that on tatami or at one of the tables. A basic soba meal costs just ¥670, but the *shun* (seasonal meal), which changes 10 times a year, is excellent and affordable. *Average main: ¥1000 2–10 Kanda Awajicho, Chiyoda-ku 03/3251–0287 No credit cards JR and Marunouchi lines, Awajicho Station (Exit A3) F2.*

$$ **MLB Café Tokyo.** Located in the shadow of Tokyo Dome, the primary
AMERICAN baseball stadium in Tokyo, this theme restaurant is filled with sports
FAMILY memorabilia, waitstaff dressed in baseball uniforms, and a menu with a lineup similar to a Hard Rock Cafe or TGI Fridays. This, or its sister branch near the Westin in Ebisu, is the perfect place for sports-loving kids. *Average main: ¥2000 1–3–61 Koraku, Bunkyo-ku 03/5840–8905 www.mlbcafe.jp JR Sobu and Toei Mita subway lines, Suidobashi Station (Exit A5) E1.*

UENO 上野

The Ueno neighborhood houses a large park near the metro station, in case you're in a picnic mood. The lively Ameyokocho market, under the train tracks, sells fresh seafood, dried goods, and freshly cut fruit skewered onto a disposable chopstick, while the streets running parallel with it are home to small eateries, lively izakaya, and low-cost standing-only bars (*tachinomiya*).

$$$$ **Sasa-no-yuki** (笹の雪). In the heart of one of Tokyo's old working-
JAPANESE class *shitamachi* (downtown) neighborhoods, Sasa-no-yuki has been serving meals based on homemade tofu for the past 325 years. The food is inspired in part by *shojin ryori* (Buddhist vegetarian cuisine), although not everything served is vegetarian. The basic set menu includes *ankake* (bean curd in sweet soy sauce), *uzumi* tofu (scrambled with rice and green tea), and *unsui* (a creamy tofu crepe filled with sea scallops, shrimp, and minced red pepper). For bigger appetites, there's also a 12-dish banquet (reservation required). There's both tatami and table seating, and the dining room includes a view of the Japanese garden complete with an ornamental waterfall. *Average main: ¥4000 2–15–10 Negishi, Ueno 03/3873–1145 Closed Mon. JR Uguisudani Station (Kita-guchi/North Exit) G1.*

$$ **Tonkatsu Musashino** (とんかつ武蔵野). The deep-fried, breaded pork
JAPANESE cutlets at this casual restaurant just south of Ueno Park's pond get rave reviews for good reason. They combine generous portions with melt-in-the-mouth tenderness, and for a great price. Set meals here are ¥1,200 and come with enough rice, miso soup, shredded cabbage, and pickles to loosen your belt a notch or two. *Average main: ¥1200 2–8–1 Ueno, Ueno 03/3831–1672 Lunch only No credit cards JR Ueno Station G1.*

0
1 mile
0
1 km
UENO
AKIHABARA
JIMBO-CHO
IMPERIAL PALACE DISTRICT
NIHOMBASHI
gastronomic magic beside izakaya establishments
SHINJUKU
solid local food in quirky digs
AKASAKA
something for every price and taste
HARAJUKU
international cuisine coupled with cafés
AOYAMA
authentic Japanese food hub
GINZA
princely meals at princely prices
SHIBUYA
ramen and light bites
ROPPONGI
diverse cuisine and family-friendly environs
SHIODOME
TSUKIJI
sushi, sushi, and more sushi
PORT OF TOKYO
ODAIBA
MEGURO
Meiji-dori
Nakasendo
Rikugien Gardens
Shinobazu-dori
Hongo-dori
Koishikawa Botanical Gardens
Mejiro-dori
Tokyo Expwy No.5
Hakusan-dori Ave.
Showa-dori
Asakusa-dori
Kasuga-dori
Kiyosu-bashi-dori
Waseda-dori
Shinjuku Gyo-en
Uchibori-dori
Aoyama-dori
Gaien-
Higashi-dori
Sakurada-dori
Shin Ohashi-dori
Sumidagawa
Kiyosumi-dori
Tokyo Expwy No.3
Tokyo Expwy No.2
Kaigan-dori
Dai-ichi-keihin
National Park for Nature Study
Meguro-dori
Sakurada-dori
Tokyo Expwy No.1
Rainbow Bridge

BEST BETS FOR TOKYO DINING

With hundreds of restaurants to choose from, how do you decide where to eat? Fodor's writers and editors have selected their favorite restaurants by price, cuisine, and experience in the Best Bets lists here. In the first column, Fodor's Choice properties represent the "best of the best" in every price category. You can also search by neighborhood for excellent eats—just peruse our reviews on the following pages.

Fodor's Choice ★

Cicada, $$$$
Enju, $$$$
Ganchan, $$$$
Harajuku Taproom, $$$
Inakaya East, $$$$
New York Grill & Bar, $$$$
Nihonbashi Yukari, $$$$
Robata, $$$$
Shin Hinomoto, $$$
Ume no Hana, $$$$

Best by Price

$

Afuri
Kanda Matsuya
Sawanoi

$$

Good Honest Grub
Heiroku-zushi
Maisen
Sakuratei

$$$

Harajuku Taproom
Roti
Shin Hinomoto

$$$$

Aquavit
Cicada
Ganchan
New York Grill & Bar
Robata
Tsukiji Edo-Gin
Ume no Hana

Best by Cuisine

AMERICAN

Homeworks, $$
Roti, $$$
Tony Roma's, $$$
Towers Modern Bistro, $$$$

RAMEN

Afuri, $
Darumaya, $
Kohmen, $

SOUTH ASIAN

Ajanta, $$
Dhaba India, $$
Sanko-en, $$$$

SUSHI

Heiroku-zushi, $$
Sushisho Masa, $$$$
Takeno Shokudo, $$$
Tsukiji Edo-Gin, $$$$

TEMPURA

Daikokuya Tempura, $$$
Tenmatsu, $$$

Best by Experience

BEST BRUNCH

Good Honest Grub, $$
Roti, $$$

CHILD-FRIENDLY

MLB Café, $$
Ninja, $$$$
Pizza Salvatore Cuomo, $$$
Tony Roma's, $$$

GREAT VIEW

Heichinrou, $$$$
New York Grill & Bar, $$$$
Towers Modern Bistro, $$$$
T.Y. Harbor Brewery, $$$$

HOTEL DINING

New York Grill & Bar, $$$$
Signature, $$$$

LATE-NIGHT DINING

Kohmen, $
Sawanoi, $
Tableaux, $$$$

MOST ROMANTIC

Aquavit, $$$$
Azure 45, $$$$

QUIRKIEST

Ninja, $$$$
Ryoma no Sora Bettei, $$$
Tachigui Sakaba buri, $$$
Tapas Molecular Bar, $$$$

ASAKUSA 浅草

Historic Asakusa is filled with restaurants serving traditional cuisine like tempura and sukiyaki. Rest and rejuvenate at a café serving Japanese sweets and green tea, or try the very casual *yakitori* restaurants that spill out onto the side streets. The walk up to the temple is lined with small shops selling small bites like *sembei* (rice crackers) and *ningyoyaki*, cakes stuffed with a sweet red bean paste.

$$$ JAPANESE **Daikokuya Tempura** (大黒家天麩羅). Although tempura is available throughout the city, the Asakusa neighborhood prides itself on its battered, deep-fried seafood and vegetables. Daikokuya, in the center of Asakusa's historic district, is a point of pilgrimage for both locals and tourists. The specialty here is shrimp tempura, and the menu choices are simple—*tendon* is tempura shrimp served over rice, and the tempura meal includes rice, pickled vegetables, and miso soup. Famished diners can add additional pieces of tempura or side dishes such as sashimi for an additional fee, or opt for a multidish course (from ¥3,300 to ¥4,700). When the line of waiting customers outside is too long, head to the shop's annex (*bekkan*) just around the corner. *Average main: ¥2500 1–38–10 Asakusa, Taitō-ku, Asakusa 03/3844–1111 www.tempura.co.jp/english No credit cards Ginza and Asakusa subway lines, Asakusa Station H1.*

$$ JAPANESE **Kamiya Bar** (神谷バー). In business since the 1880s, this is a very welcoming locals hangout famed as the home of Denki Bran ("electric brandy"), a very potent and syrupy mix of brandy and other spirits. The upper floors serve more in the way of food, but the atmosphere is best on the ground floor, where you can share one of the large wooden tables, strike up a conversation, and sample the Denki Bran along with beer and simple snacks such as sausages, breaded cutlets, and other beer hall fare. To order, go to the counter and get a ticket, and the suited waitstaff will deliver to your table. *Average main: ¥2000 1–1–1 Asakusa, Asakusa 03/3841–5400 www.kamiya-bar.com Closed Tues. No credit cards Ginza and Asakusa subway lines, Asakusa Station H1.*

$$$ JAPANESE **Tatsumiya** (たつみ屋). Here's a restaurant that's run like a formal *ryotei* (traditional Japanese restaurant focused on luxury) but has the feel of a rough-cut izakaya (Japanese pub). Neither inaccessible nor outrageously expensive, Tatsumiya is adorned—nay, cluttered—with antique chests, braziers, clocks, lanterns, bowls, utensils, and craft work, some of it for sale. The evening meal is in the *kaiseki* style, meaning multiple courses are served; tradition demands that the meal include something raw, something boiled, something vinegary, and something grilled. The kaiseki dinner is served only until 8:30, and you must reserve ahead for it. Tatsumiya also serves a light lunch, plus a variety of *nabe* (one-pot seafood and vegetable stews, prepared at your table) until 10. The pork nabe is the house specialty. *Average main: ¥3000 1–33–5 Asakusa, Taitō-ku, Asakusa 03/3842–7373 www.kiwa-group.co.jp/restaurant/264 No credit cards Ginza and Asakusa subway lines, Asakusa Station (Exits 1 and 3) H1.*

TSUKIJI 築地

The world's largest seafood market is here, in the heart of the city. A visit to the outer market is a must-see for anyone interested in food. Browse the small stalls serving sushi, ramen, and other quick bites as well as shops selling food and kitchenware. But visit soon, as the market will be relocating in late 2016.

$$$ JAPANESE ✕ **Takeno Shokudo** (多け乃食堂). Just a stone's throw from the Tokyo fish market, Takeno Shokudo is a neighborhood restaurant that tends to fill up at noon with the market's wholesalers and auctioneers and personnel from the nearby Asahi newspaper offices. There's nothing here but the freshest and the best—big portions of it, at very reasonable prices. Sushi and sashimi are the staples, but there's also a wonderful *tendon* bowl for ¥1,000 with shrimp and eel tempura on rice. Prices are not posted because they vary with the costs that morning in the market. Reservations can only be made for large parties, or if you plan to dine before 6:30 pm. *Average main: ¥3000* *6–21–2 Tsukiji, Tsukiji* *03/3541–8698* *No credit cards* *Closed Sun.* *Hibiya subway line, Tsukiji Station (Exit 1); Oedo subway line, Tsukiji-shijo Station (Exit A1)* *F5.*

$$$$ SUSHI ✕ **Tsukiji Edo-Gin** (築地江戸銀). In an area that teems with sushi bars, this one maintains its reputation as one of the best. Tsukiji Edo-Gin drapes generous slabs of fish over the vinegared rice rather than perching them demurely on top. The centerpiece of the main room is a huge tank where the day's ingredients swim about until required; it doesn't get any fresher than this. Set menus here are reasonable, especially for lunch, but a big appetite for specialties like sea urchin and *otoro* tuna can put a dent in your budget. *Average main: ¥4000* *4–5–1 Tsukiji, Tsukiji* *03/3543–4401* *No credit cards* *Hibiya subway line, Tsukiji Station (Exit 1); Oedo subway line, Tsukiji-shijo Station (Exit A1)* *F5.*

$$ JAPANESE ✕ **Yumeya** (夢や). Not far from Tsukiji, Yumeya Tsukishima ("moon island") is a large man-made island known as the birthplace of delicious *monjayaki*: a thin batter is mixed with shredded cabbage and other ingredients, fried on a griddle built into the table, and eaten directly from the grill with metal spatulas. The main street in Tsukishima is filled with dozens of monjayaki establishments, but Yumeya is one of the best, an obvious fact when you spot the line of waiting patrons. Tried-and-true monjayaki eaters make it themselves at the table, but it can be a tricky endeavor—you need to form a ring of dry ingredients on the grill and pour the batter into the middle. If you're not feeling confident, servers can also make it for you at your table. *Average main: ¥2000* *3–18–4 Tsukishima, Tsukiji* *03/3536–7870* *Closed Mon and 3rd Tues. No lunch weekdays* *Oedo and Yuraku-cho subway lines, Tsukishima Station (Exit 7)* *G5.*

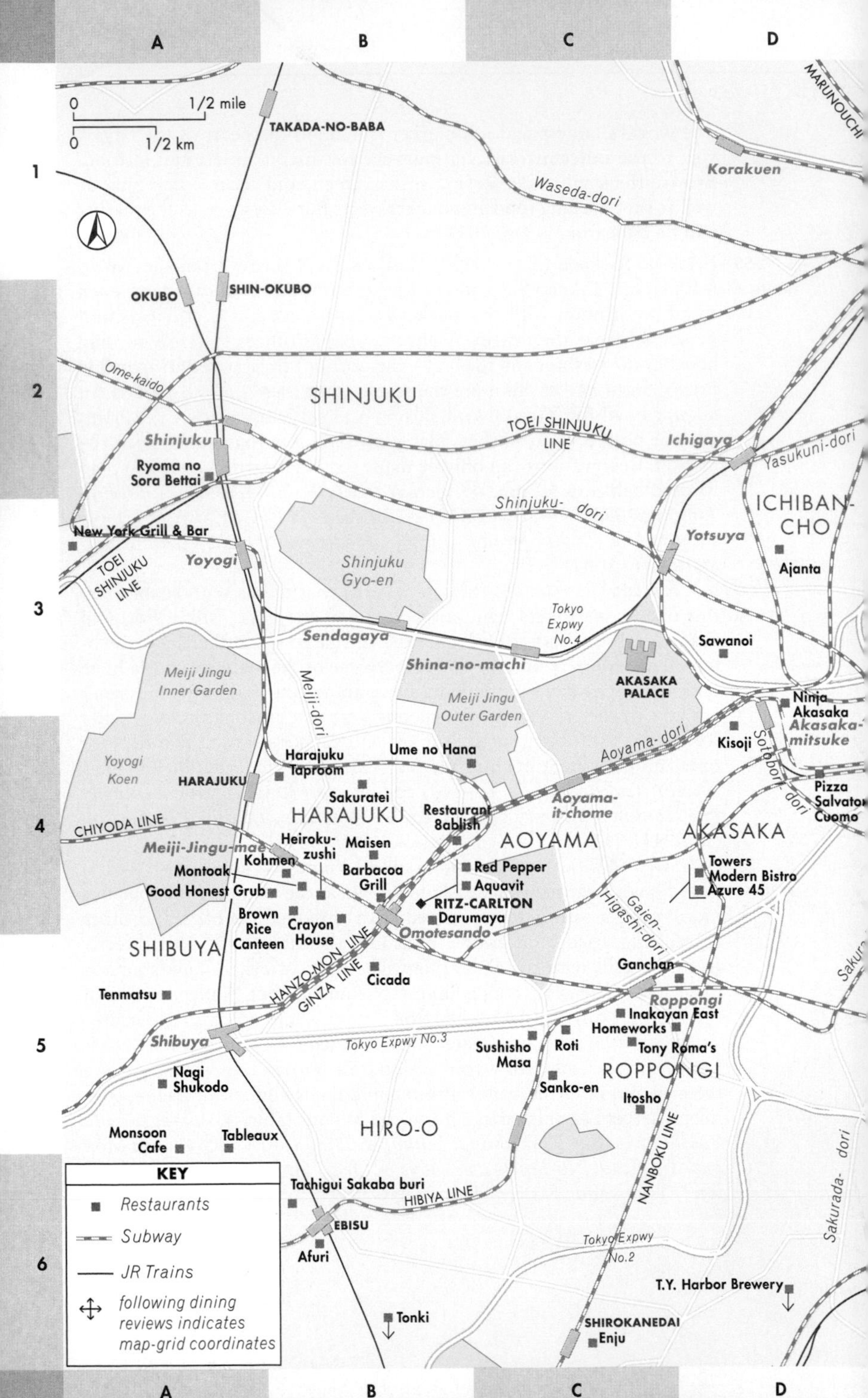
A
B
C
D
1
2
3
4
5
6
0
1/2 mile
0
1/2 km
TAKADA-NO-BABA
MARUNOUCHI
Korakuen
Waseda-dori
OKUBO
SHIN-OKUBO
Ome-kaido
SHINJUKU
TOEI SHINJUKU LINE
Ichigaya
Yasukuni-dori
Shinjuku
Ryoma no Sora Bettai
Shinjuku-dori
ICHIBAN-CHO
New York Grill & Bar
Yotsuya
Ajanta
TOEI SHINJUKU LINE
Yoyogi
Shinjuku Gyo-en
Tokyo Expwy No.4
Sendagaya
Shina-no-machi
Sawanoi
Meiji Jingu Inner Garden
Meiji-dori
Meiji Jingu Outer Garden
AKASAKA PALACE
Ninja Akasaka
Akasaka-mitsuke
Aoyama-dori
Kisoji
Sotobori-dori
Yoyogi Koen
HARAJUKU
Harajuku Taproom
Ume no Hana
Sakuratei
Aoyama-it-chome
Pizza Salvatore Cuomo
HARAJUKU
Restaurant 8ablish
CHIYODA LINE
AOYAMA
AKASAKA
Meiji-Jingu-mae
Heiroku-zushi
Maisen
Kohmen
Montoak
Barbacoa Grill
Red Pepper
Aquavit
Towers
Modern Bistro
Azure 45
Good Honest Grub
RITZ-CARLTON
Darumaya
Gaien-Higashi-dori
Brown Rice Canteen
Crayon House
Omotesando
SHIBUYA
HANZO-MON LINE
GINZA LINE
Cicada
Ganchan
Tenmatsu
Roppongi
Inakaya East
Homeworks
Shibuya
Tokyo Expwy No.3
Sushisho Masa
Roti
Tony Roma's
ROPPONGI
Nagi Shukodo
Sanko-en
Itosho
HIRO-O
Monsoon Cafe
Tableaux
NANBOKU LINE
Sakurada-dori
KEY
Restaurants
Subway
JR Trains
following dining reviews indicates map-grid coordinates
Tachigui Sakaba buri
HIBIYA LINE
EBISU
Afuri
Tokyo Expwy No.2
T.Y. Harbor Brewery
Tonki
SHIROKANEDAI
Enju

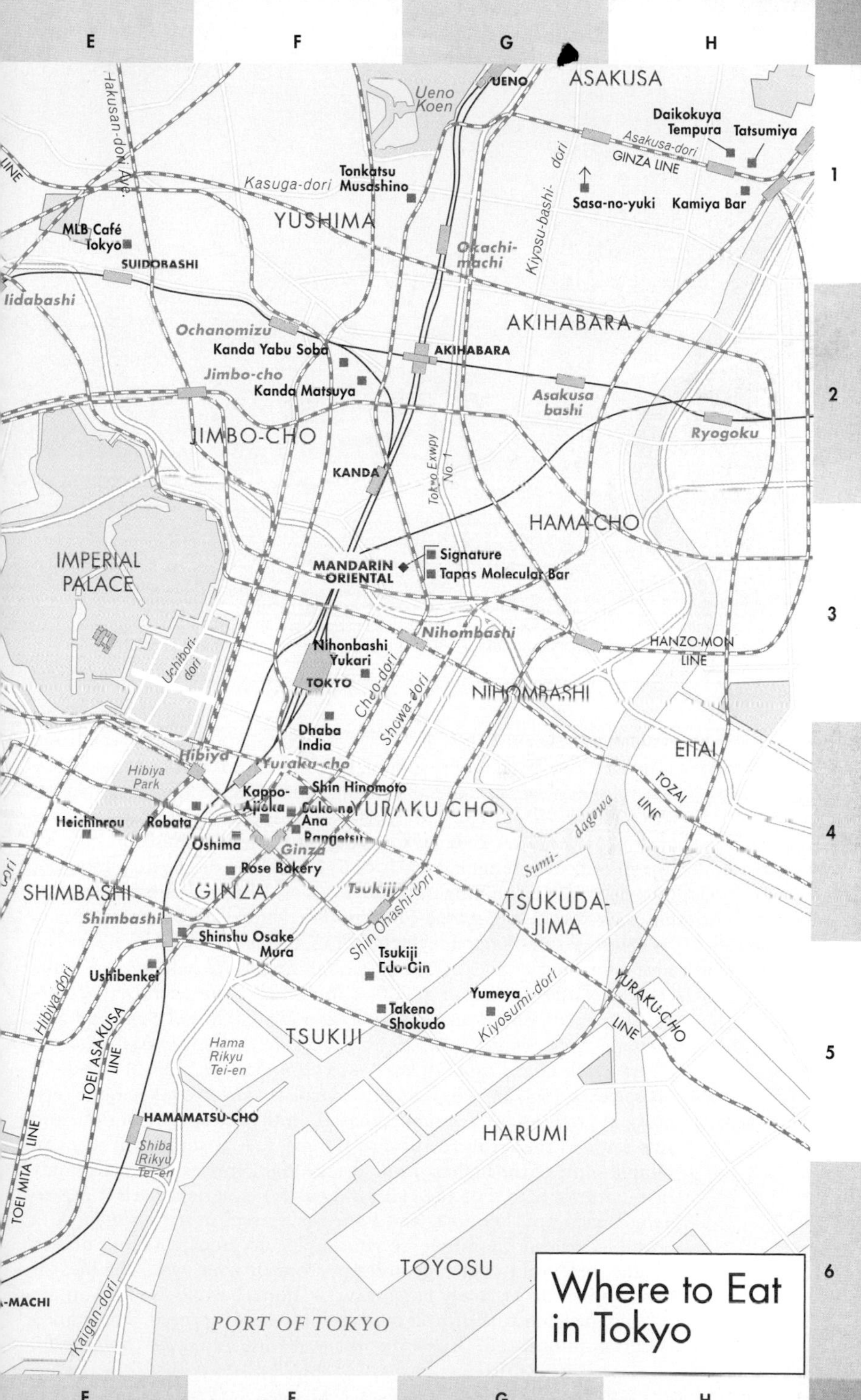

E
F
G
H
1
2
3
4
5
6
Where to Eat in Tokyo
ASAKUSA
UENO
Ueno Koen
Daikokuya Tempura
Tatsumiya
Asakusa-dori
GINZA LINE
Sasa-no-yuki
Kamiya Bar
Kiyosu-bashi-dori
Tonkatsu Musashino
Kasuga-dori
YUSHIMA
Hakusan-dori Ave.
MLB Café Tokyo
SUIDOBASHI
Iidabashi
Okachi-machi
AKIHABARA
Ochanomizu
Kanda Yabu Soba
AKIHABARA
Jimbo-cho
Kanda Matsuya
Asakusa bashi
Ryogoku
JIMBO-CHO
KANDA
Tokyo Exwpy No. 1
HAMA-CHO
IMPERIAL PALACE
MANDARIN ORIENTAL
Signature
Tapas Molecular Bar
Nihombashi
HANZO-MON LINE
Uchibori-dori
Nihonbashi Yukari
TOKYO
Chuo-dori
Showa-dori
NIHOMBASHI
Dhaba India
EITAI
Hibiya
Yuraku-cho
TOZAI LINE
Hibiya Park
Kappo-Ajioka
Shin Hinomoto
YURAKU-CHO
Sumi-dagawa
Heichinrou
Robata
Ana
Oshima
Ginza
Rose Bakery
SHIMBASHI
GINZA
Tsukiji
TSUKUDA-JIMA
Shimbashi
Shinshu Osake Mura
Shin Ohashi-dori
Tsukiji Edo-Gin
Ushibenkei
Hibiya-dori
Yumeya
Takeno Shokudo
Kiyosumi-dori
YURAKU-CHO LINE
TSUKIJI
TOEI ASAKUSA LINE
Hama Rikyu Tei-en
HAMAMATSU-CHO
HARUMI
Shiba Rikyu Tei-en
TOEI MITA LINE
TOYOSU
-MACHI
Kaigan-dori
PORT OF TOKYO

As microbrews become more ubiquitous in Tokyo, restaurants like T.Y. Brewery grow more popular.

SHIODOME 汐留

$$
JAPANESE

Shinshu Osake Mura (信州おさけ村). A sake and beer store specializing in drinks from Nagano prefecture, this standing-room-only place also functions as a very casual bar where you can sample approximately 40 kinds of sake (from ¥350 to ¥1,100 per 110-millileter glass), several craft beers from brewers such as Shiga Kogen, and interesting snacks like spiced cow's tongue. It's tricky to find, being on the first floor of a very dated office building opposite the west exit of Shimbashi Station, but look for the big statue of a *tanuki* (racoon dog) with extremely large testicles that's outside the building, then go in and turn right. The staff are very friendly and speak enough English to help with the sake choices. [$] *Average main: ¥2000* ✉ *Shimbashi Ekimae Bldg. 1, 2–20–15 Shimbashi, Shiodome* ☎ *03/3572–5488* ⏲ *Closed Sun. and Sat. evenings* ▭ *No credit cards* [M] *JR Yamanote Line, Shimbashi Station (West Exit); Ginza subway line, Shimbashi Station (Exit A3)* ✥ *E4.*

$$$$
JAPANESE

Ushibenkei (牛弁慶). High-quality marbleized beef is taken quite seriously in Japan—cuts are ranked based on the ratio, distribution, and sweetness of the fat in relation to the meat. At Ushibenkei, you can sample some of the highest rank at reasonable prices in a charmingly rustic atmosphere. For the full (and easier) experience select a *gyunabe* ("beef pot") course, and your server will move a *shichirin* (a portable coal-burning stove) to your table and prepare a range of cow tongue, beef, tofu, and vegetables in front of your eyes. The meat is fresh enough to be safely eaten raw, so don't be surprised if you are given paper-thin cuts of beef that are only lightly seared. There are à la carte options, too. [$] *Average main: ¥5500* ✉ *3–18–7 Shimbashi,*

Shiodome ☎ *03/4540–6582* ⊙ *No lunch weekends* Ⓜ *JR Yamanote Line, Shimbashi Station (Kasumori Exit); Ginza subway line, Shimbashi Station (Exit A1)* ✥ *E5.*

NIHOMBASHI 日本橋

This historic district is all about legacy and tradition. It was home to the original seafood market in Tokyo before it moved to its current location in Tsukiji. Some of the restaurants here have been passed down through generations. And Japan's oldest department store, Mitsukoshi, is also here; its basement *depachika* is filled with prepared foods for a quick bite.

$$$$ JAPANESE Fodor's Choice ★ ✕ **Nihonbashi Yukari** (日本橋ゆかり). Anyone looking to experience Japanese haute cuisine in a more relaxed atmosphere should look to this *kappō*-style restaurant, where diners eat and order at the counter. Third-generation chef—and 2002 Iron Chef champion—Kimio Nonaga displays his artistry in every element of Nihonbashi Yukari's menu. Dinner here is a multicourse affair, with each dish showcasing the freshness and quality of the seasonal ingredients. To witness him at work, and get the full *kappō* dining experience, be sure to request a counter seat when making reservations. As a bonus, Nihonbashi Yukari also offers a lunch setting for around ¥3,500, which is unusual for this kind of restaurant. $ *Average main: ¥15000* ✉ *3–2–14 Nihonbashi, Chuo-ku* ☎ *03/3271–3436* 🌐 *www.nihonbashi-yukari.com* ⊙ *Closed Sun.* ✍ *Reservations essential* ✥ *F3.*

$$$$ FRENCH ✕ **Signature** (シグネチャー). This elegant French restaurant on the 37th floor of the Mandarin Oriental Hotel has wonderful views of the Tokyo skyline as well an open kitchen, where diners can see the masterful chef Nicolas Boujéma and his staff at work. Boujéma has an impressive résumé, having worked in kitchens such as La Tour d'Argent, Le Balzac, and most recently with Pierre Gagnaire. And his cuisine does not disappoint. Inspired by Japanese kaiseki, the menu changes with the seasons. There is also a fine wine list here that includes biodynamic and organic selections. $ *Average main: ¥15000* ✉ *37F Mandarin Oriental Tokyo, 2–1–1 Nihonbashi, Chuo-ku* ☎ *03/3270–8188* 🌐 *www.mandarinoriental.com/tokyo/dining/signature* ✍ *Reservations essential* Ⓜ *Ginza subway line, Mitsukoshi-mae Station (Exit A7)* ✥ *G3.*

$$$$ JAPANESE ✕ **Tapas Molecular Bar** (タパス モレキュラーバー). Occupying a mysterious place between traditional sushi counter, tapas bar, science lab, and magic show, this award-winning restaurant breaks new ground. In full view of diners, the team of chefs assemble a small parade of bite-size morsels in surprising texture and flavor combinations. There are only eight seats, and seatings are at 6 and 8:30 only (plus 1 pm on weekends), so reserve as early as possible. $ *Average main:* ✉ *38F Mandarin Oriental Tokyo, 2–1–1 Nihonbashi, Chuo-ku* ☎ *03/3270–8188* 🌐 *www.mandarinoriental.com/tokyo/dining/molecular* ✍ *Reservations essential* Ⓜ *Ginza subway line, Mitsukoshi-mae Station (Exit A7)* ✥ *G3.*

GINZA 銀座

Tokyo's famous shopping district is a short walk from Tsukiji Market that supplies a wide variety of restaurants. At night neon lights fill the skies with the names of eateries and clubs. For a quick bite head into the basement of one of the department stores and select from the dizzying array of prepared foods.

$$ INDIAN ✕ **Dhaba India** (ダバ インデェア). With a focus on South India cuisine, Dhaba has built a reputation as having some of the best Indian flavors in town. A specialty here are the dosas (from ¥1,200), a kind of stuffed crepe, but the curries, whether the spicy black pepper mutton or the fragrant fish and shrimp masala, are just as good. It can get very busy with office workers from noon to 1 on a weekday, so it's best to come before or after that. *Average main: ¥1500 ✉ 2–7–9 Yaesu, Ginza ☎ 03/3272–7160 ⊕ www.dhabaindia.com Ⓜ Ginza subway line, Kyobashi Station (Exit 5) ✣ F4.*

$$$$ JAPANESE ✕ **Kappo-Ajioka** (割烹味岡). When prepared incorrectly, fugu, the highly poisonous puffer fish, is fatal, yet this doesn't stop people from trying it at this Tokyo branch of the Kansai fugu ryotei (puffer-fish restaurant). Licensed chefs prepare the fish in every way imaginable—raw, fried, stewed—using the fresh catch flown in straight from Shimonoseki, a prime fugu-fishing region. The overall flavor is subtle and somewhat nondescript—people are drawn more to the element of danger than the taste (fatalities are rare, but a few people in Japan die each year from fugu poisoning, usually from trying to prepare it at home). Try the house specialty of *suppon* (Japanese turtle) and fugu nabe, fugu sashimi, or fugu *no arayaki* (grilled head and cheeks). Reservations must be made two days in advance to order fugu. *Average main: ¥12000 ✉ 6F New Comparu Bldg., 7–7–12 Ginza, Chuo-ku ☎ 03/3574–8844 ⏲ Closed Sun. No lunch ✍ Reservations essential Ⓜ Ginza, Hibiya, and Marunouchi subway lines, Ginza Station (Exit A5) ✣ F4.*

$$$$ JAPANESE ✕ **Oshima** (大志満). The main draw at Oshima is sampling the *Kaga ryori* cooking of Kanazawa, a small city on the Sea of Japan known for its rich craft traditions. Waitresses dress the part in kimonos of Kanazawa's famous Yuzen dyed silk, and Kutani porcelain and Wajima lacquerware grace the exquisite table settings. As you'd expect from waterfront cuisine, seafood at Oshima is superb, but don't ignore the specialty of the house: a stew of duck and potatoes called *jibuni*. Kaiseki full-course meals are pricey (up to ¥12,960), but there's a reasonable lunchtime set menu for ¥2,700. *Average main: ¥9000 ✉ 9F Ginza Core Bldg., 5–8–20 Ginza, Chuo-ku ☎ 03/3574–8080 Ⓜ Ginza, Hibiya, and Marunouchi subway lines, Ginza Station (Exit A5) ✣ F4.*

$$$$ JAPANESE ✕ **Rangetsu** (らん月). Japan enjoys a special reputation for its lovingly raised, tender, marbled domestic beef, and if your budget can bear the weight, Rangetsu serves excellent dishes with this beef as a star ingredient. Try the signature shabu-shabu or sukiyaki course for a primer. For a blowout celebration, call ahead to reserve a private alcove, where you can cook for yourself, or have a kaiseki meal brought to your table by kimono-clad attendants. While dinner can damage the wallet, there is also a good variety of lunch sets available from ¥1,750. The location, opposite the Matsuya Department Store, is just

as elegant as the restaurant itself. *Average main: ¥10000 ✉ 3–5–8 Ginza, Chuo-ku ☎ 03/3567–1021 Ⓜ Marunouchi and Ginza subway lines, Ginza Station (Exits A9 and A10) ✣ F4.*

$$$$ JAPANESE Fodor's Choice ★ ✕ **Robata** (炉端). Old, funky, and more than a little cramped, Robata is a bit daunting at first. But fourth-generation chef-owner Takao Inoue holds forth here with an inspired version of Japanese home cooking. He's also a connoisseur of pottery and serves his food on pieces acquired at famous kilns all over the country. There's no menu; just tell Inoue-san (who speaks some English) how much you want to spend, and leave the rest to him. A meal at Robata—like the pottery—is simple to the eye but subtle and fulfilling. Typical dishes include steamed fish with vegetables, stews of beef or pork, and seafood salads. *Average main: ¥5000 ✉ 1–3–8 Yuraku-cho, Ginza ☎ 03/3591–1905 ▭ No credit cards ⏲ Closed some Sun. each month. No lunch Ⓜ JR Yuraku-cho Station (Hibiya Exit); Hibiya, Chiyoda, and Mita subway lines, Hibiya Station (Exit A4) ✣ F4.*

$$ INTERNATIONAL ✕ **Rose Bakery** (ローズベーカリー). Satisfying the need for light, healthy food that is neither raw nor fried, this airy but rather nondescript bakery and café, which also has branches in Paris and London, serves up a tasty selection of salads, quiches, vegetables, and other deli-style dishes. Although the interior's rows of tables and blank white walls can feel a bit too much like a hip reinterpretation of a school cafeteria, Rose Bakery is a good bet for a quick lunch or pastry while out wandering the Ginza area. It's also good for breakfast (from 9 am), especially if you crave a full English. *Average main: ¥2000 ✉ 6–9–5 Ginza, Ginza Komatsu West Wing 7F, Chuo-ku ☎ 03/5537–5038 ⊕ www.rosebakery.jp ▭ No credit cards ✍ Reservations not accepted ✣ E4.*

$$$$ JAPANESE ✕ **Sake no Ana** (酒の穴). With roughly 130 varieties of sake from all over Japan available by the carafe, Sake no Ana (literally, "the sake hole") does seem to feature a bottomless variety of the drink. The restaurant has its own sake sommelier, Sakamoto-san, who can help diners sort (or drink) through the restaurant's immense selection. Though most sake-specialty restaurants are open only for dinner, Sake no Ana is also open for lunch, good for those who want to space out their sampling of Japan's unofficial national drink. The food is classic izakaya fare, and at lunchtime there are hearty donburi dishes, large bowls of rice topped with seasonal sashimi or beef simmered in a sweet soy broth. *Average main: ¥5000 ✉ 3–5–8 Ginza, Chuo-ku ☎ 03/3567–1133 ✣ F4.*

$$$ JAPANESE Fodor's Choice ★ ✕ **Shin Hinomoto** (新日の基). Aka "Andy's," this izakaya is located directly under the tracks of the Yamanote Line, making the wooden interior shudder each time a train passes overhead. It's a favorite with local and foreign journalists, as the Foreign Correspondents Club is just across the street and is actually run by a Brit, Andy, who travels down the road to Tsukiji Market every morning to buy seafood. Don't miss the fresh sashimi and buttered scallops. It fills up very quickly, so call at least the day in advance to make a reservation. *Average main: ¥3000 ✉ 2–4–4 Yuraku-cho, Ginza ☎ 03/3214–8021 ⊕ www.andysfish.com/shin-hinomoto ▭ No credit cards ⏲ Closed Sun. No lunch ✍ Reservations essential Ⓜ JR Yuraku-cho Station (Hibiya Exit); Hibiya, Chiyoda, and Mita subway lines, Hibiya Station (Exits A2 and A6) ✣ F4.*

AOYAMA AND AKASAKA 青山 赤坂

High-end boutiques, cafés, and restaurants fill the streets of upscale Aoyama. People-watching is a sidewalk sport here, easily done from the venues that line the streets.

A business area by day, nearby Akasaka turns into an entertainment district in the evening. There is a wide variety of restaurants here and lunch bargains abound.

$$ INDIAN

Ajanta (アジャンタ). In the mid-20th century, the founder of Ajanta came to Tokyo to study electrical engineering. He ended up changing careers and establishing what is today one of the oldest and best Indian restaurants in town. There's no decoration to speak of at this restaurant, which stays open until 2 am (Tuesday–Saturday). The emphasis instead is on the variety and intricacy of South Indian cooking—and none of its dressier rivals can match Ajanta's menu for sheer depth. The curries are hot to begin with, but you can order them even hotter. Try the *masala dosa* (a savory crepe), *keema* (minced beef), or mutton curry. A small boutique in one corner sells saris and imported Indian foodstuffs. *Average main: ¥2000* *3–11 Niban-cho, Akasaka* *03/3264–6955* *www.ajanta.com* *No credit cards* *Yuraku-cho subway line, Kojimachi Station (Exit 5)* *E2.*

$ RAMEN

Darumaya (だるまや). The classic bowl of ramen is topped with slices of pork, but Darumaya, in the fashion district of Omotesando, has a slightly different take, topping its noodles with grilled vegetables. In the summertime be sure to order the *hiyashi soba*, a bowl of chilled noodles topped with vegetables and ham in a sesame dressing. Another shop specialty is the *tsukemen*, where the noodles and broth are served in separate bowls. Dip (don't drop) the ramen into the broth. Despite the focus on veggies, vegetarians should note, the soups and sauces are not meat-free. *Average main: ¥850* *1F Murayama Bldg., 5–9–5 Minami-Aoyama, Minato-ku* *03/3499–6295* *No credit cards* *Closed Sun. and 1st and 3rd Mon.* *Ginza, Chiyoda, and Hanzo-mon subway lines, Omotesando Station (Exit B1)* *B4.*

$$$$ JAPANESE

Kisoji (木曽路). The specialty here is shabu-shabu: thin slices of beef cooked in boiling water at your table and dipped in sauce. Normally, despite the price, this is an informal, no-frills sort of meal. Kisoji, which has been serving the dish for more than 60 years, elevates the experience, with all the tasteful appointments of a traditional *ryotei*—private dining rooms with tatami seating (at a 10% surcharge), elegant little rock gardens, and alcoves with flower arrangements. There are branches in Ginza, Shimbashi, Shinjuku and Ueno, as well. *Average main: ¥6500* *3–10–4 Akasaka, 2nd fl., Minato-ku* *03/3588–0071* *Ginza and Marunouchi subway lines, Akasaka-mitsuke Station (Belle Vie Akasaka Exit)* *D4.*

$$$$ JAPANESE FAMILY

Ninja Akasaka (忍者赤坂). In keeping with the air of mystery you'd expect from a ninja-themed restaurant, a ninja-costumed waiter leads you through a dark underground maze to your table in an artificial cave. The menu has more than 100 choices, including some elaborate set courses that are extravagant in both proportion and price. Among the impressively presented dishes are "jack-in-the-box"

Outdoor restaurants around Tokyo offer casual meals and camaraderie among diners.

seafood salad—a lacquerware box overflowing with seasonal seafood and garnished with mustard, avocado tartar, and miso paste—and the life-size bonsai-tree dessert made from cookies and green-tea ice cream. Magical tricks are performed at your table during dinner—it's slightly kitschy but entertaining nonetheless, especially for kids. $ *Average main:* ✉ *Akasaka Tokyu Plaza, 2–14–3 Nagata-cho, Minato-ku* ☎ *03/5157–3936* 🌐 *www.ninjaakasaka.com* *Reservations essential* Ⓜ *Ginza and Marunouchi subway lines, Akasaka-mitsuke Station (Tokyu Plaza Exit)* ✣ *D4.*

$$$ ITALIAN FAMILY ✕ **Pizza Salvatore Cuomo** (ピッツアサルヴァトーレクオモ). Swing open the door to Pizza Salvatore Cuomo and you'll catch a rich aroma wafting from the wood-burning oven—the centerpiece of this homey, spacious restaurant. As with Cuomo's other branches around town, the chefs here adhere to traditional Neapolitan methods, while updating recipes with dough infused with spinach, herbs, and even squid ink. Lunch courses are filling, affordable (around ¥1,000), and quick. Though seating space is ample, expect a full house on weekdays. For dinner, classic antipasto dishes such as Caprese make for an authentic Italian meal. Branches are found throughout the city. $ *Average main: ¥2500* ✉ *Prudential Plaza Bldg., 2–13–10 Nagata-cho, Chiyoda-ku* ☎ *03/3500–5700* 🌐 *www.salvatore.jp* Ⓜ *Chiyoda and Marunouchi subway lines, Akasaka-mitsuke Station* ✣ *D4.*

$ JAPANESE ✕ **Sawanoi** (澤乃井). The homemade udon noodles, served in a broth with seafood, vegetables, or chicken, make a perfect light meal or midnight snack. Try the *inaka* (country-style) udon, which has bonito, seaweed flakes, radish shavings, and a raw egg dropped into the hot broth to cook. For a heartier meal, chose the *tenkama* set: hot udon and shrimp tempura with a delicate soy-based sauce. A bit run-down, Sawanoi is one of the last remaining neighborhood shops in what is now an upscale business and entertainment district. (Dash up a short flight of stairs to get to the dining room.) It stays open until 3 am, and a menu is available in English. *Average main: ¥1000* *1F Shimpo Bldg., 3–7–13 Akasaka, Minato-ku* *03/3582–2080* *No credit cards* *Closed Sun.* *Ginza and Marunouchi subway lines, Akasaka-mitsuke Station (Belle Vie Akasaka Exit)* *D3.*

$$$$ JAPANESE Fodor's Choice ★ **Ume no Hana** (梅の花). The exclusive specialty here is tofu, prepared in more ways than you can imagine—boiled, steamed, stir-fried with minced crabmeat, served in a custard, or wrapped in thin layers around a delicate whitefish paste. Tofu is touted as the perfect high-protein, low-calorie health food; at Ume no Hana it's raised to the elegance of haute cuisine. Remove your shoes when you step up to the lovely central room. Latticed wood screens separate the tables, and private dining rooms with tatami seating are available. Prix fixe meals include a complimentary aperitif. Ume no Hana shops in Ueno and Ginza are also worth visiting. *Average main: ¥5000* *2F Aoyama M's Tower, 2–27–18 Minami-Aoyama, Minato-ku* *03/5412–0855* *www.umenohana.co.jp* *Ginza Line, Gaien-mae Station (Exit 1A)* *C4.*

HARAJUKU 原宿

Young kids flock to Harajuku on the weekends to shop for clothes and accessories along Takeshita Dori street. In nearby Omotesando the upscale Omotesando Hills has several restaurants on the upper floors.

$$$$ SCANDINAVIAN **Aquavit** (アクアビット). If you'd like to take a detour from Tokyo's kaiseki- and sushi-centric fine dining, consider this unexpected alternative. One of a handful of authentic Swedish restaurants in Tokyo, Aquavit serves a reasonably priced prix fixe lunch and dinner. A great introduction to the cuisine is the herring sampler, which includes pickled and sweet varieties that change seasonally. Entrées like the dry-cured gravlax or the foie gras with shallot marmalade, fig, and elderflower continue the Scandinavian theme. But don't ask for the tab before sampling dessert in the form of scrumptious Swedish pancakes served with ginger confit, fresh cream, and raspberries. The ultraromantic dining room manages to be both inviting and modern, thanks to design and furniture by Fritz Hansen of Denmark. *Average main: ¥10000* *1F Shimizu Bldg., 2–5–8 Kita-Aoyama, Minato-ku* *03/5413–3300* *www.aquavit-japan.com* *Reservations essential* *Ginza subway line, Gaien-mae Station (Exit 1B)* *B4.*

$$$$ BRAZILIAN **Barbacoa Grill** (バルバッコアグリル). Carnivores flock here for the great-value, all-you-can-eat Brazilian grilled chicken and barbecued beef, which the efficient waiters keep bringing to your table on skewers until you tell them to stop. Those with lighter appetites can choose the less expensive salad buffet and *feijoada* (pork stew with black beans); both are bargains. Hardwood floors, lithographs of bull motifs, warm lighting, and salmon-color tablecloths provide the backdrop. The drink menu provides the chance to try a selection of Brazilian cocktails. Look for the entrance just off Omotesando-dori on the Harajuku 2-chome

shopping street (on the north side of Omotesando-dori), about 50 yards down on the left. There's also a Barbacoa near Tokyo Station, as well as others in Roppongi, Shibuya, and Shinjuku. *Average main: ¥5400* ✉ *4–3–2 Jingu-mae, Shibuya-ku* ☎ *03/3796–0571* 🌐 *www.barbacoa.jp/aoyama* Ⓜ *Ginza, Chiyoda, and Hanzo-mon subway lines, Omotesando Station (Exit A2)* ✣ *B4.*

$$ VEGETARIAN

✕ **Brown Rice Canteen** (ブラウンライス 食堂). Run by Neal's Yard Remedies, this laid-back café has all-natural wooden interiors and natural produce on the menu. If shopping in Harajuku, it's a great place to stop for a tempeh burger, stuffed tofu pouch, or other vegetarian fare. *Average main: ¥1200* ✉ *5–1–8 Jingu-mae, Shibuya-ku* ☎ *03/5778–5416* 🌐 *www.nealsyard.co.jp/brownrice* Ⓜ *Ginza and Hanzo-mon subway lines, Omotesando Station (Exit A1)* ✣ *B4.*

$$$$ MEDITERRANEAN Fodor's Choice ★

✕ **Cicada** (シカダ). Offering up high-end Mediterranean cuisine in an incredibly stylish setting, Cicada's resortlike atmosphere feels a world away from Omotesando's busy shopping streets. In the warmer months, the outdoor patio is especially relaxing. The menu ranges from Spanish tapas and Middle Eastern mezze to hearty grilled meats and seafood. An expansive wine list and craft beers complement the range of cuisine, and the outdoor bar makes a great spot for a nightcap. Though spacious, this popular restaurant fills up quickly, so dinner reservations are recommended. *Average main: ¥3500* ✉ *5–7–28, Minami-Aoyama, Minato-ku* ☎ *03/6434–1255* 🌐 *www.tysons.jp/cicada* ✣ *B5.*

$$$ JAPANESE Fodor's Choice ★

✕ **Harajuku Taproom** (原宿タップルーム). Founded by American Bryan Baird in 2000, Baird Brewing has become one of the leaders in Japan's now booming craft beer movement, with a range of year-round brews, such as the hop-heavy Suruga Bay IPA, and creative seasonal beers that use local ingredients such as yuzu citrus and even wasabi. The Harajuku Taproom combines Baird's excellent lineup of microbrews with Japanese izakaya (pub) fare like yakitori (grilled chicken skewers), *gyoza* (dumplings), and curry rice. The Taproom's rotation of 15 beers on tap, plus two hand-pumped ales, as well as its quality food and friendly atmosphere make it a must for beer lovers and dispel any notion that all Japanese beers taste the same. There are other branches in Naka Meguro and Yokohama. *Average main: ¥3000* ✉ *1–20–13, Jingumae, No Surrender Bldg. 2F, Shibuya-ku* ☎ *03/6438–0450* 🌐 *www.bairdbeer.com/en/tap/harajuku* ▭ *No credit cards* ⏲ *No lunch weekdays* ✣ *B4.*

$$ SUSHI FAMILY

✕ **Heiroku-zushi** (平禄寿司). Often, a meal of sushi is a costly indulgence. The rock-bottom alternative is a *kaiten-zushi*, where it is literally served assembly-line style: chefs inside the circular counter place a constant supply of dishes on the revolving belt with plates color-coded for price; just choose whatever takes your fancy as the sushi parades by. A cheerful, bustling example of this genre is the Heiroku-zushi chain's branch opposite Omotesando Hills; it's all about the fresh fish here (and clearly not the design). When you're done, the server counts up your plates and calculates your bill. Expect ¥130 for staples like tuna and squid to ¥490 for delicacies like high-grade *toro* cuts of tuna and sea urchin. *Average main: ¥2000* ✉ *5–8–5 Jingu-mae, Shibuya-ku*

CLOSE UP

The Essentials of a Japanese Meal

The basic formula for a traditional Japanese meal is deceptively simple. It starts with soup, followed by raw fish, then the entrée (grilled, steamed, simmered, or fried fish, chicken, or vegetables), and ends with rice and pickles, with perhaps fresh fruit for dessert, and a cup of green tea. It's as simple as that—almost.

There are, admittedly, a few twists to the story. Beyond the raw fish, it's the incredible variety of vegetation used in Japanese cooking that still surprises the Western palate: *take-no-ko* (bamboo shoots), *renkon* (lotus root), and the treasured *matsutake* mushrooms (which grow wild in jealously guarded forest hideaways and sometimes sell for more than $60 apiece), to name a few.

There are also ground rules. Absolute freshness is first. To a Japanese chef, this is an unparalleled virtue, and much of a chef's reputation relies on the ability to obtain the finest ingredients at the peak of season: fish brought in from the sea this morning (not yesterday) and vegetables from the earth (not the hothouse), if at all possible.

Simplicity is next. Rather than embellishing foods with heavy spices and rich sauces, the Japanese chef prefers flavors au naturel. Flavors are enhanced, not elaborated, accented rather than concealed. Without a heavy sauce, fish is permitted a degree of natural fishiness—a garnish of fresh red ginger is provided to offset the flavor rather than to disguise it.

The third prerequisite is beauty. Simple, natural foods must appeal to the eye as well as to the palate. Green peppers on a vermilion dish, perhaps, or an egg custard in a blue bowl. Rectangular dishes for a round eggplant. So important is the seasonal element in Japanese cooking that maple leaves and pine needles are used to accent an autumn dish. Or two small summer delicacies, a pair of freshwater *ayu* fish, are grilled with a purposeful twist to their tails to make them "swim" across a crystal platter and thereby suggest the coolness of a mountain stream on a hot August night.

Not to be forgotten is mood, which can make or break the entire meal. Japanese connoisseurs go to great lengths to find the perfect yakitori stand—a smoky, lively place—an environment appropriate to the occasion, offering a night of grilled chicken, cold beer, and camaraderie. In fancier places, mood becomes a fancier problem, to the point of quibbling over the proper amount of "water music" trickling in the basin outside your private room.

☎ *03/3498–3968* Ⓜ *Ginza, Chiyoda, and Hanzo-mon subway lines, Omotesando Station (Exit A1)* ✥ *B4.*

$ RAMEN ✕ **Kohmen** (光麺). With a polished interior, this always-busy ramen shop may be usual, but the food is still completely authentic and tasty. Kohmen is known for its *tonkotsu* (pork bone) soup, and yelling "tonkotsu" over the counter gets you a basic bowl of soup with noodles topped with a slice of barbecued pork. Adding *zen bu no say* (with the works) gets you a side dish of hard-boiled egg, vegetables, dried seaweed, and other goodies you dump over your soup before eating. Alternatively, opt for the *tsukemen* (where you dip the noodles into a separate broth) or a spicy, sesame-heavy bowl of *tantanmen* noodles. There are several other branches around Tokyo. *Average main: ¥1000 ✉ 6–2–8 Jingu-mae, Shibuya-ku ☎ 03/5468–6344 🌐 www.kohmen.com/en ▭ No credit cards ✥ B4.*

$$ JAPANESE ✕ **Maisen** (まい泉). Converted from a *sento* (public bathhouse), Maisen still has the old high ceiling (built for ventilation) and the original signs instructing bathers where to change, but now bouquets of seasonal flowers transform the large, airy space into a pleasant dining room. Maisen's specialty is the *tonkatsu* set: tender, juicy, deep-fried pork cutlets served with a spicy sauce, shredded cabbage, miso soup, and rice. Combine with sashimi, if feeling especially hungry. There is usually a long line, but it moves quickly. Solo diners can jump the line to sit at the counter. Those who want to keep their taste buds sharp should try for the nonsmoking rooms upstairs. There's also a branch in Hikarie building in Shibuya. *Average main: ¥1800 ✉ 4–8–5 Jingu-mae, Shibuya-ku ☎ 03/3470–0071 ▭ No credit cards Ⓜ Ginza, Chiyoda, and Hanzo-mon subway lines, Omotesando Station (Exit A2) ✥ B4.*

$$ CAFÉ ✕ **Montoak** (モントーク). For an afternoon of people-watching, head to this three-story café on Omotesando street in the heart of one of the most fashion-conscious areas of Tokyo. It's the perfect place to relax and indulge. Order one of the scrumptious homemade tarts or cakes, sip a coffee, and watch the trendiest Tokyoites stroll by the full-length windows. *Average main: ¥1500 ✉ 6–1–9 Jingu-mae, Shibuya-ku ☎ 03/5468–5928 🌐 www.montoak.com ▭ No credit cards ✥ B4.*

$$ FRENCH ✕ **Red Pepper** (レッドペッパー). A short walk down a narrow alley from Omotesando Crossing, this cozy bistro is in the trendy shopping district. Guests squeeze into tiny antique school chairs and desks topped with candles in the homey dining room. The cuisine is constantly changing, but most diners ignore the printed menu in favor of the daily recommendations chalked on blackboards (mainly in Japanese) propped up here and there. Previous specials lean toward French-accented comfort food, like button mushrooms grilled in garlic and olive oil, or porcini-and-cream-sauce fettuccine. *Average main: ¥2000 ✉ 1F Shimizu Bldg., 3–5–25 Kita-Aoyama, Shibuya-ku ☎ 03/3478–1264 🌐 www.take-5.co.jp/redpepper/omotesando Ⓜ Ginza, Chiyoda, and Hanzo-mon subway lines, Omotesando Station (Exit A3) ✥ B4.*

$$ VEGETARIAN ✕ **Restaurant 8blish** (レストランエイタブリッシュ). Stop along a backstreet in the upscale fashion hub of Omotesando for a daily changing menu of salads, soups, sandwiches, and other nutritious fare for breakfast, lunch, and dinner. *Average main: ¥2000 ✉ 5–10–17 Minami-Aoyama, Minato-ku ☎ 03/6805–0597 🌐 http://eightablish.com ▭ No credit cards Ⓜ Ginza and Hanzo-mon subway lines, Omotesando Station (Exit B3) ✥ B4.*

$$ JAPANESE ✕ **Sakuratei** (さくら亭). Tucked away between the two buildings of the cutting-edge (yet very laid-back) Design Festa Gallery, Sakuratei also defies conventions—namely, that eating out doesn't mean you don't have to cook. At this do-it-yourself restaurant for *okonomiyaki* (a kind of savory pancake made with egg, meat, and vegetables), you choose ingredients and cook them on the *teppan* (grill). Okonomiyaki

4

is generally easy to make, but flipping the pancake to cook the other side can be challenging—potentially messy but still fun. Fortunately, you're not expected to wash the dishes. Okonomiyaki literally means "as you like it," so experiment with your own recipe. But if you're feeling uninspired, you can always default to the house special, *sakurayaki* (with pork, squid, and onions) or *monjayaki* (a watered-down Tokyo variation of okonomiyaki from the Kanto region). *Average main: ¥1500 ✉ 3–20–1 Jingu-mae, Shibuya-ku ☎ 03/3479–0039 🌐 www.sakuratei.co.jp ▭ No credit cards Ⓜ Chiyoda subway line, Meiji-Jingu-mae (Harajuku) Station (Exit 5) ✣ B4.*

SHIBUYA 渋谷

Shibuya is a shopper's paradise. Here you will find everything from fashion to housewares. Restaurants, however, are on the cheap side, catering to the young clientele.

$ RAMEN

Afuri (阿夫利/あふり). Ramen is the quintessential Japanese fast food: thick Chinese noodles in a savory broth, with sliced leeks, grilled *chashu* (pork loin), and spinach in a bowl. Each neighborhood in Tokyo has its favorite, and in Ebisu the hands-down favorite is Afuri. Using the picture menu, choose your ramen by inserting coins into a ticket machine, find a seat, and hand over your ticket to the cooks, who prepare your ramen then and there. There's limited seating, and at lunch and dinner, the line of waiting customers extends down the street, but as expected, the ramen is worth it. *Average main: ¥880 ✉ 1–1–7 Ebisu, Shibuya-ku ☎ 03/5795–0750 ▭ No credit cards Ⓜ JR Yamanote Line (Nishi-guchi/West Exit) and Hibiya subway line (Exit 1), Ebisu Station ✣ B6.*

$$ JAPANESE FUSION

Crayon House (クレヨンハウス). Connected to a natural-foods store, and with natural airy wooden interiors to match, Crayon House serves Japanese and Western dishes with a common theme—it's all very healthy. Ninety-five percent of ingredients are organic and the mixture of curries, pastas, salads, and other dishes are all wholesome. The lunchtime buffet is good value at ¥1,500. The desserts taste as if the notion of health has been thrown out the window. *Average main: ¥1500 ✉ 3–8–15 Kita-Aoyama ☎ 03/3406–6409 🌐 www.crayonhouse.co.jp ▭ No credit cards Ⓜ Omotesando Station (Chiyoda, Ginza, and Hanzomon lines; Exit A1 and B2) ✣ B4.*

$$ CAFÉ

Good Honest Grub (グッドオネストグラブ). This airy, laid-back restaurant has the feel of enjoying a home-cooked meal at a friend's house. Brunch is generously served 10:30–4 on weekends and national holidays, and includes Greek omelets, wraps, and perhaps the best eggs Benedict in town. True to its name, everything comes from the restaurant's own organic farm. *Average main: ¥2000 ✉ 2–20–8 Higashi, Shibuya-ku ☎ 03/3797–9877 🌐 www.goodhonestgrub.com ▭ No credit cards ◷ No dinner ✍ Reservations not accepted Ⓜ JR Yamanote, Shibuya Station (South Exit) ✣ B4.*

$$ ASIAN ✕ **Monsoon Cafe** (モンスーンカフェ). With a dozen locations (including Shinjuku and Omotesando), Monsoon Cafe meets the demand in Tokyo for "ethnic" food—which by local definition means spicy and primarily Southeast Asian. Complementing the eclectic Pan-Asian food are rattan furniture, brass tableware from Thailand, colorful papier-mâché parrots on gilded stands, Balinese carvings, and ceiling fans. Here, at the original Monsoon, the best seats in the house are on the balcony that runs around the four sides of the atrium-style central space. Try the satay (grilled, skewered cubes of meat) platter, steamed shrimp dumplings, or *nasi goreng* (Indonesian fried rice). *Average main: ¥2000 ✉ 15–4 Hachiyama-cho, Shibuya-ku ☎ 03/5489–3789 ⊕ www.monsoon-cafe.jp Ⓜ Tokyu Toyoko private rail line, Daikanyama Station (Kita-guchi/North Exit) ✣ A5.*

$$ VEGETARIAN ✕ **Nagi Shokudo** (なぎ食堂). This small restaurant hidden away on a little side street a short walk from Shibuya Station has mismatched chairs and tables and a selection of books and magazines you can read over a vegan meal. The ¥1,200 prix fixe lunch includes a choice of three dishes, which change daily, rice, miso soup, and a drink. In the evening, it's a great place to enjoy a light dinner in an arty atmosphere. *Average main: ¥2000 ✉ 15–10 Uguisudani-cho, Shibuya-ku ☎ 050/1043–7751 ⊕ nagishokudo.com ▭ No credit cards ⏲ Closed Sun. evenings and holidays Ⓜ JR Yamanote Line, Shibuya Station (South Exit) ✣ A5.*

$$$$ ECLECTIC ✕ **Tableaux** (タブロー). This restaurant may lay on more glitz than necessary—the mural in the bar depicts the fall of Pompeii, the banquettes are upholstered in red leather, and the walls are papered in antique gold—but the service is cordial and professional and the food, which is centered on Italian cuisine and U.S. steaks, is superb. The wine list is one of the most varied in town, with everything from affordable house wines (¥1,000 per glass) to rarities that will set you back upward of ¥100,000 a bottle. *Average main: ¥8000 ✉ B1 Sunroser Daikanyama Bldg., 11–6 Sarugaku-cho, Shibuya-ku ☎ 03/5489–2201 ⊕ www.tableaux.jp ⏲ No lunch Jacket and tie Ⓜ Tokyu Toyoko private rail line, Daikanyama Station (Kita guchi/North Exit) ✣ A5.*

$$$ JAPANESE ✕ **Tachigui Sakaba buri** (立食酒場buri). "One cup" sake—a single serving of sake in what looks a bit like a small mason jar—is usually bottom-of-the-barrel convenience store swill. Buri, however, turns the concept on its head by offering tasty *ji-zake* (local sake) from around Japan in the one-cup style, pairing it with a range of tapas-like servings of sashimi, yakitori, salads, and prosciutto. They also have beer on tap. Just a five-minute walk from Ebisu Station, this casual, standing-only restaurant/bar fills up quickly on weekends, so it's best to stop in early if you want to grab a table. *Average main: ¥3000 ✉ 1–14–1 Ebisu-Nishi, Shibuya-ku ☎ 03/3496–7744 ▭ No credit cards ✣ B6.*

$$$ JAPANESE ✕ **Tenmatsu** (天松). The best seats in the house at Tenmatsu, as in any tempura- *ya,* are at the counter, where your selections are taken straight from the oil and served immediately. At this vantage point, you also get to watch the chef in action, and the good-natured, hospitable chefs and staff add to the experience. Here you can rely on a

4

CLOSE UP

On the Menu

SUSHI

Sushi—slices of raw fish or shellfish on hand-formed portions of vinegared rice, with a dab of wasabi for zest—is probably the best-known Japanese dish in the Western world. The best sushi restaurants in Tokyo send buyers early every morning to the Central Wholesale Market in Tsukiji for the freshest ingredients: *maguro* (tuna), *hamachi* (yellowtail), *tako* (octopus), *ika* (squid), *ikura* (salmon roe), *uni* (sea urchin), *ebi* (shrimp), and *anago* (conger eel).

SASHIMI

Sushi's cousin sashimi consists of fresh, thinly sliced seafood served with soy sauce, wasabi paste, and a simple garnish like shredded daikon or fresh shiso leaves. Though most seafood is served raw, some sashimi ingredients, like octopus, may be cooked. Less common ingredients are vegetarian items such as cucumbers.

TEMPURA

Another Japanese dish that may be familiar to you is tempura: fresh fish, shellfish, and vegetables delicately batter-fried in oil. Tempura dates to the mid-16th century, with the earliest influences of Spanish and Portuguese culture on Japan, and you'll find it today all over the world. But nowhere is it better than in Tokyo, and nowhere in Tokyo is it better than in the tempura stalls and restaurants of shitamachi—the older commercial and working-class districts of the eastern wards—or in the restaurants that began there in the 19th century and moved upscale. Typical ingredients are shrimp, *kisu* (smelt), *shirauo* (whitebait), shiitake mushrooms, lotus root, and green peppers. To really enjoy tempura, sit at the counter in front of the chef: these individual portions should be served and eaten the moment they emerge from the oil.

SUKIYAKI

Sukiyaki is a popular beef dish that is sautéed with vegetables in an iron skillet at the table. The tenderness of the beef is the determining factor here, and many of the best sukiyaki houses also run their own butcher shops so that they can control the quality of the beef they serve—the Japanese are justifiably proud of their notorious beer-fed and hand-massaged beef.

SHABU-SHABU

Shabu-shabu is another possibility, though this dish has become more popular with tourists than with the Japanese. It's similar to sukiyaki because it's prepared at the table with a combination of vegetables, but the cooking methods differ: shabu-shabu is swished briefly in boiling water (the word *shabu-shabu* is onomatopoeic for this swishing sound), whereas sukiyaki is sautéed in oil and, usually, a slightly sweetened soy sauce.

NABEMONO

Nabemono (one-pot dishes), commonly known as nabe, may not be familiar to Westerners, but the possibilities are endless. Simmered in a light, fish-based broth, these stews can be made of almost anything: *mizutaki* (chicken), *kaki-nabe* (oysters), or the sumo wrestler's favorite, the hearty *chanko-nabe*—with something in it for everyone. Nabemono is a popular family or party dish. The restaurants specializing in nabemono often have a casual, country atmosphere.

set menu or order à la carte tempura delicacies like lotus root, shrimp, *unagi* (eel), and *kisu* (smelt). There is also a branch in Nihonbashi. *Average main: ¥3000 Tokyu Department Store, 9F, 2–24–1 Shibuya, Shibuya-ku 03/3477–4584 www.tenmatsu.com JR Yamanote Line, Shibuya Station; Ginza and Hanzo-mon subway lines, Shibuya Station (connected to the station) A5.*

ROPPONGI 六本木

The opulent Roppongi has outgrown its disco days and matured into a district with Western hotels and business skyscrapers. Restaurants run the gamut from lunch spots to quick bites to upscale options in the evening.

$$$$ FRENCH

Azure 45 (アジュール フォーティーファイブ). French restaurants in Japan have the luxury of using Japanese beef, poultry, and fresh seafood as well as vegetables that are plentiful throughout the country. On the 45th floor of the Ritz-Carlton, the restaurant makes the most of this bounty, buying seafood not only from Tsukiji Market, but also at the local Kanazawa fish port for a broader range of delicacies. Prix fixe lunch courses (from ¥5,000) come with a choice of four or five dishes from a changing monthly menu. For dinner there is a chef's tasting menu, which is paired with wine selected by the hotel's sommelier. The dining room, decorated in soft beige, white, and black, and crowned with a city skyline view, provides the appropriate tony ambience. *Average main: ¥15000 Tokyo Midtown, 9–7–1 Akasaka, Minato-ku 03/6434–8711 www.ritzcarlton.com Hibiya subway line, Roppongi Station (Exit 4A); Toei Oedo Line, Roppongi Station (Exit 7) D4.*

$$$$ JAPANESE Fodor's Choice ★

Ganchan (がんちゃん). Smoky, noisy, and cluttered, Ganchan is exactly what the Japanese expect of their yakitori joints—restaurants that specialize in bits of charcoal-broiled chicken and vegetables. The counter here seats barely 15, and you have to squeeze to get to the chairs in back. Festival masks, paper kites, lanterns, and greeting cards from celebrity patrons adorn the walls. The cooks yell at each other, fan the grill, and serve up enormous schooners of beer. Try the *tsukune* (balls of minced chicken) and the fresh asparagus wrapped in bacon. Otherwise opt for a mixed eight-skewer set that also comes with several small side dishes (¥2,625). The place stays open until 1:30 am (midnight on Sunday). *Average main: ¥4000 6–8–23 Roppongi, Minato-ku 03/3478–0092 r.gnavi.co.jp/g898300 No lunch Hibiya subway line, Roppongi Station (Exit 1A) D5.*

$$ AMERICAN

Homeworks (ホームワークス). Every so often, even on foreign shores, you've got to have a burger. When the urge strikes, the Swiss-and-bacon special at Homeworks is an incomparably better choice than anything you can get at one of the global chains. Hamburgers come in three sizes on white or wheat buns, with a variety of toppings. You also find hot teriyaki chicken sandwiches, pastrami sandwiches, and vegetarian options like a soybean veggie burger or a tofu sandwich. Desserts, alas, are so-so. With its hardwood banquettes and French doors open to the street in good weather, Homeworks is a pleasant place to linger over lunch. There are also branches in Hiro-o and Shinagawa. *Average main: ¥1500 ✉ 1F Vesta Bldg., 1–5–8 Azabu Juban, Minato-ku ☎ 03/3405–9884 🌐 www.homeworks-1.com Ⓜ Namboku and Oedo subway lines, Azabu Juban Station (Exit 4) ⊕ D5.*

$$$$ JAPANESE Fodor's Choice ★ ✕ **Inakaya East** (田舎屋東). The style here is *robatayaki*, a dining experience that segues into pure theater. Inside a large U-shape counter, two cooks in traditional garb sit on cushions behind a grill, with a cornucopia of food spread out in front of them: fresh vegetables, seafood, skewers of beef and chicken. You point to what you want, and your server shouts out the order. The cook in back plucks your selection up out of the pit, prepares it, and hands it across on an 8-foot wooden paddle. Inakaya is open from 5 pm and fills up fast after 7. If you can't get a seat here, there is now another branch, Inakaya West, on the other side of Roppongi Crossing. *Average main: ¥9000 ✉ 1F Reine Bldg., 5–3–4 Roppongi, Minato-ku ☎ 03/3408–5040 🌐 www.roppongiinakaya.jp/en ⊗ No lunch ⚠ Reservations not accepted Ⓜ Hibiya subway line, Roppongi Station (Exit 3) ⊕ C5.*

$$$$ VEGETARIAN ✕ **Itosho** (いと正). At this Zen restaurant near Zenpuku temple, food arrives in a procession of 13 tiny dishes, each selected according to season, texture, and color. Dinner costs between ¥8,000 and ¥10,000, and reservations must be made at least two days in advance. *Average main: ¥10000 ✉ 3–4–7 Azabu Juban, Minato-ku ☎ 03/3454–6538 ▭ No credit cards ⚠ Reservations essential Ⓜ Namboku and Oedo subway lines, Azabu Juban Station (Exit 1) ⊕ C5.*

$$$ AMERICAN ✕ **Roti** (ロティ). Billing itself a "modern American brasserie," Roti takes pride in the creative use of simple, fresh ingredients fused with Eastern and Western elements. For an appetizer, try the falafel and char-grilled vegetables on flat bread, or shoestring french fries with white truffle oil and Parmigiano-Reggiano cheese. Don't neglect dessert: the espresso-chocolate tart is outrageously good. Other indulgences include some 60 California wines, microbrewed ales from the famed Rogue brewery in Oregon, and Cuban cigars. There is also a fantastic weekend brunch menu and a great-value kids set menu (¥900). The best seats in the house are, in fact, outside, at one of the dozen tables around the big glass pyramid on the terrace. *Average main: ¥3000 ✉ 1F Piramide Bldg., 6–6–9 Roppongi, Minato-ku ☎ 03/5785–3671 🌐 www.roti.jp/en Ⓜ Hibiya subway line, Roppongi Station (Exit 1A); Toei Oedo Line, Roppongi Station (Exit 1A) ⊕ C5.*

$$$$ KOREAN ✕ **Sanko-en** (三幸園). In a neighborhood thick with Korean-barbecue joints, Sanko-en stands out as the best of the lot. Korean barbecue is a smoky affair; you cook your own food, usually thin slices of beef and vegetables, on a gas grill at your table. The *karubi* (brisket), which is accompanied by a great salad, is the best choice on the menu. If you like kimchi (spicy pickled cabbage), Sanko-en's is considered by some to be the best in town. Customers from all over agree, including those from the South Korean embassy a few blocks away. And they line up at all hours (from 11:30 am to midnight) to get in. *Average main: ¥6000 ✉ 1–8–7 Azabu Juban, Minato-ku ☎ 03/3585–6306 ⊗ Closed Wed. ⚠ Reservations not accepted Ⓜ Namboku and Oedo subway lines, Azabu Juban Station (Exit 4) ⊕ C5.*

$$$$ SUSHI ✕ **Sushisho Masa** (すし匠 まさ). Diners here need a dose of luck—there are only seven counter seats and reservations fill up fast. You also need a full wallet, as high-end sushi comes at a pretty price. But for the few that manage to cross those two hurdles, Sushiso Masa gives a sublime experience. The interior is unpretentious, putting the focus squarely on the gorgeous presentations for each course. But what really sets this apart from other upscale sushi spots is the extreme quality of the cuts of fish, and the garnishes that use incredibly rare ingredients, such as *zha cai* (pickled stem of the mustard plant). *Average main: ¥20000 ⊠ B1F Seven Nishi-Azabu Bldg., 4–1–15 Nishi-Azabu, Minato-ku ☎ 03/3499–9178 ⏲ Closed Mon. No lunch ✍ Reservations essential Ⓜ Hibiya subway line, Roppongi Station (Exit 1B); Toei Oedo Line, Roppongi Station (Exit 1A) ✥ C5.*

4

$$$ AMERICAN FAMILY ✕ **Tony Roma's** (トニーローマ). If your kids flee in terror when a plate of sushi is placed in front of them, you may want to take them for a taste of home at this American chain world-famous for its barbecued ribs. Started in Miami in the 1970s, this casual place serves kid-sized (and much larger) portions of ribs, burgers, chicken strips, and fried shrimp. There's another branch in the Hanzomon area. *Average main: ¥3000 ⊠ 5–4–20 Roppongi, Minato-ku ☎ 03/3408–2748 ⊕ www.tonyromas.jp/en ⏲ No lunch weekdays Ⓜ Hibiya subway line, Roppongi Station (Exit 3); Toei Oedo Line, Roppongi Station (Exit 3) ✥ C5.*

$$$$ AMERICAN ✕ **Towers Modern Bistro** (タワーズグリル.). When you're looking for a break from all the ramen, tempura, and yakitori, this restaurant on the 45th floor of the Ritz-Carlton Hotel serves a mix of international flavors that range from American to Southeast Asian to Mediterranean. A prix fixe lunch includes a choice of three items from a seasonally changing menu, and there are dinners with three, four, and five courses. A plush brunch (¥7,000) is also available weekends and holidays. Best of all, the dining room overlooks a panorama of the Tokyo Sky Tree and Tokyo Tower, which is where the eatery gets its name. *Average main: ¥11000 ⊠ Tokyo Midtown, 9–7–1 Akasaka, Minato-ku ☎ 03/6434–8711 ⊕ www.ritzcarlton.com Ⓜ Hibiya subway line, Roppongi Station (Exit 4A); Toei Oedo Line, Roppongi Station (Exit 7) ✥ D4.*

SHINJUKU 新宿

This skyscraper district is also home to the city's busiest train station. Aside from the area's restaurants, several department stores in the area have wonderful food in the basement depachika.

$$$$ INTERNATIONAL Fodor's Choice ★ ✕ **New York Grill & Bar** (ニューヨーク グリル&バー). The Park Hyatt's 52nd-floor bar and restaurant may have come to international fame thanks to Sofia Coppola's *Lost in Translation*, but expats and locals have long known that it's one of the most elegant places to take in Tokyo's nighttime cityscape over a steak or cocktail. The restaurant menu showcases excellent steaks and grilled seafood in the evening, and has one of the city's best lunch buffets during the day. If the restaurant is out of your budget, come instead to the bar when it opens (before a ¥2,200 cover charge is added to your bill) and enjoy a drink

as the sun sets over the city. The cover charge for the bar starts at 8 pm every day but Sunday, when it starts at 7 pm. *Average main: ¥20000 ✉ Park Hyatt Tokyo, 52nd fl., 3–7–1 Nishi-Shinjuku, Shinjuku-ku ☎ 03/5322–3458 🌐 www.tokyo.park.hyatt.com Reservations essential ✥ A3.*

$$$ JAPANESE **Ryoma no Sora Bettei** (龍馬の空別邸). Tokyoites love unique dining experiences and their own history—they can revel in both in this eatery, which is a tribute to Ryoma Sakamoto, a young hero who died while helping overthrow the feudal Tokugawa Shogunate in the 1860s. When you enter from the ultramodern streets of Shinjuku, slide off your shoes, stash them in a wooden locker, and walk by a statue of the sword-wielding Sakamoto as you step into the Japan of the past. You can sit in the main dining hall, which resembles a bustling historic inn, or you can phone ahead to reserve a private tatami-mat dining room. The cuisine also harkens back to the traditional rural cooking, popular before Japan opened up to the West. The house specialty is *seiro-mushi*, a bamboo box filled with carefully arranged seafood, poultry, or meat, steamed over a pot, served piping hot, and quickly shared with everyone at the table. *Average main: ¥4000 ✉ B2 141 Shinjuku Bldg., 1–4–2 Nishi-Shinjuku, Shinjuku-ku ☎ 03/3347–2207 No lunch Ⓜ JR Shinjuku Station (Nishi-guchi/West Exit) ✥ A2.*

GREATER TOKYO

A calm, residential area, Meguro has a few universities and historic temples in the neighborhood, not to mention a parasite museum that's best avoided before eating. Among its restaurants, this neighborhood houses one of the city's most famous *tonkatsu* shops.

Shinagawa is a major train station and transportation hub near Tokyo Bay with plenty of large office buildings and hotels and a variety of restaurants that cater to hungry travelers and office workers.

$$$$ JAPANESE Fodor's Choice ★ **Enju** (槐樹). The grand exterior and pristine banquet rooms are somewhat uninviting and overly formal at this upscale restaurant in the quiet surroundings of Shirokanedai (five minutes by taxi from Shinagawa), but the tables overlooking the 300-year-old Japanese garden provide a tranquil backdrop for an unforgettable meal. Yes, the views are stunning, but it's the food that draws locals and visitors again and again. Among the costly, seasonally changing prix fixe dinners are kaiseki, shabu-shabu, sukiyaki, and tempura, and there's also a buffet dinner. Go in the afternoon for more affordable options, such as the set sushi lunch (¥2,200) and green tea service (¥1,200). For more casual dining, the organic-focused Café Thrush, in the same complex, has an open-air terrace with a stunning view of the garden. *Average main: ¥10000 ✉ 1–1–1 Shirokanedai, Minato-ku ☎ 03/3443–3125 🌐 www.happo-en.com/restaurant/enju Reservations essential Ⓜ Mita and Namboku subway lines, Shirokanedai Station (Exit 2) ✥ C6.*

$$ JAPANESE **Tonki** (とんき). A family joint, with Formica-top tables, Tonki is a success that never went conglomerate or added frills to what it does best: deep-fried pork cutlets, soup, raw-cabbage salad, rice, pickles, and tea. That's the standard course, and almost everybody orders it, with good

CLOSE UP

What's a Vegetarian to Do?

Tokyo has had a reputation of being difficult for vegetarians, but as more Japanese opt to forgo meat, the number of truly vegetarian restaurants is rising. Organic produce has also become more in demand, and many nonvegetarian restaurants now serve organic meals that very often are vegetarian. The city's numerous Indian eateries are a safe bet, as are the handful of restaurants (such as Sasa-no-yuki in Ueno, which also serves nonvegetarian) that specialize in *shojin ryori*, traditional Zen vegetarian food that emphasizes natural flavors and fresh ingredients without using heavy spices or rich sauces. However, you should always inquire when making reservations at these restaurants, as some still use *dashi*, a stock made with smoked skipjack tuna and kelp. The variety and visual beauty of a full-course shojin ryori meal opens new dining dimensions to the vegetarian gourmet. *Goma-dofu*, or sesame-flavored bean curd, for example, is a tasty treat, as is *nasu-dongaku*, grilled eggplant covered with a sweet miso sauce.

Take note that a dish may be described as meat-free even if it contains fish, shrimp, or chicken. And one should assume that salads, pastas, and soups in nonvegetarian restaurants are garnished with ham or bacon.

Deva Deva Café

(デヴァデヴァカフェ). Near the picturesque Inokashira Park, Deva Deva Café is an organic oasis. Don't be surprised to see pizza, burgers, and grilled chicken on the menu of this vegan restaurant. But don't worry—the pizza is made with soy cheese; the burgers are meat-free, made with chickpeas, veggies, and herbs; and the chicken is made from soy protein. ✉ *2-14-7 Kichijoji Honcho* ☎ *042/221-6220* ▭ *No credit cards* Ⓜ *JR Chuo Line, Kichijoji Station (North Exit)*

If you plan to stay in town long-term, check out **Alishan** 阿里山 (🌐 *www.alishan-organics.com*), a vegetarian mail-order specialist.

4

reason—it's utterly delicious. Just listen to customers in line as they put in their usual orders while a server comes around to take it. Then go ahead and join in; the wait is only about 10 minutes, but the line continues every night until the place closes at 10:45. Ⓢ *Average main: ¥1900* ✉ *1-1-2 Shimo-Meguro, Meguro-ku* ☎ *03/3491-9928* ▭ *No credit cards* ⊙ *Closed Tues. and 3rd Mon. of month. No lunch* Ⓜ *JR Yamanote and Namboku subway lines, Meguro Station (Nishi-guchi/West Exit)* ✥ *B6.*

$$$$ ECLECTIC ✕ **T. Y. Harbor Brewery** (T.Y.ハーバーブルワリーレストラン). A converted warehouse on the waterfront houses this restaurant, a Tokyo hot spot for private parties. Chef David Chiddo refined his signature California-Thai cuisine at some of the best restaurants in Los Angeles and now incorporates Japanese twists into some of the dishes here. Don't miss his Thai-style red curry chicken skewers, or the shrimp cocktail with *yuzu kosho* mayonaisse. True to its name, T. Y. Harbor brews six of its own year-round beers (plus seasonal specials) in a tank that

reaches all the way to the 46-foot-high ceiling. The best seats in the house are on the bay-side deck, open from May to October. Reservations are a good idea on weekends. $ *Average main: ¥4000* ✉ *2–1–3 Higashi-Shinagawa, Shinagawa-ku* ☎ *03/5479–4555* 🌐 *www.tysons.jp/tyharbor* Ⓜ *Tokyo Monorail or Rinkai Line, Ten-nozu Isle Station (Exit B)* ✥ *D6.*

5

WHERE TO STAY

Updated by Brett Bull

Japan may have experienced more than two decades of stagnation following the collapse of the asset-inflated "bubble" economy of the late '90s, but one wouldn't know it from the steadily increasing number of high-end hotels throughout the metropolis. As land prices subsequently fell, Tokyo's developers seized the chance to construct centrally located skyscrapers. Oftentimes hotels from international brands were installed on the upper floors of these glimmering towers. This boom has complemented the spare-no-expense approach taken by many of the domestic hoteliers a decade earlier, when soaring atriums, elaborate concierge floors, and oceans of marble were all the rage. The result: Tokyo's present luxury accommodations rival those of any big city in the world.

Are there bargains to be had? Absolutely, but you'll have to do your homework, which has become an easier task with Tokyo set to host the Olympic Games in 2020, as operators are now increasingly aware of the foreign traveler on a budget. Lower-profile business hotels are decent bets for singles or couples who do not need a lot of space, and, in addition to hostels, exchanges, and rentals, the budget-conscious traveler can utilize plenty of Japanese accommodations: *ryokan, minshuku,* "capsule" hotels, homes, and temples.

A number of boutique hotels—typified by small rooms, utilitarian concepts, and quirky, stylish elements—have popped up in Tokyo. Modern room furnishings of neutral hues are prevalent, but so are such Japanese touches as paper lanterns and tatami flooring. Reception areas are simple spaces bathed in dim lights and surrounded by earth-tone wall panels. Given that these accommodations often contain only a few floors, their locations are likely not easy to find. But when priced at around ¥20,000 a night, they can offer some of the best bargains in a city known for being incredibly expensive.

LODGING PLANNER

WHAT TO EXPECT

There are three things you can take for granted almost anywhere you set down your bags in Tokyo: cleanliness, safety, and good service. Unless otherwise specified, all rooms at the hotels listed in this book have private baths and are Western style.

PRICES

Deluxe hotels charge a premium for good-size rooms, lots of perks, great service, and central locations. More affordable hotels aren't always in the most convenient places and have disproportionately small rooms, as well as fewer amenities. That said, a less-than-ideal location should be the least of your concerns. Many moderately priced accommodations are still within the central hubs; some have an old-fashioned charm and a personal touch the upscale places can't provide. However, wherever you're staying, Tokyo's subway and train system—comfortable (except in rush hours), efficient, inexpensive, and safe—gets you back and forth.

TIMING

We highly recommend making your Tokyo hotel reservation before you arrive, especially if traveling during Japan's peak holiday periods—late April to early May, August, and the New Year period.

WHAT IT COSTS IN YEN

	$	$$	$$$	$$$$
Hotels	under ¥15,000	¥15,000–¥30,000	¥30,001–¥45,000	over ¥45,000

Prices in the reviews are the lowest cost of a standard double room in high season.

WESTERN-STYLE LODGING OPTIONS

If culture shock has taken its toll, or you're simply looking for the standard amenities you associate with a hotel stay, try booking one of these options.

INTERNATIONAL HOTELS

Japan's international hotels resemble their counterparts the world over—expect Western-style quarters, English-speaking staff, and high room rates—and they are among the most expensive, tending to fall into the higher price categories.

Most major Western hotel chains, including Hilton, Hyatt, and Sheraton, have built hotels across Japan. Virtually all these properties have Western and Japanese restaurants, room service, Wi-Fi, minibars, *yukata* (cotton robes), concierge services, porters, and business and fitness centers. A few also have swimming pools. And a handful offer

WHERE SHOULD I STAY?

	Neighborhood Vibe	Pros	Cons
Ueno	Entertainment area with rail hub	Large park in area; convenient access to Narita Airport	Few entertainment options in surrounding area
Asakusa	Historic temple area with quaint shops and restaurants	Plenty of shops selling souvenirs; historic area	Not exactly central
Shiodome	Bay-side district of office towers	Numerous hotel options; nearby park	Access for pedestrians can be confusing
Ginza	High-end area with shopping and restaurants	Numerous gallery, restaurant, and shopping options	Can be expensive; a bit sterile
Nihombashi	Historic district that has grown into a trendy dining and shopping spot	Traditional area with numerous restaurant choices	Quiet on weekends
Marunouchi	Business area with numerous shopping and restaurant options	Convenient access to transportation; plenty of shops and restaurants	Business area with a businesslike feel
Aoyama and Akasaka	Business area with lively nightlife scene	Located in central Tokyo; many restaurant and bar choices	Can be noisy and crowded
Shibuya	Shopping and dining playground for young people	Fashionable; many shops, bars, and restaurants	Can be noisy and crowded; Ebisu section can be pricey
Roppongi	Entertainment and business district	Plenty of bars and restaurants; central location	Oftentimes crowded and noisy
Shinjuku	Large business and entertainment area	Lively entertainment; many hotel choices; convenient access to transportation	Can be noisy and crowded
Mejiro	Residential area	Pleasant, often overlooked area of Tokyo	Surrounding neighborhoods might offer little of interest
Odaiba	Man-made island popular with tourists	Amusement parks in area; views of Tokyo Bay	Not located in a central location; touristy

Japanese-style rooms—with tatami mats and futons—but these are more expensive.

BUSINESS HOTELS

Business hotels are for travelers who need only a place to leave luggage, sleep, and change. Rooms are small; a lone traveler often takes a double, as singles can feel claustrophobic. Each room has a phone, desk, TV (rarely with English-language channels), slippers, yukata, and bath with a prefabricated plastic tub, shower, and sink. These bathrooms are usually clean, but if you're basketball-player size, you might have trouble standing up in them. Other than those facilities, you'll probably only find a restaurant and perhaps a 24-hour receptionist, who probably doesn't speak English. Business hotels are generally near railway stations. Most fall into the more moderate price categories.

JAPANESE-STYLE LODGING OPTIONS

Looking for someplace to rest your head that echoes the Japanese experience? There are numerous options: ryokan, capsule hotels, home visits, or a stay in a traditional temple.

RYOKAN

There are two kinds of ryokan. One is an expensive traditional inn, where you're served dinner and breakfast in your room and given lots of personal attention. Rates at such places can be exorbitant—more than ¥30,000 per person per night with two meals. The other type is an inexpensive hostelry, whose rooms come with futon beds, tatami floor mats, a scroll or a flower arrangement in its rightful place, and, occasionally, meal service.

Tokyo ryokan fall in the latter category. They're often family-run, and service is less a matter of professionalism than of goodwill. Many have rooms either with or without baths (where tubs are likely to be plastic rather than cedarwood) as well as street, rather than garden, views. Because they have few rooms and the owners are usually on hand to answer questions, these small ryokan are as hospitable as they are affordable (from ¥5,000 for a single room to ¥7,000 for a double). Younger travelers love them. ■**TIP→ Many modern hotels with Japanese-style rooms are now referring to themselves as ryokan, and though meals may be served in the guests' rooms, they are a far cry from the traditional ryokan.**

Note that some ryokan do not like to have foreign guests because the owners worry that they might not be familiar with traditional-inn etiquette. ⇨ *For more information on what's expected of guests at traditional ryokan, see the Ryokan Etiquette feature in Chapter 2.*

CAPSULE HOTELS

Capsule hotels consist of plastic cubicles stacked one atop another. "Rooms" are a mere 3½ feet wide, 3½ feet high, and 7¼ feet long, and they're usually occupied by junior business travelers, backpackers, late-night revelers, or commuters who have missed the last train home. Each capsule has a bed, an intercom, an alarm clock, and a TV. Washing and toilet facilities are shared. Although you may want to try sleeping in a capsule, you probably won't want to spend a week in one. ■**TIP→ Capsule hotels have single accommodations only and most have no women-only facilities.**

TEMPLES

Accommodations in Buddhist temples provide a taste of traditional Japan. Some have instruction in meditation or allow you to observe their religious practices, while others simply provide a room. The Japanese-style rooms are very simple and range from beautiful, quiet havens to not-so-comfortable, basic cubicles. JNTO has lists of temples that accept guests. A stay generally costs ¥3,000–¥9,000 per night, which includes two meals.

5

RESERVATIONS

The Japanese Inn Group is a nationwide association of small ryokan and family-owned tourist hotels. Because they tend to be slightly out of the way and provide few amenities, these accommodations are priced to attract budget-minded travelers. The association has the active support of JNTO.

The JNTO Tourism Information Center publishes a listing of some 700 reasonably priced accommodations in Tokyo and throughout Japan. To be listed, properties must meet Japanese fire codes and charge less than ¥8,000 per person without meals. For the most part, the properties charge ¥5,000–¥6,000. These properties welcome foreigners. Properties include business hotels, ryokan of a very rudimentary nature, and minshuku. It's the luck of the draw whether you choose a good or less-than-good property. In most cases rooms are clean but very small. Except in business hotels, shared baths are the norm, and you are expected to have your room lights out by 10. The JNTO's downtown Tokyo office is open daily 9 to 5.

Contacts IACE Travel. ✉ *Tokyo* ☎ *877/489–4223* 🌐 *www.iace-asia.com.* **JNTO Tourist Information Center.** ✉ *Tokyo* 🌐 *www.jnto.go.jp.*

Japan Travel Agents JTB Global Marketing & Travel. ✉ *Tokyo* ☎ *03/5796–5454* 🌐 *www.jtb-sunrisetours.jp.* **Nippon Travel Agency.** ✉ *Tokyo* ☎ *03/6895–8355* 🌐 *www.ntainbound.com.*

Online Accommodations Japan Hotel.net. ✉ *Tokyo* 🌐 *www.japanhotel.net.* **Japan-Hotel-Reserve.** ✉ *Tokyo* 🌐 *www.japan-hotel-reserve.jp.* **Rakuten Travel.** ✉ *Tokyo* 🌐 *travel.rakuten.com.*

LODGING REVIEWS

Hotel reviews have been shortned. For full information, visit Fodors.com. Use the coordinate (✣ B2) at the end of each listing to locate a site on the Where to Stay in Tokyo map.

IMPERIAL PALACE 皇居近辺

$$$$
HOTEL
Fodor's Choice ★

Aman Tokyo (アマン東京). Mixing modern design with Japanese aesthetics, the Aman Tokyo is more than a hotel; it is an experience in the center of the city. **Pros:** immaculate; blend of Japanese aesthetics and modernity; wonderful views. **Cons:** expensive. *$ Rooms from: ¥90000 ✉ The Otemachi Tower, 1–5–6 Otemachi, Chiyoda-ku ☎ 03/5224–3333 🌐 www.amanresorts.com 52 guest rooms, 32 suites No meals Ⓜ Hanzomon, Chiyoda, Tozai, and Marunouchi subway lines, Otemachi Station (Exits C11 and C8) ✣ F3.*

BEST BETS FOR TOKYO LODGING

Fodor's offers a selective listing of quality lodging in every price range, from Tokyo's best budget beds to its most sophisticated luxury hotels. Here, we've compiled our top picks by price and experience.

Fodor's Choice★

Aman Tokyo, $$$$
Andaz Tokyo Toranomon Hills, $$$$
The Capitol Hotel Tokyu, $$$
Four Seasons Hotel Tokyo at Marunouchi, $$$$
The Gate Hotel Kaminarimon, $$
Hotel Ryumeikan Tokyo, $$
Mandarin Oriental Tokyo, $$$$
Palace Hotel Tokyo, $$$
Park Hotel Tokyo, $$
Park Hyatt Tokyo, $$$$
The Ritz-Carlton Tokyo, $$$$

Best by Price

$

the b akasaka
Hotel Asia Center of Japan
Hotel Niwa Tokyo
nine hours
Ryokan Mikawaya Honten

$$

Citadines Shinjuku Tokyo
Claska
The Gate Hotel Kaminarimon
Hotel Ryumeikan Tokyo
Mitsui Garden Hotel Ginza Premier
Park Hotel Tokyo
The Prince Park Tower Tokyo

$$$

ANA InterContinental Tokyo
The Capitol Hotel Tokyu
Palace Hotel Tokyo
The Strings by InterContinental Tokyo
Tokyo Station Hotel

$$$$

Aman Tokyo
Andaz Tokyo Toranomon Hills
Four Seasons Hotel Tokyo at Marunouchi
Mandarin Oriental Tokyo
Park Hyatt Tokyo
The Ritz-Carlton Tokyo

Best by Experience

BEST CONCIERGE

Four Seasons Hotel Tokyo at Marunouchi, $$$$
Mandarin Oriental Tokyo, $$$$
The Ritz-Carlton Tokyo, $$$$
Shangri-La Hotel Tokyo, $$$$
The Strings by InterContinental Tokyo, $$$
Westin Tokyo, $$

BEST HOTEL BARS

Andaz Tokyo Toranomon Hills, $$$$
The Gate Hotel Kaminarimon, $$
Grand Hyatt Tokyo at Roppongi Hills, $$$$
Imperial Hotel, $$$
Park Hyatt Tokyo, $$$$

BEST-KEPT SECRETS

Citadines Shinjuku Tokyo, $$
The Gate Hotel Kaminarimon, $$
Hotel Century Southern Tower, $$$$
Hotel Ryumeikan Tokyo, $$$
The Strings by InterContinental Tokyo, $$$$

BEST LOCATION

Courtyard by Marriott Tokyo Station, $$$
Four Seasons Hotel Tokyo at Marunouchi, $$$$
Hotel Century Southern Tower, $$
The Peninsula Tokyo, $$$$
Shibuya Excel Hotel Tokyu, $$

BEST FOR ROMANCE

Aman Tokyo, $$$$
Andaz Tokyo Toranomon Hills, $$$$
Grand Pacific Le Daiba, $$
Park Hyatt Tokyo, $$$$
The Ritz-Carlton Tokyo, $$$$

MOST KID-FRIENDLY

Asakusa View Hotel, $$
Prince Hotel Shinagawa, $$
The Prince Park Tower Tokyo, $$
Tokyo Dome Hotel, $$

5

$$$ HOTEL **Imperial Hotel** (帝国ホテル). Though not as fashionable or as spanking-new as its neighbor, the Peninsula, the venerable Imperial can't be beat for traditional elegance. **Pros:** an old Japanese hotel with a long history; great service; large rooms. **Cons:** layout can be confusing; some rooms have dated interiors. *Rooms from: ¥31000 ✉ 1–1–1 Uchisaiwai-cho, Chiyoda-ku ☎ 03/3504–1111 🌐 www.imperialhotel.co.jp 875 rooms, 56 suites No meals Ⓜ Hibiya subway line, Hibiya Station (Exit 5) ✥ E4.*

$$$ HOTEL Fodor's Choice ★ **Palace Hotel Tokyo** (パレスホテル東京). This hotel has a handsome, refined look that sets the stage for a luxury experience. **Pros:** great location; tasteful design; wonderful service; complimentary in-room Wi-Fi. **Cons:** on the pricey side; charge to use the pool. *Rooms from: ¥45000 ✉ 1–1–1 Marunouchi, Chiyoda-ku ☎ 03/3211–5211 🌐 www.en.palacehoteltokyo.com 278 guest rooms, 12 suites No meals Ⓜ Chiyoda, Tozai, Hanzomon subway lines, Otemachi Station (Exit C13) ✥ F3.*

$$$$ HOTEL **The Peninsula Tokyo** (ザ・ペニンシュラ東京). From the staff in caps and sharp suits, often assisting guests from a Rolls-Royce shuttling to and from Narita, to the shimmering gold glow emitting from the top floors, the 24-floor Peninsula Tokyo exudes elegance and grace. **Pros:** first-class room interiors; luxurious details; wonderful spa; great service. **Cons:** high prices; public areas can be crowded. *Rooms from: ¥52000 ✉ 1–8–1 Yuraku-cho, Chiyoda-ku ☎ 03/6270–2888 🌐 www.peninsula.com 267 rooms, 47 suites No meals Ⓜ JR Yamanote Line, Yuraku-cho Station (Hibiya-guchi/Hibiya Exit); Mita, Chiyoda, and Hibiya subway lines, Hibiya Station (Exits A6 and A7) ✥ F4.*

AKIHABARA 秋葉原

Located in the middle of the city, nearby Suido-bashi has loads of rail options and proximity to Tokyo Dome and other nearby attractions.

$ HOTEL **Hotel Niwa Tokyo** (庭のホテル 東京). Traditional and contemporary elements come together to make the Niwa Tokyo a prized little boutique hotel in the middle of the city. **Pros:** affordable; quiet area; central location; charming Japanese touches. **Cons:** small rooms; finding entrance is a bit challenging. *Rooms from: ¥11000 ✉ 1–1–16 Misaki-cho, Chiyoda-ku ☎ 03/3293–0028 🌐 www.hotelniwa.jp 238 rooms No meals Ⓜ JR Chuo or Sobu lines, Suido-bashi Station (East Exit); Mita subway line, Suido-bashi Station (Exit A1) ✥ E2.*

$$ HOTEL FAMILY **Tokyo Dome Hotel** (東京ドームホテル). Next to the city's most popular sports facility, the Tokyo Dome Hotel has a great location for sports fans at a comfortable price. **Pros:** convenient location; solid value; great for kids. **Cons:** no gym; in-room amenities are limited. *Rooms from: ¥17000 ✉ 1–3–61 Koraku, Bunkyo-ku ☎ 03/5805–2111 🌐 www.tokyodome-hotels.co.jp/e 978 guest rooms, 28 suites No meals Ⓜ JR lines, Suidobashi Station (East Exit); Namboku and Marunouchi subway lines, Korakuen Station ✥ E1.*

UENO 上野

One of Tokyo's largest rail hubs, Ueno is considered old-fashioned compared to other neighborhoods, and as such, it contains a number of ryokans.

$ B&B/INN **Ryokan Katsutaro** (旅館勝太郎). Established four decades ago, this small, simple, economical inn is a five-minute walk from the entrance to Ueno Koen (Ueno Park) and a 10-minute walk from the Tokyo National Museum. **Pros:** a traditional and unique Japanese experience; reasonably priced room rates; free Wi-Fi. **Cons:** no breakfast served; small baths; some rooms have shared Japanese baths. *Rooms from: ¥10000 ✉ 4–16–8 Ikenohata, Taito-ku ☎ 03/3821–9808 🌐 www.katsutaro.com 8 Japanese-style rooms, 4 with bath No meals Ⓜ Chiyoda subway line, Nezu Station (Exit 2) ✣ F1.*

$ B&B/INN **Sawanoya Ryokan** (澤の屋旅館). The shitamachi sub-area of Ueno is known for its down-to-earth friendliness, which you get in full measure at Sawanoya. **Pros:** traditional Japanese experience; affordable rates; friendly management. **Cons:** rooms somewhat small; a bit of a hike to the subway station; must book well in advance; many rooms share Japanese baths. *Rooms from: ¥10000 ✉ 2–3–11 Yanaka, Taito-ku ☎ 03/3822–2251 🌐 www.sawanoya.com 10 rooms, 2 with bath No meals Ⓜ Chiyoda subway line, Nezu Station (Exit 1) ✣ F1.*

ASAKUSA 浅草

Thanks to its historic attractions, Asakusa mainly caters to tourists. Standard hotels are available, but many come here for its selection of ryokan inns.

$$ HOTEL FAMILY **Asakusa View Hotel** (浅草ビューホテル). The box-shape Asakusa View is the largest Western-style hotel in the traditional Asakusa area. **Pros:** affordable, located in a historic temple area, , free in room Wi-Fi. **Cons:** room interiors generally basic; not near central Tokyo; only one key provided per room. *Rooms from: ¥16000 ✉ 3–17–1 Nishi-Asakusa, Asakusa ☎ 03/3847–1111 🌐 www.viewhotels.co.jp/asakusa 323 rooms, 3 suites No meals Ⓜ Ginza subway line, Tawara-machi Station (Exit 3) ✣ I11.*

$$ HOTEL Fodor's Choice ★ **The Gate Hotel Kaminarimon** (ザ・ゲートホテル雷門). This relative newcomer to the historic Asakusa area presents a certain stylish flair, starting from the entrance, where an elevator whisks you up 13 floors to the beautiful, glass-walled lobby. **Pros:** historic area; surrounded with great dining options; lovely views. **Cons:** rooms small by Western standards; not exactly a central location; can be crowded on weekends. *Rooms from: ¥16000 ✉ 2–16–11 Kaminarimon, Taito-ku ☎ 03/5826–3877 🌐 www.gate-hotel.jp 134 guest rooms, 3 suites No meals Ⓜ Ginza and Asakusa subway lines, Asakusa Station (Exit 2) ✣ H1.*

$$ B&B/INN **Ryokan Asakusa Shigetsu** (旅館浅草 指月). Just off Nakamise-dori and inside the Senso-ji grounds, this small inn, with both Japanese- and Western-style rooms, could not be better located for a visit to the temple. **Pros:** affordable rooms; located in a historic temple area; close to subway station. **Cons:** not convenient to central Tokyo; some guests may feel uncomfortable with futon beds and communal Japanese bathing.

5

Rooms from: ¥16000 ✉ 1–31–11 Asakusa, Asakusa ☎ 03/3843–2345 🌐 www.shigetsu.com/e/index.html 15 Japanese-style rooms, 6 Western-style rooms No meals Ⓜ Ginza subway line, Asakusa Station (Exit 1/Kaminari-mon Exit) ✥ H1.

$ B&B/INN **Ryokan Mikawaya Honten** (旅館三河屋本店). In the heart of Asakusa, this concrete ryokan is just behind the Kaminari-mon, the gateway leading to the Senso-ji complex. **Pros:** affordable accommodations; traditional Japanese experience; interesting shopping in the area. **Cons:** futons and tatami might not be suitable for those accustomed to Western-style beds; small rooms; friendly staff struggles with English. *Rooms from: ¥9700 ✉ 1–30–12 Asakusa, Asakusa ☎ 03/3841–8954 🌐 www.asakusamikawaya.com 15 rooms No meals Ⓜ Ginza subway line, Asakusa Station (Exit 1/Kaminari-mon Exit) ✥ H1.*

SHIODOME 汐留

Located between Shinagawa and Tokyo stations, Shiodome has a number of medium- and high-end lodging options. Hotels stay perched above the city, on the upper floors of the area's skyscrapers.

$$$$ HOTEL **Conrad Tokyo** (コンラッド東京). The Conrad, part of the Hilton family, welcomes you to the space age with a Japanese twist. **Pros:** modern design; fantastic bay view; fine restaurants. **Cons:** very expensive; finding the entrance to the elevator is troublesome; charge to use pool and gym. *Rooms from: ¥50000 ✉ 1–9–1 Higashi-Shimbashi, Minato-ku, Shiodome ☎ 03/6388–8000 🌐 www.conradtokyo.co.jp 222 rooms, 68 suites No meals Ⓜ JR Yamanote Line, Shimbashi Station (Shiodome Exit); Oedo subway line, Shiodome Station (Exit 9) ✥ F5.*

$$ HOTEL Fodor's Choice ★ **Park Hotel Tokyo** (パークホテル東京). Comfortable beds, large bathrooms, and sweeping panoramas of Tokyo or the bay—it's easy to see why the guest rooms of this reasonably priced "artist" hotel remain a tourist favorite. **Pros:** great value; guest rooms and public areas are stylish; excellent concierge service. **Cons:** small rooms; few in-room frills; no pool or gym. *Rooms from: ¥17000 ✉ 1–7–1 Higashi Shimbashi, Minato-ku ☎ 03/6252–1111 🌐 www.parkhoteltokyo.com 272 rooms, 1 suite No meals Ⓜ JR Yamanote Line, Shimbashi Station (Shiodome Exit); Oedo subway line, Shiodome Station (Exit 10) ✥ E5.*

NIHOMBASHI 日本橋

A historic area to the east, Nihombashi is primarily a stopover for business travelers. Some high-end accommodations are available, but you can also find good budget options.

$$$$ HOTEL Fodor's Choice ★ **Mandarin Oriental, Tokyo** (マンダリン オリエンタル 東京). Occupying the top nine floors of the glistening Nihombashi Mitsui Tower, this hotel is a blend of harmony and outright modernity. **Pros:** wonderful spa and concierge service; nice city views; attractive room interiors. **Cons:** pricey; quiet area on the weekends; no pool. *Rooms from: ¥50000 ✉ 2–1–1 Nihombashi Muromachi, Chuo-ku ☎ 03/3270–8800 🌐 www.mandarinoriental.com/tokyo 157 rooms, 21 suites No meals Ⓜ Ginza and Hanzo-mon subway lines, Mitsukoshi-mae Station (Exit A7) ✥ G3.*

$$ HOTEL **Royal Park Hotel** (ロイヤルパークホテル). A passageway connects this hotel to the Tokyo City Air Terminal, where you can easily catch a bus to Narita Airport, making the Royal Park a great one-night stopover option. **Pros:** convenient airport access; nice lobby; warm, friendly service. **Cons:** not located near downtown; immediate area deserted on weekends. *Rooms from: ¥18000 2–1–1 Nihombashi, Kakigara-cho, Chuo-ku 03/3667–1111 www.rph.co.jp 398 rooms, 9 suites No meals Hanzo-mon subway line, Suitengu-mae Station (Exit 4) H3.*

$ HOTEL **Sumisho Hotel** (住庄ほてる). Set in a down-to-earth, friendly neighborhood, this hotel is popular with budget-minded foreign visitors who prefer to stay near the small Japanese restaurants and bars of the Ningyo-cho area of Nihombashi. **Pros:** nicely priced; friendly staff; neighborhood restaurants and pubs have great food for a good price. **Cons:** small rooms and baths; not particularly stylish; quiet area on weekends. *Rooms from: ¥8000 9–14 Nihombashi-Kobunacho, Chuo-ku 03/3661–1603 www.sumisho-hotel.co.jp 83 rooms No meals Hibiya and Asakusa subway lines, Ningyo-cho Station (Exit A5) G3.*

5

GINZA 銀座

The ritzy Ginza area is a blend of business and entertainment. Domestic chain hotels are a visitor's sure bet here.

$ HOTEL **Hotel Monterey Ginza** (ホテルモントレー銀座). Yes, the faux-stone exterior that attempts to replicate 20th century Europe is a bit cheesy, but the Monterey remains a bargain in the middle of Ginza. **Pros:** multiple shopping choices in area; central location; reasonable prices considering the area. **Cons:** design lacks elegance; rooms are a tad small and a bit outdated; in-hotel dining options are limited. *Rooms from: Y10000 1–10–18 Ginza, Chuo-ku 03/3544–7111 www.hotelmonterey.co.jp/ginza 224 rooms No meals Ginza subway line, Ginza Station (Exit A13) F4.*

$$ HOTEL **Mitsui Garden Hotel Ginza Premier** (三井ガーデンホテル銀座プレミア). A winning combination—chic and reasonable—this hotel occupies the top of the 38-floor Nihonbashi Mitsui Tower at the edge of bustling Ginza. **Pros:** affordable; sharp design; convenient location; plenty of nearby shopping. **Cons:** small rooms; in-hotel restaurant a tad pricey; geared toward business rather than leisure travelers. *Rooms from: ¥19000 8–13–1 Ginza, Chūō-ku, Ginza 03/3543–1131 www.gardenhotels.co.jp/eng/ginzapremier 361 rooms No meals Ginza subway line, Ginza Station (Exit A3) or JR Shimbashi Station (Ginza Exit) F4.*

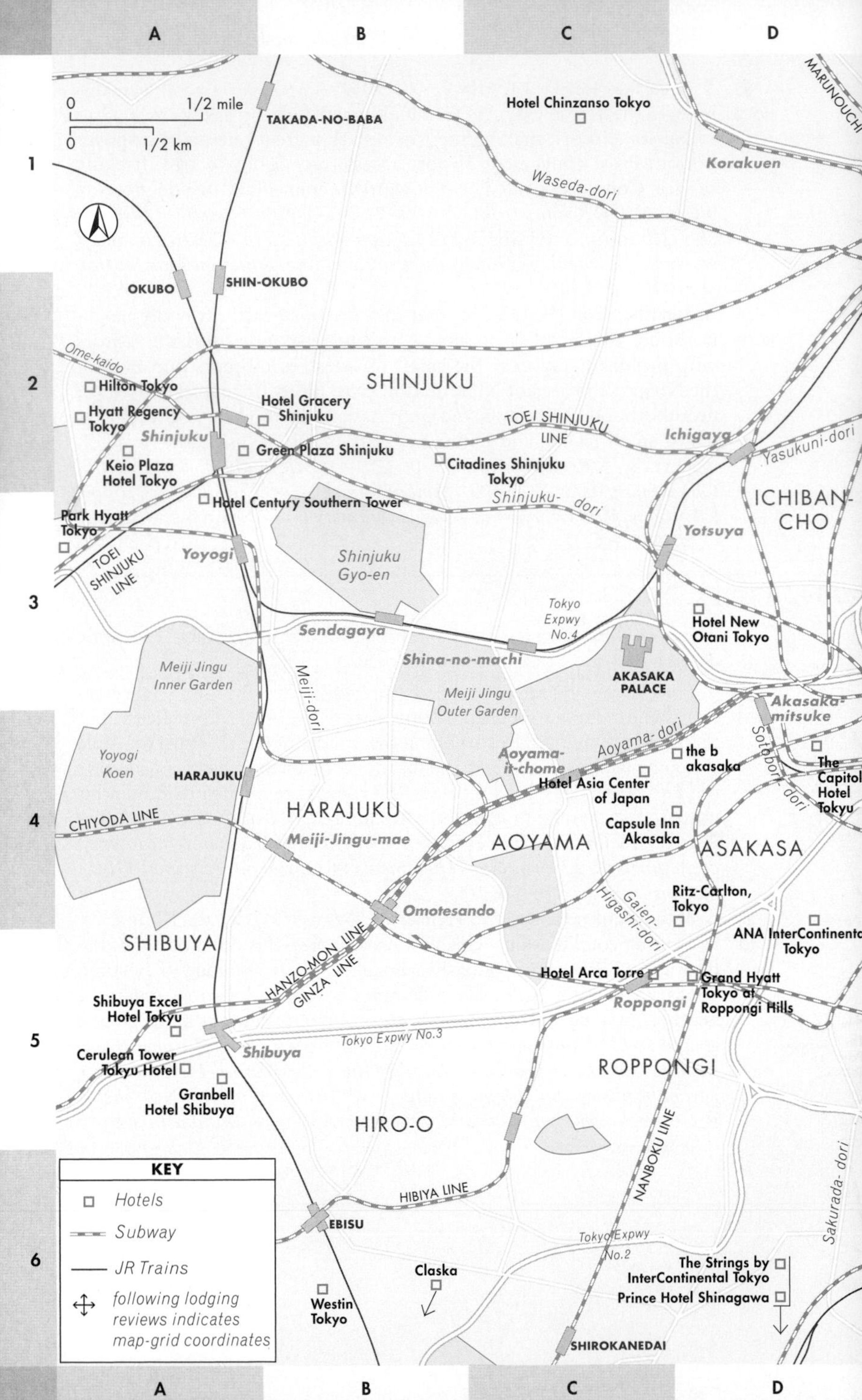

A
B
C
D
1
2
3
4
5
6
0
1/2 mile
0
1/2 km
TAKADA-NO-BABA
Hotel Chinzanso Tokyo
MARUNOUCHI
Korakuen
Waseda-dori
OKUBO
SHIN-OKUBO
Ome-kaido
Hilton Tokyo
Hyatt Regency Tokyo
Shinjuku
Keio Plaza Hotel Tokyo
Hotel Gracery Shinjuku
Green Plaza Shinjuku
SHINJUKU
TOEI SHINJUKU LINE
Citadines Shinjuku Tokyo
Ichigaya
Yasukuni-dori
Hotel Century Southern Tower
Shinjuku-dori
Park Hyatt Tokyo
ICHIBAN-CHO
Yotsuya
TOEI SHINJUKU LINE
Yoyogi
Shinjuku Gyo-en
Tokyo Expwy No.4
Hotel New Otani Tokyo
Sendagaya
Shina-no-machi
Meiji Jingu Inner Garden
Meiji-dori
AKASAKA PALACE
Meiji Jingu Outer Garden
Akasaka-mitsuke
Yoyogi Koen
HARAJUKU
Aoyama-itchome
Aoyama-dori
the b akasaka
Sotobori-dori
The Capitol Hotel Tokyu
Hotel Asia Center of Japan
HARAJUKU
CHIYODA LINE
Capsule Inn Akasaka
Meiji-Jingu-mae
AOYAMA
ASAKASA
Omotesando
Gaien-Higashi-dori
Ritz-Carlton, Tokyo
ANA InterContinental Tokyo
SHIBUYA
HANZO-MON LINE
GINZA LINE
Hotel Arca Torre
Grand Hyatt Tokyo at Roppongi Hills
Roppongi
Shibuya Excel Hotel Tokyu
Cerulean Tower Tokyu Hotel
Shibuya
Tokyo Expwy No.3
ROPPONGI
Granbell Hotel Shibuya
HIRO-O
NANBOKU LINE
Sakurada-dori
KEY
Hotels
Subway
JR Trains
following lodging reviews indicates map-grid coordinates
HIBIYA LINE
EBISU
Tokyo Expwy No.2
Claska
Westin Tokyo
The Strings by InterContinental Tokyo
Prince Hotel Shinagawa
SHIROKANEDAI

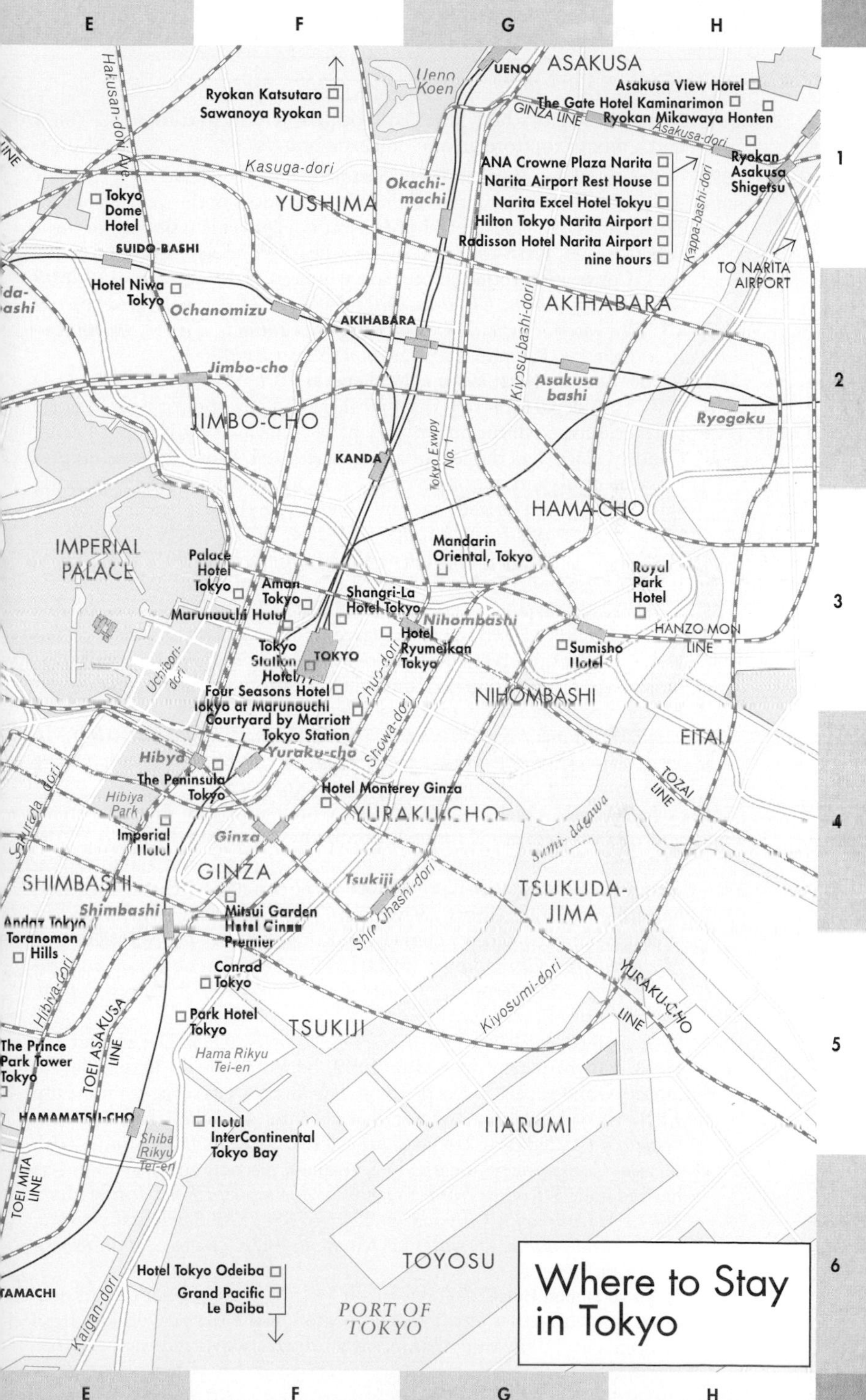

E
F
G
H
1
2
3
4
5
6
Where to Stay in Tokyo
Ryokan Katsutaro
Sawanoya Ryokan
Ueno Koen
UENO
ASAKUSA
Asakusa View Hotel
The Gate Hotel Kaminarimon
GINZA LINE
Ryokan Mikawaya Honten
Asakusa-dori
Ryokan Asakusa Shigetsu
Hakusan-dori Ave.
Kasuga-dori
ANA Crowne Plaza Narita
Narita Airport Rest House
Narita Excel Hotel Tokyu
Hilton Tokyo Narita Airport
Radisson Hotel Narita Airport
nine hours
Kappa-bashi-dori
TO NARITA AIRPORT
Tokyo Dome Hotel
YUSHIMA
Okachi-machi
SUIDO-BASHI
Hotel Niwa Tokyo
Ochanomizu
AKIHABARA
AKIHABARA
Kiyosu-bashi-dori
Jimbo-cho
Asakusa bashi
Ryogoku
JIMBO-CHO
KANDA
Tokyo Exwpy No. 1
HAMA-CHO
IMPERIAL PALACE
Palace Hotel Tokyo
Aman Tokyo
Mandarin Oriental, Tokyo
Shangri-La Hotel Tokyo
Royal Park Hotel
Marunouchi Hotel
Nihombashi
Hotel Ryumeikan Tokyo
HANZO MON LINE
Tokyo Station Hotel
TOKYO
Sumisho Hotel
Uchibori-dori
Chuo-dori
Four Seasons Hotel Tokyo at Marunouchi
Courtyard by Marriott Tokyo Station
NIHOMBASHI
Showa-dori
EITAI
Hibiya
Yuraku-cho
The Peninsula Tokyo
TOZAI LINE
Hotel Monterey Ginza
Sakurada-dori
Hibiya Park
YURAKUCHO
Imperial Hotel
Ginza
Sumi-dagawa
GINZA
Tsukiji
SHIMBASHI
TSUKUDA-JIMA
Shimbashi
Shin Ohashi-dori
Mitsui Garden Hotel Ginza Premier
Andaz Tokyo Toranomon Hills
Conrad Tokyo
Hibiya-dori
Kiyosumi-dori
YURAKU-CHO LINE
Park Hotel Tokyo
TSUKIJI
TOEI ASAKUSA LINE
The Prince Park Tower Tokyo
Hama Rikyu Tei-en
HAMAMATSU-CHO
Hotel InterContinental Tokyo Bay
HARUMI
Shiba Rikyu Tei-en
TOEI MITA LINE
TOYOSU
Hotel Tokyo Odeiba
Grand Pacific Le Daiba
TAMACHI
Kaigan-dori
PORT OF TOKYO

MARUNOUCHI 丸の内

Some of the city's best hotels are located here in Marunouchi. You'll find a mix of top foreign and domestic brands.

$$$ HOTEL **Courtyard by Marriott Tokyo Station** (コートヤード・バイ・マリオット東京ステーション). Situated on the first four floors of the sleek Kyobashi Trust Tower, the Courtyard by Marriott is a convenient option for business travelers. **Pros:** convenient; many nearby dining options; attentive staff. **Cons:** small rooms; closet space limited. *Rooms from: ¥32000* ✉ *2–1–3 Kyobashi, Chuo-ku* ☎ *03/5488–3923* 🌐 *www.cytokyo.com* *150 guest rooms* *No meals* Ⓜ *Ginza subway line, Kyobashi Station (Exit 1); JR lines, Tokyo Station (Yaesu Exit)* ✣ *F4.*

$$$$ HOTEL Fodor's Choice ★ **Four Seasons Hotel Tokyo at Marunouchi** (フォーシーズンズホテル丸の内東京). A departure from the typical grand scale of most Four Seasons properties, the Marunouchi branch, set within the glistening Pacific Century Place, has the feel of a boutique hotel. **Pros:** supreme luxury; convenient airport access; central location; helpful, English-speaking staff. **Cons:** high priced; the only views are those of nearby Tokyo Station. *Rooms from: ¥50000* ✉ *1–11–1 Marunouchi, Chiyoda-ku* ☎ *03/5222–7222* 🌐 *www.fourseasons.com/marunouchi* *48 rooms, 9 suites* *No meals* Ⓜ *JR Tokyo Station (Yaesu South Exit)* ✣ *F3.*

$$ HOTEL Fodor's Choice ★ **Hotel Ryumeikan Tokyo** (ホテル龍名館東京). One of the most affordable hotels near Tokyo Station (a mere three-minute walk away), the Ryumeikan is a great option for the business traveler or those making side trips outside the city. **Pros:** great, convenient location; wonderful restaurant; English-speaking staff. **Cons:** busy area during the week; rooms can feel small. *Rooms from: ¥19000* ✉ *1–3–22 Yaesu, Chuo-ku* ☎ *03/3271–0971* 🌐 *www.ryumeikan-tokyo.jp/english* *134 guest rooms, 1 suite* *No meals* Ⓜ *JR Tokyo Station (Yaesu North Exit)* ✣ *F3.*

$$ HOTEL **Marunouchi Hotel** (丸ノ内ホテル). Convenience is one reason to choose the Marunouchi Hotel, occupying the upper 11 floors of the Marunouchi Oazo Building and joining Tokyo Station via an underground walkway. **Pros:** convenient airport access; central location; helpful concierge. **Cons:** designed for business travelers; rooms are smallish; limited dining choices. *Rooms from: ¥24000* ✉ *1–6–3 Marunouchi, Chiyoda-ku* ☎ *03/3217–1111* 🌐 *www.marunouchi-hotel.co.jp* *204 rooms, 1 suite* *No meals* Ⓜ *JR Tokyo Station (Marunouchi North Exit)* ✣ *F3.*

$$$$ HOTEL **Shangri-La Hotel Tokyo** (シャングリ・ラ ホテル 東京). The Shangri-La Hotel Tokyo, which opened in 2009, boasts high-end luxury, lavish interiors, and superb views of Tokyo Bay and the cityscape from the top 11 floors of Marunouchi Trust Tower Main, a 37-floor building conveniently located near Tokyo Station. **Pros:** convenient location; lavish service. **Cons:** pricey; located in a business district; entrance might be hard to find. *Rooms from: ¥51000* ✉ *Marunouchi Trust Tower Main, 1–8–3 Marunouchi, Chiyoda-ku* ☎ *03/6739–7888* 🌐 *www.shangri-la.com* *184 rooms, 16 suites* *No meals* Ⓜ *JR Tokyo Station (Yaesu North Exit)* ✣ *F3.*

$$$ HOTEL **Tokyo Station Hotel** (東京ステーションホテル). Convenience and nostalgia come together at this hotel, located inside the busy Tokyo train station, a grand building that recently refurbished its redbrick exterior.

Pros: convenient location; easy access to shopping; lovely, historic setting; helpful English-speaking staff. **Cons:** rooms on the small side; views from some rooms limited. *Rooms from: ¥45000 ✉ 1–9–1 Marunouchi, Chiyoda-ku ☎ 03/5220–1111 ⊕ www.tokyostationhotel.jp ⇒ 145 guest rooms, 5 suites No meals Ⓜ JR Line, Tokyo Station (South Exit) ✥ F3.*

AOYAMA AND AKASAKA 青山

An entertainment and business district in the middle of the city, Akasaka is buzzing around the clock. Accommodations can range from high-end international brands to pared-down capsule hotels.

$$$ HOTEL **ANA InterContinental Tokyo** (インターコンチネンタルホテル東京 *ANA*). With a central location and modest pricing, the ANA is a great choice for the business traveler, and its ziggurat-atrium points to the heyday of the power lunch: the mid-1980s. **Pros:** great concierge; wonderful city views; spacious lobby. **Cons:** charge for in-room Internet; room bathrooms a bit small. *Rooms from: ¥31000 ✉ 1–12–33 Akasaka, Minato-ku ☎ 03/3505–1111 ⊕ www.anaintercontinental-tokyo.jp ⇒ 801 rooms, 43 suites No meals Ⓜ Ginza and Namboku subway lines, Tameike-Sanno Station (Exit 13); Namboku subway line, Roppongi-itchome Station (Exit 3) ✥ D4.*

$$$$ HOTEL Fodor's Choice ★ **Andaz Tokyo Toranomon Hills** (アンダーズ東京). In 2014, Hyatt brought its high-end boutique brand Andaz to the Toranomon Hills complex with great fanfare. **Pros:** great bar; amazing views; huge bathrooms. **Cons:** finding entrance can be troublesome; expensive. *Rooms from: ¥49000 ✉ 1–23–4 Toranomon, Minato-ku ☎ 03/6830–1234 ⊕ www.tokyo.andaz.hyatt.jp ⇒ 156 guest rooms, 8 suites No meals Ⓜ Ginza subway line, Toranomon Station (Exit 1) ✥ E5.*

$ HOTEL **the b akasaka** (ザ・ビー赤坂). Part of a boutique chain that promotes its ability to deliver the five *bs*—bed, breakfast, balance, business, and benefits—the b akasaka is a simple, stylish option with great value. **Pros:** near large entertainment area; affordable. **Cons:** difficult to find; single rooms can feel confining. *Rooms from: ¥14000 ✉ 7–6–13 Akasaka, Minato-ku ☎ 03/3586–0811 ⊕ www.theb-hotels.com ⇒ 156 rooms No meals Ⓜ Chiyoda subway line, Akasaka Station (Exit 3B) ✥ D4.*

$$$ HOTEL Fodor's Choice ★ **The Capitol Hotel Tokyu** (ザ・キャピトルホテル東急). Everything old is new again: the Capitol, once a boxy 29-floor commercial complex designed by architect Kengo Kuma and run by Hilton, has a long history that includes hosting The Beatles. **Pros:** convenient location; beautiful and spacious pool; no charge for Wi-Fi throughout hotel. **Cons:** pricey; government district might not appeal to tourists. *Rooms from: ¥33000 ✉ 2–10–3 Nagata-cho, Minato-ku ☎ 03/3503–0109 ⊕ www.capitolhoteltokyu.com ⇒ 238 rooms, 13 suites No meals Ⓜ Ginza and Namboku subway lines, Tameike-Sanno Station (Exit 5) ✥ D4.*

5

$ HOTEL **Capsule Inn Akasaka** (かぷせるイン赤坂). Travelers looking for a budget option—or adventurous souls wanting a full-immersion experience—seek out the Capsule Inn. **Pros:** Wi-Fi; convenient location; unique experience. **Cons:** not for the claustrophobic; few services; women not allowed. *Rooms from: ¥3500 6–14–1 Akasaka, Minato-ku 03/3588–1811 www.marroad.jp/capsule 201 capsules No meals Chiyoda subway line, Akasaka Station (Exit 6) ↔ D4.*

$$ HOTEL **Hotel New Otani Tokyo** (ホテルニューオータニ東京). A bustling complex in the center of Tokyo—restaurants and shopping arcades beneath the sixth-floor lobby swarm with crowds—the New Otani can feel frantic, but its best feature, a spectacular 10-acre Japanese garden, readily visible from the appropriately named Garden Lounge, helps guests find sanctuary. **Pros:** beautiful garden; first-rate concierge; outdoor pool. **Cons:** complex layout could be off-putting; public areas a bit dated. *Rooms from: ¥20000 4–1 Kioi-cho, Chiyoda-ku 03/3265–1111 www.newotanihotels.com/tokyo 1,418 rooms, 61 suites No meals Ginza and Marunouchi subway lines, Akasaka-mitsuke Station (Exit 7) ↔ D3.*

SHIBUYA 渋谷

Shibuya is a shopping and entertainment Mecca for teens and twenty-somethings. Travelers appreciate the convenience of the multiple train lines and the central location.

$$$ HOTEL **Cerulean Tower Tokyu Hotel** (セルリアンタワー東急ホテル). Perched on a slope above Shibuya's chaos, the Cerulean Tower has a cavernous yet bustling lobby filled with plenty of attentive, English-speaking staffers. **Pros:** friendly, attentive service; great city views; convenient location. **Cons:** pricey rates; Shibuya is one of Tokyo's more crowded areas; building fronts a very busy street. *Rooms from: ¥31000 26–1 Sakuragaoka-cho, Shibuya-ku 03/3476–3000 www.ceruleantower-hotel.com 402 rooms, 9 suites No meals JR Shibuya Station (South Exit) ↔ A5.*

$ HOTEL **Granbell Hotel Shibuya** (渋谷グランベルホテル). Location, location, location—that's the Granbell, and with a minimalist pop-art style to boot. **Pros:** reasonable rates; great location; funky, fun design; free Wi-Fi throughout property. **Cons:** small rooms; neighborhood can be noisy; difficult to find hotel entrance. *Rooms from: ¥14000 15–17 Sakuragaoka–cho, Shibuya-ku 03/5457–2681 www.granbellhotel.jp 98 rooms, 7 suites No meals JR Shibuya Station (West Exit) ↔ A5.*

$$ HOTEL **Shibuya Excel Hotel Tokyu** (渋谷エクセル東急). The key to this unremarkable but very convenient hotel within the towering Mark City complex is access: local shopping and cheap dining options are aplenty, Shinjuku is a five-minute train ride to the north, and the Narita Express departs from nearby Shibuya Station frequently each morning. **Pros:** affordable; convenient location; friendly staff. **Cons:** small, uninspired rooms; crowds in the area can be intimidating. *Rooms from: ¥24000 1–12–2 Dogenzaka, Shibuya-ku 03/5457–0109 shibuya-e.tokyuhotels.com 407 rooms, 1 suite No meals JR Shibuya Station (Hachiko Exit) ↔ A5.*

ROPPONGI 六本木

A boisterous entertainment district, Roppongi has hotels for travelers who want to be in the thick of the action. Lodgings run the gamut from low-end budget inns to some of the world's top brands.

$$$$ **HOTEL** **Grand Hyatt Tokyo at Roppongi Hills** (グランドハイアット東京). Japanese refinement and a contemporary design come together perfectly at the Grand Hyatt—a tasteful and well-appointed hotel in the middle of Roppongi, one of Tokyo's top entertainment areas. **Pros:** great spa; wide range of restaurants; stunning rooms. **Cons:** pricey; easy to get lost in the building's complicated layout. *Rooms from: ¥50000 ✉ 6–10–3 Roppongi, Minato-ku, Roppongi ☎ 03/4333–1234 www.tokyo.grand.hyatt.com 359 rooms, 28 suites No meals Ⓜ Hibiya subway line, Roppongi Station (Exit 1A); Oedo subway line, Roppongi Station (Exit 3) ✣ D5.*

$$ **HOTEL** **Hotel Arca Torre** (ホテルアルカトーレ). Sitting on a coveted location in the heart of one of Tokyo's premier nightlife quarters, this European-inspired hotel is just a few minutes' walk from the Tokyo Midtown and Roppongi Hills shopping-and-entertainment complexes. **Pros:** affordable; convenient access to nightlife; free Wi-Fi. **Cons:** no room service; no closets; small rooms; neighborhood's bars and clubs make the area noisy. *Rooms from: ¥15000 ✉ 6–1–23 Roppongi, Minato-ku, Roppongi ☎ 03/3404–5111 www.arktower.co.jp/arcatorre 76 rooms No meals Ⓜ Hibiya and Oedo subway lines, Roppongi Station (Exit 3) ✣ C5.*

$ **HOTEL** **Hotel Asia Center of Japan** (ホテルアジア会館). Established mainly for Asian students and travelers on limited budgets, these accommodations have become popular due to their good value and easy access (a 15-minute walk) to the nightlife of Roppongi. **Pros:** affordable; great area for those who love the nightlife; free Wi-Fi. **Cons:** just one restaurant; no room service; small rooms. *Rooms from: ¥12000 ✉ 8–10–32 Akasaka, Minato-ku, Roppongi ☎ 03/3402–6111 www.asiacenter.or.jp 173 rooms No meals Ⓜ Ginza and Hanzo-mon subway lines, Aoyama-itchome Station (Exit 4) ✣ C4.*

$$ **HOTEL** **FAMILY** **The Prince Park Tower Tokyo** (ザ・プリンス パークタワー東京). The surrounding parkland and the absence of any adjacent buildings make the Park Tower a peaceful retreat in the middle of the city. **Pros:** park nearby; well-stocked convenience store on first floor; fun extras like a bowling alley and pool. **Cons:** a tad isolated; extra fee for pool and fitness center; few dining options in immediate area. *Rooms from: ¥18000 ✉ 4–8–1 Shiba-koen, Minato-ku ☎ 03/5400–1111 www.princehotels.com/en/parktower 580 rooms, 23 suites No meals Ⓜ Oedo subway line, Akabanebashi Station (Akabanebashi Exit) ✣ E5.*

$$$$ HOTEL Fodor's Choice ★ **The Ritz-Carlton, Tokyo** (ザ・リッツ・カールトン東京). Installed in the top floors of the 53-story Midtown Tower, the Ritz-Carlton provides Tokyo's most luxurious accommodations squarely in the middle of the city. **Pros:** great views of Tokyo; romantic setting; convenient access to nightlife; stunning rooms loaded with luxurious goodies. **Cons:** high prices; immediate area is somewhat grungy. *Rooms from: ¥51000 9–7–1 Akasaka, Minato-ku 03/3423–8000 www.ritzcarlton.com 212 rooms, 36 suites No meals Hibiya subway line, Roppongi Station (Exit 4); Oedo subway line, Roppongi Station (Exit 7) ✣ D4.*

SHINJUKU 新宿

Known to be the world's busiest train hub, Shinjuku attracts business and leisure travelers. The west side of the station includes numerous big-name international chains, while the opposite side offers a number of domestic chains.

$$ HOTEL **Citadines Shinjuku Tokyo** (シタディーン新宿). Part hotel, part serviced apartments catering to short- or long-term travelers, the Citadines Shinjuku is a sunny venue of superb value. **Pros:** away from the congestion of Shinjuku Station; sizable rooms; very clean; cheerful design. **Cons:** a little difficult to find; dining options limited on the premises. *Rooms from: ¥16000 1–28–13 Shinjuku, Shinjuku-ku 03/5379–7208 www.citadines.jp 160 apartments No meals Marunouchi subway line, Shinjuku Gyoemmae Station (Exit 2) ✣ B2.*

$ HOTEL **Green Plaza Shinjuku** (グリーンプラザ新宿). Budget travelers in Shinjuku willing to throw claustrophobia to the wind can settle in for a night at the Green Plaza, a capsule hotel in the entertainment district of Kabuki-cho. **Pros:** a top choice for a capsule hotel as it's fairly priced; convenient location; public bath area has mineral baths and saunas. **Cons:** small and limited accommodations; noisy neighborhood. *Rooms from: ¥4500 1–29–2 Kabuki-cho, Shinjuku-ku 03/3207–5411 www.hgpshinjuku.jp No credit cards 660 capsules (630 for men, 30 for women) No meals Shinjuku Station (Higashi-guchi/East Exit) ✣ A2.*

$$ HOTEL **Hilton Tokyo** (ヒルトン東京). A short walk from the megalithic Tokyo Metropolitan Government Office, the Hilton is a particular favorite of Western business travelers. **Pros:** great gym; convenient location; free shuttle to Shinjuku Station. **Cons:** hotel lobby can get busy; restaurants are pricey. *Rooms from: ¥26000 6–6–2 Nishi-Shinjuku, Shinjuku-ku 03/3344–5111 www3.hilton.com 683 rooms, 128 suites No meals Shinjuku Station (Nishi-guchi/West Exit); Marunouchi subway line, Nishi-Shinjuku Station (Exit C8); Oedo subway line, Tocho-mae Station (all exits) ✣ A2.*

$$ HOTEL **Hotel Century Southern Tower** (小田急ホテルセンチュリーサザンタワー). The sparse offerings at the Century (i.e., no room or bell service, empty refrigerators) are more than compensated for by the hotel's reasonable prices and wonderful location atop the 35-floor Odakyu Southern Tower, minutes by foot from Shinjuku Station. **Pros:** affordable; convenient location; great views; simple but tasteful rooms. **Cons:** room amenities are basic; no room service or pool. *Rooms from: ¥19000 2–2–1 Yoyogi,*

Shibuya-ku ☎ 03/5354–0111 ⊕ www.southerntower.co.jp ⇐ 375 rooms ⊙ No meals Ⓜ Shinjuku Station (Minami-guchi/South Exit); Oedo and Shinjuku subway lines, Shinjuku Station (Exit A1) ⊕ A3.

$$ HOTEL **Hotel Gracery Shinjuku** (ホテルグレイスリー新宿). Paying tribute to Godzilla with a location in the center of the city, the Gracery is a good choice for tourists who want to get up close to the screen's top monster. **Pros:** convenient to Shinjuku Station; easy access to bars and restaurants; affordable. **Cons:** seedy area; kitsch might not appeal to everyone; rooms on small side. Ⓢ *Rooms from: ¥16000 ✉ 1–19–1 Kabukicho, Shinjuku-ku ☎ 03/6833–2489 ⊕ shinjuku.gracery.com ⇐ 970 rooms ⊙ No meals Ⓜ JR subway lines, Shinjuku Station (East Exit) ⊕ B2.*

$$ HOTEL **Hyatt Regency Tokyo** (ハイアットリージェンシー東京). Set amid Shinjuku's skyscrapers, this hotel has the trademark Hyatt atrium-style lobby: seven stories high, with open-glass elevators soaring upward and three huge chandeliers suspended from above. **Pros:** friendly staff; affordable room rates; spacious rooms. **Cons:** rather generic exteriors and common areas; restaurant options are limited outside hotel. Ⓢ *Rooms from: ¥23000 ✉ 2–7–2 Nishi-Shinjuku, Shinjuku-ku ☎ 03/3348–1234 ⊕ tokyo.regency.hyatt.com ⇐ 726 rooms, 18 suites ⊙ No meals Ⓜ Marunouchi subway line, Nishi-Shinjuku Station (Exit C8); Oedo subway line, Tocho-mae Station (all exits) ⊕ A2.*

$$ HOTEL **Keio Plaza Hotel Tokyo** (京王プラザホテル). Composed of two cereal-box-shape towers, this hotel has a reputation as a business destination that serves its guests with a classic touch. **Pros:** nice pools; affordable nightly rates; convenient location. **Cons:** bland exteriors and common areas; restaurant options outside hotel limited; crowded if there are conventions or large groups in residence. Ⓢ *Rooms from: ¥18000 ✉ 2–2–1 Nishi-Shinjuku, Shinjuku-ku ☎ 03/3344–0111 ⊕ www.keioplaza.com ⇐ 1,414 rooms, 22 suites ⊙ No meals Ⓜ Shinjuku Station (Nishi-guchi/West Exit) ⊕ A2.*

$$$$ HOTEL Fodor's Choice ★ **Park Hyatt Tokyo** (パークハイアット東京). Sofia Coppola's classic film *Lost in Translation* was a love letter to this hotel, and when the elevator inside the sleek, Kenzo Tange–designed Shinjuku Park Tower whisks you to the atrium lounge with a panorama of Shinjuku through floor-to-ceiling windows, you may feel smitten as well. **Pros:** city icon that stays relevant; wonderful room interiors; great skyline views; top-class restaurants. **Cons:** pricey; somewhat remote; taxi is best way to get to Shinjuku Station. Ⓢ *Rooms from: ¥52000 ✉ 3–7–1–2 Nishi-Shinjuku, Shinjuku-ku ☎ 03/5322–1234 ⊕ www.tokyo.park.hyatt.com ⇐ 154 rooms, 23 suites ⊙ No meals Ⓜ JR Shinjuku Station (Nishi-guchi/West Exit) ⊕ A3.*

ODAIBA お台場

Thanks to its secluded destination, the Odaiba area is a lovely place to stay on a romantic getaway. (The hotels line Tokyo Bay and are known for their views.) At the same time, business travelers also stay here to be close to the convention center grounds, and they appreciate resting their eyes and gazing over the sea.

5

$$ HOTEL FAMILY **Grand Pacific Le Daiba** (グランパシフィックル ダイバ). A sprawling complex at the tip of a human-made peninsula in Tokyo Bay, the Grand Pacific is a good choice for conventioneers at the nearby Tokyo Big Site. **Pros:** great views of Tokyo Bay; large, nicely appointed rooms; romantic setting. **Cons:** isolated location; numerous weddings booked on weekends; wait for breakfast can be long. *Rooms from: ¥16000 ✉ 2–6–1 Daiba, Minato-ku ☎ 03/5500–6711 www.grandpacific.jp/eng 860 rooms, 24 suites No meals Ⓜ Yurikamome rail line, Daiba Station ✣ F6.*

$$ HOTEL **Hilton Tokyo Odaiba** (ヒルトン東京お台場). With a facade that follows the curve of the Tokyo Bay shoreline, the 16-story Hilton Tokyo Odaiba presents itself as an "urban resort" with European style. **Pros:** great views of Tokyo Bay; friendly staff; romantic setting. **Cons:** isolated location might not be ideal for the sightseer; room interiors are a tad bland. *Rooms from: ¥18000 ✉ 1–9–1 Daiba, Minato-ku ☎ 03/5500–5500 www.hilton.com 435 rooms, 18 suites No meals Ⓜ Yurikamome rail line, Daiba Station ✣ F6.*

GREATER TOKYO

It may have a station on the Yamanote Line, but Meguro is a relatively residential area, and guests staying at hotels here appreciate the seclusion that affords.

Meanwhile, on the south end of the Yamanote metro line loop, Shinagawa is a destination for the business traveler. Hotels are clustered on either side of Shinagawa Station.

Located just south of Ikebukuro, Mejiro is a quiet residential area. Travelers staying here are seeking a break from the frenetic, urban pace of central Tokyo.

$$ HOTEL **Claska** (クラスカ). Hip, modern, and utterly Japanese, the Claska provides a premier boutique hotel experience. **Pros:** stylish Japanese aesthetics in a modern setting; great staff; cool gift shop. **Cons:** five minutes by taxi from Meguro Station; dining options in immediate area are limited; often fully booked. *Rooms from: ¥21000 ✉ 1–3–18 Chuo-cho, Meguro-ku ☎ 03/3719–8121 www.claska.com 15 rooms, 3 suites No meals Ⓜ Toyoko Line, Gakugeidaigaku Station (Higashi-guchi/East Exit); 5 mins by taxi from JR Meguro Station ✣ B6.*

$$$ HOTEL **Hotel Chinzanso Tokyo** (ホテル椿山荘東京). Set inside a 17-acre garden, the elegant and European Hotel Chinzanso is a sheltered haven in Tokyo's busy metropolis and a former estate of an imperial prince. **Pros:** gorgeous, sprawling grounds; huge bathrooms; glamorous pool. **Cons:** limited dining options in immediate area; isolated location; room interiors a tad dated. *Rooms from: ¥32000 ✉ 2–10–8 Sekiguchi, Bunkyo-ku ☎ 03/3943–1111 www.hotel-chinzanso-tokyo.com 219 rooms, 41 suites No meals Ⓜ Yuraku-cho subway line, Edogawa-bashi Station (Exit 1A) ✣ C1.*

$$ HOTEL FAMILY **Prince Hotel Shinagawa** (品川プリンスホテル). Just a three-minute walk from JR Shinagawa Station, the Prince is a sprawling complex that's part hotel (with four towers) and part entertainment village, featuring everything from a bowling alley to tennis courts to a 10-screen movie

theater. **Pros:** affordable rates; multiple entertainment choices, including a bowling alley and an IMAX theater; nice view of Tokyo Bay from lounge. **Cons:** complicated layout; crowded on weekends; rooms can be small. *Rooms from: ¥16000 ✉ 4–10–30 Takanawa, Minato-ku ☎ 03/3440–1111 🌐 www.princehotels.com/en/shinagawa ⇨ 3,331 rooms 🍽 No meals Ⓜ JR Yamanote Line, Shinagawa Station (Nishi-guchi/West Exit) ✥ D6.*

$$$ HOTEL **The Strings by InterContinental Tokyo** (ストリングスホテル東京インターコンチネンタル). Beautifully blending modernity with traditional Japanese aesthetics, the Strings is one of Shinagawa's top-tier hotels. **Pros:** great lobby; convenient location; nice view of the Tokyo skyline. **Cons:** expensive rates; finding elevator entrance can be challenging; no pool or spa. *Rooms from: ¥31000 ✉ 2–16–1 Konan, Minato-ku, Shinagawa-ku ☎ 03/5783–1111 🌐 www.intercontinental-strings.jp ⇨ 206 rooms, 6 suites 🍽 No meals Ⓜ JR Yamanote Line, Shinagawa Station (Konan Exit) ✥ D6.*

$$ HOTEL **Westin Tokyo** (ウェスティンホテル東京). In the Yebisu Garden Place development, the Westin provides easy access to Mitsukoshi department store, the Tokyo Metropolitan Museum of Photography, the elegant Ebisu Garden concert hall, and the Taillevent-Robuchon restaurant (in a full-scale reproduction of a Louis XV château). **Pros:**"Heavenly Beds"; large rooms; great concierge. **Cons:** walk from station is more than 10 minutes; rooms can feel stuffy to some; charge for Internet. *Rooms from: ¥28000 ✉ 1–4–1 Mita, Meguro-ku ☎ 03/5423–7000 🌐 www.westin-tokyo.co.jp ⇨ 418 rooms, 20 suites 🍽 No meals Ⓜ JR Yamanote Line and Hibiya subway line, Ebisu Station (Higashi-guchi/East Exit) ✥ B6.*

$$ HOTEL **Hotel InterContinental Tokyo Bay** (ホテルインターコンチネンタル東京ベイ). Wedged between Tokyo Bay and an expressway, the InterContinental boasts lovely views, albeit in a slightly isolated setting. **Pros:** sweeping views of the Rainbow Bridge and Tokyo Bay; large, nicely appointed rooms; quiet area. **Cons:** no pool; might be too out of the way for the sightseer; the gym is small. *Rooms from: ¥27000 ✉ 1–16–2 Kaigan, Minato-ku ☎ 03/5404–2222 🌐 www.interconti-tokyo.com ⇨ 332 rooms, 7 suites 🍽 No meals Ⓜ Yurikamome rail line, Takeshiba Station ✥ F5.*

NEAR NARITA AIRPORT

Transportation between Narita Airport and Tokyo proper takes at least an hour and a half. In heavy traffic, a limousine bus or taxi ride, which could set you back ¥30,000, can stretch to two hours or more. A sensible strategy for visitors with early-morning flights home would be to spend the night before at one of the hotels near the airport, all of which have courtesy shuttles to the departure terminals; these hotels are also a boon to visitors en route elsewhere with layovers in Narita. Many of them have soundproof rooms to block out the noise of the airplanes.

$ HOTEL **ANA Crowne Plaza Narita** (ANAクラウンプラザホテル成田). With its brass-and-marble detail in the lobby, this hotel replicates the grand style of other hotels in the ANA chain. **Pros:** convenient location; pleasant staff; airport shuttle. **Cons:** small rooms; charge to use pool; in-house restaurants are the only dining options in the area. *Rooms from: ¥14000 ✉ 68 Hori-no-uchi, Chiba-ken, Narita ☎ 0476/33–1311, 0120/029–501 toll-free 🌐 www.anacrowneplaza-narita.jp 389 rooms, 7 suites No meals ✢ H1.*

$$ HOTEL **Hilton Tokyo Narita Airport** (ヒルトン成田). Given its proximity to the airport (a 10-minute drive), this C-shape hotel is a reasonable choice for a one-night visit. **Pros:** reasonably priced rooms; spacious lobby; airport shuttle. **Cons:** charge to use the pool and gym; common areas a bit worn; in-room Wi-Fi is not free. *Rooms from: ¥15000 ✉ 456 Kosuge, Chiba-ken, Narita ☎ 0476/33–1121 🌐 www.hilton.com 537 rooms, 11 suites No meals ✢ H1.*

$ HOTEL **Narita Airport Rest House** (成田エアポートレストハウス). This basic business hotel doesn't have much in the way of frills. **Pros:** day rooms available; some of the closest rooms to the airport; hotel provides a shuttle to the airport. **Cons:** few dining choices outside the hotel; dated in-room furnishings. *Rooms from: ¥8000 ✉ Narita International Airport, Chiba-ken, Narita ☎ 0476/32–1212 🌐 www.apo-resthouse.com 187 rooms No meals ✢ H1.*

$ HOTEL **Narita Excel Hotel Tokyu** (成田エクセル東急). Airline crews rolling their bags through the lobby are a common sight at the Excel, a hotel with reasonable prices and friendly service. **Pros:** nice concierge; view of runway from bar; nice Japanese garden. **Cons:** small bathrooms; no outside dining options in immediate area. *Rooms from: ¥9000 ✉ 31 Oyama, Chiba-ken, Narita ☎ 0476/33–0109 🌐 narita.tokyuhotels.com 704 rooms, 2 suites No meals ✢ H1.*

$ HOTEL **nine hours** (ナインアワーズ). For a layover at Narita, this capsule hotel's location can't be beat—it's inside Terminal 2. **Pros:** convenient; reasonably priced. **Cons:** tight confines; limited services; can be noisy. *Rooms from: ¥3900 ✉ 1–1 Furugome, Terminal 2 ☎ 0476/33–5109 🌐 ninehours.co.jp 129 capsules (71 for men, 58 for women) No meals ✢ H1.*

$ HOTEL **Radisson Hotel Narita Airport** (ラディソンホテル成田). Set on 28 spacious, green acres, this modern hotel feels somewhat like a resort, with massive indoor and outdoor pools. **Pros:** reasonably priced rooms; high-quality bathroom toiletries by Shiseido; nice-size rooms; airport shuttle available. **Cons:** a 15-minute drive by car to the airport; no outside restaurants in the immediate area. *Rooms from: ¥9000 ✉ 650–35 Nanae, Chiba-ken, Tomisato ☎ 0476/93–1234 🌐 www.radissonnarita.jp 488 rooms, 2 suites No meals ✢ H1.*

6

NIGHTLIFE

Updated by Noriko Kitano

The sheer diversity of nightlife in Tokyo is breathtaking. Rickety street stands sit yards away from luxury hotels, and wallet-crunching hostess clubs can be found next to cheap and raucous rock bars. Whatever your style, you'll find yourself in good company if you venture out after dark.

Most bars and clubs in the main entertainment districts have printed price lists, often in English. Drinks generally cost ¥800–¥1,200, although some small exclusive bars and clubs can set you back a lot more. Be wary of establishments without visible price lists. Hostess clubs and small backstreet bars known as "snacks" or "pubs" can be particularly treacherous territory for the unprepared. That drink you've just ordered could set you back a reasonable ¥1,000; you might, on the other hand, have wandered unknowingly into a place that charges you ¥30,000 up front for a whole bottle—and slaps a ¥20,000 cover charge on top. If the bar has hostesses, it's often unclear what the companionship of one will cost you, but you can bet a lot. Ignore the persuasive shills on the streets of Roppongi and Kabuki-cho, who will try to hook you into their establishment. There is, of course, plenty of safe ground: in hotel lounges, jazz clubs, Irish-themed pubs, sake bars, and sedate retreats where the social lubricant flows past millions of tonsils nightly.

Major nightlife districts in Tokyo include Aoyama, Ginza, Roppongi, Shibuya, Shinbashi, and Shinjuku. Each has a unique atmosphere, clientele, and price level.

ASAKUSA 浅草

BARS

Fodor's Choice ★

Kamiya Bar. Tokyo's oldest Western-style bar hasn't had a face-lift for decades (the main building is registered as a tangible cultural property) and that's part of what draws so many drinkers to this bright, noisy venue. The other major attraction is the Denki Bran, a delicious but hangover-inducing liquor (comprising gin, red wine, brandy, and curaçao) that was invented here about 100 years ago and is now stocked by bars throughout Japan. ✉ *1–1–1 Asakusa,*

1 mile
1 km
Meiji-dori
Nakasendo
Rikugien Gardens
Shinobazu-dori
Mejiro-dori
Koishikawa Botanical Gardens
Hongo-dori
Hakusan dori Ave
Tokyo Expwy No.5
UENO
Showa-dori
ASAKUSA
from view-filled bars to dark jazz clubs, the key word is sophistication
Asakusa-dori
Kasuga-dori
Waseda-dori
Kiyosu-bashi-dori
AKIHABARA
JIMBO-CHO
SHINJUKU
it's all here: a red light district, gay bars, and bohemian boites
IMPERIAL PALACE DISTRICT
NIHOMBASHI
Uchibori-dori
Shinjuku Gyo-en
ARAJUKU
AOYAMA
dress well, think young, and bring a credit card or two
Aoyama dori
Meiji-dori
Gaien-
GINZA
high rollers, expensive drinks, and kimono-clad waitresses
Shin Ohashi-dori
SHIBUYA
araoke boxes, cheap cafés, cocktail lounges for the young young at heart
Sakurada-dori
SHIODOME
Sumidagawa
TSUKIJI
Kiyosumi-dori
Tokyo Expwy No.3
ROPPONGI
something for everyone, from boisterous bars to luxurious lounges
Sakurada-dori
Tokyo Expwy No.2
Kaigan-dori
PORT OF TOKYO
ODAIBA
National Park for Nature Study
EGURO
Meguro-dori
Sakurada-dori
Dai-ichi-keihin
Tokyo Expwy No.1
Rainbow Bridge

Taitō-ku, Asakusa ☎ 03/3841–5400 ⏲ Closed Tues. Ⓜ Asakusa and Ginza subway lines, Asakusa Station (Exit 3 and A5).

FAMILY **Top of Tree.** Perched on the top of the Soramachi complex, this bar-restaurant attracts locals and tourists for overwhelming, breathtaking views of Tokyo Sky Tree. Signature drinks include Amaou-brand strawberry cocktails. The music's mostly jazz, and spacious and cushy seats, with sprawling views of Tokyo through the oversized glass windows and ceiling, make you want to linger. ✉ *31F Soramachi, Tokyo Skytree Town, 1–1–2 Oshiage, Sumida-ku, Asakusa ☎ 03/5809–7377.*

BEER HALLS AND PUBS

World Beer Museum. As the name suggests, beers from around the world are for sale, including 300 kinds in bottles and 20 more on tap. The large outdoor terrace with low-key downtown views is quiet and pleasant. The English-speaking German staff, when available, can help you choose the right beer. ✉ *7F Soramachi, Tokyo Skytree Town, 1–1–2 Oshiage, Sumida-ku, Asakusa ☎ 03/5610–2648 🌐 www.world-liquor-importers.co.jp/en/index.html.*

AOYAMA 青山

BARS

Radio. Koji Ozaki is the closest thing Tokyo has to a superstar bartender. This demure septuagenarian, who still works one week per month, has been crafting cocktails for half a century, and he's known for both his perfectionism and creativity. Ozaki designed not only the bar he works behind, but the glasses he serves his creations in (some of the best in the city). All bartenders arrange the bar's flowers. You need to dress up (avoid short pants or flip-flops by all means), and remember, this is a place for quiet relaxation. ✉ *3–10–34 Minami-Aoyama, Aoyama ☎ 03/3402–2668 🌐 www.bar-radio.com ⏲ Closed Sun. and holidays Ⓜ Chiyoda, Ginza, and Hanzomon subway lines, Omotesando Station (Exit A4).*

Two Rooms. Aoyama's dressed-up drinkers hang out on the stylish terrace. Drinks are big, pricey, and modern—think martinis in multiple fresh fruit flavors such as kiwi. The terrace overlooking Shinjuku area is particularly comfortable in spring and summer. ✉ *5F AO Building, 3–11–7 Kita-Aoyama, Aoyama ✥ Chiyoda, Ginza, and Hanzomon subway lines, Omotesando Station (Exit B2) ☎ 03/3498–0002 🌐 www.tworooms.jp.*

DANCE CLUBS

Le Baron de Paris. The Tokyo branch of the Paris and New York club is partly owned by superstar designer Marc Newson and as you might expect, draws a fashionable crowd of fashion designers, models, editors, stylists, and actors. Expect an eclectic mix of nostalgic and modern party music from the '80s plus hip-pop, disco, and rock. ✉ *B1, 3–8–40 Minami-Aoyama, Minato-ku, Aoyama ☎ 03/3408–3665 🌐 www.lebaron.jp/en Ⓜ Chiyoda, Ginza, and Hanzomon subway lines, Omotesando Station (Exit A4/A3).*

CLOSE UP

What to Drink in Tokyo

Whether you're out with friends, with clients, or belting out a tune at the local karaoke bar, you're sure to have a drink at least once during your stay. Things may look a little different, even before you start knocking back a few, so take note of the liquors of this island nation. And remember, shout *Kanpai!* (sounds like "kaan-pie") instead of *Cheers!* when you raise your glass.

SAKE

Sake, pronounced *sa*-kay, is Japan's number-one alcoholic beverage. There are more than 2,000 different brands of sake produced throughout Japan. Like other kinds of wine, sake comes in sweet (*amakuchi*) and dry (*karakuchi*) varieties; these are graded *tokkyu* (superior class), *ikkyu* (first class), and *nikkyu* (second class) and are priced accordingly. (Connoisseurs say this ranking is for tax purposes and is not necessarily a true indication of quality.)

Best drunk at room temperature (*nurukan*) so as not to alter the flavor, sake is also served heated (*atsukan*) or very rarely with ice (*rokku de*) in summer. It's poured from *tokkuri* (small ceramic vessels) into tiny cups called *guinomi.* The diminutive size of these cups shouldn't mislead you into thinking you can't drink too much. The custom of making sure that your companion's cup never runs dry often leads the novice astray.

Junmaishu is the term for pure rice wine, a blend of rice, yeast, and water to which no extra alcohol has been added. Junmaishu sake has the strongest and most distinctive flavor, compared with various other methods of brewing, and is preferred by the sake *tsu,* as connoisseurs are known.

Apart from the *nomiya* (bars) and restaurants, the place to sample sake is the *izakaya,* a drinking establishment that usually serves dozens of different kinds of sake, including a selection of *jizake,* the kind produced in limited quantities by small regional breweries throughout the country.

HEAVENLY SPIRITS

Shochu is made from a variety of base ingredients such as buckwheat, sweet potatoes, or rice, and is particularly associated with the southern island of Kyushu. It's served either on the rocks or mixed with water and can be hot or cold. Sometimes a wedge of lemon or a small pickled apricot, known as *umeboshi,* is added as well. It can also be mixed with club soda and served cold as a popular drink called *chuhai.*

HAVIN' A BIIRU

Japan has four large breweries: Asahi, Kirin, Sapporo, and Suntory. Asahi and Kirin are the two heavyweights, constantly battling for the coveted title of "Japan's No. 1 Brewery," but many beer fans rate Suntory's Malts brand and Sapporo's Yebisu brand as the tastiest brews in the land. In recent years, Belgian beers have grown in popularity and are available in specialty shops and even supermarkets; the products of Japanese microbreweries have also become easier to find. Most recently, domestic craft beer (*ji bi ru*) has become very popular, and it's appearing on tap at restaurants and bars around the city. Yona Yona Ale is a refreshing and light beer that pairs with most foods and is available at many places.

JAZZ CLUBS

Blue Note Tokyo. This premier live jazz venue isn't for everyone: prices are high, sets short, and patrons packed in tight, sometimes sharing a table with strangers. But if you want to catch Pat Metheny and Natalie Cole in a relatively small venue, this is the place. Expect to pay upward of ¥11,000 to see major acts. ✉ *Raika Bldg., 6–3–16 Minami-Aoyama, Minato-ku, Aoyama* ☎ *03/5485–0088* 🌐 *www.bluenote.co.jp* Ⓜ *Chiyoda, Ginza, and Hanzo-mon subway lines, Omotesando Station (Exit A5).*

HARAJUKU 原宿

BARS

Harajuku Taproom. Expat Bryan Baird runs an acclaimed microbrewery in a Shuzenji area of Izu, and he serves his range of brews in this casual and friendly place, along with decent and inexpensive Japanese-style pub grub such as *yakitori* (chicken skewers). ✉ *2F No Surrender Bldg., 1–20–13 Jingu-mae, Shibuya* ☎ *03/6438–0450* 🌐 *bairdbeer.com/en.*

Montoak. Positioned halfway down the prestigious shopping street Omotesando-dori, within spitting distance of such fashion giants as Gucci, Louis Vuitton, and Tod's, this hip restaurant-bar is a great place to rest after testing the limits of your credit card. With smoky floor-to-ceiling windows and cushy armchairs, the place attracts a hipper-than-thou clientele and young fashionistas. The bar food consists of proscuitto, salads, cheese plates, and the like. ✉ *6–1–9 Jingu-mae, Shibuya* ☎ *03/5468–5928* 🌐 *www.montoak.com* Ⓜ *Chiyoda subway line, Meiji-Jingu-mae Station (Exit 4).*

SHIBUYA 渋谷

BARS

Akaoni. The emphasis here is *nama*, unrefined, unpasteurized sake. About 80 kinds from 60 brewing companies are available daily. You may want to sample this unique beverage while in Tokyo, since you won't find it at home: nama is short-lived, too delicate and fresh to transport or export, so it's not widely available overseas. You can accompany your choice with authentic Japanese fare, served here as small bites. Reservations are necessary. ✉ *2–15–3 Sangenjaya, Shibuya* ✥ *Denenchofu-sen and Tokyu Setagaya lines, Sagenjaya Station* ☎ *03/3410–9918* 🌐 *www.akaoni39.com.*

BEER HALLS AND PUBS

What the Dickens. This spacious pub in the Ebisu feels like "grandma's house" and more authentically British than many of its rivals, thanks partly to a menu of traditional pub grub, including hearty pies. Using aged logs, the second floor feels like a nice tree house. The place hosts regular live music (funk, folk, jazz, rock, reggae—anything goes here) and other events, so it can be very loud, particularly on Friday and Saturday. ✉ *4F Roob 6 Bldg., 1–13–3 Ebisu-Nishi, Shibuya* ☎ *03/3780–2099* 🌐 *www.whatthedickens.jp* ⏲ *Closed Mon.* Ⓜ *Hibiya subway line, Ebisu Station (Nishi-guchi/West Exit).*

CLOSE UP

Tokyo-Style Nightlife

Tokyo has a variety of nightlife options, so don't limit yourself to your hotel bar in the evenings. Spend some time relaxing the way the locals do at *izakaya*, karaoke, and live houses—three unique forms of contemporary Japanese entertainment.

IZAKAYA

Izakaya (literally "drinking places") are Japanese pubs that can be found throughout Tokyo. If you're in the mood for elegant decor and sedate surroundings, look elsewhere; these drinking dens are often noisy, bright, and smoky. But for a taste of authentic Japanese-style socializing, a visit to an izakaya is a must—this is where young people start their nights out, office workers gather on their way home, and students take a break to grab a cheap meal and a drink.

Typically, izakaya have a full lineup of cocktails, a good selection of sake, draft beer, and lots of cheap, greasy Japanese and Western food; rarely does anything cost more than ¥1,000. Picture menus make ordering easy, and because most cocktails retain their Western names, communicating drink preferences shouldn't be difficult.

KARAOKE

In buttoned-down, socially conservative Japan, karaoke is one of the safety valves. Employees, employers, teenage romancers, and good friends all drop their guard when there's a microphone in hand. The phenomenon started in the 1970s when cabaret singer Daisuke Inoue made a coin-operated machine that played his songs on tape so that his fans could sing along. Unfortunately for Inoue, he neglected to patent his creation, thereby failing to cash in as karaoke became one of Japan's favorite pastimes. Nowadays it's the finale of many an office outing, a cheap daytime activity for teens, and a surprisingly popular destination for dates.

Unlike most karaoke bars in the United States, in Japan the singing usually takes place in the seclusion of private rooms that can accommodate groups. Basic hourly charges vary and are almost always higher on weekends, but are usually less than ¥1,000. Most establishments have a large selection of English songs, stay open late, and serve inexpensive food and drink, which you order via a telephone on the wall. Finding a venue around one of the major entertainment hubs is easy—there will be plenty of young touts eager to escort you to their employer. And unlike with most other touts in the city, you won't end up broke by following them.

LIVE HOUSES

Tokyo has numerous small music clubs known as "live houses." These range from the very basic to miniclub venues, and they showcase the best emerging talent on the local scene. Many of the best live houses can be found in the Kichijoji and Koenji areas, although they are tucked away in basements citywide. The music could be gypsy jazz one night and thrash metal the next, so it's worth doing a little research before you turn up. Cover charges vary depending on who's performing but are typically ¥3,000–¥5,000.

DANCE CLUBS

Womb. Well-known techno and break-beat DJs make a point of stopping by this Shibuya überclub on their way through town. The turntable talent, local and international, and four floors of dance and lounge space make Womb Tokyo's most consistently rewarding club experience. Drawing adults from their late twenties to forties, the place gets packed sometimes after 1 in the morning. Entry costs around ¥3,500. ⊠ *2–16 Maruyama-cho, Shibuya* ☎ *03/5459–0039* ⊕ *www.womb.co.jp* Ⓜ *JR Yamanote Line, Ginza and Hanzo-mon subway lines, Shibuya Station (Hachiko Exit for JR and Ginza, Exit 3A for Hanzo-mon).*

IZAKAYA

Tatemichiya. The concrete walls are adorned with rock musicians' autobiographies and posters of the Sex Pistols and Ramones, who also provide the sound track. Artist Yoshitomo Nara shows up here, so if you're lucky, you can drink with him and watch him draw on the walls. ⊠ *B1, 30–8 Sarugaku-cho, Shibuya* ☎ *03/5459–3431* Ⓜ *Tokyu Toyoko Line, Daikanyama Station.*

KARAOKE

Shibuya Shidax Village Club. Next to the corporate headquarters of Shidax, Japan's largest karaoke chain, this facility has 80 private karaoke rooms and a restaurant. Weekday rates run about ¥620 per hour and double on weekends and holidays. ⊠ *1–12–13 Jinnan, Shibuya* ☎ *03/3461–9356* ⊕ *www.shidax.co.jp/sc/index.html* Ⓜ *JR, Ginza, and Hanzo-mon subway lines, Shibuya Station (Hachiko Exit).*

Smash Hits. If karaoke just isn't karaoke for you without drunken strangers to sing to, this expat favorite is the place to be. It has about 50,000 international songs, including about 28,000 English, Spanish, and French choices, and a central performance stage. The ¥3,500 cover charge gets you two drinks. ⊠ *B1F M2 Bldg., 5–2–26 Hiro-o, Shibuya* ☎ *03/3444–0432* ⊕ *www.smashhits.jp* ⊙ *Closed Sun. and Mon.* Ⓜ *Hibiya Line, Hiroo Station (Exit B2).*

GINZA 銀座

BARS

Peter. Like most of Tokyo's high-end hotels, the Peninsula has a high-rise bar. But unlike many staid hotel bars, this 24th-floor spot with a forest of chrome trees, designed by Yabu Pushelberg, is lots of fun. ⊠ *24F Peninsula Tokyo, 1–8–1 Yuraku-cho, Chiyoda-ku, Ginza* ☎ *03/6270–2763* ⊕ *tokyo.peninsula.com/en/fine-dining/peter-lounge-bar* Ⓜ *Hibiya and Mita subway lines, Hibiya Station (Exit A6).*

Star Bar. It's often said that Ginza has all the best bars, and Star Bar may be the best of the lot. Owner and bartender Hisashi Kishi is the president of the Japan Bartenders Association, and his attention to detail in the narrow, dark, and calm room is staggering. ⊠ *B1, 1–5–13 Ginza, Chūō-ku, Ginza* ☎ *03/3535–8005* ⊕ *starbar.jp/english.shtml* Ⓜ *JR Yamanote Line, Yuraku-cho Station (Kyobashi Exit).*

BEER HALLS AND PUBS

FAMILY **Ginza Lion.** This bar, in business since 1899 and occupying the same stately Chuo-dori location since 1934, is remarkably inexpensive for one of Tokyo's toniest addresses. Ginza shoppers and office workers alike drop by for beer and ballast—anything from Japanese-style fried chicken to spaghetti. Beers start at ¥600. ✉ *7–9–20 Ginza, Chūō-ku, Ginza* ☎ *03/3571–2590, 0120/84–8136 for customer service center* 🌐 *www.ginzalion.jp* Ⓜ *Ginza, Hibiya, and Marunouchi subway lines, Ginza Station (Exit A3).*

MARUNOUCHI 丸の内

JAZZ CLUBS

Cotton Club. In these intimate and luxurious surroundings you can listen to not only jazz but also a diverse range of music: soul, R&B, J-pop, and world music. The club has such an excellent sound system that musicians such as Ron Carter record here. Fine French cuisine lures music lovers for special nights out and important business entertaining. ✉ *2F Tokia, 2–7–3 Marunouchi, Chiyoda-ku, Marunouchi* ✥ *JR and subway lines, Tokyo Station, directly connected to the Tokia bldg.* ☎ *03/3215–1555* 🌐 *www.cottonclubjapan.co.jp/en.*

JAZZ FESTIVALS

Tokyo Jazz Festival. On the first weekend in September, the festival takes over the Tokyo International Forum and Cotton Club Tokyo in Marunouchi. Though the forum's 5,000-seat hall lacks the intimacy you might seek in a jazz show, the lineup is usually an impressive mix of local talent and international stars. ✉ *3–5–1 Marunouchi, Chiyoda-ku* ☎ *03/5777–8600* 🌐 *www.tokyo-jazz.com.*

ROPPONGI 六本木

BARS

Agave. In this authentic Mexican cantina, your palate will be tempted by a choice of more than 400 kinds of tequilas and mescals—making this the world's largest selection. Most of the varieties here aren't available anywhere else in Japan, so the steep prices may be worth paying. Foods are mostly Mexican appetizers. ✉ *B1 Clover Bldg., 7–15–10 Roppongi, Minato-ku, Roppongi* ☎ *03/3497–0229* 🌐 *agave.jp* ⏲ *Closed Sun. and holiday Mon.* Ⓜ *Hibiya and Oedo subway lines, Roppongi Station (Exit 3).*

DANCE CLUBS

Super-Deluxe. This isn't quite a dance club. You could call it an experimental party space, with almost each night hosting a different kind of event. It's a birthplace of Pecha Kucha, a popular evening of presentations by creative types, but you might also find a techno night, a Japanese drums concert, or a performance-art event. ✉ *B1, 3–1–25 Nishi-Azabu, Minato-ku, Roppongi* ☎ *03/5412–0515* 🌐 *www.super-deluxe.com* ⏲ *Closed during mid-Aug. Obon holiday and Golden Week in May* Ⓜ *Hibiya and Oedo subway lines, Roppongi Station (Exit 3 or 1C).*

In such a dense city, narrow bars crop up anywhere they can find space, including under a railway arch.

JAZZ CLUBS

Billboard Live Tokyo. With everything from rock and J-pop to soul and funk, this three-story joint makes one of the best food-and-live music experiences in Tokyo, all with panoramic views of Roppongi. Patrons love this venue partly because they're so close to performers like George Clinton, Dicky Betts, and Gen Hoshino; they often end up on the stage dancing and singing or shaking hands. Shows usually kick off at 7 and 9:30 pm on weekdays, 6 and 9 pm on Saturday and 4:30 and 7:30 pm on Sunday. ⊠ *4F Tokyo Midtown Garden Terr., 9–7–4 Akasaka, Minato-ku, Roppongi* ☎ *03/3405–1133.*

KARAOKE

Pasela Resort Roppongi. This 10-story entertainment complex on the main Roppongi drag of Gaien-Higashi-dori has seven floors of karaoke rooms, some Bali-themed, with more than 10,000 foreign-song titles. Both large and small groups can be accommodated. A Mexican-theme darts bar and a restaurant are also on-site. Rates run ¥500–¥1,300 per hour. ⊠ *4F–10F, 5–16–3 Roppongi, Minato-ku, Roppongi* ☎ *0120/911–086* 🌐 *www.pasela.co.jp* Ⓜ *Hibiya and Oedo subway lines, Roppongi Station (Exit 4A).*

SHINJUKU 新宿

BARS

Albatross G. This tiny, artsy bar and its red walls, hung with paintings and deer head, and many chandeliers attracts crowds with its friendliness and affordability. The clientele is a nice mix of local Japanese and foreign travelers. ⊠ *5th Ave., 1–1–7 Kabuki-cho, Shinjuku*

CLOSE UP

All That Tokyo Jazz

The Tokyo jazz scene is one of the world's best, far surpassing that of Paris and New York with its number of venues playing traditional, swing, bossa nova, rhythm and blues, and free jazz. Though popular in Japan before World War II, jazz really took hold of the city after U.S. forces introduced Charlie Parker and Thelonius Monk in the late 1940s. The genre had been banned in wartime Japan as an American vice, but even at the height of the war, fans were able to listen to their favorite artists on Voice of America radio. In the 1960s Japan experienced a boom in all areas of the arts, and jazz was no exception. Since then, the Japanese scene has steadily bloomed, with several local stars—such as Sadao Watanabe in the 1960s and contemporary favorites Keiko Lee and Hiromi Uehara—gaining global attention. Today there are more than 120 bars and clubs that host live music, plus hundreds that play recorded jazz. Shinjuku, Takadanobaba, and Kichijoji are the city's jazz enclaves. Famous international acts regularly appear at big-name clubs such as the Blue Note, but the smaller, lesser-known joints usually have more atmosphere. With such a large jazz scene, there's an incredible diversity to enjoy, from Louis Armstrong tribute acts to fully improvised free jazz—sometimes on successive nights at the same venue.

If you time your visit right, you can listen to great jazz at one of the city's more than 20 annual festivals dedicated to this adopted musical form. The festivals vary in size and coverage, but two to check out are the Tokyo Jazz Festival and the Asagaya Jazz Street Festival.

6

☎ *03/3203–3699* 🌐 *www.alba-s.com* Ⓜ *JR and Marunouchi subway lines, Shinjuku Station (East Exit).*

Donzoko. This venerable bar claims to be Shinjuku's oldest—established in 1951—and has hosted Yukio Mishima and Akira Kurosawa among many other luminaries. It's also one of several bars that claim to have invented the popular *chu-hai* cocktail (*shochu* with juice and soda). The vibrant atmophere feels more like a pub, and the four floors are almost always packed. ✉ *3–10–2 Shinjuku, Shinjuku* ☎ *03/3354–7749* 🌐 *www.donzoko.co.jp* Ⓜ *Marunouchi and Shinjuku subway lines, Shinjuku-san-chome Station (Exit C3).*

La Jetée. It should come as no surprise that French cinema is the proprietor's big passion: a film lover's paradise, La Jetée is covered in Euro-cinema posters and was named after a French movie. It struggles to seat 10–12 customers, but that means intimate conversations—in Japanese, French, and sometimes English—usually about movies. If you want to discuss European cinema with Wim Wenders or sit toe-to-toe with Quentin Tarantino, this is your best bet. The music, naturally, comes exclusively from film sound tracks. ✉ *2F, 1–1–8 Kabuki-cho, Shinjuku* ☎ *03/3208–9645* 🌐 *www.lajetee.net* ⏲ *Closed Sun. and holidays* Ⓜ *JR and Marunouchi subway lines, Shinjuku Station (East Exit).*

TOKYO'S GAY BARS

Gay culture is a little different in Japan than it is in the West. Though the gay presence on TV is increasing, most gay life still takes place well under the radar. Even so, there's less prejudice than you might experience elsewhere. People are more likely to be baffled than offended by gay couples, and some hotels may "not compute" that a same-sex couple would like a double bed. But with a little digging you'll find a scene more vibrant than you—or many Tokyoites—might expect. The city's primary LGBT hub is Ni-chome in the Shinjuku district (take the Shinjuku or Marunouchi subway line to Shinjuku-Sanchome Station; Exit C7). Ni-chome is sometimes likened to its more notorious neighbor Kabuki-cho, and the name is also spoken in hushed tones and accompanied by raised eyebrows. Ni-chome, however, is more subtle in its approach. Gay and gay-friendly establishments can be found sprinkled in other areas, too, among them Shibuya, Asakusa, Ueno, and, surprisingly, Shinbashi, where a cluster of gay bars near Shinbashi Station are cheek-by-jowl with establishments that cater to hard-drinking businessmen out for a night on the town.

Fodor'sChoice ★ **New York Bar.** Even before *Lost in Translation* introduced the Park Hyatt's signature lounge to filmgoers worldwide, New York Bar was a local Tokyo favorite. All the style you would expect of one of the city's top hotels combined with superior views of Shinjuku's skyscrapers and neon-lighted streets make this one of the city's premier nighttime venues. The quality of the jazz and service equals that of the view. With the largest selection of U.S. wines in Japan, drinks start at ¥1,200, and there's a cover charge of ¥2,200 after 8 pm (7 pm on Sunday). Local jazz bands play on Sunday. ✉ *52F Park Hyatt Hotel, 3–7–1–2 Nishi-Shinjuku, Shinjuku* ☎ *03/5322–1234* 🌐 *tokyo.park.hyatt.jp/en/hotel/dining/NewYorkBar.html* Ⓜ *JR Shinjuku Station (West Exit for the shuttle bus service, South Exit for walk-in).*

GAY BARS

Aiiro Cafe. Almost every great gay night out begins at this welcoming street-corner pub with a large red shrine gate, where the patrons spill out onto the street. This is the perfect place to put back a few cocktails, meet new people, and get a feeling for where to go next. The crowd is mixed and very foreigner-friendly. ✉ *2–18–1 Shinjuku, Shinjuku* ☎ *03/6273–0740* 🌐 *aliving.net/english.html.*

ArcH. The spacious basement joint hosts a wide range of events for gays and lesbians every night. The events include thirtysomething nights and underwear-only nights. Cover charge depends on the event. ✉ *B1 Casa Verde, 2–11–2 Shinjuku, Shinjuku* ☎ *03/6380–6966* 🌐 *aliving.net.*

Arty Farty. Cheap and cheesy, Arty Farty is a fun club, complete with a ministage and stripper pole. Those with aversions to Kylie or Madonna need not bother. The crowd is mixed and foreigner-friendly. ✉ *2F Kyutei Bldg., 2–11–7 Shinjuku, Shinjuku* ☎ *03/5362–9720* 🌐 *www.arty-farty.net.*

CLOSE UP

Golden Gai

Tucked away on the eastern side of Tokyo's sordid Kabuki-cho district (near Shinjuku), Golden Gai is a ramshackle collection of more than 200 Lilliputian bars that survived the rampant construction of Japan's bubble-economy years, thanks to the passion of its patrons. In the 1980s when the *yakuza*, Japan's crime syndicate, was torching properties to sell the land to big-thinking developers, Golden Gai's supporters took turns guarding the area each night.

Each bar occupies a few square yards, and some accommodate fewer than a dozen drinkers. With such limited space, many of the bars used to rely on their regulars—along with their name-written bottles kept behind the counter—and gave a frosty welcome and exorbitant bill to the casual visitor. But times are changing, as are leases, and a new generation of owners is gradually emerging to offer the same intimate drinking experience and cold beers without the unwelcome reception.

—Nicholas Coldicott

6

Dragon Men. Despite the name, Tokyo's swankiest gay lounge also welcomes women. The neon-lighted space would look right at home in New York or Paris. ✉ *1F Stork Nagasaki, 2–11–4 Shinjuku, Shinjuku* ☎ *03/3341–0606* Ⓜ *Marunouchi subway line, Shinjuku-san-chome Station.*

GB. This men-only club carries a whiff of the old days when things were less mainstream. Video monitors show contemporary music hits. On weekends the place is packed with rather quiet and reserved gentlemen, mostly in their thirties and forties, and cruising via strategically placed mirrors. Women are welcome, too. ✉ *B1 Shinjuku Plaza Bldg., 2–12–3 Shinjuku, Shinjuku* ☎ *03/3352–8972* 🌐 *www.gb-tokyo.com/index.php/en* ⏲ *Closed Mon.* Ⓜ *Marunouchi subway line, Shinjuku-san-chome Station.*

Gold Finger. This relaxed bar for "women who love women" is a cozy den of vintage lamps and cafélike ambience. Men are welcome on Friday; Saturdays are women-only. ✉ *Hayashi Bldg., 2–12–11 Shinjuku, Shinjuku* ☎ *03/6383–4649* 🌐 *www.goldfingerparty.com* ⏲ *Closed Tues. and Wed.* Ⓜ *Marunouchi subway line, Shinjuku-san-chome Station.*

JAZZ CLUBS

Hot House. This could very well be the world's smallest jazz club. An evening here is like listening to live jazz in your living room. Live acts are trios at most, with no space for a full set of drums or amplifiers. Simple, homemade Japanese cooking (free of charge) helps make this a truly intimate experience. With 10 seats and no standing allowed, reservations are recommended. Entry costs ¥3,500–¥4,500. ✉ *B1 Liberal Takadanobaba, 3–23–5 Takadanobaba, Shinjuku* ☎ *03/3367–1233* Ⓜ *JR Takadanobaba Station (Waseda Exit).*

Kabukicho, in Shinjuku, is a brightly lighted hub for izakaya pachinko parlors, and karaoke, as well as tattooed yakuza.

Intro. This small basement jazz joint is home to one of the best jazz experiences in Tokyo, with a Saturday "12-hour jam session" that stretches until 5 am. Live sessions run throughout the week except Monday and Friday, when the regulars enjoy listening to the owner's extensive vinyl and CD collection. Italian food is available. ✉ *B1 NT Bldg., 2–14–8 Takadanobaba, Shinjuku* ☎ *03/3200–4396* Ⓜ *JR Takadanobaba Station (Waseda Exit).*

Shinjuku Pit Inn. Most major jazz musicians have played at least once in this classic Tokyo club. The veteran club stages mostly mainstream fare with the odd foray into the avant-garde. The emphasis here is strictly on jazz—and the place resembles a small concert hall. Entry runs ¥1,400–¥5,000. ✉ *B1 Accord Shinjuku Bldg., 2–12–4 Shinjuku, Shinjuku* ☎ *03/3354–2024* 🌐 *www.pit-inn.com/index_e.html* Ⓜ *Marunouchi subway line, Shinjuku-san-chome Station.*

GREATER TOKYO

BARS

Kuri. Specializing in seasonal sake, this little bar serves about 100 varieties from around 40 breweries. Food is limited to appetizers that include salted squid, pickled cheese, and sea urchin. Dim lighting creates a nice mood, and the staff is happy to help you choose the right sake. Note that the surrounding Shinbashi district is a popular nighttime hangout for businessmen, so don't be surprised to encounter wandering hordes of inebriated accountants on the streets. ✉ *2F Sakurai Bldg., 3–19–4 Shinbashi, Minato-ku, Greater Tokyo* ☎ *03/3438–3375* ⏲ *Closed Sun.*

BEER HALLS AND PUBS

Craft Beer Market. This craft beer specialist serves nearly 30 Japanese beers on tap, with regional variations from around the country, at reasonable prices. The wide selection of foods includes roast chicken and carpaccio. This loftlike space with plenty of elbow room will make you comfortable, as will the easygoing ambience. A drink menu is available in English. ✉ *1F Sumitomo-shoji Jinbochobil, 2–11–15 Jinbocho, Kanda, Chiyoda-ku, Greater Tokyo* ☎ *03/6272–5652* 🌐 *www.craftbeermarket.jp/store_jimbo.html* ⏲ *Closed Sun.*

Popeye. Of the staggering 70 beers on tap here, 70% are top-quality Japanese microbrews, from pilsners to IPAs to barley wines. The owner is one of Japan's leading authorities on beer, and his passion is reflected in the quality of the brews. The convivial, sports-bar-like atmosphere attracts a mature clientele, making this a great option for a post-sumo spot. The menu includes chicken ale stew, beer cake, and beer ice cream. ✉ *2–18–7 Ryogoku, Sumida-ku, Greater Tokyo* ✥ *JR Ryogoku Station (West Exit)* ☎ *03/3633–2120* 🌐 *www.40beersontap.com* ⏲ *Closed Sun.*

DANCE CLUBS

Ageha. This massive, bay-side Ageha is probably the Japan's largest club venue with the city's best sound system and most diverse musical lineup. The arena hosts well-known house and techno DJs, the bar plays hip-hop, a summer-only swimming-pool area has everything from reggae to break beats, and inside a chill-out tent "Box," there's usually ambient or trance music according to programs. Because of its far-flung location and enormous capacity, Ageha can look like either a throbbing party or an embarrassingly empty hall, depending on the caliber of the DJ. Free buses to Ageha depart about every half hour or 45 minutes between midnight and 4 am from a stop opposite the Shibuya police station on Roppongi-dori, a one-minute walk from Shibuya Station (there are also return buses about every half hour or 45 minutes from midnight to 5 am). For gay nights, shuttles also depart from Shibuya. Entry costs around ¥3,500. ✉ *2–2–10 Shin-Kiba, Kōtō-ku, Greater Tokyo* ☎ *03/5534–2525* 🌐 *www.ageha.com* Ⓜ *Yuraku-cho subway line, Shin-Kiba Station.*

6

JAZZ FESTIVALS

Asagaya Jazz Street Festival. Held the last weekend of October, this predominantly mainstream festival takes places in some less-than-mainstream venues, ranging from a Shinto shrine to a Lutheran church (most within walking distance of Asagaya Station). More than 200 bands and 1,300 musicians play, and previous headliners include the Mike Price Jazz Quintet and pianist Yosuke Yamashita. The festival gets crowded, so come early to ensure entry. ✉ *4F, Wagafurusato-kan, 1–36–10 Asagaya-Minami, Suginami-ku, Greater Tokyo* ☎ *03/5305–5075* 🌐 *www.asagayajazzst.com.*

LIVE MUSIC

Manda-la 2. Relaxed, quiet, and intimate, this local favorite in the bustling western suburb of Kichijoji attracts an eclectic group of performers. Cover charges range from ¥2,200 to ¥3,300. ✉ *2–8–6 Kichijoji-Minami-cho, Musashino* ☎ *0422/42–1579* Ⓜ *Keio Inokashira* *private rail line, JR Chuo and JR Sobu lines, Kichijoji Station (Koen-guchi/Park Exit and South Exit).*

Shelter. An ever-popular, long-running venue attracts everyone from their late teens to early forties. This is a great place to catch promising local rock bands. Admission runs ¥2,000–¥4,000. ✉ *B1F, Senda Bldg., 2–6–10 Kitazawa, Setagaya-ku, Shibuya* ☎ *03/3466–7430* 🌐 *www.loft-prj.co.jp/SHELTER* Ⓜ *Keio Inokashira, Odakyu private rail lines, Shimo-Kitazawa Station (South Exit).*

Showboat. A small, basic venue in western Tokyo that's been going strong for more than a decade, Showboat attracts semiprofessional and professional performers. Entry runs ¥2,000–¥5,000. ✉ *B1 Oak Hill Koenji, 3–17–2 Koenji Kita, Suginami-ku, Greater Tokyo* ☎ *03/3337–5745* 🌐 *showboat1993.wix.com/showboat1993* Ⓜ *JR Sobu and JR Chuo lines, Koenji Station (Kita-guchi/North Exit).*

7

THE PERFORMING ARTS

Updated by Noriko Kitano

Tokyo's rich cultural history entwines itself with an influx of foreign influences, so Tokyoites get the best of both worlds. An astonishing variety of dance and music, both classical and popular and much of it Western, can be found in Tokyo, alongside the must-see traditional Japanese arts of Kabuki and Noh.

The city is a proving ground for local talent and a magnet for orchestras and concert soloists from all over the world. Tokyo also has modern theater—in somewhat limited choices, to be sure, unless you can follow dialogue in Japanese, but Western repertory companies can always find receptive audiences here for plays in English. And it doesn't take long for a hit show from New York or London to open. Musicals such as *Mamma Mia!* have found enormous popularity here—although the protagonists speak Japanese.

Among about 10 professional dance troupes in Japan, the best known are the New National Ballet, which usually performs at the New National Theater, and the K-Ballet Company and the Tokyo Ballet, both of which stage performances at the Bunka Kaikan in Ueno and Orchard Hall of the Bunkamura complex in Shibuya. Tokyo has plenty of venues for opera, and few groups to perform in them, so touring companies like the Metropolitan, the Bolshoi, Sadler's Wells, and the Bayerische Staatsoper find Tokyo a very compelling venue—as well they might when even seats at ¥30,000 or more sell out far in advance.

Tokyo movie theaters screen a broad range of films—everything from big Asian hits to American blockbusters and Oscar nominees. The diversity brought by smaller distributors and an increased appetite for Korean, Middle Eastern, South American, and Aussie cinema have helped develop vibrant small theaters that cater to art-house fans. New multiplexes have also brought new screens to the capital, providing a more comfortable film-going experience than some of the older Japanese theaters.

Metropolis, a free English-language weekly magazine, and *Weekend Scene,* published for free by *The Japan Times on Friday,* have up-to-date listings of what's going on in the city; they are available at hotels, book and music stores, some restaurants and cafés, and other locations. *The Japan News* also has entertainment features and listings in the Friday edition.

Ticket Pia. If your hotel can't help you with concert and performance bookings, call Ticket Pia or visit their shops around Tokyo, including two at Narita Airport. Beware, though, that except at the airport and Asakusa Culture Tourist Information Center, few people speak English here. Note that credit cards issued overseas are often not accepted, so bring cash. ⊠ *2–18–9 Kaminarimon, Taito-ku* ☎ *0570/02–9111, 03/5774–5200 customer service center.*

FILM

Bunkamura. This complex has two movie theaters that tend to screen French and foreign films; a concert, opera, and classic ballet auditorium (Orchard Hall); a performance space (Theater Cocoona, often used for ballet and other dance); a gallery; and a museum. ⊠ *2–24–1 Dogenzaka* ☎ *03/3477–9111* ⊕ *www.bunkamura.co.jp* Ⓜ *JR Yamanote Line, Ginza and Hanzo-mon subway lines, and private rail lines, Shibuya Station (Exit 3A).*

Eurospace. One of the best venues for art-house films in Japan screens independent European and Asian hits and small-scale Japanese movies. Directors and actors often appear on the stage, greeting fans on opening days. Occasionally Japanese films run with English subtitles. ⊠ *3F Kinohaus, 1–5 Maruyama-cho* ✣ *JR, Ginza subway lines, Shibuya Station (Hachiko Exit)* ☎ *03/3461–0211* ⊕ *www.eurospace.co.jp.*

TOHO Cinemas Chanter. This three-screen cinema complex shows many European and American films by independent producers but also showcases fine work by filmmakers from Asia and the Middle East. ⊠ *1–2–2 Yuraku-cho, Chiyoda-ku* ☎ *03/6868–5001* ⊕ *www.tohotheater.jp/theater/034/institution04.html* Ⓜ *Hibiya, Chiyoda, and Mita subway lines, Hibiya Station (Exit A5).*

FAMILY **TOHO Cinemas Roppongi Hills.** This complex provides good comfort along with its nine screens, and about 2,100 seats that include "First-Class" VIP seats. It also has an extra-large screen and MediaMation MX4D technology. It's the principal venue for the Tokyo International Film Festival held each fall. There are plenty of bars in the area for post-movie discussions. Late shows screen on weekends. ⊠ *Keyakizaka Complex, 6–10–2 Roppongi, Minato-ku* ☎ *03/6868–5024* ⊕ *www.tohotheater.jp/theater/009/access.html* 🎫 *Regular theater ¥1,800, premier theater ¥4,800* Ⓜ *Hibiya and Oedo subway lines, Roppongi Station (Roppongi Hills Exit).*

MODERN THEATER

Takarazuka. Japan's all-female theater troupe was founded in the Osaka suburb of Takarazuka in 1913 and has been going strong ever since. Today it has not one but five companies, one of which has a permanent home in Tokyo at the 2,069-seat Takarazuka Theater. Where else but at the Takarazuka could you see *Gone With the Wind,* sung in Japanese, with a young woman in a mustache and a frock coat playing Rhett Butler? Same-day tickets are sold at the box office at either 9:30 am or 10 am for later shows. Advance tickets are available through ticketing agencies and the theater's website. Any remaining tickets are sold at the theater box office. ✉ *1–1–3 Yuraku-cho, Chiyoda-ku* ☎ *03/5251–2001* 🌐 *kageki.hankyu.co.jp/english* 🎫 *¥2,500–¥8,800* Ⓜ *JR Yamanote Line, Yuraku-cho Station (Hibiya Exit); Hibiya subway line, Hibiya Station (Exit A5); Chiyoda and Mita subway lines, Hibiya Station (Exit A13).*

FAMILY **Tokyo Dome.** A 45,852-seat sports arena, the dome also hosts big-name Japanese pop acts as well as the occasional international star. ✉ *1–3–61 Koraku, Bunkyō-ku* ☎ *03/5800–9999* 🌐 *www.tokyo-dome.co.jp/e* Ⓜ *Marunouchi and Namboku subway lines, Koraku-en Station (Exit 2); Mita subway line, Suido-bashi Station (Exit A5); JR Suido-bashi Station (Nishi-guchi/West Exit).*

MUSIC

Akasaka Blitz. Eclectic performances at this artsy music venue range from Japanese rock to Korean and Japanese pop to visual-kei (visual-style) groups, who wear elaborate makeup and stage costumes. ✉ *Akasaka Sacas, 5–3–2 Akasaka, Minato-ku* ✥ *Chiyoda subway line, Akasaka Station* ☎ *03/3584–8811* 🌐 *www.tbs.co.jp/blitz.*

FAMILY **Kioi Hall.** Behind Hotel New Otani stands this relatively small concert venue, which showcases both performances of Western classical music, such as piano and violin recitals, and Japanese works, including *shakuhachi* flute music. It hosts programs for families to learn how to play such traditional Japanese instruments. ✉ *6–5 Kioi-cho, Chiyoda-ku* ✥ *JR, Marunouchi and Nanboku subway lines, Yotsuya Station (Koujimachi Exit); Yurakucho subway line, Koujimachi Station (Exit 2)* ☎ *03/3237–0061* 🌐 *www.kioi-hall.or.jp.*

New National Theater. With its 1,632-seat main auditorium, this venue nourishes Japan's fledgling efforts to make a name for itself in the world of opera. The Opera City Concert Hall has a massive pipe organ and hosts a free concert on Friday from 11:45 to 12:30, as well as visiting orchestras and performers. Ballet and large-scale operatic productions such as *Carmen* draw crowds at the New National Theater's Opera House, while the Pit and Playhouse theaters showcase dance and more-intimate dramatic works. The complex also includes an art gallery. ✉ *1–1–1 Hon-machi, Shibuya-ku, Shinjuku* ☎ *03/5352–9999* 🌐 *www.nntt.jac.go.jp/* 🎫 *¥3,000–¥21,000* Ⓜ *Keio Shin-sen private rail line, Hatsudai Station (Higashi-guchi/East Exit).*

NHK Hall. The home base for the Japan Broadcasting Corporation's NHK Symphony Orchestra, known as N-Kyo, is probably the auditorium most familiar to Japanese lovers of classical music, as performances here are routinely rebroadcast on the national TV station. The concerts also sometimes take place in adjoining Suntory Hall. ✉ *2–2–1 Jinnan* ☎ *03/3465–1751, 03/3465–1780 for N-kyo* 🌐 *www.nhk-sc.or.jp/nhk_hall* Ⓜ *JR Yamanote Line, Harajuku Station (Exit Omotesando-guchi).*

In the spring, Noh performances can take place outdoors lighted by torchlight, just as they did in the 14th century.

Suntory Hall. This lavishly appointed concert auditorium in the Ark Hills complex has probably the best acoustics in the city, and its great location allows theatergoers to extend their evening out: there's an abundance of great restaurants and bars nearby. ✉ *1–13–1 Akasaka, Minato-ku, Roppongi* ☎ *03/3505–1001* 🌐 *www.suntory.com/culture-sports/suntoryhall* Ⓜ *Ginza subway line, Tameike-Sanno Station (Exit 13); Namboku subway line, Roppongi-Ichome Station (Exit 3).*

Tokyo Metropolitan Festival Hall (*Tokyo Bunka Kaikan*). In the 1960s and '70s this hall was one of the city's premier showcases for classical ballet, orchestral music, and visiting soloists. It still gets major bookings. ✉ *5–45 Ueno Koen, Taitō-ku* ☎ *03/3828–2111* 🌐 *www.t-bunka.jp/en* Ⓜ *JR Yamanote line, Ueno Station (Koen-guchi/Park Exit).*

PERFORMING ARTS CENTERS

Bunkyo Civic Hall. This three-story, city-run performance hall showcases classical music and ballet, opera, dance, and drama. Visitors might be especially interested in performances of local interest featuring puppets, wind music, and Japanese Kabuki dance. ✉ *1–16–21 Kasuga, Bunkyō-ku* ✥ *Marunouchi and Nanboku subway lines, Kourakuen Station (Exit 5)* ☎ *03/5803–1100, 03/5803–1111 tickets only* 🌐 *bunkyocivichall.jp.*

Tokyo Opera City (東京オペラシティ). This mixed-use office and entertainment complex is home to the New National Theater, Tokyo (Shin Kokuritsu Gekijo Tokyo), consisting of the 1,814-seat Opera House, the 1,010-seat Playhouse, and an intimate performance space called the Pit, with seating for up to 438. Architect Helmut Jacoby's design

CLOSE UP

The Red Lights of Kabuki-cho

Tokyo has more than its fair share of red-light districts, but the leader of the pack is unquestionably Kabuki-cho, located just north of Shinjuku Station. The land was once a swamp, although its current name refers to an aborted post–World War II effort to bring culture to the area in the form of a landmark Kabuki theater. Nowadays, most of the entertainment is of the insalubrious kind, with strip clubs, love hotels, host and hostess clubs, and thinly disguised brothels all luridly advertising their presence.

The area's also home to throngs of Japanese and Chinese gangsters, giving rise to its image domestically as a danger zone. But in truth, Kabuki-cho poses little risk even to the solo traveler. The sheer volume of people in the area each night, combined with a prominent security-camera presence, means that crime stays mostly indoors.

Despite its sordid reputation, Kabuki-cho does have attractions beyond the red lights. There are eateries galore ranging from chain diners to designer restaurants.

for this building, with its reflecting pools, galleries, and granite planes of wall, deserves real plaudits.

Its east side consists of a 54-story office tower flanked by a sunken garden and art gallery on one side and a concert hall on the other. The museum focuses rather narrowly on post–World War II Japanese abstract painting, with its 3,000-piece Terada Collection. The 1,632-seat concert hall is arguably the most impressive classical-music venue in Tokyo, with tiers of polished-oak panels, and excellent acoustics despite the venue's daring vertical design. ✉ *3–20–2 Nishi-Shinjuku, Shinjuku* ☎ *03/5353–0788 concert hall, 03/5351–3011 New National Theater* 🌐 *www.tokyooperacity.co.jp* Ⓜ *Keio Shinsen line, Hatsudai Station (Higashi-guchi/East Exit).*

TRADITIONAL THEATER

⇨ *For descriptions and background on traditional Japanese theater, see Chapter 2, A Japanese Cultural Primer.*

KABUKI

FAMILY **Kabuki-za.** This legendary theater opened in 1889 was rebuilt after an earthquake in 1923, air raids in 1945, and again a few years ago. The new theater retains the original style and architecture and includes a *hanamichi* (runway) passing diagonally through the audience to a revolving stage, which looks out to 1,800 seats. Depending on programs, matinees usually begin at 11 and end at 3:30; evening performances start at 4:30 and end at 9. You can buy an unreserved ticket that allows you to see one act of a play from the topmost gallery. Bring binoculars—the gallery is very far from the stage. You might also want to rent an earphone set to follow the play in English. ✉ *4–12–15 Ginza, Chūō-ku* ☎ *03/3545–6800,* 🌐 *www.kabuki-bito.jp/eng* 🎫 *Reserved seats ¥4,000–¥20,000, topmost* *gallery ¥500–¥2,000* Ⓜ *Hibiya and Asakusa subway lines, Higashi-Ginza Station (station directly connected to the theater).*

National Theater (国立劇場 *Kokuritsu Gekijo*). Architect Hiroyuki Iwamoto's winning entry in the design competition for the National Theater building (1966) is a rendition in concrete of the ancient *azekura* (storehouse) style, invoking the 8th-century Shosoin Imperial Repository in Nara. The large hall seats 1,610 and presents primarily Kabuki theater, ancient court music, and dance. The small hall seats 590 and is used mainly for *bunraku* puppet theater and traditional music. Performances are in Japanese, but English-translation headsets are available for many shows. Debut performances, called *kao-mise,* are worth watching to catch the stars of the next generation. Tickets can be reserved until the day of the performance by calling the theater box office between 10 and 6. ✉ *4–1 Hayabusa-cho, Chiyoda-ku, Imperial Palace* ☎ *03/3265–7411* 🌐 *www.ntj.jac.go.jp* 🎫 *Varies depending on performance* Ⓜ *Hanzo-mon subway line, Hanzo-mon Station (Exit 1).*

Shimbashi Enbujo. Dating to 1925, this theater was built for the geisha of the Shimbashi quarter to present their spring and autumn performances of traditional music and dance. This is the top spot in Tokyo to see the nation's favorite traditional performing art. The theater is also the home of "Super Kabuki," a faster, jazzier modern version. Seats commonly run ¥3,000–¥16,500, and there's no gallery. ✉ *6–18–2 Ginza, Chūō-ku* ☎ *03/3541–2600* 🌐 *www.shochiku.co.jp/play/enbujyo* Ⓜ *Hibiya and Asakusa subway lines, Higashi-Ginza Station (Exit 6).*

7

NOH

FAMILY **National Noh Theater.** One of the few public halls to host Noh performances, this theater provides basic English-language summaries of the plots at performances. Individual screens placed in front of each seat also give an English translation. ✉ *4–18–1 Sendagaya, Shibuya* ☎ *03/3423–1331, 03/3230–3000 reservations* 🌐 *www.ntj.jac.go.jp/nou.html* 🎫 *¥2,700–¥6,700* Ⓜ *JR Chuo Line, Sendagaya Station (Minami-guchi/South Exit); Oedo subway line, Kokuritsu-Kyogijo Station (Exit A4).*

FAMILY **Sumida Triphony Hall.** Home to New Japan Philharmonic, the venue is mostly for Western classical music, chamber music, and piano recitals. It has many programs by amateur orchestras and ensembles, as well. The 1,800-seat hall is thought to have the best acoustics in Tokyo. ✉ *1–2–3 Kinshicho, Sumida-ku* ✥ *JR, Hanzomon subway lines, Kinshicho Station (Exit North for JR, Exit 3 for Hanzomon subway line)* ☎ *03/5608–5404, 03/5608–1212 tickets/reservations only* 🌐 *www.triphony.com.*

8

SHOPPING

Updated by Misha Janette

Tokyo is Japan's showcase. The crazy clothing styles, obscure electronics, and new games found here are capable of setting trends for the rest of the country—and perhaps the rest of Asia, and even Europe and America.

Part of the Tokyo shopping experience is simply to observe, and on Saturday especially, in districts like the Ginza and Shinjuku, you will notice that the Japanese approach to shopping can be nothing short of feverish. You'll probably want to resist the urge to join in the fray, especially since many of the wildly trendy clothes and accessories for sale will already be "uncool" by the time you get home. But shopping in Tokyo can also be an exercise in elegance and refinement, especially if you shop for items that are Japanese-made for Japanese people and sold in stores that don't cater to tourists. With brilliantly applied color, balance of form, and superb workmanship, crafts items can be exquisite and well worth the price you'll pay—and some can be quite expensive.

Note the care taken with items after you purchase them, especially in department stores and boutiques. Goods will be wrapped, wrapped again, bagged, and sealed. Sure, the packaging can be excessive—does anybody really need three plastic bags for one croissant?—but such a focus on presentation has deep roots in Japanese culture.

This focus on presentation also influences salespeople who are invariably helpful and polite. In the larger stores they greet you with a bow when you arrive, and many of them speak at least enough English to help you find what you're looking for. There's a saying in Japan: *o-kyaku-sama wa kami-sama,* "the customer is a god"—and since the competition for your business is fierce, people do take it to heart.

Horror stories abound about prices in Japan—and some of them are true. Yes, European labels can cost a fortune here, but did you really travel all the way to Tokyo to buy an outfit that would be cheaper in the designer mall at home? True, a gift-wrapped melon from a department-store gourmet counter can cost $150. But you can enjoy gawking even if you don't want to spend like that. And if you shop around, you can find plenty of gifts and souvenirs at fair prices.

Japan has finally embraced the use of credit cards, although some smaller mom-and-pop shops may still take cash only. So when you go souvenir hunting, be prepared with a decent amount of cash; Tokyo's low crime rates make this a low-risk proposition. The dishonor associated with theft is so strong, in fact, that it's considered bad form to conspicuously count change in front of cashiers.

Japan has an across-the-board 8% value-added tax (V.A.T.) imposed on luxury goods. This tax can be avoided at some duty-free shops in the city (don't forget to bring your passport). It's also waived in the duty-free shops at the international airports, but because these places tend to have higher profit margins, your tax savings there are likely to be offset by the higher markups.

Stores in Tokyo generally open at 10 or 11 am and close at 8 or 9 pm.

AKIHABARA 秋葉原

Akihabara was at one time the only place Tokyoites would go to buy cutting-edge electronic gadgets, but the area has lost its aura of exclusivity thanks to the Internet and the big discount chains that have sprung up around the city. Still, for sheer variety of products and foreigner-friendliness, Akihabara has the newcomers beat—and a visit remains essential to any Tokyo shopping spree. Salesclerks speak decent English at most of the major shops (and many of the smaller ones), and the big chains offer duty-free and export items. Be sure to poke around the backstreets for smaller stores that sell used and unusual electronic goods. The area has also become the center of the *otaku* (nerd) boom, with loads of shops selling enough video games and *manga* (sophisticated comic books) to satisfy even the most fastidious geek.

8

ANTIQUES

Yasukuni Jinja (靖国神社 *Yasukuni Shrine*). Most Sundays, from sunrise to sunset, antiques-hunters can search and explore this flea market, which boasts 30–50 booths run by professional collectors. It's located within the controversial Yasukuni Jinja grounds, so when you're finished shopping, stroll through the shrine that pays respect to dead Japanese soldiers. ✉ *3–1–1 Kudan-Kita, Chiyoda-ku* ☎ *03/3261–8326* 🌐 *www.yasukuni.or.jp/english/index.html* Ⓜ *Hanzo-mon and Shinjuku subway lines, Kudanshita Station (Exit 1).*

COSTUMES

Cospa Gee Store (ジーストア). Fans of anime will enjoy this zany Japanese costume-shop experience. It's like no other in the world and a good place to pick up an original costume for Halloween. ✉ *2F MN Bldg., 3–15–5 Soto-Kanda, Chiyoda-ku, Akihabara* ☎ *03/3526–6877* Ⓜ *JR Yamanote Line, Akihabara Station (Akihabara Electric Town Exit).*

DOLLS

Kyugetsu (九月). In business for more than a century, Kyugetsu sells every kind of doll imaginable, from the East and the West. ✉ *1–20–4 Yanagibashi, Taitō-ku* ☎ *03/5687–5176* 🌐 *www.kyugetsu.com/e/index.html* Ⓜ *Asakusa subway line, JR Sobu Line, Asakusa-bashi Station (Exit A3).*

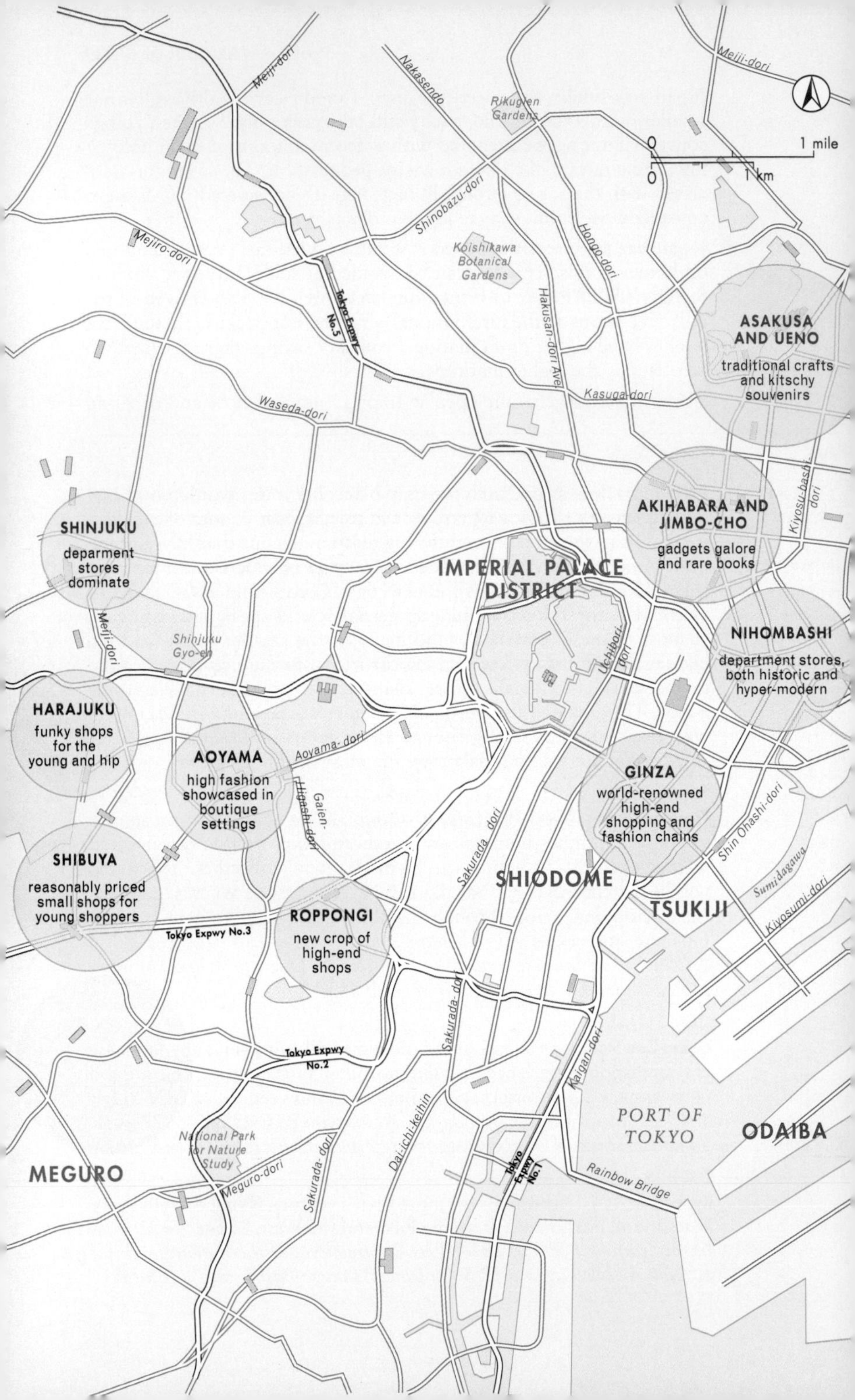

ASAKUSA AND UENO
traditional crafts and kitschy souvenirs
AKIHABARA AND JIMBO-CHO
gadgets galore and rare books
IMPERIAL PALACE DISTRICT
NIHOMBASHI
department stores, both historic and hyper-modern
SHINJUKU
deparment stores dominate
HARAJUKU
funky shops for the young and hip
AOYAMA
high fashion showcased in boutique settings
SHIBUYA
reasonably priced small shops for young shoppers
ROPPONGI
new crop of high-end shops
GINZA
world-renowned high-end shopping and fashion chains
SHIODOME
TSUKIJI
PORT OF TOKYO
ODAIBA
MEGURO
Rikugien Gardens
Koishikawa Botanical Gardens
Shinjuku Gyo-en
National Park for Nature Study
Meiji-dori
Nakasendo
Shinobazu-dori
Hongo-dori
Hakusan-dori Ave.
Mejiro-dori
Tokyo Expwy No.5
Waseda-dori
Kasuga-dori
Kiyosu-bashi-dori
Uchibori-dori
Aoyama-dori
Gaien-Higashi-dori
Sakurada-dori
Shin Ohashi-dori
Sumidagawa
Kiyosumi-dori
Tokyo Expwy No.3
Tokyo Expwy No.2
Dai-ichi-keihin
Kaigan-dori
Tokyo Expwy No.1
Rainbow Bridge
Meguro-dori
0
1 mile
0
1 km

ELECTRONICS

LAOX (ソフマップ). One of the big Akihabara department stores, LAOX has several locations and the largest and most comprehensive selection in the district, with four buildings. The seven-story main branch is duty-free, with three floors dedicated to electronic gadgets, such as lightweight vacuum cleaners and eco-friendly humidifiers, that come with English instruction booklets. English-speaking staff members are on call. LAOX has annexes—one exclusively for musical instruments, another for duty-free appliances—and outlets in Ginza, Odaiba and Narita Airport. This is a good place to find the latest in digital cameras, watches, and games. ✉ *1–2–9 Soto-Kanda, Chiyoda-ku, Akihabara* ☎ *03/3253–7111* 🌐 *www.laox.co.jp* Ⓜ *JR Yamanote Line, Akihabara Station (Electric Town Exit).*

Radio Kaikan (ラジオ会館). Eight floors featuring a variety of independent vendors selling mini-spy cameras, cell phones disguised as stun guns, manga comics, adult toys, gadgets, and oddball hobby supplies draw otaku, other shoppers, and visitors alike. And that's just the main building. Start browsing from the top floor and work your way down. There are two annexes across the street as well. ✉ *1–15–16 Soto-Kanda, Chiyoda-ku, Akihabara* ☎ *03/3251–3711 office* Ⓜ *JR Yamanote Line, Akihabara Station (Akihabara Electric Town Exit).*

Sofmap (ソフマップ). One Akihabara retailer that actually benefited from the bursting of Japan's economic bubble in the early '90s is this electronics chain, once known as a used-PC and software chain with a heavy presence in Tokyo. Now its multiple branches also sell all sorts of new electronics, music, and mobile phones. Most are open daily until 8. ✉ *4–1–1 Soto-Kanda, Chiyoda-ku, Akihabara* ☎ *03/3253–1111* Ⓜ *JR Yamanote Line, Akihabara Station (Electric Town Exit).*

Thanko (サンコー). As the king of wacky electronics from Japan, Thanko sells everything from bamboo smartphone cases and smokeless ashtrays to wireless charging stations diguised as jewelry. This showroom and its other branches are a must-see for gadget geeks. ✉ *3–14–8 Soto-Kanda, Chiyoda-ku* ☎ *03/5297–5783* 🌐 *www.raremonoshop.jp* Ⓜ *JR Yamanote Line, Akihabara Station (Akihabara Electric Town Exit).*

PAPER

Origami House (おりがみ会館 *Origami Kaikan*). There's more than just shopping for paper goods at this mini-tower dedicated to the art of folding, open since 1885. You can also tour a papermaking workshop and learn the art of origami in the shop's gallery. ✉ *1–7–14 Yushima, Bunkyo-ku, Akihabara* ☎ *03/3811–4025* 🌐 *www.origamihouse.jp* 🕓 *Closed Sun.* Ⓜ *JR Chuo and Sobu lines, Ochanomizu Station (West Exit); Chiyoda subway line, Yushima Station (Exit 5).*

UENO 上野

Ueno is known for its temples and traditional crafts shops, and recently small modern boutiques have added a fresh dimension to the neighborhood.

SPECIALTY STORES

Nakata Shoten Okachimachi (中田商店 御徒町店). This store probably has more shades of green than the average Tokyo park. Stuffed with cargo pants, camouflage jackets, military uniforms, and ammo boxes, Nakata Shoten is more about outfitting its customers in funky fashion than resurrecting Imperial militarism. The watches make interesting souvenirs. ✉ *6–2–14 Ueno, Taitō-ku, Ueno* ☎ *03/3839–6866* 🌐 *www.nakatashoten.com* Ⓜ *JR lines, Okachi-machi Station (North Exit); Toei Oedo subway line, Ueno Okachi-machi Station (Exit A7).*

Jusan-ya (十三や). A samurai who couldn't support himself as a feudal retainer launched this business selling handmade boxwood combs in 1736. It has been in the same family ever since. Jusan-ya is on Shinobazu-dori, a few doors west of its intersection with Chuo-dori in Ueno. ✉ *2–12–21 Ueno, Taitō-ku* ☎ *03/3831–3238* 🌐 *www.kyoto-wel.com/shop/S81004* ⏲ *Closed Sun.* Ⓜ *Ginza subway line, Ueno Hiroko-ji Station (Exit 3); JR Yamanote Line, Ueno Station (Shinobazu Exit).*

Roots Shakuhachi: The Bamboo Way (ルーツ尺八). Once carried by itinerant Buddhist priests, the *shakuhachi*, a long bamboo flute, is one of Japan's most hauntingly soothing musical instruments. It is a testament to Japan's traditional aesthetic of elegant simplicity. At Roots Shakuhachi, customers can make their own shakuhachi. Budget ¥5,000 and 30 minutes to an hour to make your shakuhachi, and a little more time to learn the basics of how to play it. ✉ *Com So Koya, 3–1–17 Yanaka, Taito-ku* 🌐 *roots-shakuhachi.weebly.com* Ⓜ *JR Yamanote Line, Nippori Station (West Exit), Chiyoda Line, Sendagi Station (Dango-zaka Exit)* ⏲ *Closed Wed.*

SHOPPING STREETS AND ARCADES

Ameyoko Market (アメヤ横丁). Everything from fresh fish to cheap import clothing is for sale at this bustling warren of side streets between Okachi-machi and Ueno stations. In the days leading up to New Year's, the area turns into mosh-pit mayhem as shoppers fight for fish and snacks to serve over the holidays. The official name of the market is Ameya-Yoko-cho but is almost always shortened to Ameyoko. ✉ *Ueno 6-chome, Taitō-ku* Ⓜ *JR Ueno Station (Hiroko-ji Exit), JR Okachi-machi Station (Exit A7).*

ASAKUSA 浅草

While visiting the Senso-ji shrine complex in Asakusa, take time to stroll through the neighborhood's many arcades. At first glance, many of the goods sold here are the kinds of souvenirs you can find in any tourist trap. Look a little harder and you can find small backstreet shops that have been making beautiful wooden combs, delicate fans, and other items of fine traditional craftsmanship for generations. Also here are the cookware shops of Kappabashi, where you can load up on everything from sushi knives to plastic lobsters.

DOLLS

FAMILY **Marugin** (人形のまるぎん). This long-standing doll emporium specializes in *Hina* dolls, or emperor and empress sets in extravagant Heian-era clothing. Young Japanese girls display these every year for one month until March 2, Girls Day. ✉ *1–18–9 Asakusa-bashi, Taitō-ku, Asakusa* ☎ *03/3862–6088* Ⓜ *JR Sobu line (West Exit), Asakusa subway line, Asakusa-bashi Station (Exit A3).*

FOOD

Kawahara Shoten (川原商店). The brightly colored bulk packages of rice crackers, shrimp-flavored chips, and other Japanese snacks sold here make offbeat gifts. ✉ *3–9–2 Nishi-Asakusa, Taitō-ku, Asakusa* ☎ *03/3842–0841* ⏲ *Closed Sun.* Ⓜ *Ginza subway line, Asakusa Station (Exit 1).*

Tokiwa-do (常盤堂). Come here to buy some of Tokyo's most famous souvenirs: *kaminari okoshi* (thunder crackers), made of rice, millet, sugar, and beans. The shop is on the west side of Asakusa's Thunder God Gate, the Kaminari-mon entrance to Senso-ji, and you can watch as they make them in front of you. ✉ *1–3–2 Asakusa, Taitō-ku, Asakusa* ☎ *03/3841–5656* 🌐 *www.tokiwado.tokyo* Ⓜ *Ginza subway line, Asakusa Station (Exit 1).*

Tsubaya Knives (つば屋包丁店). This shop's remarkable selection of high-quality cutlery for professionals is designed for every imaginable use, as the art of food presentation in Japan requires a great variety of cutting implements. The best of these carry the Traditional Craft Association seal: hand-forged tools of tempered blue steel, set in handles banded with deer horn to keep the wood from splitting. Be prepared to pay the premium for these items. A cleaver just for slicing soba can cost as much as ¥50,000. ✉ *3–7–2 Nishi-Asakusa, Taito-ku, Asakusa* ☎ *03/3845–2005* Ⓜ *Ginza subway line, Asakusa (Exit 1).*

SHOPPING STREETS AND ARCADES

Nakamise Market (仲見世通り *Nakamise-dori*). This narrow street is heaven for those seeking out traditional knickknacks and souvenirs. It is just as lively as it was when it was established in the Edo period, although now shops sells cheap sushi key chains and T-shirts alongside traditional hairpieces and silk screens. The entrance is marked by the giant red lantern at the Kaminari-mon, and ends at the grounds of the Senso-ji Complex. ✉ *Asakusa 1-chome, Taito-ku* ☎ *03/3844–3350* Ⓜ *Ginza subway line, Asakusa Station (Exit 1).*

Nishi-Sando Arcade (西参道商店街 *Nishi-Sando Shoten-gai*). Kimono and *yukata* (cotton kimono) fabrics, traditional accessories, swords, and festival costumes at very reasonable prices are all for sale at this Asakusa arcade. It runs east of the area's movie theaters, between Rok-ku and the Senso-ji Complex. ✉ *Asakusa 2-chome, Taito-ku* Ⓜ *Ginza subway line, Asakusa Station (Exit 1).*

SPECIALTY STORES

Kondo Bamboo (竹製品専門の近藤商店). Bamboo is the name of the game here, and a plethora of goods range from baskets to display stands made of the resilient, natural material. ✉ *3–1–13 Matsugaya,*

Taitō-ku, Asakusa ☎ 03/3841–3372 ⊙ Closed Sun. Ⓜ Ginza subway line, Tawara-machi Station (Exit 3).

SWORDS AND KNIVES

Ichiryo-ya Hirakawa (一両屋平川). This small, cluttered souvenir shop in the Nishi-Sando arcade carries antique swords and reproductions and has some English-speaking salesclerks. ✉ *2–7–13 Asakusa, Taitō-ku, Asakusa* ☎ *03/3843–0052* ⊙ *Closed Thurs.* Ⓜ *Ginza subway line, Asakusa Station (Exit 1) or Tawara-machi Station (Exit 3).*

TRADITIONAL WARES

Fuji-ya (ふじ屋). Master textile creator Keiji Kawakami is an expert on the hundreds of traditional towel motifs that have come down from the Edo period: geometric patterns, plants and animals, and scenes from Kabuki plays and festivals. His cotton *tenugui* (teh- *noo*-goo-ee) hand towels are collector's items, often framed instead of used as towels. When Kawakami feels he has made enough of one pattern of his own design, he destroys the stencil. The shop is near the corner of Dembo-in Dori, on the street that runs parallel behind Naka-mise dori. ✉ *2–2–15 Asakusa, Taitō-ku, Asakusa* ☎ *03/3841–2283* ⊙ *Closed Thurs.* Ⓜ *Ginza subway line, Asakusa Station (Exit 1).*

Hyaku-suke (百助). This is the last place in Tokyo to carry government-approved skin cleanser made from powdered nightingale droppings. Ladies of the Edo period—especially the geisha—swore by the cleanser. These days this 300-year-old-plus cosmetics shop sells little of the nightingale powder, but its theatrical makeup for Kabuki actors, geisha, and traditional weddings—as well as unique items like seaweed shampoo, camellia oil, and handcrafted combs and cosmetic brushes—makes it a worthy addition to your Asakusa shopping itinerary. ✉ *2–2–14 Asakusa, Taitō-ku, Asakusa* ☎ *03/3841–7058* ⊙ *Closed Tues.* Ⓜ *Ginza subway line, Asakusa Station (Exit 6).*

FAMILY **Maizuru** (まいづる). This perennial tourist favorite manufactures the plastic food that's displayed outside almost every Tokyo restaurant. Ersatz sushi, noodles, and even beer cost just a few thousand yen. You can buy tiny plastic key holders and earrings, or splurge on a whole Pacific lobster, perfect in coloration and detail down to the tiniest spines on its legs. ✉ *1–5–17 Nishi-Asakusa, Taitō-ku, Asakusa* ☎ *03/3843–1686* Ⓜ *Ginza subway line, Asakusa Station (Exit 6).*

Naka-ya (中屋). If you want to equip yourself for the neighborhood's annual Sanja Festival in May, this is the place to come for traditional costumes. Best buys here are *sashiko hanten;,* which are thick, woven firemen's jackets; and *happi* coats, cotton tunics printed in bright colors with Japanese characters. Some items are available in children's sizes. ✉ *2–2–12 Asakusa, Taitō-ku, Asakusa* ☎ *03/3841–7877* 🌐 *www.nakaya.co.jp* Ⓜ *Ginza subway line, Asakusa Station (Exit 6).*

Soi Interior & Style Design. The selection of lacquerware, ceramics, and antiques sold at this Kappabashi shop is modest, but Soi displays the items in a primitivist setting of stone walls and wooden floor planks, with up-tempo jazz in the background. ✉ *3–25–11 Nishi-Asakusa, Taitō-ku, Asakusa* ☎ *03/3843–7200* 🌐 *www.soi-2.jp* Ⓜ *Ginza subway line, Asakusa Station (Exit 6).*

Continued on page 253

SHOP TOKYO

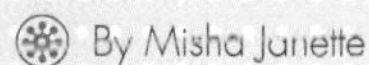

Tokyo, the most retail-dense city in the world, lures even the most reluctant shoppers with promises of every product imaginable. Travel back in time at department and specialty stores selling traditional ceramics and lacquerware, or leap into the future in Akihabara and other gadget-oriented neighborhoods. Fashionistas watch trends in Harajuku morph before their eyes, while those with more highbrow sensibilities browse the jewelry at stalwarts like Mikimoto.

Each Tokyo neighborhood has its own specialty, style, mood, and type of customer. Local production still thrives in the city's backstreets despite an influx of global chains and mega-corporations. Keep in mind, however, that nearly all of the locally produced goods will cost a pretty penny; the Japanese are meticulous in design and quality, and tend to prefer small-scale production to large output. Here in Tokyo you will find that one-offs and limited-edition items are often the norm rather than the exception.

For clothing, sizing is still the biggest roadblock to really getting the most from Tokyo boutiques. But with the abundance of quirky trends sometimes it's enough just to window-shop.

Above: Shoppers mill around the entrance to Tokyo's Louis Vuitton.

WHAT TO BUY

MANGA

Manga, or Japanese comic books, have had an incredible influence on pop culture around the world. The inherently Japanese-style illustrations are fun to look at, and the simple language is great for studying. Book-Off, a well-known used manga chain, sells comics at rock-bottom prices, sometimes ¥100 each.

INNERWEAR

The Japanese are known for their electronics, but did you know their textile and fiber industry is also one of the most advanced in the world? The sweat-repelling, heat-conducting, UBAV/UVB-blocking and aloe-vera dispensing underthings available at Tokyo department stores are probably already in every Japanese person's top drawer at home.

FLAVORED SNACKS

Japan is the land of limited-edition products, and every season brings new, adventurous flavors in finite quantities. All it takes is a trip to the local convenience store to find melon- or Sakura-flavored Kit-Kat bars, or sweet Mont Blanc-flavored Pepsi. We dare you to try them.

PHONE ACCESSORIES

Cell phones and their accoutrement have become a fashion statement all their own. Phone straps, small plastic models that hang from one's phone, are the most popular. They come in all forms, from Asahi beer bottles to Hello Kitty dolls. There are also matching plastic "no peek" sheets that prevent others from spying on your phone's screen.

HOUSEWARES

Tokyoites appreciate fine design, and this passion is reflected in the exuberance of the city's *zakka* shops—retailers that sell small housewares. The Daikanyama and Aoyama areas positively brim with these stores, but trendy zakka can be found throughout the city. Handmade combs, chopsticks, and towels are other uniquely Japanese treasures to consider picking up while in Tokyo.

RECORDS

Tokyo's small specialty music stores are a real treat: local music and imports from around the world are usually available on both vinyl and CD. Out-of-print or obscure vinyl editions can run well over ¥10,000, but collectors will find the condition of the jackets to be unmatched.

SOCKS

As it's customary in Japanese houses to remove one's shoes, socks are more than mere padding between foot and shoe. It's no surprise, then, that the selection of socks goes well beyond black and white. Stripes, polka-dots, Japanese scenery, and monograms are just some of the depictions you'll find at the high-end sock boutiques. The complicated weaving techniques mean they will also cost more than the average cotton pair.

WASHLETTE TOILET SEATS

It may seem ludicrous, but the Japanese "washlette" toilet seat is perhaps the best innovation of this millennium. The seats are heated, come with deodorizers, and may even play music to mask any "rude" sounds. Even better, some can be retrofitted to old toilets—just be sure to check your seat measurements before leaving home.

SAKE SETS

Sake is a big deal here, and the type of sake presented to another can make or break business deals and friendships. Better than just a bottle are the gift sets that include the short sake glasses and oversized bottles in beautiful packaging fit for royalty.

CHARCOAL

Japanese women have been using charcoal, or *takesumi*, in their beauty routines for centuries, believing it cleans out the pores and moisturizes the skin. Charcoal-infused formulas are used in soaps, cleansers, cremes, and masques, and often are naturally colored pitch-black like squid ink.

JEWELRY

Japan has always been known for its craftsmen who possess the ability to create finely detailed work. Jewelry is no exception, especially when cultured pearls are used. Pearls, which have become something of a national symbol, are not inexpensive, but they are much cheaper in Japan than elsewhere.

FOLK CRAFTS

Japanese folk crafts, called *mingei*—among them bamboo vases and baskets, fabrics, paper boxes, dolls, and toys—achieve a unique beauty in their simple and sturdy designs. Be aware, however, that simple does not mean cheap. Long hours of labor go into these objects, and every year there are fewer craftspeople left, producing their work in smaller and smaller quantities. Include these items in your budget ahead of time: The best—worth every cent—can be fairly expensive.

EXPERIENCING JAPANESE DEPATO

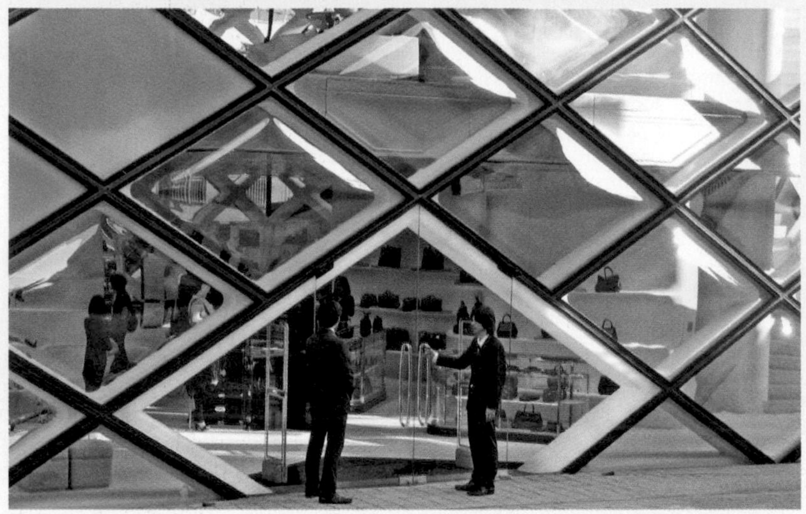

The impressive architecture at the Prada flagship matches the designer wares inside.

A visit to a Japanese *depato* (department store) is the perfect Cliff's Notes introduction to Japanese culture. Impeccable service combines with the best luxury brands, gourmet food, and traditional goods—all displayed as enticing eye candy.

These large complexes are found around major train stations and are often owned by the conglomerate rail companies who make their profit when visitors take the train to shop there. The stores themselves commonly have travel agencies, theaters, and art galleries on the premises, as well as reasonably priced and strategically placed restaurants and cafés.

ARRIVE EARLY

The best way to get the full experience is to arrive just as the store is opening. Err on the early side: Tokyo's department stores are exacting in their opening times. White-gloved ladies and gents bow to waiting customers when the doors open on the hour. Early birds snatch up limited-edition food and goods before they sell out. There's never a dearth of reasons to come: local celebrity appearances, designer Q&A sessions, and fairs.

ANATOMY OF A DEPATO

The first floors typically house cosmetics, handbags, and shoes, with the next few floors up going to luxury import brands. On many a top floor you'll find gift packages containing Japan's best-loved brands of sake, rice crackers, and other foods. Department stores also typically devote one floor to traditional Japanese crafts, including ceramics, paintings, and lacquerware.

Don't miss the *depachika* (food departments) on the basement levels, where an overwhelming selection of expensive Japanese and Western delicacies are wrapped with the utmost care. More affordable versions come packed deli-style to be taken home for lunch or dinner.

Shibuya's depato attract trendsetters.

BEST DEPATO FOR . . .

Most department stores are similar and house the same brands. But some have distinctive characteristics.

The Trendy Dresser: Seibu in Shibuya and Ikebukuro is known for its collection of fashion-forward tenants.

Emerging Designers: Isetan in Shinjuku oozes style and has ample space on the fourth floor dedicated to up-and-coming designers.

Gifts: Shinjuku's Takashimaya is the place to buy souvenirs for discerning friends back home.

Traditional Crafts: Mitsukoshi in Nihombashi will leave those looking for a bit of Old Japan wide-eyed.

Depato interiors are often dramatic.

TIPS FOR DEPATO SHOPPING

■ Major department stores accept credit cards and provide shipping services.

■ It's important to remember that, unlike most of the Western world, goods must be purchased in the department where they were found. This goes for nearly every multilevel shop in Japan.

■ Nowadays, most salesclerks speak some English. If you're having communication difficulties, someone will always come to the rescue.

■ On the first floor you'll invariably find a general information booth with maps of the store in English.

■ Some department stores close one or two days a month. To be on the safe side, call ahead.

FASHIONABLE TOKYO

The Japanese fashion scene has gone through many changes since Yohji Yamamoto's solemn, deconstructed garments and Rei Kawakubo's Comme des Garçons clothing lines challenged norms in the 1980s. While these designers and their ilk are still revered, it's Tokyo's street fashion that keeps the city on the world's radar.

Clockwise from top left: An orange-haired Harajuku Girl; manga-influenced street fashion; Sailor Moon-inspired Harajuku girls.

Thanks to Gwen Stefani's "Harajuku Girls" and Quentin Tarantino's *Kill Bill*, images of the Gothic Lolita—a fashion subculture typified by a Victorian porcelain-doll look punctuated by dark makeup and macabre accessories—have seeped into Western popular culture. New subcultures, or "tribes," like the Harajuku Girls emerge, take hold in Tokyo, and evolve (or get thrown aside) with blazing speed. The "forest girl" tribe's aesthetic draws from sources such as the American prairie and traditional German attire in loose layers, often in organic and vintage materials. The "skirt boys" are among the mens' tribes. These cool boys stomp around in boots and skirts that Japanese menswear designers have been favoring on the runway in recent years.

Japanese fashion continues to awe and inspire; international designers come to Tokyo for ideas. This means you might already be wearing something from Tokyo without even knowing it!

SIZING UP JAPANESE SIZES

Japanese garments, even if they are not a troublesome and common "one-size-fits-all," run considerably smaller than American items. The female aesthetic tends to favor loose and roomy shapes so is far more forgiving than the menswear, which is often cut impossibly small and tight.

Shibuya brands often carry items in nothing more than an arbitrary "one-size-only" on the racks that may not fit many Westerners at all. Many designers, in deference to the growing foreign market, are starting to offer larger sizes. The internationally recognized brands, department stores, and bigger boutiques, including Opening Ceremony in Shibuya, are the best bets for finding a range of sizes.

Shoes tend to run small, often stopping at 27 cm (U.S. size 9) for men and 24 cm (U.S. size 8) for women. What's more, Japanese shoes are often made a little wider than their Western counterparts.

Above: Harajuku Girls wear dramatic costume like outfits.

A TALE OF TWO NEIGHBORHOOD STYLES

You don't need to be an industry insider attending Japan's Fashion Week shows to get a sense of Tokyo's multiple styles; you just need to stroll the neighborhoods where every sidewalk is a catwalk.

Japanese street fashion begins and ends along the maze-like backstreets of **Harajuku**, referred to as "Ura-Hara." You'll find many of Tokyo's most popular and promising up-and-coming brands' boutiques, although it might take sharp eyes to spot the often-obstructed store signs. Tokyo's youngest shoppers come for the newest fashions and to show off their costume-like vestments. Visit on a Sunday to see them in full regalia. If the throngs of tweens prove too much, there are other incredible street-fashion shopping areas. Shimokitazawa and Koenji are known for their used-clothing shops and a young fashion scene that's just as lively as that of Harajuku.

For a different take, go to **Shibuya**, where women and men have cultivated a distinctive fashion and lifestyle. The so-called Shibuya style is vivid, brash, and hyper, and comes with its own idols, models, and magazines. Malls such as 109, which is the center of this movement's universe, dedicate their retail space wholly to this world.

More than 50,000 people, including many visitors to Tokyo, attend the biannual **Tokyo Girls Collection**, daylong events of Shibuya-style fashion shows and musical performances by pop big acts. JTB offers full package tours around the event starting at ¥8,000 per person.

FIVE EMERGING DESIGNERS

Limi Feu: Limi, Yohji Yamamoto's daughter, takes a hint from him in her loose, monotone, punk attire, but injects it with a cool, feminine touch. 🌐 *www.limifeu.com*

Matohu: This unisex brand creates looks based on traditional and colorful Japanese clothing, namely robes, by incorporating ancient dye and weaving techniques into 21st-century designs. 🌐 *www.matohu.com/en*

N. Hoolywood: Daisuke Obana's menswear line has been on the top of Japanese editors' lists since 2002. He adds contemporary design elements to used clothing, and his attire tends to be loose and casual. 🌐 *www.n-hoolywood.com*

Phenomenon: This is one of the most exciting menswear brands to come out since A Bathing Ape. Expect a combo of hip-hop, 80s, and bespoke tailoring with pitch-perfect styling. 🌐 www.phenomenon.tv

Somarta: This brand is known for its intricate, seamless knitwear and other experimental textiles developed using Japanese technology. The menswear line called Molfic follows the same innovative ethos in its seasonless designs. 🌐 *www.somarta.jp*

Top to bottom: Limi Feu, N. Hoolywood, Somarta

CLOSE UP

Shopping in Kappabashi

A wholesale-restaurant-supply district might not sound like a promising shopping destination, but Kappabashi, about a 10-minute walk west of the temples and pagodas of Asakusa, is worth a look. Ceramics, cutlery, cookware, folding lanterns, and even kimonos can all be found here, along with the kitschy plastic food models that appear in restaurant windows throughout Japan. The best strategy is to stroll up and down the 1-km (½-mile) length of Kappabashi-dogu-machi-dori and visit any shop that looks interesting. Most stores here emphasize function over charm, but some manage to stand out for their stylish spaces as well. Most Kappabashi shops are open until 5:30; some close Sunday. To get here, take the Ginza subway line to Tawara-machi Station.

NIHOMBASHI 日本橋

To the north of Tokyo Station is Nihombashi, which sees historic department stores facing off with 21st-century malls; only a few mom-and-pop shops still stand their ground.

BOOKS

Yaesu Book Center (八重洲ブックセンター). English-language paperbacks, art books, and calendars are available on the seventh floor of this celebrated bookstore. ✉ *2–5–1 Yaesu, Chūō-ku, Marunouchi* ☎ *03/3281–0811* Ⓜ *JR Yamanote Line, Tokyo Station (Yaesu South Exit 5).*

DEPARTMENT STORES

Fodor'sChoice ★ **Mitsukoshi** (三越). Founded in 1673 as a dry-goods store, Mitsukoshi later played one of the leading roles in introducing Western merchandise to Japan. It has retained its image of quality and excellence, with a particularly strong representation of Western fashion designers. The store also stocks fine traditional Japanese goods—don't miss the art gallery and the crafts area on the sixth floor. With its own subway stop, bronze lions at the entrance, and an atrium sculpture of the Japanese goddess Magokoro, this flagship store merits a visit even if you're not planning on buying anything. ✉ *1–4–1 Nihombashi Muro-machi, Chūō-ku, Nihombashi* ☎ *03/3241–3311* Ⓜ *Ginza and Hanzo-mon subway lines, Mitsukoshi-mae Station (Exits A3 and A5).*

FOOD

Yamamoto Seaweed (山元海苔店 *Yamamoto Noriten*). The Japanese are resourceful in their uses of products from the sea. Nori, the paper-thin dried seaweed used to wrap maki sushi and *onigiri* (rice balls), is the specialty here. If you plan to bring some home with you, buy unroasted nori and toast it yourself at home; the flavor will be far better than that of the preroasted sheets. ✉ *1–6–3 Nihombashi Muro-machi, Chūō-ku, Nihombashi* ☎ *03/3241–0290* 🌐 *www.yamamoto-noriten.co.jp/english* Ⓜ *Hanzo-mon and Ginza subway lines, Mitsukoshi-mae Station (Exit A1).*

MALLS AND SHOPPING CENTERS

Coredo (コレド). Unlike other big stores in the Nihombashi area, this sparkling mall feels contemporary thanks to an open layout and extensive use of glass. Neighboring it are three more new glittery towers: Coredo Muromachi 1, 2, and 3, which fuse traditional housewares stores with modern fashion boutiques. The in-house Nihombashi Tourist Center runs workshops on everything from dressing like a Geisha to cooking food. ✉ *1–4–1 Nihombashi, Chūō-ku, Nihombashi* ☎ *03/3242–0010* 🌐 *31urban.jp/en/index.html* Ⓜ *Ginza, Tozai, and Asakusa subway lines, Nihombashi Station (Exit B12).*

PAPER

Ozu Washi (小津和紙). This shop, which was opened in the 17th century, has one of the largest *washi* showrooms in the city and its own gallery of antique papers. Best to check ahead of time, but they sometimes have classes for just ¥500 on how to make your own washi paper. ✉ *3–6–2 Nihombashi-Honcho, Chūō-ku, Nihombashi* ☎ *03/3662–1184* 🌐 *www.ozuwashi.net/english* ⏲ *Closed Sun.* Ⓜ *Ginza and Hanzo-mon subway lines, Mitsukoshi-mae Station (Exit A4).*

SWORDS AND KNIVES

Kiya Blades (木屋刃物 *kiya hamono*). Workers shape and hone blades in one corner of this shop, which carries cutlery, pocketknives, saws, and more. Scissors with handles in the shape of Japanese cranes are among the many unique gift items sold here, and custom-made knives are available, too. Kiya is located in the Coredo Muro-machi complex. ✉ *2–2–1 Nihombashi-Muromachi, Chuo-ku, Nihombashi* ☎ *03/3241–0110* 🌐 *www.kiya-hamono.co.jp* Ⓜ *Ginza subway line, Mitsukoshi-mae Station (Exit A6).*

GINZA 銀座

This world-renowned entertainment and shopping district dates back to the Edo period (1603–1868), when it consisted of long, willow-lined avenues. The willows have long since gone, and the streets are now lined with department stores and boutiques. The exclusive shops in this area—including flagship stores for major jewelers like Tiffany & Co., Harry Winston, and Mikimoto—sell quality merchandise at high prices. Now many affordable fashion and goods chains have built towers in the area, creating a mix of high- and low-brow style that defines modern Tokyo's taste. On Sunday the main strip of Chuo-dori is closed to car traffic, and umbrella-covered tables dot the pavement; it's a great place to rest your weary feet.

CLOTHING

Fodor's Choice ★ **Dover Street Market.** This multistory fashion playhouse is a shrine to exclusives, one-offs, and other hard-to-find pieces from luxury brands all over the world. Curated by Comme des Garçons, the selection may leave all but the most dedicated fashion fans scratching their heads, but the unique interior sculptures and rooftop shrine with Japanese garden alone warrant a visit. ✉ *6–9–5 Ginza, Chūō-ku, Ginza* ☎ *03/6228–5080* 🌐 *ginza.doverstreetmarket.com* Ⓜ *Ginza, Hibiya, and Marunouchi subway lines, Ginza Station (Exit A2).*

FAMILY **Uniqlo** (ユニクロ). Customers can wrap themselves in simple, low-price items from the company's own brand. This 12-story location is the world's largest, and sells men's, women's, and children's clothing right on the main Ginza drag. ✉ *6–9–5 Ginza, Chuo-ku, Ginza* ☎ *03/6252–5181* Ⓜ *Ginza, Hibiya, and Marunouchi subway lines, Ginza Station (Exit A2).*

DEPARTMENT STORES

Fodor's Choice ★ **Matsuya** (松屋). On the fourth floor, this gleaming department store houses an excellent selection of Japanese fashion, including Issey Miyake and Yohji Yamamoto. The European-designer boutiques on the second floor are particularly popular with Tokyo's brand-obsessed shoppers. The rooftop terrace is a welcome respite for the weary. ✉ *3–6–1 Ginza, Chūō-ku, Ginza* ☎ *03/3567–1211* 🌐 *www.matsuya.com/visitor/en* Ⓜ *Ginza, Marunouchi, and Hibiya subway lines, Ginza Station (Exit A12).*

Mitsukoshi (三越). The Ginza branch of Japan's first department-store chain has been open since 1930 and remains the largest department store in the area, with a sprawling grass-covered terrace on the ninth floor that provides a respite from the shopping bustle. On the third floor is an area called "Le Place" that sells only local designer fashion, and the two basement floors have an impressive selection of delicacies. ✉ *4–6–16 Ginza, Chūō-ku, Ginza* ☎ *03/3562–1111* 🌐 *mitsukoshi.mistore.jp.e.bm.hp.transer.com/store/ginza/index.html* Ⓜ *Ginza, Marunouchi, and Hibiya subway lines, Ginza Station (Exits A6, A7, and A8).*

FAMILY Fodor's Choice ★ **Muji** (無印良品). This chain sells generically branded housewares and clothing at reasonable prices. At the massive Ginza store is a large selection of furniture, appliances, bedding, and clothes for the whole family, all in the signature Bauhaus-inspired simplified designs. If you're a bit overwhelmed by the options, relax at the dining area that boasts—what else?—Muji meals. ✉ *3–8–3 Marunouchi, Chiyoda-ku, Ginza* ☎ *03/5208–8241* Ⓜ *JR Yamanote Line, Yuraku-cho subway line, Yuraku-cho Station (JR Kyobashi Exit, subway Exit D9).*

Wako (和光). This grand old department store is well known for its high-end watches, glassware, and jewelry, as well as having some of the most sophisticated window displays in town. The clock atop the curved 1930s-era building is illuminated at night, making it one of Tokyo's more recognized landmarks. ✉ *4–5–11 Ginza, Chūō-ku, Ginza* ☎ *03/3562–2111* 🌐 *www.wako.co.jp* Ⓜ *Ginza, Marunouchi, and Hibiya subway lines, Ginza Station (Exits A9 and A10).*

ELECTRONICS

Apple Store. Like its counterparts in cities around the world, this very stylish showroom displays the newest models from Apple's line of computer products. The Genius Bar on the second floor provides consulting services should you need to resuscitate a comatose iPad or MacBook while traveling. ✉ *3–5–12 Ginza, Chūō-ku, Ginza* ☎ *03/5159–8200* 🌐 *www.apple.com/jp/retail/ginza* Ⓜ *Ginza, Hibiya, and Marunouchi subway lines, Ginza Station (Exit A13).*

FAMILY **Sony Building** (ソニービル). Test-drive the latest Sony gadgets at this retail and entertainment space in the heart of Ginza. The first- to fourth-floor showrooms allow parents to fiddle with digital cameras and computers from Japan's electronics leader, while kids can enjoy interactive displays of electric trains and weight-sensitive musical stairs. The Opus theater on the eighth floor shows movie trailers on a super-high-definition 4K screen and hosts games and events to coincide with movie releases. Take a break by browsing the Internet for free or at one of the cafés or pubs on the floors above the showroom. ✉ *5–3–1 Ginza, Chūō-ku, Ginza* ☎ *03/3573–2371* 🌐 *www.sonybuilding.jp/e* Ⓜ *JR Yamanote Line, Yuraku-cho Station (Ginza Exit); Ginza, Hibiya, and Marunouchi subway lines, Ginza Station (Exit B9).*

Sukiya Camera (スキヤカメラ). The cramped Nikon House branch of this two-store operation features so many Nikons—old and new, digital and film—that it could double as a museum to the brand. Plenty of lenses and flashes are available as well. ✉ *4–2–13 Ginza, Chūō-ku, Ginza* ☎ *03/3561–6000* Ⓜ *JR Yamanote Line, Yuraku-cho Station (Ginza Exit); Ginza, Hibiya, and Marunouchi subway lines, Ginza Station (Exit B10).*

JEWELRY

Ginza Tanaka (銀座田中). One of the finest jewelers in Japan was founded in 1892. The store specializes in precious metals and diamond jewelry. It also sells a wide variety of art objects in gold, like those found on Buddhist altars. ✉ *1–7–7 Ginza, Chūō-ku, Ginza* ☎ *03/5561–0491* 🌐 *www.ginzatanaka.co.jp/en* Ⓜ *Yuraku-cho subway line, Ginza 1-chome Station (Exit 7).*

Fodor's Choice ★ **Mikimoto.** Kokichi Mikimoto created his technique for cultured pearls in 1893. Since then his name has been associated with the best quality in the industry. Mikimoto's tower in Ginza is a boutique devoted to nature's ready-made gems; the building, like the pearls it holds, dazzles visitors with a facade that resembles Swiss cheese. ✉ *2–4–12 Ginza, Chūō-ku, Ginza* ☎ *03/3562–3130* 🌐 *www.mikimoto.com* Ⓜ *Ginza, Hibiya, and Marunouchi subway lines, Ginza Station (Exit C8).*

Tasaki Pearls (田崎). Tasaki sells pearls at slightly lower prices than Mikimoto. The brand opened this glittery flagship tower in Ginza that moved them from the old guard into the contemporary big leagues. There's a large collection of pearl and gem items, from costume to bridal and fine jewelry. On the fifth floor is an event space that holds numerous art exhibits. ✉ *5–7–5 Ginza, Chūō-ku, Ginza* ☎ *03/3289–1111* 🌐 *www.tasaki.co.jp* Ⓜ *Ginza, Hibiya, and Marunouchi subway lines, Ginza Station (Exit A2).*

KIMONOS

Tansu-ya (たんす屋). This small but pleasant Ginza shop has attractive used kimonos, yukata, and other traditional clothing in many fabrics, colors, and patterns. The helpful staff can acquaint you with the somewhat complicated method of putting on the garments. There are tax-free locations scattered throughout the city, including Shibuya, Asakusa, Aoyama, and Shibuya. ✉ *3–4–5 Ginza, Chūō-ku, Ginza* ☎ *03/3561–8529* 🌐 *tansuya.jp* Ⓜ *Ginza, Hibiya, and Marunouchi subway lines, Ginza Station (Exit A13).*

PAPER

Itoya (伊東屋). Completely remodeled in 2015, this huge paper emporium is brimming with locally crafted and imported stationery, much of which is designed to translate traditional motifs onto contemporary office tools. ✉ *2–7–15 Ginza, Chūō-ku, Ginza* ☎ *03/3561–8311* 🌐 *www.ito-ya.co.jp* Ⓜ *Ginza, Hibiya, and Marunouchi subway lines, Ginza Station (Exit A13).*

Kyukyodo (鳩居堂). Kyukyodo has been in business since 1663—and in this spacious Ginza location since 1880—selling wonderful handmade Japanese papers, paper products, incense, brushes, and other materials for calligraphy. ✉ *5–7–4 Ginza, Chūō-ku, Ginza* ☎ *03/3571–4429* 🌐 *www.kyukyodo.co.jp* Ⓜ *Ginza, Hibiya, and Marunouchi subway lines, Ginza Station (Exit A2).*

SWORDS AND KNIVES

Fodor's Choice ★ **Nippon Token** (日本刀剣 *Japan Sword*). Wannabe samurai can learn how to tell their *toshin* (blades) from their *tsuka* (sword handles) with help from the English-speaking staff at this small shop, which has been open since the Meiji era (1868–1912). Items that range from a circa-1390 samurai sword to inexpensive or decorative reproductions allow you to take a trip back in time. ✉ *3–8–1 Toranomon, Minato-ku, Ginza* ☎ *03/3434–4321* 🌐 *www.japansword.co.jp* ⏲ *Closed Sun.* Ⓜ *Hibiya and Ginza subway lines, Tora-no-mon Station (Exit 2).*

Token Shibata (刀剣柴田). This tiny, threadbare shop incongruously situated near Ginza's glittering department stores sells expensive well-worn antique swords. They can also sharpen your blade for you, if you happen to be packing while traveling. ✉ *5–6–8 Ginza, Chūō-ku, Ginza* ☎ *03/3573–2801* ⏲ *Closed Sun.* Ⓜ *Ginza, Hibiya, and Marunouchi subway lines, Ginza Station (Exit A1).*

SHOPPING STREETS AND ARCADES

International Shopping Arcade (インターナショナルアーケード). A ragtag collection of shops holds a range of goods, including cameras, electronics, pearls, and kimonos in a retro passageway. The shops are duty-free, and most of the sales staff speaks decent English. If you listen carefully you'll hear the rumble of cars passing above on the freeway that forms the roof of the building. ✉ *1–7–23 Uchisaiwai-cho, Chiyoda-ku, Ginza* Ⓜ *Chiyoda and Hibiya subway lines, Hibiya Station (Exit A13).*

MARUNOUCHI 丸の内

To the west of Tokyo Station, which for all intents and purposes is the entranceway to the city, is Marunouchi, a high-rise forest that is all about modernity. The arcades and shops attract sophisticated professionals who look for no-fuss quality. They also know how to let loose at the neighborhood's lounges and bars when the workday is done.

BOOKS

FAMILY **Maruzen** (丸善書店). In this flagship branch of the Maruzen chain in the Oazo building, there are English titles on the fourth floor as well as art books; the store also hosts occasional art exhibits. ✉ *1–6–4 Marunouchi, Chiyoda-ku* ☎ *03/5288–8881* 🌐 *www.maruzen.co.jp*

8

Ⓜ *JR Yamanote Line, Tokyo Station (North Exit); Tozai subway line, Otemachi Station (Exit B2C).*

HOUSEWARES

Pass the Baton (パスザバトン). *Zakka* is what the Japanese call small knickknacks and gifts, and this eccentric store is brimming with zakka from the coffers of local fashion designers, artists, magazine editors, celebrities, and other stylish Tokyo denizens. The carefully curated goods are fixed up and resold, with an option to give a portion of the profit to charity. It is tucked inside the Brick Square complex, next to an English rose garden. ✉ *2–6–1 Marunouchi, Chiyoda-ku* ☎ *03/6269–9555* 🌐 *www.pass-the-baton.com* Ⓜ *Marunouchi subway line, Tokyo Station (Marunouchi Bldg. Exit); JR Yamanote Line, Tokyo Station (Marunouchi Minami-guchi/South Exit).*

MALLS AND SHOPPING CENTERS

Marunouchi Buildings (丸の内ビル). Bringing some much-needed retail dazzle to the area are these six shopping, office, and dining mega-complexes called Marunocuhi, Shin-marunouchi, Oazu, Iiyo, Brick Square, and Tokia. Highlights include the fifth-floor open terrace on the Marunouchi building, with its view of Tokyo Station, and Bricksquare, which has its own oasislike European garden on the ground floor to rest in between bouts of shopping at the luxury and everyday boutiques. ✉ *2–4–1 Marunouchi, Chiyoda-ku, Marunouchi* ☎ *03/5218–5100* 🌐 *www.marunouchi.com/e* Ⓜ *Marunouchi subway line, Tokyo Station (Marunouchi Bldg. Exit); JR Yamanote Line, Tokyo Station (Marunouchi Minami-guchi/South Exit).*

AOYAMA 青山

You'll find boutiques by many of the leading Japanese and Western designers in Aoyama, as well as elegant, but pricey, antiques shops on Kotto-dori. Aoyama tends to be a showcase not merely of high fashion but also of the latest concepts in commercial architecture and interior design. Omotesando, a long, wide avenue running from Aoyama-dori into Meiji Jingu, is known as the Champs-Elysées of Tokyo. The sidewalks are lined with cafés, designer boutiques, and antiques and souvenir shops. Omotesando is perfect for browsing, window-shopping, and lingering over a café au lait.

ANTIQUES

Fuji-Torii (富士鳥居). An English-speaking staff, a central Omotesando location, and antiques ranging from ceramics to swords are the big draws at this shop, in business since 1948. In particular, Fuji-Torii has an excellent selection of folding screens, lacquerware, painted glassware, and *ukiyo-e* (woodblock prints). You can also pick up contemporary gifts, such as reading glasses with frames wrapped in traditional fabric. ✉ *6–1–10 Jingu-mae, Shibuya-ku, Aoyama* ☎ *03/3400–2777* 🌐 *www.fuji-torii.com* ⏲ *Closed Tues. and 3rd Mon. of every month* Ⓜ *Chiyoda and Fukutoshin subway lines, Meiji-Jingu-mae Station (Exit 4).*

Komingei Morita (古民芸もりた *Traditional Crafts Morita*). Antiques and new *mingei* (Japanese folk crafts) are on display alongside a large

CLOSE UP

The Power of Tea

Green tea is ubiquitous in Japan. But did you know that besides being something of a national drink, it's also good for you? Green tea contains antioxidants twice as powerful as those in red wine; these help reduce high blood pressure, lower blood sugar, and fight cancer. A heightened immune system and lower cholesterol are other benefits attributed to this beverage.

Whether drinking green tea for its healing properties, good taste, or as a manner of habit, you'll have plenty of choices in Japan. Pay attention to tea varietals, which are graded by the quality and parts of the plant used, because price and quality runs the spectrum within these categories. For the very best Japanese green tea, take a trip to the Uji region of Kyoto.

Bancha (common tea). This second harvest variety ripens between summer and fall, producing leaves larger than those of sencha and a weaker-tasting tea.

Genmai (brown rice tea). This is a mixture, usually in equal parts, of green tea and roasted brown rice.

Genmaicha (popcorn tea). This is a blend of bancha and genmai teas.

Gyokuro (jewel dew). Derived from a grade of green tea called *tencha* (divine tea), the name comes from the light-green color the tea develops when brewed. Gyokuro is grown in the shade, an essential condition to develop just this type and grade.

Hojicha (panfried tea). A panfried or oven-roasted green tea.

Kabusecha (covered tea). Similar to gyokuro, kabusecha leaves are grown in the shade, though for a shorter period, giving it a refined flavor.

Kukicha (stalk tea). A tea made from stalks by harvesting one bud and three leaves.

Matcha (rubbed tea). Most often used in the tea ceremony, matcha is a high-quality, hard-to-find powdered green tea. It has a thick, paintlike consistency when mixed with hot water. It is also a popular flavor of ice cream and other sweets in Japan.

Sencha (roasted tea). This is the green tea you are most likely to try at the local noodle or bento shop. Its leaves are grown under direct sunlight, giving it a different flavor from cousins like gyokuro.

stock of textiles from throughout Asia. An easy-to-transport gift would be *furoshiki*, which is rather inexpensive wood-blocked cloth used as decorative covers in daily life. ✉ *5–12–2 Minami-Aoyama, Minato-ku, Aoyama* ☎ *03/3407–4466* 🌐 *www.aoyama-omotesandou.com/global/english.html* Ⓜ *Ginza, Chiyoda, and Hanzo-mon subway lines, Omotesando Station (Exit B1).*

CERAMICS

Tsutaya Kakichaki (つたや花器茶器 *Tsutaya Ikebana and Tea*). *Ikebana* (flower arrangement) and *sado* (tea ceremony) goods are the only items sold at this shop, but they come in such stunning variety that a visit is definitely worthwhile. Colorful vases in surprising shapes and traditional ceramic tea sets make unique souvenirs. ✉ *5–10–5 Minami-Aoyama,*

Mix with Tokyo's most glamorous residents at Prada's architecturally dazzling Omotesando store.

Minato-ku, Aoyama ☎ *03/3400–3815* Ⓜ *Ginza, Chiyoda, and Hanzo-mon subway lines, Omotesando Station (Exit B1).*

CLOTHING

Bapexclusive Aoyama. Since the late 1990s, no brand has been more coveted by Harajuku scenesters than the BATHING APE label (shortened to BAPE) founded by DJ–fashion designer NIGO. At the height of the craze, hopefuls would line up outside NIGO's well-hidden boutiques for the chance to plop down ¥7,000 for a T-shirt festooned with a simian visage or *Planet of the Apes* quote. BAPE has since gone aboveground, with the brand expanding across the globe. You can see what the fuss is all about in this spacious two-story shop with an upstairs conveyor belt of sneakers that is always a draw. ✉ *5–5–8 Minami-Aoyama, Minato-ku, Aoyama* ☎ *03/3407–2145* 🌐 *www.bape.com* Ⓜ *Ginza and Hanzo-mon subway lines, Omotesando Station (Exit A5).*

Fodor's Choice ★ **Comme des Garçons** (コムデギャルソン). Sinuous low walls snake through Comme des Garçons founder Rei Kawakubo's flagship store, a minimalist labyrinth that houses the designer's signature clothes, shoes, and accessories. Staff members do their best to ignore you, but that's no reason to stay away from one of Tokyo's funkiest retail spaces. ✉ *5–2–1 Minami-Aoyama, Minato-ku, Aoyama* ☎ *03/3406–3951* 🌐 *www.comme-des-garcons.com* Ⓜ *Ginza, Chiyoda, and Hanzo-mon subway lines, Omotesando Station (Exit A5).*

Fodor's Choice ★ **Issey Miyake** (イッセイミヤケ). The otherworldly creations of internationally renowned brand Issey Miyake are on display at his flagship store in Aoyama, which carries the full Paris line. Keep walking on the

THE ARCHITECTURE OF OMOTESANDO

With Tokyo's impressive array of high-end fashion and jewelry stores has come an equally astonishing collection of beautiful buildings. A 20-minute walk along the Omotesando promenade from Aoyama to Harajuku takes you past several standout structures. Start at the **Prada** flagship on the southeast end of Omotesando. The Swiss-based Herzog & de Meuron team created this building of concave and protruding diamond-shape glass panels, which give it a honeycomblike effect. Across the street they reprised their hit with the new Miu Miu flagship in 2015, made of aluminum and brass. Next door are glittery buildings for **Chloé** and **Cartier**. Part of Chloé's facade is hidden behind wooden bamboolike slits that tilt and jut high into the air at random.

Walk toward Shibuya on Aoyama dori—on the right is the Ao Building. At night, the glass exterior becomes a curtain of blue, green, and purple lights, recalling the aurora borealis. Or proceed on Omotesando toward Harajuku, where you'll find the "squeezed" building that is Hugo Boss. Farther along is the white translucent box that is **Dior**, designed by Pritzker Architecture Prize recipients Kazuyo Sejima and Ryue Nishizawa of SANAA. Moving projections play on the building during most of the year. Hang a left on Meiji-dori and you won't miss the **Audi Forum's** "Iceberg" Building. The sharp geometry of the blue glass structure was inspired by ice, crystal, and plastic bottles. Finally, just on the north side of Meiji-jingu crossing is the **H&M** building, which appears to be a tower of stacked ice cubes. The cubes glow softly from day to night and reflect the dynamic design of the city that surrounds it.

8

same street away from Omotesando Station and also find a string of other Miyake stores just a stone's throw away, including Issey Miyake Men and Pleats Please. At the end of the street is the Reality Lab with a barrage of Miyake's most experimental lines like BaoBao, In-Ei, and incredible origamilike clothing from 132 5. ✉ *3–18–11 Minami-Aoyama, Minato-ku, Aoyama* ☎ *03/3423–1408* 🌐 *www.isseymiyake.com* Ⓜ *Ginza, Chiyoda, and Hanzo-mon subway lines, Omotesando Station (Exit A4).*

Maison Kitsune. The half-Japanese, half-French duo who make this brand are former DJs and music producers, which may explain why the cashmere V-neck sweaters and silk shift dresses have such a cool edge to them. The Kitsune Café, in a traditional Japanese home just one block east, carries more casual street wear and serves some of the best coffee in the area. ✉ *3–15–13 Minami-Aoyama, Minato-ku, Aoyama* ☎ *03/5786–4842* 🌐 *www.kitsune.fr* Ⓜ *Ginza, Chiyoda, and Hanzo-mon subway lines, Omotesando Station (Exit A4).*

Fodor's Choice ★ **Prada.** This fashion "epicenter," designed by Herzog & de Meuron, is one of the most buzzed-about architectural wonders in the city. Its facade is made up of a mosaic of green glass "bubble" windows: alternating convex and concave panels create distorted reflections of the surrounding area. Many world-renowned, nearby boutiques have tried to replicate the significant impact the Prada building has had on the Omotesando, but none have been unable to match this tower. Most visitors opt for a photo in front of the cavelike entrance that leads into the basement floor. ✉ *5–2–6 Minami-Aoyama, Minato-ku, Aoyama* ☎ *03/6418–0400* Ⓜ *Ginza, Chiyoda, and Hanzo-mon subway lines, Omotesando Station (Exit A5).*

Sou-Sou (そうそう). *Tabi* are the traditional cloth socks and shoes with a cleft-toe shape. This Kyoto-based brand is the last of the artisanal tabi makers, and yet the graphic, cute, and funky patterns are so ready for this era, you'd never know they were traditional. There is a café that serves tea and traditional Japanese sweets inspired by its textile patterns. ✉ *5–4–24 Minami-Aoyama, Minato-ku, Aoyama* ☎ *03/3407–7877* Ⓜ *Ginza, Hanzo-mon, and Chiyoda subway lines, Omotesando Station (Exit B1).*

Undercover (アンダーカバー). This stark shop houses Paris darling Jun Takahashi's cult clothing. Racks of men's and women's punkish duds sit under a ceiling made of a sea of thousands of hanging lightbulbs. ✉ *5–3–22 Minami-Aoyama, Minato-ku, Aoyama* ☎ *03/3407–1232* 🌐 *www.undercoverism.com* Ⓜ *Ginza, Chiyoda, and Hanzo-mon subway lines, Omotesando Station (Exit A5).*

CRAFTS

Oriental Bazaar (オリエンタルバザー). The three floors of this popular tourist destination are packed with just about anything you could want as a traditional Japanese handicraft souvenir: painted screens, pottery, chopsticks, dolls, and more, all at very reasonable prices. ✉ *5–9–13 Jingu-mae, Shibuya-ku, Aoyama* ☎ *03/3400–3933* 🌐 *www.orientalbazaar.co.jp* 🕑 *Closed Thurs.* Ⓜ *Chiyoda and Fukutoshin subway lines, Meiji-Jingu-mae Station (Exit 4).*

FOOD

FAMILY Fodor's Choice ★ **Ginza Natsuno** (銀座夏野). This two-story boutique sells an incredible range of chopsticks, from traditional to pop motifs, and wooden to crystal-encrusted sticks that can be personalized. Children's chopsticks and dishes are housed in their own boutique behind it, but it's a must-see no matter your age. ✉ *4–2–17 Jingu-mae, Aoyama* ☎ *03/3403–6033* 🌐 *www.e-ohashi.com* Ⓜ *Ginza, Chiyoda, and Hanzo-mon subway lines, Omotesando Station (Exit A2).*

HOUSEWARES

Franc Franc Lounge (フランフランラウンジ). This branch of the popular chain sells very reasonably priced interior goods that are trendy among young, urban Tokyoites. Think candles shaped like desserts and crystal-encrusted photo frames among one-off customized chaises. There's a Taschen Books shop-in-shop and a MUG café in here to boot. ✉ *3–1–3 Minami-Aoyama, Minato-ku, Aoyama* ☎ *03/5785–2111* 🌐 *www.francfranc.com* Ⓜ *Ginza subway line, Gaienmae Station (Exit 1A).*

Sempre (センプレ). Playful, colorful, and bright describe both the products and the space of this Kotto-dori housewares dealer. Among the great finds here are interesting tableware, glassware, lamps, and jewelry. ✉ *5–13–3 Minami-Aoyama, Minato-ku, Aoyama* ☎ *03/5464–5655* 🌐 *www.sempre.jp* Ⓜ *Ginza, Chiyoda, and Hanzo-mon subway lines, Omotesando Station (Exit B1).*

KIMONO

Gallery Kawano (ギャラリー川野). Kawano sells kimonos and kimono fabric in a variety of patterns. A satchel made of crepe fabric called *kinchaku* is the bag traditionally held when wearing a kimono, and cute little patchwork ones here make a unique find. ✉ *4–4–9 Jingu-mae, Shibuya-ku, Aoyama* ☎ *03/3470–3305* 🌐 *gallery-kawano.com* Ⓜ *Ginza, Chiyoda, and Hanzo-mon subway lines, Omotesando Station (Exit A2).*

MALLS AND SHOPPING CENTERS

Glassarea (グラッセリア). Virtually defining Aoyama elegance is this small cobblestone shopping center, which draws well-heeled young professionals to its handful of fashion boutiques, spa, and a specialty store of Japanese crafts from Fukui prefecture. ✉ *5–4–41 Minami-Aoyama, Minato-ku, Aoyama* ☎ *03/5778–4450* 🌐 *www.glassarea.com* Ⓜ *Ginza, Chiyoda, and Hanzo-mon subway lines, Omotesando Station (Exit B1).*

Gyre (ジャイル). Near the Harajuku end of Omotesando, this mall houses luxury-brand shops such as Chanel and Maison Martin Margiela, three concept shops by Comme des Garçons, and one of only two Museum of Modern Art Design Stores outside New York City ✉ *5–10–1 Jingu-mae, Shibuya-ku, Harajuku* ☎ *03/5400–5801* 🌐 *gyre-omotesando.com* Ⓜ *Chiyoda and Fukutoshin subway lines, Meiji-Jingumae Station (Exit 4).*

Omotesando Hills (表参道ヒルズ). Architect Tadao Ando's adventure in concrete is also one of Tokyo's monuments to shopping. Despised and adored with equal zeal, the controversial project demolished the charming yet antiquated Dojunkai Aoyama Apartments along Omotesando Avenue. Six wedge-shape floors include some brand-name heavy hitters (Saint Laurent and Harry Winston) and a wide range of smaller stores whose shelves showcase mid- to high-end shoes and bags. It's worth a stroll to see the latest in Japanese haute couture, and restaurants and cafés can also be found here—but beware of long lines. ✉ *4–12–10 Jingu-mae, Shibuya-ku, Aoyama* ☎ *03/3497–0310* 🌐 *www.omotesandohills.com* Ⓜ *Hanzo-mon, Ginza, and Chiyoda subway lines, Omotesando Station (Exit A2), Chiyoda and Fukutoshin subway lines, Meiji-Jingumae Station (Exit 4).*

HARAJUKU 原宿

The average shopper in Harajuku is under 20; a substantial percentage is under 16. Most stores focus on moderately priced clothing and accessories, with a lot of kitsch mixed in. This shopping and residential area extends southeast from Harajuku Station along both sides of Omotesando and Meiji-dori; the shops that target the youngest consumers concentrate especially on the narrow street called Takeshita-dori.

8

CLOSE UP

Traditional Crafts

The Japanese take pride in their *monozukuri*: a gift for making things. Well they might, with traditions of craftsmanship centuries old to draw on: an itch for perfection, a loving respect for materials, and a profound aesthetic sense of what can be done with them. Each region has its own traditional crafts, but you can find exquisite pieces from all over the country with some focused shopping in Tokyo.

CERAMICS

Most Japanese pottery, apart from some porcelain and earthenware, is stoneware—formed into a wonderful variety of vases, cups, bowls, and platters and fired in climbing kilns on the slopes of hills. At first glance, Japanese ceramics seem priced for a prince's table, but keep an eye out for seasonal sales; you can often find affordable pieces. Department stores have extensive selections of these and other wares.

DOLLS

Traditional dolls, meant primarily for display and not as playthings, come in many different styles: the long, cylindrical Kokeshi; red, round papier-mâché Daruma; and ceramic figurines in the traditional costumes of geisha, samurai, and festival dancers, called Hakata. The best area to shop for dolls in Tokyo is **Asakusa-bashi**, by the Sumida River.

PRINTED FABRICS

Stencil-dyed fabrics date to the Edo period and survive in a range of motifs and intricate geometric designs—especially suitable for light summer kimonos, room dividers, and cushion covers. *Furoshiki*—large cotton squares for wrapping, storing, and carrying things—make great wall hangings, as do the smaller cotton hand towels called *tenugui*. Look for the latter at **Fuji-ya**, in Asakusa *(see Asakusa shopping)*.

KIMONOS

A new kimono, in brocaded silk, can cost ¥1 million or more. Consider a secondhand version—about ¥10,000 in a flea market, for one in decent condition—or look instead for cotton summer kimonos, called *yukata*, in a wide variety of colorful designs, which you can buy new for ¥7,000–¥10,000. In Tokyo browse the **Gallery Kawano** *(see Aoyama shopping)*.

LACQUERWARE

For its history, diversity, and fine workmanship, lacquerware rivals ceramics as the traditional Japanese craft nonpareil. Cheaper pieces usually have plastic rather than wood underneath, and because these won't shrink and crack in dry climates, they make safer—but no less attractive—buys.

PAPER

The Japanese make *washi* (handmade paper, usually of mulberry fibers) in myriad colors, textures, and designs and fashion it into an astonishing number of useful and decorative objects. Look for stationery, greeting cards, single sheets for gift wrapping and origami, and washi-covered jewelry boxes, at **Kyukyodo** *(see Ginza shopping)*.

FIND IT ALL

The **Japan Traditional Craft Center** *(see Roppingi shopping)* sells the best of the craft work from all over the country, in most of the important categories, from paper to tools to pottery.

Tokyo's most exciting neighborhood for youth fashion and design lies beyond that, in the maze of backstreets called Ura-hara.

CLOTHING

Fodor's Choice ★ **Beams** (ビームス). Harajuku features a cluster of no fewer than 10 Beams stores that provide Japan's younger men and women with extremely hip threads. With branches ranging from street wear to high-end import brands, as well as a record store, uniform gallery, funky "from Tokyo" souvenir shop that sells anime figurines, and one that sells manga alongside designer-made T-shirts inspired by comic books, shopping here ensures that you or your kids will be properly stocked with the coolest wares from the city. ✉ *3–24–7 Jingu-mae, Shibuya-ku, Harajuku* ☎ *03/3470–3947* 🌐 *www.beams.co.jp* Ⓜ *JR Harajuku Station (Takeshita-Dori Exit); Chiyoda and Fukutoshin subway lines, Meiji-Jingu-mae Station (Exit 5).*

6% Doki Doki. If there's one shop that is the epitome of crazy, *kawaii* (cute) Harajuku fashion, it's this pastel dollhouselike shop on the second floor of a nondescript building. The acid-color tutus and glittery accessories are part of a style called "kawaii anarchy" and may be the most unique shopping experience in Tokyo. The colorful shopgirls alone are an attraction, and if asked nicely they will happily pose for photos. ✉ *4–28–16 Jingu-mae, Shibuya-ku, Harajuku* ☎ *03/3479–6116* 🌐 *www.dokidoki6.com* Ⓜ *Chiyoda and Fukutoshin subway lines, Meiji-Jingu-mae Station (Exit 5).*

MALLS AND SHOPPING CENTERS

Laforet (ラフォーレ). This mall is so earnest about staying on the tip of Harajuku fashion trends that it changes out stores every six months. While shop genres vary, from Gothic Lolita to bohemian chic, they all target fashion-conscious teenagers. Rumor has it that many of the West's top fashion designers still come here to look for inspiration for their next collections. ✉ *1–11–6 Jingu-mae, Shibuya-ku, Harajuku* ☎ *03/3475–0411* 🌐 *www.laforet.ne.jp/en* Ⓜ *Chiyoda and Fukutoshin subway lines, Meiji-Jingu-mae Station (Exit 5).*

8

SHIBUYA 渋谷

This is primarily an entertainment and retail district geared toward teenagers and young adults. The shopping scene caters to these groups with many reasonably priced smaller shops and a few department stores that are casual yet chic. You may notice that many neighborhood denizens are neither young nor chic—Shibuya is also a popular entertainment district and loaded with restaurants, karaoke lounges, bars, and nightclubs. At the southern edges of the neighborhood you can unleash your inner fashionista in Daikanyama, a boutique heaven with stacks of retro T-shirts, assortments of skate-punk wear, and a concentration of premium denim shops that makes jeans fans giddy. Just beyond, the sakura-tree-lined banks of the Meguro River explodes with pink blossoms in spring. The riverbanks attract an organic-living-oriented crowd, whose aesthetic is reflected in the bohemian clothing sold at the laid-back shops.

BOOKS

Fodor's Choice ★ **Daikanyama T-Site.** This oasis within the metropolis is a calming respite with a Zen garden, trendy terrace eatery, gallery, and, of course, the main business, a shop selling books, music, and videos with a focus on art and design. Almost all of the 30,000 books here can be taken to the lounge to read, as can a large selection of foreign magazines. Many locals come here to be seen, bringing along their lapdogs dressed in designer duds from the store's pet boutique. ✉ *17–5 Sarugaku-cho, Meguro-ku, Shibuya* ☎ *03/3770–2525* 🌐 *tsite.jp/daikanyama/* Ⓜ *Toyoko line, Daikanyama Station (Central Exit).*

CLOTHING

Aquvii Tokyo. The doodads and thingamajiggies at this cozy shop are by local designers. Silver chopstick earrings, "Banzai"-printed handbags, imaginative phone cases, and other unique items—perfect for souvenirs—topple the shelves from floor to ceiling. ✉ *6–19–16 Jingu-mae, Shibuya* ☎ *03/6427–1219* 🌐 *www.aquvii.com* Ⓜ *JR Yamanote Line, Hanzo-mon, Fukutoshin, and Ginza subway lines, Shibuya Station (Hachiko Exit for JR, Exit 13 for subway).*

Harcoza (ハルコ座). This is one of those "only in Tokyo" shops, with a quirky selection of clothing and accessories such as a bonsai tree watch and rings made of solidified croissants and desserts. Even the changing room is a statement: it's a replicated stage for Japanese idols of the '70s and '80s, replete with a disco ball. ✉ *2–15–9 Ebisu-nishi, Shibuya* ☎ *03/6416–0725* 🌐 *www.harcoza.com* ⏲ *Closed Tues.* Ⓜ *Tokyu Toyoko Line, Daikanyama Station (West Exit).*

Journal Standard (ジャーナルスタンダード). This is not a chain dedicated to outfitting office workers in shirts and ties. In fact, this branch is frequented by young couples looking for the season's *it* fashions, with the signature JS uber-casual aesthetic. The neighboring boutiques follow in the same vein, so take a stroll down the street as well. ✉ *1–5–6 Jinnan, Shibuya* ☎ *03/5457–0700* 🌐 *journal-standard.jp* Ⓜ *JR Yamanote Line, Ginza, Fukutoshin, and Hanzo-mon subway lines, Shibuya Station (Hachiko Exit for JR, Exits 6 and 7 for subways).*

HOUSEWARES

FAMILY Fodor's Choice ★ **Tokyu Hands** (東急ハンズ). This chain carries a wide and varied assortment of goods, including hobby and crafts materials, art supplies, and knitting and sewing materials, as well as jewelry, household goods, stationery, even cosmetics. There's a new café and exhibit space on the seventh floor with an ever-changing selection of small goods from local artisans for sale. It's not unusual to see Japanese hobbyists spending an entire afternoon browsing in here. ✉ *12–18 Udagawa-cho, Shibuya* ☎ *03/5489–5111* 🌐 *www.tokyu-hands.co.jp/foreign.html* Ⓜ *JR Yamanote Line, Ginza, Fukutoshin, and Hanzo-mon subway lines, Shibuya Station (Hachiko Exit for JR, Exits 6 and 7 for subway).*

Zero First Design. Kyu-Yamate-dori at Daikanyama is a well-known hub of interior goods stores, and this one is full of unique and modern pieces from both local and international designers. ✉ *2–3–1 Aobadai, Meguro-ku, Shibuya* ☎ *03/5489–6101* 🌐 *01st.com* Ⓜ *Tokyu Toyoko Line, Daikanyama Station (Komazawa-dori Exit).*

JEWELRY AND ACCESSORIES

B Jirushi Yoshida. This Beams boutique's main draw is the limited-edition Porter bag for men and women, plus other collaborations of savvy daily goods, including brands such as Monocle, Wonderwall, and Wacko Maria. ✉ *2F, 19–6 Sarugakucho, Shibuya* ☎ *03/5428–5952* 🌐 *www.bjirushi.com* Ⓜ *Tokyu Toyoko Line, Daikanyama Station (Komazawa-dori Exit).*

LACQUERWARE

Fodor's Choice ★ **Yamada Heiando** (山田平安堂). With a spacious, airy layout and lovely lacquerware goods, this fashionable shop is a must for souvenir hunters—and anyone else who appreciates fine design. Rice bowls, sushi trays, *bento* lunch boxes, *hashioki* (chopstick rests), and jewelry cases come in traditional blacks and reds, as well as patterns both subtle and bold. Prices are fair—many items cost less than ¥10,000—but these are the kinds of goods for which devotees of Japanese craftsmanship would be willing to pay a lot. ✉ *Hillside Terrace G Block #202, 18–12 Sarugakucho, Shibuya* ☎ *03/3464–5541* 🌐 *www.heiando1919.com* Ⓜ *Tokyu Toyoko Line, Daikanyama Station (Komazawa-dori Exit).*

MALLS AND SHOPPING CENTERS

Parco (渋谷パルコ). These vertical malls filled with small retail shops and boutiques are all within walking distance of one another in the commercial heart of Shibuya. Parco Part 1 caters to a young crowd and stocks many trendy "it" brands from the local runways, though Comme des Garçons Black and the curiously conceptual Pyaruco are less expensive options. Part 3 also sells a mixture of casual fashion and hip interior goods that won't break the bank. ✉ *15–1 Udagawa-cho, Shibuya* ☎ *03/3464–5111* 🌐 *www.parco.co.jp/customer* Ⓜ *Ginza, Fukutoshin, and Hanzo-mon subway lines, Shibuya Station (Exits 6 and 7).*

Shibuya 109 This nine floor outlet is a teenage girl's dream, especially if they follow the *gyaru* tribe, a particularly gaudy and brash fashion genre born in Shibuya. The place is filled with small stores whose merchandise screams kitsch and trend. Here, the fashionable sales assistants are the stars, and their popularity in this mall can make them media superstars. On weekends, dance concerts and fashion shows are often staged at the front entrance. ✉ *2–29–1 Dogenzaka, Shibuya* ☎ *03/3477–5111* 🌐 *www.shibuya109.jp/en* Ⓜ *JR Yamanote Line, Ginza, Fukutoshin, and Hanzo-mon subway lines, Shibuya Station (Hachiko Exit for JR, Exit 3A for subway lines).*

MUSIC

Manhattan Records (マンハッタンレコード). The hottest hip-hop, reggae, house, and R&B vinyl can be found here, and a DJ booth pumps out the jams from the center of the room. Don't expect a lot of advice from the staff—no one can hear you over the throbbing tunes. ✉ *10–1 Udagawa-cho, Shibuya* ☎ *03/3477–7166* 🌐 *manhattanrecords.jp* Ⓜ *JR Yamanote Line, Ginza, Fukutoshin, and Hanzo-mon subway lines, Shibuya Station (Hachiko Exit for JR, Exits 6 and 7 for subway).*

Tower Records (タワーレコード). This huge emporium carries one of the most diverse selections of CDs and DVDs in the world. Take a rest at the café after visiting the second floor, which houses books,

8

with a large selection of English-language publications. ✉ *1–22–14 Jinnan, Shibuya* ☎ *03/3496–3661* 🌐 *tower.jp/store/kanto/shibuya* Ⓜ *JR Yamanote Line, Hanzo-mon, Fukutoshin, and Ginza subway lines, Shibuya Station (Hachiko Exit for JR, Exit 7 for subway).*

WORD OF MOUTH

"[My son likes] shopping in Harajuku and Shibuya, which are youth-oriented and can be a surprisingly good value. Tower Records (in Shibuya) . . . [has a] vast collection of CDs/DVDs of every genre, including albums only released in Japan. . . . There is also a vast guitar shop in Shinjuku, which is also a good place to find out about gigs, with a fair chance of an English speaker to assist." —Alec

TOYS

FAMILY Fodor's Choice ★ **Kiddy Land** (キディランド). The Omotesando landmark commonly regarded as Tokyo's best toy store carries the cutest and most kitschy of everyday goods that draw in even the most hardened of souls. This is the leader in making or breaking the popularity of the myriad character goods that Japan spits out seasonally. Like caterpillars with salaryman faces, some of the items may be odd or surprising, but they're never boring. ✉ *6–1–9 Jingu-mae, Shibuya-ku, Harajuku* ☎ *03/3409–3431* 🌐 *www.kiddyland.co.jp/en/stores.html* Ⓜ *JR Yamanote Line, Harajuku Station (Omotesando Exit); Chiyoda and Fukutoshin subway lines, Meiji-Jingu-mae Station (Exit 4).*

ROPPONGI 六本木

Roppongi's reputation has traditionally been marred by being a vortex of riffraff populating the neighborhood day or night, and there certainly are a number of dingy clubs and bars. But in recent years it has seen shopping complexes, luxury condominiums, and parks pop up that have given it a new high-end image. What's more, the addition of a handful of grade-A museums such as the new National Art Center with its undulating all-glass facade, the Mori Art Museum on the 50th floor of Roppongi Hills, the Suntory Museum of Art, and the Issey Miyake–produced 21_21 Design Sight in the Midtown Tokyo complex has transformed this into an area to see and be seen in.

CERAMICS

Savoir Vivre (サボアービブレ). In the swanky Axis Building, this store sells contemporary and antique tea sets, cups, bowls, and glassware. ✉ *3F Axis Bldg., 5–17–1 Roppongi, Minato-ku, Roppongi* ☎ *03/3585–7365* 🌐 *savoir-vivre.co.jp* ⏲ *Closed Wed.* Ⓜ *Hibiya and Oedo subway lines, Roppongi Station (Exit 3).*

CLOTHING

Restir (レスティアー). Next to the Midtown Tokyo complex, this is possibly the most exclusive and fashion-forward boutique in the city. It's made up of a cluster of stores, from luxury stores for men and women to a surf and activewear store, a café, and another store dedicated to high-end lifestyle gadgets like headphones, toy cameras, and stylish mobile peripherals. ✉ *9–6–17 Akasaka, Minato-ku, Roppongi*

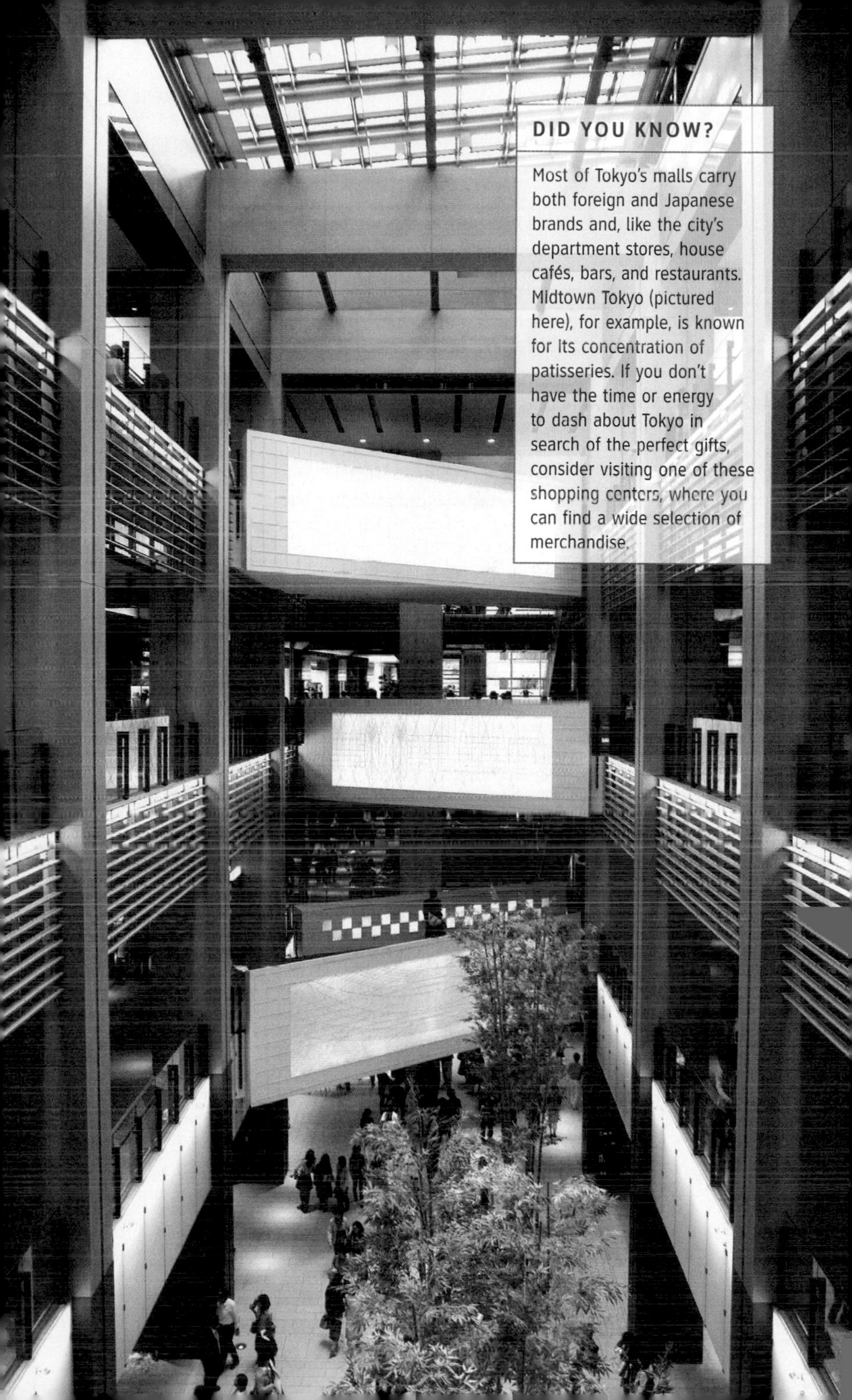

DID YOU KNOW?

Most of Tokyo's malls carry both foreign and Japanese brands and, like the city's department stores, house cafés, bars, and restaurants. Midtown Tokyo (pictured here), for example, is known for its concentration of patisseries. If you don't have the time or energy to dash about Tokyo in search of the perfect gifts, consider visiting one of these shopping centers, where you can find a wide selection of merchandise.

☎ *03/5413–3708* 🌐 *restir-holdings.com/section/index.html* Ⓜ *Hibiya and Oedo subway lines, Roppongi Station (Exit 8); Chiyoda subway line, Nogizaka Station (Exit 3).*

CRAFTS

Japan Traditional Craft Center. On show is the best craft work from all over the country, from paper to tools to pottery. Some of the prices in the shop can be deservedly high, but this is an excellent place to find one-of-a-kind, high-quality items. In addition to the gift shop, the center houses rotating crafts exhibits and hosts workshops and demonstrations. ✉ *8–1–22 Akasaka, Minato-ku, Roppongi* ☎ *03/5785–1301* 🌐 *kougeihin.jp.*

MALLS AND SHOPPING CENTERS

Axis (アクシス). Classy and cutting-edge furniture, electronics, fabrics, ceramics, and books are sold at this multistory design center on the main Roppongi drag of Gaien-Higashi-dori. Savoir Vivre has an excellent selection of ceramics, and automobile-philes love the Garage shop for its array of accessories for high-end cars. On the fourth floor, the JIDA Gallery shows the best of what's current in Japanese industrial design. ✉ *5–17–1 Roppongi, Minato-ku, Roppongi* ☎ *03/3587–2781* 🌐 *www.axisinc.co.jp* ⊗ *Closed Sun.* Ⓜ *Hibiya and Oedo subway lines, Roppongi Station (Exit 3); Namboku subway line, Roppongi Itchome Station (Exit 1).*

FAMILY **Roppongi Hills** (六本木ヒルズ). You could easily spend a whole day exploring the retail areas of this minicity, a complex of shops, restaurants, residential and commercial towers, a nine-screen cineplex, the Grand Hyatt Tokyo hotel, and the Mori Art Museum—all wrapped around the TV Asahi studios and sprawled out in five zones located between the Roppongi intersection and Azabu Juban. The shops here emphasize eye-catching design and chichi brands. The world's only Alexander McQueen accessories store, modern kimono brand Jotaro Saito, and Estnation, with its often-occurring pop-up shops, are good destinations. Finding a particular shop, however, can be a hassle given the building's Escher-like layout. To navigate, go to the information center to retrieve a floor guide with color-coded maps in English; most of the staff members speak English as well. ✉ *6–10–1 Roppongi, Minato-ku, Roppongi* ☎ *03/6406–6000* 🌐 *www.roppongihills.com* Ⓜ *Hibiya and Oedo subway lines, Roppongi Station (Roppongi Hills Exit).*

Tokyo Midtown (東京ミッドタウン). This huge complex is an architectural statement with sweeping glass roofs and a large walkable garden in the back. The airy, open spaces house exclusive boutiques, hotels, and a concentration of cafés by the world's top pâtissiers on the first few floors. ✉ *9–7–3 Akasaka, Minato-ku, Roppongi* ☎ *03/3475–3100* 🌐 *www.tokyo-midtown.com/en* Ⓜ *Hibiya and Oedo subway lines, Roppongi Station (Exit 8); Chiyoda subway line, Nogizaka Station (Exit 3).*

SPAS

May's. It's all about personalized service at this so-called garden spa, which has been in business for more than 80 years and is now located in the swanky Roppongi Hills complex. Big-name clients have included the Japanese Royal Family, Grace Kelly, and Mariah Carey.

Herbs used in the footbath are from the facility's own herb gardens right outside the windows, and among the long roster of services are facial treatments, body treatments, waxing, aroma massage, and aroma and geranium baths, as well as bridal prep and kimono dressing services. ✉ *6–4–1 Roppongi, Minato-ku, Roppongi* ☎ *03/3408–1613* 🌐 *www.hollywoodsalon.co.jp/mgs/mgs_e/index_e.html* Ⓜ *Hibiya and Oedo subway lines, Roppongi Station (Roppongi Hills Exit).*

WORD OF MOUTH

"I lived in Tokyo and Yodobashi was about 30 minutes or so from my apartment. I used to frequent the place all the time on the weekends. Not just for camera gear, but, also for stereo equipment as well." —gearsau

SHINJUKU 新宿

Shinjuku is not without its honky-tonk and sleaze, but it also has some of the city's most popular department stores. The shopping crowd is a mix of Tokyo youth and office workers. Surrounding the Shinjuku Station are several discount electronics and home-appliance outlets. The area's abundant array of shopping, business, politics, and entertainment forms a microcosm of Tokyo culture. Just north is Ikebukuro, a bustling neighborhood that is the nearest urban center to the northern outlying suburbs of Tokyo. Because of this, many Shinjuku stores have set up shop in Ikebukuro, but here they are often supersized to accommodate the weekend crowds.

BOOKS

Kinokuniya (紀伊国屋). This mammoth bookstore, an annex of Takashimaya, devotes most of its sixth floor to English titles, with an excellent selection of travel guides, magazines, and books on Japan. ✉ *Takashimaya Times Sq., 5–24–2 Sendagaya, Shibuya-ku, Shinjuku* ☎ *03/5361–3301* 🌐 *www.kinokuniya.co.jp* Ⓜ *JR Yamanote Line, Shinjuku Station (Minami-guchi/South Exit); Fukutoshin subway line, Shinjuku Sanchome Station (Exit E8).*

CLOTHING

Don Quixote (ドンキホーテ). This 24-hour discount store has chains all around the country. The generally tight quarters aren't recommended for those with claustrophobia, but bargain-hunters love the costumes, odd cosmetics, family-size bags of Japanese snacks, and used luxury handbags and watches. It's all haphazardly stacked from the floor to the ceiling. ✉ *1–16–5 Kabuki-cho, Shinjuku-ku, Shinjuku* ☎ *03/5291–9211* 🌐 *www.donki.com* Ⓜ *Marunouchi, Oedo, and Shinjuku subway lines, JR Yamanote Line, Keio and Odakyu lines, Shinjuku Station (Higashi-guchi/East Exit).*

CRAFTS

Bingo-ya (備後屋). This tasteful four-floor shop allows you to complete your souvenir shopping in one place. The store carries traditional handicrafts—including ceramics, toys, lacquerware, Noh masks, fabrics, and lots more—from all over Japan. ✉ *10–6 Wakamatsu-cho, Shinjuku-ku,*

8

Shinjuku ☎ *03/3202–8778* 🌐 *www.quasar.nu/bingoya* ⏲ *Tues.–Sun. 10–7* ⏲ *Closed Mon. and every 3rd weekend of the month* Ⓜ *Oedo subway line, Wakamatsu Kawada Station (Kawada Exit).*

DEPARTMENT STORES

Isetan (伊勢丹). Established in 1886, "The Bergdorf's of Tokyo" is known for its high-end fashions both local and foreign, including a selection of larger sizes not found in most Tokyo stores. The second and third floors have champagne bars and snazzy store design that rival the world's best shops, making this one of the most pleasant shopping experiences in Tokyo, or anywhere, for that matter. The basement food court, which includes both traditional and modern prepared cuisine, is one of the city's largest in a department store. ✉ *3–14–1 Shinjuku, Shinjuku-ku, Shinjuku* ☎ *03/3225–2514* 🌐 *isetan.mistore.jp/store/shinjuku* Ⓜ *JR Yamanote Line, Marunouchi subway line, Shinjuku Station (Higashi-guchi/East Exit for JR, Exits B2, B3, B4, and B5 for subway line).*

Fodor's Choice ★ **Marui O1O1** (O1O1 マルイ). Easily recognized by its red-and-white "O1" logo, Marui burst onto the department store scene in the 1980s by introducing an in-store credit card—one of the first stores in Japan to do so. The four Marui buildings—Marui Honkan, Marui Annex, Marui One, and Marui Mens—comprise the largest department store in the area by a large margin. Women flock to the stores in search of petite clothing, and you can find the largest concentration of Gothic and Lolita clothing in the city at the Annex. ✉ *3–30–13 Shinjuku, Shinjuku-ku, Shinjuku* ☎ *03/3354–0101* 🌐 *www.0101.co.jp/stores/language/en* Ⓜ *JR Yamanote Line, Shinjuku Station (Higashi-guchi/East Exit); Marunouchi, Shinjuku, and Fukutoshin subway lines, Shinjuku San-chome Station (Exit A1).*

Seibu (西武デパート池袋本店). Even Japanese customers have been known to get lost in this mammoth department store; the main branch is in Ikebukuro, a bustling neighborhood just north of Shinjuku. Seibu has an excellent selection of household goods, from furniture to lacquerware and quirky interior design pieces in its stand-alone Loft shops (which you'll find throughout the city next to Seibu branches, or occasionally in the department store itself). ✉ *1–28–1 Minami Ikebukuro, Toshima-ku, Shinjuku* ☎ *03/3981–8569* 🌐 *www.sogo-seibu.jp.e.ld.hp.transer.com/foreign/en/ikebukuro/index.html* Ⓜ *JR Yamanote Line, Marunouchi, Fukutoshin, and Yurakucho subway lines, Ikebukuro Station (Minami-guchi/South Exit); Seibu Ikebukuro Line, Seibu Ikebukuro Station (Seibu Department Store Exit); Tobu Tojo Line, Tobu Ikebukuro Station (Minami-guchi/South Exit).*

Takashimaya (高島屋). In Japanese, *taka* means "high"—a fitting word for this store, which is beloved for its superior quality and prestige. Gift-givers all over Japan seek out this department store; a present that comes in a Takashimaya bag makes a statement regardless of what's inside. Like most department stores each floor is dedicated to stores with similar price points, but here the north half is for women and south for men, so couples and families can shop on the same floors. The basement-level food court carries every gastronomic delight imaginable, from Japanese crackers and Miyazaki beef to one of the largest gourmet dessert courts in the city. The annexes boast a large-scale Tokyu Hands and Kinokuniya bookstore as well. ✉ *Takashimaya Times Sq., 5–24–2 Sendagaya, Shibuya-ku, Shinjuku* ☎ *03/5361–1111* 🌐 *www.takashimaya.co.jp* Ⓜ *JR Yamanote Line, Shinjuku Station (Minami-guchi/South Exit); Fukutoshin subway line, Shinjuku Sanchome Station (Exit E8).*

ELECTRONICS

Bic Uniqlo (ビックロ). Dubbed "Bicqulo" for short, this is Japanese experimental shopping at its best. Bic is a discount electronics retailer and Uniqlo sells basic clothing pieces. Together, they present stylish outfits on mannequins that vacuum and display all sorts of other unique "fusion" items. Boasting the tag line "all messed up," this shop has become a destination in itself. Native English speakers are on hand at all hours. ✉ *3–29–1 Shinjuku, Shinjuku-ku, Shinjuku* ☎ *03/5363–5741* 🌐 *www.uniqlo.com/jp/community/store_news/store.php?poi=10101424* Ⓜ *Marunouchi, Oedo, and Shinjuku subway lines, JR Yamanote Line, Keio and Odakyu lines, Shinjuku Station (Higashi-guchi/East Exit).*

Yodobashi Camera (ヨドバシカメラ). This discount-electronics superstore near Shinjuku Station carries a selection comparable to that of Akihabara's big boys. It is made up of a number of annexes, including a watch, hobby, and professional camera building, that together span several blocks. ✉ *1–11–1 Nishi-Shinjuku, Shinjuku-ku, Shinjuku* ☎ *03/3346–1010* 🌐 *www.yodobashi.com* Ⓜ *Marunouchi, Shinjuku, and Oedo subway lines, JR Yamanote Line, Keio and Odakyu lines, Shinjuku Station (Nishi-guchi/West Exit).*

8

MUSIC

Fodor's Choice ★ **Disk Union** (ディスクユニオン). Vinyl junkies rejoice. The Shinjuku flagship of this chain sells Latin, rock, and indie at 33 rpm. Be sure to grab a store flyer that lists all of the branches, since each specializes in one music genre. Oh, and for digital folk, CDs are available, too. ✉ *3–31–4 Shinjuku, Shinjuku-ku, Shinjuku* ☎ *03/5919–4565* 🌐 *diskunion.net* Ⓜ *Marunouchi, Oedo, and Shinjuku subway lines, JR Yamanote Line, Keio and Odakyu lines, Shinjuku Station (Higashi-guchi/East Exit).*

PAPER

Kami-no-Takamura (紙のたかむら). Specialists in washi and other papers printed in traditional Japanese designs, this shop also carries brushes, inkstones, and other tools for calligraphy. At the entrance is a gallery showcasing seasonal traditional stationery and the work of local artists. ✉ *1–1–2 Higashi-Ikebukuro, Toshima-ku, Shinjuku* ☎ *03/3971–7111* 🌐 *www.wagami-takamura.com* Ⓜ *JR Yamanote Line, Marunouchi and Fukutoshin subway lines, Ikebukuro Station (East Exit for JR, Exit 35 for subway).*

ODAIBA お台場

MALLS AND SHOPPING CENTERS

FAMILY
Fodor's Choice
★

Decks Tokyo Beach (デックス東京ビーチ). Overlooking the harbor, this seven-story complex of shops, restaurants, and boardwalks is really two connected malls: Island Mall and Seaside Mall. Daiba Little Hong Kong, on the sixth and seventh floors of the Island Mall, has a collection of Cantonese restaurants and dim sum joints on neon-lighted "streets" designed to evoke the real Hong Kong. For kids (or nostalgic adults), check out the Lego Discovery Center, the Joypolis mega arcade, a fun house, and a Madame Tussaud's. At the Seaside Mall, a table by the window in any of the restaurants looks out to a delightful view of the harbor, especially at sunset, when the *yakatabune* (traditional-roofed pleasure boats) drift down the Sumida-gawa from Yanagibashi and Ryogoku. ✉ *1–6–1 Daiba, Minato-ku, Odaiba* ☎ *03/3599–6500* 🌐 *www.odaiba-decks.com* Ⓜ *Rinkai Line, Tokyo Teleport Station; Yurikamome Line, Odaiba-kaihin Koen Station.*

9

SIDE TRIPS FROM TOKYO

WELCOME TO SIDE TRIPS FROM TOKYO

TOP REASONS TO GO

★ **Peer at Fuji:** Climb Japan's tallest mountain or catch a glimpse of it from Fuji-Hakone-Izu National Park.

★ **Escape into rustic Japan:** The endless modernity of Tokyo seems worlds away in Nikko, where the Tosho-gu area shrines and temples transport you centuries back into the country's past and the Kegon Falls just transport you.

★ **Get into a Zen-like state:** Kita-Kamakura is home to two preeminent Zen temples, Engaku and Kencho. In Hase, gaze on the Great Buddha or explore inside the giant statue.

★ **Go to China without boarding a plane:** In Yokohama, a port city, sample authentic Chinese goods, spices, and crafts in Chinatown. For a bit of whimsy and a great view, ride Yokohama's Ferris wheel.

1 Fuji-Hakone-Izu National Park and Mt. Fuji. Fuji-Hakone-Izu National Park lies southwest of Tokyo. Its chief attraction, of course, is Mt. Fuji. South of it, the Izu Peninsula projects out into the Pacific, with Suruga Bay to the west and Sagami Bay to the east. The beaches and rugged shoreline of Izu and its numerous hot-springs inns and resorts make the region a favorite destination for the Japanese.

2 Nikko. Nikko is not simply the site of the Tokugawa Shrine but also of a national park, Nikko Kokuritsu Koen, on the heights above it. The centerpiece of the park is Chuzenji-ko, a deep lake some 21 km (13 miles) around, and the 318-foot-high Kegon Falls, Japan's most famous waterfall.

3 Kamakura. Kamakura is an ancient city—the birthplace, one could argue, of the samurai way of life. Minamoto no Yoritomo, the country's first shogun, chose this site, with its rugged hills and narrow passes, as the seat of his military government. The warrior elite took much of their ideology—and their aesthetics—from Zen Buddhism, endowing splendid temples that still exist today.

4 Yokohama. Yokohama is Japan's largest port and has an international character that rivals—if not surpasses—that of Tokyo. Its waterfront park and its ambitious Minato Mirai bay-side development project draw visitors from all over the world.

GETTING ORIENTED

Kamakura and Yokohama are close enough to Tokyo to provide ideal day trips, and as it's unlikely that you'll stay overnight in either city, no accommodations are listed for them. Nikko is something of a toss-up: you can easily see Tosho-gu and be back in Tokyo by evening. But when the weather turns glorious in spring or autumn, why not spend some time in the national park, staying overnight at Chuzenji and returning to the city the next day? Mt. Fuji and Hakone, on the other hand—and especially the Izu Peninsula—are pure resort destinations. Staying overnight is an intrinsic part of the experience, and it makes little sense to go without hotel reservations confirmed in advance.

Updated by Robert Morel

As diverse and exciting as the neighborhoods of Tokyo are, a short day trip or overnight away from the city offers a refreshingly different perspective on Japan. The city is a great base for numerous day trips, including visits to the iconic Fuji-san (Mt. Fuji) in Fuji-Hakone-Izu National Park, one of Japan's most popular resort areas; Nikko, a popular vacation destination for Tokyo residents and the home of Tosho-gu, the astonishing shrine to the first Tokugawa shogun Ieyasu; the ancient city of Kamakura, which has great historical and cultural sights; and Yokohama, a port city with an international character all its own—it's home to the country's largest Chinatown.

One caveat: the term "national park" does not quite mean what it does elsewhere in the world. In Japan, pristine grandeur is hard to come by; there are few places in this country where intrepid hikers can go to contemplate the beauty of nature for very long in solitude. If a thing's worth seeing, it's worth developing. This worldview tends to fill Japan's national parks with bus caravans, ropeways, gondolas, scenic overlooks with coin-fed telescopes, signs that tell you where you may or may not walk, fried-noodle joints and vending machines, and shacks full of kitschy souvenirs. That's true of Nikko, and it's true as well of Fuji-Hakone-Izu National Park.

PLANNING

RESTAURANTS

The local specialty in Nikko is a soybean-based concoction known as *yuba* (tofu skin); dozens of restaurants in Nikko serve it in a variety of dishes you might not have believed possible for so prosaic an ingredient. Other local favorites are *soba* (buckwheat) and *udon* (wheat-flour) noodles—both inexpensive, filling, and tasty options for lunch.

Three things about Kamakura make it a good place to dine. It's on the ocean (properly speaking, on Sagami Bay), which means that fresh seafood is everywhere; it's a major tourist stop; and it has long been a prestigious place to live among Japan's worldly and well-to-do (many successful writers, artists, and intellectuals call Kamakura home). On a day trip from Tokyo, you can feel confident picking a place for lunch almost at random.

Yokohama, as befits a city of more than 3 million people, lacks little in the way of food: from quick-fix lunch counters to elegant dining rooms, you'll find almost every imaginable cuisine. Your best bet is Chinatown—Japan's largest Chinese community—with more than 100 restaurants representing every regional style. If you fancy Italian, Indian, or even Scandinavian, this international port is still guaranteed to provide an eminently satisfying meal.

HOTELS

In both Nikko and the Fuji-Hakone-Izu area, there are modern, Western-style hotels that operate in a fairly standard international style. More common, however, are the traditional *ryokan* (inns). The main difference between these lodging options is that Western-style hotels are situated in prime tourist locations whereas ryokans stick strictly to Japanese-style rooms and are found in less touristy locations. The undisputed pleasure of a ryokan is to return to it at the end of a hard day of sightseeing, luxuriate for an hour in a hot bath with your own garden view, put on the *yukata* (cotton kimono) provided for you (remember to close your right side first and then the left), and sit down to a catered private dinner party. There's little point to staying at a Western-style hotel: these places do most of their business with big, boisterous tour groups; the turnover is ruthless; and the cost is way out of proportion to the service they provide.

The price categories listed here are for double occupancy, but you'll find that most normally quote per-person rates, which include breakfast and dinner. Remember to stipulate whether you want a Japanese or Western breakfast. If you don't want dinner at your hotel, it's usually possible to renegotiate the price, but the management will not be happy about it; the two meals are a fixture of their business. The typical ryokan takes great pride in its cuisine, usually with good reason: the evening meal is an elaborate affair of 10 or more different dishes, based on the fresh produce and specialties of the region, served to you—nay, *orchestrated*—in your room on a wonderful variety of trays and tableware designed to celebrate the season. *Hotel reviews have been shortened. For full information, visit Fodors.com.*

	WHAT IT COSTS IN YEN			
	$	$$	$$$	$$$$
Restaurants	Under ¥1,000	¥1,000–¥2,000	¥2,001–¥3,000	over ¥3,000
Hotels	Under ¥12,000	¥12,000–¥18,000	¥18,001–¥22,000	over ¥22,000

Restaurant prices are the average cost of a main course at dinner, or if dinner is not served, at lunch. Hotel prices are the lowest cost of a standard double room in high season.

FUJI-HAKONE-IZU NATIONAL PARK
富士箱根伊豆国立公園

This region, southwest of Tokyo between Suruga and Sagami bays, is one of Japan's most popular resort areas. The main attraction, of course, is Mt. Fuji, a dormant volcano—it last erupted in 1707—rising to a height of 12,388 feet. The mountain is truly beautiful; utterly captivating in the ways it can change in different light and from different perspectives. Its symmetry and majesty have been immortalized by poets and artists for centuries. Keep in mind that in spring and summer, Mt. Fuji often hides behind a blanket of clouds—worth noting if seeing the mountain is an important part of your trip.

Apart from Mt. Fuji itself, each of the three areas of the park—the Izu Peninsula, Hakone and environs, and the Five Lakes—has its own unique appeal. The Izu Peninsula is popular for its beaches and scenically rugged coastline. Hakone has mountains, volcanic landscapes, and lake cruises, plus *onsen* (hot springs) of its own. The Five Lakes form a recreational area with some of the best views of Mt. Fuji. And in each of these areas there are monuments to Japan's past.

Although it's possible to make a grand tour of all three areas at one time, most people make each of them a separate excursion from Tokyo.

Trains serve you well in traveling to major points anywhere in the northern areas of the national-park region and down the eastern coast of the Izu Peninsula. For the west coast and central mountains of Izu, there are no train connections; unless you are intrepid enough to rent a car, the only way to get around is by bus.

Especially in summer and fall, most towns and resorts have local visitor information centers. Few of them have staff members who speak fluent English, but you can still pick up local maps and pamphlets, as well as information on low-cost inns, pensions, and guesthouses.

FUJI-SAN (MT. FUJI) 富士山

Fodor's Choice ★

Mt. Fuji is the crown jewel of the national park. There are six routes to the summit of the 12,388-foot-high mountain but only two, both accessible by bus, are recommended: from Go-gome (Fifth Station), on the north side, and from Shin-Go-gome (New Fifth Station), on the south.

Continued on page 290

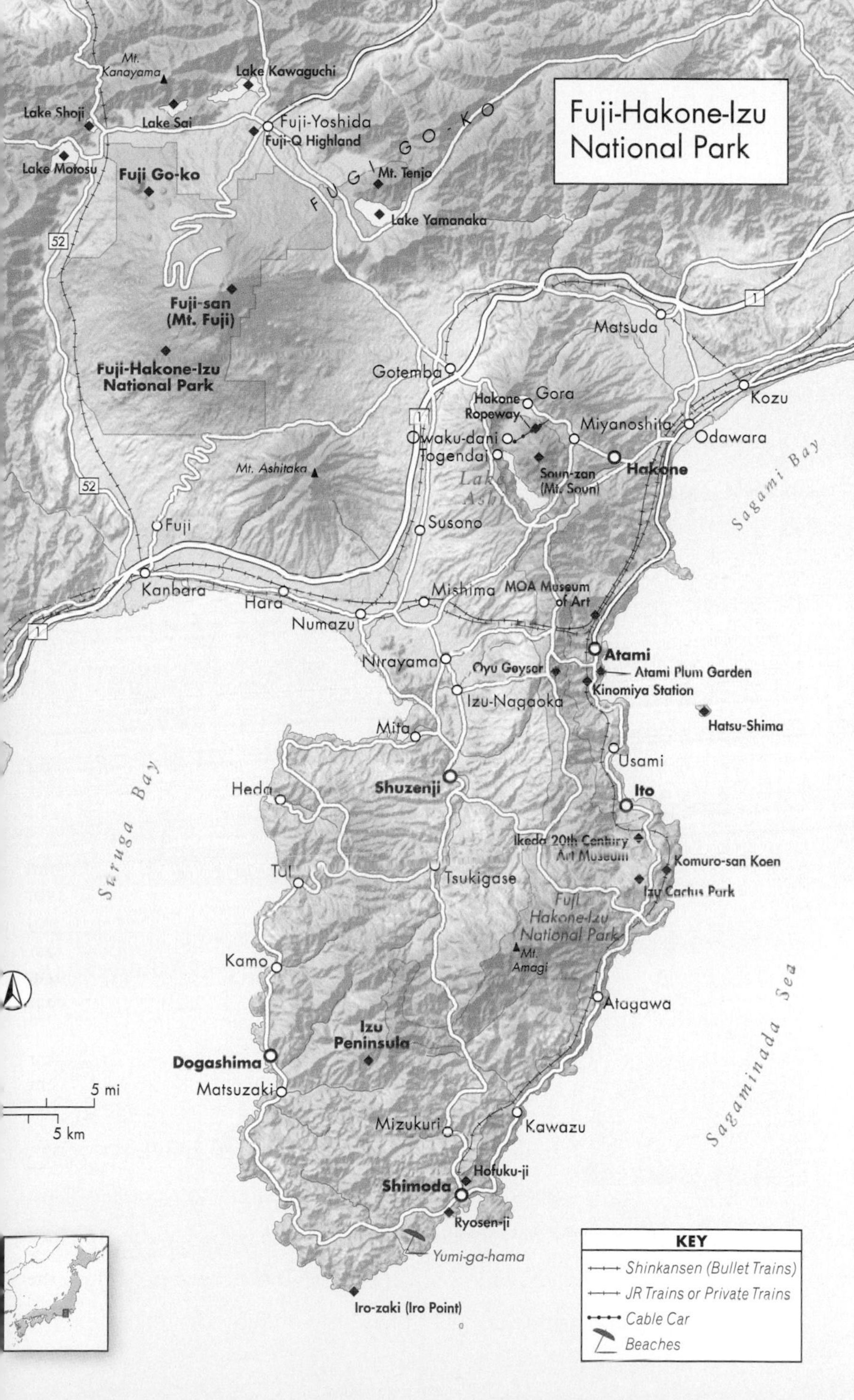
Fuji-Hakone-Izu National Park
Mt. Kanayama
Lake Kawaguchi
Lake Shoji
Lake Sai
Fuji-Yoshida
Fuji-Q Highland
Lake Motosu
Fuji Go-ko
FUJI GO-KO
Mt. Tenjo
Lake Yamanaka
52
Fuji-san (Mt. Fuji)
Fuji-Hakone-Izu National Park
1
Matsuda
Gotemba
Gora
Hakone Ropeway
Miyanoshita
Kozu
Owaku-dani
Odawara
Togendai
Hakone
Mt. Ashitaka
Soun-zan (Mt. Soun)
Lake Ashi
Sagami Bay
Fuji
Susono
Kanbara
Hara
Mishima
MOA Museum of Art
Numazu
Atami
Nirayama
Oyu Geyser
Atami Plum Garden
Kinomiya Station
Izu-Nagaoka
Hatsu-Shima
Mita
Usami
Suruga Bay
Heda
Shuzenji
Ito
Ikeda 20th Century Art Museum
Komuro-san Koen
Tsukigase
Izu Cactus Park
Toi
Fuji Hakone-Izu National Park
Mt. Amagi
Kamo
Atagawa
Sagaminada Sea
Izu Peninsula
Dogashima
5 mi
Matsuzaki
5 km
Mizukuri
Kawazu
Hofuku-ji
Shimoda
Ryosen-ji
Yumi-ga-hama
Iro-zaki (Iro Point)
KEY
Shinkansen (Bullet Trains)
JR Trains or Private Trains
Cable Car
Beaches

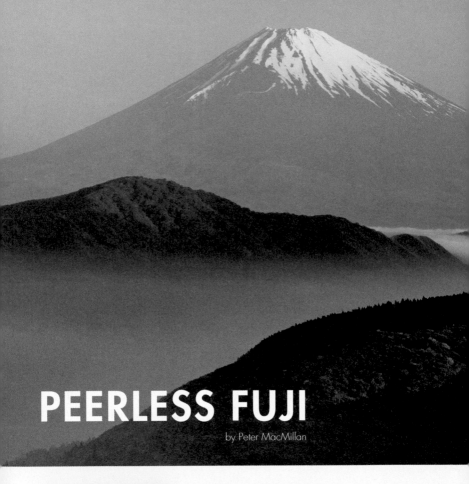

PEERLESS FUJI

by Peter MacMillan

Climbing Mt. Fuji

Mount Fuji greets hikers who arrive at its summit just before dawn with the *go-raiko,* or the Honorable Coming of the Light. The reflection of this light shimmers across the sky just before the sun first appears, giving the extraordinary sunrise a mystical feel. Fuji-san's early morning magic is just one of the characteristics of the mountain that has captured the collective imagination of the Japanese, along with its snowy peak, spiritual meaning, and propensity to hide behind clouds. The close-to-perfectly symmetrical cone is an object to conquer physically and to admire from afar.

Japan is more than 70% mountainous, and Fuji is its tallest mountain. It appears in literature, art, and culture from the highest level to the most ordinary in countless ways. In a word, Fuji is ubiquitous.

Since ancient times Mt. Fuji has been an object of worship for both Shinto and Buddhist practitioners. Shrines devoted to Konohana-Sakuya Hime, Mt. Fuji's goddess, dot the trails. So sacred is Fuji that the mountaintop torii gate at the Okumiya of Sengen Taisha Shrine (though at Fuji's foot, the shrine also encompasses the mountain above the 8th station) states that this is the greatest mountain in the world. Typically the gate would provide the shrine's name. Here, the torii defines not the shrine but the sacred space of the mountain.

Rising to 12,385 feet (3,776 meters) Mt. Fuji is an active volcano, but the last eruption was in 1707. Located on the boundaries of Shizuoka and Yamanashi prefectures, the mountain is an easy day trip west of Tokyo, and on clear days you can see the peak from the city. In season, hikers clamber to the peak, but it is gazing upon Fuji that truly inspires awe and wonder. No visit to Japan would be complete without at least a glimpse of this beautiful icon.

(top left) Mt. Fuji's famous morning light draws visitors, (top right) the summit is often surrounded by clouds, (bottom right) the trails are rocky and rugged at tiimes.

THE SYMBOLISM OF FUJI-SAN

ARTISTIC FUJI

Mt. Fuji is one of the world's most painted and photographed mountains. But rising above all the visual depictions are Katsushika Hokusai's *Thirty-six Views of Mt. Fuji* and his *One Hundred Views of Mt. Fuji*. The latter is a stunning work and considered his masterpiece. However, the *Thirty-Six Views* is more famous because the images were printed in full color, while the *One Hundred Views* was printed in monochrome black and gray. His *Great Wave off Kanagawa* is one of the most famous prints in the history of art.

Hokusai believed that his depictions would get better and better as he got older, and they did; his *One Hundred Views* was completed when he was 75. He was also obsessed with achieving immortality. In creating the *One Hundred Views of Mt. Fuji*, a mountain always associated with immortality, he hoped to achieve his own. History proved him right.

LITERARY FUJI

There are thousands of literary works related to Fuji, including traditional and modern poems, haiku, Noh dramas, novels, and plays. In the Man'yoshu, 8th-century poet Yamabe no Akahito famously extolled Fuji: "When I sail out/on the Bay of Tago/every where's white-/Look! Snow's piling up/ on the peak of Fuji." Matsuo Basho, in another well known poem, wrote about not being able to see the mountain: "How lovely and intriguing!/ Covered in drifting fog,/ the day I could not see Fuji." There are many times of the year when Fuji hides behind the clouds, so don't be disappointed if you miss it. Like the great haiku poet, see the mountain in the eye of your heart.

(top) Katsushika Hokusai's *Red Fuji*, (bottom) *Great Wave off Kanagawa* by Katsushika Hokusai

SEE FUJI-SAN FROM AFAR

Like the poets and artists who have found inspiration in gazing at Fuji-san, you, too, can catch a glimpse of the snow-capped cone on the horizon. On a clear day, most likely in winter when the air is dry and the clouds lift, the following experiences provide some of the best Fuji views.

SEE FUJI

Atop Tokyo. Visit the Tokyo City View observation promenade on the 52nd floor of the Mori Tower in Roppongi. You can walk all around this circular building and take in the spectacular views of Tokyo and, when the weather is fine, Fuji. While you're here, don't miss the sky-high Mori Art Museum, a contemporary art space on the 52nd and 53rd floors. The evening view of the city is also splendid, but Fuji will be slumbering under the blanket of nightfall.

From Hakone. Part of Fuji-Hakone-Izu National Park, the same park Fuji calls home, and an easy day trip from Tokyo, Hakone is a playground of hiking trails, small art museums, an onsen, and more. Head to the beautiful garden at Hakone Detached Palace for scenic views of Fuji-san. Early morning and late evening will provide the best chance for clear skies.

Speeding out of town. The classic view of Fuji is from the Shinkansen traveling from Tokyo to Kyoto. Some of the world's fastest transportation technology hums beneath you when, suddenly, the world's most beautiful and sacred mountain appears on the left. This striking combination of the ancient and cutting-edge is at the heart of understanding Japan. Make sure not to fall asleep!

(top) Shinkansen speeding past Fuji, (bottom) Fuji from inside Hakone National Park i

CLIMBING FUJI-SAN
FROM KAWAGUCHIKO TRAIL

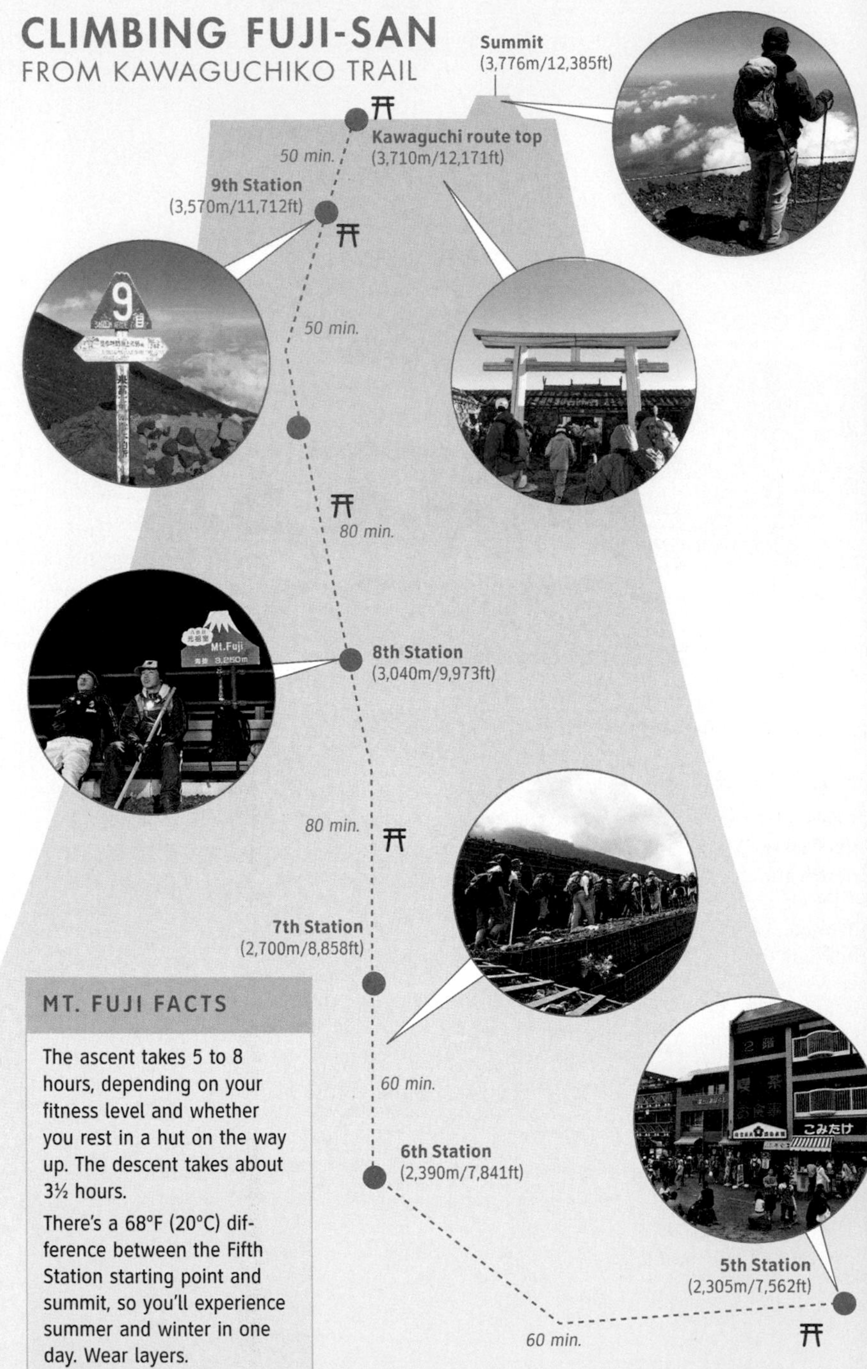

MT. FUJI FACTS

The ascent takes 5 to 8 hours, depending on your fitness level and whether you rest in a hut on the way up. The descent takes about 3½ hours.

There's a 68°F (20°C) difference between the Fifth Station starting point and summit, so you'll experience summer and winter in one day. Wear layers.

A photographer capturing view from Mt. Fuji

Although many Japanese like to climb Mt. Fuji once in their lives, there's a saying in Japanese that only a fool would climb it twice. You, too, can make a once-in-a-lifetime climb during the mountain's official open season from July through August. Unless you're an experienced hiker, do not attempt to make the climb at another time of year.

TRAIL CONDITIONS

Except for the occasional cobblestone path, the routes are unpaved and at times steep, especially toward the top. Near the end of the climb there are some rope banisters to steady yourself, but for the most part you'll have to rely on your own balance.

Fuji draws huge crowds in season, so expect a lot of company on your hike. The throngs grow thicker in August during the school break and reach their peak during the holiday Obon week in mid-August; it gets so crowded that hikers have to queue up at certain passes. Trails are less crowded overnight. Go during the week and in July for the lightest crowds (though the weather is less reliable). Or accept the crowds and enjoy the friendships that spring up among strangers on the trails.

TRAILS OVERVIEW

If you're in good health you should be able to climb from the base to the summit. That said, the air is thin, and it can be humbling to struggle for oxygen while some 83-year-old Japanese grandmother blithely leaves you in her dust (it happens).

Most visitors take buses as far as the Fifth Station and hike to the top from there (⇨ *See Mt. Fuji listing in this chapter for more information on buses*). The paved roads end at this halfway point.

Four routes lead to Mt. Fuji's summit—the **Kawaguchiko, Subashiri, Gotemba,** and **Fujinomiya**—and each has a corresponding Fifth Station that serves as the transfer point between bus and foot. Depending on which trail you choose, the ascent takes between 5 and 10 hours. Fujinomiya is closest to the summit; Gotemba is the farthest.

We recommend Kawaguchiko (Fuji-Yoshida) Trail in Yamanashi, as its many first-aid centers and lodging facilities (huts) ensure that you can enjoy the climb. **■ TIP→ Those interested in experiencing Fuji's religious and spiritual aspects should walk this trail from the mountain's foot. Along the way are small shrines that lead to the torii gate at the top, which signifies Fuji's sacred status.** While the food and cleanliness standards at mountain huts are subpar, they provide valuable rest spots and even more valuable camaraderie and good will among travelers.

AT THE TOP

Once you reach the top of Mt. Fuji, you can walk along the ridge of the volcano. A torii gate declares that Fuji is the greatest mountain in the world. It also marks the entrance to the **Fuji-san Hon-miya Sengen Taisha Shrine** (at the foot of the mountain near the Kawaguchiko Trail is the shrine's other facility). Inside the shrine, head to the post office where you can mail letters and postcards with a special Mt. Fuji stamp. There's also a chalet at the top for those captivated enough to stay the night.

NIGHT HIKES

The most spectacular way to hike Mt. Fuji is to time the climb so that you arrive at sunrise. Not only is the light famously enchanting, but the sky is also more likely to be clear, allowing for views back to Tokyo. Those who choose this have a few options. Start from the Kawaguchiko Fifth Station on the Kawaguchi Trail around 10 PM (or later, depending on the sunrise time) and hike through the night, arriving at the summit between 4:30 and 5 AM, just as the sun begins to rise. A better alternative is to begin in the afternoon or evening and hike to the Seventh or Eighth Station, spend a few hours resting there, and then depart very early in the morning to see the sun rise. ■ **TIP→ The trail isn't lit at night, so bring a headlamp to illuminate the way. Avoid carrying flashlights, though, as it is important to keep your hands free in case of a fall.**

(top) First glimpse of the go-raiko, (bottom) Mt. Fuji at dawn

COMMEMORATE YOUR VISIT

Purchase a walking stick at the base of Mt. Fuji and, as you climb, have it branded at each station. By the time you reach the top you'll have the perfect souvenir to mark your achievement.

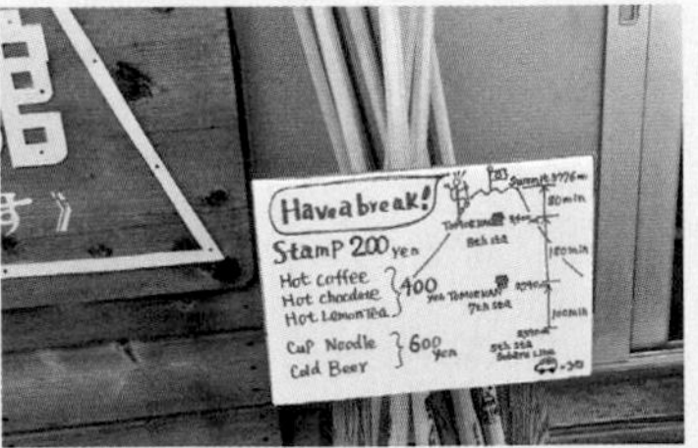

Walking sticks for sale

DID YOU KNOW?

Although earlier meanings of the word *Fuji* include "peerless," and "immortal one," the current way of writing Fuji implies "wealthy persons of military status." The mountain called *fuji-san* (not *fuji-yama*) in Japanese.

GETTING HERE AND AROUND

Take one of the daily buses directly to Go-gome from Tokyo; they run July through August and leave from Shinjuku Station. The journey takes about two hours and 40 minutes from Shinjuku and costs ¥2,600. Reservations are required; book seats through the Fuji Kyuko Highway Bus Reservation Center, the Keio Highway Bus Reservation Center, the Japan Travel Bureau (which should have English-speaking staff), or any major travel agency.

Although the buses are more affordable and convenient, if you need to return from Mt. Fuji to Tokyo by train, take an hour-long bus ride from Shin-Go-gome to Gotemba (¥1,500). From Gotemba take the JR Tokaido and Gotemba lines to Tokyo Station (¥1,940), or take the JR Asagiri express train from Gotemba to Shinjuku station (¥2,810).

ESSENTIALS

Buses from Tokyo Fuji Kyuko Highway Bus Reservation Center. ☎ *03/5376-2222* 🌐 *highway-buses.jp/fuji.* **JTB Sunrise Tours.** ☎ *03/5796-5454* 🌐 *www.jtb-sunrisetours.jp.* **Keio Highway Bus Reservation Center.** ☎ *03/5376-2222* 🌐 *highway-buses.jp.* **Tokai Bus Company** (東海バス). ☎ *0557/36-1112 main office, 0558/22-2514 Shimoda Information Center.*

EXPLORING

Fuji-san (Mt. Fuji). ✉ *Fuji-Hakone-Izu National Park* 🌐 *www.fujisan-climb.jp* 🕓 *Official hiking season: July 1–Aug. 26* ⇨ *For more information, see the highlighted listing in this chapter.*

IZU PENINSULA 伊豆半島

Izu is defined by its dramatic rugged coastline, beaches, and onsen (hot springs).

GETTING HERE AND AROUND

Having your own car makes sense only for touring the Izu Peninsula, and only then if you're prepared to cope with less-than-ideal road conditions, lots of traffic (especially on holiday weekends), and the paucity of road markers in English. It takes some effort—but exploring the peninsula *is* a lot easier by car than by public transportation. From Tokyo take the Tomei Expressway as far as Oi-matsuda (about 84 km [52 miles]); then pick up Routes 255 and 135 to Atami (approximately 28 km [17 miles]). From Atami drive another 55 km (34 miles) or so down the east coast of the Izu Peninsula to Shimoda.

■ **TIP→ One way to save yourself some trouble is to book a car through the Nippon or Toyota rental agency in Tokyo and arrange to pick it up at the Shimoda branch.** You can then simply take a train to Shimoda and use it as a base. From Shimoda you can drive back up the coast to Kawazu (35 minutes) and then to Shuzenji (30 minutes). It is possible to drop off the car in Tokyo, but only at specific branches, so visit your rental-car company's website or call them in advance.

Once you are on the Izu Peninsula itself, sightseeing excursions by boat are available from several picturesque small ports. From Dogashima, you can take the Dogashima Marine short (20 minutes, ¥1,200) or long (50 minutes, ¥2,300) tours of Izu's rugged west coast.

The Fuji Kyuko company operates a daily ferry to Hatsu-shima from Atami (25 minutes, ¥2,400 round-trip) and another to the island from Ito (23 minutes, ¥1,200 one-way). Izukyu Marine offers a 40-minute tour (¥1,400) by boat from Shimoda to the coastal rock formations at Iro-zaki.

JTB Sunrise Tours operates a tour to Hakone, including a cruise across Lake Ashi and a trip on the gondola over Owaku-dani (¥15,000 includes lunch and return to Tokyo by Shinkansen; ¥12,000 includes lunch and return to Tokyo by bus). **■TIP→ These tours are an economical way to see the main sights all in one day and are ideal for travelers with limited time.** Sunrise tours depart daily from Tokyo's Hamamatsu-cho Bus Terminal and some major hotels.

Trains are by far the easiest and fastest ways to get to the Izu Peninsula and the rest of the Fuji-Hakone-Izu National Park area. The gateway station of Atami is well served by comfortable express trains from Tokyo, on both JR and private railway lines. These in turn connect to local trains and buses that can get you anywhere in the region you want to go. Call the JR Higashi-Nihon Info Line (10–6 daily, except December 31–January 3) for assistance in English.

The *Kodama* Shinkansen from JR Tokyo Station to Atami costs ¥4,190 and takes 45 minutes; JR (Japan Railways) passes are valid. The JR local from Atami to Ito takes 25 minutes and costs ¥320. Ito and Atami are also served by the JR Odoriko Super Express (not a Shinkansen train) also departing from Tokyo Station; check the schedule display board for the correct platform. The Tokyo–Ito run takes 1¾ hours and costs ¥4,190; you can also use a JR Pass. The privately owned Izukyu Railways, on which JR Passes are not valid, makes the Ito–Shimoda run in one hour for ¥1,620.

The Izu–Hakone Railway Line runs from Tokyo to Mishima (one hour, 36 minutes; ¥4,090), with a change at Mishima for Shuzenji (31 minutes, ¥500); this is the cheapest option if you don't have a JR Pass. With a JR Pass, a Shinkansen–Izu Line combination saves about 35 minutes and is the cheapest option. The Tokyo–Mishima Shinkansen leg (62 minutes) costs ¥4,400; the Mishima–Shuzenji Izu Line leg (31 minutes) costs ¥500.

ESSENTIALS

Rental-Car Contacts Nippon Rent-a-Car. ☎ *03/3485–7196* 🌐 *www.nipponrentacar.co.jp.* **Toyota Rent-a-Car.** ☎ *0800/7000–815 toll-free in Japan; English operator available, 03/5954–8020 international* 🌐 *rent.toyota.co.jp/eng.*

Tour Contacts Dogashima Marine (堂ヶ島マリン). ☎ *0558/52–0013* 🌐 *www.izudougasima-yuransen.com.* **Fuji Kyuko** (富士急行). ☎ *0557/81–0541* 🌐 *www.fujikyu.co.jp/en/.* **Izukyu Marine** (伊豆急マリン). ☎ *0558/22–1151.*

Tourist Information Atami City Tourist Association. ✉ *Shinsui Park, 2018-8 Nagisa-cho, Atami* ☎ *0557/85–2222.* **Shimoda Tourist Association** (伊豆下田観光ガイド). ✉ *1-4-27 Shimoda, Shimoda* ☎ *0558/22–1531* 🌐 *www.shimoda-city.info.*

9

CLOSE UP

A Healing Headache

While earthquakes are an annoying, everyday fact of life in Japan, they also provide one of the country's greatest delights: thermal baths. Wherever there are volcanic mountains—and there are a lot—you're sure to find springs of hot water, called *onsen,* which are rich in all sorts of restorative minerals. Any place where lots of spas have tapped these sources is an *onsen chiiki* (hot-springs resort area). The Izu Peninsula is particularly rich in onsen. It has, in fact, one-fifth of the 2,300-odd officially recognized hot springs in Japan.

Spas take many forms, but the ne plus ultra is that small secluded Japanese mountain inn with a *rotemburo* (an open-air mineral-spring pool). For guests only, these pools are usually in a screened-off nook with a panoramic view. A room in one of these inns on a weekend or in high season should be booked months in advance. (High season is late December to early January, late April to early May, the second and third weeks of August, and the second and third weeks of October.) More typical is the large resort hotel, geared mainly to groups, with one or more large indoor mineral baths of its own. Where whole towns and villages have developed to exploit a local supply of hot water, there will be several of these large hotels, an assortment of smaller inns, and probably a few modest public bathhouses, with no accommodations, where you just pay an entrance fee for a soak of whatever length you wish.

Train Information Izukyu Corporation (伊豆急). ☎ *0557/53–1115 main office, 0558/22–3202 Izukyu Shimoda Station* 🌐 *www.izukyu.co.jp.* **JR Higashi-Nihon Info Line** (JR東日本お問い合わせ先 *JR East Info Line*). ☎ *050/2016–1603 English info line.* **Odakyu Sightseeing Service Center.** ✉ *Shinjuku Station 1F, Odakyu Railway West Exit* ☎ *03/5321–7887* 🌐 *www.odakyu.jp/english/center.*

ATAMI 熱海

100 km (60 miles) southwest of Tokyo Station.

The gateway to the Izu Peninsula is Atami. Most Japanese travelers make it no farther into the peninsula than this town on Sagami Bay, so Atami itself has a fair number of hotels and traditional inns.

When you arrive, collect a map from the **Atami Tourist Information Office** at the train station.

GETTING HERE AND AROUND

From JR Tokyo Station, take the Tokaido Line to Atami, which is the last stop (one hour, 34 minutes, ¥1,990) or the Kodama Shinkansen (49 minutes, ¥4,190).

EXPLORING

Atami Plum Garden (熱海梅園 *Atami Bai-en*). The best time to visit the garden is in late January or early February, when its 850 trees bloom. If you do visit, also stop by the small shrine that's in the shadow of an enormous old camphor tree. The shrine is more than 1,000 years old and is popular with people who are asking the gods for help with alcoholism. The tree is more than 2,000 years old and has been designated a

National Monument. It's believed that if you walk around the tree once, another year will be added to your life. Atami Bai-en is always open to the public and is 15 minutes by bus from Atami or an eight-minute walk from Kinomiya Station, the next stop south of Atami served by local trains. ✉ *8–11 Baien-cho* ☎ *0557/85–2222* *Free.*

Hatsu-shima (初島). If you have the time and the inclination for a beach picnic, it's worth taking the 25-minute high-speed ferry (round-trip ¥2,400) from the pier. There are five departures daily between 7:30 and 5:20 from both Atami and Ito, though the times vary by season. You can easily walk around the island, which is only 4 km (2½ miles) in circumference, in less than two hours. Use of the **Picnic Garden** (open daily 10–3) is free. ✉ *Atami Port, 6–11 Wadahama Minamicho* ☎ *0557/81–0541 ferry* 🌐 *www.hatsushima.jp.*

MOA Museum of Art (美術館 *MOA Bijutsukan*). This museum houses the private collection of the messianic religious leader Mokichi Okada (1882–1955), who founded a movement called the Sekai Kyusei Kyo (Religion for the Salvation of the World). He also acquired more than 3,000 works of art; some are from the Asuka period (6th and 7th centuries). Among these works are several particularly fine *ukiyo-e* (Edo-era wood-block prints) and ceramics. On a hill above the station and set in a garden full of old plum trees and azaleas, the museum also affords a sweeping view over Atami and the bay. ✉ *26–2 Momoyama* ☎ *0557/84–2511* 🌐 *www.moaart.or.jp/en* ¥*1,600* ⏲ *Fri.–Wed. 9:30–4:30.*

Oyu Geyser (大湯間欠泉 *Oyu Kanketsusen*). Located just a 15-minute walk southeast from Atami Station, the geyser used to gush on schedule once every 24 hours but stopped after the Great Kanto Earthquake of 1923. Not happy with this, the local chamber of commerce rigged a pump to raise the geyser every five minutes. ✉ *3 Kamijuku-cho.*

WHERE TO STAY

$$$$ B&B/INN **Atami Taikanso** (熱海大観荘). The views of the sea must have been the inspiration for Yokoyama Taikan, the Japanese artist who once owned this villa that is now a traditional Japanese inn with exquisite furnishings and individualized service. **Pros:** seaside rooms have beautiful views. **Cons:** eating dinner may take most of your evening. *Rooms from: ¥45000* ✉ *7–1 Hayashigaoka-cho* ☎ *0557/81–8137* *44 Japanese-style rooms with bath* *Some meals.*

$$$$ HOTEL **Hotel Micuras** (ホテルミクラス). Style, comfort, ocean views, and natural hot springs make this hotel one of Atami's best. **Pros:** stylish, modern. **Cons:** lacks the history or charm of a traditional inn. *Rooms from: ¥40,000* ✉ *3–19 Higashikaigan-cho* ☎ *0577/86–111* 🌐 *www.micuras.jp* *62 rooms (55 ocean-view, 7 mountain-view)* *No meals.*

ITO 伊東

16 km (10 miles) south of Atami.

There are some 800 thermal springs in the resort area surrounding Ito. These springs—and the beautiful, rocky, indented coastline nearby—remain the resort's major attractions, although there are plenty of interesting sights here. Some 150 hotels and inns serve the area.

Ito traces its history of associations with the West to 1604, when William Adams (1564–1620), the Englishman whose adventures served as the basis for James Clavell's novel *Shogun,* came ashore.

Four years earlier Adams had beached his disabled Dutch vessel, *De Liefde,* on the shores of the southwestern island of Kyushu and become the first Englishman to set foot on Japan. The authorities, believing that he and his men were Portuguese pirates, put Adams in prison, but he was eventually befriended by the shogun Ieyasu Tokugawa, who brought him to Edo (present-day Tokyo) and granted him an estate. Ieyasu appointed Adams his adviser on foreign affairs. The English castaway taught mathematics, geography, gunnery, and navigation to shogunate officials and in 1604 was ordered to build an 80-ton Western-style ship. Pleased with this venture, Ieyasu ordered the construction of a larger oceangoing vessel. These two ships were built at Ito, where Adams lived from 1605 to 1610.

This history was largely forgotten until British Commonwealth occupation forces began coming to Ito for rest and recuperation after World War II. Adams's memory was revived, and since then the Anjin Festival (the Japanese gave Adams the name *anjin,* which means "pilot") has been held in his honor every August. A monument to the Englishman stands at the mouth of the river.

GETTING HERE AND AROUND

From JR Tokyo Station or Shinagawa Station, take the Tokaido Line (two hours, 15 minutes, ¥2,210) or the Super Odoriko Express (one hour, 40 minutes, ¥4,190) to Ito Station.

ESSENTIALS

Visitor Information Ito Tourist Association (伊東観光協会 *Ito Kanko Kyoukai*). ✉ *1–8–3 Yukawa* ☎ *0557/37–6105* 🌐 *itospa.com/ito-city-english-tour-guide.*

EXPLORING

Ikeda 20th-Century Art Museum (池田20世紀美術館 *Ikeda 20-Seiki Bijutsukan*). The museum, which overlooks Lake Ippeki, houses works by Picasso, Dalí, Chagall, and Matisse, plus a number of wood-block prints. The museum is a 15-minute walk northwest from Izu Cactus Park. ✉ *614 Totari* ☎ *0557/45–2211* 🎫 *¥1,000* 🕓 *Thurs.–Tues. 10–4:30.*

Izu Cactus Park (伊豆シャボテン公園 *Izu Shaboten Koen*). The park consists of a series of pyramidal greenhouses that contain 5,000 kinds of cacti from around the world. At the base of Komuro-san (Mt. Komuro), the park is 20 minutes south of Ito Station by bus. ✉ *1317–13 Futo* ☎ *0557/51–1111* 🎫 *¥2,300* 🕓 *Mar.–Oct., daily 9–5; Nov.–Feb., daily 9–4.*

Komuro-san Koen (小室山公園 *Mt. Komuro Park*). Some 3,000 cherry trees of 35 varieties bloom at various times throughout the year. You can take a cable car to the top of the mountain, which has a lovely view of the sea below. The park is about 20 minutes south of Ito Station by bus. ✉ *1428 Komuro-cho* ☎ *0557/37–6105* 🎫 *Free; round-trip cable car to mountaintop ¥500* 🕓 *Daily 9–4.*

WHERE TO STAY

$$$$ B&B/INN **Hanafubuki** (花吹雪). This traditional Japanese inn, which is located in the Jogasaki forest, has modern, comfortable rooms, but still retains classic elements like tatami mats, sliding screen doors, and *chabudai* (low dining tables) with *zabuton* (cushion seating). **Pros:** an authentic Japanese experience. **Cons:** meals are available to nonguests, so the dining room can be a bit crowded. *Rooms from: ¥45,000* ✉ *1041 Yawatano* ☎ *0557/54–1550* 🌐 *www.hanafubuki.co.jp* *12 Japanese-style rooms with bath, 2 Western-style rooms with bath, 3 family rooms with bath* *Some meals.*

$$$$ HOTEL **Hatoya Sun Hotel** (ホテルサンハトヤ). A scenic coastline provides a backdrop for traditional-style lodgings and such amenities as open-air hot springs that look out to the ocean and mountains beyond. **Pros:** live entertainment at dinner. **Cons:** a lot of guests with children make this a bit noisy. *Rooms from: ¥40,000* ✉ *572–12 Yukawa* ☎ *0557/36–4126* *187 Japanese-style rooms with bath, 3 Western-style rooms with bath, 1 mixed Western-Japanese-style room with bath* *Some meals.*

EN ROUTE **Atagawa.** South of Ito the coastal scenery is lovely—each sweep around a headland reveals another picturesque sight of a rocky, indented shoreline. There are several spa towns en route to Shimoda. Higashi-Izu (East Izu) has numerous hot-springs resorts, of which Atagawa is the most fashionable. South of Atagawa is **Kawazu**, a place of relative quiet and solitude, with pools in the forested mountainside and waterfalls plunging through lush greenery. ✉ *Ito.*

SHIMODA 下田

35 km (22 miles) south of Ito city.

Of all the resort towns south of Ito along Izu's eastern coast, none can match the distinction of Shimoda. The town's encounter with the West began when Commodore Matthew Perry anchored his fleet of black ships off the coast here in 1853. To commemorate the event, the three-day Black Ship Festival (Kurofune Matsuri) is held here every year in mid-May. Shimoda was also the site, in 1856, of the first American consulate.

The **Shimoda Tourist Office,** in front of the station, has the easiest of the local English itineraries to follow. The 2½-km (1½-mile) tour covers most major sights. On request, the tourist office will also help you find local accommodations.

GETTING HERE AND AROUND

From JR Shinagawa Station, take the Tokaido Line to Atami, change to the Ito Line, and take it to the final stop, Izukyu Shimoda Station (three hours, 45 minutes, ¥3,883).

ESSENTIALS

Shimoda Tourist Office. ✉ *1–1 Sotogaoka* ☎ *0558/22–1531.*

EXPLORING

Hofuku-ji (宝福寺). The first American consul to Japan was New York businessman Townsend Harris. Soon after his arrival in Shimoda, Harris asked the Japanese authorities to provide him with a female servant; they sent him a young girl named Okichi Saito, who was engaged to be married. The arrangement brought her a new name, Tojin (the

Foreigner's) Okichi, much disgrace, and a tragic end. When Harris sent her away, she tried, but failed, to rejoin her former lover. The shame brought upon her for working and living with a Westerner and the pain of losing the love of her life drove Okichi to drown herself in 1892. Her tale is recounted in Rei Kimura's biographical novel *Butterfly in the Wind* and inspired Puccini's *Madame Butterfly,* although some skeptics say the story is more gossip than fact. Hofuku-ji was Okichi's family temple. The museum annex displays a life-size image of her, and just behind the temple is her grave—where incense is still kept burning in her memory. The grave of her lover, Tsurumatsu, is at Toden-ji, a temple about midway between Hofuku-ji and Shimoda Station. ✉ *18–26–1 Shimoda* ☎ *0558/22–0960* 🎫 *¥300* ⏲ *Daily 8–5.*

Ryosen-ji (了仙寺). This is the temple in which the negotiations took place that led to the United States–Japan Treaty of Amity and Commerce of 1858. The **Treasure Hall** (Homotsu-den) contains more than 300 original artifacts relating to Commodore Perry and the "black ships" that opened Japan to the West. ✉ *3–12–12 Shimoda* ☎ *0558/22–0657* 🌐 *www.izu.co.jp/~ryosenji* 🎫 *Treasure Hall ¥500* ⏲ *Daily 8:30–5.*

OFF THE BEATEN PATH

Yumi-ga-hama (弓ケ浜). If you love the sun, make sure you stop at Yumi-ga-hama. It's one of the nicest sandy beaches on the whole Izu Peninsula. Although the water is usually warm enough to swim from June, the crowds come out during Japan's beach season in July and August. The bus from Shimoda Station stops here before continuing to Irozaki, the last stop on the route. **Amenities:** food and drink (July and August); lifeguards (July and August); toilets; parking. **Best for:** swimming (June–August); solitude (September–June). ✉ *Shimoda* ✣ *11 km (7 miles) southwest of Shimoda, just south of highway 136.*

WHERE TO STAY

$ B&B/INN **Pension Sakuraya** (ペンションン桜家). The best lodgings at this family-run inn just a few minutes' walk from Shimoda's main beach are the Japanese-style corner rooms, which have nice views of the hills surrounding Shimoda. **Pros:** very homey atmosphere. **Cons:** rooms are a bit cramped. Ⓢ *Rooms from: ¥10000* ✉ *2584–20 Shira-hama* ☎ *0558/23–4470* 🌐 *izu-sakuraya.jp/english* ⇨ *4 Western-style rooms with bath, 5 Japanese-style rooms without bath* 🍴 *Some meals.*

$$$$ HOTEL **Shimoda Prince Hotel** (下田プリンスホテル). At this modern V-shape resort hotel that faces the Pacific, the decor is more functional than aesthetic, but a white-sand beach is just steps away, and there's a panoramic view of the ocean from the picture windows in the dining room. **Pros:** an excellent view of the sea; one of the best hotels in town. **Cons:** restaurants are on the pricey side. Ⓢ *Rooms from: ¥32000* ✉ *1547–1 Shira-hama* ☎ *0558/22–2111* 🌐 *www.princehotels.com* ⇨ *70 Western-style rooms with bath, 6 Japanese-style rooms with bath* 🍴 *Some meals.*

$$$$ HOTEL **Shimoda Tokyu Hotel** (下田東急ホテル). Perched just above the bay, the Shimoda Tokyu has impressive views of the Pacific from one side (where rooms cost about 10% more) and mountains from the other. **Pros:** nice views of the ocean. **Cons:** restaurants are expensive for Tokyo standards. Ⓢ *Rooms from: ¥40000* ✉ *5–12–1 Shimoda* ☎ *0558/22–2411*

shimoda.tokyuhotels.com *107 Western-style rooms with bath, 8 Japanese-style rooms with bath* *Breakfast.*

DOGASHIMA 堂ヶ島

16 km (10 miles) northeast of Mishima.

The sea has eroded the coastal rock formations into fantastic shapes near the little port town of Dogashima, including a tombolo, or a narrow band of sand, that connects the mainland to a small peninsula with a scenic park.

GETTING HERE AND AROUND

Dogashima is not directly accessible by train but buses run from Shinjuku and Tokyo Stations. From Tokyo Station, take the JR Shinkansen to Mishima (44 minutes, ¥3,890), change to the Izu Hakone Line to Shuzenji (35 minutes, ¥500), and take the Tokai bus to the Dogashima stop. There is also an express Tokai Bus, Minami Izu Line, which takes you from Shimoda Station to Dogashima (55 minutes).

TOURS

Dogashima Marine Sightseeing Boat. Sightseeing boats from Dogashima Pier make 20-minute runs to see the rocks (¥1,200). In an excess of kindness, a recorded loudspeaker—which you can safely ignore—recites the name of every rock you pass on the trip. *0558/52–0013* *www.izudougasima-yuransen.com.*

WHERE TO STAY

$$$$ HOTEL **Dogashima New Ginsui** (堂ヶ島ニュー銀水). Perched above the water and a secluded beach, every Japanese-style guest room overlooks the sea. **Pros:** by far the best luxury resort on Izu's west coast; stunning views; concierge. **Cons:** a bit far from sightseeing spots. *Rooms from: ¥46000* *2977–1 Nishina, Nishi-Izu-cho* *0558/52–2211* *www.dougashima-newginsui.jp* *121 Japanese-style rooms with bath* *Some meals.*

SHUZENJI 修善寺

25 km (15 miles) south of Mishima by Izu-Hakone Railway.

Shuzenji—a hot-springs resort in the center of the peninsula, along the valley of the Katsura-gawa (Katsura River)—enjoys a certain historical notoriety as the place where the second Kamakura shogun, Minamoto no Yoriie, was assassinated in the early 13th century. Don't judge the town by the area around the station; most of the hotels and hot springs are 2 km (1 mile) to the west.

GETTING HERE AND AROUND

The train is by far the easiest way to get to Shuzenji. The JR Tokaido Line runs from Tokyo to Mishima (two hours, 10 minutes, ¥2,270), with a change at Mishima for Shuzenji (31 minutes, ¥510); this is the cheapest option if you don't have a JR Pass. With a JR Pass, a Kodama Shinkansen–Izu Line combination saves an hour. The Tokyo–Mishima Shinkansen leg (62 minutes) costs ¥4,520; the Mishima–Shuzenji Izu Line leg (31 minutes) costs ¥510.

CLOSE UP

Ryokan Etiquette

Guests are expected to arrive at ryokan in the late afternoon. When you do, put on the slippers that are provided and a maid will escort you to your room. Remember to remove your slippers before entering your room; never step on the tatami (straw mats) with shoes or slippers. Each room will be simply decorated—one small, low table, cushions on the tatami, and a scroll on the wall—which will probably be shoji (sliding paper-paneled walls).

In ryokan with thermal pools, you can take to the waters anytime, although the pool doors are usually locked from 11 pm to 6 am. In ryokan without thermal baths or private baths in guest rooms, visits must be staggered. Typically the maid will ask what time you would like to bathe and fit you into a schedule. Make sure you wash and rinse off entirely before getting into the bath. Do not get soap in the tub. Other guests will be using the same bathwater, so it is important to observe this custom. After your bath, change into the yukata provided in your room. Don't worry about walking around in it—other guests will be doing the same.

Dinner is served around 6. At the larger, newer ryokan, meals will be in the dining room; at smaller, more personal ryokan, it is served in your room. When you are finished, a maid will clear away the dishes and lay out your futon. In Japan *futon* means bedding, and this consists of a thin cotton mattress and a heavy, thick comforter, which is replaced with a thinner quilt in summer. The small, hard pillow is filled with grain. Some of the less expensive ryokan (under ¥7,000 per person) have become slightly lackadaisical in changing the quilt cover with each new guest; in as inoffensive a way as possible, feel free to complain—just don't shame the proprietor. Around 8 am, a maid will gently wake you, clear away the futon, and bring in your Japanese-style breakfast, which will probably consist of fish, pickled vegetables, and rice. If this isn't appealing, politely ask if it's possible to have coffee and toast. Checkout is at 10 am.

Make sure you call or email as far in advance as possible for a room—inns are not always willing to accept foreign guests because of language and cultural barriers. It is nearly impossible to get a room in July or August. Many top-level ryokan require new guests to have introductions and references from a respected client of the inn to get a room; this goes for new Japanese guests, too. On the other hand, inns that do accept foreigners without introduction sometimes treat them as cash cows, which means they might give you cursory service and a lesser room. If you don't speak Japanese, try to have a Japanese speaker reserve a room for you.

WHERE TO STAY

$$$$ B&B/INN **Goyokan** (五葉館). This family-run ryokan on Shuzenji's main street has rooms that look out on the Katsura-gawa, plus gorgeous stone-lined (for men) and wood-lined (for women) indoor hot springs. **Pros:** unique, modern take on a ryokan. **Cons:** lacks cozy feel of a true ryokan. *Rooms from: ¥32000* ✉ *765–2–1 Shuzenji-cho* ☎ *0558/72–2066* 🌐 *www.goyokan.co.jp* *11 Japanese-style rooms without bath* *Breakfast.*

$$$$ **B&B/INN** **Kyorai-An Matsushiro-kan** (去来庵 松城館). Although this small family-owned inn is nothing fancy, the owners make you feel like a guest in their home. **Pros:** nice shared hot-spring bath. **Cons:** rather dated design throughout. *Rooms from: ¥34000* *55 Kona, Izunokuni* *055/948–0072* *No credit cards* *16 Japanese-style rooms, 14 with bath* *Some meals.*

$$$$ **B&B/INN** **Ochiairou Murakami** (落合楼村上). This traditional ryokan was built in the Showa period, and though it has been renovated and modernized, the main wooden structure remains true to its original design, with spacious and comfortable rooms that look out into the gardens. **Pros:** free pickup from Yugashima bus terminal; lovely garden on the grounds. **Cons:** rather expensive. *Rooms from: ¥38000* *1887–1 Yugashima, Izu* *055/885–0014* *15 Japanese-style rooms with bath* *Some meals.*

$$$$ **B&B/INN** **Ryokan Sanyoso** (旅館三養荘). At the former villa of the Iwasaki family, founders of the Mitsubishi conglomerate, museum-quality antiques furnish the rooms. The best rooms have traditional baths made of fragrant cypress wood and overlook exquisite little private gardens. **Pros:** authentic ryokan and furnishings; Japanese bath available; as luxurious and beautiful a place as you'll find on the Izu Peninsula. **Cons:** most expensive ryokan in the area. *Rooms from: ¥60000* *270 Mamanoue, Izunokuni* *055/947–1111* *www.princehotels.com/en/sanyo-so* *3 Western-style, 30 Japanese-style, and 7 mixed Western-Japanese-style rooms with bath* *Some meals.*

HAKONE 箱根

The national park and resort area of Hakone is a popular day trip from Tokyo and a good place for a close-up view of Mt. Fuji (assuming the mountain is not swathed in clouds, as often happens in summer). **■ TIP→ On summer weekends it often seems as though all of Tokyo has come out to Hakone with you. Expect long lines at cable cars and traffic jams everywhere.**

9

TIMING

You can cover the best of Hakone in a one-day trip out of Tokyo, but if you want to try the curative powers of the thermal waters or do some hiking, then stay overnight. Two of the best areas are around the old hot-springs resort of Miyanoshita and the western side of Koma-ga-take-san (Mt. Koma-ga-take).

GETTING HERE AND AROUND

The typical Hakone route, outlined here, may sound complex, but this is in fact one excursion from Tokyo so well defined that you really can't get lost—no more so, at least, than any of the thousands of Japanese tourists ahead of and behind you. The first leg of the journey is from Odawara or Hakone-Yumoto by train and cable car through the mountains to Togendai, on the north shore of Ashi-no-ko (Lake Ashi). The long way around, from Odawara to Togendai by bus, takes about an hour—in heavy traffic, an hour and a half. The trip over the mountains, on the other hand, takes about two hours. Credit the difference to the Hakone Tozan Tetsudo Line—possibly the slowest train you'll ever ride.

Using three switchbacks to inch its way up the side of the mountain, the train takes 54 minutes to travel the 16 km (10 miles) from Odawara to Gora (38 minutes from Hakone-Yumoto). The steeper it gets, the grander the view.

Trains do not stop at any station en route for any length of time, but they do run frequently enough to allow you to disembark, visit a sight, and catch another train.

Within the Hakone area, buses run every 15 to 30 minutes from Hakone-machi to Hakone-Yumoto Station on the private Odakyu Line (40 minutes, ¥960), and Odawara Station (one hour, ¥1,180), where you can take either the Odakyu Romance Car back to Shinjuku Station or a JR Shinkansen to Tokyo Station.

Hakone Sightseeing Cruise. This ride is free with your Hakone Free Pass; otherwise, buy a ticket (¥1,480 round-trip) at the office in the terminal. A few ships of conventional design ply Lake Ashi; the rest are astonishingly corny Disney knockoffs. One, for example, is rigged like a 17th-century warship. ✉ *181 Hakone, Ashigarashimo District* ☎ *0460/83–6325* 🌐 *www.hakone-kankosen.co.jp* 🎫 *¥1,840 round-trip (without Hakone Free Pass)* ⏲ *Summer, 40-min intervals; winter, 50-min intervals. Mar.–Nov., daily 9:30–5; Dec.–Feb., daily 9:30–4.*

Odakyu Sightseeing Service Center. Many places in Hakone accept the Hakone Free Pass. It's valid for three days and issued by the privately owned Odakyu Railways. The pass covers the train fare to Hakone and allows you to use any mode of transportation, including the Hakone Tozan Cable Car, the Hakone Ropeway, and the Hakone Cruise Boat. In addition to transportation, Free Pass holders get discounts at museums such as the Hakone Museum of Art, restaurants, and shops. The list of participants is pretty extensive and it always changes, so it's a good idea to check out the website for a complete list of participating companies and terms and conditions.

The Hakone Free Pass (¥5,640) and the Fuji-Hakone Pass (¥7,400) can be purchased at the Odakyu Sightseeing Service Center inside JR Shinjuku Station in Tokyo, near the West Exit, or by credit card over the phone. Allow a couple of days for delivery to your hotel. If you have a JR Pass, it's cheaper to take a Kodama Shinkansen from Tokyo Station to Odawara and buy the Hakone Free Pass there (¥4,500) for travel within the Hakone region only. ✉ *JR Shinjuku Station, 3–8 Shinjuku, near the West Exit* ☎ *03/5321–7887* 🌐 *www.odakyu.jp.*

ESSENTIALS

Tourist Information Hakone Tourist Association (箱根観光協会 *Hakone Kanko Kyoukai*). ✉ *698 Yumoto, Hakone* ☎ *0460/85–7177* 🌐 *www.hakone.or.jp/en.*

EXPLORING

TOP ATTRACTIONS

Fodor's Choice ★ **Hakone Kowakien Yunessun** (箱根小涌園 ユネッサン). This complex on the hills overlooking Hakone has more than the average onsen. In addition to all the water-based attractions, there is a shopping mall modeled on a European outdoor market, swimsuit rental shop, massage salon, and game center. The park is divided into two main zones, called Yunessun

CLOSE UP

The Road to the Shogun

In days gone by, the town of Hakone was on the Tokaido, the main highway between the imperial court in Kyoto and the shogunate in Edo (present-day Tokyo). The road was the only feasible passage through this mountainous country, which made it an ideal place for a checkpoint to control traffic. The Tokugawa Shogunate built the Hakone-machi here in 1618; its most important function was to monitor the *daimyo* (feudal lords) passing through—to keep track, above all, of weapons coming into Edo, and womenfolk coming out.

When Ieyasu Tokugawa came to power, Japan had been through nearly 100 years of bloody struggle among rival coalitions of daimyo. Ieyasu emerged supreme because some of his opponents had switched sides at the last minute, in the Battle of Sekigahara in 1600. The shogun was justifiably paranoid about his "loyal" barons—especially those in the outlying domains—so he required the daimyo to live in Edo for periods of time every two years. When they did return to their own lands, they had to leave their wives behind in Edo, hostages to their good behavior. A noble lady coming through the Hakone Sekisho without an official pass, in short, was a case of treason.

The checkpoint served the Tokugawa dynasty well for 250 years. It was demolished only when the shogunate fell, in the Meiji Restoration of 1868. An exact replica, with an exhibition hall of period costumes and weapons, was built as a tourist attraction in 1965.

and Mori no Yu ("Forest Bath"). In the Yunessun side, you need to wear a swimsuit, and can visit somewhat tacky re-creations of Turkish and ancient Roman baths. You can also take a dip in coffee, green tea, sake, or red wine. It is all a bit corny, but fun. Younger visitors enjoy the waterslides on "Rodeo Mountain." In the more secluded Mori no Yu side, you can go au naturel in a variety of indoor and outdoor, single-sex baths. When signing in at reception, get a waterproof digital wristband that allows you to pay for lockers and drink machines within the complex. ✉ *1297 Ninotaira Hakone-machi, Ashigarashimo-gun* ☎ *0460/82–4126* 🌐 *www.yunessun.com* 💴 *Yunessun zone ¥2,900, Mori no Yu zone ¥1,900, both for ¥4,100* ⏲ *Mar.–Oct., Yunessun daily 9–7, Mori no Yu daily 11–9; Nov.–Feb., Yunessun daily 9–6, Mori no Yu daily 11–9.*

Hakone Open-Air Museum (箱根彫刻の森美術館 *Hakone Chokoku-no-mori Bijutsukan*). Only a few minutes' walk from the Miyanoshita Station (directions are posted in English), the museum houses an astonishing collection of 19th- and 20th-century Western and Japanese sculpture, most of it on display in a spacious, handsome garden. There are works here by Rodin, Moore, Arp, Calder, Giacometti, Takashi Shimizu, and Kotaro Takamura. One section of the garden is devoted to Emilio Greco. Inside are works by Picasso, Léger, and Manzo, among others. ✉ *1121 Ni-no-taira* ☎ *0460/82–1161* 🌐 *www.hakone-oam.or.jp* 💴 *¥1,600* ⏲ *Mar.–Nov., daily 9–5; Dec.–Feb., daily 9–4.*

Hakone Ropeway. At the cable-car terminus of Soun-zan, a gondola called the Hakone Ropeway swings up over a ridge and crosses the valley called **Owaku-dani,** also known as "Great Boiling Valley," on its way to Togendai. The landscape here is desolate, with sulfurous billows of steam escaping through holes from some inferno deep in the earth—yet another reminder that Japan is a chain of volcanic islands. At the top of the ridge is one of the two stations where you can leave the gondola. From here, a ¾-km (½-mile) walking course wanders among the sulfur pits in the valley. Just below the station is a restaurant; the food here is truly terrible, but on a clear day the view of Mt. Fuji is perfect. Remember that if you get off the gondola at any stage, you—and others in the same situation—will have to wait for someone to make space on a later gondola before you can continue down to Togendai and Ashi-no-ko (but the gondolas come by every minute). ✉ *1–15–1 Shiroyama, Odawara* ☎ *0460/32–2205* 🎫 *¥1,510 round-trip Sounzan Station to Owakudani Station* ⏲ *Mar.–Nov., daily 8:45–5:15; Dec.–Feb., daily 9:15–4:15.*

Miyanoshita (宮ノ下). The first stop on the train route from Hakone-Yumoto, this is a small but very pleasant and popular resort. As well as hot springs, this village has antiques shops along its main road and several hiking routes up the ¾-km- (½-mile-) tall Mt. Sengen. If you get to the top, you'll be rewarded with a great view of the gorge. ✉ *Hakone.*

WORTH NOTING

Ashi-no-ko (芦ノ湖 *Lake Ashi*). From Owaku-dani, the descent by gondola to Togendai on the shore of Lake Ashi takes 25 minutes. There's no reason to linger at Togendai; it's only a terminus for buses to Hakone-Yumoto and Odawara and to the resort villages in the northern part of Hakone. Head straight for the pier, a few minutes' walk down the hill, where boats set out on the lake for Hakone-machi. With still water and good weather, you'll get a breathtaking reflection of the mountains in the waters of the lake as you go. ✉ *Hakone.*

Gora (強羅). This small town is at the end of the train line from Odawara and at the lower end of the Hakone Tozan Cable Car. It's a good jumping-off point for hiking and exploring. Ignore the little restaurants and souvenir stands here: get off the train as quickly as you can and make a dash for the cable car at the other end of the station. If you let the rest of the passengers get there before you, and perhaps a tour bus or two, you may stand 45 minutes in line. ✉ *Hakone.*

Hakone Museum of Art (箱根美≠術館 *Hakone Bijutsukan*). A sister institution to the MOA Museum of Art in Atami, Hakone Museum of Art is at the second stop of the Hakone Tozan Cable Car. The museum, which consists of two buildings set in a garden, houses a modest collection of porcelain and ceramics from China, Korea, and Japan. ✉ *1300 Gora* ☎ *0460/2–2623* 🌐 *www.moaart.or.jp/hakone* 🎫 *¥900* ⏲ *Apr.–Nov., Fri.–Wed. 9:30–4:30; Dec.–Mar., Fri.–Wed. 9:30–4.*

Hakone Sekisho (箱根町). This barrier, a checkpoint on the road with a guardhouse and lookout tower, was built in 1618 to inspect incoming and outgoing traffic until it was demolished during the Meiji Restoration of 1868. An exact replica was built as a tourist attraction in 1965

Passengers floating over the Owaku-dani valley on the Hakone Ropeway can see Fuji looming—on a clear day, of course.

and is only a few minutes' walk from the pier, along the lakeshore in the direction of Moto-Hakone. ✉ *1 Hakone-machi* ☎ *0460/83–6635* 🎫 *¥500* ⏱ *Mar.–Nov., daily 9–5; Dec.–Feb., daily 9–4:30, last entry 30 mins before closing.*

Soun-zan (早雲山 *Mt. Soun*). The Hakone Tozan Cable Car travels from Gora to Soun-zan, departing every 20 minutes; it takes 10 minutes (¥410; free with the Hakone Free Pass) to get to the top. It provides a good launch for an ideal day of hiking. There are four stops en route, and you can get off and reboard the cable car at any of them if you've paid the full fare. ✉ *Hakone.*

9

WHERE TO STAY

$$$$ HOTEL **Fujiya Hotel** (富士屋ホテル). Built in 1878, this Western-style hotel with modern additions is showing signs of age, but that somehow adds to its charm. **Pros:** wonderful, friendly service. **Cons:** rooms and bath design are rather dated. $ *Rooms from: ¥50000* ✉ *359 Miyanoshita, Hakone-machi* ☎ *0460/82–2211* 🌐 *www.fujiyahotel.jp* *149 Western-style rooms with bath* 🍽 *Some meals.*

$ HOTEL **Fuji-Hakone Guest House** (富士箱根ゲストハウス). This small, family-run Japanese inn has simple tatami rooms with the bare essentials. **Pros:** friendly staff; inexpensive rates. **Cons:** difficult to access from nearest transportation, especially at night. $ *Rooms from: ¥10000* ✉ *912 Sengoku-hara (103 Moto-Hakone for Moto-Hakone Guest House), Hakone-machi* ☎ *0460/84–6577 Fuji-Hakone, 0460/83–7880 Moto-Hakone* 🌐 *fujihakone.com/en* *14 Japanese-style rooms without bath in Fuji-Hakone, 5 Japanese-style rooms without bath in Moto-Hakone* 🍽 *Some meals.*

$$$$ B&B/INN **Gora Tensui** (強羅天翠). Upon entering this cross between a luxury Western-style hotel and traditional inn, guests remove their shoes and socks, sit at a counter bar with their tired feet resting in the hot-mineral-spring bath under the bar, and enjoy a tea or beer as they check in. **Pros:** four rooms have a private onsen on a terrace. **Cons:** no Japanese food in the restaurant. *Rooms from: ¥50000 1320–276 Gora, Ashigarashimo-gun 0460/86–1411 www.gora-tensui.com 10 Western-style rooms, 7 Japanese-style rooms, all with bath Some meals.*

WHAT THE . . . ?

No, your eyes are not playing tricks on you. Those are in fact local entrepreneurs boiling eggs in the sulfur pits in Owaku-dani. Locals make a passable living selling the eggs, which turn black, to tourists at exorbitant prices. A popular myth suggests that eating one of these eggs can extend your life by seven years.

$$$$ HOTEL **Hakone Prince Hotel Ashinoko** (箱根プリンスホテル芦ノ湖). You have a choice of hotel rooms or cozy cottages at this resort complex, with the lake in front and the mountains of Koma-ga-take in back. **Pros:** lovely quaint cottages surrounded by nature. **Cons:** a bit remote from sightseeing spots; popular with groups and business conferences. *Rooms from: ¥50000 144 Moto-Hakone, Hakone-machi 0460/83–1111 www.princehotels.com 142 Western-style rooms with bath, 116 Western-style cottages with bath Breakfast.*

FUJI GO-KO (FUJI FIVE LAKES) 富士五湖

To the north of Mt. Fuji, the Fuji Go-ko area affords an unbeatable view of the mountain on clear days and makes the best base for a climb to the summit. With its various outdoor activities, such as skating and fishing in winter and boating and hiking in summer, this is a popular resort area for families and business conferences.

The five lakes are, from the east, Yamanaka-ko, Kawaguchi-ko, Sai-ko, Shoji-ko, and Motosu-ko. Yamanaka and Kawaguchi are the largest and most developed as resort areas, with Kawaguchi more or less the centerpiece of the group.

TIMING

You can visit this area on a day trip from Tokyo, but unless you want to spend most of it on buses and trains, plan on staying overnight.

GETTING HERE AND AROUND

Direct bus service runs daily from Shinjuku Station in Tokyo to Lake Kawaguchi every hour between 7:10 am and 11:20 pm. Buses go from Kawaguchi-ko Station to Go-gome (the fifth station on the climb up Mt. Fuji) in about an hour; there are eight departures a day until the climbing season (July and August) starts, when there are 15 departures or more, depending on demand. The cost is ¥1,750.

The transportation hub, as well as one of the major resort areas in the Fuji Five Lakes area, is Kawaguchi-ko. Getting there from Tokyo requires a change of trains at Otsuki. The JR Chuo Line Kaiji and Azusa express trains leave Shinjuku Station for Otsuki on the half hour from 7 am to 8 pm (more frequently in the morning) and take approximately one hour. At Otsuki, change to the private Fuji-Kyuko Line for Kawaguchi-ko, which takes another 50 minutes. The total traveling time is about two hours, and you can use your JR Pass as far as Otsuki; otherwise, the fare is ¥1,490. The Otsuki–Kawaguchi-ko leg costs ¥1,140.

The Holiday Kaisoku Fuji train, available on weekends and national holidays, has direct express service from Shinjuku, leaving at 8:14 and arriving at Kawaguchi-ko Station at 10:26. Coming back, you have a choice of late-afternoon departures from Kawaguchi-ko that arrive at Shinjuku in the early evening. Check the express timetables before you go; you can also call either the JR Higashi-Nihon Info Line or Fujikyuuko Kawaguchi-ko Station for train information.

ESSENTIALS

Visitor Information Fuji-Kawaguchiko Tourist Association (富士河口湖観光協会 *Fuji Kawaguci-ko Kanko Kyoukai*). ✉ *364–1 Funatsu, Fujikawaguchiko-machi, Minami-Tsuru-gun* ☎ *0555/72–6700* 🌐 *www.fujisan.ne.jp.*

EXPLORING

FAMILY **Fuji-Q Highland** (富士急ハイランド). The largest of the recreational facilities at Lake Kawaguchi has an impressive assortment of rides, roller coasters, and other amusements, but it's probably not worth a visit unless you have children in tow. In winter there's superb skating here, with Mt. Fuji for a backdrop. Fuji-kyu Highland is about 15 minutes' walk east from Kawaguchi-ko Station. In addition to the entry fee, there are charges for various attractions, so it's best to get the one-day free pass. ✉ *5–6–1 Shin Nishihara, Fujiyoshida* ☎ *0555/23–2111* 🌐 *www.fujiq.jp/en* 💴 *1 day free pass ¥5,200, entrance only ¥1,400* 🕐 *Weekdays 9–5, weekends 9–8.*

Lake Kawaguchi (河口湖 *Kawaguchi-ko*). A 5- to 10-minute walk from Kawaguchi-ko Station, this is the most developed of the five lakes. It's ringed with weekend retreats and vacation lodges—many of them maintained by companies and universities for their employees. Excursion boats depart from a pier here on 30-minute tours of the lake. The promise, not always fulfilled, is to have two views of Mt. Fuji: one of the mountain itself and the other inverted in its reflection on the water.

Lake Motosu (本栖湖 *Motosu-ko*). Lake Motosu is the farthest west of the five lakes. It's also the deepest and clearest of the Fuji Go-ko. It takes about 50 minutes to get here by bus.

Lake Sai (西湖 *Sai-ko*). Between Lakes Shoji and Kawaguchi, Lake Sai is the third-largest lake of the Fuji Go-ko, with only moderate development. From the western shore there is an especially good view of Mt. Fuji. Near Sai-ko there are two natural caves, an ice cave and a wind cave. You can either take a bus or walk to them.

Lake Shoji (精進湖 *Shoji-ko*). Many consider Lake Shoji, the smallest of the lakes, to be the prettiest. There are still remnants of lava flow jutting out from the water, which locals perch upon while fishing. The Shoji Trail leads from Lake Shoji to Mt. Fuji's fifth station through Aoki-ga-hara (Sea of Trees). This forest has an underlying magnetic lava field that makes compasses go haywire. Be prepared with a good trail map before taking this hike.

THE SHOJI TRIANGLE

The Aoki-ga-hara Jukai (Sea of Trees) seems to hold a morbid fascination for the Japanese. Many people go into Aoki-ga-hara every year and never come out, some of them on purpose. If you're planning to climb Mt. Fuji from this trail, go with a guide.

Lake Yamanaka (山中湖 *Yamanaka-ko*). The largest lake of the Fuji Go-ko, Yamanaka is 35 minutes by bus to the southeast of Kawaguchi. It's also the closest lake to the popular trail up Mt. Fuji that starts at Go-gome, and many climbers use this resort area as a base.

Mt. Tenjo (天上山 *Tenjo-san*). From the shore of Lake Kawaguchi (near the pier) the Kachikachi Ropeway quickly brings you to the top of the 3,622-foot-tall mountain. From the observatory here the whole of Lake Kawaguchi lies before you, and beyond the lake is a classic view of Mt. Fuji. ✉ *1163–1 Azagawa, Fuji-Kawaguchiko-machi* ☎ *0555/72–0363 Ropeway* 🌐 *www.kachikachiyama-ropeway.com* 🎫 *Round-trip ¥700, one-way ¥400* ⏲ *Daily Mar.–Nov. 9–5; Dec.–Feb, 9–4:30 (every 5 mins).*

WHERE TO STAY

$$$$ HOTEL — **Fuji View Hotel** (富士ビューホテル). Accommodations are a little threadbare but comfortable and right on the lakefront, and the terrace lounge affords fine views of the lake and of Mt. Fuji beyond. **Pros:** comparatively inexpensive lodgings. **Cons:** rooms are rather small. $ *Rooms from: ¥34000* ✉ *511 Katsuyama-mura, Fuji-Kawaguchiko-machi* ☎ *0555/83–2211* 🌐 *www.fujiview.jp* *40 Western-style rooms with bath, 30 Japanese-style rooms with bath* 🍽 *Some meals.*

$$$$ HOTEL — **Hotel Mount Fuji** (富士山ホテル). This is the best resort hotel on Lake Yamanaka, with European-style rooms and all the facilities for a recreational holiday, including on-site game and karaoke rooms and a nature walk on the grounds. **Pros:** comfortable rooms; many activities on the hotel grounds. **Cons:** one of the more expensive options in the area; convenient location and large banquet halls make it a favorite among tour groups. $ *Rooms from: ¥30000* ✉ *1360–83 Yamanaka, Yamanaka-ko-mura* ☎ *0555/62–2111* 🌐 *mountfujihotels.jp* *150 Western-style rooms with bath, 1 Japanese-style room with bath* 🍽 *Some meals.*

$ B&B/INN — **Inn Fujitomita** (旅館ふじとみた). One of the closest lodging options to the Mt. Fuji hiking trails is not much to look at from the outside, but the interior is spacious and homey. **Pros:** spacious rooms; pleasant surrounding grounds. **Cons:** very crowded during climbing season. $ *Rooms from: ¥10000* ✉ *3235 Shibokusa, Oshinomura, Minami-Tsuru-gun* ☎ *0555/84–3359* 🌐 *www.tim.hi-ho.ne.jp/innfuji* 💳 *No credit cards* *9 Japanese-style rooms, 2 with bath* 🍽 *Some meals.*

NIKKO 日光

130 km (81 miles) north of Tokyo.

"Think nothing is splendid," asserts an old Japanese proverb, "until you have seen Nikko." Nikko, which means "sunlight," is a popular vacation spot for the Japanese, for good reason: its gorgeous sights include a breathtaking waterfall and one of the country's best-known shrines. In addition, Nikko combines the rustic charm of a countryside village (complete with wild monkeys that have the run of the place) with a convenient location not far from Tokyo.

THE UBIQUITOUS TORII

Wondering what those gatelike structures are with two posts and two crosspieces? They are torii and are used as gateways to Japanese Shinto temples.

GETTING HERE AND AROUND

The limited express train of the Tobu Railway has two direct connections from Tokyo to Nikko every morning, starting at 7:30 am from Tobu Asakusa Station, a minute's walk from the last stop on Tokyo's Ginza subway line (one hour, 48 minutes, ¥2,800) with additional trains on weekends, holidays, and in high season. All seats are reserved. Bookings are not accepted over the phone and can be bought only at Asakusa Station. During summer, fall, and weekends, buy tickets a few days in advance. Alternatively, the rapid train takes only a bit longer at half the price and requires no reservations (two hours, 10 minutes, ¥1,360). If you're visiting Nikko on a day trip, note that the last return train is at 7:43 pm, requiring a quick and easy change at Shimo-Imaichi, and arrives at Asakusa at 9:35 pm. If you have a JR Pass, use JR (Japan Railways) service, which connects Tokyo and Nikko, from Ueno Station. Take the Tohoku Honsen Line limited express to Utsunomiya (about 1½ hours) and transfer to the train for JR Nikko Station (45 minutes). The earliest departure from Ueno is at 5:10 am; the last connection back leaves Nikko at 9:02 pm and brings you into Ueno at 11:38 pm. (If you're not using the JR Pass, the one-way fare costs ¥2,590.)

More expensive, but faster, is taking the Shinkansen to Utsunomiya and changing for the JR train to Nikko Station; the one-way fare, including the surcharge for the express, is ¥5,370. The first train leaves Tokyo Station at 6:04 am (or Ueno at 6:10) and takes about 1 hour, 30 minutes to Nikko. To return, take the 9:46 pm train from Nikko to Utsunomiya and catch the last Shinkansen back at 10:38 pm.

It's possible, but unwise, to travel by car from Tokyo to Nikko. The trip takes at least three hours, and merely getting from central Tokyo to the toll-road system can be a nightmare. Coming back, especially on a Saturday or Sunday evening, is even worse.

Buses and taxis can take you from Nikko to the village of Chuzenji and nearby Lake Chuzenji; one-way cab fare from Tobu Nikko Station to Chuzenji is about ¥7,000. ■**TIP→ There is no bus service between Tokyo and Nikko.** Local buses leave Tobu Nikko Station for Lake Chuzenji, stopping just above the entrance to Tosho-gu, approximately every 30 minutes from 6:15 am until 7:01 pm. The fare to Chuzenji is ¥1,150, and the ride takes about 40 minutes. The last return bus from the lake leaves at 7:39 pm, arriving back at Tobu Nikko Station at 9:17 pm.

VISITOR INFORMATION

You can do a lot of preplanning for your visit to Nikko with a stop at the Japan National Tourist Organization office in Tokyo, where the helpful English-speaking staff will ply you with pamphlets and field your questions about things to see and do. Closer to the source is the Tourist Information and Hospitality Center in Nikko itself, about halfway up the main street of town between the railway stations and Tosho-gu, on the left; don't expect too much in the way of help in English, but the center does have a good array of English information about local restaurants and shops, registers of inns and hotels, and mapped-out walking tours.

ESSENTIALS

Tourist Information Nikko Tourist Information Center (日光観光案内所). ✉ *591 Gokou-machi* ☎ *0288/54–2496.*

EXPLORING

The town of Nikko is essentially one long avenue—Sugi Namiki (Cryptomeria Avenue)—extending for about 2 km (1 mile) from the railway stations to Tosho-gu. You can easily walk to most places within town. Tourist inns and shops line the street, and if you have time, you might want to make this a leisurely stroll. The antiques shops along the way may turn up interesting—but expensive—pieces like armor fittings, hibachi, pottery, and dolls. The souvenir shops here sell ample selections of local wood carvings.

TOSHO-GU 東照宮

Fodor's Choice ★

The Tosho-gu area encompasses three UNESCO World Heritage sites—Tosho-gu Shrine, Futarasan Shrine, and Rinnoji Temple. These are known as *nisha-ichiji* (two shrines and one temple) and are Nikko's main draw. Signs and maps clearly mark a recommended route that will allow you to see all the major sights, which are within walking distance of each other. You should plan for half a day to explore the area.

A multiple-entry ticket is the best way to see the Tosho-gu precincts. The ¥1,300 pass gets you entrance to Rinno-ji (Rinno Temple), the Taiyu-in Mausoleum, and Futara-san Jinja (Futara-san Shrine); for an extra ¥400 you can also see the Sleeping Cat and Ieyasu's tomb at Taiyu-in (separate fees are charged for admission to other sights). There are two places to purchase the multiple-entry ticket: one is at the entrance to Rinno Temple, in the corner of the parking lot, at the top of the path called the Higashi-sando (East Approach) that begins across the highway from the Sacred Bridge; the other is at the entrance to Tosho-gu, at the top of the broad Omote-sando (Central Approach), which begins about 100 yards farther west.

CLOSE UP

Ieyasu's Legacy

In 1600, Ieyasu Tokugawa (1543–1616) won a battle at a place in the mountains of south-central Japan called Seki-ga-hara that left him the undisputed ruler of the archipelago. He died 16 years later, but the Tokugawa Shogunate would last another 252 years.

The founder of such a dynasty required a fitting resting place. Ieyasu (ee-eh- *ya*-su) had provided for one in his will: a mausoleum at Nikko, in a forest of tall cedars, where a religious center had been founded more than eight centuries earlier. The year after his death, in accordance with Buddhist custom, he was given a *kaimyo*—an honorific name to bear in the afterlife. Thenceforth, he was Tosho-Daigongen: the Great Incarnation Who Illuminates the East. The Imperial Court at Kyoto declared him a god, and his remains were taken in a procession of great pomp and ceremony to be enshrined at Nikko.

The dynasty he left behind was enormously rich. Ieyasu's personal fief, on the Kanto Plain, was worth 2.5 million *koku* of rice. One koku, in monetary terms, was equivalent to the cost of keeping one retainer in the necessities of life for a year. The shogunate itself, however, was still an uncertainty. It had only recently taken control after more than a century of civil war. The founder's tomb had a political purpose: to inspire awe and to make manifest the power of the Tokugawas. It was Ieyasu's legacy, a statement of his family's right to rule.

Tosho-gu was built by his grandson, the third shogun, Iemitsu (it was Iemitsu who established the policy of national isolation, which closed the doors of Japan to the outside world for more than 200 years). The mausoleum and shrine required the labor of 15,000 people for two years (1634–36). Craftsmen and artists of the first rank were assembled from all over the country. Every surface was carved and painted and lacquered in the most intricate detail imaginable. Tosho-gu shimmers with the reflections of 2,489,000 sheets of gold leaf. Roof beams and rafter ends with dragon heads, lions, and elephants in bas-relief; friezes of phoenixes, wild ducks, and monkeys; inlaid pillars and red-lacquer corridors: Tosho-gu is everything a 17th-century warlord would consider gorgeous, and the inspiration is very Chinese.

TOP ATTRACTIONS

Futara-san Jinja (二荒山神社 *Futara-san Shrine*). Nikko's holy ground is far older than the Tokugawa dynasty, in whose honor it was improved upon. Founded in 782, Futara-san Jinja (Futura-san Shrine) is a peaceful contrast to the more elaborate Toshogu Shrine. Futara-san actually has three locations: the Main Shrine at Tosho-gu; the Chugu-shi (Middle Shrine), at Chuzenji-ko; and the Okumiya (Inner Shrine), on top of Mt. Nantai.

The bronze torii at the entrance to the shrine leads to the gilded and elaborately carved **Kara-mon** (Chinese Gate); beyond it is the **Hai-den,** the shrine's oratory. The Hai-den, too, is richly carved and decorated, with a dragon-covered ceiling. The Chinese lions on the panels at the rear are by two distinguished painters of the Kano school. From the

9

oratory of the Taiyu-in a connecting passage leads to the **Hon-den** (Sanctum)—the present version of which dates from 1619. Designated a National Treasure, it houses a gilded and lacquered Buddhist altar some 9 feet high, decorated with paintings of animals, birds, and flowers, in which resides the object of all this veneration: a seated wooden figure of Iemitsu himself. ✉ *Take the avenue to the left as you're standing before the stone torii at Tosho-gu and follow it to the end, 2307 Sannai* 🎫 *Shrine only ¥200, multiple-entry ticket (includes Rinno Temple and Taiyu-in Mausoleum) ¥1,300* ⏲ *Apr.–Oct., daily 8–5; Nov.–Mar., daily 9–4.*

SEEKING YOUR FORTUNE?

Make sure you visit **Gohoten-do,** in the northeast corner of Rinno Temple, behind the Sanbutsu-do. Three of the Seven Gods of Good Fortune, derived from Chinese folk mythology, are enshrined here. These three Buddhist deities are Daikoku-ten and Bishamon-ten, who bring wealth and good harvests, and Benzai-ten, patroness of music and the arts.

Rinno-ji (輪王寺 *Rinno Temple*). This temple belongs to the Tendai sect of Buddhism, the head temple of which is Enryaku-ji, on Mt. Hiei near Kyoto. The main hall of Rinno Temple, called the **Sanbutsu-do,** is the largest single building at Tosho-gu; it enshrines an image of Amida Nyorai, the Buddha of the Western Paradise, flanked on the right by Senju (Thousand-Armed) Kannon, the goddess of mercy, and on the left by Bato-Kannon, regarded as the protector of animals. These three images are lacquered in gold and date from the early part of the 17th century. The original Sanbutsu-do is said to have been built in 848 by the priest Ennin (794–864), also known as Jikaku-Daishi. The present building dates from 1648.

In the southwest corner of the Rinno Temple compound, behind the abbot's residence, is an especially fine Japanese garden called **Shoyo-en,** created in 1815 and thoughtfully designed to present a different perspective of its rocks, ponds, and flowering plants from every turn on its path. To the right of the entrance to the garden is the Homotsu-den (Treasure Hall) of Rinno Temple, a museum with a collection of some 6,000 works of lacquerware, painting, and Buddhist sculpture. The museum is rather small, and only a few of the pieces in the collection—many of them designated National Treasures and Important Cultural Properties—are on display at any given time. ✉ *2300 Yamauchi* ☎ *0288/54–0531* 🎫 *Taiyu-in Mausoleum and Futara-san Shrine ¥1,300, Shoyo-en and Homotsu-den ¥400* ⏲ *Apr.–Oct., daily 8–5, last entry at 4; Nov.–Mar., daily 8–4, last entry at 3.*

Taiyu-in Mausoleum (大猷院廟). This grandiose building is the resting place of the third Tokugawa shogun, Iemitsu (1604–51), who imposed a policy of national isolation on Japan that was to last more than 200 years. Iemitsu, one suspects, had it in mind to upstage his illustrious grandfather; he marked the approach to his own tomb with no fewer than six different decorative gates. The first is another Nio-mon—a Gate of the Deva Kings—like the one at Tosho-gu. The dragon painted on the ceiling is by Yasunobu Kano. A flight of stone steps leads from

Nikko Area

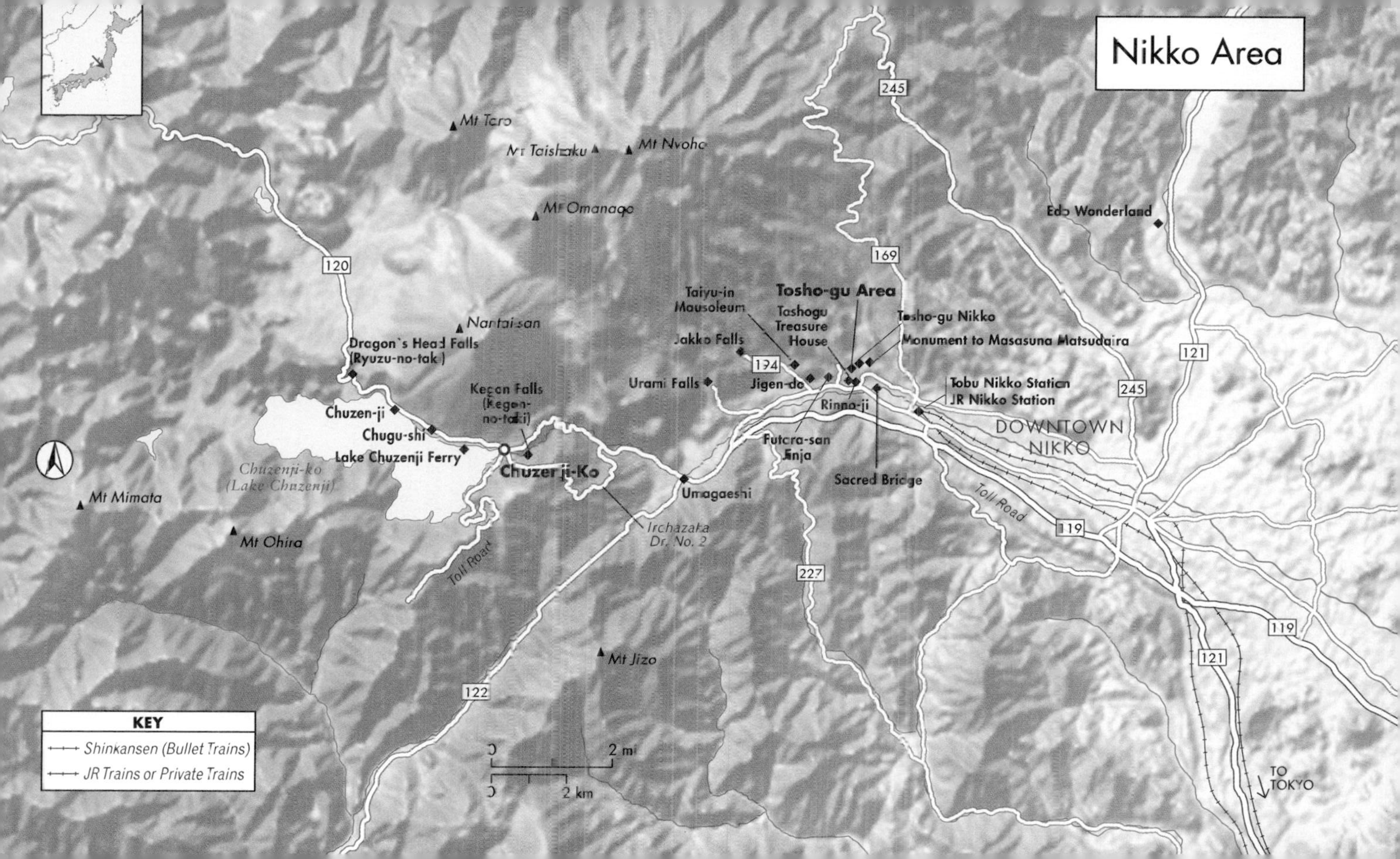

Nikko Area
Mt Taro
Mt Taishaku
Mt Nyoho
Mt Omanago
Edo Wonderland
245
169
120
Nantai-san
Dragon's Head Falls (Ryuzu-no-taki)
Taiyu-in Mausoleum
Tosho-gu Area
Toshogu Treasure House
Tosho-gu Nikko
Monument to Masasuna Matsudaira
Jakko Falls
194
Urami Falls
Jigen-do
Rinno-ji
Tobu Nikko Station
JR Nikko Station
121
DOWNTOWN NIKKO
Kegon Falls (Kegon-no-taki)
Chuzen-ji
Chugu-shi
Lake Chuzenji Ferry
Chuzenji-Ko
Chuzenji-ko (Lake Chuzenji)
Futara-san Jinja
Sacred Bridge
Umagaeshi
Mt Mimata
Mt Ohira
Irohazaka Dr. No. 2
Toll Road
119
227
Mt Jizo
122
KEY
Shinkansen (Bullet Trains)
JR Trains or Private Trains
0
2 mi
0
2 km
TO TOKYO

The gold-leaf detailing at Rinno Ji complements the gold on the three famed Buddhas in Sanbutsudoh Hall.

here to the second gate, the Niten-mon, a two-story structure protected front and back by carved and painted images of guardian gods. Beyond it, two more flights of steps lead to the middle courtyard. As you climb the last steps to Iemitsu's shrine, you'll pass a bell tower on the right and a drum tower on the left; directly ahead is the third gate, the remarkable **Yasha-mon,** so named for the figures of *yasha* (she-demons) in the four niches. This structure is also known as the Peony Gate (Botan-mon) for the carvings that decorate it.

As you exit the shrine, on the west side, you come to the fifth gate: the **Koka-mon,** built in the style of the late Ming dynasty of China. The gate is normally closed, but from here another flight of stone steps leads to the sixth and last gate—the cast copper **Inuki-mon,** inscribed with characters in Sanskrit—and Iemitsu's tomb. ✉ *2300 Sannai* 🎫 *¥1,300, includes admission to Rinno Temple and Futara-san Shrine* ⏲ *Apr.–Oct., daily 8–5; Nov.–Mar., daily 8–4.*

Fodor's Choice ★ **Tosho-gu Nikko** (東照宮). With its riot of colors and carvings, inlaid pillars, red-lacquer corridors, and extensive use of gold leaf, this 17th-century shrine to Ieyasu Tokugawa is one of the most elaborately decorated shrines in Japan.

The **Hon-den (Main Hall)** of Tosho-gu is the ultimate purpose of the shrine. You approach it from the rows of lockers at the far end of the enclosure; here you remove and store your shoes, step up into the shrine, and follow a winding corridor to the Oratory (Hai-den)—the anteroom, resplendent in its lacquered pillars, carved friezes, and coffered ceilings bedecked with dragons. Over the lintels are paintings by

Tosa Mitsuoki (1617–91) of the 36 great poets of the Heian period, with their poems in the calligraphy of Emperor Go-Mizunoo. Deeper yet, at the back of the Oratory, is the Inner Chamber (Nai-jin)—repository of the Sacred Mirror that represents the spirit of the deity enshrined here. The hall is enclosed by a wall of painted and carved panel screens; opposite the right-hand corner of the wall, facing the shrine, is the **Kito-den**, a hall where annual prayers were once offered for the peace of the nation.

Behind the Inner Chamber is the Innermost Chamber (Nai-Nai-jin). No visitors come this far. Here, in the very heart of Tosho-gu, is the gold-lacquer shrine where the spirit of Ieyasu resides—along with two other deities, whom the Tokugawas later decided were fit companions. One was Toyotomi Hideyoshi, Ieyasu's mentor and liege lord in the long wars of unification at the end of the 16th century. The other was Minamoto no Yoritomo, brilliant military tactician and founder of the earlier (12th-century) Kamakura Shogunate (Ieyasu claimed Yoritomo for an ancestor).

Between the Goma-do and the Kagura-den (a hall where ceremonial dances are performed to honor the gods) is a passage to the Sakashita-mon (Gate at the Foot of the Hill). Above the gateway is another famous symbol of Tosho-gu, the Sleeping Cat—a small panel said to have been carved by Hidari Jingoro (Jingoro the Left-handed), a late-16th-century master carpenter and sculptor credited with important contributions to numerous Tokugawa-period temples, shrines, and palaces. A separate admission charge (¥520) is levied to go beyond the Sleeping Cat, up the flight of 200 stone steps through a forest of cryptomeria to **Ieyasu's tomb**. The climb is worth it for the view of the Yomei-mon and Kara-mon from above; the tomb itself is unimpressive.

The centerpiece of Tosho-gu is the **Yomei-mon** (Gate of Sunlight), at the top of the second flight of stone steps. A designated National Treasure, it's also called the **Higurashi-mon** (Twilight Gate)—implying that you could gape at its richness of detail all day, until sunset. And rich it is indeed: 36 feet high and dazzling white, the gate has 12 columns, beams, and roof brackets carved with dragons, lions, clouds, peonies, Chinese sages, and demigods, painted vivid hues of red, blue, green, and gold. On one of the central columns, there are two carved tigers; the natural grain of the wood is used to bring out the "fur." As you enter the Yomei-mon, there are galleries running east and west for some 700 feet; their paneled fences are also carved and painted with nature motifs.

The portable shrines that appear in the Tosho-gu Festival, held yearly on May 17–18, are kept in the **Shinyo-sha,** a storeroom to the left as you come through the Twilight Gate into the heart of the shrine. The paintings on the ceiling, of *tennin* (Buddhist angels) playing harps, are by Tan-yu Kano (1602–74).

Mere mortals may not pass through the Chinese Gate (Kara-mon), which is the "official" entrance to the Tosho-gu inner shrine. Like its counterpart, the Yomei-mon, on the opposite side of the courtyard, the Kara-mon is a National Treasure—and, like the Yomei-mon, is carved

Tosho-gu honors Ieyasu Tokugawa, the first shogun and founder of Tokyo.

and painted in elaborate detail with dragons and other auspicious figures. ✉ *2301 Sannai* ☎ *0288/54–0560* 🎫 *Free* ⏲ *Apr.–Oct., daily 9–5; Nov.–Mar., daily 9–4.*

OFF THE BEATEN PATH

Located on the northern shore of peaceful Yunoko (Lake Yuno), these isolated **hot springs** were once a popular destination for 14th-century aristocrats. Today, the area is still known for its hot springs—being able to soak in an onsen (hot springs) all year long, even when temperatures drop below zero, will always be a major plus—but they are now controlled by separate resorts. Besides the healing and relaxing effects of the baths, visitors come for the hiking trails, fishing, camping, skiing, birdwatching, and mountain-climbing opportunities. **■ TIP→ Try to avoid the fall season, as it's peak visitor time and there are always delays.** You can get to the Yumoto onsen by taking the Tobu Operated Buses, which leave Tobu Nikko and JR Nikko stations. There are one or two services an hour, depending on the time of the day. A one-way trip from central Nikko takes about 80 minutes and costs ¥1,700.

WORTH NOTING

FAMILY **Edo Wonderland** (日光江戸村 *Nikko Edo Mura*). Edo Wonderland, a living-history theme park a short taxi ride from downtown, re-creates an 18th-century Japanese village. The complex includes sculpted gardens with waterfalls and ponds and 22 vintage buildings, where actors in traditional dress stage martial arts exhibitions, historical theatrical performances, and comedy acts. You can even observe Japanese tea ceremony rituals in gorgeous tatami-floor houses, as well as people dressed as geisha and samurai. Strolling stuffed animal characters and acrobatic ninjas keep kids happy. Nikko Edo Mura has one large restaurant and 15 small food stalls serving period cuisine like *yakisoba* (fried soba) and *dango* (dumplings). ✉ *470–2 Karakura* ☎ *0288/77–1777* 🌐 *www.edowonderland.net* 🎫 *¥4,700 unlimited day pass includes rides and shows* 🕘 *Mid-Mar.–Nov., daily 9–5; Dec.–mid-Mar., daily 9:30–4.*

Monument to Masasuna Matsudaira (松平正綱の杉並木寄進碑). Opposite the Sacred Bridge, at the east entrance to the grounds of Tosho-gu, this monument pays tribute to one of the two feudal lords charged with the construction of Tosho-gu. Matsudaira's great contribution was the planting of the wonderful cryptomeria trees (Japanese cedars) surrounding the shrine and along all the approaches to it. The project took 20 years, from 1628 to 1648, and the result was some 36 km (22 miles) of cedar-lined avenues—planted with more than 15,000 trees in all. Fire and time have taken their toll, but thousands of these trees still stand in the shrine precincts, creating a setting of solemn majesty the buildings alone could never have achieved. Thousands more line Route 119 east of Nikko on the way to Shimo-Imaichi. ✉ *Moritomo.*

DID YOU KNOW?

Under the policy of national seclusion, only the Dutch retained trading privileges with Japan. Even then, they were confined to the tiny artificial island of Dejima, in the port of Nagasaki. They regularly sent tokens of their esteem to the shogunate to keep their precarious monopoly, including the two bronze items found in the Sacred Stable, which were sent in 1636. The 200-year-plus monopoly was dissolved when Japan decided to open its borders to other Western countries in 1858.

Sacred Bridge (神橋 *Shinkyo*). Built in 1636 for shoguns and imperial messengers visiting the shrine, the original bridge was destroyed in a flood; the present red-lacquer wooden structure dates to 1907. Buses leaving from either railway station at Nikko go straight up the main street to the bridge, opposite the first of the main entrances to Tosho-gu. The Sacred Bridge is just to the left of a modern bridge, where the road curves and crosses the Daiya-gawa (Daiya River). ✉ *2307 Sannai* 🕘 *Apr.–Oct., daily 9–5; Nov.–Mar., daily 9–4.*

Toshogu Treasure House (宝物館 *Homotsu-kan*). An unhurried visit to the precincts of Tosho-gu should definitely include the Treasure House, as it contains a collection of antiquities from its various shrines and temples. From the west gate of Rinno Temple, turn left off Omote-sando, just below the pagoda, onto the cedar-lined avenue to Futara-san Jinja. A minute's walk brings you to the museum, on the left. ✉ *2280 Sannai* ☎ *0288/54–2558* 🎫 *¥500* 🕘 *Apr.–Oct., daily 9–5; Nov.–Mar., daily 9–4.*

CHUZENJI-KO 中禅寺湖

More than 3,900 feet above sea level, at the base of the volcano known as Nantai-san, is Chuzenji-ko (Lake Chuzenji), renowned for its clean waters and fresh air. People come to boat and fish on the lake and to enjoy the surrounding scenic woodlands, waterfalls, and hills.

TOP ATTRACTIONS

Fodor's Choice ★ **Kegon Falls** (華厳滝 *Kegon-no-taki*). More than anything else, the country's most famous falls are what draw the crowds of Japanese visitors to Chuzenji. Fed by the eastward flow of the lake, the falls drop 318 feet into a rugged gorge; an elevator takes you to an observation platform at the bottom. The volume of water over the falls is carefully regulated, but it's especially impressive after a summer rain or a typhoon. In winter the falls do not freeze completely but form a beautiful cascade of icicles. The elevator is just a few minutes' walk east from the bus stop at Chuzenji village, downhill and off to the right at the far end of the parking lot. ✉ *2479–2 Chugushi* ☎ *0288/55–0030* 🎫 *Elevator ¥550* ⏲ *Daily 8–5.*

THREE LITTLE MONKEYS

While in the Sacred Stable, make sure to look at the second panel from the left. The three monkeys, commonly known as "Hear no evil, Speak no evil, See no evil," have become something of a Nikko trademark; the image has been reproduced on plaques, bags, and souvenirs. While the phrase's true origins are uncertain, scholars and legend suggest it originated from this shrine as a visual interpretation of the religious phrase, "If we do not hear, see, or speak evil, we ourselves shall be spared all evil." As for the monkeys, it's been said that a Chinese Buddhist monk introduced the image to Japan in the 8th century.

NEED A BREAK?

Ryuzu-no-taki Chaya (竜頭滝茶屋). Take a breather at this charming, but rustic, tea shop near the waterfalls. Enjoy a cup of green tea, a light meal, or Japanese sweets like rice cakes boiled with vegetables and dango (sweet dumplings) while you gaze at the falling waters. ✉ *2485 Chugushi* ☎ *0288/55–0157*.

Lake Chuzenji Ferry (中禅寺湖機船 *Chuzenjiko Kisen*). Explore Lake Chuzenji on chartered 60-minute boat rides. ✉ *2478–21 Chugushi* ☎ *0288/55–0360* 🎫 *¥150–¥1,500 depending on route* ⏲ *Dec.–Mar., daily 9:30–3:30.*

Urami Falls (裏見滝 *Urami-no-taki*). A poetic description says it all and still holds true: "the water," wrote the great 17th-century poet Basho, "seemed to take a flying leap and drop a hundred feet from the top of a cave into a green pool surrounded by a thousand rocks. One was supposed to inch one's way into the cave and enjoy the falls from behind." The falls and the gorge are striking—but you should make the climb only if you have good hiking shoes and are willing to get wet in the process. ✉ *The steep climb to the cave begins at the Arasawa bus stop, with a turn to the right off the Chuzenji road.*

WORTH NOTING

Chugu-shi (中宮祠). A subshrine of the Futara-san Shrine at Tosho-gu, this is the major religious center on the north side of Lake Chuzenji, about 1½ km (1 miles) west of the village. The Homotsu-den (Treasure House) contains an interesting historical collection, including swords, lacquerware, and medieval shrine palanquins. ✉ *Nikko* 🎫 *Homotsu-Den ¥300; Shrine free* ⏲ *Apr.–Oct., daily 8–5; Nov.–Mar., daily 9–4.*

The three monkeys, who "hear no evil, speak no evil, see no evil," perch on the paneling of Tosho-gu's Sacred Stable.

Chuzen-ji (中禅寺 *Chuzen Temple*). A subtemple of Rinno Temple, at Tosho-gu, the principal object of worship here is the **Tachi-ki Kannon,** a 17-foot-tall standing statue of the Buddhist goddess of mercy, said to have been carved more than 1,000 years ago by the priest Shodo from the living trunk of a single Judas tree. The bus trip from Nikko to the national park area ends at Chuzenji village, which shares its name with the temple established here in 784. ✉ *2578 Chugushi* ✣ *1½ km (1 mile) south of Chugu-shi village along the eastern shore of the lake* 🎫 *¥500* ⏲ *Apr.–Oct., daily 8–5; Mar. and Nov., daily 8–4; Dec.–Feb., daily 8–3:30.*

Dragon's Head Falls (竜頭滝 *Ryuzu-no-taki*). If you've budgeted an extra day for Nikko, you might want to consider a walk around the lake. A paved road along the north shore extends for about 8 km (5 miles), one-third of the whole distance, as far as the "beach" at Shobu-ga-hama. Here, where the road branches off to the north for Senjogahara, are the lovely cascades of Dragon's Head Falls. To the left is a steep footpath that continues around the lake to Senju-ga-hama and then to a campsite at Asegata. The path is well marked but can get rough in places. From Asegata it's less than an hour's walk back to Chuzenji village. ✉ *Nikko.*

Jakko Falls (寂光滝 *Jakko-no-taki*). Falling water is one of the special charms of the Nikko National Park area; people going by bus or car from Tosho-gu to Lake Chuzenji often stop off en route to see these falls, which descend in a series of seven terraced stages, forming a sheet of water about 100 feet high. About 1 km (½ mile) from the shrine precincts, at the Tamozawa bus stop, a narrow road to the right leads to an uphill walk of some 3 km (2 miles) to the falls. ✉ *Nikko.*

Umagaeshi (馬返し). In the old days, the road became too rough for horse riding, so riders had to alight and proceed on foot; the lake is 4,165 feet above sea level. From Umagaeshi the bus climbs a one-way toll road up the pass; the old road has been widened and is used for the traffic coming down. The two roads are full of steep hairpin turns, and on a clear day the view up and down the valley is magnificent—especially from the halfway point at **Akechi-daira** (Akechi Plain), from which you can see the summit of **Nantai-san** (Mt. Nantai), reaching 8,149 feet. Hiking season lasts from May through mid-October; if you push it, you can make the ascent in about four hours. Wild monkeys make their homes in these mountains, and they've learned the convenience of mooching from visitors along the route. Be careful—they have a way of not taking no for an answer. Do not give in to the temptation to give them food—they will never leave you alone if you do. ✉ *About 10 km (6 miles) from Tobu Station in Nikko, or 8 km (5 miles) from Tosho-gu.*

FEELING ADVENTUROUS?

Akechi-daira Ropeway (明智平ロープウェイ). If you want to avoid the hairpin turns, try the ropeway that runs from Akechi-daira Station directly to the Akechi-daira lookout. It takes three minutes and the panoramic views of Nikko and Kegon Falls are priceless. ✉ *703 Hosomachi* ☎ *0288/55–0331* 🎫 *¥400* ⏲ *Apr.–Oct., daily 8:30–4; Nov.–Mar., daily 9–3.*

WHERE TO EAT

DOWNTOWN NIKKO

$$$$ JAPANESE FUSION ✕ **Gyoshintei** (堯心亭). This is the only restaurant in Nikko devoted to *shojin ryori,* the Buddhist-temple vegetarian fare that evolved centuries ago into haute cuisine. Gyoshintei is decorated in the style of a *ryotei* (traditional inn), with all-tatami seating. It differs from a ryotei in that it has one large, open space where many guests are served at once, rather than a number of rooms for private dining. Dinner is served until 7. $ *Average main: ¥4000* ✉ *2339–1 Sannai* ☎ *0288/53–3751* ⏲ *Closed Thurs.*

$$$$ JAPANESE ✕ **Masudaya** (ゆば亭ますだや). Masudaya started out as a sake maker more than a century ago, but for four generations now, it has been the town's best-known restaurant. The specialty is yuba, which the chefs transform, with the help of local vegetables and fresh fish, into sumptuous high cuisine. The building is traditional, with a lovely interior garden; but meals here are prix fixe, and the assembly-line-style service detracts from the ambience. $ *Average main: ¥5000* ✉ *439–2 Ishiya-machi* ☎ *0288/54–2151* ⏲ *Closed Thurs. No dinner* ✍ *Reservations essential.*

$$$$ EUROPEAN ✕ **Meiji-no-Yakata** (明治の館). Not far from the east entrance to Rinno Temple, Meiji-no-Yakata is an elegant 19th-century Western-style stone house, originally built as a summer retreat for an American diplomat. The food, too, is Western-style; specialties of the house include fresh

DID YOU KNOW?

The 320-foot-high Kegon Falls draws visitors from all over Japan and the world. The spectacular sight near Lake Chuzenji is also home to 12 other waterfalls. Behind and next to Kegon, these falls drip out of cracks in the volcano, Nantai-san. Try to spot a few of them once you've taken in Kegon's grandeur.

rainbow trout from Lake Chuzenji, roast lamb with pepper sauce, and melt-in-your-mouth filet mignon made from local Tochigi beef. High ceilings, hardwood floors, and an air of informality make this a very pleasant place to dine. *Average main: ¥5000* ✉ *2339–1 Sannai* ☎ *0288/53–3751* *No credit cards.*

$$$$ JAPANESE ✕ **Sawamoto** (澤本). Charcoal-broiled *unagi* (eel) is an acquired taste, and there's no better place in Nikko to acquire it than at this small and unpretentious place with only five plain-wood tables. Service can be lukewarm, but Sawamoto is reliable for a light lunch or dinner of unagi on a bed of rice, served in an elegant lacquered box. Eel is considered a stamina builder: just right for the weary visitor on a hot summer day. *Average main: ¥4000* ✉ *1037–1 Kamihatsuishi-machi* ☎ *0288/54–0163* *No dinner.*

CHUZENJI-KO

$$$ JAPANESE ✕ **Nantai** (なんたい). The low tables, antiques, and pillows scattered on tatami flooring make visitors feel like they're dining in a traditional Japanese living room. Try the Nikko specialty, yuba (tofu skin), which comes with the *nabe* (hot pot) for dinner. It's the quintessential winter family meal. The seafood here is fresh and both the trout and salmon are recommended. Each meal comes with rice, pickles, and selected side dishes like soy-stewed vegetables, tempura, udon, and a dessert. *Average main: ¥3000* ✉ *2478–4 Chugushi* ☎ *0288/55–0201.*

WHERE TO STAY

DOWNTOWN NIKKO

$ HOTEL **Turtle Inn Nikko** (タートルイン日光). Modest, cost-conscious Western- and Japanese-style accommodations come with or without a private bath. **Pros:** cozy atmosphere; English-speaking staff. **Cons:** rooms a bit on the small side. *Rooms from: ¥10000* ✉ *2–16 Takumi-cho* ☎ *0288/53–3168* *www.turtle-nikko.com* *No credit cards* *7 Western-style rooms, 3 with bath; 5 Japanese-style rooms without bath* *No meals.*

CHUZENJI-KO

$$$$ RESORT **Chuzenji Kanaya** (中禅寺金谷ホテル). Pastel colors decorate the simple, tasteful rooms of this outpost of the Nikko Kanaya on the road from the village to Shobu-ga-hama, and floor-to-ceiling windows overlook the lake or grounds. **Pros:** relaxing resort feel; spacious rooms. **Cons:** the most expensive hotel in the area. *Rooms from: ¥54000* ✉ *2482 Chugu-shi* ☎ *0288/51–0001* *www.kanayahotel.co.jp/english/chuzenji/index.html* *60 rooms, 54 with bath* *Some meals.*

KAMAKURA 鎌倉

40 km (25 miles) southwest of Tokyo

As a religious center, Kamakura presents an extraordinary legacy. Most of its temples and shrines are in settings of remarkable beauty; many are designated National Treasures. If you can afford the time for only one day trip from Tokyo, you should probably spend it here.

For the aristocrats of the Heian-era Japan (794–1185), life was defined by the Imperial Court in Kyoto. Who in their right mind would venture elsewhere? In Kyoto there was grace and beauty and poignant affairs of the heart; everything beyond was howling wilderness. By the 12th century two clans—the Taira (*ta*-ee-ra) and the Minamoto, themselves both offshoots of the imperial line—had come to dominate the affairs of the court and were at each other's throats in a struggle for supremacy. The rivalry between the two clans became an all-out war, and by 1185 the Minamoto were masters of all Japan. Yoritomo no Minamoto forced the Imperial Court to name him shogun; he was now de facto and de jure the military head of state. The emperor was left as a figurehead in Kyoto, and the little fishing village of Kamakura, a superb natural fortress surrounded on three sides by hills and guarded on the fourth by the sea, became—and for 141 years remained—the seat of Japan's first shogunal government.

After 1333, when the center of power returned to Kyoto, Kamakura reverted to being a sleepy backwater town on the edge of the sea. After World War II, it began to develop as a residential area for the well-to-do. Though the religious past is much in evidence, nothing secular survives from the shogunal days; there wasn't much there to begin with. The warriors of Kamakura had little use for courtiers, or their palaces and gardened villas; the shogunate's name for itself, in fact, was the Bakufu—literally, the "tent government."

9

GETTING HERE AND AROUND

A bus from Kamakura Station (Sign 5) travels to most of the temples and shrines in the downtown Kamakura area, with stops at most access roads to the temples and shrines. However, you may want to walk out as far as Hokoku-ji and take the bus back; it's easier to recognize the end of the line than any of the stops in between. You can also go by taxi to Hokoku-ji—any cabdriver knows the way—and walk the last leg in reverse.

Bus companies in Kamakura don't conduct guided English tours. However, if your time is limited or you don't want to do a lot of walking, the Japanese tours hit the major attractions. These tours depart from Kamakura Station eight times daily, starting at 9 am; the last tour leaves at 1 pm. Purchase tickets at the bus office to the right of the station.

The KSGG Club Volunteer Guides has a free guide service. Arrangements must be made in advance through the group's website.

JTB Sunrise Tours runs daily English-language trips from Tokyo to Kamakura; these tours are often combined with trips to Hakone. You can book through, and arrange to be picked up at, any of the major hotels. Check to make sure that the tour covers everything you want to see, as many include little more than a passing view of the Great Buddha in Hase. Given how easy it is to get around—most sights are within walking distance of each other, and others are short bus or train rides apart—you're better off seeing Kamakura on your own.

> **TIMING TIP**
>
> If your time is limited, you may want to visit only Engaku Temple and Tokei Temple in Kita-Kamakura before riding the train one stop to Kamakura. If not, follow the main road all the way to Tsuru-ga-oka Hachiman-gu and visit four additional temples en route.

Traveling by train is by far the best way to get to Kamakura. Trains run from Tokyo Station (and Shimbashi Station) every 10 to 15 minutes during the day. The trip takes 56 minutes to Kita-Kamakura and one hour to Kamakura. Take the JR Yokosuka Line from Track 1 downstairs in Tokyo Station (Track 1 upstairs is on a different line and does not go to Kamakura). The cost is ¥800 to Kita-Kamakura, ¥920 to Kamakura (or use your JR Pass). It's now also possible to take a train from Shinjuku, Shibuya, or Ebisu to Kamakura on the Shonan-Shinjuku Line, but these trains depart less frequently than those departing from Tokyo Station. Local train service connects Kita-Kamakura, Kamakura, Hase, and Enoshima.

To return to Tokyo from Enoshima, take a train to Shinjuku on the Odakyu Line. There are 11 express trains daily from here on weekdays, between 8:38 am and 8:45 pm; 9 trains daily on weekends and national holidays, between 8:39 am and 8:46 pm; and even more in summer. The express takes about 70 minutes and costs ¥1,250. Or you can retrace your steps to Kamakura and take the JR Yokosuka Line to Tokyo Station.

VISITOR INFORMATION

Both Kamakura and Enoshima have their own tourist associations, although it can be problematic getting help in English over the phone. Your best bet is the Kamakura Station Tourist Information Center, which has a useful collection of brochures and maps. And since Kamakura is in Kanagawa Prefecture, visitors heading here from Yokohama can preplan their excursion at the Kanagawa Prefectural Tourist Association office in the Silk Center, on the Yamashita Park promenade.

ESSENTIALS

Tour Contacts **KSGG Club Volunteer Guides.** 🌐 *www.ksgg.org.*

Tourist Information **Fujisawa City Tourist Association.** ☎ *0466/22-4141* 🌐 *www.fujisawa-kanko.jp.* **Kamakura Station Tourist Information Center.** ✉ *1-1-1 Komachi* ☎ *0467/22-3350.* **Kamakura Tourist Association** (鎌倉観光協会 *Kamakura Kanko Kyoukai*). ✉ *1-12 Onarimachi* ☎ *0467/23-3050* 🌐 *kamakura-info.jp.* **Kanagawa Prefectural Tourist Association.** ☎ *045/681-0007* 🌐 *www.kanagawa-kankou.or.jp.*

EXPLORING

There are three principal areas in Kamakura, and you can easily get from one to another by train. From Tokyo head first to Kita-Kamakura for most of the important Zen temples, including Engaku-ji (Engaku Temple) and Kencho-ji (Kencho Temple). The second area is downtown Kamakura, with its shops and museums and the venerated shrine Tsuru-ga-oka Hachiman-gu. The third is Hase, a 10-minute train ride southwest from Kamakura on the Enoden Line. Hase's main attractions are the great bronze figure of the Amida Buddha, at Kotoku-in, and the Kannon Hall of Hase-dera. There's a lot to see in Kamakura, and even to hit just the highlights takes you most of a busy day.

KITA-KAMAKURA 北鎌倉

Hierarchies were important to the Kamakura Shogunate. In the 14th century it established a ranking system called Go-zan (literally, "Five Mountains") for the Zen Buddhist monasteries under its official sponsorship. These are clustered in the Kita-Kamakura district.

TOP ATTRACTIONS

Engaku-ji (円覚寺 *Engaku Temple*). The largest of the Zen monasteries in Kamakura, Engaku-ji (Engaku Temple) was founded in 1282 and ranks second in the Five Mountains hierarchy. Here, prayers were to be offered regularly for the prosperity and well-being of the government; Engaku Temple's special role was to pray for the souls of those who died resisting the Mongol invasions in 1274 and 1281. The temple complex currently holds 18 buildings, but once contained as many as 50. Often damaged in fires and earthquakes, it has been completely restored.

Engaku Temple belongs to the Rinzai sect of Zen Buddhism. Introduced into Japan from China at the beginning of the Kamakura period (1192–1333), the ideas of Zen were quickly embraced by the emerging warrior class. The samurai especially admired the Rinzai sect, with its emphasis on the ascetic life as a path to self transcendence. The monks of Engaku Temple played an important role as advisers to the shogunate in matters spiritual, artistic, and political.

Among the National Treasures at Engaku Temple is the **Hall of the Holy Relic of Buddha** (Shari-den), with its remarkable Chinese-inspired thatched roof. Built in 1282, it was destroyed by fire in 1558 but rebuilt in its original form soon after, in 1563. The hall is said to enshrine a tooth of the Gautama Buddha himself, but it's not on display. In fact, except for the first three days of the New Year, you won't be able to go any farther into the hall than the main gate. Such is the case, alas, with much of the Engaku Temple complex: this is still a functioning monastic center, and many of its most impressive buildings are not open to the public. The accessible National Treasure at Engaku Temple is the **Great Bell** (Kosho), on the hilltop on the southeast side of the complex. The bell—Kamakura's most famous—was cast in 1301 and stands 8 feet tall. It's rung only on special occasions, such as New Year's Eve. Reaching the bell requires a trek up a long staircase, but once you've made it to the top you can enjoy tea and traditional Japanese sweets at a small outdoor café. The views of the entire temple grounds and surrounding cedar forest from here are tremendous.

The two buildings open to the public at Engaku Temple are the **Butsu-nichi-an**, which has a long ceremonial hall where you can enjoy *sado* (Japanese tea ceremony), and the **Obai-in.** The latter is the mausoleum of the last three regents of the Kamakura Shogunate: Tokimune Hojo, who led the defense of Japan against the Mongol invasions; his son Sadatoki; and his grandson Takatoki. Off to the side of the mausoleum is a quiet garden with apricot trees, which bloom in February. As you exit Kita-Kamakura Station, you'll see the stairway to Engaku Temple just in front of you. ✉ *409 Yama-no-uchi, Kita-Kamakura* ☎ *0467/22-0478* 🎫 *¥300* ⏲ *Nov.–Mar., daily 8–4; Apr.–Oct., daily 8–5.*

Enno-ji (円応寺 *Enno Temple*). In the feudal period, Japan acquired from China a belief in Enma, the lord of hell, who, with his court attendants, judged the souls of the departed and determined their destination in the afterlife. Kamakura's otherwise undistinguished Enno-ji (Enno Temple) houses some remarkable statues of these judges—as grim and merciless a court as you're ever likely to confront. To see them is enough to put you on your best behavior, at least for the rest of your excursion. Enno Temple is a minute's walk or so from Kencho Temple, on the opposite (south) side of the main road to Kamakura. ✉ *1543 Yama-no-uchi, Kita-Kamakura* ☎ *0467/25-1095* 🎫 *¥200* ⏲ *Mar.–Nov., daily 9–4; Dec.–Feb., daily 9–3.*

Kencho-ji (建長寺 *Kencho Temple*). Founded in 1250, Kencho-ji (Kencho Temple) was the foremost of Kamakura's five great Zen temples, and it lays claim to being the oldest Zen temple in all of Japan. It was modeled on one of the great Chinese monasteries of the time and built for a distinguished Zen master who had just arrived from China. Over the centuries, fires and other disasters have taken their toll on Kencho-ji, and although many buildings have been authentically reconstructed, the temple complex today is half its original size. Near the Main Gate (San-mon) is a bronze bell cast in 1255; it's the temple's most important treasure. The Main Gate and the Lecture Hall (Hatto) are the only two structures to have survived the devastating Great Kanto Earthquake of 1923. Like Engaku-ji, Kencho-ji is a functioning temple of the Rinzai sect, where novices train and laypeople can come to take part in Zen meditation. Nearly hidden at the back of the temple is a long stairway and hiking trail that leads to Zuisen-ji, another of Kamakura's major temples. The hike takes about 90 minutes. ✉ *8 Yama-no-uchi* ✣ *The entrance to Kencho Temple is about halfway along the main road from Kita-Kamakura Station to Tsuru-ga-oka Hachiman-gu, on the left* ☎ *0467/22-0981* 🌐 *www.kenchoji.com* 🎫 *¥300* ⏲ *Daily 8:30–4:30.*

Tokei-ji (東慶寺 *Tokei Temple*). A Zen temple of the Rinzai sect, Tokei-ji holds special significance for the study of feminism in medieval Japan. More popularly known as the Enkiri-dera, or Divorce Temple, it was founded in 1285 by the widow of the Hojo regent Tokimune as a refuge for the victims of unhappy marriages. Under the shogunate, a husband of the warrior class could obtain a divorce simply by sending his wife back to her family. Not so for the wife: no matter what cruel and unusual treatment her husband meted out, she was stuck with him. If she ran away, however, and managed to reach Tokei Temple without

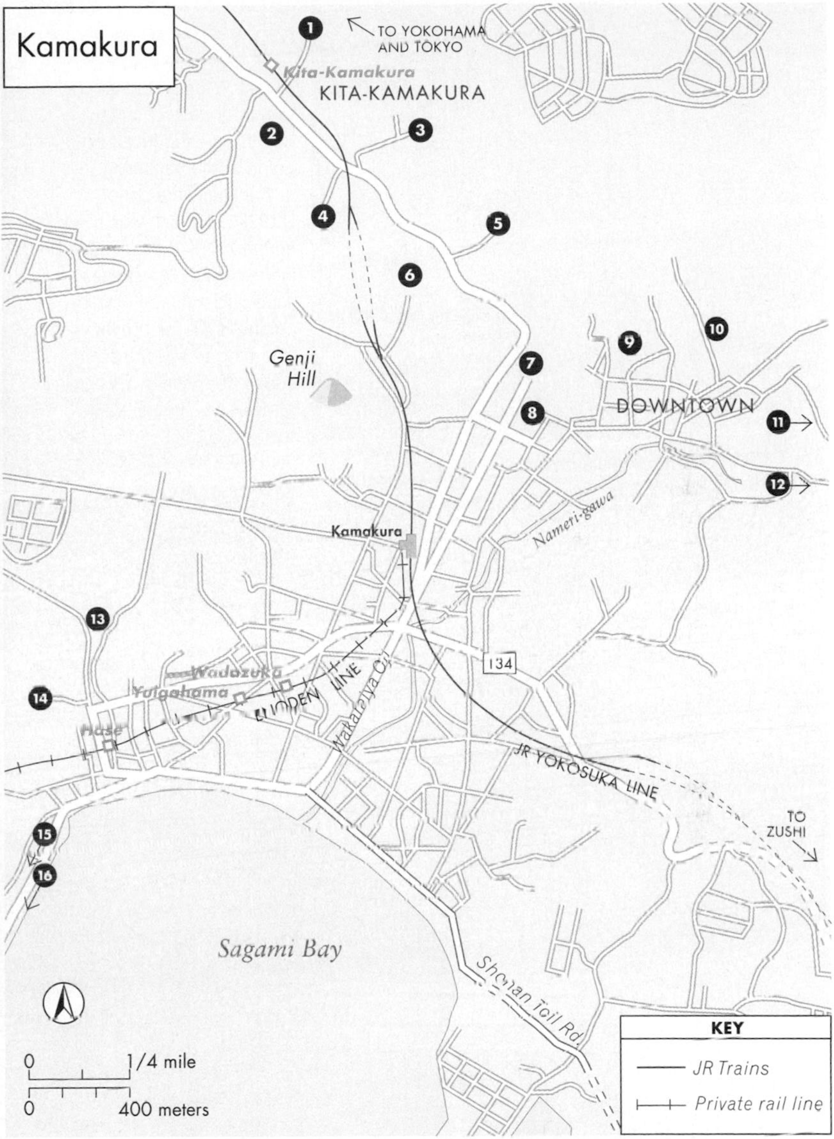

Kamakura
TO YOKOHAMA AND TOKYO
Kita-Kamakura
KITA-KAMAKURA
Genji Hill
DOWNTOWN
Nameri-gawa
Kamakura
134
Wakamiya Oji
ENODEN LINE
Wadazuka
Yuigahama
Hase
JR YOKOSUKA LINE
TO ZUSHI
Sagami Bay
Shonan Toll Rd.
1
2
3
4
5
6
7
8
9
10
11
12
13
14
15
16
0
1/4 mile
0
400 meters
KEY
JR Trains
Private rail line

Engaku-ji (Engaku Temple) 1
Enno-ji (Enno Temple) 6
Enoshima 16
Hase-dera 14
Hokoku-ji (Hokoku Temple) 12
Jochi-ji (Jochi Temple) 4
Jomyo-ji (Jomyo Temple) 11
Kamakura Great Buddha (Daibutsu) 13
Kamakura-gu (Kamakura Shrine) 10
Kamakura Museum of National Treasures (Kamakura Kokuhokan) 8
Kencho-ji (Kencho Temple) 5
Meigetsu-in (Meigetsu Temple) 3
Ryuko-ji (Ryuko Temple) 15
Tokei-ji (Tokei Temple) 2
Tsurugaoka Hachimangu 7
Yoritomo's Tomb 9

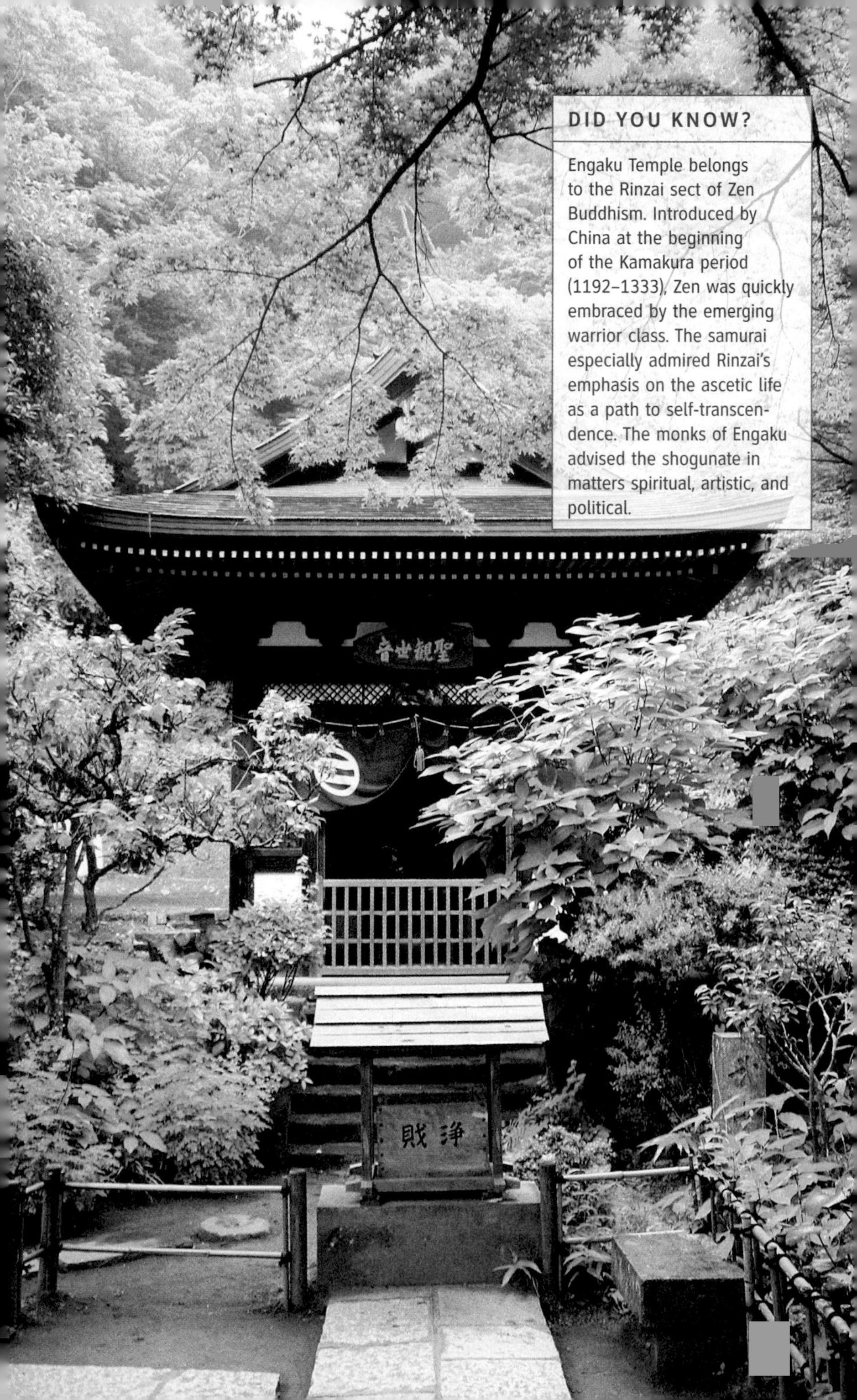

DID YOU KNOW?

Engaku Temple belongs to the Rinzai sect of Zen Buddhism. Introduced by China at the beginning of the Kamakura period (1192–1333), Zen was quickly embraced by the emerging warrior class. The samurai especially admired Rinzai's emphasis on the ascetic life as a path to self-transcendence. The monks of Engaku advised the shogunate in matters spiritual, artistic, and political.

being caught, she could receive sanctuary at the temple and remain there as a nun. After three years (later reduced to two), she was officially declared divorced. The temple survived as a convent through the Meiji Restoration of 1868. The last abbess died in 1902; her headstone is in the cemetery behind the temple, beneath the plum trees that blossom in February. Tokei Temple was later reestablished as a monastery.

The **Matsugaoka Hozo** (Treasure House) of Tokei Temple displays several Kamakura-period wooden Buddhas, ink paintings, scrolls, and works of calligraphy, some of which have been designated by the government as Important Cultural Objects. The library, called the Matsugaoka Bunko, was established in memory of the great Zen scholar D. T. Suzuki (1870–1966).

Tokei Temple is on the southwest side of the JR tracks (the side opposite Engaku Temple), less than a five-minute walk south from the station on the main road to Kamakura (Route 21—the Kamakura Kaido), on the right. ✉ *1367 Yama-no-uchi, Kita-Kamakura* ☎ *0467/22–1663* 🌐 *www.tokeiji.com* 💴 *Tokei Temple ¥200, Matsugaoka Hozo additional ¥400* ⏲ *Tokei Temple: Apr.–Oct., daily 8:30–5; Nov.–Mar., daily 8:30–4. Matsugaoka Treasure House: Mon.–Thurs. 9:30–3:30.*

WORTH NOTING

Jochi-ji (浄智寺 *Jochi Temple*). In the Five Mountains hierarchy, Jochi-ji (Jochi Temple) was ranked fourth. The buildings now in the complex are reconstructions; the Great Kanto Earthquake of 1923 destroyed the originals. The garden here is exquisite. Jochi-ji is on the south side of the railway tracks, a few minutes' walk farther southwest of Tokei-ji in the direction of Kamakura. ✉ *1402 Yama-no-uchi, Kita-Kamakura* ✥ *Turn right off the main road (Rte. 21) and cross over a small bridge; a flight of moss-covered steps leads up to the temple* ☎ *0467/22–3943* 💴 *¥200* ⏲ *Daily 9–4:30.*

Meigetsu-in (明月院 *Meigetsu Temple*). This temple is also known as Ajisai-dera (the hydrangea temple), and when the flowers bloom in June, it becomes one of the most popular places in Kamakura. The gardens transform into a sea of color—pink, white, and blue—and visitors can number in the thousands. A typical Kamakura light rain shouldn't deter you; it only showcases this incredible floral display to its best advantage. Meigetsu-in features Kamakura's largest *yagura* (a tomb cavity enclosing a mural) on which 16 images of Buddha are carved. ✉ *189 Yama-no-uchi, Kita-Kamakura* ✥ *To reach Meigetsu-in from Tokei-ji, walk along Route 21 toward Kamakura for about 20 minutes until you cross the railway tracks; take the immediate left turn onto the narrow side street that doubles back along the tracks. This street bends to the right and follows the course of a little stream called the Meigetsu-gawa to the temple gate* ☎ *0467/24–3437* 💴 *¥300* ⏲ *Nov.–May and July–Oct., daily 9–4; June, daily 8:30–5.*

DOWNTOWN KAMAKURA 鎌倉市

Downtown Kamakura is a good place to stop for lunch and shopping. Restaurants and shops selling local crafts, especially the carved and lacquered woodwork called Kamakura-bori, abound on Wakamiya Oji and the street parallel to it, Komachi-dori.

When the first Kamakura shogun, Minamoto no Yoritomo, learned he was about to have an heir, he had the tutelary shrine of his family moved to Kamakura from nearby Yui-ga-hama and ordered a stately avenue to be built through the center of his capital from the shrine to the sea. Along this avenue would travel the procession that brought his son—if there were a son—to be presented to the gods. Yoritomo's consort did indeed bear him a son, Yoriie (yo- *ree*-ee-eh), in 1182; Yoriie was brought in great pomp to the shrine and then consecrated to his place in the shogunal succession. Alas, the blessing of the gods did Yoriie little good. He was barely 18 when Yoritomo died, and the regency established by his mother's family, the Hojo, kept him virtually powerless until 1203, when he was banished and eventually assassinated. The Minamoto were never to hold power again, but Yoriie's memory lives on in the street that his father built for him: Wakamiya Oji, "the Avenue of the Young Prince."

TOP ATTRACTIONS

Hokoku-ji (報国寺 *Hokoku Temple*). Visitors to Kamakura tend to overlook this lovely little Zen temple of the Rinzai sect that was built in 1334, but it's worth a look. Over the years it had fallen into disrepair and neglect, until an enterprising priest took over, cleaned up the gardens, and began promoting the temple for meditation sessions, calligraphy exhibitions, and tea ceremony. Behind the main hall are a thick grove of bamboo and a small tea pavilion—a restful oasis and a fine place to go for *matcha* (green tea). The temple is about 2 km (1 mile) east on Route 204 from the main entrance to Tsuru-ga-oka Hachiman-gu; turn right at the traffic light by the Hokoku Temple Iriguchi bus stop and walk about three minutes south to the gate. ✉ *2–7–4 Jomyo-ji* ☎ *0467/22–0762* 🌐 *www.hokokuji.or.jp* 🎫 *¥200, tea ceremony ¥500* ⏲ *Daily 9–4.*

Tsurugaoka Hachimangu (鶴岡八幡宮 *Minamoto Shrine*). This shrine is dedicated to the legendary emperor Ojin, his wife, and his mother, from whom Minamoto no Yoritomo claimed descent. At the entrance, the small, steeply arched, vermilion **Taiko-bashi** (Drum Bridge) crosses a stream between two lotus ponds. The ponds were made to Yoritomo's specifications. His wife, Masako, suggested placing islands in each. In the larger **Genji Pond,** to the right, filled with white lotus flowers, she placed three islands. Genji was another name for clan, and three is an auspicious number. In the smaller **Heike Pond,** to the left, she put four islands. Heike (*heh*-ee-keh) was another name for the rival Taira clan, which the Minamoto had destroyed, and four—homophonous in Japanese with the word for "death"—is very unlucky indeed.

On the far side of the Drum Bridge is the **Mai-den.** This hall is the setting for a story of the Minamoto celebrated in Noh and Kabuki theater. Beyond the Mai-den, a flight of steps leads to the shrine's Hon-do (Main Hall). To the left of these steps is a ginkgo tree that—according to legend—was witness to a murder that ended the Minamoto line in 1219. From behind this tree, a priest named Kugyo leapt out and beheaded his uncle, the 26-year-old Sanetomo, Yoritomo's second son and the last Minamoto shogun. The priest was quickly apprehended, but Sanetomo's head was never found. As at all other Shinto shrines,

CLOSE UP

An Ancient Soap Opera

Once a year, during the Spring Festival (early or mid-April, when the cherry trees are in bloom), the Mai-den hall at Tsuru-ga-oka Hachiman-gu is used to stage a heartrending drama about Minamoto no Yoritomo's brother, Yoshitsune. Although Yoritomo was the tactical genius behind the downfall of the Taira clan and the establishment of the Kamakura Shogunate in the late 12th century, it was his dashing half brother who actually defeated the Taira in battle. In so doing, Yoshitsune won the admiration of many, and Yoritomo came to believe that his sibling had ambitions of his own. Despite Yoshitsune's declaration of allegiance, Yoritomo had him exiled and sent assassins to have him killed. Yoshitsune spent his life fleeing from one place to another until, at the age of 30, he was betrayed in his last refuge and took his own life.

Earlier in his exile, Yoshitsune's lover, the dancer Shizuka Gozen, had been captured and brought to Yoritomo and his wife, Masako. They commanded her to dance for them as a kind of penance. Instead she danced for Yoshitsune. Yoritomo was furious, and only Masako's influence kept him from ordering her death. When he discovered, however, that Shizuka was carrying Yoshitsune's child, he ordered that if the child were a boy, he was to be killed. A boy was born. Some versions of the legend have it that the child was slain; others say he was placed in a cradle, like Moses, and cast adrift in the reeds.

the Hon-do is unadorned; the building itself, an 1828 reconstruction, is not particularly noteworthy. ✉ *2–1–31 Yuki-no-shita* ✥ *To reach Tsuru-ga-oka Hachiman-gu from the east side of Kamakura Station, cross the plaza, turn left, and walk north along Wakamiya Oji. Straight ahead is the first of three arches leading to the shrine, and the shrine itself is at the far end of the street* ☎ *0467/22–0315* 🎫 *Free* ⏲ *Daily 9–4.*

Yoritomo's tomb (頼朝の墓). The man who put Kamakura on the map, so to speak, chose not to leave it when he died: it's only a short walk from Tsuru-ga-oka Hachiman-gu to the tomb of the man responsible for its construction, Minamoto no Yoritomo. If you've already been to Nikko and have seen how a later dynasty of shoguns sought to glorify its own memories, you may be surprised at the simplicity of Yoritomo's tomb. ✉ *2–5–2 Nishimi-kaido* ✥ *Exit Tsuru-ga-oka Hachiman-gu, turn left and then left again, and follow the small road up to Yoritomo's tomb* 🎫 *Free* ⏲ *Daily 9–4.*

WORTH NOTING

Jomyo-ji (浄明寺 *Jomyo Temple*). Founded in 1188, this is one of the Five Mountains Zen monasteries. Though this modest single-story monastery belonging to the Rinzai sect lacks the grandeur and scale of the Engaku and Kencho, it still merits the status of an Important Cultural Property. It is nestled inside an immaculate garden that is particularly beautiful in spring, when the cherry trees bloom. A tea ceremony with Japanese green tea takes place in this lovely setting. The monastery's only distinctive features are its green roof and the statues of Shaka

Nyorai and Amida Nyorai, who represent truth and enlightenment, in the main hall. ✉ *3–8–31 Jomyo-ji* ✣ *From Hokoku-ji, cross the main street (Route 204) that brought you the mile or so from Tsuru-ga-oka Hachiman-gu, and take the first narrow street north. The monastery is about 100 yards from the corner* ☎ *0467/22–2818* 🎫 *Jomyo Temple ¥100, tea ceremony ¥500* ⏲ *Daily 9–4.*

Kamakura-gu (鎌倉宮 *Kamakura Shrine*). This Shinto shrine was built after the Meiji Restoration of 1868 and was dedicated to Prince Morinaga (1308–36), the first son of Emperor Go-Daigo. When Go-Daigo overthrew the Kamakura Shogunate and restored Japan to direct imperial rule, Morinaga—who had been in the priesthood—was appointed supreme commander of his father's forces. The prince lived in turbulent times and died young: when the Ashikaga clan in turn overthrew Go-Daigo's government, Morinaga was taken into exile, held prisoner in a cave behind the present site of Kamakura Shrine, and eventually beheaded. The **Homotsu-den** (Treasure House), on the northwest corner of the grounds, next to the shrine's administrative office, is of interest mainly for its collection of paintings depicting the life of Prince Morinaga. ✉ *154 Nikaido* ✣ *From Yoritomo's tomb walk to Route 204 and turn left; at the next traffic light, a narrow street on the left leads off at an angle to the shrine, about 5 minutes' walk west* ☎ *0467/22–0318* 🎫 *Kamakura Shrine free, Treasure House ¥300* ⏲ *Daily 9–4.*

Kamakura Museum of National Treasures (鎌倉国宝館 *Kamakura Kokuhokan*). This museum was built in 1928 as a repository for many of the most important objects belonging to the shrines and temples in the area; many of these are designated Important Cultural Properties. Located along the east side of the Tsuru-ga-oka Hachiman-gu shrine precincts, the museum has an especially fine collection of devotional and portrait sculpture in wood from the Kamakura and Muromachi periods; the portrait pieces may be among the most expressive and interesting in all of classical Japanese art. ✉ *2–1–1 Yuki-no-shita* ☎ *0467/22–0753* 🎫 *¥400* ⏲ *Tues.–Sun. 9–4.*

HASE 長谷

On hydrangea-clad hillsides just outside downtown Kamakura are two of the town's main attractions, the Great Buddha and Hase-dera Temple.

TOP ATTRACTIONS

Fodor's Choice ★ **Hase-dera** (長谷寺). The only temple in Kamakura facing the sea, this is one of the most beautiful, and saddest, places of pilgrimage in the city. On a landing partway up the stone steps that lead to the temple grounds are hundreds of small stone images of Jizo, one of the bodhisattvas in the Buddhist pantheon. Jizo is the savior of children, particularly the souls of the stillborn, aborted, and miscarried; the mothers of these children dress the statues of Jizo in bright red bibs and leave them small offerings of food, heartbreakingly touching acts of prayer.

The **Kannon Hall** (Kannon-do) at Hase-dera enshrines the largest carved-wood statue in Japan: the votive figure of Juichimen Kannon, the 11-headed goddess of mercy. Standing 30 feet tall, the goddess bears a crown of 10 smaller heads, symbolizing her ability to search out in all directions for those in need of her compassion. No one knows for certain when the figure was carved. According to the temple records, a monk named Tokudo Shonin carved two images of the Juichimen Kannon from a huge laurel tree in 721. One was consecrated to the Hase-dera in present-day Nara Prefecture; the other was thrown into the sea in order to go wherever the sea decided that there were souls in need, and that image washed up on shore near Kamakura. Much later, in 1342, Takauji Ashikaga—the first of the 15 Ashikaga shoguns who followed the Kamakura era—had the statue covered with gold leaf.

The **Amida Hall** of Hase-dera enshrines the image of a seated Amida Buddha, who presides over the Western Paradise of the Pure Land. Minamoto no Yoritomo ordered the creation of this statue when he reached the age of 42; popular Japanese belief, adopted from China, holds that your 42nd year is particularly unlucky. Yoritomo's act of piety earned him another 11 years—he was 53 when he was thrown by a horse and died of his injuries. The Buddha is popularly known as the *yakuyoke* (good-luck) Amida, and many visitors—especially students facing entrance exams—make a point of coming here to pray. To the left of the main halls is a small restaurant where you can buy good-luck candy and admire the view of Kamakura Beach and Sagami Bay. ✉ *3–11–2 Hase* ✣ *From Hase Station, walk north about 5 minutes on the main street (Rte. 32) toward Kotoku-in and the Great Buddha, and look for a signpost to the temple on a side street to the left* ☎ *0467/22–6300* 🌐 *www.hasedera.jp* 🎫 *¥300* ⏲ *Mar.–Sept., daily 8–5:30; Oct.–Feb., daily 8–4:30.*

NEED A BREAK?

Kaiko-an (海光庵). A spacious tearoom inside the temple grounds offers dango (sweet rice dumplings on a stick), green tea, and sweets. Rest your feet, grab a table by the windows, and take in the breathtaking views of the ocean. ✉ ***3–11–2 Hase, Hase*** ☎ ***0467/22–6300.***

Fodor's Choice ★

Kamakura Great Buddha (鎌倉大仏 *Kamakura Daibutsu*). The single biggest attraction in Hase is the Great Buddha—sharing the honors with Mt. Fuji, perhaps, as the quintessential picture-postcard image of Japan. The statue of the compassionate Amida Buddha sits cross-legged in the temple courtyard, the drapery of his robes flowing in lines reminiscent of the sculpture of ancient Greece, his expression profoundly serene. The 37-foot bronze figure was cast in 1292, three centuries before Europeans reached Japan; the concept of the classical Greek lines in the Buddha's robe must have come over the Silk Route through China during the time of Alexander the Great. The casting was probably first conceived in 1180, by Minamoto no Yoritomo, who wanted a statue to rival the enormous Daibutsu in Nara. Until 1495 the Amida Buddha was housed in a wooden temple, which washed away in a great tidal wave. Since then the loving Buddha has stood exposed, facing the cold winters and hot summers, for more than five centuries.

It may seem sacrilegious to walk inside the Great Buddha, but for ¥20 you can enter the figure from a doorway in the right side and explore his stomach, with a stairway that leads up to two windows in his back, offering a stunning view of the temple grounds (open until 4:15 pm).

9

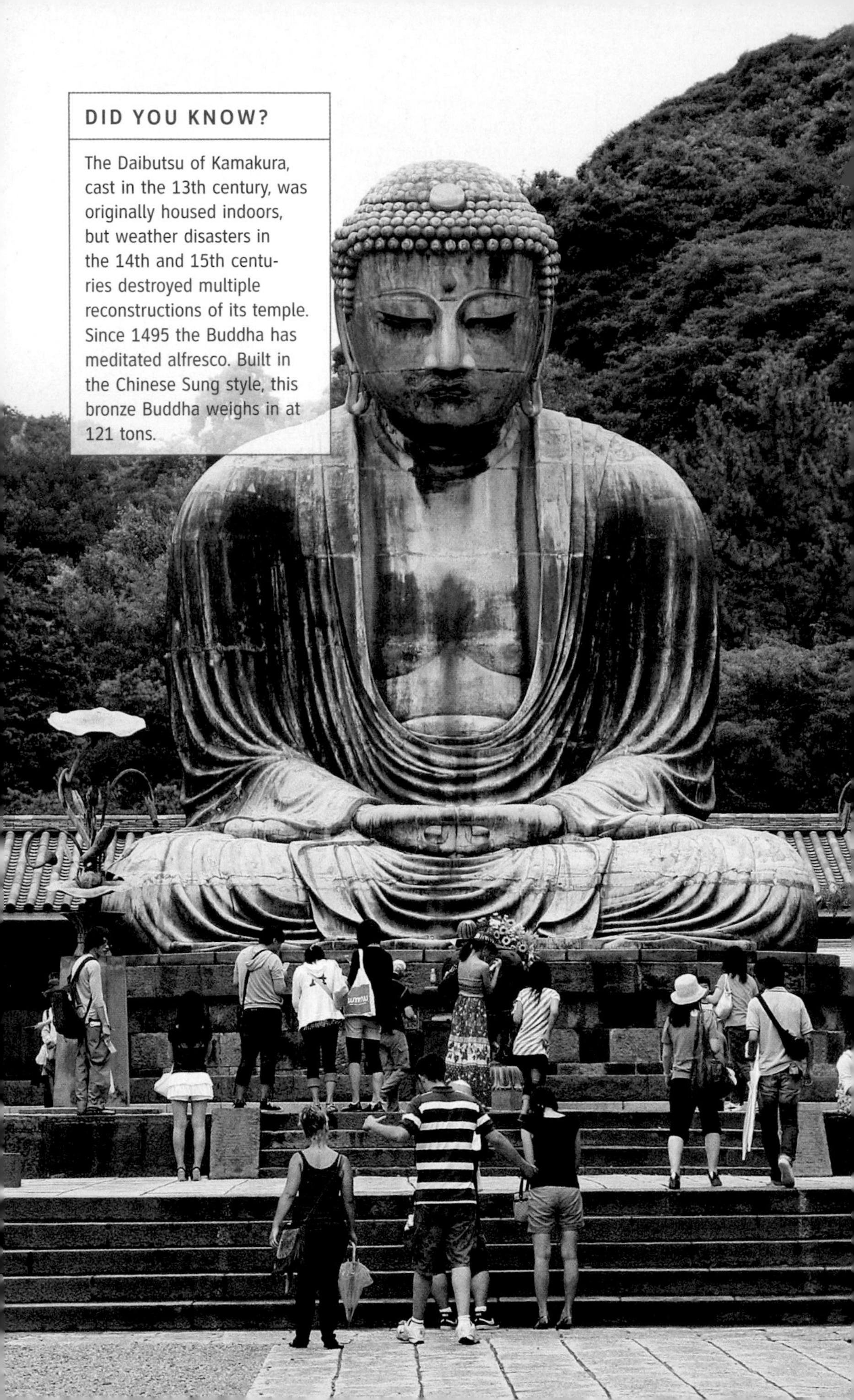

DID YOU KNOW?

The Daibutsu of Kamakura, cast in the 13th century, was originally housed indoors, but weather disasters in the 14th and 15th centuries destroyed multiple reconstructions of its temple. Since 1495 the Buddha has meditated alfresco. Built in the Chinese Sung style, this bronze Buddha weighs in at 121 tons.

To reach Kotoku-in and the Great Buddha, take the Enoden Line from the west side of JR Kamakura Station three stops to Hase. From the East Exit, turn right and walk north about 10 minutes on the main street (Route 32). ✉ *4–2–28 Hase* ☎ *0467/22–0703* 🌐 *www.kotoku-in.jp* 🎫 ¥200 ⏲ *Apr.–Sept., daily 7–6; Oct.–Mar., daily 7–5:30.*

Ryuko-ji (龍口寺 *Ryuko Temple*). The Kamakura story would not be complete without the tale of Nichiren (1222–82), the monk who founded the only native Japanese sect of Buddhism and is honored here. Nichiren's rejection of both Zen and Jodo (Pure Land) teachings brought him into conflict with the Kamakura Shogunate, and the Hojo regents sent him into exile on the Izu Peninsula in 1261. Later allowed to return, he continued to preach his own interpretation of the Lotus Sutra—and to assert the "blasphemy" of other Buddhist sects, a stance that finally persuaded the Hojo regency, in 1271, to condemn him to death. The execution was to take place on a hill to the south of Hase. As the executioner swung his sword, legend has it that a lightning bolt struck the blade and snapped it in two. Taken aback, the executioner sat down to collect his wits, and a messenger was sent back to Kamakura to report the event. On his way he met another messenger, who was carrying a writ from the Hojo regents commuting Nichiren's sentence to exile on the island of Sado-ga-shima.

Followers of Nichiren built Ryuko Temple in 1337, on the hill where he was to be executed, marking his miraculous deliverance from the headsman. There are other Nichiren temples closer to Kamakura—Myohon-ji and Ankokuron-ji, for example. But Ryuko has not only the typical Nichiren-style main hall, with gold tassels hanging from its roof, but also a beautiful pagoda, built in 1904. ✉ *3–13–37 Katase, Fujisawa* ✥ *Take the Enoden train line west from Hase to Enoshima—a short, scenic ride that cuts through the hills surrounding Kamakura to the shore. From Enoshima Station walk about 100 yards east, keeping the train tracks on your right* ☎ *0466/25–7357* 🎫 *Free* ⏲ *Daily 6–4.*

9

OFF THE BEATEN PATH

Enoshima (江ノ島). The Sagami Bay shore in this area has some of the closest beaches to Tokyo, and in the hot, humid summer months it seems as though all of the city's teeming millions pour onto these beaches in search of a vacant patch of rather dirty gray sand. Pass up this mob scene and press on instead to Enoshima. The island is only 4 km (2½ miles) around, with a hill in the middle. Partway up the hill is a shrine where the local fisherfolk used to pray for a bountiful catch—before it became a tourist attraction. Once upon a time it was quite a hike up to the shrine; now there's a series of escalators, flanked by the inevitable stalls selling souvenirs and snacks. The island has several cafés and restaurants, and on clear days some of them have spectacular views of Mt. Fuji and the Izu Peninsula. To reach the causeway from Enoshima Station to the island, walk south from the station for about 3 km (2 miles), keeping the Katase-gawa (Katase River) on your right. To return to Tokyo from Enoshima, take a train to Shinjuku on the Odakyu line. From the island walk back across the causeway and take the second bridge over the Katase-gawa. Within five minutes you'll come to Katase-Enoshima Station. Or you can retrace your steps to Kamakura and take the JR Yokosuka Line to Tokyo Station. ✉ *Kamakura.*

Hase-dera, in Kamakura, is dedicated to unborn children. The beautiful temple faces the sea.

WHERE TO EAT

KITA-KAMAKURA

$$$$ JAPANESE ✕ **Hachinoki Kita-Kamakura-ten** (鉢の木北鎌倉店). Traditional shojin ryori (the vegetarian cuisine of Zen monasteries) is served in this old Japanese house on the Kamakura Kaido (Route 21) near the entrance to Jochi Temple. The seating is mainly in tatami rooms with beautiful antique wood furnishings. If you prefer table seating, visit the annex building. Allow plenty of time; this is not a meal to be hurried through. *Average main: ¥3500 ✉ 350 Yama-no-uchi, Kita-Kamakura ☎ 0467/23–3723 ⏲ Closed Wed.*

$$$ JAPANESE FUSION ✕ **Kyorai-an** (去来庵). A traditional Japanese structure houses this restaurant known for its excellent Western-style beef stew. Also on the menu are pasta dishes, rice bouillon, homemade cheesecake, and wine produced in the Kita-Kamakura wine region. Half the seats are on tatami mats and half are at tables, but all look out on a peaceful patch of greenery. Kyorai-an is on the main road from Kita-Kamakura to Kamakura on the left side; it's about halfway between Meigetsu Temple and Kencho Temple, up a winding flight of stone steps. *Average main: ¥2500 ✉ 157 Yamanouchi ☎ 0467/24–9835 ▭ No credit cards ⏲ Closed Fri. No dinner Mon.–Thurs.*

DOWNTOWN KAMAKURA

$ CAFÉ ✕ **Bergfeld** (ベルグフェルド). If you need to take a break during your walking tour of Kamakura, you may want to stop by this quaint café and bakery. It serves German cakes and cookies that are surprisingly authentic—the baker trained in Germany. There are a few small tables outside, and cozy tables inside where you can enjoy coffee and cakes before resuming your tour. Many Japanese who visit from other parts of the country bring back the bakery's butter cookies as souvenirs. *Average main: ¥700* ✉ *3–9–24 Yukinoshita* ☎ *0467/24–2706* *No credit cards* *Closed Tues. and 3rd Thurs. of the month.*

$$ SUSHI **Kaisen Misaki-ko** (海鮮三崎港). This *kaiten-zushi* (sushi served on a conveyor belt that lets you pick the dishes you want) restaurant serves eye-poppingly large fish portions that hang over the edge of their plates. All the standard sushi creations, including tuna, shrimp, and egg, are prepared here. As in any kaiten-zushi joint, simply stack up your empty dishes to the side. When you are ready to leave, the dishes will be counted and you will be charged accordingly. The restaurant is on the right side of the road just as you enter Komachi-dori from the East Exit of Kamakura Station. *Average main: ¥1500* ✉ *1–7–1 Komachi* ☎ *0467/22–6228* *No credit cards.*

THE POWER OF THE JAPANESE BLADE

In the corner of the enclosure where the Chinese Gate and Sanctum are found, an antique bronze lantern stands some 7 feet high. Legend has it that the lantern would assume the shape of a goblin at night; the deep nicks in the bronze were inflicted by swordsmen of the Edo period—on guard duty, perhaps, startled into action by a flickering shape in the dark. This proves, if not the existence of goblins, the incredible cutting power of the Japanese blade, a peerlessly forged weapon.

HASE

$$$$ CHINESE **Kaiserro** (華正樓). This establishment, in an old Japanese house, serves the best Chinese food in the city. The dining-room windows look out on a small, restful garden. Make sure you plan for a stop here on your way to or from the Great Buddha at Kotoku-in. *Average main: ¥8000* ✉ *3–1–14 Hase* ☎ *0467/22–0280* *Reservations essential.*

9

YOKOHAMA 横浜

20 km (12½ miles) southwest of Tokyo

In 1853, a fleet of four American warships under Commodore Matthew Perry sailed into the bay of Tokyo (then Edo) and presented the reluctant Japanese with the demands of the U.S. government for the opening of diplomatic and commercial relations. The following year Perry returned and first set foot on Japanese soil at Yokohama—then a small fishing village on the mudflats of Tokyo bay.

Two years later New York businessman Townsend Harris became America's first diplomatic representative to Japan. In 1858 he was finally able to negotiate a commercial treaty between the two countries; part of the deal designated four locations—one of them Yokohama—as treaty ports. In 1859 the shogunate created a special settlement in Yokohama for the growing community of merchants, traders, missionaries, and other assorted adventurers drawn to this exotic new land of opportunity.

The foreigners (predominantly Chinese and British, plus a few French, Americans, and Dutch) were confined here to a guarded compound about 5 square km (2 square miles)—placed, in effect, in isolation—but not for long. Within a few short years the shogunal government collapsed, and Japan began to modernize. Western ideas were welcomed, as were Western goods, and the little treaty port became Japan's principal gateway to the outside world. In 1872 Japan's first railway was built, linking Yokohama and Tokyo. In 1889 Yokohama became a city; by then the population had grown to some 120,000. As the city prospered, so did the international community and by the early 1900s Yokohama was the busiest and most modern center of international trade in all of East Asia.

Then Yokohama came tumbling down. On September 1, 1923, the Great Kanto Earthquake devastated the city. The ensuing fires destroyed some 60,000 homes and took more than 40,000 lives. During the six years it took to rebuild the city, many foreign businesses took up quarters elsewhere, primarily in Kobe and Osaka, and did not return.

Over the next 20 years Yokohama continued to grow as an industrial center—until May 29, 1945, when in a span of four hours, some 500 American B-29 bombers leveled nearly half the city and left more than half a million people homeless. When the war ended, what remained became—in effect—the center of the Allied occupation. General Douglas MacArthur set up headquarters here, briefly, before moving to Tokyo; the entire port facility and about a quarter of the city remained in the hands of the U.S. military throughout the 1950s.

By the 1970s Yokohama was once more rising from the debris; in 1978 it surpassed Osaka as the nation's second-largest city, and the population is now inching up to the 3.5-million mark. Boosted by Japan's postwar economic miracle, Yokohama has extended its urban sprawl north to Tokyo and south to Kamakura—in the process creating a whole new subcenter around the Shinkansen Station at Shin-Yokohama.

The development of air travel and the competition from other ports have changed the city's role in Japan's economy. The great liners that once docked at Yokohama's piers are now but a memory, kept alive by a museum ship and the occasional visit of a luxury vessel on a Pacific cruise. Modern Yokohama thrives instead in its industrial, commercial, and service sectors—and a large percentage of its people commute to work in Tokyo. Is Yokohama worth a visit? Not, one could argue, at the expense of Nikko or Kamakura. But the waterfront is fun and the museums are excellent.

GETTING HERE AND AROUND

From Narita Airport, a direct limousine-bus service departs once or twice an hour between 7:05 am and 10:25 pm for Yokohama City Air Terminal (YCAT). YCAT is a five-minute taxi ride from Yokohama Station. JR Narita Express trains going on from Tokyo to Yokohama leave the airport every hour from 7:44 am to 9:44 pm. The fare is ¥4,290 (¥5,830 for the first-class Green Car coaches). Or you can take the limousine-bus service from Narita to Tokyo Station and continue on to Yokohama by train. Either way, the journey takes more than two hours—closer to three, if traffic is heavy.

The Airport Limousine Information Desk phone number provides information in English daily 9 to 6; you can also get timetables on its website. For information in English on Narita Express trains, call the JR Higashi-Nihon Info Line, available daily 10 to 6.

Most of the things to see in Yokohama are within easy walking distance of a JR or subway station, but this city is so much more negotiable than Tokyo that exploring by bus is a viable alternative. The city map available in the visitor centers in Yokohama has most major bus routes marked on it, and the important stops on the tourist routes are announced in English. The fixed fare is ¥210. One-day passes are also available for ¥600. Contact the Sightseeing Information Office at Yokohama Station (JR, East Exit) for more information and ticket purchases.

One subway line connects Azamino, Shin-Yokohama, Yokohama, Totsuka, and Shonandai. The basic fare is ¥200. One-day passes are also available for ¥740. The Minato Mirai Line, a spur of the Tokyu Toyoko Line, runs from Yokohama Station to all the major points of interest, including Minato Mirai, Chinatown, Yamashita Park, Motomachi, and Basha-michi. The fare is ¥180–¥200, and one-day unlimited-ride passes are available for ¥450. On weekends Yokohama has the 1-Day Green Family Pass, allowing up to five members of the same family to travel on all city buses for ¥1,000 in total.

There are taxi stands at all the train stations, and you can always flag a cab on the street. ■ **TIP→ Vacant taxis show a red light in the windshield.** The basic fare is ¥730 for the first 2 km (1 mile), then ¥80 for every additional 350 meters (0.2 mile). Traffic is heavy in downtown Yokohama, however, and it's often faster to walk.

JR trains from Tokyo Station leave approximately every 10 minutes, depending on the time of day. Take the Yokosuka, the Tokaido, or the Keihin Tohoku Line to Yokohama Station (the Yokosuka and Tokaido lines take 30 minutes; the Keihin Tohoku Line takes 40 minutes and cost ¥470). From there the Keihin Tohoku Line (Platform 3) goes on to Kannai and Ishikawa-cho, Yokohama's business and downtown areas. If you're going directly to downtown Yokohama from Tokyo, the blue commuter trains of the Keihin Tohoku Line are best.

The private Tokyu Toyoko Line, which runs from Shibuya Station in Tokyo directly to Yokohama Station, is a good alternative if you leave from the western part of Tokyo. ■ **TIP→ The term "private" is important because it means that the train does not belong to JR and is not a subway line. If you have a JR Pass, you'll have to buy a separate ticket.** Depending on which Tokyu Toyoko Line you catch—the Limited Express, Semi Express, or Local—the trip takes between 25 and 44 minutes and costs ¥270.

Yokohama Station is the hub that links all the train lines and connects them with the city's subway and bus services. Kannai and Ishikawa-cho are the two downtown stations, both on the Keihin Tohoku Line; trains leave Yokohama Station every two to five minutes from Platform 3. From Sakuragi-cho, Kannai, or Ishikawa-cho, most of Yokohama's points of interest are within easy walking distance; the one notable exception is Sankei-en, which you reach via the JR Keihin Tohoku Line to Negishi Station and then a local bus.

VISITOR INFORMATION

The Yokohama Tourist Office, in the central passageway of Yokohama Station, is open daily 9 to 7 (closed December 28–January 3). The head office of the Yokohama Convention & Visitors Bureau, open weekdays 9 to 5 (except national holidays and December 29–January 3), is in the Sangyo Boeki Center Building, across from Yamashita Koen.

ESSENTIALS

Airport Transportation Airport Limousine Information Desk. ☎ *03/3665-7220* 🌐 *www.limousinebus.co.jp.*

EXPLORING

Large as Yokohama is, the central area is very negotiable. As with any other port city, much of what it has to offer centers on the waterfront—in this case, on the west side of Tokyo Bay. The downtown area is called Kannai (literally, "within the checkpoint"); this is where the international community was originally confined by the shogunate. Though the center of interest has expanded to include the waterfront and Ishikawa-cho, to the south, Kannai remains the heart of town.

Think of that heart as two adjacent areas. One is the old district of Kannai, bounded by Basha-michi on the northwest and Nippon-odori on the southeast, the Keihin Tohoku Line tracks on the southwest, and the waterfront on the northeast. This area contains the business offices of modern Yokohama. The other area extends southeast from Nippon-odori to the Moto-machi shopping street and the International Cemetery, bordered by Yamashita Koen and the waterfront to the northeast; in the center is Chinatown, with Ishikawa-cho Station to the southwest. This is the most interesting part of town for tourists. ■ **TIP→ Whether you're coming from Tokyo, Nagoya, or Kamakura, make Ishikawa-cho Station your starting point. Take the South Exit from the station and head in the direction of the waterfront.**

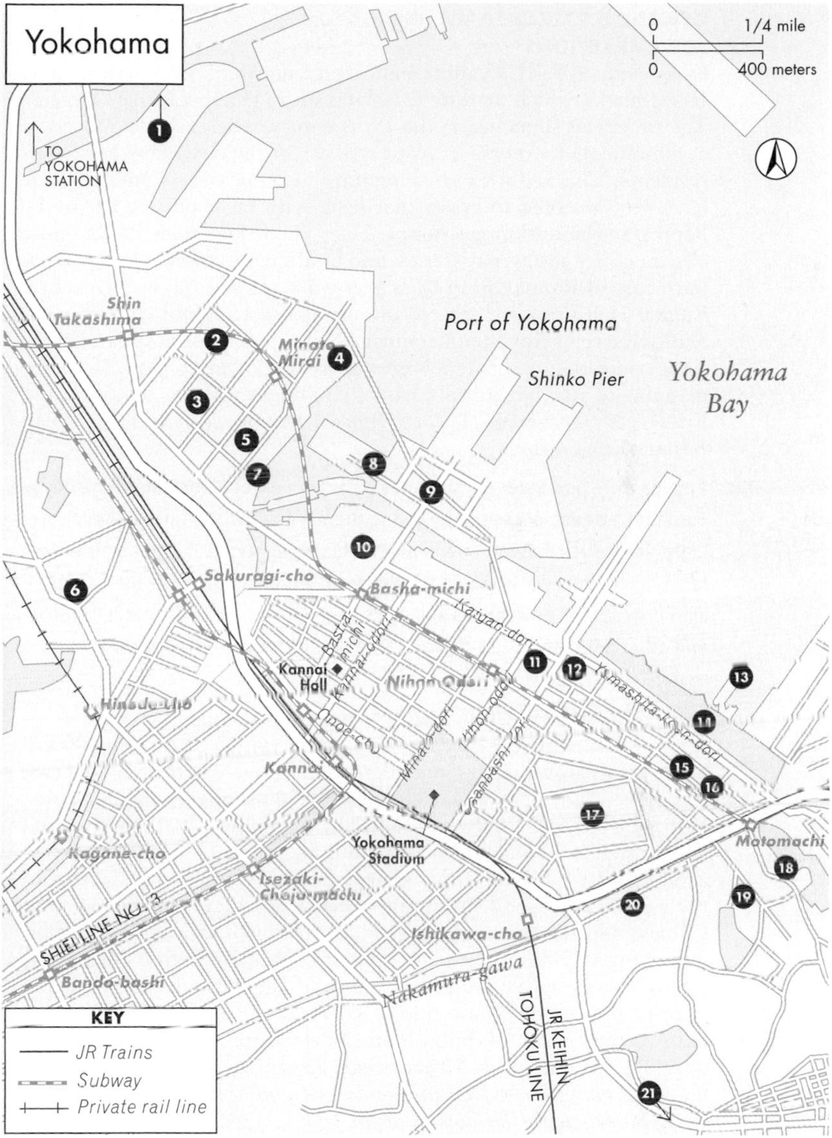

Yokohama

0 1/4 mile
0 400 meters

TO YOKOHAMA STATION

Port of Yokohama

Shinko Pier

Yokohama Bay

Shin Takashima

Minato Mirai

Sakuragi-cho

Basha-michi

Kaigan-dori

Basha-michi

Kannai-odori

Kannai Hall

Nihon Odori

Yamashita-koen-dori

Minato-dori

Nihon-odori

Sambashi-dori

Kannai

Yokohama Stadium

Motomachi

Kagane-cho

Isezaki-Chojamachi

Ishikawa-cho

SHIEI LINE NO. 3

Bando-bashi

Nakamura-gawa

JR KEIHIN TOHOKU LINE

KEY

- JR Trains
- Subway
- Private rail line

Basha-michi **10**
Chinatown **17**
Harbor View Park **18**
Hikawa-maru **13**
Iseyama Kotai Jingu **6**
Landmark Tower **5**
Marine Tower **15**
Minato Mirai 21 .... **2**
Mitsubishi Minatomirai Industrial Museum **4**
Moto-machi **20**
Nippon-maru Memorial Park **7**
Sankei-en **21**
Silk Museum **12**
Soji-ji **1**
World Porters **9**
Yamashita Koen **14**
Yokohama Archives of History **11**
Yokohama Cosmo World **8**
Yokohama Doll Museum **16**
Yokohama Foreign General Cemetery **19**
Yokohama Museum of Art **3**

CENTRAL YOKOHAMA 横浜市街

TOP ATTRACTIONS

Basha-michi (馬車道). Running southwest from Shinko Pier to Kannai is Basha-michi, which literally translates into "Horse-Carriage Street." The street was so named in the 19th century, when it was widened to accommodate the horse-drawn carriages of the city's new European residents. This redbrick thoroughfare and the streets parallel to it have been restored to evoke that past, with faux-antique telephone booths and imitation gas lamps. Here you'll find some of the most elegant coffee shops, patisseries, and boutiques in town. On the block northeast of Kannai Station, as you walk toward the waterfront, is **Kannai Hall** (look for the red-orange abstract sculpture in front), a handsome venue for chamber music, Noh, classical recitals, and occasional performances by such groups as the Peking Opera. If you're planning to stay late in Yokohama, you might want to check out the listings. ✉ *Naka-ku* Ⓜ *JR Line, Kannai Station; Minato Mirai Line, Basha-michi Station.*

NEED A BREAK?

Keyuca Café and Sweets. Japanese pâtissiers excel at making exquisite European sweets, occasionally giving them a new twist with Japanese ingredients such as sweet bean paste. This elegant café is a good place to taste these skills while taking a break from your walking tour. The cappuccino is excellent, and there's a daily changing menu of bagel sandwiches and other light fare. ✉ ***B1 Queen's East, 2–3–2 Minato-Mirai, Nishi-ku*** ☎ ***045/640–1361.***

Chinatown (中華街 *Chuka-gai*). The largest Chinese settlement in Japan—and easily the city's most popular tourist attraction—Yokohama's Chinatown draws more than 18 million visitors a year. Its narrow streets and alleys are lined with some 350 shops selling foodstuffs, herbal medicines, cookware, toys and ornaments, and clothing and accessories. If China exports it, you'll find it here. Wonderful exotic aromas waft from the spice shops. Even better aromas drift from the quarter's 160-odd restaurants, which serve every major style of Chinese cuisine: this is the best place for lunch in Yokohama. Chinatown is a 10-minute walk southeast of Kannai Station. When you get to Yokohama Stadium, turn left and cut through the municipal park to the top of Nihon-odori. Then take a right, and enter Chinatown through the Gembu-mon (North Gate), which leads to the dazzling red-and-gold, 50-foot-high Zenrin-mon (Good Neighbor Gate). ✉ *Naka-ku* Ⓜ *JR Line, Ishikawa-cho Station; Minato Mirai Line, Motomachi-Chukagai Station.*

Harbor View Park (港の見える丘公園 *Minato-no-Mieru-Oka Koen*). The park—a major landmark in this part of the city, known, appropriately enough, as the Bluff (*yamate*)—was once the barracks of the British forces in Yokohama. Come here for spectacular nighttime views of the waterfront, the floodlit gardens of Yamashita Park, and the Bay Bridge. Foreigners were first allowed to build here in 1867, and it has been prime real estate ever since—an enclave of consulates, churches,

Get a taste of China in Japan with a visit to the restaurants and shops of Yokohama's Chinatown.

international schools, private clubs, and palatial Western-style homes. ✉ *Naka-ku* Ⓜ *JR Line, Ishikawa-cho Station; Minato Mirai Line, Motomachi-Chukagai Station.*

Hikawa-maru (氷川丸). Moored on the waterfront, more or less in the middle of Yamashita Park, is the *Hikawa-maru*. The ocean liner was built in 1929 by Yokohama Dock Co. and launched on September 30, 1929. For 31 years, she shuttled passengers between Yokohama and Seattle, Washington, making a total of 238 trips. A tour of the ship evokes the time when Yokohama was a great port of call for the transpacific liners. The ship has a French restaurant, and in summer there's a beer garden on the upper deck. ✉ *Yamashita-koen, Naka-ku* ☎ *045/641–4362* 🎫 *¥500* 🕓 *Apr.–June, Sept., and Oct., daily 9:30–7; July and Aug., daily 9:30–7:30; Nov.–Mar., daily 9:30–6:30* Ⓜ *JR Line, Ishikawa-cho Station; Minato Mirai Line, Motomachi-Chukagai Station.*

Silk Museum (シルク博物館 *Shiruku Hakubutsukan*). From the opening of its borders to the beginning of the 20th century, silk was Japan's most sought-after export and nearly all of it went through Yokohama. The museum, which pays tribute to this period, houses an extensive collection of silk fabrics and an informative exhibit on the silk-making process. People on staff are very happy to answer questions. In the same building, on the first floor, are the main offices of the Yokohama International Tourist Association and the Kanagawa Prefectural Tourist Association. The museum is at the northwestern end of the Yamashita Park promenade, on the second floor of the Silk Center

Building. ✉ *1 Yamashita-cho, Naka-ku* ☎ *045/641–0841* 🌐 *www.silkmuseum.or.jp* 🎟 *¥500* ⏲ *Tues.–Sun. 9–4* Ⓜ *Minato Mirai Line, Nihon Odori Station (Exit 3).*

WORTH NOTING

Marine Tower (マリンタワー). For an older generation of Yokohama residents, the 348-foot-high decagonal tower, which opened in 1961, was the city's landmark structure; civic pride prevented them from admitting that it falls lamentably short of an architectural masterpiece. The tower has a navigational beacon at the 338-foot level and purports to be the tallest lighthouse in the world. At the 328-foot level, an observation gallery provides 360-degree views of the harbor and the city, and on clear days in autumn or winter, you can often see Mt. Fuji in the distance. Marine Tower is in the middle of the second block northwest from the end of Yamashita Park, on the left side of the promenade. ✉ *15 Yamashita-cho, Naka-ku* ☎ *045/641–7838* 🌐 *www.marinetower.jp* 🎟 *¥750* ⏲ *Daily 10–10* Ⓜ *JR Line, Ishikawa-cho Station; Minato Mirai Line, Motomachi-Chukagai Station.*

Moto-machi (元町). Within a block of Ishikawa-cho Station is the beginning of this street, which follows the course of the Nakamura-gawa (Nakamura River) to the harbor where the Japanese set up shop 100 years ago to serve the foreigners living in Kannai. The street is now lined with smart boutiques and jewelry stores that cater to fashionable young Japanese consumers. ✉ *Naka-ku* Ⓜ *JR Line, Ishikawa-cho Station; Minato Mirai Line, Motomachi-Chukagai Station.*

Yamashita Koen (山下公園 *Yamashita Park*). This park is perhaps the only positive legacy of the Great Kanto Earthquake of 1923. The debris of the warehouses and other buildings that once stood here were swept away, and the area was made into a 17-acre oasis of green along the waterfront. The fountain, representing the Guardian of the Water, was presented to Yokohama by San Diego, California, one of its sister cities. ✉ *279 Yamashita-cho, Naka-ku* ✢ *From Harbor View Park, walk northwest through neighboring French Hill Park and cross the walkway over Moto-machi. Turn right on the other side and walk one block down toward the bay to Yamashita-Koen-dori, the promenade along the park* Ⓜ *JR Line, Ishikawa-cho Station; Minato Mirai Line, Motomachi-Chukagai Station.*

Yokohama Archives of History (横浜開港資料館 *Yokohama Kaiko Shiryokan*). Within the archives, housed in what was once the British Consulate, are some 140,000 items recording the history of Yokohama since the opening of the port to international trade in the mid-19th century. Across the street is a monument to the U.S.–Japanese Friendship Treaty. ✉ *3 Nihon-odori, Naka-ku* ✢ *To get here from the Silk Center Building, at the end of the Yamashita Park promenade, walk west to the corner of Nihon-odori; the archives are on the left* ☎ *045/201–2100* 🌐 *www.kaikou.city.yokohama.jp/en* 🎟 *¥200* ⏲ *Tues.–Sun. 9:30–5* Ⓜ *Minato Mirai Line, Nihon-odori Station.*

FAMILY **Yokohama Doll Museum** (横浜人形の家 *Yokohama Ningyo-no-ie*). This museum houses a collection of roughly 3,500 dolls from all over the world. In Japanese tradition, dolls are less to play with than to display—either in religious folk customs or as the embodiment of some spiritual quality. Japanese visitors to this museum never seem to outgrow their affection for the Western dolls on display here, to which they tend to assign the role of timeless "ambassadors of goodwill" from other cultures. The museum is worth a quick visit, with or without a child in tow. It's just across from the southeast end of Yamashita Park, on the left side of the promenade. ✉ *18 Yamashita-cho, Naka-ku* ☎ *045/671–9361* 🌐 *www.doll-museum.jp* 🎫 *¥400* 🕙 *Tues.–Sun., 9:30–5* Ⓜ *JR Line, Ishikawa-cho Station; Minato Mirai Line, Motomachi-Chukagai Station.*

Yokohama Foreign General Cemetery (横浜山手外国人墓地 *Yokohama Yamate Gaikokujin Bochi*). This Yokohama landmark is a reminder of the port city's heritage. It was established in 1854 with a grant of land from the shogunate; the first foreigners to be buried here were Russian sailors assassinated by xenophobes in the early days of the settlement. Most of the 4,500 graves on this hillside are English and American, and about 120 are of the Japanese wives of foreigners; the inscriptions on the crosses and headstones attest to some 40 different nationalities whose citizens lived and died in Yokohama. ✉ *96 Yamate-cho, Naka-ku* ✣ *From Moto-machi Plaza, it's a short walk to the north end of the cemetery* 🌐 *www.yfgc-japan.com* 🕙 *No entry after 4 pm* Ⓜ *JR Line, Ishikawa-cho Station; Minato Mirai Line, Motomachi-Chukagai Station.*

AROUND YOKOHAMA

TOP ATTRACTIONS

Iseyama Kotai Jingu (伊勢山皇大神宮 *Iseyama Kotai Shrine*). A branch of the nation's revered Grand Shrines of Ise, this is the most important Shinto shrine in Yokohama—but it's worth a visit only if you've seen most everything else in town. ✉ *64 Miyazaki-cho, Nishi-ku* ✣ *The shrine is a 10-minute walk west of Sakuragi-cho Station* ☎ *045/241–1122* 🎫 *Free* 🕙 *Daily 9–7* Ⓜ *JR Line, Sakuragi-cho Station; Minato Mirai Line, Minato Mirai Station.* 9

FAMILY **Landmark Tower** (ランドマークタワー). Although no longer Japan's tallest building—that title now goes to Osaka's brand-new Abeno Harukas—this 70-story tower in Yokohama's Minato Mirai is the tallest in Greater Tokyo. The observation deck on the 69th floor has a spectacular view of the city, especially at night; you reach it via a high-speed elevator that carries you up at an ear-popping 45 kph (28 mph). The complex's **Dockyard Garden,** built in 1896, is a restored dry dock with stepped sides of massive stone blocks. The long, narrow floor of the dock, with its water cascade at one end, makes a wonderful year-round open-air venue for concerts and other events; in summer (July–mid-August), the beer garden installed here is a perfect refuge from the heat. The Yokohama Royal Park Hotel occupies the top 20 stories of the building,

Landmark Tower and the Ferris wheel create a lovely skyline along Yokohama Bay.

and the courtyard on the northeast side connects to **Queen's Square,** a huge atrium-style vertical mall with dozens of shops (mainly for clothing and accessories) and restaurants. ✉ *2–2–1 Minato Mirai, Nishi-ku* ☎ *045/222–5015* 🌐 *www.yokohama-landmark.jp* 🎫 *Elevator to observation deck ¥1,000* 🕑 *Daily 10–9* Ⓜ *JR Line, Sakuragi-cho Station; Minato Mirai Line, Minato Mirai Station.*

Minato Mirai 21 (みなとみらい21). If you want to see Yokohama urban development at its most self-assertive, then this is a must. The aim of this project, launched in the mid-1980s, was to turn some three-quarters of a square mile of waterfront property, lying east of the JR Negishi Line railroad tracks between the Yokohama and Sakuragi-cho stations, into a model "city of the future." As a hotel, business, international exhibition, and conference center, it's a smashing success. ✉ *Nishi-ku* 🌐 *www.minatomirai21.com* Ⓜ *JR Line, Sakuragi-cho Station; Minato Mirai Line, Minato Mirai Station.*

Sankei-en (三渓園). Opened to the public in 1906, this was once the estate and gardens of Tomitaro Hara (1868–1939), one of Yokohama's wealthiest men, who made his money as a silk merchant before becoming a patron of the arts. On the extensive grounds of the estate he created is a kind of open-air museum of traditional Japanese architecture, some of which was brought here from Kamakura and the western part of the country. Especially noteworthy is **Rinshun-kaku,** a villa built for the Tokugawa clan in 1649. There's also a tea pavilion, Choshukaku, built by the third Tokugawa shogun, Iemitsu. Other buildings include a small temple transported from Kyoto's famed Daitoku-ji and a farmhouse from the Gifu district in the Japan Alps (around

Takayama). ✉ 58–1 Honmoku San-no-tani, Naka-ku ☎ 045/621–0634 🌐 www.sankeien.or.jp 🎫 Inner garden ¥500 ⏲ Inner garden: daily 9–4. Outer garden and farmhouse: daily 9–4:30 Ⓜ JR Keihin Tohoku Line to Negishi Station and a local bus (number 58, 99, or 101) bound for Honmoku; Yokohama Station (East Exit) and take the bus (number 8 or 148) to Honmoku Sankei-en Mae (the trip takes about 35 mins).

BLOOMIN' SEASON

Walking through Sankei-en is especially delightful in spring, when the flowering trees are at their best: plum blossoms in February and cherry blossoms in early April. In June come the irises, followed by the water lilies. In autumn the trees come back into their own with tinted golden leaves.

WORTH NOTING

FAMILY **Mitsubishi Minatomirai Industrial Museum.** Filling galleries on the first floor of the Landmark Tower are rocket engines, power plants, a submarine, various gadgets, and displays that simulate piloting helicopters—great fun for kids. *✉ 3-3–1 Minato Mirai, Nishi-ku 🎫 ¥500 ⏲ Wed.–Mon. 10–5 Ⓜ JR Line, Sakuragi-cho Station; Minato Mirai Line, Minato Mirai Station.*

Nippon-maru Memorial Park (日本丸メモリアルパーク). The centerpiece of the park, which is on the east side of Minato Mirai 21, where the O-oka-gawa (O-oka River) flows into the bay, is the *Nippon-maru,* a full-rigged three-masted ship popularly called the "Swan of the Pacific." Built in 1930, it served as a training vessel. The *Nippon-maru* is now retired, but it's an occasional participant in tall-ships festivals and is open for guided tours. Adjacent to the ship is the **Yokohama Port Museum,** a two-story collection of ship models, displays, and archival materials that celebrate the achievements of the Port of Yokohama from its earliest days to the present. *✉ 2–1–1 Minato Mirai, Nishi-ku ☎ 045/221–0280 🌐 www.nippon-maru.or.jp 🎫 ¥600 ⏲ Tues.–Sun. 10–5 Ⓜ JR Line, Sakuragi-cho Station; Minato Mirai Line, Minato Mirai Station.*

World Porters (ワールドポーターズ). This shopping center, on the opposite side of Yokohama Cosmo World, is notable chiefly for its restaurants that overlook the Minato Mirai area. Try arriving at sunset; the spectacular view of twinkling lights and the Landmark Tower, the Ferris wheel, and hotels occasionally include Mt. Fuji in the background. Walking away from the waterfront area from World Porters leads to **Aka Renga** (Redbrick Warehouses), two more shopping-and-entertainment facilities. *✉ 2–2–1 Shinko, Naka-ku ☎ 045/222–2121 🌐 www.yim.co.jp 🎫 Free ⏲ Daily 10–9, restaurants 10 am–11 pm Ⓜ JR Line, Sakuragi-cho Station; Minato Mirai Line, Minato Mirai Station.*

FAMILY **Yokohama Cosmo World** (よこはまコスモワールド). This amusement-park complex claims—among its 30 or so rides and attractions—the world's largest water-chute ride, four stories high. The Ferris wheel towers over Yokohama. The park is west of Minato Mirai and Queen's Square, on both sides of the river. *✉ 2–8–1 Shinko, Naka-ku*

☎ *045/641–6591* 🎫 *Park free, rides ¥300–¥700 each* ⏲ *Mid-Mar.–Nov., weekdays 11–9, weekends 11–10; Dec.–mid-Mar., weekdays 11–8, weekends 11–9* Ⓜ *JR Line, Sakuragi-cho Station; Minato Mirai Line, Minato Mirai Station.*

Yokohama Museum of Art (横浜美術館 *Yokohama Bijutsukan*). Designed by Kenzo Tange and housed at Minato Mirai 21, the museum has 5,000 works in its permanent collection. Visitors will see paintings by both Western and Japanese artists, including Cézanne, Picasso, Braque, Klee, Kandinsky, Ryusei Kishida, and Taikan Yokoyama. ✉ *3–4–1 Minato Mirai, Nishi-ku* ☎ *045/221–0300* 🌐 *yokohama.art.museum/eng* 🎫 *¥500, ¥1,000–¥1,500 for special exhibits* ⏲ *Mon.–Wed. and weekends 10–5:30* Ⓜ *JR Line, Sakuragi-cho Station; Minato Mirai Line, Minato Mirai Station.*

OFF THE BEATEN PATH

Soji-ji (総持寺). One of the two major centers of the Soto sect of Zen Buddhism, Soji-ji, in Yokohama's Tsurumi ward, was founded in 1321. The center was moved here from Ishikawa, on the Noto Peninsula (on the Sea of Japan, north of Kanazawa), after a fire in the 19th century. There's also a Soji-ji monastic complex at Eihei-ji in Fukui Prefecture. The Yokohama Soji-ji is one of the largest and busiest Buddhist institutions in Japan, with more than 200 monks and novices in residence. The 14th-century patron of Soji-ji was the emperor Go-Daigo, who overthrew the Kamakura Shogunate; the emperor is buried here, but his mausoleum is off-limits to visitors. However, you can see the **Buddha Hall,** the **Main Hall,** and the **Treasure House.** ✉ *2–1–1 Tsurumi, Tsurumi-ku* ✣ *Take the JR Keihin Tohoku Line 2 stops from Sakuragi-cho to Tsurumi. From the station walk 5 mins south (back toward Yokohama), passing Tsurumi University on your right. Look out for the stone lanterns that mark the entrance to the temple complex* ☎ *045/581–6021* 🎫 *¥300* ⏲ *Daily dawn–dusk; Treasure House Tues.–Sun. 10–4.*

WHERE TO EAT

$$$$ JAPANESE

✕ **Chano-ma** (茶の間). This stylish eatery serves modern Japanese cuisine that you enjoy while lounging on bedlike seats as a house DJ spins tunes. Make sure you try the miso sirloin steak or grilled scallops with tasty citron sauce drizzled on top, served with a salad. It gets crowded here on the weekends, so come early to avoid a long wait. Try coming at lunchtime and you can take advantage of the set-lunch special. Ⓢ *Average main: ¥3500* ✉ *3F Red Brick Warehouse Bldg. 2, 1–1–2 Shinkou, Naka-ku* ☎ *045/650–8228* Ⓜ *Minato Mirai Line, Basha-michi Station; JR Negishi Line, Sakuragi-cho and Kannai stations.*

$$$$ CHINESE

✕ **Kaseiro** (華正樓). Surprisingly, Chinese food can be hit-or-miss in Japan, but not at Kaseiro. This elegant restaurant, with red carpets and gold-tone walls, is the best of its kind in the city, serving authentic Beijing cuisine, including, of course, Peking Duck and shark-fin soup. The consistently delicious dishes, combined with the fact that both the owner and chef are from Beijing, make this restaurant a well-known favorite among locals and travelers alike. *Average main: ¥10000 ✉ 186 Yamashita-cho, Chinatown, Naka-ku ☎ 045/681–2918 Jacket and tie.*

$$$$ JAPANESE ✕ **Motomachi Bairin** (元町梅林). The area of Motomachi is known as the wealthy, posh part of Yokohama; restaurants here tend to be exclusive and expensive, though the service and quality justify the price. This restaurant is an old-style Japanese house complete with a Japanese garden and five private tatami rooms. For a real feast, try the 27-course banquet that includes traditional Japanese delicacies such as sashimi, shiitake mushrooms, and chicken in white sauce; deep-fried burdock; and broiled sea bream. *Average main: ¥12000 ✉ 1–55 Motomachi, Naka-ku ☎ 045/662–2215 Closed Mon. Reservations essential.*

$$$$ JAPANESE ✕ **Rinka-en** (隣花苑). If you visit the gardens of Sankei-en, you might want to have lunch or dinner at this traditional country restaurant, which serves kaiseki-style cuisine. The owner is the granddaughter of Hara Tomitaro, who donated the gardens to the city. *Average main: ¥7000 ✉ 52–1 Honmoku San-no-tani, Naka-ku ☎ 045/621–0318 No credit cards Closed Wed. and Aug. Reservations essential Jacket and tie.*

$$$$ ITALIAN ✕ **Roma Statione** (ローマステーション). Opened more than 40 years ago, this popular venue between Chinatown and Yamashita Park is Yokohama's source for Italian food. The owner, whose father studied cooking in Italy before returning home, is also the head chef and has continued using the original recipes. The house specialty is seafood: the spaghetti *vongole* (with clam sauce) is particularly good, as is the spaghetti *pescatora* and the seafood pizza. An added bonus is the impressive selection of Italian wines. *Average main: ¥3500 ✉ 26 Yamashita-cho, Naka-ku ☎ 045/681–1818 Ⓜ Minato Mirai Line, Motomachi-Chukagai Station (Exit 1).*

$$$$ SCANDINAVIAN ✕ **Scandia** (スカンディア). This Scandinavian restaurant near the Silk Center and the business district is known for its smorgasbord. It's popular for business lunches as well as for dinner. Scandia stays open until midnight, later than many other restaurants in the area. Expect dishes like steak tartare, marinated herring, and fried eel, and plenty of rye bread. While dinner is pricey, lunches are a relative bargain. *Average main: ¥9000 ✉ 1–1 Kaigan-dori, Naka-ku ☎ 045/201–2262 No credit cards.*

$$$$ STEAKHOUSE ✕ **Serina Romanchaya** (瀬里奈 浪漫茶屋). The hallmarks of this restaurant are *ishiyaki* steak, which is grilled on a hot stone, and shabu-shabu—thin slices of beef cooked in boiling water at your table and dipped in one of several sauces; choose from sesame, vinegar, or soy. Fresh vegetables, noodles, and tofu are also dipped into the seasoned broth for a filling yet healthful meal. *Average main: ¥10000 ✉ B1 Shin-Kannai Bldg., 4–45–1 Sumiyoshi-cho, Naka-ku ☎ 045/681–2727.*

9

$$$$ ITALIAN FAMILY

Yokohama Cheese Cafe (横浜チーズカフェ). This is a cozy and inviting casual Italian restaurant, whose interior looks like an Italian country home. There are candles on the tables and an open kitchen where diners can watch the cooks making pizza. On the menu: 18 kinds of Napoli-style wood-fire–baked pizzas, 20 kinds of pastas, fondue, and other dishes that include—you guessed it—cheese. The set-course menus are reasonable, filling, and recommended. *Average main: ¥3500* *2–1–10 Kitasaiwai, Nishi-ku* *045/290–5656* *No lunch* *JR Yokohama Station.*

UNDERSTANDING JAPANESE

ABOUT JAPANESE

ESSENTIAL PHRASES

MENU GUIDE

ABOUT JAPANESE

To read and write Japanese you need a command of some 2,000 *kanji* (ideogram characters derived from Chinese) and two syllabic alphabets, called *hiragana* and *katakana*. The pronunciation of all the *kanji* and their various inflections can be rendered in either alphabet, although *katakana* is normally used for the spelling of foreign loan-words, making it the most immediately useful for visitors.

The alphabets are made up of four types of syllables: the single vowels *a, i, u, e,* and *o* (pronounced ah, ee, ooh, eh, and oh); vowel-consonant pairs like *ka, ni, hu,* or *ro*; the single consonant *n* (which punctuates, for example, the upbeats of the word for bullet train, *Shinkansen: shee*-n- *ka*-n- *se*-n); and compounds like *kya, chu,* and *ryo*—also each one syllable. Thus Tokyo, the capital city, has only two syllables—*tō* and *kyō*—not three. Likewise pronounce Kyōto *kyō-to*, not *kee-oh-to*. The Japanese *r* is rolled so that it sounds like a bounced *d*. There is no *l*-sound in the language, and the Japanese have great difficulty in distinguishing *l* from *r*, whether spoken or written.

No diphthongs. Paired vowels in Japanese words are not slurred together, as in the English *brain* or *stein*. The Japanese separate them, as in *mae* (*ma*-eh), which means "in front of"; *kōen* (*ko*-en); and *tokei* (to- *keh*-ee), which means "clock" or "watch."

Macrons. Many Japanese words, when rendered in *romaji* (Roman letters) use a macron, or bar, over certain vowels to indicate whether it is pronounced long or short. The macrons in *Tokyo*, for example, direct you to double the length of the *o*: *to*-o- *kyo*-o. Likewise, when you see double consonants, as in the city name Nikkō, double up on the *k*s—as you would with "bookkeeper"—and elongate the *o*. (Note, however, that macrons are often omitted recently.)

Emphasis. Some books state that the Japanese emphasize all syllables in their words equally. This is not true. Take the words *sayōnara* and *Hiroshima*. Americans are likely to stress the downbeats: *sa*-yo-*na*-ra and *hi*-ro- *shi*-ma. The Japanese actually emphasize the second beat in each case: sa- *yō*-na-ra (note the macron) and hi- *ro*-shi-ma. Metaphorically speaking, the Japanese don't so much stress syllables as pause over them or race past them: emphasis is more a question of speed than weight. In the vocabulary below, we indicate emphasis by italicizing the syllable that you should stress.

Note also the unstressed pronunciations. The word *desu* roughly means "is." It looks like it has two syllables, but the Japanese race past the final *u* and just say "dess." Likewise, some verbs end in *-masu,* which is pronounced "mahss." Similarly, the character *shi* is often quickly pronounced "sh," as in the phrase meaning "pleased to meet you": *ha*-ji-me- *mash(i)*-te.

Hyphens. Throughout this book we have hyphenated certain words to help you recognize meaningful patterns and vocabulary elements. This isn't conventional; it is practical. Seeing *Eki-mae-dōri* (literally "Station Front Avenue) this way instead of run together in a single word, for example, makes it easier to register the terms for "station" and "avenue" for use elsewhere. You'll also run across a number of sight names that end in *-jingu* or *-jinja* or *-taisha,* all of which mean "Shinto shrine."

Structure. Japanese sentences are structured quite differently, subject-object-verb, instead of subject-verb-object as in English. "I am going to Tokyo" would translate literally in Japanese as "Tokyo to I'm going."

Note: placing an "o" before words like *tera* (*otera*) and *shiro* (*oshiro*) makes the word honorific. The meaning is clear enough without it, but omitting the polite form would be exceedingly un-Japanese.

ESSENTIAL PHRASES

ENGLISH	PRONUNCIATION	JAPANESE
BASICS		
Yes/No	*ha*-i / *ii*-e	はい / いいえ
Please	o-ne- *gai* shi-masu	お願いします
Thank you (very much).	(*do*-mo) a- *ri*-ga-to go- *zai*-ma su	(どうも) ありがとうございます
You're welcome.	*dō* i-ta-shi- *mashi*-te	どういたしまして
Excuse me.	su-mi-ma- *sen*	すみません
Sorry	go- *men* na- *sai*	ごめんなさい
Good morning.	o- *ha*-yō go- *zai*-ma-su	おはようございます
Good day/afternoon.	kon- *ni*-chi wa	こんにちは
Good evening.	kom- *ban*-wa	こんばんは
Good night.	o-ya- *su*-mi na- *sai*	おやすみなさい
Good-bye	sa- *yō*-na-ra	さようなら
Mr./Mrs./Miss	-san	～さん
Pleased to meet you.	*ha*-ji-me- *mashi*-te	はじめまして
How do you do?	*dō*-zo yo- *ro*-shi-ku o-ne- *gai* shi-masu	どうぞよろしくお願いします

NUMBERS

The first reading is used for reading numbers, as in telephone numbers, and the second is often used for counting things.

1	*i*-chi / hi- *to*-tsu	一 / 一つ
2	ni / fu- *ta*-tsu	二 / 二つ
3	san / *mit*-tsu	三 / 三つ
4	yon (shi) / *yot*-tsu	四 / 四つ
5	go / i- *tsu*-tsu	五 / 五つ
6	*ro*-ku / *mut*-tsu	六 / 六つ
7	*na*-na (*shi*-chi)/ na- *na*-tsu	七 / 七つ
8	*ha*-chi / *yat*-tsu	八 / 八つ
9	kyū / ko-ko- *no*- tsu	九 / 九つ
19	*jū*-kyū	十九
20	*ni*-jū	二十

ENGLISH	PRONUNCIATION	JAPANESE
21	*ni*-jū-i-chi	二十一
30	*san*-jū	三十
40	*yon*-jū	四十
50	*go*-jū	五十
60	*ro*-ku-jū	六十

DAYS OF THE WEEK

Sunday	*ni*-chi *yō*-bi	日曜日
Monday	*ge*-tsu *yō*-bi	月曜日
Tuesday	*ka* yō-bi	火曜日
Wednesday	*su*-i *yō*-bi	水曜日
Thursday	*mo*-ku *yō*-bi	木曜日
Friday	*kin* yō-bi	金曜日
Saturday	*dō* yō-bi	土曜日
weekday	*hei*-ji-tsu	平日
weekend	*shū*-ma-tsu	週末

MONTHS

January	*i*-chi *ga*-tsu	一月
February	*ni* ga-tsu	二月
March	*san* ga-tsu	三月
April	*shi* ga-tsu	四月
May	*go* ga-tsu	五月
June	*ro*-ku *ga*-tsu	六月
July	*shi*-chi *ga*-tsu	七月
August	*ha*-chi *ga*-tsu	八月
September	*ku* ga-tsu	九月
October	*jū* ga-tsu	十月
November	*jū*-i-chi *ga*-tsu	十一月
December	*jū*-ni *ga*-tsu	十二月

ENGLISH	PRONUNCIATION	JAPANESE

USEFUL EXPRESSIONS, QUESTIONS, AND ANSWERS

Do you speak English?	*ei*-go ga wa- *ka*-ri-ma-su *ka*	英語がわかりますか。
I don't speak Japanese.	ni- *hon*-go ga wa- *ka*-ri-ma- *sen*	日本語がわかりません。
I don't understand.	wa- *ka*-ri-ma- *sen*	わかりません。
I understand.	wa- *ka*-ri-ma-shi- *ta*	わかりました。
I don't know.	*shi*-ri-ma- *sen*	知りません。
I'm American (British).	wa- *ta*-shi wa a- *me*-ri-ka (i- *gi*-ri-su) jin *desu*	私はアメリカ(イギリス)人です。
What's your name?	o- *na*-ma-e wa *nan* desu *ka*	お名前はなんですか。
My name is [name].	[name] to *mo*-shi- *ma*-su	~と申します。
What time is it?	i-ma *nan*-ji desu *ka*	今何時ですか。
How?	*dō* yat-te	どうやって。
When?	*i*-tsu	いつ。
yesterday/today/ tomorrow	ki- *nō* /kyō/ *ashi*-ta	昨日 / 今日 / 明日
this morning	*ke*-sa	けさ
this afternoon	*kyō* no *go*-go	今日の午後
tonight	*kom*-ban	今晩
Excuse me, what?	su- *mi*-ma- *sen*, *nan* desu *ka*	すみません、何ですか。
What is this/that?	*ko*-re/ *so*-re wa *nan* desu *ka*	これ / それは何ですか。
Why?	*na*-ze desu *ka*	なぜですか。
Who?	*da*-re desu *ka*	だれですか。
I am lost.	*mi*-chi ni ma-yo-i- *mashi*-ta	道に迷いました。
Where is the [place]	[place] wa *do*-ko desu *ka*	はどこですか
.. train station?	e-ki	駅
.. subway station?	chi- *ka*-te-tsu-no eki	地下鉄の駅
.. bus stop?	*ba*-su *no*-ri- *ba*	バス乗り場

ENGLISH	PRONUNCIATION	JAPANESE
.. taxi stand?	*ta*-ku-shi-i *no*-ri- *ba*	タクシー乗り場
.. airport?	*kū*-kō	空港
.. post office?	*yū*-bin- *kyo*-ku	郵便局
.. bank?	*gin*-kō	銀行
.. [name] hotel?	[name] ho- *te*-ru	ホテル
.. elevator?	e-re- *bē*-tā	エレベーター
Where are the restrooms?	*to*-i-re wa *do*-ko desu *ka*	トイレはどこですか。
here/there/over there	*ko*-ko/ *so*-ko/ *a*-so-ko	ここ / そこ / あそこ
left/right	hi- *da*-ri/ *mi*-gi	左 / 右
straight ahead	mas- *su*-gu	まっすぐ
Is it near (far)?	chi- *ka*-i (*tō*-i) desu *ka*	近い（遠い）ですか。
Are there any rooms?	*he*-ya ga a-ri- *ma*-su *ka*	部屋がありますか。
I'd like [item].	[item] ga ho- *shi*-i no desu ga	がほしいのですが。
.. newspaper	*shim*-bun	新聞
.. stamp	*kit*-te	切手
.. key	*ka*-gi	鍵
I'd like to buy [item].	[item] o kai- *ta*-i no desu ga	を買いたいのですが。
.. a ticket to [destination].	[destination] *ma*-de no *kip*-pu	までの切符
map	*chi*-zu	地図
How much is it?	i- *ku*-ra desu *ka*	いくらですか。
It's expensive (cheap).	ta- *ka*-i (ya- *su*-i) de su *ne*	高い（安い）ですね。
a little (a lot)	su- *ko*-shi (*ta*-ku-san)	少し（たくさん）
more/less	*mot*-to ō-ku/ su-ku-na-ku	もっと多く / 少なく
enough/too much	*jū*-bun/ō- *su*-gi-ru	十分 / 多すぎる
I'd like to exchange	*ryō*-ga e shi-te i- *ta*-da-ke-masu *ka*	両替していただけますか。
.. dollars to yen	*do*-ru o *en* ni	ドルを円に
.. pounds to yen	*pon*-do o *en* ni	ポンドを円に

ENGLISH	PRONUNCIATION	JAPANESE
How do you say [word] in Japanese?	ni- *hon*-go de wa [word] wa *dō* *i*-i-masu *ka*	日本語で.はどう言いますか。
I am ill/sick.	wa- *ta*-shi wa *byō*-ki desu	私は病気です。
Please call a doctor/an ambulance.	*i*-sha/kyū-kyū-sha o *yon*-de ku-da- *sa*-i	医者/救急車を呼んでください。
Please call the police.	*ke*-i-sa-tsu o *yon*-de ku da *sa* i	警察を呼んでください。
Help!	*ta*-su- *ke*-te	助けて!

USEFUL WORDS

airport	*kū* kō	空港
bay	wan	湾
beach	*ha*-ma	浜
behind	*u* shi-ro	後ろ
bridge	*ha*-shi or - *ha*-shi	橋
bullet train, literally "new trunk line"	*Shin*-kan-sen	新幹線
castle	o- *shi*-ro or -jo	城
cherry blossoms	*sa*-kura	桜
city or municipality	-shi	市
department store	de- *pā*-to	デパート
district	-gun	郡
east	hi- *ga*-shi	東
exit	*de*-guchi or -guchi	出口
festival	*ma*-tsuri	祭
foreigner	*gai*-jin (more politely: gai- *ko*-ku-jin)	外人
garden	*ni*-wa	庭
gate	mon or torii	門 / 鳥居
hill	oka	丘
hot-spring spa	*on*-sen	温泉
in front of	*ma*-e	前

ENGLISH	PRONUNCIATION	JAPANESE
island	shima or -jima/-tō	島
Japanese words rendered in roman letters	*rō*maji	ローマ字
lake	*mi*-zu- *u*-mi or -ko	湖
main road	*kai*-dō or *kō*-dō	街道 / 公道
morning market	asa- *i*-chi	朝市
mountain	yama or –san	山
museum	bi- *ju*-tsu-kan for art; haku- *bu*-tsu-kan for natural history, etc.	美術館・博物館
north	kita	北
park	*kō*-en	公園
peninsula	-hantō	半島
plateau	*kō*-gen	高原
pond	ike or -ike	池
prefecture	-ken/-fu	県 / 府
pub (Japanese-style)	iza- *ka*-ya	居酒屋
river	kawa or -gawa	川 / 河
sea	*u*-mi or -kai	海
section or ward	-ku	区
shop	*mi*-se or -ya	店 / 屋
shrine	jinja or -gu	神社 / 宮
south	mi- *na*-mi	南
street	michi or -dō	道
subway	chi- *ka*-tetsu	地下鉄
temple	tera or -ji/-in	寺 / 院
town	*ma*-chi	町
train	*den*-sha	電車
train station	eki	駅
valley	*ta*-ni	谷
west	*ni*-shi	西

MENU GUIDE

BASICS AND USEFUL EXPRESSIONS

a bottle of	*ip*-pon	一本
a glass/cup of	*ip*-pai	一杯
ashtray	*ha*-i- *za*-ra	灰皿
bill/check	kan- *jō*	勘定
bread	pan	パン
breakfast	*chō*-sho-ku	朝食
butter	ba- *tā*	バター
cheers!	kam- *pai*	乾杯!
chopsticks	*ha*-shi	箸
cocktail	*ka*-ku- *te*-ru	カクテル
Does that include dinner?	*Yū*-sho-ku gatsu-ki- *ma*-su-ka	夕食が付きますか。
fork	*fō*-ku	フォーク
I am diabetic.	wa- *ta*-shi wa tō-*nyō*-byō de su	私は糖尿病です。
I am dieting.	*da*-i-et-to *chū* desu	ダイエット中です。
I am a vegetarian.	*saisho*-ku shu- *gi*-sha/ beji- *tari*-an de-su	菜食主義者 / ベジタリアンです。
I cannot eat [item].	[item] wa *ta*-be-ra- re-ma- *sen*	は食べられません。
I'd like to order.	*chū*-mon o shi- *tai* desu	注文をしたいです。
I'd like [item].	[item] o o-ne- *gai*-shi-ma su	をお願いします。
I'm hungry.	o-na-ka ga *su*-i-te i- *ma*-su	お腹が空いています。
I'm thirsty.	*no*-do ga ka- *wa*-i-te i- *ma*-su	喉が渇いています。
It's tasty.	o-i-shi-i (ma- *zu*-i) desu	おいしい(まずい)です。
knife	*na*-i-fu	ナイフ
lunch	*chū*-sho-ku	昼食
menu	me-nyū	メニュー
napkin	*na*-pu- *kin*	ナプキン

pepper	ko- *shō*	こしょう
plate	*sa*-ra	皿
Please give me [item].	[item] o ku-da- *sa*-i	をください。
salt	*shi*-o	塩
set menu	*te*-i-sho-ku	定食
spoon	su- *pūn*	スプーン
sugar	sa-tō	砂糖
wine list	*wa*-i-n *ri*-su-to	ワインリスト
What do you recommend?	o-su-su-me *ryō*-ri wa *nan* desu *ka*	おすすめ料理は何ですか。

MEAT DISHES

gyō-za	minced pork spiced with ginger and garlic in a Chinese wrapper and fried or steamed	ギョウザ
hayashi *rai*-su	beef flavored with tomato and brown sauce with onions and peas over rice	ハヤシライス
kara- *a*-ge	deep-fried chicken	から揚げ
karē- *rai*-su	curried rice: thick curry gravy typically containing beef over white rice	カレーライス
katsu- *ka*-rē	curried rice with tonkatsu	カツカレー
niku- *ja*-ga	beef and potatoes stewed together with sweetened soy sauce	肉じゃが
okonomi- *ya*-ki	a Japanese pancake made from a batter of flour, egg, cabbage, and meat or seafood, griddle-cooked and sprinkled with green onions and a Worcestershire-soy-based sauce	お好み焼き

o-yako- *dom*-buri (*o*-yako-don)	literally, "mother and child bowl": cooked chicken and egg in broth over rice	親子どんぶり(親子丼)
rōru *kya*-betsu	rolled cabbage; beef or pork rolled in cabbage and cooked	ロールキャベツ
shabu-shabu	thin slices of beef swirled for an instant in boiling water flavored with soup stock and then dipped into a thin sauce	しゃぶしゃぶ
shō-ga-yaki	pork cooked with ginger	しょうが焼き
shū-mai	shrimp or pork wrapped in a light dough and steamed (originally Chinese)	シュウマイ
su- *bu*-ta	sweet-and-sour pork, originally a Chinese dish	酢豚
suki- *ya*-ki	one-pot meal of thinly sliced beef, green onions, mushrooms, thin noodles, and tofu simmered in a mixture of soy sauce, mirin, and a little sugar	すき焼き
su- *tē*-ki	steak	ステーキ
tanin- *dom*-buri (*ta*-nin-don)	literally, "strangers in a bowl": similar to oyako-domburi, but with beef instead of chicken	他人どんぶり(他人丼)
ton- *ka*-tsu	breaded deep-fried pork cutlets	トンカツ
yaki- *ni*-ku	thin slices of beef marinated then barbecued over an open fire at the table	焼き肉

yaki- *to*-ri	bits of chicken on skewers with green onions, marinated in sweet soy sauce and grilled	焼き鳥

SEAFOOD DISHES

a-ge- *za*-kana	deep-fried fish	揚げ魚
a-ji	horse mackerel	あじ
a- *sa*-ri no *sa*-kamushi	clams steamed with rice wine	あさりの酒蒸し
bu-ri	yellowtail	ぶり
do- *jō* no yana- *ga*-wa-nabe	loach cooked with burdock root and egg in an earthen dish	どじょうの柳川鍋
ebi fu- *ra*-i	deep-fried breaded prawns	海老フライ
ika	squid	イカ
i- *wa*-shi	sardines	いわし
karei fu- *ra*-i	deep-fried breaded flounder	かれいフライ
ka-tsuo no ta- *ta*-ki	bonito lightly braised, eaten with chopped ginger and scallions and thin soy sauce	かつおのたたき
ma-guro	tuna	まぐろ
ni- *za*-kana	soy-simmered fish	煮魚
sa-ba no *mi*-so-ni	mackerel stewed with soybean paste	さばの味噌煮
sam-ma	saury pike	さんま
sa-shimi	fresh raw fish served sliced thin on a bed of white radish with a saucer of soy sauce and horseradish	刺身
sa- *wa*-ra	Spanish mackerel	さわら
sha-ke / *sā*-mon	salmon	しゃけ / サーモン
shime- *sa*-ba	mackerel marinated in vinegar	しめさば

shio- *ya*-ki	fish sprinkled with salt and broiled until crisp	塩焼き
tako	octopus	たこ
ten-jū	deep-fried prawns served over rice with sauce	天重
teri- *ya*-ki	fish basted in soy sauce and broiled	照り焼き
u-na-jū	eel marinated in a slightly sweet soy sauce, charcoal-broiled, and served over rice	うな重
yaki- *za*-kana	broiled fish	焼き魚

SUSHI

a-ji	horse mackerel	あじ
ama- *e*-bi	sweet shrimp	甘えび
a-nago	conger eel	あなご
ao- *ya*-gi	round clam	あおやぎ
chirashi *zu*-shi	a variety of seafood arranged on the top of a bowl of rice	ちらし寿司
e-bi	shrimp	えび
futo- *ma*-ki	big roll with egg and pickled vegetables	太巻き
hamachi	yellowtail	はまち
hirame	flounder	ひらめ
ho- *ta*-te-gai	scallop	ほたて貝
ika	squid	いか
i kura	salmon roe	いくら
ka-ni	crab	かに
kappa- *ma*-ki	cucumber roll	かっぱ巻き
kariforunia- *ma*-ki	California roll, with crabmeat and avocado (originally American)	カリフォルニア巻き
ka-zuno- *ko*	herring roe	数の子

ko- *ha*-da	shad	こはだ
ma-guro	tuna	まぐろ
ma-ki *zu*-shi	raw fish, vegetables, or other ingredients rolled in sushi rice and wrapped in dried seaweed	巻き寿司
mi-ru-gai	giant clam	みる貝
nigiri *zu*-shi	rice shaped by hand into bite-size cakes and topped with raw or cooked fish or other ingredients	にぎり寿司
sa-ba	mackerel	さば
sha-ke / *sā*-mon	salmon	しゃけ / サーモン
shinko- *ma*-ki	a type of pickle rolled in rice and wrapped in seaweed	新香巻き
tai	red snapper	たい
tako	octopus	たこ
ta-mago	egg	玉子
tekka- *ma*-ki	small bits of tuna rolled in rice and wrapped in seaweed	鉄火巻き
to-ro	fatty tuna	とろ
u-ni	sea urchin	うに

VEGETABLE DISHES

ae- *mo*-no	vegetables dressed with sauces	和えもの
daigaku *i*-mo	fried yams in a sweet syrup	大学いも
go-bō	burdock root	ごぼう
hō- *ren*-so	spinach	ほうれん草
ka-bocha	pumpkin	かぼちゃ
kim-pira *go*-bō	carrots and burdock root, fried with soy sauce	きんぴらごぼう

kyū-ri	cucumber	きゅうり
ne-gi	green onions	ねぎ
ni- *mo*-no	vegetables simmered in a soy- and sake-based sauce	煮物
o- *den*	street food of various types of fish cakes, vegetables, and boiled eggs simmered in a soy fish stock	おでん
o-hi- *ta*-shi	boiled vegetables with soy sauce and dried shaved bonito or sesame seeds	おひたし
ren-kon	lotus root	れんこん
sato- *i*-mo	taro root	さといも
su-no- *mo*-no	vegetables seasoned with vinegar	酢の物
ta-kenoko	bamboo shoots	タケノコ
tem-pura	vegetables, shrimp, or fish deep-fried in a light batter and dipped into a thin sauce with grated white radish	天ぷら
tsuke- *mo*-no	Japanese pickles made from white radish, eggplant, or other vegetables	漬け物
ya- *sai* i- *ta*-me	stir-fried vegetables	野菜炒め

EGG DISHES

cha-wan *mu*-shi	vegetables, shrimp, etc., steamed in egg custard	茶碗蒸し
medama- *ya*-ki	fried eggs, sunny-side up	目玉焼き
omu- *rai*-su	omelet with rice inside	オムライス
yude *ta*-mago	boiled eggs	ゆで卵

TOFU DISHES

agedashi *dō*-fu	deep-fried plain tofu garnished with spring onions, dipped in hot broth	揚げだし豆腐
hiya- *yak*-ko	cold tofu with soy sauce and grated ginger	冷やっこ
mābō *dō*-fu	tofu and ground pork in a spicy sauce (originally Chinese)	マーボー豆腐
tō-fu no *den*-gaku	tofu broiled on skewers and flavored with miso	豆腐の田楽
yu- *dō*-fu	boiled tofu with green onions	湯豆腐

RICE DISHES

chā-han	fried rice with vegetables and pork	チャーハン(炒飯)
chi- *ma*-ki	sticky rice wrapped in bamboo skin	ちまき
gohan	steamed white rice	ご飯
o- *ka*-yu	rice porridge	お粥
oni- *gi*-ri	triangular balls of rice with fish or vegetables inside and wrapped in sheets of dry seaweed	おにぎり

SOUPS

miso *shi*-ru	thin broth containing tofu, mushrooms, or other ingredients in a soup flavored with miso or soybean paste	みそ汁
sui- *mo*-no	clear broth, often including fish and tofu	吸い物
ton- *ji*-ru	pork soup with vegetables	豚汁

NOODLES

hiya- *mu*-gi	similar to sōmen, but thicker	ひやむぎ

rā-men	Chinese noodles in soy sauce, miso, or salt-flavored broth, often with chāshū (roast pork)	ラーメン
so-ba	buckwheat noodles served in a broth or, during the summer, cold on a bamboo mesh (called *za*-ru soba)	そば
sō-men	summer dish of very thin wheat noodles, usually served cold with a tsuyu or thin sauce	そうめん
u-don	broad flour noodles that can be lunch in a light broth, or a meal (nabe- *ya*-ki *u*-don) when meat, chicken, egg, and vegetables are added	うどん
yaki- *so*-ba	noodles fried with beef and cabbage, garnished with pickled ginger and vegetables	焼きそば

FRUIT

an-zu	apricot	あんず
bu *dō*	grapes	ぶどう
i-chigo	strawberries	いちご
ichi- *ji*-ku	figs	いちじく
kaki	persimmon	柿
kuri	chestnuts	栗
ku-rumi	walnuts	くるみ
mi- *kan*	tangerine (mandarin orange)	みかん
mo-mo	peach	桃
nashi	Japanese pear	梨
ringo	apple	リンゴ

saku- *ram*-bo	cherry	さくらんぼ
sui-ka	watermelon	西瓜

DESSERT

aisu	ice cream	アイス
kōhii *ze*-rii	coffee-flavored gelatin	コーヒーゼリー
pu-rin	caramel pudding	プリン
wa- *ga*-shi	sweet bean-paste confection	和菓子
yō-kan	sweet bean-paste jelly	ようかん

DRINKS

Alcoholic

bii-ru	beer	ビール
chū-hai	shōchū mixed with soda water, lemon juice, or other flavoring	チューハイ
nama *bii*-ru	draft beer	生ビール
sa-ke	rice wine, also called Ni- *hon*-shu, which can be semi-sec (*a*-makuchi) or dry (*ka*-rakuchi), usually served warm (atsukan), although purists prefer it cold	酒, 日本酒
shō-chū	spirit distilled from potatoes	焼酎

Nonalcoholic

ja-sumin cha	jasmine tea	ジャスミン茶
jū-su	juice, but can also mean any soft drink	ジュース
kō-cha	black tea	紅茶
kōhii	coffee	コーヒー
ni- *hon* cha	Japanese green tea, also called simply o-cha	日本茶
ū-ron cha	Oolong tea	ウーロン茶

TRAVEL SMART TOKYO

GETTING HERE AND AROUND

AIR TRAVEL

Flying time to Japan is 14 hours from New York, 13 hours from Chicago, and 10 hours from Los Angeles. The trip east, because of tailwinds, can be about 45 minutes shorter, and the trip west that much longer because of headwinds.

Most major U.S. airports offer multiple direct flights to Tokyo each day.

Flights to Osaka or Nagoya usually involve a transfer, though some West Coast hubs like San Francisco and Los Angeles run direct flights. Because of the distance, fares to Japan tend to be expensive, usually around $1,200 for a seat in coach.

Both of Japan's major carriers have reduced prices for flights within the country. JAL offers the Oneworld Yokoso Visit Japan Fare; ANA has the Experience Japan Fare. These are real cost-savers if your trip includes destinations such as Kyushu or Hokkaido, though tickets must be booked outside Japan, and there are restrictions on use in peak times.

All domestic flights in Japan are no-smoking.

Airline Security Issues Transportation Security Administration. *www.tsa.gov.*

Air Pass Information

ANA Experience Japan Fare. *800/235-9262 All Nippon Airways in U.S. www.ana.co.jp.*

Oneworld Yokoso Visit Japan Fare. *800/525-3663 Japan Airlines www.jal.co.jp/yokosojapan.*

TRAVEL TIMES FROM TOKYO

To	By Air	By Car or Bus	By Train
Osaka	1¼ hours	7–8 hours	2½ hours
Hiroshima	1½ hours	10 hours	4 hours
Kyoto	1¼ hour	7 hours	2 hours
Fukuoka	2 hours	14 hours	5 hours
Sapporo	1½ hours	15 hours	9 hours

TIP→ Ask the local tourist board about hotel and local transportation packages that include tickets to major museum exhibits or other special events.

AIRPORTS

The major gateway to Japan is Tokyo's Narita Airport (NRT), 80 km (50 miles) northeast of the city. The Haneda Airport International Terminal also has flights to major international cities and is only 20 km (12 miles) south of central Tokyo.

Most domestic flights to and from Tokyo are out of Haneda Airport.

There are three terminals at Narita Airport. Terminals 1 and 2 are for international flights, while the newly opened Terminal 3 is for flights on domestic and international low-cost carriers. Terminal 1 has two adjoining wings, north and south. When you arrive, your first task should be to convert your money into yen; you need it for transportation into Tokyo. In both wings, ATMs and money-exchange counters are in the wall between the customs inspection area and the arrival lobby. All three terminals have a Japan National Tourism Organization information center, where you can get free maps, brochures, and other visitor information. Ticket counters for airport limousine buses and express trains to Tokyo are directly across from the customs-area exits at Terminals 1 and 2.

If you have time to kill at Narita, take a local Keisei Line train into Narita town

15 minutes away, where a traditional shopping street and the beautiful Narita-san Shinsho Temple are a peaceful escape from airport noise.

Flying into Haneda provides visitors with quicker access to downtown Tokyo, which is a short monorail ride away. Stop by the currency exchange and Tourist Information Desk in the second-floor arrival lobby before taking a train into the city. There are also numerous jade-uniformed concierge staff on hand to help passengers with any questions.

Airport Information Haneda Airport (HND). ☎ *03/5757–8111* 🌐 *www.haneda-airport.com.* **Narita Airport (NRT).** ☎ *0476/34–8000* 🌐 *www.narita-airport.jp.*

GROUND TRANSPORTATION

Known as "The Gateway to Japan," Narita is about 90 minutes—dependent on city traffic—by taxi or bus from central Tokyo. The Keisei Skyliner and Japan Railways NEX are the easiest ways to get into the city.

Directly across from the customs-area exits at both terminals are the ticket counters for buses to Tokyo. Buses leave from platforms just outside terminal exits, exactly on schedule, the departure time is on the ticket. The Airport Limousine has shuttle-bus service from Narita to Tokyo starting at ¥2,900. Cheaper options include The Access Narita (¥1,000) and Tokyo Shuttle (¥900).

Japan Railways trains stop at Narita Airport Terminals 1 and 2. The fastest and most comfortable is the Narita Limited Express (NEX). Trains from the airport go directly to the central Tokyo Station in just about an hour, then continue to Yokohama and Ofuna. Daily departures begin at 7:44 am; the last train is at 9:44 pm. In addition to regular seats, there is a first-class Green Car and private four-person compartments. All seats are reserved, and you need to reserve one for yourself in advance, as this train fills quickly.

The Keisei Skyliner train runs every 20–30 minutes between the airport terminals and Keisei-Ueno Station. The trip takes around 40 minutes. The first Skyliner leaves Narita for Ueno at 7:28 am, the last at 10:30 pm. From Ueno to Narita the first Skyliner is at 5:58 am, the last at 6:20 pm. Keisei's slightly slower Access Express service also runs between Narita and Keisei-Ueno. If you are arriving with a Japan Rail Pass and staying in Tokyo for a few days, it is best to pay for the transfer into the city and wait to activate the rail pass for travel beyond Tokyo.

Contacts The Access Narita. 🌐 *accessnarita.jp.* **Airport Limousine.** ☎ *03/3665–7232* 🌐 *www.limousinebus.co.jp.* **Japan Railways.** ☎ *050/2016–1603 for JR East InfoLine* 🌐 *www.jreast.co.jp/e.* **Keisei Railway.** ☎ *03/3831–0131 for Ueno information counter, 0476/32–8505 at Narita Airport* 🌐 *www.keisei.co.jp/keisei/tetudou/skyliner/us.* **Tokyo Shuttle.** 🌐 *www.keiseibus.co.jp/en/kousoku/nrt16.html.*

TRANSFERS BETWEEN AIRPORTS

Transfer between Narita and Haneda, the international and domestic airports, is easiest by the Airport Limousine Bus, which should take 75 minutes and costs ¥3,000. The Keisei Access Express also runs between the two airports but requires one transfer at Aoto Station.

FLIGHTS

Japan Airlines (JAL), United Airlines American Airlines, Delta Airlines, and All Nippon Airways (ANA) link North American cities with Tokyo's Haneda and Narita airports. Most of these airlines also fly in and out of Japan's two other international airports, Kansai International Airport, located south of Osaka and Centrair, near Nagoya.

Airline Contacts All Nippon Airways. ☎ *800/235–9262 in U.S., 03/6741–1120 in Japan for domestic flights, 03/3239–0298 in Japan for international flights* 🌐 *www.ana.co.jp.* **American Airlines.** ☎ *800/433–7300 in U.S., 03/3298–7677 in Japan* 🌐 *www.aa.com.* **Delta Airlines.** ☎ *800/241–4141 in U.S., 0570/077–733 in Japan* 🌐 *www.delta.com.* **Japan Airlines.** ☎ *800/525–3663 in U.S., 03/6733–3062 in Japan,* 🌐 *www.jal.co.jp/en.* **United Airlines.** ☎ *800/864–8331 in U.S., 03/6732–5011 in Japan* 🌐 *www.united.com.*

TRAVEL TIMES INTO TOKYO

From Narita	To	Fares	Times	Notes
Airport Limousine (buses)	Various $$$$ hotels in Tokyo and JR Tokyo and Shinjuku train stations	¥3,100	Every hr until 9 pm	70–90 mins, can be longer in traffic
Airport Limousine (buses)	Tokyo City Air Terminal (TCAT)	¥2,900	Every 10–20 mins, 7 am–10:55 pm	
The Access Narita	Ginza, Tokyo Station	¥1,000	Every 10–20 mins, 7:25 am–10:45 pm	
Tokyo Shuttle	Tokyo Station	¥900	Every 20 mins, 7 am–11:15 pm	
Narita Limited Express (NEX)	Central Tokyo Station, then continue to Yokohama and Ofuna	One-way fare ¥3,020; Green Car from ¥4,560	Daily departures begin at 7:44 am; last train is at 9:44 pm	All seats are reserved.
Keisei Skyliner train	Keisei-Ueno Station	¥2,470	Every 20–30 mins, 7:28 am–10:30 pm	All seats are reserved.
Keisei Access Express	Keisei-Ueno Station	¥1,240	Every 20–30 mins, 5:46 am–10:34 pm	No seats are reserved.
Taxi	Central Tokyo	¥20,000 or more		
From Haneda	**To**	**Fares**	**Times**	**Notes**
Tokyo Monorail	Central Tokyo	¥490	Every 20 mins, 5:13 am–midnight	Trip takes 25–30 mins. Connect to other major stations via the Yamanote Line at Hamamatsucho Station.
Taxi	Central Tokyo	¥5,000–¥6,000		

BOAT TRAVEL

Ferries connect most of the islands of Japan. Some of the more popular routes are from Tokyo to Tomakomai or Kushiro in Hokkaido; from Tokyo to Shikoku; and from Tokyo or Osaka to Kyushu. You can purchase ferry tickets in advance from travel agencies or at offices on the piers before boarding. The ferries are inexpensive and a pleasant, if slow, way of traveling. Private cabins are available, but most passengers travel in the economy class, where they sleep on the carpeted floor in one large room and eat, drink, and enjoy themselves in a convivial atmosphere. There is little English information for local ferries, apart from four companies serving the Inland Sea between Osaka/Kobe and Kyushu. ⇨ *For information on local ferries, see the Essentials sections for individual towns within each chapter.*

Information Ferry Sunflower. 🌐 *www.ferry-sunflower.co.jp.* **Hankyu Ferry.** 🌐 *www.han9f.co.jp.* **Meimon Taiyo Ferry.** 🌐 *www.cityline.co.jp.*

BUS TRAVEL

Japan Railways (JR) has a number of long-distance buses that are comfortable and inexpensive and also runs short-distance buses in some areas that have limited rail service. You can use Japan Rail Passes *(Train Travel, below)* on some, but not all, of these buses. Japan Rail Passes are not accepted by private bus companies. Bus routes and schedules are constantly changing, but tourist information offices have up-to-date details. It's now possible to travel from Osaka to Tokyo for as little as ¥5,000 one-way. Buses are generally modern and very comfortable, though overnight journeys are best avoided. Nearly all are now no-smoking. Daytime highway buses are often an excellent way to get to many interesting out-of-the-way destinations.

City buses, especially outside of Tokyo, are quite convenient, but be sure of your route and destination, because the bus driver probably won't speak English. Local buses usually have a set cost, anywhere from ¥100 to ¥200, depending on the route and municipality that operates them, in which case you board at the front of the bus and pay as you get on. On some buses cost is determined by the distance you travel. You take a ticket when you board at the rear door of the bus; it bears the number of the stop at which you boarded. Your fare depends on your destination and is indicated by a board at the front of the bus. Bus schedules can be hard to fathom if you don't read Japanese, however, so it's best to ask for help at a tourist information office. The Nihon Bus Association has information about routes and which companies have English Web information.

Reservations on long-distance routes are not always essential except at peak holiday times and on the most popular routes, like Tokyo–Osaka.

Bus Information Nihon Bus Association. 🌐 *www.bus.or.jp/en.* **Willer Express.** ☎ *050/5805–0383* 🌐 *willerexpress.com/en.*

CAR TRAVEL

You need an international driving permit (IDP) to drive in Japan. IDPs are available from the American Automobile Association. These international permits, valid only in conjunction with your regular driver's license, are universally recognized; having one may save you a problem with local authorities. Drivers must be 18 years of age. Driving is on the left, and bear in mind that this adjustment may be difficult for some drivers.

Major roads in Japan are sufficiently marked in English, and on country roads there's usually someone to ask for help. However, it's a good idea to have a detailed map with town names written in *kanji* (Japanese characters) and *romaji* (romanized Japanese).

Car travel along the Tokyo–Kyoto–Hiroshima corridor and in other built-up areas of Japan is not as convenient as the trains. Roads are congested, gas is expensive, and highway tolls are exorbitant (tolls between Tokyo and Kyoto amount to ¥10,550). In major cities, with the exception of main arteries, English signs are few and far between, one-way streets often lead you off the track, and parking is often hard to find.

Car-rental rates in Tokyo begin at around ¥5,500 a day and ¥37,800 a week, including tax, for an economy car with unlimited mileage.

Local Agencies Nippon Rent-A-Car. ☎ *03/6859–6234* 🌐 *www.nipponrentacar.co.jp/english.* **Nissan Rent A Car.** 🌐 *nissan-rentacar.com/english.* **Toyota Rent a Car.** ☎ *03/5954–8020 in Tokyo, 0800/7000–815 toll-free in Japan* 🌐 *rent.toyota.co.jp/eng/.*

GASOLINE

Gas stations are plentiful along Japan's toll roads, and prices are fairly uniform across the country. Prices are high—roughly ¥150 per liter. Credit cards are accepted everywhere and are even encouraged—there are discounts for them at some places. Self-service stations have recently become legal, so if you pump your own gas you may get a small discount. Often you pay after putting in the gas, but there are also machines where you put money in first and then use the receipt to get change back. Staff will offer to take away trash and clean car windows. Tipping is not customary.

PARKING

There is little on-street parking in Japan. Parking is usually in staffed parking lots or in parking towers within buildings. Expect to pay upward of ¥300 per hour. Parking regulations are strictly enforced, and illegally parked vehicles are towed away. Recovery fees start at ¥30,000 and increase hourly.

ROAD CONDITIONS

Roads in Japan are often narrower than those in the United States, but they're well maintained in general. Driving in cities can be troublesome, as there are many narrow, one-way streets and little in the way of English road signs except on major arteries. Japanese drivers stick to the speed limit, but widely ignore bans on mobile phone use and dashboard televisions.

ROADSIDE EMERGENCIES

Emergency telephones along highways can be used to contact the authorities. Car-rental agencies generally provide roadside assistance services. Mobile phones are now so widespread that local drivers can call for help from the middle of nowhere.

Emergency Services Police. ☎ *110.*

RULES OF THE ROAD

In Japan driving is on the left. Speed limits vary, but generally the limit is 100 kph (60 mph) on motorways, 40 kph (25 mph) in cities. Penalties for speeding are severe. By law, car seats must be installed if the driver is traveling with a child under six, while the driver and all passengers in cars must wear seat belts at all times. Driving while using handheld phones is illegal.

Many smaller streets lack sidewalks, so cars, bicycles, and pedestrians share the same space. Fortunately, considering the narrowness of the streets and the volume of traffic, most Japanese drivers are technically skilled. However, they may not allow quite as much distance between cars as you're used to. Be prepared for sudden lane changes by other drivers. When waiting at intersections after dark, many drivers, as a courtesy to other drivers, turn off their main headlights to prevent glare. Since 2006 there has been a nationwide crackdown on drunk driving, following a spate of horrific, headline-grabbing accidents, so it's wisest to avoid alcohol entirely if you plan to drive.

CRUISE SHIP TRAVEL

Japan is a popular cruise ship destination, particularly for upscale and luxury cruise lines, many of which do an annual around-Japan cruise. In fact, you might very well find yourself visiting more off-the-beaten-path destinations on a cruise than on a land-based tour, though the trade-off often means spending considerably less time in each place.

Hakodate, Hiroshima, Kobe, Nagasaki, Osaka, and Yokohama are among the Japanese ports welcoming foreign cruise ships.

MOTORCYCLE TRAVEL

With its super-narrow roads and alleyways, a fantastic way to tool around Tokyo is with a scooter, while the rest of the country—with its rolling hills, mountains, and shoreline—is also a pleasure to see via motorcycle. There are many bikers in Japan, so highways, rest stops, and campgrounds are all equipped to handle whatever bike you choose to tour with. Japan Bike Rentals is run by a *gaijin* (foreigner) so you can drop your dictionaries and do all the paperwork in English—and online. All riders need a passport, a valid unrestricted motorcycle license from their own country, and an International Driving Permit. Japan Bike Rentals is open seven days a week, but you need to make your booking online first, whether to rent a bike, rent a GPS for a self-guided tour, or join a guided tour. It's closed in January and February. Rental819 has a number of branches in Tokyo featuring Harley-Davidson, Ducati, and Triumph motorcycles.

Contacts Japan Bike Rentals. ☎ *03/3584–5185* 🌐 *japanbikerentals.com.* **Rental819.** ☎ *0120/819–147* 🌐 *www.rental819.com/english.*

SUBWAY TRAVEL

Tokyo Metro and Toei operate separate subway lines in Tokyo, with Tokyo Metro operating the majority of them. The companies charge separate fares—that is, a ticket from one company is not valid on a train operated by the other, so you want to complete a journey on lines operated by one company rather than switching. Some especially useful lines for visitors are the Ginza Line, which moves between Asakusa and Shibuya, and the Oedo and Marunouchi lines, which loop around the city center.

Contacts Toei. 🌐 *www.kotsu.metro.tokyo.jp/eng.* **Tokyo Metro.** 🌐 *www.tokyometro.jp/en.*

PURCHASING TICKETS

Basic train and subway fares within Tokyo are between ¥130 and ¥310, depending on how far you travel. Purchase tickets from machines that take coins or cash near the gates. Maps above each machine—usually in Japanese and English in central Tokyo—list destinations and fares. **TIP→ Sometimes the station map will be written only in Japanese. In that case, buy the lowest-priced ticket and adjust the fare upon arrival.**

PREPAID CARDS AND PASSES

Suica is a rechargeable debit card that can be used on JR and non-JR trains and also subways. It's also accepted for payment at convenience stores and some vending machines. **PASMO,** another rechargeable prepaid card, operates the same way. You need to pay a nonreturnable ¥500 to be issued a Suica or PASMO card, but it's worth it to avoid buying tickets and worrying about fares and have the flexibility to flit between all of Tokyo's transportation networks. The **Tokyo Tour Ticket (Tokyo Furii Kippu)** is a one-day pass for unlimited travel on JR lines, subways, and buses within Tokyo's 23 wards; it costs ¥1,590 and is available at subway stations and JR ticket offices.

Contacts PASMO. 🌐 *www.pasmo.co.jp/en.* **Suica.** 🌐 *www.jreast.co.jp/e/pass/suica.html.* **Tokyo Tour Ticket.** 🌐 *www.jreast.co.jp/e/pass/tokyo_free.html.*

TAXI TRAVEL

Taxis are an expensive way of getting around cities in Japan, although nascent deregulation moves are easing the market a little. In Tokyo, for instance, the first 2 km (1 mile) cost ¥730 and it's ¥90 for every additional 280 meters (400 yards). Between 10 pm and 5 am there is a 20% service charge on top of that. If possible, avoid using taxis during rush hours (7:30 am–9:30 am and 5 pm–7 pm).

In general, it's easy to hail a cab: do not shout or wave wildly—simply raise your hand if you need a taxi. Japanese taxis have automatic door-opening systems, so do not try to open the taxi door. Stand back when the cab comes to a stop—if you are too close, the door may slam into you. When you leave the cab, do not try to close the door; the driver will do it automatically. Only the curbside rear door opens. A red light on the dashboard (visible through the front window) indicates an available taxi, and a green light indicates an occupied taxi.

Drivers are for the most part courteous, though not necessarily chatty. Unless you're going to a well-known destination such as a major hotel, it's advisable to have a Japanese person write out your destination in Japanese. Your hotel concierge can do this for you. Remember, there is no need to tip.

TRAIN TRAVEL

Riding Japanese trains is one of the pleasures of travel in the country. Efficient and convenient, trains run frequently and on schedule. The Shinkansen (bullet train), one of the fastest trains in the world, connects major cities north and south of Tokyo. It is only slightly less expensive than flying, but is in many ways more convenient because train stations are more centrally located than airports (if you have a Japan Rail Pass, it's extremely affordable).

Other trains, though not as fast as the Shinkansen, are just as convenient and substantially cheaper. There are three types of train services: *futsu* (local service), *tokkyu* (limited express service), and *kyuko* (express service). Many tokkyu and kyuko trains have a first-class compartment known as the Green Car. Smoking is allowed only in designated carriages on long-distance and Shinkansen trains. Local and commuter trains are entirely no-smoking.

Because there are no porters or carts at train stations, it's a good idea to travel light when getting around by train. Every train station, however small, has luggage lockers, which cost about ¥300 for 24 hours.

If you plan to travel by rail, get a Japan Rail Pass, which provides unlimited travel on Japan Railways (JR) trains (covering most destinations in Japan) but not on lines owned by other companies. For the Sanyo, Tokaido, and Kyushu Shinkansen lines, the pass is valid on any trains except the Nozomi and Mizuho, which stop infrequently. However, it is valid on all trains on the Yamagata, Tohoku, Joetsu, Akita, and Hokuriku Shinkansen lines.

The JR Pass is also valid on some local buses operated by Japan Railways, though not on the long-distance JR highway buses. You can make seat reservations without paying a fee on all trains that have reserved-seat coaches, usually long-distance trains. The Japan Rail Pass does not cover the cost of sleeping compartments on overnight trains (called blue trains).

You can purchase one-, two-, or three-week passes. A one-week pass is about as expensive as a regular round-trip ticket from Tokyo to Kyoto on the Shinkansen. You must obtain a rail pass voucher prior to arrival in Japan (you cannot buy them in Japan), and the pass must be used within three months of purchase. The pass is available only to people with tourist visas, as opposed to business, student, and diplomatic visas.

When you arrive in Japan, you exchange your voucher for the Japan Rail Pass. You can do this at the Japan Railways desk in the arrivals hall at Narita Airport or at JR stations in major cities. When you make this exchange, you determine the day that you want the rail pass to begin, and, accordingly, when it ends. You do not have to begin travel on the day you make the exchange; instead, pick the starting date to maximize use.

Japan Rail Passes are available in coach class and first class (Green Car), and as the difference in price between the two is relatively small, it's worth the splurge for first-class luxury, especially on the Shinkansen. A one-week pass costs ¥29,110 coach class, ¥38,800 first class; a two-week pass costs ¥46,390 coach class, ¥62,950 first class; and a three-week pass costs ¥59,350 coach class, ¥81,870 first class. The one-week pass pays for itself after one Tokyo–Kyoto round-trip Shinkansen ride. Contact a travel agent or Japan Airlines to purchase the pass.

Many travelers assume that rail passes guarantee them seats on the trains they wish to ride. Not so. If you're using a rail pass, you should book seats ahead. You can reserve up to two weeks in advance or just minutes before the train departs. If you fail to make a train, there's no penalty, and you can reserve again.

Seat reservations for any JR route may be made at any JR station except those in the tiniest villages. The reservation windows or offices, *midori-no-madoguchi,* have green signs in English and green-stripe windows. If you're traveling without a Japan Rail Pass, there's a surcharge of approximately ¥500 (depending upon distance traveled) for seat reservations, and if you miss the train, you'll have to pay for another reservation. When making your seat reservation you may request a no-smoking or smoking car. Your reservation ticket shows the date and departure time of your train as well as your car and seat number. Notice the markings painted on the platform or little signs above the platform; ask someone which markings correspond to car numbers. If you don't have a reservation, ask which cars are unreserved. Unreserved tickets can be purchased at regular ticket windows. There are no reservations made on local service trains. For traveling short distances, tickets are usually sold at vending machines. A platform ticket is required if you go through the wicket gate onto the platform to meet someone coming off a train. The charge is between ¥120 and ¥160, depending on the station.

Most clerks at train stations know a few basic words of English and can read roman script. Moreover, they are invariably helpful in plotting your route. The complete railway timetable is a mammoth book written only in Japanese; however, you can get an English-language train schedule from the Japan National Tourism Organization *(See JNTO in Visitor Information, below)* that covers the Shinkansen and a few of the major JR Limited Express trains. JNTO's booklet *The Tourist's Language Handbook* provides helpful information about purchasing tickets in Japan. The Jorudan Train Route Finder is a good online source for searching train times and prices.

Information **East Japan Railway Company.** ☎ *050/2016–1603* 🌐 *www.jreast.co.jp/e.* **Jorudan Train Route Finder.** ☎ *03/5369–4051* 🌐 *www.jorudan.co.jp/english.*

Buying a Pass **Japan Rail Pass.** 🌐 *www.japanrailpass.net.*

ESSENTIALS

ACCOMMODATIONS

Overnight accommodations in Japan run from luxury hotels to *ryokan* (traditional inns) to youth hostels and even capsules. Western-style rooms with Western-style bathrooms are widely available in large cities, but in smaller, out-of-the-way towns it may be necessary to stay in a Japanese-style room—an experience that can only enhance your stay.

Large chain and business hotels usually quote prices based on rooms and occupancy. Traditional ryokan prices are generally per person and include dinner and breakfast. If you do not want dinner at your hotel, it is usually possible to renegotiate the price. Stipulate, too, whether you wish to have Japanese or Western breakfasts, if any. Japanese-style rooms generally have tatami flooring and a futon instead of a bed. Rarely do they have a private bath or shower; guests bathe in communal baths, following a particular etiquette, and baths are frequently open only a few hours a day. When you make reservations at a hotel outside a city, you are usually expected to take breakfast and dinner at the hotel—this is the rate quoted to you unless you specify otherwise. In this guide, properties are assigned price categories based on the price of a double room at high season (excluding holidays).

A top-notch agent planning your trip to Japan will make sure you have all the necessary domestic travel arrangements reserved in advance and check ahead for reservations for sumo tournaments, geisha shows, or the one-day-a-month temple opening. And when things don't work out the way you hoped, it's nice to have an agent to put things right.

Online Accommodations Japan Hotel.net. ☎ *877/477–7441* 🌐 *www.japanhotel.net.* **Rakuten Travel.** 🌐 *www.travel.rakuten.co.jp/en*

.Japan Travel Agents IACE Travel. ✉ *Nihombashi* ☎ *03/5825–2030 in Japan, 877/489–4223 in U.S.* 🌐 *www.iace-usa.com.* **JTB (Japan Travel Bureau).** ✉ *Tokyo* ☎ *03/5796–5454* 🌐 *www.jtbcorp.jp/en.* **Nippon Travel Agency.** ☎ *310/768–3119* 🌐 *www.ntaamerica.com*

APARTMENT AND HOUSE RENTALS

In addition to the agents listed here, English-language newspapers, magazines, and online sites such as the *Japan Times, Metropolis*, or *Gaijinpot.com* may be helpful in locating a rental property. Note that renting apartments or houses in Japan is not a common way to spend a vacation, and weekly studio-apartment rentals may be fully booked by local business travelers.

The range of online booking services for Japan is expanding, although most of the accommodations booked this way are large and impersonal and staff in the hotel may not speak any English. Also check the location carefully to avoid incurring unforeseen extra costs and hassles in trying to reach the sights from a suburban hotel.

Contacts Fontana. ☎ *03/3382–0289* 🌐 *www.tokyocityapartments.net.* **Ichii.** ☎ *03/5437–5233* 🌐 *www.japt.co.jp.* **Sakura House.** ☎ *03/5330–5250* 🌐 *www.sakura-house.com.*

Rental Listings Gaijinpot.com. 🌐 *www.gaijinpot.com.* **Metropolis.** ☎ *03/3423–6932* 🌐 *metropolisjapan.com.*

HOME VISITS

Through the home-visit system, travelers can get a sense of domestic life in Japan by visiting a local family in their home. The program is voluntary on the homeowner's part, and there's no charge for a visit. To make a reservation, apply in writing for a home visit at least a day in advance to the local tourist information office of the place you are visiting. Contact the Japan National Tourism

Organization *(Visitor Information, below)* before leaving for Japan for more information on the program.

ADDRESSES

The simplest way to decipher a Japanese address is to break it into parts. For example: 6-chome 8–19, Chuo-ku, Fukuoka-shi, Fukuoka-ken. In this address the "chome" indicates a precise area (a block, for example), and the numbers following chome indicate the building within the area. Note that buildings aren't always numbered sequentially; numbers are often assigned as buildings are erected. Only local police officers and mail carriers in Japan seem to be familiar with the area defined by the chome. Sometimes, instead of chome, "machi" (town) is used. Written addresses in Japan also have the opposite order of those in the West, with the city coming before the street. "Ku" refers to a ward (a district) of a city, "shi" refers to a city name, and "ken" indicates a prefecture, which is roughly equivalent to a state in the United States. It's not unusual for the prefecture and the city to have the same name, as in the above address. There are a few geographic areas in Japan that are not called ken. One is greater Tokyo, which is called Tokyo-to. Other exceptions are Kyoto and Osaka, which are followed by the suffix "-fu"—Kyoto-fu, Osaka-fu. Hokkaido, Japan's northernmost island, is also not considered a ken. Not all addresses conform exactly to the above format. Rural addresses, for example, might use "gun" (county) where city addresses have "ku" (ward). Even Japanese people cannot find a building based on the address alone. If you get in a taxi with a written address, do not assume the driver will be able to find your destination. Usually, people provide very detailed instructions or maps to explain their exact locations. It's always good to know the location of your destination in relation to a major building or department store.

BUSINESS SERVICES AND FACILITIES

Kinko's outlets throughout Japan help with business services, and the Japan Convention Service can arrange interpretation and conference planning. Printing and copying can also be done at most convenience stores. The Japan National Tourism Office (JNTO) has extensive contacts for business travelers. Major hotels have business centers.

Contacts Japan Convention Service. ☎ *03/3508–1211* 🌐 *www.jcs-pco.com.* **Kinko's.** 🌐 *www.kinkos.co.jp.*

COMMUNICATIONS

INTERNET

Phone jacks are the same in Japan as in the United States. Many hotels have LAN and Wi-Fi connections for high-speed Internet access. Ethernet cables are usually available at hotels if you don't bring your own. Wireless Internet access (Wi-Fi) is increasingly available for free at certain coffee shops (Starbucks, after free registration), convenience stores (like 7-Eleven), and various tourist sites throughout the country; some higher-end hotels charge an extra fee for in-room Internet access. There are Internet cafés in many cities, but they tend to be dark, cavelike halls focused more on *manga* (comic books) and computer games than staying in touch with people back home. Although free Wi-Fi access is not as widespread as in the United States, free services allow tourists to access a number of Wi-Fi hot spots around the country. Two of the most useful are Travel Japan Wi-Fi (for hot spots throughout Japan) and Free Wi-Fi Japan (mainly in the Tokyo area and surrounding tourist sites). Visitors needing consistent Internet access when out and about may want to rent a pocket Wi-Fi router.

Free Wi-Fi Japan. This service provides access to many hot spots in Tokyo and the surrounding areas. It just requires getting a free log-in and password online or at a tourist center. ⊕ *flets.com/freewifi/index.html.*

Travel Japan Wi-Fi. For Wi-Fi access at up to 200,000 hot spots throughout Japan using iOS or Android devices, register online with this service. ⊕ *wi2.co.jp/tjw/english.html.*

PHONES

The good news is that you can now make a direct-dial telephone call from virtually any point on Earth. The bad news? You can't always do so cheaply. Calling from a hotel is almost always the most expensive option; hotels usually add huge surcharges to all calls, particularly international ones. Calling cards usually keep costs to a minimum, but only if you purchase them locally.

The country code for Japan is 81. When dialing a Japanese number from outside Japan, drop the initial "0" from the local area code.

CALLING WITHIN JAPAN

Public telephones are a dying species in cell-phone-happy Japan. But there are some public telephones in train and subway stations, and in hotel lobbies. Phones accept ¥100 coins as well as prepaid telephone cards. Operator assistance at 104 is in Japanese only. Weekdays 9–5 (except national holidays) English-speaking operators can help you at the toll-free NTT Information Customer Service Centre.

Contacts Directory Assistance. ☎ *104.* **NTT Information Customer Service Centre.** ☎ *0120/36–4463.*

CALLING OUTSIDE JAPAN

With pay phones that can be used for international calls becoming a rarity, and high rates calling from hotels, the best way to call abroad is using a Wi-Fi–based service like Skype or Google Voice. There are still a few telephone cards such as the KDDI Super World Card that can be used for international calls. Each card has a different access code, so follow the included instructions. Major U.S. cellular carriers also have international voice and data plans. Check yours for details.

The country code for the United States is 1.

Japan has several telephone companies for international calls, so make a note of all the possible access code numbers to use to connect to your U.S. server before departure.

Access Codes AT&T Travel Information. ⊕ *www.att.com/esupport/traveler.jsp.* **MCI WorldPhone.** ☎ *800/955–0925* ⊕ *consumer.mci.com/international/english/resources/accessnos.jsp.* **Sprint International Access.** ☎ *866/866–7509* ⊕ *shop.sprint.com.*

CALLING CARDS

Telephone cards, sold in vending machines, hotels, and a variety of stores, are tremendously convenient. Cards for ¥1,000 can be used in virtually all public telephones. For international calls, look for phones that accept KDDI and Softbank prepaid cards valued between ¥1,000 and ¥7,000.

MOBILE PHONES

Japan is the world leader in mobile-phone technology, but overseas visitors cannot easily use their handsets in Japan because it is a non-GSM country. It is best to rent a phone from one of the many outlets at Narita, Kansai, and Nagoya airports. Softbank sells 3G SIM cards so you can use your own number in Japan. Most company rental rates start at ¥525 a day, excluding insurance. Check the airport websites for the current companies.

Contacts JAL ABC Rental Phone. ☎ *0120/086–072* ⊕ *www.jalabc.com/english/index3.html.* **Softbank.** ☎ *030/3560–7730* ⊕ *www.softbank-rental.jp.*

CUSTOMS AND DUTIES

Japan has strict regulations about bringing firearms, pornography, and narcotics into the country. Anyone caught with drugs is liable to be detained, refused reentry into Japan, and deported. Certain fresh fruits, vegetables, plants, and animals are also illegal. Nonresidents are allowed to bring in duty-free: (1) 400 cigarettes or 100 cigars or 500 grams of tobacco; (2) three 760-milliliter bottles of alcohol; (3) 2 ounces of perfume; (4) other goods up to ¥200,000 value.

Getting through customs at a Japanese airport goes more smoothly if you are well dressed, clean-shaven, and as conventional looking as possible. Visitors arriving off flights from other Asian countries are particularly scrutinized for narcotics.

Japan Information Ministry of Finance, Customs and Tariff Bureau. *03/3581-4111* *www.customs.go.jp.*

U.S. Information U.S. Customs and Border Protection. *877/227-5511 in U.S., 202/325-8000 outside U.S.* *www.cbp.gov.*

DAY TOURS AND GUIDES

The Japan National Tourism Organization (JNTO) sponsors a Volunteer Guide program in which local citizens volunteer to show visitors around; this is a great way to meet Japanese people. These are not professional guides; they usually volunteer both because they enjoy welcoming foreigners, and because they want to practice their English. You have to negotiate the itinerary with the guide. The services of Volunteer Guides are free, but you should pay for their travel costs, admission fees, and any meals you eat with them. To participate in this program, make arrangements for a Volunteer Guide in advance through JNTO in the United States or through the tourist office in the area where you want the guide to meet you. The program operates in 75 towns and cities, including Tokyo, Kyoto, Nara, Nagoya, Osaka, and Hiroshima. Bookings can be made through the Volunteer Guides website.

The Japan National Tourism Organization can also put you in touch with various local volunteer groups that conduct tours in English; you need only pay for the guide's travel expenses, admission fees to cultural sites, and meals if you eat together. Assume that the fee will be ¥25,000–¥45,000 for a full eight-hour day.

Contacts Japan Guide Association. *03/3863-2895* *www.jga21c.or.jp.* **Volunteer Guides.** *www.jnto.go.jp/eng/arrange/travel/guide/guideservice.html.*

ELECTRICITY

The electrical current in Japan is 100 volts, 50 cycles alternating current (AC) in eastern Japan, and 100 volts, 60 cycles in western Japan; the United States runs on 110 volt, 60-cycle AC current. Wall outlets in Japan accept plugs with two flat prongs, as in the United States, but do not accept U.S. three-prong plugs.

Most laptops and mobile phone chargers are dual voltage (i.e., they operate equally well on 110 and 220 volts), so require only an adapter. These days the same is true of small appliances such as hair dryers. Always check labels and manufacturers' instructions to be sure. Don't use 110-volt outlets marked for shavers only for high-wattage appliances such as hair dryers.

EMERGENCIES

Assistance in English is available 24 hours a day on the toll-free Japan Helpline.

The U.S. embassy and consulate is open weekdays, with one- to two-hour closings for lunch. Call for exact hours.

Contacts U.S. Embassy and Consulate. *1-10-5 Akasaka, Minato-ku* *03/3224-5000* *japan.usembassy.gov* M *Namboku Line, Tameike-Sanno Station (Exit 13).*

General Emergency Contacts Ambulance and Fire. *119.* **Japan Helpline.** *0120/46-1997 toll-free, 0570/000-911 in Japan* *www.jhelp.com/en/jhlp.html.*

HEALTH

Japan is a safe, clean country for travelers with good drinking water and no major water- or insect-borne diseases. Drugs and medications are widely available at drugstores, although the brand names and use instructions are in Japanese, so if you're on regular medication, take along enough supplies to cover the trip. As with any international travel, be sure to bring your prescription or a doctor's note just in case. Condoms are sold widely, but they may not have the brands you're used to. Speak with your physician and/or check the CDC or World Health Organization websites for health alerts, particularly if you're pregnant or traveling with children or have a chronic illness.

SPECIFIC ISSUES IN JAPAN

Japan is basically a safe country for travelers. But there is chance of being caught up in an earthquake. Information on earthquakes is broadcast (in Japanese) as news flashes on television within minutes, and during major disasters national broadcaster N.H.K. broadcasts information in English on radio and television. Minor tremors occur nearly every month, and sometimes train services are temporarily halted. Check emergency routes at hotels and higher ground if staying near coastal areas.

Tap water is safe everywhere in Japan. Medical treatment varies from highly skilled and professional at major hospitals to somewhat less advanced in small neighborhood clinics. At larger hospitals you have a good chance of encountering English-speaking doctors who have been partly educated in the West.

Mosquitoes can be a minor irritation during the rainy season, though you are never at risk of contracting anything serious like malaria. If you're staying in a ryokan or any place without air-conditioning, anti-mosquito coils or an electric-powered spray will be provided. Dehydration and heatstroke could be concerns if you spend a long time outside during the summer months, but isotonic sports drinks are readily available from the nation's ubiquitous vending machines.

OVER-THE-COUNTER REMEDIES

It may be difficult to buy the standard over-the-counter remedies you're used to, so it's best to bring with you any medications (in their proper packaging) you may need. Medication can be bought only at pharmacies in Japan, but every neighborhood seems to have at least one. Ask for the *yakyoku*. Pharmacists in Japan are usually able to manage at least a few words of English and certainly able to read some, so have a pen and paper ready, just in case. In Japanese, aspirin is *asupirin* and Tylenol is *tairenoru*. Following national regulations, Japanese drugs contain less potent ingredients than foreign brands, so the effects can be disappointing; check advised dosages carefully.

HOURS OF OPERATION

General business hours in Japan are weekdays 9–5. Most offices are closed on Saturday and Sunday.

Banks are open weekdays from 9 am until 4 or 5 pm. As with shops, there's a trend toward longer and later opening hours.

Gas stations follow usual shop hours, though 24-hour stations can be found near major highways.

Museums generally close Monday and the day following national holidays. They are also closed the day following special exhibits and during the weeklong New Year's celebrations.

Department stores are usually open 10–7, but close one day a week, varying from store to store. Other stores are open from 10 or 11 to 8 or 9. There's a trend toward longer and later opening hours in major cities, and 24-hour convenience stores, most of which have ATM facilities, can be found across the entire country.

HOLIDAYS

As elsewhere, peak times for travel in Japan tend to fall around holiday periods. Avoid traveling during the few days before and after New Year's; during Golden Week, which follows Greenery

Day (April 29); and in mid-July and mid-August, at the time of Obon festivals, when many Japanese return to their hometowns (Obon festivals are celebrated July or August 13–16, depending on the location). Note that when a holiday falls on a Sunday, the following Monday is a holiday.

Japan's national holidays are January 1 (*Ganjitsu,* New Year's Day); the second Monday in January (*Senjin-no-hi,* Coming of Age Day); February 11 (*Kenkoku Kinen-bi,* National Foundation Day); March 20 or 21 (*Shumbun-no-hi,* Vernal Equinox); April 29 (*Showa-no-hi,* Showa Day); May 3 (*Kempo Kinen-bi,* Constitution Memorial Day); May 4 (*Midori-no-hi,* Greenery Day; May 5 (*Kodomo-no-hi,* Children's Day); the third Monday in July (*Umi-no-hi,* Marine Day); the third Monday in September (*Keiro-no-hi,* Respect for the Aged Day); September 23 or 24 (*Shubun-no-hi,* Autumnal Equinox); the second Monday in October (*Taiiku-no-hi,* Sports Day); November 3 (*Bunka-no-hi,* Culture Day); November 23 (*Kinro Kansha-no-hi,* Labor Thanksgiving Day); December 23 (*Tenno Tanjobi,* Emperor's Birthday).

MAIL

The Japanese postal service is very efficient. Airmail between Japan and the United States takes between five and eight days. Surface mail can take anywhere from four to eight weeks. Express service is also available through post offices.

Although there are numerous post offices in every city, it's probably best to use the central post office near the main train station, because the workers speak English and can handle foreign mail. Some of the smaller post offices are not equipped to send packages. Post offices are open weekdays 9–5 and Saturday 9–noon. Some central post offices have longer hours, such as the one in Tokyo, near Tokyo Station, which is open 9–9 on weekdays and until 7 on weekends. Most hotels and many convenience stores also sell stamps.

The Japanese postal service has implemented the use of three-numeral-plus-four postal codes, but its policy is similar to that in the United States regarding ZIP-plus-fours; that is, addresses with the three-numeral code still arrive at their destination, albeit perhaps one or two days later. Mail to rural towns may take longer.

It costs ¥110 to send a letter by air to North America. An airmail postcard costs ¥70.

To get mail, have parcels and letters sent "poste restante" to the central post office in major cities; unclaimed mail is returned after 30 days.

SHIPPING PACKAGES

FedEx has many drop-off locations inside large business centers around Tokyo. It would cost about ¥10,000 to send a 1-kilogram (2.20 pound) package from central Tokyo to California, and delivery would be within four days. Two-day shipping is available at a higher rate.

To ship a 5-kilogram (11-pound) parcel to the United States costs ¥10,150 if sent by airmail, ¥7,300 by SAL (economy airmail), and ¥4,000 by sea. Allow a week for airmail, two to three weeks for SAL, and up to six weeks for packages sent by sea. Large shops usually ship domestically, but not overseas.

Express Services FedEx. ☎ *0120/003–200 toll-free, 043/298–1919* 🌐 *www.fedex.com/jp_english.*

MONEY

Japan can be expensive, but there are ways to cut costs. This requires, to some extent, an adventurous spirit and the courage to stray from the standard tourist paths. One good way to hold down expenses is to avoid taxis (they tend to get stuck in traffic anyway) and try the inexpensive, efficient subway and bus systems; instead of going to a restaurant with menus in English and Western-style food, go to places where you can rely on your good old index finger to point to the dish you want, and try food that the Japanese eat.

ITEM	AVERAGE COST
Cup of Coffee	¥250–¥600
Glass of Wine	¥600–¥1,000
Glass of Beer	¥500–¥800
Sandwich (convenience store)	¥300
1-Mile Taxi Ride in Capital City	¥700
Museum Admission	¥1,000

■ TIP→ Banks never have every foreign currency on hand, and it may take as long as a week to order. If you're planning to exchange funds before leaving home, don't wait until the last minute.

ATMS AND BANKS

Your own bank probably charges a fee for using ATMs abroad; the foreign bank you use may also charge a fee. Nevertheless, you usually get a better rate of exchange at an ATM than at a currency-exchange office or even in a bank. Plus, extracting funds as you need them is a safer option than carrying around a large amount of cash.

■ TIP→ PINs with more than four digits are not recognized at ATMs in many countries. If yours has five or more, remember to change it before you leave.

The easiest way to withdraw money is at convenience-store ATMs. 7-Eleven stores and Seven Bank ATMs accept most internationally branded cards. ATMs at many regular Japanese banks do not accept foreign-issue cash or credit cards. UFJ and Shinsei banks are members of the Plus network. Post offices have ATMs that accept Visa, MasterCard, American Express, Diners Club, and Cirrus cards. In more rural areas, it can be difficult to find suitable ATMs, so it is best to get cash before venturing into the countryside. PIN numbers in Japan are made up of four digits. In Japanese an ATM is commonly referred to by its English initialism, while a PIN is *ansho bango*. Most machines also have English on-screen instructions.

CREDIT CARDS

It's a good idea to inform your credit-card company before you travel, especially if you're going abroad and don't travel internationally very often. Otherwise, the credit-card company might put a hold on your card owing to unusual activity—not a good thing halfway through your trip. Record all your credit-card numbers—as well as the phone numbers to call if your cards are lost or stolen—in a safe place, so you're prepared should something go wrong. Both MasterCard and Visa have general numbers you can call (collect if you're abroad) if your card is lost, but you're better off calling the number of your issuing bank, since MasterCard and Visa usually just transfer you to your bank; your bank's number is usually printed on your card.

If you plan to use your credit card for cash advances, you'll need to apply for a PIN at least two weeks before your trip. Although it's usually cheaper (and safer) to use a credit card abroad for large purchases (so you can cancel payments or be reimbursed if there's a problem), note that some credit-card companies *and* the banks that issue them add substantial percentages to all foreign transactions, whether they're in a foreign currency or not. Check on these fees before leaving home, so there won't be any surprises when you get the bill.

■ TIP→ Before you charge something, ask the merchant whether or not he or she plans to do a dynamic currency conversion (DCC). In such a transaction the credit-card processor (shop, restaurant, or hotel, not Visa or MasterCard) converts the currency and charges you in dollars. In most cases you'll pay the merchant a 3% fee for this service in addition to any credit-card company and issuing-bank foreign-transaction surcharges.

Dynamic currency conversion programs are becoming increasingly widespread. Merchants who participate in them are supposed to ask whether you want to be charged in dollars or the local currency, but they don't always do so. And even if they do offer you a choice, they may well avoid mentioning the additional surcharges. The good news is that you *do* have a choice. And if this practice really gets your goat, you can avoid it entirely thanks to American Express; with its cards, DCC simply isn't an option.

MasterCard and Visa are the most widely accepted credit cards in Japan. When you use a credit card, you'll be asked if you intend to be charged in one installment as most locals do. Say *hai-ikkai* (Yes, one time) since being charged in installments won't work for most U.S.-issued cards. Cash is still king, especially at Tokyo's smaller businesses.

Reporting Lost Cards American Express. ☎ *03/3220-6100 in Japan* 🌐 *www.americanexpress.com.* **Diners Club** ☎ *0120/074-024 in Japan* 🌐 *www.dinersclub.com.* **MasterCard.** ☎ *00531/113-886 in Japan* 🌐 *www.mastercard.us.* **Visa.** ☎ *00531/111-555 in Japan* 🌐 *www.visa.com.*

CURRENCY AND EXCHANGE

The unit of currency in Japan is the yen (¥). There are bills of ¥10,000, ¥5,000, ¥2,000, and ¥1,000. Coins are ¥500, ¥100, ¥50, ¥10, ¥5, and ¥1. Japanese currency floats on the international monetary exchange, so changes can be dramatic.

TIP→ Even if a currency-exchange booth has a sign promising no commission, rest assured that there's some kind of huge, hidden fee. And as for rates, you're almost always better off getting foreign currency at an ATM or exchanging money at a bank.

RESTROOMS

The most hygienic restrooms are found in hotels and department stores, and are usually clearly marked with international symbols. You may encounter Japanese-style toilets, with bowls recessed into the floor, over which you squat facing the top of the tank. This may take some getting used to, but it's completely sanitary, as you don't come into direct contact with the facility. If you want to avoid squatting, check out the last cubicle in the row, because it may be a Western-style toilet.

In many homes and Japanese-style public places, there will be a pair of slippers at the entrance to the restroom. Change into these before entering the room, and change back when you exit.

Toilets in some train stations don't have toilet paper, though there are dispensers where packets can be purchased for ¥50 or so. Many locals accept the free tissue packets that are handed out as advertisements in the center of town for this reason. Similarly, paper towel dispensers and hand dryers are not always installed, so bring a small handkerchief or washcloth with you, as well as some hand sanitizer.

PACKING

Pack light, because porters can be hard to find and storage space in hotel rooms may be tiny. What you pack depends more on the time of year than on any dress code. Pack for Tokyo as you would for any American or European city. At more expensive restaurants and nightclubs men usually need to wear a jacket and tie. Wear conservative-color clothing at business meetings. Casual clothes are fine for sightseeing. Jeans are as popular in Japan as they are in the United States, and are perfectly acceptable for informal dining and sightseeing.

Although there are no strict dress codes for visiting temples and shrines, you will be out of place in immodest outfits. For sightseeing leave sandals and open-toe shoes behind; you'll need sturdy walking shoes for the gravel pathways that surround temples and fill parks. Make sure to bring comfortable clothing that isn't too tight to wear in traditional Japanese restaurants, where you may need to sit on tatami-matted floors.

Japanese do not wear shoes in private homes or in any temples or traditional inns. Having shoes you can quickly slip in and out of is a decided advantage. Take wool socks (checking first for holes!) to help you through those shoeless occasions in winter.

All lodgings provide a thermos of hot water and bags of green tea in every room. For coffee you can call room service, buy very sweet coffee in a can from a vending machine, or purchase packets of instant coffee at local convenience stores. If you're staying in a Japanese inn, they probably won't have coffee.

Sunglasses, sunscreen lotions, and hats are readily available, and these days they're not much more expensive in Japan than they are in the United States. It's a good idea to carry a couple of plastic bags to protect your camera and clothes during sudden cloudbursts.

Take along small gift items, such as scarves or perfume sachets, to thank hosts (on both business and pleasure trips), whether you've been invited to their home or out to a restaurant.

PASSPORTS

Hotels in Japan require foreign guests to show passports at check-in, but police are unlikely to ask foreign visitors for on-the-spot identification, although crime crackdowns on nightlife areas of big cities and political tensions with North Korea or Russia can alter local circumstances in some areas.

U.S. Passport Information U.S. Department of State. ☎ *877/487–2778* 🌐 *travel.state.gov/passport.*

U.S. Passport and Visa Expediters A. Briggs Passport & Visa Expeditors. ☎ *800/806–0581* 🌐 *www.abriggs.com.* **American Passport Express.** ☎ *800/455–5166,* 🌐 *www.americanpassport.com.*

SAFETY

Even in its major cities Japan is a very safe country, with one of the lowest crime rates in the world. You should, however, keep an eye out for pickpockets and avoid unlighted roads at night like anywhere else. The greatest danger is the possibility of being caught up in an earthquake and its resulting tsunami. Earthquake information is broadcast (in Japanese) as news flashes on television within minutes, and during major disasters national broadcaster N.H.K. broadcasts information in English on radio and television. Minor tremors occur nearly every month, and sometimes train services are temporarily halted. Check emergency routes at hotels and how to get to higher ground if staying near coastal areas.

TIP→ Distribute your cash, credit cards, IDs, and other valuables between a deep front pocket, an inside jacket or vest pocket, and a hidden money pouch. Don't reach for the money pouch once you're in public.

TAXES

An 8% national consumption tax is added to all hotel bills. There is also a local Tokyo tax of ¥100 per night for bills between ¥10,000 and ¥14,999 and ¥200 for bills over ¥15,000.

At first-class, full-service, and luxury hotels, a 10% service charge is added to the bill in place of individual tipping. At more expensive ryokans, where individualized maid service is provided, the service charge is usually 15%. At business hotels, minshuku, youth hostels, and economy inns, no service charge is added to the bill.

There's an across-the-board, nonrefundable 8% consumption tax levied on all sales. Authorized tax-free shops knock the tax off purchases over ¥10,000 if you show your passport and a valid tourist visa. A large sign is displayed at such shops. An 8% tax is also added to all restaurant bills. At more expensive restaurants a 10%–15% service charge can be added to the bill. Tipping is not customary.

TIME

All of Japan is in the same time zone, which is 14 hours ahead of New York, and 17 hours ahead of San Francisco. Daylight saving time is not observed.

TIPPING

Tipping is not common in Japan. It's not necessary to tip taxi drivers, or at hair salons, barbershops, bars, or nightclubs. A chauffeur for a hired car usually receives a tip of ¥500 for a half-day excursion and ¥1,000 for a full-day trip. It's not customary to tip employees of hotels, even porters, unless a special service has been rendered. In such cases, a gratuity of ¥2,000–¥3,000 should be placed in an envelope and handed to the staff member discreetly. It is not customary to tip hotel maids.

TOURS

Tokyo features on almost every tour of Japan. Read brochures carefully and try to see through the inevitable pictures of cherry trees and geisha to check whether what is planned fits your idea of a holiday. Is it temple after temple? Does the tour include experiences such as sushi and sumo or are these only pricey options? Is the domestic travel by bullet train, plane, or bus? Japan can be quite a culture shock, so resist the temptation to pack in too much, and go for tours that include half days of freedom, because just stepping outside the hotel into the local streets is likely to provide some unexpected sights and experiences.

Japan can be daunting for first-time visitors and anyone without Japanese-language skills, so a package tour is a great way to get into the country and find your feet. However, beware of expensive optional tours such as tea ceremonies, Kabuki tours, and night views. Local tourist offices can probably tell you how to have the same experience more economically.

Recommended Companies **Explorient Travel Services.** ☎ *800/785–1233 in U.S.* 🌐 *www.explorient.com.* **General Tours.** ☎ *800/221–2216 in U.S.* 🌐 *www.generaltours.com.* **Kintetsu.** ☎ *630/250–8840 in U.S.* 🌐 *www.kintetsu.com.*

SPECIAL-INTEREST TOURS

ART

Japan, Tokyo included, is overflowing with art—from pottery and painting to the precise skills of flower arranging and calligraphy. Many tours include museums and art galleries, but only some get you right into the artists' studios with English-language help to understand their skills and the chance to try your hand.

Contacts **Absolute Travel.** ☎ *212/627–1950 in U.S.* 🌐 *www.absolutetravel.com.* **Smithsonian Journeys.** ☎ *855/330–1542 in U.S.* 🌐 *www.smithsonianjourneys.org.*

LANGUAGE PROGRAMS

There is no better way to learn the language than to immerse yourself by studying Japanese in Japan, with classes, a homestay, and cultural tours on which to put the newfound skills into action. The Japanese Information and Culture Center (JICC) website has good links to schools and procedures for study-abroad programs.

Contacts **Japan Information and Culture Center (JICC).** ☎ *202/238–6900 in U.S.* 🌐 *www.us.emb-japan.go.jp/jicc.*

VISITOR INFORMATION

The Japan National Tourism Organization (JNTO) has an office in Tokyo. The JNTO-affiliated International Tourism Center of Japan also has more than 140 counters/offices nationwide. Look for the sign showing a red question mark and the word "information" at train stations and city centers.

Japan National Tourism Organization (JNTO) Contacts Japan National Tourism Organization/Tokyo. ✉ *Tokyo* ☎ *03/3502–1461 in Japan, 212/757–5640 New York branch, 213/623–1952 Los Angeles branch* 🌐 *www.jnto.go.jp/eng.*

Tourist Information Centers (TIC) Tourist Information Center Kansai International Airport. ✉ *Kansai International Airport Terminal 1, Bldg. 1, Osaka* ☎ *072/456–6160* **Tourist Information Center Marunouchi.** ✉ *1st fl., Shin-Tokyo Bldg., 3–3–1 Marunouchi, Chiyoda-ku* ☎ *03/3201–3331* 🌐 *www.jnto.go.jp* ✉ *Arrival Floor, Terminals 1 & 2, Narita* ☎ *0476/30–3383 Terminal 1, 0476/34–5877 Terminal 2.* **Tourist Information Center Narita Terminals 1 & 2.** ✉ *Arrival Floor, Terminals 1 & 2, Narita* ☎ *0476/30–3383 Terminal 1, 0476/34–5877 Terminal 2.*

ONLINE TRAVEL TOOLS

Online cultural resources and travel-planning tools abound for travelers to Japan. Aside from the expected information about regions, hotels, and festivals, Web Japan has offbeat info such as the location of bargain-filled ¥100 shops in Tokyo and buildings designed by famous architects. Another good source for all-Japan information and regional sights and events is Japan-guide.com.

Urban Rail maintains a useful subway navigator, which includes the subway systems in Tokyo and the surrounding areas. The Metropolitan Government website is an excellent source of information on sightseeing and current events in Tokyo.

Check out the websites of Japan's three major English-language daily newspapers: the *Asahi Shimbun*, *The Japan News*, and the *Japan Times*. Entertainment information is available on the sites of Metropolis and *Time Out Tokyo*; both have up-to-date arts, events, and dining listings. In the Kansai region, *Kansai Scene* is definitely worth a look.

Avoid being lost in translation with the help of Japanese-Online, a series of online language lessons that can help you pick up a bit of Japanese before your trip. (The site also, inexplicably, includes a sampling of typical Japanese junior-high-school math problems.) Order Japan's tastiest dishes with confidence by checking translations on Bento.com.

All About Japan Web Japan. 🌐 *web-jpn.org.*

Currency Conversion XE.com. 🌐 *www.xe.com.*

English-Language Media Sources *Asahi Shimbun AJW.* 🌐 *ajw.asahi.com.* **Bento.com.** 🌐 *www.bento.com.* ***The Japan News.*** 🌐 *www.the-japan-news.com.* ***Japan Times.*** 🌐 *www.japantimes.co.jp.* **Metropolis.** 🌐 *metropolisjapan.com.* ***Time Out Tokyo.*** 🌐 *www.timeout.jp.*

Learn Japanese Japanese-Online. 🌐 *www.japanese-online.com.*

Transportation Hitachi's Hyperdia-timetable. 🌐 *www.hyperdia.com.* **Jorudan Train Route Finder.** 🌐 *www.jorudan.co.jp/english.* **Tokyo Metropolitan Government.** 🌐 *www.metro.tokyo.jp.* **Urban Rail.** 🌐 *www.urbanrail.net.*

INDEX

D

E

F

G

H

R

S

T

PHOTO CREDITS

Front cover: Jon Arnold/ AWL Images [Description: Sushi in a Japanese restaurant, Tokyo, Japan]. Back cover, from left to right: Valeria73 I Dreamstime.com; Nikada/iStockphoto; Y. Shimizu, JNTO. Spine: tungtopgun / Shutterstock.1, Jochen Tack / age fotostock. 2-3, Chad Ehlers / age fotostock. 5, Kimtaro / Flick. Chapter 1: Experience Tokyo: 8-9 Sepavo I Dreamstime.com.15 (top), Yasufumi Nishi / JNTO. 15 (bottom), Gavin Hellier / age fotostock. 16, Y. Shimizu, JNTO. 17, alvarez / iStockphoto. 27, Steve Vidler / age fotostock. 28 (top left), 663highland / Wikimedia Commons. 28 (bottom left), public domain. 28 (right), Javier Larrea / age fotostock. 29 (top left), Fedor Selivanov / Shutterstock. 29 (bottom), Razvan Radu-Razvan Photography / iStockphoto, 29 (center), Rachelle Burnside / Shutterstock. 29 (top right), CAN BALCIOGLU / Shutterstock. 30 (left), Neale Cousland / Shutterstock. 30 (top right), Ilya D. Gridnev / Shutterstock. 30 (bottom right), Wikimedia Commons. 31 (left), Yasufumi Nishi / JNTO. 31 (top right), Dr Flash / Shutterstock. 31 (bottom right), Tataroko / Wikimedia Commons. 32 (top left), tci / age fotostock. 32 (bottom left), Tibor Bognar / age fotostock. 32 (right), Jochen Tack / age fotostock. Chapter 2: A Japanese Culture Primer: 33, Sergii Rudiuk / Shutterstock. 34, thinboyfatter/Flickr. 35, Kagawa Prefecture/JNTO. 35 (inset), sevenke/Shutterstock. 36, JNTO. 37, Payless Images/Shutterstock. 38 (top), JNTO. 38 (bottom), Saga Prefecture/JNTO. 39 (all), Hokkaido Tourism Organization/JNTO. 40 (top and bottom), Nagano Prefecture/JNTO. 41 (top), JNTO. 41 (bottom), Jill Battaglia/iStockphoto. 42 (top), Tondo Soesanto Soegondo/Shutterstock. 42 (bottom), svry/Shutterstock. 43, Kanazawa City/JNTO. 44 and 45 (top), JNTO. 45 (bottom), Photo Japan / age fotostock. 46, Okinawa Convention & Visitors Bureau/JNTO. 47, Ishikawa Prefecture/ JNTO. 48, Ishikawa Prefecture Tourist Association and Kanazawa Convention Bureau/ JNTO. 49 (left), su.bo/ Flickr. 49 (right), Nagano Prefecture/ JNTO. 50, Jim Epler/iStockphoto. 51, Iwate Prefecture/JNTO. 52, Iain Masterton / age fotostock. 53 (bottom left), JNTO. 53 (top right), Nagano Prefecture/ JNTO. 54, Christophe Boisvieux / age fotostock. 55, chrisho/ iStockphoto. 56, John Warburton-Lee Photography / Alamy. 57 (bottom left), Juri Pozzi/iStockphoto. 57 (top right), Japan Ryokan Association/ JNTO. 58, ton koene / age fotostock. 59 (top), luisvilla/Flickr. 59 (bottom), Lukas Kurtz/Flickr. 60, Steve Silver / age fotostock. 61 (bottom left), FOTOSEARCH RM / age fotostock. 61 (top right), _Yuki_K_ /Flickr. 62, Steve Silver / age fotostock. 62 (bottom left), Kodokan/ JNTO. 62 (top right), Steve Silver / age fotostock. 64, Kevin O'Hara / age fotostock. 65 (bottom left), strikeael/Flickr. 65 (top right), Oote Boe / age fotostock. 66, Kanazawa City/ JNTO. 67 (bottom left), simonhn/Flickr. 67 (top right), jonrawlinson/Flickr. 68, Mitchell Coster / age fotostock. 69 (bottom left), Okayama Prefecture/JNTO. 69 (top right), Noriko Kitano. 70 and 71 (bottom), Yasufumi Nishi/ JNTO. 71 (top), thinboyfatter/Flickr. 72, Y.Shimizu/ JNTO. 73 (bottom left), Yasufumi Nishi/ JNTO. 73 (top right), JNTO. 74, PSno7/Shutterstock. 75, Yasufumi Nishi/ JNTO. 76, Christopher Heschong/Flickr. Chapter 3: Exploring Tokyo: 77, JNTO. 78, Y. Shimizu. 80, Yasufumi Nishi / JNTO. 83, Atsuo Baba / iStockphoto. 85, Tibor Bognar / age fotostock. 88 and 91, Chic Ushio. 92, Sylvain Grandadam / age fotostock. 93, heiwa4126 / Flickr. 97, JNTO. 98, Cristian Baitg/iStockphoto. 100, np&djjewell / Flickr. 102, JTB Photo / age fotostock. 103, mypokcik / Shutterstock. 106, MeeRok / Shutterstock. 109, Chie Ushio. 110, senso-ji. 111, Scirocco340/Shutterstock. 113, alvarez / iStockphoto. 114, Tifonimages / Shutterstock. 117, bizmac / Flickr. 118, Ryan KC Wong / iStockphoto. 120, MIKI Yoshihito / Flickr. 123, Roberto A Sanchez / iStockphoto. 124, Y.Shimizu / JNTO. 126, ehnmark / Flickr. 129, EverJeanEverJean / Flickr. 130, VH / age fotostock. 133, Yasufumi Nishi / JNTO. 134, TommL / iStockphoto. 137, yury zaporozhchenko / iStockphoto. 138, Sylvain Grandadam / age fotostock. 139, Tokyo Convention & Visitors Bureau. 140, Iain Masterton / age fotostock. 143, Itinerant Lens / Shutterstock. 144, José Fuste Raga / age fotostock. 146, William Fawcett fotoVoyager.com / iStockphoto. 149, Cristina CIOCHINA / Shutterstock. 150, JTB Photo / age fotostock. 151, J. Henning Buchholz/Shutterstock. 152, SeanPavonePhoto/Shutterstock. 155, William Fawcett fotoVoyager.com/iStockphoto. Chapter 4: Where to Eat. 161, Ronnarong Thanuthattaphong/Shutterstock. 160, Christian Kober/age fotostock. 161 (top), Karl Baron / Flickr 161 (bottom), jetalone / Flickr. 162, Tokyo Convention & Visitors Bureau. 172, T.Y. Express. 177, Luciano Lepre / age fotostock. Chapter 5: Where to Stay: 191, Courtesy of the Palace Hotel Tokyo. 192, George Apostolidis/ Mandarin Oriental, Tokyo. Chapter 6: Nightlife: 213, dat'/Flickr, [CC BY-ND 2.0]. 214, Lukas Kurtz/Flickr. 222, Mark Henley / age fotostock. 226, Jose Fuste Raga /age fotostock. Chapter 7: The Performing Arts: 229, Travel Pix Collection / age fotostock. 230, JNTO. 233, JNTO. Chapter 8: Shopping: 237, aluxum/iStockphoto. 238 and 245, JNTO. 246 (top left), ton koene/age fotostock. 246 (bottom left), idealisms/Flickr. 246 (top right), Andrew Currie/Flickr. 246 (bottom right), JTB Photo / age fotostock. 247 (top left), robcocquyt/Shutterstock. 247 (top), Sylvain Grandadam / age fotostock. 247, (bottom left), Mie Prefecture, JNTO. 247 (right), bptakoma/Flickr. 248, Kimtaro/Flickr. 249 (top), JNTO. 249 (bottom), dichohecho/Flickr. 250 (top left), Ron Koeberer / age fotostock. 250 (top right), ton koene / age fotostock. 250 (bottom), SeanPavonePhoto/iStockphoto. 251, Boaz Rottem

/ age fotostock. 252 (top), LIMI Feu SS 2010 Collection. 252 (center), N. Hoolywood. 252 (bottom), Somarta. 260, Edmund Sumner/VIEW/age fotostock. 269, Dorian Weber / age fotostock. Chapter 9: Side Trips from Tokyo: 275, Yujiro | Dreamstime.com. 276 and 277 (top left), Aschaf/Flickr. 277 (top right), Yasufumi Nishi/JNTO. 277 (bottom), H.L.I.T./Flickr. 278, ototadana/Flickr. 282-83, JTB Photo/ age fotostock. 282 (bottom), Banzai Hiroaki/Flickr. 283 (top and bottom), flickr.com/diloz. 284 (top and bottom), Wikimedia Commons. 285 (top), Vidler Steve / age fotostock. 285 (bottom), Odakyu Electric Railway/JNTO. 286 (top left, right 3, and right 4), jetalone/Hajime NAKANO/Flickr. 286 (bottom left), flickr.com/diloz. 286 (right 2), imgdive/Banzai Hiroaki/Flickr. 286 (top right), skyseeker/ Flickr. 287, Azlan DuPree/Flickr. 288 (top), diloz/Flickr. 288 (center), jetalone/Hajime NAKANO/ Flickr. 288 (bottom), imgdive/BanzaiHiroaki/Flickr. 289, JTB Photo / age fotostock. 303 and 312, JTB Photo / age fotostock. 314, Vladimir Khirman/iStockphoto. 317, Imre Cikajlo/iStockphoto. 319, Tony Waltham / age fotostock. 326, 332 and 334, Aschaf/Flickr. 341, Yasufumi Nishi/ JNTO. 344, matteusus/iStockphoto. About Our Writers: All photos are courtesy of the writers except for the following: Misha Janette, courtesy of Celia Humphries.

NOTES

NOTES

NOTES

NOTES

ABOUT OUR WRITERS

When he's not hitting the pavement for the entertainment business newspaper *Variety* or his online news site, *The Tokyo Reporter*, **Brett Bull** can be found working away behind a drafting table at a Japanese construction company, his occupation since arriving in Tokyo from California over a decade ago. For this edition he worked on the Where to Stay chapter.

Nagoya updater **Rob Goss** has lived in Tokyo since 1999. Writing Japan-related features on topics ranging from travel to sustainability, Rob is a contributor to *Time*, *National Geographic Traveler*, and many other publications around the world. He has also written and updated a dozen books on Japan. For this edition, he worked on the Experience and Where to Eat chapters.

Noriko Kitano is a Tokyo-based freelance journalist and a stringer to the Associated Press and *The New York Times* covering politics and culture. She also works as a translator and translated Alice Waters's *The Art of Simple Food* into Japanese. When not writing, she enjoys chamber music, playing the piano, and walking her pug in the park. For this edition, she revised the Nightlife and the Performing Arts chapters.

Born in the great state of Washington, **Misha Janette** moved to Japan in 2004 to study at Tokyo's Bunka Fashion College. She is a regular fashion columnist for *The Japan Times* and CNNgo, and contributes to *Numero Tokyo, Vogue Girl Japan,* and *Racked* on top of being a wardrobe stylist for musicians and magazines. For this edition she updated the Shopping chapter and wrote the Shop Tokyo feature.

Robert Morel has been exploring Japan since 2003 and still thinks the best way to get from Hokkaido to Okinawa is by bicycle. He currently writes about, photographs, and lives in Tokyo's historic Yanaka neighborhood. For this edition he updated the Exploring, Side Trips, and Travel Smart chapters.

Annemarie Sasagawa grew up in the wilds of northern British Columbia and now lives in Tokyo's Shinjuku ward. After years on the road as a tour leader in Japan, she hung up her backpack to get a PhD in cultural anthropology at the University of Tokyo. Annemarie updated our Japanese Cultural Primer this edition.

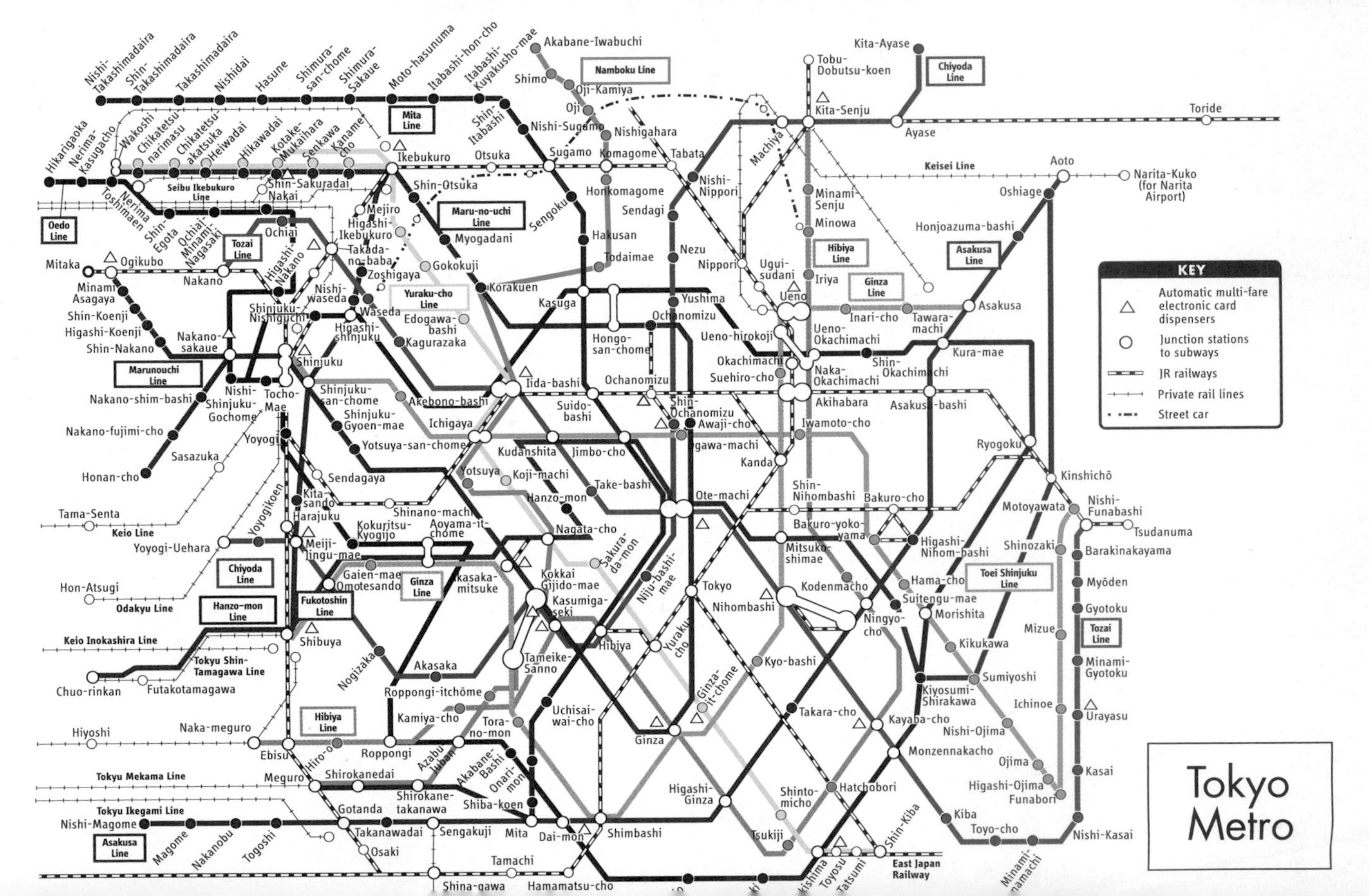
Tokyo Metro
KEY
Automatic multi-fare electronic card dispensers
Junction stations to subways
JR railways
Private rail lines
Street car
Mita Line
Namboku Line
Chiyoda Line
Keisei Line
Seibu Ikebukuro Line
Oedo Line
Tozai Line
Maru-no-uchi Line
Hibiya Line
Ginza Line
Asakusa Line
Yuraku-cho Line
Marunouchi Line
Keio Line
Odakyu Line
Hanzo-mon Line
Fukotoshin Line
Keio Inokashira Line
Tokyu Shin-Tamagawa Line
Toei Shinjuku Line
Tokyu Mekama Line
Tokyu Ikegami Line
East Japan Railway
Nishi-Takashimadaira
Shin-Takashimadaira
Takashimadaira
Nishidai
Hasune
Shimura-san-chome
Shimura-Sakaue
Moto-hasunuma
Itabashi-hon-cho
Itabashi-Kuyakusho-mae
Shin-Itabashi
Akabane-Iwabuchi
Shimo
Oji-Kamiya
Oji
Nishi-Sugamo
Nishigahara
Kita-Ayase
Tobu-Dobutsu-koen
Kita-Senju
Ayase
Toride
Hikarigaoka
Nerima-Kasugacho
Wakoshi
Chikatetsu-narimasu
Chikatetsu-akatsuka
Heiwadai
Hikawadai
Kotake-Mukaihara
Senkawa
Kaname-cho
Ikebukuro
Otsuka
Sugamo
Komagome
Tabata
Machiya
Aoto
Narita-Kuko (for Narita Airport)
Nerima
Toshimaen
Shin-Egota
Ochiai-Minami-Nagasaki
Shin-Sakuradai
Nakai
Shin-Otsuka
Honkomagome
Sendagi
Nishi-Nippori
Minami-Senju
Minowa
Oshiage
Honjoazuma-bashi
Mejiro
Higashi-Ikebukuro
Myogadani
Sengoku
Hakusan
Nezu
Nippori
Ochiai
Takada-no-baba
Gokokuji
Todaimae
Ugui-sudani
Iriya
Mitaka
Ogikubo
Nakano
Higashi-Nakano
Zoshigaya
Korakuen
Kasuga
Yushima
Ueno
Inari-cho
Tawara-machi
Asakusa
Minami-Asagaya
Shin-Koenji
Higashi-Koenji
Shin-Nakano
Nishi-waseda
Shinjuku-Nishiguchi
Waseda
Edogawa-bashi
Higashi-shinjuku
Kagurazaka
Ochanomizu
Hongo-san-chome
Ueno-hirokoji
Ueno-Okachimachi
Kura-mae
Nakano-sakaue
Shinjuku
Okachimachi
Naka-Okachimachi
Shin-Okachimachi
Nishi-Shinjuku-Gochome
Tocho-Mae
Shinjuku-san-chome
Akebono-bashi
Iida-bashi
Suehiro-cho
Akihabara
Asakusa-bashi
Nakano-shim-bashi
Shinjuku-Gyoen-mae
Ichigaya
Suido-bashi
Shin-Ochanomizu
Awaji-cho
Iwamoto-cho
Nakano-fujimi-cho
Yoyogi
Yotsuya-san-chome
Kudanshita
Jimbo-cho
Ogawa-machi
Kanda
Ryogoku
Honan-cho
Sasazuka
Yotsuya
Koji-machi
Take-bashi
Shin-Nihombashi
Bakuro-cho
Kinshichō
Sendagaya
Hanzo-mon
Ote-machi
Motoyawata
Nishi-Funabashi
Tsudanuma
Tama-Senta
Kita-sando
Harajuku
Shinano-machi
Kokuritsu-Kyogijo
Aoyama-it-chome
Nagata-cho
Bakuro-yoko-yama
Higashi-Nihom-bashi
Shinozaki
Barakinakayama
Yoyogikoen
Yoyogi-Uehara
Meiji-Jingu-mae
Sakura-da-mon
Mitsuko-shimae
Myōden
Gaien-mae
Omotesando
Akasaka-mitsuke
Kokkai Gijido-mae
Kasumiga-seki
Niju-bashi-mae
Tokyo
Nihombashi
Kodenmacho
Hama-cho
Suitengu-mae
Morishita
Gyotoku
Hon-Atsugi
Ningyo-cho
Mizue
Shibuya
Hibiya
Yuraku-cho
Kikukawa
Minami-Gyotoku
Tameike-Sanno
Kyo-bashi
Sumiyoshi
Chuo-rinkan
Futakotamagawa
Nogizaka
Akasaka
Roppongi-itchōme
Kiyosumi-Shirakawa
Ichinoe
Urayasu
Ginza-it-chome
Takara-cho
Kamiya-cho
Tora-no-mon
Uchisai-wai-cho
Kayaba-cho
Nishi-Ojima
Hiyoshi
Naka-meguro
Ginza
Ebisu
Hiro-o
Roppongi
Azabu-Juban
Akabane-Bashi
Onari-mon
Monzennakacho
Ojima
Kasai
Meguro
Shirokanedai
Higashi-Ginza
Shinto-micho
Hatchobori
Higashi-Ojima
Funabori
Shirokane-takanawa
Shiba-koen
Kiba
Nishi-Magome
Gotanda
Takanawadai
Sengakuji
Mita
Dai-mon
Shimbashi
Tsukiji
Toyo-cho
Nishi-Kasai
Magome
Nakanobu
Togoshi
Osaki
Tamachi
Toyosu
Tatsumi
Shin-Kiba
Minami-Sunamachi
Shina-gawa
Hamamatsu-cho